I0699741

# ARISTOTLE

# ARISTOTLE

New light on his life and on
some of his lost works

Volume II

*Observations on some of Aristotle's
lost works*

Anton-Hermann Chroust

University of Notre Dame Press

*American edition 1973*
*University of Notre Dame Press*
*Notre Dame, Indiana 46556*

*First published in 1973*
*by Routledge & Kegan Paul Ltd,*
*Broadway House, 68–74 Carter Lane*
*London EC4V 5EL*
*Printed in Great Britain by*
*Richard Clay (The Chaucer Press) Ltd, Bungay, Suffolk*
*© 1973 by Anton-Hermann Chroust*

**Library of Congress Cataloging in Publication Data**

Chroust, Anton-Hermann.
    Observations on some of Aristotle's lost works.

    (His Aristotle: new light on his life and on some of his lost works, v. 2)
    Includes bibliographical references.
    1. Aristoteles. I. Title. II. Series.
B481.C56 vol. 2      185 [B]s [185]      73–8895
ISBN 0-268-00518-4

*To the Memory of*
*Roscoe Pound*
*Teacher, Friend, Scholar*

# Contents

CONTENTS

# Abbreviations

DL  Diogenes Laertius, *The Lives and Opinions of Eminent Philosophers*

DH  Dionysius of Halicarnassus, *I. Epistola ad Ammaeum*

VH  *Vita Aristotelis Hesychii* (*Vita Menagiana, Vita Menagii*)

VM  *Vita Aristotelis Marciana*

VV  *Vita Aristotelis Vulgata* (*Vita Pseudo-Ammoniana, Vita Pseudo-Elias*)

VL  *Vita Aristotelis Latina*

I VS  *I Vita Aristotelis Syriaca* (author unknown), Cod. Berol. Sachau 226

II VS  *II Vita Aristotelis Syriaca* (author unknown), Cod. Vat. Syriacus 158

I VA  *I Vita Aristotelis Arabica* (Ibn Abi Yaqub an-Nadim, *Kitab al-Fihrist*)

II VA  *II Vita Aristotelis Arabica* (Abu-l-Wafa al-Mubassir (or Mubashir) Ibn Fatik, *Kitab Mukhtar al-Hikam wa-Mahasin al-Kilam—The Book of Selections from Wisdom and Beautiful Sayings*)

III VA  *III Vita Aristotelis Arabica* (Al-Qifti Gamaladdin al-Qadi al-Akram, *Tabaqat al-Hukama—Schools of Wise Men*)

IV VA  *IV Vita Aristotelis Arabica* (Ibn Abi Usaibia, *Uyun al-Anba fi Tabaqat al-Atibba—Book of Sources of Information About the Schools of Doctors*)

In the Arabic names and titles, the 'accents' have been omitted. The *Vitae Aristotelis* mentioned above have been compiled and are easily accessible in I. Düring, *Aristotle in the Ancient Biographical Tradition*, Studia Graeca et Latina Gothoburgensia, vol. 63, no. 2 (Göteborg, 1957).

# Introduction*

It is a matter of common knowledge that the first scholarly compilation of the many fragments,[1] rightly or wrongly credited to the lost or early works of Aristotle, was made by Valentin Rose in his *Aristoteles Pseudepigraphus* (Leipzig, 1863). Nine years earlier, in his unusual but very influential *De Aristotelis Librorum Ordine et Auctoritate Commentatio* (Berlin, 1854), Rose, aside from citing some fragments of the lost Aristotelian compositions, laid down a number of basic and somewhat unusual canons concerning the writings of Aristotle: (i) barring a few minor and insignificant titles, the traditional *Corpus Aristotelicum*, as it has been handed down by Andronicus of Rhodes, contains all, or almost all, the authentic writings of Aristotle; (ii) of the authentic works of Aristotle, the only significant losses are the *Problemata*,[2] the *Collection of the 158 Constitutions*,[3] some minor parts of the *Metaphysics*, some parts of the *Poetics* and some parts of the *Politics*; (iii) aside from the works incorporated in the *Corpus Aristotelicum* (and the missing *Problemata* and *Collection*), there never existed any authentic compositions of the Stagirite; and (iv) because there never existed any 'lost works' of Aristotle, the so-called 'fragments,' 'excerpts' or 'reports' of such lost works as they are found in ancient and patristic authors, are unquestionably spurious.

When discarding in this radical and uncompromising manner all the fragments of the lost works as wholly apocryphal, Rose used what may be called a sweeping *a priori* approach. In regard to their form and doctrinal content, Rose insisted that these alleged fragments have a decidedly Platonic flavor. But since Aristotle was always an 'Aristotelian' and as such was fundamentally opposed to Plato and Platonic teachings, these fragments clearly must be spurious.[4] Rose further expounded and expanded these basic canons in his *Aristoteles Pseudepigraphus* of 1863. In this work, for reasons difficult to understand, he also collected whatever alleged *pseudepigrapha* he believed to have been unearthed. Hence, the first modern, scholarly collection of Aristotelian fragments actually owes its origin to Rose's determined effort to prove these fragments apocryphal. Rose also maintained this intransigent position in his *Aristoteles Qui Ferebantur Librorum Fragmenta*, which in 1870 came to be incorporated into the fifth volume of I. Bekker's deservedly famous *Corpus Aristotelicum*. This work of Rose was printed separately as well as enlarged in 1886.[5] It has become a standard work, still used and cited in our time.

Certain aspects of Rose's methods and opinions were quite unusual. He started out with the assumption that the 'catalogue' of Aristotelian works preserved by Diogenes Laertius (DL V. 22–7) contained a great many apocryphal writings, and that especially the first nineteen titles are, and undoubtedly must be, entirely spurious. This being established, he rather arbitrarily assigned, without further investigation or evidence, the fragments he had already determined to be spurious to those allegedly spurious titles or works. In other words, he decreed, in a somewhat high-handed manner, frequently without much supporting evidence,[6] that such-and-such fragment should be listed under such-and-such title. In so doing, he also proclaimed that a fragment chosen and assigned in this arbitrary manner is declaratory of the philosophic content or message of the composition to which it was thus assigned. To what possible confusion and errors such an utterly capricious method may lead can easily be gathered from the following examples chosen at random: Fragments 37–48 (Rose), all concerned with the soul or the nature of the soul, are directly and uncompromisingly assigned to the *Eudemus or On the Soul*.[7] At the same time, he credits fragments 59–61 (Rose), taken from Iamblichus, *Protrepticus* 47, 5–48, 21 (Pistelli), to the Aristotelian *Protrepticus*;[8] fragment 15 (Rose), to the Aristotelian *On Philosophy*; fragment 193 (Rose), to the Aristotelian *On the Pythagoreans*; and fragments 177–8 (Rose), to the Aristotelian *Homeric Questions*—although all these fragments likewise discuss problems related to the soul and, hence, might as well be assigned to the *Eudemus or On the Soul*. This particular example, which could be multiplied many times, supports the contention that Rose's assignments and identifications, on the whole, are rather capricious and therefore must be considered somewhat unreliable. Nevertheless, no one will seriously deny that in terms of an authoritative collection of fragments from Aristotle's lost works, Rose's *Aristotelis Qui Ferebantur Librorum Fragmenta* (Leipzig, 1886) is of immense and lasting value as a starting point, if used with care, for scholarly investigations into the many and often desperately involved problems connected with these lost works.

By decisively influencing the vast majority of later scholars, Rose's unusual method has had a lasting and, in some instances, an almost fatal effect upon all subsequent efforts to deal effectively with the lost (early) compositions of Aristotle. Later scholars, as evidenced by the collection of fragments compiled by R. Walzer in his *Aristoteles: Dialogorum Fragmenta in Usum Scholarum* of 1934, W. D. Ross in his *Select Fragments* of 1952, I. Düring in his *Aristotle's Protrepticus: An Attempt at Reconstruction* of 1961 (Düring limits himself to the fragments traditionally assigned to the Aristotelian *Protrepticus*), M. Untersteiner in his *Aristotele: Della Filosofia* of 1963 (Untersteiner limits himself to the fragments commonly ascribed to the Aristotelian *On Philosophy*), and by A.-H. Chroust in his *Aristotle: Protrepticus—A Reconstruction* of 1964 (Chroust restricts himself to the fragments conventionally credited to the Aristotelian *Protrepticus*), did not really inquire into the reasons—if any—why a particular fragment had been, or should be, credited to a specific work or listed under a particular title. It appears, therefore, that these later scholars, who most certainly made some original contributions of their own, were simply under the spell of Rose's peculiar assignments which they apparently accepted without reservations.[9] In this unusual fashion, Rose's original collection, though meritorious and useful as a mere collection, has had a lasting influence on subsequent Aristotelian scholarship.

A further result of Rose's unusual editorial method was that his unique compilation came to be regarded almost unanimously as a collection of real, that is, *verbatim* 'citations' from Aristotle's lost works, rather than as mere excerpts, references or doxographical reports made by later and, at times, rather poorly informed authors. In their own clumsy way, some of these authors garbled, misunderstood and even deliberately falsified the original Aristotelian text or texts.[10] While Rose's collection or compilation included, with few reservations, practically everything which ancient reporters and critics had ascribed to Aristotle, recent and certainly more critical scholarship has come to the sound conclusion that most of these fragments must be treated with much discrimination. It is now realized that many of the fragments contain the true, though in some instances badly mutilated and poorly reported, remnants of Aristotle's authentic early compositions. As might be expected, each ancient reporter altered, or tried to alter, Aristotle's original thought so as to integrate or reconcile it with his own peculiar philosophic conviction. Moreover, each reporter recasts it in his own particular language, which in all likelihood differed considerably from the language and terminology used by Aristotle. This seems to be the case, for instance, with Iamblichus' *Protrepticus*, which has been relied upon as a true 'report' on the essential content of Aristotle's *Protrepticus*.

The influence of Rose's method and prejudice, for example, is still strongly felt in Jaeger's work on the intellectual development of Aristotle's philosophic thought.[11] Without minimizing Jaeger's matchless scholarship, it must be conceded that he accepted without reservation Rose's collection as essentially a 'fragmentary outline' of some of Aristotle's lost writings—a compendium of those Aristotelian compositions which have survived only in the form of fragments, excerpts or doxographical reports. Proceeding on this assumption, Jaeger attempted to reconstruct and interpret the philosophy propagated in these early works. In the pursuit of this complex undertaking he relied upon the surviving fragments of the *Eudemus*, the *Protrepticus* and the *On Philosophy*, as they had been compiled and identified by Rose.[12] However, in so doing, Jaeger went far beyond Rose. He included in his discussions what he believed to be genuine excerpts from the Aristotelian *Protrepticus*, although these excerpts had not been incorporated into Rose's collection.[13] It must always be realized that Jaeger was not primarily interested in retrieving, reconstructing or in listing ancient *testimonia*, but rather in establishing Aristotle's intellectual development from an early Platonism to a later 'Aristotelianism.' Accordingly, his selections and attributions were determined to a large extent by the manner and degree to which certain excerpts lent support to his major thesis.[14] Considering the fact that for his enterprise Jaeger was forced to use the inadequate collection of Aristotelian fragments compiled by Rose, his scholarly attainments are truly remarkable.

Despite all learned discussions and conjectures of the past fifty years, the main problem still confronting modern Aristotelian scholarship is simply this: although in recent times much valuable material has been gathered and collated by a host of competent and enterprising scholars, and although, on the whole, this was done with much care, much effort and astounding acumen, we can never be certain whether this material may in fact be credited to Aristotle in general or to definite Aristotelian lost works in particular. Neither the more recent collection of fragments compiled by R. Walzer in 1934, who, under the influence of Jaeger's pioneering work, limited himself to the *Eudemus*, the *Protrepticus* and to the *On Philosophy*; nor that of W. D. Ross of 1952; nor that of I. Düring, who made a new compilation of the fragments of Aristotle's *Protrepticus*,[15] nor that of M. Untersteiner, who compiled the fragments of Aristotle's *On Philosophy*[16]—none have succeeded in resolving this nagging problem. Undoubtedly, these new collections are vastly superior to Rose's compilation. However, it must be conceded that these more recent and certainly more scholarly collections—and for that matter, all our present scholarship regarding the lost works of Aristotle—in the final analysis are still based on, and decisively influenced by, Rose's collection which was originally meant to be a survey of alleged Aristotelian *pseudepigrapha*. Thus, as paradoxical or ironical as it may seem, Rose's materials, which originally had been collated as instances of alleged *apocrypha*, still constitute the basis as well as the starting point of all modern investigations into the lost authentic compositions of Aristotle.[17] It must be conceded, therefore, that recent investigations are but a refinement of Rose's original and utterly negative method and intent. The basic scholarly attitude towards Aristotle's lost works still is determined and, hence, prejudiced by what Rose had said in support of his unusual (and questionable) thesis contrived about one hundred years ago. In keeping with this fatal traditionalism, a fragment or excerpt only too frequently is deemed to be a remnant of a certain lost composition of Aristotle simply because Rose had listed it under the title of this lost work. From this rather shaky foundation, more recent Aristotelian scholarship is making a determined effort to enlarge our knowledge of a particular lost composition of Aristotle; to seek out, wherever possible, additional fragments; to determine the doctrinal or philosophic content of this composition; and to retrieve and reconstruct this whole composition.[18]

It is obvious that such a procedure does not, and cannot, always distinguish between purely doxographical reports (which possibly misinterpret, misunderstand or distort the original text or texts) and actual fragments or concise excerpts. Barring a few isolated instances, the present status of the many problems connected with the lost works of Aristotle does not permit us to establish with any degree of certainty which particular texts are genuine fragments or excerpts, and which are merely doxographical accounts of frequently doubtful value. Neither does it really enable us to determine with any degree of certainty which texts may be safely credited to Aristotle or, perhaps, to a particular composition or title.[19] All this compounds the difficulties inherent in any attempt to reconstruct these lost works of Aristotle or present an adequate account of their philosophic content.

It must be remembered that we possess only a negligibly small number of direct quotations or excerpts which may safely be assigned to a definite work. Every other assignment is at best an intelligent or persuasive conjecture, but nothing more than a conjecture. Undoubtedly, whenever we are in possession of a fragment or excerpt (or doxographical report) which ancient tradition or ancient *testimonia* univocally credit to a particular composition, we may safely accept this assignment. The same holds true when, as in Simplicius, *Comment. in Aristotelis De Caelo (Comment. in Arist. Graec.*, vol. VII), p. 485, lines 19-22, the reporter 'pinpoints' the place where this particular passage was to be found in the original Aristotelian work (*On Prayer*), expressly credits this passage to Aristotle, mentions the title of this composition and, by implication, indicates the number of books which constituted the original work. Such information supplies us with a relatively reliable starting point. Beyond that we have to rely upon reasonable conjecture, trying to add those texts or materials which have not yet been identified or expressly assigned to a specific title by ancient authority, but which manifest some reasonable connection with a fragment vouched for by the ancients. But here, too, we must remember that within such a procedure 'reason' or 'logic' is frequently an elusive, and even a deceptive thing. For such a 'logic'—a 'logic of the situation' or a 'logic of persuasion and justification'—is often strongly prejudiced by a whole series of unfounded conjectures regarding the alleged doctrinal content of a certain work and 'what it must have been.'[20] Proceeding further along these lines, we shall make two rather disconcerting discoveries: first, those fragments which can be assigned to a definite work with any degree of assurance are discouragingly few; and, second, the number of fragments or excerpts for which we are unable to discover the proper title or place, or which could be assigned with equal persuasiveness to two or more different works, is fatally plentiful.

This desperate situation has induced many sincere and competent scholars simply to write off, and even to deprecate, any and all efforts to deal successfully with the lost works of Aristotle. In other words, the extremely limited amount of materials which are available to us, as well as the obvious unreliability of most of these materials, has prompted some scholars to proclaim that it is simply impossible to arrive at any positive results as regards the lost works of Aristotle, and that it is sheer folly to pursue this kind of investigation which, in their opinion, is bound to end in utter and wasteful failure. In another place, the present author has attempted to answer these critics—an answer which might be appropriate to an introduction to a work discussing the lost compositions of Aristotle:[21]

> It is preferable to have tried, in a spirit of disciplined and
> competent optimism, and with the aid of whatever relevant
> materials one may reasonably muster, to recover . . . any and all

of the lost work of the early Aristotle—no matter how far one may actually go astray—than not to try at all. Perhaps such a suggestion is too 'revolutionary' with some timid, 'conservative' or unimaginative souls who always shy away from novel conjectures and reasonable hypotheses. It should be borne in mind, however, that every bit of decent human progress throughout the ages has ultimately been the result of some 'revolutionary recklessness' proceeding along lines of valiant though educated and intelligent conjectures. Those who are perennially opposed to novel ideas and adventurous undertakings may not gloat whenever one of the 'reckless optimists' should stumble or commit errors. Those who never 'get off the ground' and who never even dream of taking the 'high road' of intellectual vistas cannot possibly take a fall. But neither will they ever experience the deep satisfaction of intellectual adventure which carries us beyond the confines of routinized knowledge. Hence, they should not belittle those who reach out for the seemingly unattainable.

Chapter I is an attempt to establish the probable dates of composition of some of the more important or, at least, better known lost works of Aristotle. Here, as in most of the following chapters, reasonable hypotheses are employed to reach certain tentative conclusions which might not be far from the actual truth. Chapter II is a short survey as well as a brief discussion of some of the so-called minor and less-known lost works of Aristotle. Because of their presumed insignificance, these particular compositions have so far received little attention.[22] Since only a few and, on the whole, relatively unimportant fragments of these so-called minor works have been uncovered—and this is probably the main reason why they are often, but undeservedly, referred to as 'minor,' 'less-known' or 'less important' lost works—little if anything can be said about their philosophic content or doctrinal significance. Chapter III deals with the *Gryllus or On Rhetoric*, in all likelihood the first major literary effort of Aristotle. The *Gryllus* is primarily a discussion of the true nature and proper use of rhetoric, while at the same time it is a polemic against Isocrates and his particular brand of rhetoric and philosophy. Chapters IV and V tackle the problems connected with the *Eudemus or On the Soul*. Chapter IV suggests that the *Eudemus* is primarily a *consolatio mortis* concerned with the immortality of the soul. Chapter V seeks to explain this immortality on the basis of the soul's substantiality. Chapter VI attempts to reconstruct the essential, or better, the likely content of the Aristotelian *On Justice*, which is probably the most extensive of all early dialogues and in all likelihood one of the most elusive and most difficult works to retrieve and interpret.

Chapters VII, VIII, IX and X discuss some of the problems connected with the *Protrepticus*, which is perhaps the best known composition from among the lost works of Aristotle. Chapter VII, in particular, recounts the many (and often conflicting) scholarly efforts to retrieve and reconstruct the *Protrepticus*. Chapter VIII insists that, contrary to a widely held opinion, fragment 13 (Walzer, Ross), which in the past has uniformly been assigned to the *Protrepticus*, probably should be credited to the Aristotelian *Politicus*. Chapter IX is an attempt to find a reasonable explanation for the puzzling problem of why Aristotle addressed so important a composition as the *Protrepticus* to Themison of Cyprus, a relatively insignificant person. Chapter X points out that in the *Protrepticus*, Aristotle makes use of the panegyric analogy as well as of the 'three basic ways of life' in order to explain and illustrate the meaning of the term 'philosopher' or 'philosophy.' Chapter XI turns upon the problem of the Absolute Good in the *Politicus* and upon the ultimate function of the Absolute Good as the final normative standard.

Chapters XII, XIII, XIV, XV and XVI attempt to analyze certain topics connected with the highly problematic *On Philosophy*. Chapter XII, in particular, tries to establish the likely date of this most important dialogue. Chapter XIII investigates the particular manner in which Aristotle essayed to prove the existence of God through the orderly and beautiful universe, thus devising the first articulate cosmological or teleological proof for the existence of God. Chapter XIV discusses in detail the Aristotelian concept of God, a difficult and somewhat confusing problem because of the obviously inadequate and distorted manner in which this involved problem has been recorded, communicated and discussed by Cicero. Chapter XV points out that in the *On Philosophy* Aristotle advances a rather unique doctrine of the soul, wholly different from, and ultimately wholly incompatible with, that expounded in the *De Anima*, as well as somewhat different from that advanced in the *Eudemus or On the Soul*. Chapter XVI investigates possible points of contact between Aristotle's *On Philosophy* (and some other writings of Aristotle) and Zoroastrian teachings. Chapter XVII not only attempts to show that in his *On Kingship* Aristotle was highly critical of Plato's notion of the 'philosopher king' but also tries to explain the particular reasons for Aristotle's rejection of Plato's utopian political ideal. Volume II ends with a brief conclusion reiterating the close interplay between Aristotle's life and philosophic work, the far-reaching impact which Plato's philosophy in general had on Aristotle, and the effects of Plato's injunction to translate intellectual achievements into reformatory action.

Under the heading of 'Werner Jaeger and the Reconstruction of Aristotle's Lost Works,' a lengthy Postscript discusses and evaluates Jaeger's contributions to the identification, retrieval and possible reconstruction of some of Aristotle's lost early works. It is only befitting that an investigation such as the present book should contain a memorial honoring the greatest Aristotelian scholar of our times and, perhaps, of all times.

But let the reader beware: like Volume I, which is not intended to be an exhaustive biography of Aristotle in the traditional sense of the term, but rather a critical discussion of certain incidents which appear to have been the salient events in the life of the Stagirite, Volume II is not a coherent and exhaustive account and analysis, nor is it a comprehensive presentation of his lost works. It is merely a somewhat eclectic collection of discussions focusing on certain limited though probably crucial problems connected with some of these lost works. In this sense, the appropriate subtitle of Volume II might well have been *Varia Aristotelica*.

Admittedly, not all of Aristotle's lost works are analyzed or discussed here in detail. Such important compositions as the *On the Good* or the *On (the) Ideas*, to mention two flagrant instances, are not investigated,[23] although in Chapter I an attempt is made to establish the approximate dates of these two works. There is only one valid explanation for such a flagrant omission, namely, the admission, already stated previously, that Volume II of this book is primarily an eclectic discussion of certain limited aspects of the almost limitless problems inherent in some of Aristotle's lost works. No attempt is made here to discuss any of the doctrinal treatises or *pragmateia* incorporated in the traditional *Corpus Aristotelicum*. In the general Preface to this work, it has already been mentioned that the *Corpus Aristotelicum* deserves renewed attention and further investigation in regard to the authenticity or Aristotelian authorship—in part or *in toto*—of some of these treatises. Such an undertaking, which would touch the very roots of Aristotelian scholarship and Aristotelian tradition in general, however, is outside the limited scope of this book. Nevertheless, the investigations presented here may perhaps contribute some useful materials or some stimulating ideas and challenges to a further inquiry into the authenticity of at least certain parts of the *Corpus Aristotelicum*. Volume I, for instance, might indicate that Aristotle's many and often prolonged involvements in some of the major political events connected with the rise of Macedonia during the reigns of King Philip and King Alexander may in fact not have been conducive to the production of so large a literary output as the *Corpus Aristotelicum* would indicate. Volume II, again, might suggest that to a significant extent (though with certain unmistakable modifications) Aristotle was a Platonist, at least until about 348 B.C., and that he might have remained a Platonist for the remainder of his life. Considering his many involvements in political matters after 348 B.C., it is conceivable that he might never have found the time or have had the intellectual leisure to become an 'Aristotelian.' Like so many views expressed in this book, this particular suggestion, too, is still pure hypothesis based upon a number of 'educated conjectures.' In the light of the present-day status of Aristotelian scholarship in general, and especially of historical scholarship in particular (not to mention the desperate paucity of reliable sources relating to the lost early works), almost everything we profess to know about Aristotle or about his writings and intellectual outlook is probably conjecture or hypothesis in one form or another.

# Chapter I

# The Probable Dates of Some of Aristotle's Lost Works*

The conjectural dating of the lost works of Aristotle is a difficult and, in a way, thankless and even dangerous undertaking. Whoever attempts this task is faced with a number of almost insurmountable obstacles: there are few surviving 'fragments' of these lost works and their content is frequently obscure. The manner as well as the form in which they have been transmitted by ancient and early Christian authors or critics is of greatly varying quality. Frequently this tends to confuse and mislead the reader, for, barring a few instances, these 'fragments' are not, as some people seem to surmise, *verbatim* citations from Aristotle's original texts. They are disjointed excerpts or doxographical references which as often as not reflect the philosophic conviction (or lack of such) of the reporter rather than the philosophy expounded by Aristotle. To further aggravate this dismal situation, many of these reporters or doxographers, due to negligence or ineptitude, badly garble, distort and even falsify (in many instances unintentionally) the Aristotelian original. Moreover, we can never be certain whether or not a particular 'fragment,' which traditionally has been credited to a particular lost work of Aristotle, actually belongs to this composition. Such are, in brief, some of the many problems anyone will face when he attempts to establish the approximate dates of some of the lost works of Aristotle.

Almost unanimous consensus recognizes the *Gryllus*[1] to be the first, or at least the first important, publication of Aristotle.[2] The dating of this particular work is greatly facilitated by a number of fairly reliable ancient sources which recount the occasion that prompted its composition. Gryllus (or Grylus), the son of Xenophon, heroically died in a cavalry skirmish which preceded the battle of Mantinea in the summer of 362 B.C.[3] In the honored memory of the young hero, as well as in order to ingratiate themselves with the rich and influential Xenophon, numerous professional rhetoricians, among them the famous Isocrates himself, wrote eulogies and epitaphs. Some of these eulogies apparently

were obsequious, intended primarily to please the father.[4] In his
*Gryllus*, we are told, Aristotle castigates these authors for having
degraded rhetoric by using and abusing it for irrational appeals to
emotion and passion. It is this information which enables us to date the
*Gryllus* fairly accurately. Gryllus died in the summer of 362 B.C., a fact
which furnishes an absolute *tempus post quod* of the composition of the
*Gryllus*. It must also be assumed that the many 'obsequious eulogies' to
which the sources allude were written a short time after Gryllus' death,
presumably one and, perhaps, two years after the event. For it was only
then that Aristotle launched his denunciations of these flatterers. Hence,
it would be reasonable to maintain that the *Gryllus* could not have been
composed much before the year 360–59 B.C., and, perhaps, a little later.

To establish the approximate *tempus ante quod* of the *Gryllus*, however, is somewhat more difficult. We know, for instance, that in the
fifties Aristotle began to teach rhetoric in the Academy.[5] It is also safe
to assume that he was entrusted with conducting such an independent
'course' because in his *Gryllus* he had demonstrated to the satisfaction
of Plato and the Academy not only his ability and willingness to
disagree publicly with the mighty Isocrates, but also the 'orthodoxy'
of his views as to what constitutes true rhetoric (as Plato had expounded
it in the *Phaedrus*). Hence, the composition of the *Gryllus* might have
been considered adequate proof of his qualification as a successful
teacher of rhetoric. F. Solmsen[6] and I. Düring[7] are of the opinion that
Aristotle offered this 'course' somewhere between the years 360 and
355. In view of the fact that Aristotle completed his 'preliminary' or
'pre-philosophical' studies about 357, it might be appropriate, however, to date this 'course' closer to the year 355. This, then, would
suggest the year 355, or thereabouts, as the most reasonable *tempus ante
quod*. But there is another piece of evidence which might assist us in
establishing the *tempus ante quod* of the *Gryllus*: Cephisodorus, the
disciple and apologist of Isocrates, composed an *Against Aristotle*, presumably also a 'rebuttal' of Aristotle's *Gryllus*.[8] In this composition,
Cephisodorus, among other matters, reprimands Aristotle for having
criticized and condemned the rhetoric of Isocrates. On the strength of the
evidence found in Dionysius of Halicarnassus, *Epistola ad Cn. Pompeium
1*, Düring assumes that the *Against Aristotle*, which was probably
provoked by the *Gryllus*, was written about 360 B.C.[9] It might be
advisable, however, to move the date of the *Against Aristotle* to *c.* 356,
or even later. Moreover, around 353–52 Isocrates wrote his *Antidosis*,
which undoubtedly was also a defense against his detractors, including
probably the young Aristotle.[10] From all these indications and 'edu-

2

cated guesses,' it might be inferred that the years between 358 and 356 constitute the *tempus ante quod,* and the year 360–59 the most likely *tempus post quod* of the *Gryllus.*[11]

The *On (the) Ideas* or *On Ideas* (in one book),[12] it is commonly believed, was in some way connected with, or stimulated by, Plato's *Parmenides* or, perhaps, by Plato's lecture or lectures 'On the Good.'[13] H. Karpp suggests that this work is anterior to Book A of the *Metaphysics,* and that it must be dated during the Academic period of Aristotle.[14] H. Philippson, on the other hand, thinks that it is prior to Plato's *Parmenides,*[15] which is commonly dated about 364–63 or 363–62 B.C.[16] Needless to say, Philippson's thesis is difficult to maintain since, aside from denying the dependence of the *On (the) Ideas* on the Platonic *Parmenides,* it would assign the *On (the) Ideas* to the earliest years of Aristotle's studies at the Academy. Conversely, P. Wilpert insists that the *On (the) Ideas* constitutes Aristotle's 'rejection' of Plato's Separate Ideas.[17] Since, according to Wilpert, in the *Eudemus* as well as in the *Protrepticus* Aristotle apparently still accepts Plato's basic teachings as regards the Separate Ideas—the *Eudemus* was composed approximately in 352 or 351, and the *Protrepticus* between 352 and 350[18]—he concludes that the *On (the) Ideas* must be posterior to the death of Plato, which occurred in 348–47 B.C., but anterior to Book A of the *Metaphysics.* Hence, Book A of the *Metaphysics,* which seems to 'cite' from the *On (the) Ideas,* would also have to be dated some time after 348–47 B.C. Some aspects of Wilpert's thesis, which also seem to ignore the fact that the *On Philosophy* is in all likelihood posterior to the *On (the) Ideas,*[19] in part had already been stressed by W. Jaeger. Jaeger insists, however, that the *On (the) Ideas* (and Book A of the *Metaphysics*) is definitely anterior to the death of Plato[20] and, hence, anterior to the *On Philosophy,* which he dates shortly after the death of Plato.

P. Moraux, who makes a determined effort to establish the exact date of the *On (the) Ideas,*[21] conjectures that this work was written before the death of Plato, but certainly after 355–54, the year in which, according to Moraux, Eudoxus of Cnidus is said to have died.[22] Likewise, D. J. Allan puts the *On (the) Ideas* prior to the death of Plato.[23] On the other hand, I. Düring suggests that in the *On (the) Ideas* Aristotle takes issue with Eudoxus, the 'acting scholarch' of the Academy during Plato's second sojourn in Syracuse (367–365/64 B.C.). At the same time, Düring maintains, the *On (the) Ideas* is related to Plato's *Parmenides,* which was composed shortly after Plato's return from Syracuse in 365–64 B.C. The *On (the) Ideas,* he alleges, is really part of that major 'intramural discussion' among the members of the Academy over the nature and function of the Platonic Separate Ideas, which probably began soon after (and perhaps even before) Plato's return, and of which the *Parmenides* is but one literary manifestation. Hence, Düring concludes, the *On (the) Ideas* must be dated in the vicinity of the year 360—an unlikely early date, although the particular occasion he assigns to the composition of this work is wholly persuasive.[24] It must be borne in mind, however, that Düring's relatively early dating is in part prompted by his determination to disprove Jaeger's 'evolutionary thesis' concerning the gradual development of Aristotle's basic philosophic thought. It is influenced by his sustained efforts to prove that practically from the very moment he entered the Academy (in 367 B.C.) Aristotle was an 'Aristotelian' and, hence, must have been critical of Plato's fundamental philosophic position.

After carefully examining the surviving fragments of the *On (the) Ideas* and evaluating the different scholarly interpretations of these fragments and the ancient references to this work, as well as after analyzing the many and often penetrating suggestions as to how this dialogue should be dated, one might propose: (a) that the *On (the) Ideas* was composed while Aristotle was still a member of the Academy, that is, prior to the year 348–47 B.C.; (b) that in all likelihood this dialogue is anterior to Book A of the *Metaphysics*;[25] (c) that since the *On (the) Ideas* is definitely related to, or, better, influenced by, Plato's *Parmenides*, it must be posterior to the latter; and (d) that the *On (the) Ideas* apparently attempts to 'replace' the traditional Platonic Separate Ideas with 'first principles.' It seems that such a 'transition' from Ideas to 'first principles' was seriously discussed among members of the Academy after (and perhaps even before) the publication of the *Parmenides* and, more likely, after the publication of Plato's *Sophist* and *Statesman*. (e) The *Sophist* and the *Statesman* can be dated about the year 360, or a little later. (f) Only about 357 did Aristotle complete his 'preparatory' or 'pre-philosophic' studies in order to tackle 'pure philosophy.' (g) In all likelihood it was only about 357 that Aristotle was admitted to the intimate circle of advanced or initiated members of the Academy who seriously, but not always approvingly, discussed certain problems connected with Plato's philosophy.

Hence, it would be quite fair to assume that the reasonable *tempus post quod* for dating the *On (the) Ideas* is probably the year 357–56. A more thorough and, incidentally, more critical 'investigation' of the foundations of Plato's philosophy was perhaps Aristotle's first advanced work in pure philosophy, carried out after his 'graduation' from his preparatory studies. Perhaps, after having been admitted to the

4

'graduate level' of philosophic inquiry, he was encouraged to take an active part in the great discussion of the Separate Ideas which enlivened the Academy during the fifties. The *On (the) Ideas* might very well be the product of this active participation. It will be remembered that in 357 Aristotle was twenty-seven years old. He had already attracted some attention by the publication of the *Gryllus*,[26] in which he struck what seems to have been a successful blow for the Academy against Isocrates, the rival of the Academy. It was, perhaps, this first literary success which entitled (and encouraged) him actively to contribute his own suggestions to the great intramural debate over the Separate Ideas of Plato. Hence, it could also be argued that the *On (the) Ideas* is, in all likelihood, the first indication of Aristotle's intellectual independence and 'philosophic secession' from Plato. For this very reason, the proper dating of the *On (the) Ideas* is of critical importance.

It is probably even more difficult to establish with any degree of certainty the likely *tempus ante quod* of the composition of the *On (the) Ideas*. We are justified in surmising that this dialogue is approximately contemporary with, though in all likelihood slightly anterior to, the *On the Good*, anterior to the *Protrepticus* and certainly anterior to the *On Philosophy*. As will be shown presently, the *On the Good* was probably written between 357 and 355; the *Protrepticus* probably between 352 and 350; and the *On Philosophy* between 350–49 (or 348) and *c.* 347.[27] Hence, it might be reasonable to date the *On (the) Ideas* about 357–56 or, perhaps, slightly later.[28] Needless to say, in view of the extreme difficulty of determining not only the *tempus post quod*, but also the *tempus ante quod* of the *On (the) Ideas*, this approximate date is highly conjectural.

Tradition has it that the composition of the *On the Good*[29] is related to, or is stimulated by, a 'lecture' on, or a public discussion of, 'the Good' or of 'the One,' delivered by Plato (in the Piraeus),[30] presumably shortly after his return from his third journey to Syracuse in 360 B.C. It is also held that Speusippus, Xenocrates, Heracleides of Pontus, Aristotle and others attended this lecture which, according to tradition, apparently disappointed many listeners, and that some of these listeners, including Aristotle, subsequently wrote essays criticizing some of the main theses advanced by Plato.[31] It seems, therefore, that the dating of Plato's lecture might supply the *tempus post quod* for establishing the date of the Aristotelian *On the Good*.[32] Unfortunately, we possess no means of ascertaining the exact date this lecture was delivered, except perhaps the unsupported surmise that this happened after Plato's return in 360. More recently, J. Stenzel has succeeded in establishing certain significant connections between Aristotle's *On the Good* and Plato's *Philebus*.[33] Stenzel's theories have found the support of W. D. Ross,[34] A. Mansion, P. Moraux[35] and H. D. Saffrey.[36] While Ross, Mansion and Moraux relate the *On the Good* to the *Philebus*, Saffrey also conjectures that it is posterior to the Platonic *Timaeus*, but certainly anterior to the Aristotelian *On Philosophy*,[37] a thesis which is corroborated by considerable ancient testimony.[38] The *Timaeus* was probably written about 360–58, while Plato's lecture 'On the Good' was in all likelihood delivered some time after the completion of the *Timaeus*,[39] presumably in 357 or 356. We possess no conclusive evidence, however, to support this assumption.[40]

Thus, it would seem reasonable to surmise that the proper *tempus post quod* for the *On the Good* is about 357–56.[41] This date, however, remains wholly conjectural. In determining the *tempus ante quod*, on the other hand, we must begin with the Aristotelian *On Philosophy* which, as shall be shown presently,[42] was probably written somewhere between *c.* 350–49 (or 348) and 347.[43] The *On Philosophy* (Book II) presupposes the *On the Good* in that the former takes up, and probably enlarges upon, some of the topics already discussed in the *On the Good*.[44] When determining the *tempus ante quod* of the *On the Good* it might, however, be better to rely on the *Protrepticus*. The *Protrepticus*, it will be pointed out later, was in all likelihood written about 352–50.[45] It has been claimed that in the *Protrepticus* Aristotle apparently resumed the discussion of some problems already treated in the *On the Good*. Hence, the *Protrepticus* would have to be posterior to the *On the Good*.[46] Furthermore, as has already been stated, the *On the Good* is approximately contemporary with, or perhaps slightly posterior to, the *On (the) Ideas*, which has tentatively been dated shortly after the year 357. Thus, it might be proper to date the *On the Good* about 357/56–355.[47]

The dating of the *On Justice*[48] appears to be particularly difficult. Undoubtedly, this dialogue was modelled on Plato's *Republic*[49] (which in antiquity had the sub-title of *On Justice*), although it seems to reject or, at least, modify some of the notions advanced by Plato.[50] On the strength of certain reasonable similarities between the psychology of the *On Justice* and the psychology underlying the Aristotelian *Protrepticus* (dated between 352 and 350) and the Aristotelian *Eudemus* (about 352), P. Moraux tries to fix the date for the composition of the *On Justice* some time after 353–52,[51] that is, in close proximity to the *Eudemus* and the *Protrepticus*. As a matter of fact, Moraux believes that in the light of its 'more realistic attitude,' the *On Justice* is actually posterior to the *Protrepticus* and, concomitantly, posterior to the *Eudemus*.[52] If Moraux's thesis were correct, then the *On Justice* would have been written after 352–50. It might be better, however, to conjecture that the *On Justice* is approximately contemporary with the *Protrepticus*, if not slightly anterior to it. I. Düring is probably correct when he tentatively dates the *On Justice* about the year 355 (or slightly later),[53] that is, some time prior to the *Protrepticus*, and approximately one or two years anterior to the *Eudemus*.[54]

In dating the *On Justice* it must be borne in mind that this dialogue was modelled after the Platonic *Republic*. Hence, the *Republic* furnishes a *tempus post quod*, although certainly not a very useful one. In addition to the Platonic *Republic*, the *On Justice* also takes account of Plato's *Statesman* which must be dated shortly after 360. Thus, one might safely locate the *On Justice* after 360–59, or after 357–56. The *tempus ante quod* of the *On Justice*, however, seems to be even more elusive. It can reasonably be asserted that there are some doctrinal similarities and, at the same time, some doctrinal differences, between the *On Justice* and the *Protrepticus*. Although P. Moraux wishes to date the *On Justice* after the *Protrepticus*,[55] it might be better to date it prior to the *Protrepticus* and, hence, closer to Plato's *Republic* and *Statesman*. If this could be proved, then the *Protrepticus* would supply the *tempus ante quod* for the *On Justice*, and the period for its composition would be the years between 357–56 and 352. Düring's tentative effort to locate the *On Justice* about 355,[56] might, after all, be the most sensible suggestion.

It will be noted that the date of Aristotle's *Eudemus or On the Soul*[57] is proximate (*pace* O. Gigon) to the death of Eudemus of Cyprus, the close friend of the young Aristotle.[58] In June (?) of 354, Dion was assassinated by Callippus, who installed himself as tyrant of Syracuse and ruled the city for a little over one year (354–53). In 354 some of Dion's friends and partisans, among them Eudemus, apparently rallied to avenge Dion and recover Syracuse. Several armed clashes occurred and in one of these encounters, which probably took place late in 354 or early in 353, Eudemus was killed.[59] The news of Eudemus' (and Dion's) death, in all likelihood reached Athens and the Academy late (?) in 353. This news prompted Aristotle to compose his *Eudemus*, which is actually a *consolatio mortis* as well as a memorial, written in a spirit reminiscent of—and probably influenced by—Plato's *Phaedo*, which likewise could be called a *consolatio mortis*.[60] Hence, it is reasonable to date the *Eudemus* about 352 B.C. (or, perhaps, a little later), although not all scholars find this date acceptable. O. Gigon, who uses an analogy with the time lapse of about ten years between the death of Socrates (in 399 B.C.) and the composition of the Platonic *Phaedo*, is of the opinion that the *Eudemus* must be dated several years after the death of Eudemus of Cyprus, and certainly much later than 353–52.[61]

According to W. Jaeger, the *Protrepticus*[62] is wholly Platonic. Jaeger contends that it was written to uphold and defend the philosophic and educational ideal or *paideia* of Plato and the Academy—an ideal which was founded on φρόνησις, (or the 'theoretic life')—against the vociferous pretensions of Isocrates and his school of rhetoric.[63] Hence, Jaeger would date the *Protrepticus* during Aristotle's 'Academic period.' The reasonableness of this assumption cannot be contested. W. Theiler, who sees in the *Protrepticus* certain unmistakable indications of Aristotle's incipient independence from Plato and Platonic teachings, would date it close to the year 348–47.[64] The proper date of the *Protrepticus* was established more accurately and more convincingly when scholars discovered the obvious connections between Aristotle's *Protrepticus* and Isocrates' *Antidosis*.[65] Since the date of the *Antidosis* can safely be placed about the year 353–52, the only major question that remained to be settled was whether the *Protrepticus* preceded the *Antidosis* or *vice versa*— whether the *Antidosis* provoked the *Protrepticus*, or whether the *Protrepticus* caused Isocrates to launch the *Antidosis*.

B. Einarson maintains that the *Protrepticus* is definitely posterior to the *Antidosis* in that it constitutes a 'rebuttal' of the latter. Hence, Einarson concludes, the *Protrepticus* must have been written shortly after 352.[66] P. von der Mühll, on the other hand, arrives at the opposite conclusion. He believes that the *Antidosis*, which he dates in 353, is a 'reply' to the *Protrepticus* and its philosophic pretensions. Thus, he would date it shortly before the year 353.[67] F. Nuyens, again, ignoring the connections between the *Antidosis* and the *Protrepticus*, claims that in the *Protrepticus* Aristotle propagates an 'instrumentalist' doctrine as regards the soul-body relation. This, according to Nuyens, indicates that the *Protrepticus* is definitely 'post-Platonic,' and that it must be dated after the death of Plato.[68] Nuyens' thesis, as has been shown, would implicitly deny that the *Protrepticus* is vitally related to, or influenced and determined by, the *Antidosis* of Isocrates.

J. Zürcher insists that the *Protrepticus* was composed some time after Aristotle had left the Academy (in 348 B.C.),[69] thus taking up the theory advanced by W. Theiler.[70] Zürcher bases his thesis on the argument that this composition reflects a very mature view on life in general, and that it is addressed to a ruling king—and no fledgling philosopher would dare personally to address a king. G. Müller likewise maintains that the *Protrepticus* is a relatively late work, composed some time after Aristotle had seceded from the Platonic Academy, in that it reflects notions very similar to, and even identical with, certain ideas expressed in the *Nicomachean Ethics*.[71] G. Reale, however, rejects Zürcher's thesis by pointing out that in 352–50 Aristotle already was in his thirties and, hence, a 'mature' thinker; that in the *Protrepticus* he spoke in the name and with the authority of the Platonic Academy rather than in his own name; and that Themison, the person to whom the *Protrepticus* is addressed, was at best an unimportant and little known 'ruler.'[72]

I. Düring and R. Stark likewise believe that the *Protrepticus* displays a 'philosophic maturity' and an independence of mind which is indicative of Aristotle's later (doctrinal) treatises. The *Protrepticus*, Düring and Stark argue, is primarily concerned with practical (political) action and issues. It does not, as Plato would have it, one-sidedly extoll theoretic (contemplative) wisdom and the 'theoretic life' at the expense of practical experience and goal-determined action.[73] Moreover, Düring insists that in the *Protrepticus* Aristotle alludes to a novel teleology which is wholly incompatible with Plato's doctrine of the Separate Ideas. According to Düring, in the *Protrepticus*, Aristotle also posits a kind of efficient cause quite similar to that advocated in Aristotle's *Physics*.[74] From all this, Düring infers that the *Protrepticus* must be posterior to the *Topics*, to Books I and II of the *Rhetoric*, to certain parts of the *Physics* and to the two *Analytics*.[75] In other words, he maintains nothing less than that the *Protrepticus* is indicative of the fact that at the time of its composition, Aristotle had already found as well as formulated his own independent and final philosophic standpoint—a philosophy substantially different from Platonism and, on the whole, incompatible with Plato's basic teachings. Düring gives special emphasis to his thesis by proclaiming that there exist no real differences between the *Protrepticus* as such and the later doctrinal treatises of Aristotle,[76] thus radically denying the basic tenets of W. Jaeger.[77] Düring concludes that the *Protrepticus* must be a fairly late work among the early compositions of the Stagirite. In arguing that the *Protrepticus* professes essentially the same ethical doctrines as does the *Nicomachean Ethics*, F. Dirlmeier seems to agree with Düring's basic views and, by implication, with Düring's chronology.[78] Similarly, there are other scholars who, either by claiming or disclaiming the Platonism of the Aristotelian *Protrepticus*, attempt to determine the proper date of this important work.[79]

Unfortunately, all these learned and penetrating discussions do not contribute very much to the proper dating of the *Protrepticus*. However, one thing seems to be rather firmly established: the *Protrepticus* is related in some way to the *Antidosis* of Isocrates, and the *Antidosis* was published about 353-52 B.C. Apparently these two important facts cannot effectively be disputed. The only problem yet to be resolved is whether the *Protrepticus* induced Isocrates to launch his *Antidosis*, or whether the publication of the *Antidosis* in 353–52 prompted Aristotle to write the *Protrepticus*.[80] The solution of this problem would determine whether the *Protrepticus* was composed before or after the year 353–52. It appears, however, that the stronger arguments are on the side of those scholars who insist that the publication of Isocrates' *Antidosis* was taken by Aristotle as a serious challenge to the Academy and the philosophy it stood for. In any event, so it appears, Aristotle responded to this challenge by writing the *Protrepticus*. Accordingly, the year 353–52 would seem to constitute the reasonable *tempus post quod* for the composition of the *Protrepticus*.

The *tempus ante quod* of the *Protrepticus*, on the other hand, is rather difficult to establish, unless one should conjecture that the appearance of the *Antidosis* forced an immediate rebuttal, which with Aristotle assumed the form of a λόγος προτρεπτικός. Perhaps the *On Philosophy* of Aristotle might supply such a *tempus ante quod* or, still better, a somewhat 'remote' *tempus ante quod*. As shall be shown presently, the *On Philosophy* was in all likelihood written between *c.* 350–49 (or 348) and *c.* 347 B.C. Since the *On Philosophy* is probably later than the *Protrepticus*, it would be reasonable to date the latter somewhere between 352 and 350 B.C., or simply about the year 352 B.C. In light of the available evidence, this date, if given a little leeway in either direction, seems to be most reasonable and most convincing.

Another possible clue for determining the date of the *Protrepticus* may be found in the fact that this composition apparently was addressed to Themison of Cyprus.[81] Isocrates, the rival and foe of the Platonic Academy, for some time had exerted a dominant intellectual influence on certain people on the island of Cyprus, and especially with the Evagorids, the powerful rulers of Cypriot Salamis. In 352–51 B.C., the Greek settlers on Cyprus revolted against their Phoenician and Persian overlords, who tried to suppress all Greek influence on the island. To the general dismay of the Greeks, the Evagorids, the friends and pupils of Isocrates, sided with the Persians. This was a most opportune moment for Aristotle and for the Academy to deal Isocrates, who had been highly embarrassed by the treasonable conduct of his friends, a crushing blow and to break his intellectual stranglehold on Cyprus. Moreover, it offered a unique chance to gain for the Academy an intellectual foothold on the island. This might well be a reasonable explanation why so significant a work as the *Protrepticus* is addressed to the Cypriot Themison, a relatively insignificant man: Themison was to play the role of a 'bridgehead' for the intellectual invasion of Cyprus by the Platonic Academy; and the proper time for launching such an invasion was the anti-Persian revolt on Cyprus in 352–51 B.C., which, thanks to the deportment of the Evagorids, had seriously damaged the position and prestige of Isocrates.[82]

The only significant passage or fragment which might give us a reasonable clue as to how the *Politicus*[83] might be dated is the statement which insists that 'in the second book of his *Politicus* Aristotle proclaims that the Good is the most exact measure or standard among all measures or standards,'[84] or 'that for all things the Good is the most exact measure or standard.'[85] If we are to accept the version 'that for all things the Good is the most exact measure or standard,' in other words, if we adopt R. Stark's translation (and interpretation), then we might also maintain that at the time he wrote the *Politicus*, Aristotle had already abandoned Plato's notion of the Separate Idea of the Good (or of the One) which, like the Idea of the One of the later Platonic dialogues, is for Plato the 'most exact Idea' among all Ideas or 'Exemplars.' Hence, the *Politicus* might well be dated after the *Protrepticus*, that is, after 352–50. It will be noted that the 'interpretation' or translation suggested by R. Stark declares the Good to be the ultimate and most exact measure or standard of all things as well as for all actions. Since the *Politicus* is a political tract, and since it was probably modelled after Plato's *Statesman*, the Good which Aristotle had in mind here might also include the common Good. If this be the case, then Aristotle also manages to bring about a rapprochement of ethics and politics in maintaining that true politics is founded on the understanding of the ethical Good or, perhaps, the common Good. Such a notion, however, is rather close to what Aristotle had to say in the *Nicomachean Ethics*, where he insists that 'virtue and the good man as such are the measure of all things.'[86] It must be borne in mind, however, that in the *Philebus* as well as in the *Statesman*, Plato had attempted to reduce ethics (and politics) to 'an art of measuring,' in which the Good constitutes the final and, concomitantly, 'the most exact' measure or standard. All individual actions are evaluated (or measured) by the way in which they correspond to the absolute Good—according to Plato, the one single and ultimate value or criterion.[87] All these considerations and arguments only seem to strengthen the thesis that the *Politicus* is slightly anterior to the *On Philosophy*. Hence, it might be reasonable to surmise that the *Politicus* was written shortly after 350, and that it is perhaps contemporary with, or slightly anterior to, the *On Philosophy*, provided we accept the translation and interpretation suggested by R. Stark. However, if we should prefer the translation and interpretation proposed by W. Jaeger, then we might be compelled to date the *Politicus* somewhat earlier, that is, approximately contemporary with the *Protrepticus*.[88]

There is, however, an additional hypothesis as to the proper dating of the *Politicus*. In the *Gryllus*, Aristotle rejects the particular rhetoric of Isocrates and his school; and in the *Protrepticus*, he defends the general philosophic ideal of the Academy against the pretensions of Isocrates. Similarly, in the *Politicus*, he might have condemned the social or political philosophy recommended by Isocrates. We know that Isocrates propagated a practical-pragmatic or utilitarian attitude towards politics, and that he ridiculed the theoretic-ethical approach to politics and political science recommended by certain philosophers, including Plato and some members of the Early Academy. It appears, therefore, that in the *Politicus*, Aristotle attempts to reassert the philosophic-ethical approach to politics. Hence, he insists that the objective or absolute Good constitutes the ultimate as well as most reliable and most exact measure or criterion of all political thought and action. Aristotle also seems to maintain that it was the task of the true philosopher—a man much maligned by Isocrates—to determine and define this absolute criterion: the ultimate and universal objective Good. It would not be amiss, then, to conjecture that the Aristotelian *Politicus* is in fact a special reply (rejoinder) to the *Antidosis* of Isocrates—a 'special rebuttal' of the politico-ethical implications contained in the *Antidosis*.[89] If our thesis could be substantiated, then we would have to conclude that Aristotle actually wrote two 'rebuttals' to Isocrates' *Antidosis*: the *Protrepticus*, which is a defense of the general 'philosophic ideal of life' advocated by Plato and the Academy, and the *Politicus*, which as a kind of 'special pleading' is the re-affirmation of the moral implications of political thought and action. Since it has been shown that the *Antidosis* was written in 353–52, and since the *Protrepticus* probably was composed between 352 and 350, it might be reasonable, therefore, to date the *Politicus* about 350 B.C. or shortly thereafter. However, if we were to accept Iamblichus, *Protrepticus*, p. 55, line 7– p. 56, line 2 (Pistelli), that is, part of frag. 13, Walzer; frag. 13, Ross; frags. 48–50, Düring; and frags. 46–48, Chroust, as a fragment of the *Politicus* rather than of the Aristotelian *Protrepticus*, then we might have to revise this date by moving it closer to the year 352 or thereabouts, especially if we were to regard the *Politicus* as a rejoinder to the *Antidosis* of Isocrates.[90]

Since the likely date of the *On Philosophy*[91] will be treated in greater detail in Chapter XII,[92] it will not be necessary to discuss this problem here. In summation, the following may be asserted as to the probable date of the *On Philosophy*: this work is certainly later than the Platonic *Timaeus*. In all likelihood, it is also later than the Aristotelian *Protrepticus*,[93] which has been dated between 352 and 350. It is also reasonable to assume that it is later than the *Politicus*. Hence, the probable *tempus post quod* of the *On Philosophy* is approximately the year 350–49 and, perhaps, the early part of the year 348. Since the *On Philosophy* seems to be anterior to the *Epinomis* (which has been dated about 346), the year 347–46 appears to be the most likely *tempus ante quod*. In addition, it might also be contended that the *On Philosophy* is approximately contemporary with the last books of the Platonic *Laws*, and that in the summer of 348 Aristotle was compelled to flee Athens for political reasons (the capture of Olynthus by the Macedonians)[94]—an upsetting incident in the life of Aristotle which most certainly was not conducive to the composition of so important and so complex a work as the *On Philosophy*, especially, since the second half of 348 and the first half of 347 were spent by Aristotle in travel and resettlement in Asia Minor.[95] Consequently, the composition of the *On Philosophy* may tentatively be dated in the years between *c.* 350–49 and *c.* 348. W. Jaeger's method of dating this dialogue as well as the reasons he advances for so doing cannot be accepted, although the date he proposes certainly comes very close to what appears to be the historical truth.

The determination of the approximate dates of the other early Aristotelian (lost) writings or dialogues is an almost impossible and certainly frustrating task. The surviving fragments of these writings or dialogues are simply too meager and often too insignificant to permit even a sensible or 'educated' guess. Those works, however, of which we still possess sufficient and sufficiently significant fragments—fragments which permit us to form an intelligent opinion—can be dated with a reasonable degree of certainty, although here, too, we will frequently have to resort to calculated conjectures and persuasive hypotheses. Thus, it appears that the following dates—dates which also take into account that fact that it was only in *c.* 357 B.C. that Aristotle completed his 'preliminary' or 'pre-philosophical' studies, and that, due to 'political pressures,' he fled from Athens in the summer or early fall of 348—might possibly be accepted: the *Gryllus* was apparently written between 360–59 and 358–57 (or 356); the *On (the) Ideas* in 357–56; the *On the Good* between 357–56 and 355; the *On Justice* in *c.* 355 or shortly thereafter; the *Eudemus* in 352 (or 351); the *Protrepticus* between 352 and 350, and probably closer to the latter date; the *Politicus* perhaps shortly after 350 (or, perhaps, around 352–51); and the *On Philosophy* between 350–49 and 348. Needless to say, all these dates are at best tentative and hypothetical They still require further and certainly more solid confirmation. But, no matter how persuasive the evidence or argument that might be introduced in support of a particular date, there always will be well-founded dissent, reasoned disagreement and justified doubt about this date.

# Chapter II

# A Note on Some of the 'Minor Lost Works' of Aristotle*

The surviving fragments of Aristotle's earliest writings were for a long time sadly neglected and, in some instances, simply ignored. Although during recent years some of the 'more important' of these works—the *Protrepticus, Gryllus, On (the) Ideas, On the Good, Eudemus or On the Soul, On Justice* and the *On Philosophy*—have received some noteworthy scholarly attention,[1] the so-called 'minor' or 'lesser' lost compositions have frequently been declared unworthy of such consideration. They are, at best, relegated to somewhat meaningless collections of fragments.[2] In some instances, these fragments are assigned arbitrarily to certain titles of the earliest (lost) works of Aristotle, as they are listed in the ancient 'catalogues' of Aristotle's writings.[3] This astonishing and deplorable neglect not only has deprived the student of ancient philosophy of a more thorough understanding as well as a correct appraisal of the intellectual development of the Stagirite but probably also has denied him a fuller and more accurate appreciation of Aristotle's later philosophic views. Moreover, it may have fostered a wholly erroneous or partially defective notion of the history of ancient philosophy in general and of the diverse philosophic issues or problems discussed during the mid-fourth century B.C. in particular.

The several works briefly discussed here are the *On Prayer, On Education, On Pleasure, On Wealth, On Noble Birth, Sophist, To Alexander* (or, *To Alexander or On Colonization*) and the *Nerinthus*. These works are listed in the 'catalogue' of Diogenes Laertius, in that of the *Vita Aristotalis Hesychii* and, at least in part, in that of Ptolemy (-el-Garib).[4] V. Rose rather arbitrarily assigned certain fragments attributed to Aristotle to some of the titles enumerated in the 'catalogue' of Diogenes Laertius.[5] Or to put it differently: Rose simply decreed that such and such a fragment should be listed under such and such title.[6] Barring a few exceptions, the assignments made by Rose, it will be noted, were accepted and, in a way, 'canonized' by later scholars. To mention just one instance: Fragment 646, Rose (frag. 1, Ross) has been assigned to Aristotle's *On Kingship*, while fragment 648, Rose (frag. 1, Ross) has been assigned to the *To Alexander*. Since both fragments discuss essentially the same problem, it cannot be denied that they may both be assigned to either the *On Kingship* or to the *To Alexander* or, perhaps, to some other work or works of Aristotle. Nevertheless, for the sake of clarity and simplicity, we shall follow here Rose's traditional assignments, although doing so does not necessarily mean acceptance of his assignments.

The only extant and apparently authentic fragment of Aristotle's *On Prayer*[7] contains the rather cryptic observation that 'Aristotle had the notion of something (that there is something) above "pure intellect" (νοῦς) and above Being. This is clearly shown by his general assertion, found towards the end of his composition *On Prayer*, namely, that God is either "pure intellect" or something even above and beyond "pure intellect."'[8] From this brief statement it may be inferred that Aristotle, as he also implies in the third Book of his *On Philosophy*,[9] believes in as well as asserts the existence of a supreme 'incorporeal' Being which he identifies with 'pure intellect.' In short, the supreme God is 'pure mind' or, perhaps, *actus purus* (the 'mind of minds')[10] and, in fact, something beyond 'mind' (including perhaps the human mind?) in that He transcends sensibility and corporeal Being in the ordinary sense of the term.[11] In the latter sense, viewed from the ontological order, God is actually beyond the intellect and as such He is also beyond the (human) intellect which seeks to comprehend Him or Being in general—a notion which does not fully coincide with what Aristotle says, for instance, in the *Metaphysics*, but rather with some views held by Plato. Hence, in a certain way, this supreme God is also ineffable and possibly the Ineffable One. An interesting aspect of this fragment, it will be noted, is the following: according to Simplicius, Aristotle stated his proposition about the nature of God in a disjunctive form, that is, in an 'either-or (ἢ . . . ἢ καί) manner.' Moreover, he uses the indefinite 'something (τὶ)' when he defines the nature of God. This Aristotelian incertitude about the true nature of God seems to reflect the general incertitude which was typical of some ancient prayers addressing God by 'whatever Thy name may be (ὁπότερον ὄνομα),' or by 'whoever Thou may be (ὅστις εἶ).' This incertitude, which also reveals a degree of fear or doubt as well as a sense of inadequacy in the mind of the person who either prays to or speaks of God, appears to be reflected in Aristotle's statement about the nature of God.

If this be the case, then we might also conjecture that Aristotle's assertion that God 'is above and beyond "pure intellect"' as well as above and beyond Being may essentially be Platonic or, to be more exact, may contain a kind of 'summary' of Plato's fundamental theological views [12] to which Aristotle apparently subscribed at the time he wrote the *On Prayer*.[13] In *Republic* 509B, it will be remembered, Plato maintained that 'of the Good it may be said that it is not only the author of the knowledge of all things known, but also the author of their Being and essence, and yet the Good is not Being or essence, but something which by far transcends Being and essence.' Hence, when composing the *On Prayer*, Aristotle must have been of the opinion that Plato believed in the existence of an ultimate 'reality' [14] which not only transcends the 'order of the intellect,' but is also superior to this 'order' as well as to the 'order of Being.' Moreover, Cicero, *De Natura Deorum* I. 13. 33, contains the information that Aristotle had called God or the divine an 'intellect' (*mens*), that he considered the cosmos to be God, and that he had put 'some other God above the cosmos.' It is possible, therefore, that this 'other God' Who is 'above the cosmos,' is identical with the God Who, according to the *On Prayer*, is 'above and beyond "pure intellect"' as well as above and beyond ordinary Being. If this be so, then we might also surmise that Aristotle speaks here of the divine intellect and, perhaps, of the 'principle' of this divine intellect which is 'above and beyond' the divine intellect, as well as above and beyond all Being (as it is expressed in the divine cosmos). Aristotle's concept of God as something above and beyond 'pure intellect' and Being subsequently seems to have become one of the main philosophic issues, not only with Middle Platonism (Albinus), Neo-Platonism and with some of the late Hellenistic authors, but also with certain early Christian authors.[15]

While stating the existence of a Supreme Being, Aristotle seems to stress the 'pure intellectuality' ('spirituality'?) of God.[16] He also emphasizes the fact that God both is and transcends 'pure intellect' or 'pure mind' and, concomitantly, is beyond the universe (although He is also 'in' the universe), beyond Being and beyond the human intellect.[17] It might also be conjectured that, in keeping with his assertion of the pure intellectuality (or 'spirituality'?) of God, in his *On Prayer* Aristotle wishes to convey the notion that mortal man may approach God 'only in spirit' and pray to him only in and through the intellect. For, consonant with the Greek notion that only like can communicate with like,[18] the divine 'pure intellect' may be reached only through the intellect, that is, through intellectual (or 'spiritual'?) truth.[19] Or, as St. John has put it: 'God is Spirit ($\pi\nu\epsilon\hat{v}\mu\alpha$); and they that worship Him must worship Him in spirit and in truth.'[20] The *On Prayer*, then, is an eloquent example of Aristotle's basic religious convictions, declaratory of his piety.[21] As such, it provides us with a deeper insight not only into Aristotle the philosopher, but also into Aristotle the man.[22]

Of the Aristotelian *On Education*[23] only two[24] rather short fragments have survived: 'Florus . . . himself was haunted by many problems, and he communicated them to his associates, bearing out Aristotle's observation that such learning causes many vexations and much confusion (ταραχάς).'[25] The second fragment contains the information that 'Protagoras invented the shoulder-pad on which porters carry their loads—at least this is what Aristotle maintains in his treatise *On Education*. For he himself [*scil.*, Protagoras] had been a porter, as Epicurus states somewhere.[26] And this is how he [*scil.*, Protagoras] was brought to the attention of Democritus, who saw how skillfully he had tied together his bundle of woods.'[27] It appears that in the *On Education* Aristotle contends that the mere—haphazard and disorganized—accumulation of purely factual information without proper intellectual training, mental discipline and without a systematic (philosophic) 'point of reference' may breed confusion and, hence, may become an unbearable burden as well as a 'dangerous thing.'

Relying on Diogenes Laertius and Aulus Gellius, it might be contended that the *On Education* dealt primarily with, and advocated, philosophically structured thought, that is, scientific method rather than general indiscriminate learning. This seems to follow from the statement that Protagoras, by systematically (geometrically?) arranging his load, successfully managed to carry a surprisingly heavy burden. Disciplined and orderly thought, relying on philosophic articulation, on the other hand, is a great and lasting asset which transforms the heavy burden of haphazard acquisition of factual knowledge into something useful and even pleasant. In a certain way, the *On Education* might reflect what Plato had said (in the *Theaetetus* and in the *Republic*)[28] extolling the undeniable advantages of 'scientific' or philosophic thought over the mere accumulation of disjointed bits of information or polymathy. In other words, in the *On Education*, Aristotle stresses the decisive differences that exist between the quantitative and the qualitative aspects of human knowledge,[29] advocating the superiority of philosophic abstraction and generalization over unrelated concrete facts. In keeping with his well attested interest in, and concern with, empirical and historical facts, Aristotle may also have maintained here that, if properly employed and adequately organized, polymathy is not so much the undoing of philosophic thought as it is the wholesome result of the proper scientific or philosophic approach or, possibly, the starting point of philosophic inquiry. Structured polymathy is often the eloquent proof of the practical efficacy of a structured philosophy. The proper philosophic approach, then, may also increase the possible number of successful intellectual avenues leading to a more adequate understanding and appreciation of the frequently bewildering diversity of empirical reality[30] in that it converts diverse sensations into true empirical knowledge.

Aristotle may also have pointed out in the *On Education* that we may learn a great lesson from observation and from watching how certain things are done. Hence, true education is both theoretic study or deliberation and practical experience. More than that, he might have attempted to convey the notion that we can learn something even from the humblest of our fellow men or from the most insignificant of daily incidents. Some scholars also insist that the *On Education* is actually an ethico-political tract and, perhaps, a sort of 'mirror for princes.'[31]

Of the Aristotelian *On Pleasure*,[32] only a questionable and rather insignificant, as well as relatively uninformative, fragment has come down to us: 'Others call Philoxenus [of Leucas] a lover of fishes, but Aristotle refers to him simply as a "lover of good food." He [*scil.*, Aristotle] also writes in some place [in the *On Pleasure* (?), *note by the present author*] as follows: "When they are making speeches to crowded audiences they spend the whole day telling about marvelous events, and they tell these events to people who have just returned from the Phasis or the Borysthenes [*scil.*, two rivers in southern Russia, flowing into the Black Sea], although they themselves have read nothing except Philoxenus' *Banquet*, and not even the whole of that book."'[33] Relying on this extremely scanty piece of evidence, we may surmise that the *On Pleasure* chastizes those who, like so many uneducated or half-educated people, display a disproportionate interest in fanciful stories, far away places, vulgar achievements and gastronomical exploits.[34] That this particular fragment has been assigned to the *On Pleasure* may probably be attributed to the fact that in the *Eudemian Ethics*,[35] Philoxenus is mentioned as a 'lover of good food,' that is, as a person who derives his main pleasure from consuming extravagant foods.[36] However, since we actually know almost nothing about the *On Pleasure*, the assignment of Athenaeus, *Epitome* I 6D, to this early work is purely conjectural.[37] W. Jaeger[38] maintains that the problem of pleasure, which was to play a key role in Aristotle's later works of ethics, during the last years of Plato's scholarchate came to be the topic of an important and, it appears, prolonged as well as animated debate within the

Academy.[39] It seems that during this debate the hedonistic views of Eudoxus of Cnidus [40] (and Antisthenes) were pitted against the radically anti-hedonistic position taken by Speusippus.[41] Plato (as evidenced by the Platonic *Philebus*), Xenocrates and Aristotle, on the other hand, seem to have assumed a kind of intermediary position.[42] Speusippus,[43] Xenocrates [44] and Aristotle, Jaeger insists, were sufficiently stimulated by this debate to compose separate treatises on the subject, and, as a result of this debate, Plato wrote the *Philebus*.[45]

Of Aristotle's *On Wealth* [46] only four (and perhaps six or seven) fragments have so far been discovered: 'Of the majority of people, as Aristotle observes, some from sheer meanness do not make any use whatever of all their wealth, while others misuse it from sheer extravagance. The latter are forever slaves of their pleasures, while the former are slaves of their business affairs.' [47] Essentially the same idea reappears in Plutarch, *De Cupiditate Divitiarum* 8 (*Moralia* 527A), a passage which likewise has been considered a fragment of the Aristotelian *On Wealth*: 'Aristotle insists that some people do not at all use their wealth, while others misuse it, implying that both are wrong. The former derive no benefit from what they possess, and the latter only incur injury and disgrace.' [48] In the two fragments preserved by Plutarch, it will be noted, one may find a distinctly pessimistic attitude: wealth, as a rule, has a deleterious effect on men, and it is the exception that men should make good use of wealth, that is, make it subservient to a noble and morally acceptable purpose. Cicero, *De Officiis* II. 16. 56–7, a report which has been assigned to the *On Wealth*, points out that 'there is much weight and truth in Aristotle's reproaching us for not wondering at the extravagant sums of money spent in order to ingratiate the masses. That men besieged by an enemy should be compelled to pay a *mina* for a pint of plain water, this [Aristotle maintains] seems incredible when we first hear of it; and we all are surprised by this. But when we consider the particular circumstances, we condone such necessary practices. In these enormous and unchecked expenditures there is really nothing that surprises us, though there is no excuse that this was done from necessity, or that there is an increase in personal dignity [through spending extravagant sums of money in order to ingratiate oneself with the masses]. The delight of the masses is of short duration and, as a rule, is derived from the meanest of objects; and when satiation is achieved, the very memory of the pleasure vanishes. He [*scil.*, Aristotle] sums up the subject well when he observes that such practices gratify children, mere women, slaves and freemen who are like slaves. But they cannot possibly meet with the approval of a serious-minded man who weighs all events on the basis of rational judgment.'[49] And finally, Philodemus, in what is considered a fragment of the *On Wealth*, relates: 'This happened to Aristotle (as Metrodorus has shown) as regards his argument in his work *On Wealth* where he attempts to show that the good man is also a good money-maker, and the bad man a bad money-maker.'[50] Thus, while the fragments from Plutarch and Cicero emphasize the proper use of wealth, the fragment from Philodemus is concerned with the manner of acquiring wealth, a topic which is also discussed in Aristotle, *Politics* 1256 a 1 ff.

The two fragments transmitted by Plutarch, it appears, refer to one and the same source, namely, to the Aristotelian *On Wealth*. In both instances two different attitudes towards wealth are stated in essentially the same terms. In the case of the *De Cupiditate Divitiarum*, however, the moral significance rather than the causes of these two attitudes are the main issue. Cicero, on the other hand, contrasts the calculating spender who spends his wealth in order primarily to gain popular acclaim and public prestige, and the generous spender who uses his wealth to perform humanitarian and noble deeds.[51] According to Philodemus, Metrodorus insists that Aristotle was of the opinion that a 'business man,' politician or 'gatherer of earthly goods' could also be a good and honest man. Perhaps it is important to note that both Philodemus and Metrodorus are Epicureans and therefore fundamentally hostile towards Aristotle. A cursory study of Aristotle's *Politics* (1257 b 1–1258 b 7), however, seems to indicate that the Stagirite did not recommend the unrestrained acquisition of wealth; that he denounced those who were completely absorbed in the gathering of wealth; that he censured those who engage in business solely for business' sake (a practice which he called unnatural); and that he condemned the 'making money out of money,' that is, the practice of usury (a practice which he described as the most unnatural among all methods of acquiring wealth). In brief, Aristotle, at least in the *Politics*, rejects the 'pure businessman' who seeks wealth for its own sake. Hence, it may be conjectured that Metrodorus' (and Philodemus') invectives are, in all probability, directed against the Aristotelian *On Wealth*.

Plato himself had admitted that wealth is one of the external goods which are compatible with true philosophic happiness. Moreover, wealthy people, he maintained, have a greater opportunity of dedicating themselves to the pursuit of philosophy.[52] Relying on the testimony of Plutarch, we might assume, therefore, that in the *On Wealth* Aristotle did not outrightly condemn wealth as such. Rather, he probably stressed the proper and intelligent use of wealth, emphasizing that the ultimate meaning of wealth consists in its relation to man's pursuit of virtue and philosophy,[53] and denouncing the vulgar and ostentatious display of riches or prodigality for selfish reasons. This is also the main theme of the fragment from Cicero's *De Officiis*, where the humanitarian and social use of wealth is extolled. As a matter of fact, the Ciceronian fragment and the two fragments from Plutarch are essentially in agreement as to the true (moral) meaning of wealth and as to its proper use. This agreement might indicate that these three fragments are the remnants of one and the same work: Aristotle's *On Wealth*. Hence, it might be surmised that, among other topics, the *On Wealth* condemns senseless prodigality for the sole purpose of satisfying one's sensuous appetites, ambitions and vanity. At the same time, it recommends, as well as praises, the intelligent and moral use of wealth. Relying on Philodemus' (Metrodorus') report, we might also conjecture that in the *On Wealth* Aristotle discussed not only the various uses of wealth (which for Aristotle seem to be of prime importance), but also the different ways by which wealth is acquired.[54] And like the use of wealth, its acquisition too, was probably subjected to a moral evaluation rather than to a mere economic analysis. This seems to follow from the statement that 'the good man is a good money-maker, and the bad man a bad money-maker.'[55] Aristotle probably essayed to demonstrate under what conditions man's varying attitudes towards wealth may be called moral or morally acceptable. In this he displayed his essential adherence to Plato's basic teachings, although he probably differed from Plato in that he viewed the problem of wealth from the standpoint of a 'realist' rather than from that of a Platonic or Utopian idealist, tempering his 'realism' with moral considerations.

In summation, it might be maintained that in the *On Wealth* Aristotle apparently insisted that the acquisition, possession and use of wealth must be controlled or determined by rational as well as moral judgments; and that uneducated (ill-informed) and evil people—judging from his last will and testament Aristotle died a fairly wealthy man—do not know how to acquire or use wealth properly or beneficially. He also seems to have pointed out that under certain circumstances extravagant expenditures are an absolute necessity and, hence, are fully justified, especially whenever and wherever they are serving a noble purpose. But to spend money recklessly merely in order to ingratiate oneself with the masses—to display one's wealth for the sole purpose of impressing people, winning their approval or gaining popularity and popular acclaim—is utter folly, plain vulgarity and outright immorality.

In this fashion, Aristotle also denounced as well as condemned the essentially vulgar practice, quite common among the newly rich both in ancient and modern times, of seeking popular recognition, public acclaim, general notoriety, political influence, or of simply gratifying sensuous appetites, by spending extravagant sums of money. And finally, Aristotle probably also distinguished between the proper and the improper ways of acquiring wealth.[56]

Of the Aristotelian *On Noble Birth* [57] apparently a fairly large number of fragments, including what appears to be a literal quotation, have been preserved.[58] This work discusses the problem of what constitutes 'nobility' (of character?) and also treats of the true significance of nobility and 'noble birth. At the outset, and by critically surveying several divergent opinions, it is admitted that it is extremely difficult to determine 'noble birth,' especially since most people, including the majority of wise men, disagree on the true meaning of the notion of 'noble birth.'[59] Lycophron, for instance, is said to have called it something wholly irrelevant, claiming that its very meaning is obscure and that it is really a matter of personal opinion, especially, since 'in truth there is no real difference between the lowly born and the well-born.'[60] This statement, which actually addresses itself to the meaning and validity of the term 'noble birth,' not only conforms to Lycophron's views about the 'contractual origin' of all social, legal or political institutions, but is also in accord with his insistence upon the natural equality of all men, as well as with his pronounced 'logical relativism.' Others, again, are reported to have maintained that the nobly born are the descendants of noble ancestors. Thus Socrates insists that because Aristides, surnamed the Just, was a virtuous man, his daughter (or descendant) Myrto was of noble birth. Simonides, on the other hand, maintains that the well-born are those whose ancestors had been wealthy over a long period of time.[61] The position taken by Simonides, Stobaeus insists, contradicts 'Theognis' caustic remark as well as that of the poet [*scil.*, Euripides] who wrote: "Mortals honor noble birth, but marry rather the rich." [62] For is not a rich man [Euripides observes] preferable to one who has a rich great-grandfather or some other rich ancestor, but is himself poor?'[63]

It appears that in keeping with a traditionalist point of view about nobility (and by injecting a moral overtone), Aristotle defined noble birth as follows: not those born of wealthy parents or, perhaps, the descendants from wealthy ancestors, but those born of or descended from virtuous parents or virtuous ancestors are nobly born,[64] provided they are capable of living up to their nobility.[65] But they may insist on being respected and regarded as noble people only as long as they act nobly.[66] Since present nobility is preferable to ancient nobility, it is better to be a virtuous man than to have virtuous ancestors. This being so, Aristotle continues, a man is virtuous, noble and well-born in virtue of the excellence that is proper to him—because his stock is good. Hence, Aristotle concludes, 'good birth is excellence of stock.'[67] It is, in other words, the 'transmission' of the ancestors' (moral) excellence to their descendants which makes people 'noble.'[68] In the *On Noble Birth*, Aristotle apparently illustrates his thesis by pointing out that in a second marriage (?) Socrates took Myrto for his wife, although she had no dowry.[69] He did so because Myrto was the daughter (or grand-daughter or great-granddaughter) of Aristides the Just.[70] But Myrto was not noble or virtuous because her grandfather or great-grandfather Aristides had been a noble and virtuous man, but because Aristides' ancestors had been noble and virtuous: 'Good stock or lineage is one in which there have been many good men. Now this happens when the stock or lineage had a good origin. . . . People are well-born . . . not if their father is well-born, but if the originator of the stock or lineage is so.'[71] Since the nobility or virtuousness of Aristides or that of his ancestors had been transmitted to Myrto, she was truly noble-born (and was expected to become the mother of noble and virtuous children). It may also be observed that Myrto had no dowry, that is, was apparently a poor person. This fact is in itself highly significant: according to Aristotle, then, a noble-born and virtuous person does not have to be a wealthy person.[72] In brief, Aristotle, following what appears to be an essentially Platonic tradition, seems to have advocated here a basically 'aristocratic' theory of descent—'aristocratic' not in a 'biological sense,' but rather in its intellectual and moral implications, that is, something related to the inheritance of noble traits of character and deportment.[73]

The Aristotelian *Sophist*,[74] of which only three meager fragments have been preserved, was probably composed in imitation of Plato's *Sophist*. In his *Sophist*, Aristotle apparently reports that Empedocles was the inventor of rhetoric, and Zeno of Elea the inventor of dialectics;[75] that Empedocles not only advocated the freedom of thought, but also was averse to any kind of rule or regulation; and that the same Empedocles, preferring the 'simple life,' declined a rulership offered to him.[76] On the basis of this rather scanty evidence, we might conjecture that in the *Sophist*, Aristotle recommended not only 'principled thought,' but also extolled a 'principled way of life' controlled by stable rules and regulations to which all people must submit. They will have to construe or accept principles and rely on 'principled thought' not only in order to exercise their reason properly and effectively so as to establish and maintain workable intercommunications, but also in order to live the proper, that is, sensible life in general. It also appears that in the *Sophist* Aristotle related that 'the first of his books which he [*scil.*, Protagoras] read in public was a work "On the Gods".... He read it at Athens in the home of Euripides or, as some maintain, in that of Megaclides [or Heraclides], while others say that this event took place in the Lyceum. His disciple, Archagoras, the son of Theodotus, read it for him.... His accusor was Euathlus.'[77] In the light of this slight evidence, it might be maintained that the Aristotelian *Sophist* was, among other topics, either a brief outline of the history of Greek philosophy or, perhaps, a work about dialectics or the history of dialectics. Aristotle's reference to Empedocles' insistence on the freedom of thought and to his general aversion to any kind of rule or regulation might possibly indicate that in the *Sophist* he stated what subsequently Timon of Phlius had to say about Empedocles, namely, that 'the principles he [*scil.*, Empedocles] chose require further principles to explain them.'[78] In so doing, Timon probably implied that Empedocles, who frequently presented his philosophic views in the obscure language of *mythos*, failed to establish an acceptable philosophic system with persuasive and coherent rules of scientific argumentation.[79]

The *Sophist* might also have contained, among other matters, a sustained condemnation of certain sophists (and some philosophers in general) as well as a sustained rejection of their intellectual ('nihilistic' or 'relativist') tendencies, pointing out that people who constantly violate accepted rules and standards, and persistently mock deeply rooted beliefs, sooner or later experience serious troubles. A more satisfactory explanation of the nature and content of the *Sophist* might possibly be found in the likely affinity of the Aristotelian *Sophist* with the Platonic *Sophist*. Aside from the fact that both dialogues bear the same title, this affinity seems to be attested to by the fact that dialectics constitute one of the main topics, if not the main topic, of both the Platonic and the Aristotelian *Sophist*.[80] Hence, it may be surmised that the Aristotelian *Sophist* likewise discusses the nature and validity of dialectics. It may also be conjectured that the Aristotelian *Sophist* was composed in fairly close proximity to the Platonic *Sophist*, which is usually dated between 364 and 361 B.C.[81]

Of the Aristotelian *To Alexander or (To) Alexander or on Coloniza-tion*,[82] only three[83] or possibly six[84] fragments appear to have survived. According to Plutarch, *De Alexandri Fortuna aut Virtute* I. 6, 'Alexander did not heed the advice of Aristotle, namely, to play the part of a leader of the Greeks, and that of a master to the barbarians—to care for the former as friends and kinsmen, and to treat the latter as animals and plants.'[85] Hence, it seems that in his *To Alexander*, Aristotle, the Macedonian and, accordingly, the semi-barbarian, counselled the king to treat conquered barbarian peoples as slaves,[86] while he should always consider Greeks his fellow humans and deal with them accordingly. Aristotle's position in this highly controversial issue apparently was not shared by all people and most certainly not by all philosophers.[87] Thus, according to Strabo I. 4. 9, 'Eratosthenes refuses to praise those who [as Aristotle had done] divided the whole of the human race into two categories, namely, Greeks and barbarians; and who [as Aristotle had done] advised Alexander to treat Greeks as friends, but barbarians as enemies.'[88] Assuming that the fragments traditionally assigned to the Aristotelian *On Kingship*[89] are in fact from the *To Alexander*, then Aristotle must also have advised Alexander on the tasks and duties of the true king,[90] 'instructing him how he should rule. This book had such an effect on the mind of Alexander that when the latter had failed to confer a benefit on anyone, he would say, "today I have not been king, for I have done good to no one."'[91] But realizing that his advice to Alexander would probably be met with strong opposition on the part of other philosophers or advisers to the king, Aristotle also pointed out to Alexander that 'it was not merely unnecessary for the king to be a philosopher, but even a distinct disadvantage. What he should do was to listen to and take the advice of true philosophers. For in so doing he would fill his reign with noble deeds rather than with good words.'[92] It may be maintained, therefore, that in certain respects the *To Alexander* (and the *On Kingship*) was a 'mirror for princes,' counselling Alexander how to rule well and how to deal with different peoples, races and cultures.

Of the Aristotelian *Nerinthus*[93] only a single and extremely meager fragment has come down to us: 'This man, after some passing association with my studies . . . had almost the same experiences as the philosopher Axiothea [of Phlius],[94] Zeno of Citium[95] and the Corinthian farmer. Axiothea, after reading a book of Plato's *Republic*, migrated from Arcadia to Athens and attended Plato's lectures for a long time without being discovered to be a woman—like Lycomedes' Achilles. The Corinthian farmer, after having become acquainted with the *Gorgias*—not [the philosopher] Gorgias himself, but with the dialogue Plato wrote attacking the sophists—forthwith gave up his farm and his vines, put his soul under the guidance of Plato and made it a seed-bed and a planting ground for Plato's philosophy. This is the man whom Aristotle honors in his *Corinthian Dialogue*.'[96] It has been suggested that the *Nerinthus* might in fact constitute a sort of auto-biographical sketch,[97] and that it might possibly contain Aristotle's own justification of his having 'transferred' from the school of Isocrates (which he apparently first attended upon his arrival in Athens in 367 B.C.) to the Academy.[98] In Plato and in the Academy, the young Aristotle found the intellectual and spiritual guide and surroundings that would lead him to a new life—the theoretic life—based on disciplined reason and philosophic insight. If this hypothesis could be substantiated, the *Nerinthus* would lend much support to Jaeger's theory that the young Aristotle, by becoming a convinced Platonist, made his soul 'a seed-bed and planting ground for Plato's philosophy.'[99] But the *Nerinthus* might also have contained the message that only the most rigorous philosophic training under the guidance of a proven master is conducive to true knowledge and right understanding.[100]

In view of the scarceness and scantiness of the surviving fragments which are ascribed to some of the minor lost works of the young Aristotle, it is virtually impossible to say anything of real significance about these works. Omitted from our list are Aristotle's *Symposium*, *Eroticus*, *On Kingship*, *On Poets*, as well as some of the other minor writings or dialogues. The *Gryllus*, *On the Good*, *On (the) Ideas*, *Eudemus or On the Soul*, *Protrepticus*, *On Justice*, *Politicus* and the *On Philosophy*, on the other hand, deserve more detailed scholarly treatment. Of these latter compositions, we apparently possess sufficient fragments to warrant, and make quite promising, such undertakings. In some instances, as in the case of the *Protrepticus* and perhaps some other early work, we might actually be in a position to determine much of their philosophic content and thus reconstruct their specific texts. As regards the so-called minor early compositions, however, we seem to be restricted to a few tentative remarks and brief comments, not infrequently based on a great amount of speculative conjecture. In view of the fact that the fragmentary remnants of these minor early works are extremely meager, it is also plainly impossible to date them with accuracy. We might note, however, that not merely the titles, but also the style and form of some of these earliest Aristotelian writings would indicate that in all likelihood they were modelled on certain Platonic dialogues. This raises the further question, difficult if not impossible to answer: whether in some of his earliest works Aristotle primarily attempted to imitate Plato; whether he tried to 'outdo' his teacher by demonstrating how the problems or topics discussed in certain Platonic dialogues could have been handled in a more satisfactory manner or, perhaps, be presented in a more methodical fashion; or whether, in a spirit of budding intellectual independence, he intended to correct, disprove or even contradict some of Plato's statements?

These brief and probably not always satisfactory remarks are perhaps useful and enlightening if they only remind us that our knowledge of the philosophic views entertained by the young Aristotle is still rather inadequate. They imply that, despite W. Jaeger's ingenious evolutionary thesis, the relationship of the philosophy propagated in the lost (early) works of Aristotle to the philosophy advanced in the doctrinal treatises collected in the traditional *Corpus Aristotelicum* is still essentially unresolved. But this dilemma shall not prevent us from attempting to offer some tentative answers to this puzzling problem which may be at the very bottom of the whole 'Aristotelian question.'

# Aristotle's First Literary Effort: The *Gryllus*— A Work on the Nature of Rhetoric*

In their respective 'catalogues' of Aristotle's writings, Diogenes Laertius,[1] Hesychius of Smyrna (the author of the *Vita Aristotelis Hesychii*)[2] and Ptolemy (-el-Garib)[3] include a composition entitled *Concerning Rhetoric or Gryllus* (generally cited as *Gryllus* or *Grylus*). With the exception of a few relatively insignificant fragments, excerpts or references, this *Gryllus*[4] has been completely lost in the course of time, as were most of the other earliest (or 'exoteric') works of Aristotle. Assuming that they actually relate to the lost *Gryllus*, these few extant fragments, however, enable us to draw certain significant conclusions concerning the original form, nature and content of this composition.

When recording the various arguments made by people who denied that rhetoric is an art (τέχνη in the Platonic sense of the term), Quintilian observes that 'Aristotle, as was his habit, advanced some tentative arguments of his own in the *Gryllus* which are indicative of his mental subtleness and ingenuity.'[5] And Diogenes Laertius relates: '[In his *Gryllus*] Aristotle maintains that there are innumerable authors of epitaphs and eulogies upon Gryllus [the son of Xenophon] who wrote, in part at least, for the purpose of ingratiating themselves to his father.'[6] These two fragments or reports, to which we might add some passages from Quintilian, *Institutio Oratoria* II. 17. 1–14, are apparently the only ancient literary remnants that make direct or indirect reference to the Aristotelian *Gryllus*.

From the brief remarks found in Quintilian and Diogenes Laertius, it might be reasonably supposed that Aristotle composed a work on rhetoric (in one book) which he apparently entitled *Gryllus*.[7] In this composition, it seems, he insisted that not every form or manner of rhetoric is an art (τέχνη). Moreover, the remarks by Quintilian and Diogenes Laertius plainly imply that the *Gryllus* was also a polemic (or critical) work. According to Diogenes Laertius, Gryllus (or Grylus), who fought on the side of Sparta against Thebes, fell in a cavalry skirmish which preceded the battle of Mantinea in the summer (June?)

of 362 B.C.[8] In the words of Diogenes Laertius, when Aristotle composed the *Gryllus*, 'a great many epitaphs and eulogies upon Gryllus' already had been written in memory of him. Several years, therefore, must have passed between the death of Gryllus and composition of the Aristotelian dialogue.[9] Hence, it might be surmised that the *Gryllus* was written about 360 B.C., or perhaps, a little later.[10] It may also be assumed that the *Gryllus* is probably the first 'published' or major composition which can safely be credited to Aristotle, and the existence of which can still be ascertained. In sum, the *Gryllus* was probably written during Aristotle's eighth or ninth year of study with Plato in the Academy, that is, when Aristotle was approximately twenty-five or twenty-six years old.[11] It is interesting to note that in what appears to be Aristotle's first major work, the young man takes to task and castigates some of the most prominent and most renowned rhetoricians of his time.

It is commonly though by no means universally [12] held that Aristotle's *Gryllus* was composed in dialogue form, although it is practically impossible to determine whether it was, in W. Jaeger's terminology, a 'dialogue of discussion' or an 'obstetric dialogue' fashioned after the earliest (Socratic) dialogues of Plato. As will be shown presently, in its content it seems to have been written in fairly close imitation of those passages in Plato's *Gorgias* which denounce certain prevailing types of rhetoric. Hence, it might be expected that the *Gryllus* would also imitate, at least to some extent, the external form of the Platonic *Gorgias*. Moreover, tradition has it that the earliest compositions of Aristotle, as they have been recorded and listed by Diogenes Laertius, the *Vita Aristotelis Hesychii*, and by Ptolemy (-el-Garib), were all dialogues [13]—in a certain sense, 'Platonic' dialogues.[14] Finally, the very title of this work likewise suggests that it was a dialogue. For this unusual title—unusual for Aristotle—seems to be an imitation of Plato's manner of entitling his own dialogues.[15] Nonetheless, as W. Jaeger has convincingly pointed out, the Aristotelian dialogues, even the earliest ones, appear to have been primarily 'expository' rather than 'dramatic' works—'dramatic' in the sense of Plato's early ('obstetric') dialogues.[16]

What, then, might be the connection between the title of this work, *Gryllus*, and its ostensible subject, rhetoric? E. Heitz,[17] among others, advances the thesis that, as is the case with Aristotle's lost dialogue, *Eudemus or On the Soul*,[18] where the title is purely dedicatory, Aristotle chose the title *Gryllus* primarily in order to commemorate and honor one of his personal friends. Just as the *Eudemus*, composed shortly (?)

after 354–53 B.C.,[19] commemorates Aristotle's close friendship with Eudemus of Cyprus (who fell in battle trying to liberate Syracuse), Heitz argues, the *Gryllus* was occasioned by the death of Gryllus in 362 B.C., and written shortly thereafter in memory of a dear friend. Hence, it would also be a sort of *consolatio mortis* or memorial. To justify the title (*Gryllus*) for a work on rhetoric, Heitz concludes that Gryllus himself must have been one of the discussants, and perhaps the main discussant, in the dialogue bearing his name.[20] P. Thillet points out, however, that Heitz's thesis is highly conjectural, not to say improbable.[21] Moreover, there is no evidence whatever that Aristotle and Gryllus ever were personal friends, or that Aristotle wished to honor the memory of Gryllus in a special dialogue. It is even doubtful that the two men knew each other. Thus, the connection between Gryllus and a discussion of the nature of rhetoric, between the young hero and the dialogue named after him, would seem to be purely accidental.

P. Thillet and F. Solmsen, on the other hand, have suggested what seems to be a more plausible and probably the only plausible explanation of this unusual combination of Gryllus' name and the subject of rhetoric. On the strength of Quintilian's remark that 'Aristotle . . . advances some tentative arguments of his own in his *Gryllus*, which are indicative of his mental subtleness and ingenuity,'[22] Thillet and Solmsen arrive at the persuasive conclusion that the *Gryllus* is primarily a polemic piece rather than a constructive or doctrinal work.[23] It is most certainly not a simple memorial, for it would be most unbefitting to turn a memorial or a *consolatio mortis* into a polemic. This seems to follow, Thillet and Solmsen maintain, from the fact that Quintilian refers to the Aristotelian *Gryllus* in the context of his lengthy discussion of 'whether rhetoric is an art.' Quintilian recalls that neither the past teachers of rhetoric nor the rhetoricians themselves ever questioned the categorization of rhetoric as an art, and that they were supported in this by many philosophers, among them the majority of the Stoics and Peripatetics.[24] As regards those philosophers who hold the opposite view—who insist that rhetoric is not an art—Quintilian continues, it must always be borne in mind that these particular philosophers, among them presumably Aristotle, did not truly affirm what they actually believed. They merely disputed involved and difficult issues in order to display their ingenuity of reasoning as well as their eristic talents.[25] Of the several arguments advanced in support of the thesis that rhetoric is not an art, Quintilian remembers those which maintained that rhetoric was a 'natural gift';[26] those which insisted that 'nothing that is based upon art can have existed before the art in question existed, whereas from time immemorial men have always spoken in their own defense or in the denunciation of others,' and long before the art or the teaching of rhetoric was invented; [27] and those which claimed that that which a man does or can do without having first formally learned or studied it cannot belong to any art—and all men are capable of speaking, even those who have never (in a technical or formal sense) learned how to speak.[28]

Some of these statements or arguments, it is believed, originally appeared in the Aristotelian *Gryllus*. According to this 'fragment,' Aristotle must have alleged that proper rhetoric, and not every form of rhetoric, has always been considered an art, and not merely a natural faculty or talent; that no one had ever seriously disputed this; and that the several arguments which attempted to deny that true rhetoric was an art, despite their acumen, may not be taken seriously in that they were purely dialectical performances or devices without any real merit—an intellectual veneer invented to enliven and dramatize the whole discussion.[29] In this the young Aristotle still seems to adhere to Plato's early 'obstetric' method of discussion as it becomes manifest, for instance, in the Platonic *Gorgias* or the *Phaedrus*. As a disciple and admirer of Plato, Aristotle probably believed that under the circumstances this particular form of eristic dialogue constituted the established and hence the only proper vehicle for adequately expressing a philosophic thought or for effectively arguing a disputed issue.

Quintilian further notes that although in his *Gryllus* Aristotle offers 'some tentative arguments of his own'[30] against the argument that rhetoric is an art, the Stagirite 'also wrote three books on the art of rhetoric. In the first book he not only admits that rhetoric is an art, but also treats it as a department of politics and of dialectics (or logic).'[31] From this remark Thillet and Solmson conclude that Aristotle's *Gryllus* must have denied that rhetoric, or at least certain types of rhetoric, constitutes an art ($\tau\acute{\epsilon}\chi\nu\eta$) in Plato's terms. They further assume that at the time he wrote the *Gryllus*, Aristotle was a Platonist and, as such, under the spell of the Platonic *Gorgias* and *Phaedrus*. In view of the change of position which becomes manifest in the first book of the Aristotelian *Rhetoric*, Quintilian apparently considers the *Gryllus* primarily a polemic not against rhetoric in general, but against a certain type of rhetoric as well as against certain rhetoricians or teachers of rhetoric who were prominent during Aristotle's time. Hence, Quintilian also implies that the *Gryllus* is not a doctrinal work or treatise. With this in mind we might better appreciate Diogenes Laertius' observation that 'Aristotle insisted that a great many people had composed epitaphs, eulogies or encomia upon Gryllus, largely for the purpose of ingratiating themselves (χαριζόμενοι) to his father [Xenophon].'[32] The expression χαρίζεσθαι is frequently used by Plato to characterize the servility or obsequiousness of certain sophists and rhetoricians who indulged in abject flattery.[33] Hence, from the fact that Aristotle calls the eulogists of Gryllus (or Xenophon) 'obsequious' (χαριζόμενοι), we may also infer that he was hostile towards these rhetoricians, and that in the *Gryllus* he gave vent to this hostility. The *Gryllus*, therefore, must be considered primarily a polemic work aimed at certain rhetoricians and teachers of rhetoric who in their performances had debased rhetoric and, hence, had aroused Aristotle's displeasure as well as provoked his scathing criticism. At the same time, it is probably also a defense of rhetoric—the proper (Platonic) rhetoric as it had been expounded in Plato's *Gorgias* and *Phaedrus*—and, in all likelihood, a lengthy statement as to what constitutes proper rhetoric.

If all this be true, then the remark of Diogenes Laertius (II. 55) can be fully harmonized with the observations made by Quintilian. The realization that the *Gryllus* is primarily a polemic against certain rhetoricians would also explain the otherwise puzzling title of this dialogue: the *Gryllus* was not written, as some scholars insist, to honor the memory of Gryllus, but to chastise those rhetoricians who, in a spirit of abject flattery, had composed many epitaphs and eulogies commemorating the heroic Gryllus.[34] The death of Gryllus became the occasion for a plethora of obsequious eulogies. These eulogies drew the ire of Aristotle and induced him to attack their composers and the kind of rhetoric they were employing.[35] This is the only possible connection between the title of this dialogue and its real subject matter—between *Gryllus* and rhetoric. Had the Aristotelian *Gryllus* actually been an epitaph or eulogy upon Gryllus, this work would have implied a serious contradiction: flattering Gryllus (or Xenophon) while condemning Gryllus' flatterers.

In sum, when composing the *Gryllus*, Aristotle was motivated not perchance by a personal admiration for Gryllus or Xenophon, but rather by his determined disapproval of the large number of eulogies upon Gryllus and the fawning tenor of these eulogies. Aristotle's ire was probably even more aroused[36] by the participation of some of the most prominent rhetoricians of the day, among them the renowned Isocrates, in the obsequious praise of Gryllus.[37] There can be little doubt that some of these eulogies were abject in tone and over-ingratiating in sentiment. On the strength of the surviving, though extremely scanty, evidence it could even be maintained that the Aristotelian *Gryllus*, as shall be shown presently, is a fierce polemic aimed at Isocrates in particular.[38] If this be so, then the *Gryllus* is also part of that anti-Isocratic literature which originated with Plato and the Academy. In particular, it is the beginning of Aristotle's protracted literary controversy with Isocrates. This controversy, it is commonly believed, was continued in Aristotle's *Protrepticus*[39] and possibly in Aristotle's *Politicus*.[40] Isocrates, in turn, seems to have answered these charges and denunciations in his *Antidosis* which, according to some scholars, preceded (and provoked) the *Protrepticus*, while according to others, it constituted Isocrates' reply to the *Protrepticus*. The *Against Aristotle*, composed about 360 B.C. or shortly thereafter by Cephisodorus, a pupil of Isocrates, among other issues also contained a defense of Isocrates against the attacks made by Aristotle in the *Gryllus*;[41] and the *Ad Demonicum*, authored by an unknown disciple of Isocrates, in turn might have been a rebuttal of the *Protrepticus*.

The excessive number of prominent eulogies and the many obsequious praises which they heaped on Gryllus (and his father) implied, at least to Aristotle and the members of the Academy, that certain rhetoricians regarded rhetoric simply as a convenient means of arousing emotions and passions. Through the deliberate efforts of certain eulogists, in order to achieve purely emotional reactions, rhetoric apparently had been degraded to an emotional appeal to the irrational part of the soul.[42] Hence, it is not surprising that Aristotle, who as a disciple of Plato was conversant with the Platonic *Gorgias* (and *Phaedrus*), should violently object to such contemptible practices, denounce the ultimate philosophic outlook underlying them, and chastise the men who engaged in and countenanced such practices. In rejecting and denouncing this type of rhetoric, Aristotle acts in full accordance with the spirit and tenets of Plato's basic teachings as regards rhetoric and philosophy in general.

Moreover, in refuting these eulogists Aristotle also wishes to re-establish the undisputed supremacy of reason over passion, the primacy of intellectual integrity (in the Platonic sense) over worldly success,[43] and perhaps the superiority of the Academy over the school of Isocrates. In short, he attempts to restore and re-affirm the supremacy of the theoretic life over the practical and pragmatic life advocated by Isocrates, a supremacy which had seriously been threatened by Isocrates and his followers. Furthermore, it is likely that Aristotle, in formulating his attacks upon the eulogists and upon Isocrates in particular, availed himself of the invectives with which Plato had chastised the sophists and rhetoricians in his *Gorgias*.[44] As a matter of fact, it would be reasonable to surmise that the *Gryllus* reiterates in substance—perhaps in a more 'expository' and 'methodical' manner—certain anti-sophistic and anti-rhetorical arguments and utterances found in the Platonic *Gorgias*. Hence, in order to reconstruct the essential tenor of the *Gryllus*, it might be appropriate to turn to this Platonic work. When comparing the *Gryllus* and the Platonic *Gorgias*, we must keep in mind, however, that in the *Gryllus*, Aristotle probably does not engage in eristic duels of verbal thrusts and counter-thrusts so characteristic of Plato's early dialogues. Rather, he might have restricted himself to more prosaic discussions and demonstrations. It was probably in this context that Aristotle, in the words of Quintilian, displayed 'his usual mental subtleness and acumen.' In this respect, the dialogues of Aristotle always differ from those of Plato.

In the *Gorgias*, Plato maintains that rhetoric 'is not an art (τέχνη) at all ... [but] something which, as I was lately reading in a work of yours [*scil.*, Polus'], you claim having turned into an art. . . . [Rhetoric] is a sort of experience ... producing a kind of emotional delight and gratification. . . . The whole, of which rhetoric is but a part, is not an art at all, but the habit of a ready and bold wit which knows how to manipulate men. And this habit I sum up under the heading of "flattery". . . .'[45] Because true art, that is, Platonic τέχνη, is exclusively concerned with that intellectual activity which always gives a rational account of empirical facts by relating them to ultimate principles and causes, rhetoric, as practiced or promulgated by certain sophists and rhetoricians, including Isocrates, in the opinion of Plato cannot possibly be a τέχνη. Therefore, Plato insists, rhetoric, like flattery, is actually something 'ignoble ... because it aims at pleasure without giving any thought to what is "best." An art I do not call it,' Plato concludes, 'but only an emotional experience, because it is unable to explain or to offer a reason for the nature of its own application. And I do not call an irrational (unprincipled) thing a τέχνη.'[46]

It is quite likely that in his *Gryllus* Aristotle uses similar arguments. However, we must not assume that Aristotle merely restates the basic theses advanced in the Platonic *Gorgias*. From Quintilian's observation that in the *Gryllus* Aristotle 'produces some tentative arguments of his own [that is, not those of Plato?] which are indicative of his mental subtleness and ingenuity,'[47] it might be inferred that in the *Gryllus* Aristotle not only adopts the basic position held by Plato, but also devises some original ideas and arguments of his own, as well as a certain original and distinct method of argument. In so doing, he apparently displays considerable acumen, ingenuity and originality.[48]

It is possible, as Thillet points out,[49] that Quintilian actually quotes some of Aristotle's own arguments, such as the statement that 'all arts have their own subject matter . . . whereas rhetoric has none';[50] that 'no art will acquiesce in false opinions, because a true art must be based on immediate perceptions . . . whereas rhetoric gives its assent to false conclusions';[51] that 'every art has some definite and proper end towards which it directs its efforts, whereas rhetoric, as a rule, has no such end, even though at times it claims to have such an end without, however, succeeding in fulfilling its promise';[52] that 'the arts know when they have attained their proper end, whereas rhetoric does not';[53] that 'rhetoric does things which no art does, namely, makes use of vices that serve its ends, inasmuch as it proclaims falsehoods and excites passions';[54] that 'rhetoricians speak indifferently on either side of an argument . . . and [whereas] no true art is self-contradictory, rhetoric does contradict itself, and whereas no true art attempts to demolish what it itself has built up, this does happen in the operations of rhetoric';[55] and that because 'rhetoric teaches either what ought to be said or what ought not to be said, it is not an art, inasmuch as it teaches also what ought not to be said, or because while it teaches what ought to be said, it also teaches precisely the opposite.'[56] These arguments, some of which are remarkably acute and subtle, could very well have been advanced or developed in Aristotle's *Gryllus* independently, though probably under the general influence of Plato's *Gorgias*, and used in support of Aristotle's contention that rhetoric—or a certain type of rhetoric—is not a τέχνη. Hence, it may also be maintained that Quintilian's *Institutio Oratoria* II. 17. 14–30, contains substantial 'fragments' of the lost Aristotelian *Gryllus*.[57] But it will be noted that many of these arguments can also be found in Plato's *Phaedrus*, *Gorgias* and elsewhere.[58]

It has already been pointed out that in all likelihood the Aristotelian *Gryllus* is a polemic directed at contemporary rhetoricians in general (or at least at those orators who appealed to emotions and passions through flattering memorials and obsequious eulogies), and at Isocrates in particular. This latter statement requires additional substantiation. We know from Diogenes Laertius that 'Isocrates likewise wrote an encomium of Gryllus.'[59] The fact that Diogenes Laertius mentions this valuable bit of information in the context of his report that 'a great many people composed epitaphs and eulogies on Gryllus,' and that Aristotle denounced these people for doing this, seems to indicate that Aristotle, in the *Gryllus*, not only refers to Isocrates by name, but probably also chastises him for his obsequious abuse of rhetoric.[60] It would plainly be unthinkable for Aristotle to take issue with these rhetoricians without engaging Isocrates, the most outstanding and most renowned orator of the time, who likewise composed an obsequious encomium on Gryllus (and who was the much detested rival of the Academy).

Quintilian relates that Isocrates was the most distinguished pupil of Gorgias of Leontini.[61] If this was the case, Isocrates' rhetorical style and standards were probably patterned after those of his renowned teacher. Gorgias, it will be remembered, was savagely denounced in Plato's *Protagoras* and *Gorgias*. As has been argued, Aristotle probably had Plato in mind when he patterned some of his own invectives against the rhetoricians (and against Isocrates) in the *Gryllus*.[62] This would lend additional support to the thesis that the *Gryllus* is under the influence of Plato's *Gorgias*.

The surmise that the *Gryllus* contains a sustained criticism of and attack upon Isocrates and the type of rhetoric he advocated also seems to be supported by Philodemus, *De Rhetorica*, col. XLXVIII, 36–col. LV, 44. This lengthy and vitriolic passage, aimed at Aristotle, seems to contain some 'fragments' of the *Gryllus* which so far have been either overlooked or simply ignored: '[Aristotle] advanced a number of reasons for engaging in politics [political rhetoric?], namely, first, that one who is not familiar with political events [and with political oratory] is frequently of the opinion that he is surrounded by general un-friendliness. Second, that philosophy will make considerable progress in a city that is well governed; and, third, that he was disappointed in most of the contemporary politicians [and political orators] who were constantly embroiled in petty party politics.'[63] It is not unreasonable to assume that Philodemus quotes here from some arguments which Aristotle used in the *Gryllus* in support of his theses as to what con-stitutes proper rhetoric or political rhetoric. The above three argu-ments are refuted by Philodemus in the following manner: 'Of the [three] reasons why he [*scil.*, Aristotle] advocates [in the *Gryllus*?] that one who has the ability to engage in politics [in political oratory?] should actually do so, the first argument applies to himself rather than to a man who takes no active interest in communal affairs. For if he was of the opinion that a man who took no part in current political events would have no [political?] friends, the plain truth is that he himself had no friends, or if he had a friend he could not keep him for any length of time. . . . Philosophy [here Philodemus takes issue with the second reason, *note by the present author*] was not prevented from making considerable progress, just as it did not prevent Aristotle. But even if it had been prevented by someone from making progress, philosophy would never have been brought into general contempt, because philosophy is independent and needs no assistance from any man.... He also stated [here Philodemus takes issue with the third reason, *note by the present author*] that he was dissatisfied with present conditions. But we cannot now, as in the golden age, expect sudden improvements, and if we do refer to the golden age of which the poets speak, we would deal with non-existing things and hunt the dreams of the ancients.' [64] All these statements of Philodemus, although in a badly garbled form, might contain allusions to what Aristotle had said in the *Gryllus* about Isocrates and the special kind of rhetoric Isocrates had recommended.

Philodemus continues: 'One who wants to make himself a popular figure among the people who despise the gifts which philosophy so graciously bestows, and who exalt rhetoric as their true benefactor ... such a person for a short time might have a number of pupils until he returns to philosophy proper....' [65] Aristotle 'did not behave like a true philosopher [when he attacked Isocrates].... For, if the rhetoric of Isocrates was of no use, the proper thing for Aristotle was to let Isocrates go on with it. If, on the other hand, it was useful [for Aristotle to speak out against Isocrates], Aristotle should have done so irrespective of whether or not Isocrates existed. If, however, it was neither of the two, Aristotle should not have devoted himself to rhetoric in order that he might not seem incompetent in the eyes of certain people or to be acting from sheer envy....' [66] When denouncing Isocrates, Aristotle 'most certainly did not understand the true purpose of rhetoric....' [67] For when attacking Isocrates, Aristotle 'was certainly less noble than the teachers of rhetoric [than Isocrates?], for they attempt to impart a certain technique and try to hand down the principles of rhetoric, not merely for the sake of one's peace of mind, but also for the health of the body, except of course those few orators who practice rhetoric for its own sake and delight in denouncing certain theses....' [68] 'If, on the other hand, he [*scil.*, Aristotle] was searching for the truth ... why did he choose the rhetoric of Isocrates—which he denounced in various ways—rather than political oratory which he considered to be different from that of Isocrates?' [69] Moreover, Aristotle 'had some strange reasons for urging young men to concentrate on political oratory: first, if they acquired practical experience and would immediately take up a practical (political) career, they would be prevented from pursuing some disinterested studies and, hence, would appear lacking the proper philosophic training. If, on the other hand, they would have no practical experience, they could not be effective statesmen unless they would study for a very long time. . . .'[70]

It is fairly reasonable to assume that Philodemus refers here to some arguments which had been made by Aristotle in the *Gryllus* against Isocrates and the kind of rhetoric that had been advocated and practiced by the latter. Hence, this part of Philodemus' *De Rhetorica*, with some reservations and alterations, may be included among the genuine fragments of the lost Aristotelian *Gryllus*. It must always be borne in mind, however, that Philodemus, the Epicurean and persistent detractor of Aristotle, quotes from the *Gryllus* in an essentially confusing manner, trying to discredit the Stagirite in the traditional Epicurean fashion. Hence, it is safe to surmise that he intentionally distorts some statements made by Aristotle. Moreover, in this lengthy and informative passage Philodemus also alludes to what Aristotle probably had said in his course of lectures on rhetoric, which he offered in the Academy between *c.* 360 and 355 B.C.[71] In any event, what is of paramount importance to us is Philodemus' report that Aristotle criticized and chastised Isocrates for the kind of rhetoric the latter had been advocating. And this is exactly what Aristotle seems to have done in the *Gryllus*.

The assumption that in his *Gryllus* Aristotle also denounces Isocrates finds further support in the fact that Cephisodorus, a disciple of Isocrates, at one time attacked Aristotle. In his *Against Aristotle*, probably published between 360 and 355 B.C.,[72] this Cephisodorus reproaches Aristotle for having criticized and wholly misunderstood Isocrates' method, educational policy and general philosophic outlook:[73] 'Cephisodorus, when he saw his master and teacher Isocrates being attacked by Aristotle . . . waged war on Aristotle.'[74] This, in turn, impels the conclusion that in the *Gryllus* Aristotle had denounced Isocrates and the kind of rhetoric or philosophy he propagated. Thus, Aristotle's denial of rhetoric's categorization as an art would seem to be aimed directly at Isocrates.[75] If this be the case, then Aristotle seems to attach to Isocrates, reputedly the greatest orator of his day, the label of dilettante and falsifier. Moreover, in Aristotle's judgment, Isocrates' brand of rhetoric is emphatically not a τέχνη.[76]

The question might now be raised as to what the particular issues were which prompted Aristotle's attack upon Isocrates. It is known that Plato had made the radical claim that henceforth all true *paideia*, including true rhetoric and true intellectual culture, must be founded exclusively on the rational knowledge of imperishable values or absolute principles and on the exclusive use of *phronesis*. In short, he recommended the purely 'theoretic life' without compromise. However, the educational and cultural ideas of the sophists, despite Plato's savage denunciations in the *Protagoras* and in the *Gorgias*, succeeded in retaining a prominent place in the educational, intellectual and cultural life of Greece.[77] This was due in no small degree to the efforts of Isocrates, who pronounced rhetoric—his brand of rhetoric—the sound foundation of all higher education or educational philosophy. More than that: Isocrates severely criticized and ridiculed not only the almost mythical importance which Plato and the Platonists attached to *phronesis*, but also the apparently exaggerated Platonic intellectualism, which held up pure intellectual knowledge as the panacea for all the ills of this world.[78] Isocrates, on the other hand, attempted to find practical solutions to man's almost infinite problems—solutions which could reasonably and effectively be translated into concrete action and, at the same time, retain some moral meaning.[79] Thus, whenever Isocrates refers to philosophy, he has in mind something radically different from what Plato would call philosophy: to Isocrates, philosophy meant nothing more, and nothing less, than a general intellectual and humanistic *paideia*.[80] Isocrates, in fact, became the founder of a literary humanism which in its general outlook was centered on the concrete conditions of life, while Plato fervently advocated a purely philosophic, theoretic and essentially abstract attitude towards man. The clash between these two basic intellectual positions constitutes one of the main events in Greek intellectual history during the fourth century B.C. Much to Plato's annoyance, Isocrates persuasively and effectively advocated his realistic approach to life, arguing it in his orations and writings, as well as teaching it in his school, which about the year 360 B.C. had acquired a considerable reputation (and an impressive enrollment) not only throughout Greece, but also beyond the Hellenic orbit. A fierce denunciation of Isocrates and of the views he expressed in the *Nicocles*, *Ad Evagoram* and in the *Ad Nicoclem* may, for instance, be found in Plato's *Republic*: 'The harsh feelings which many people entertain towards philosophy originates with certain pretenders [*scil.*, Isocrates], who rush in uninvited and are always abusing those, and find fault with those, who [*scil.*, like Plato] make persons instead of things the theme of their philosophic discussions.'[81]

One is led, therefore, to assume further that in the *Gryllus* Aristotle discusses and criticizes the very principles (or lack of principles) which Isocrates proposed in his rhetoric and, indeed, in his whole philosophy of life.[82] It is here that Aristotle for the first time openly confronts and violently opposes Isocrates' philosophic and educational ideals.[83] The attacks which Aristotle launches against Isocrates and his whole school also reveal something about the intellectual outlook of the young Aristotle, who around 360 B.C. still professed most enthusiastically the intellectual ideals so eloquently propagated by his teacher and mentor Plato, as he would for several years to come. As a faithful and, one might assume, ambitious student of Plato, he was fully convinced that Plato's lofty ideals of the 'theoretic life' were infinitely superior to the intellectual and cultural (humanistic) notions advocated by Isocrates, the most successful and, at the same time, the most dangerous rival of Plato and the Platonic Academy in the Greek orbit.

Finally, Isocrates' eulogy of Gryllus (and Xenophon) probably presented a unique opportunity for Aristotle to participate actively in the 'great conflict of ideas' which separated the school of Plato from that of Isocrates—to take part in the crucial contemporary 'dialogue' between the two most outstanding men of the time on problems touching upon the ultimate foundations, the final significance and the very heart of the truly intellectual life.[84] Moreover, this was also a splendid opportunity to 'strike a telling blow' for the cause of the Academy and thereby earn the attention, and perhaps the admiration and gratitude, of his teacher Plato and the entire Academy. By championing in his *Gryllus* the Platonic-Academic views in the bitter and prolonged debate with Isocrates over the constitution of the truly intellectual and philosophic life, Aristotle probably displayed all the uncompromising enthusiasm characteristic of youth. At the same time he employed, in the words of Quintilian, all the dialectical acumen, intellectual subtleness and mental ingenuity he could possibly muster, making it a brilliant display of his philosophic (and dialectical) talents. With the sense that he was supporting and furthering the work of his teacher and of his associates in the Academy, Aristotle could not but condemn the cultural and intellectual ideals advocated by Isocrates.

This clash between Aristotle (who here completely subscribes to Plato's philosophic standpoint) and Isocrates—a clash which in all likelihood constituted the main theme of the *Gryllus*—might be reduced to a conflict between an uncompromisingly 'principled philosophy' and a less principled 'practical and result-oriented philosophy of life' which, in a humanistic flair, takes into account worldly success, practical effectiveness and the general human condition within an existential rather than ideal (Platonic) world.

It also appears that the *Gryllus* produced certain practical or tangible results—rewards for which Aristotle had perhaps hoped when composing this polemic. As a consequence of, or reward for, his *Gryllus*,

Aristotle was permitted—perhaps even urged—to offer a course of lectures on rhetoric in the Academy. Certainly, this signal honor can at least partially be attributed to this demonstration of his qualification as a teacher and advocate of Platonic rhetoric, and to his loyalty to the Academy in standing up to the mighty Isocrates, a man much condemned and much disliked (and maligned) by Plato and the Academy.[85]

In summation,[86] it may be maintained that Aristotle's *Gryllus* was not perchance a 'memorial' honoring Gryllus, but rather a composition on the nature of rhetoric; that its title, *Gryllus*, is purely incidental; that it was probably written in dialogue form; that it was composed shortly after the death of Gryllus, presumably about 360 B.C. or shortly thereafter; that it adhered in substance to the rhetorical and philosophic standards which Plato had established in the *Protagoras* and *Gorgias* (and in the *Phaedrus*); that it contained a sustained and, presumably, violent attack upon certain contemporary rhetoricians and, especially, on Isocrates; that it denounced Isocrates' alleged indifference or opposition to true—Platonic—philosophy and its attendant rigoristic educational ideals; that it made a strong and impressive case in support of a rhetoric (and philosophy) based upon a comprehensive grasp of ultimate and absolute moral as well as intellectual (theoretic) values; that in the *Gryllus* the youthful Aristotle already displayed the logical, dialectic and eristic acumen for which he later gained much renown; and that in consequence of the *Gryllus*, Aristotle was judged qualified to offer a course of lectures on rhetoric in the Academy.

# Chapter IV

# Eudemus or On the Soul:
# An Aristotelian Dialogue on the
# Immortality of the Soul*

The 'catalogues' of Aristotle's writings listed by Diogenes Laertius and by the author of the *Vita Aristotelis Hesychii* enumerate among his earliest compositions a work entitled *On the Soul*, in one book.[1] Modeled, without doubt, on the early dialogues of Plato, this *On the Soul*, which apparently also carried the subtitle of *Eudemus*, was a dialogue. In any event, one extant fragment of the *Eudemus*, preserved by Plutarch,[2] clearly indicates that in this composition Aristotle makes use of the 'Socratic technique' of question and answer so characteristic of the early Platonic dialogues. As a pupil of Plato[3]—according to tradition Aristotle was Plato's disciple for about twenty years—it is only natural that the Stagirite should have imitated the literary style and technique of his teacher and, hence, should have made use of the dialogue form, the classical literary medium through which Plato gave expression to his philosophic message.[4]

Aside from a few and on the whole rather scanty and frequently not very informative fragments, references or excerpts found in some ancient authors, critics or commentators, the *Eudemus* has in the course of time been completely lost.[5] Nevertheless, with the help of these ancient reporters, scholars are able to retrieve and perhaps even reconstruct with a fair degree of accuracy the essential content or 'message' of this composition.[6] Judging from the impact it made on certain subsequent authors, the *Eudemus* must have acquired some literary renown throughout antiquity. This is evidenced, for instance, by the fact that the *Eudemus* apparently furnished the model for several subsequent *consolationes mortis*. It is also permissible to assume that the *Eudemus* was dedicated to the memory of Eudemus of Cyprus, apparently a close personal friend and possibly a 'classmate' of Aristotle in the Platonic Academy.[7]

According to the testimony of Cicero (who probably quotes directly from Aristotle's *Eudemus*), Eudemus of Cyprus while on a journey to Macedonia came to the city of Pherae in Thessaly, which at that time was ruled by the tyrant Alexander (of Pherae), a person of considerable renown. Here Eudemus fell gravely ill and the physicians attending him gave up all hope of saving his life. In a dream, brought on by high fever, Eudemus had an apparition which prophesied to him that he would recover within a few days, that Alexander would die (or be assassinated) within a short time, and that he, Eudemus, would return to his native land (Cyprus, from which he apparently had been banished) in five years. The first two prophecies actually came true: Eudemus recovered unexpectedly and Alexander was assassinated (in 359–58 B.C.) by his wife's brothers. Five years later, in 354–53 B.C., Eudemus, who had hoped that by this time he would be back in Cyprus,[8] died in battle near the city of Syracuse on the island of Sicily. Hence, the dream did not signify that Eudemus would return to his native land, but that he would die in five years: on leaving the body, Eudemus' soul would return to its true ('heavenly') home[9]—a thoroughgoing Platonic notion.

Plutarch, on his part, narrates that in 357 B.C. Eudemus took part in the military campaign of Dion of Syracuse which was intended to liberate Syracuse from the tyrannical rule of Dionysius the Younger. Eudemus fell in battle and, in the words of Plutarch, 'Aristotle composed in his honor a dialogue entitled *On the Soul.*'[10] If Plutarch's account should prove to be correct—some of its details are definitely not in accord with the historical facts—then the composition of the *Eudemus or On the Soul* would have been occasioned by Eudemus' death in battle, fighting by the side of Dion in 357 in the hope of upholding the political ideals of the Platonic Academy. It should also be remembered that according to Plutarch, other members of the Platonic Academy, but not Plato, approved of and joined Dion's action against Dionysius the Younger; and that it was Speusippus who persuaded Dion that the people of Syracuse were ready and eager to revolt against Dionysius and, hence, prevailed upon Dion to join this enterprise.[11]

In order to determine the precise date of Eudemus' death and, incidentally, in order to establish the likely date or at least the *tempus post quod* of the composition of Aristotle's *Eudemus*, it will be necessary briefly to review certain incidents in the history of Syracuse. In (June?) 354 B.C., Dion, who had succeeded temporarily in driving out Dionysius the Younger (in 357 B.C.), was treacherously assassinated by Callippus, a former member of the Platonic Academy. This Callippus, whose foul deed 'scandalized fortune and upbraided the gods,' subsequently made himself tyrant of Syracuse, ruling the city for a little over one year (354–353/52 B.C.). Some of the friends and partisans of Dion, who opposed and resented Callippus, attempted to retake the city of Syracuse and remove Callippus by force of arms. Eudemus, a partisan of Dion, apparently was killed in one of the ensuing armed clashes between the partisans of Callippus and those of Dion. These clashes or skirmishes lasted from the late summer of 354 until the end of 353 and, perhaps, into the early part of 352. According to these facts, then, Eudemus would have died in the course of the prolonged struggle which ultimately drove out Callippus in 353–52 B.C.,[12] rather than in connection with Dion's seizure of Syracuse in 357 B.C. Hence, it would appear that Eudemus died sometime around 354 or 353 B.C., and that in consequence the *Eudemus* was written about 352–51 B.C. or shortly thereafter. Plutarch's statement, it will be noted, also does not fully coincide with Cicero's report that Eudemus died five years after the assassination of Alexander of Pherae. Now it is fairly certain that Alexander was murdered in 359–58 B.C.[13] If, therefore, Eudemus' death occurred five years after this event, he must have died in 354 or 353 B.C. and not, as Plutarch suggests, in 357 B.C. Cicero's report, then, would lend support to the story that Eudemus was slain in battle, presumably in the vicinity of Syracuse, either late in 354 or, more likely, in 353 B.C.[14]

The news of Eudemus' death, it may be surmised, reached Athens and the Academy probably late in 353 (assuming that Eudemus died in 353) or early in 352 B.C. This prompted Aristotle to compose the *Eudemus*.[15] Hence, it is also reasonably safe to conjecture that this dialogue was written in 352 or, perhaps, shortly thereafter.[16] In any event, the year 352 B.C. may confidently (*pace* Gigon) be regarded as the likely *tempus post quod* of the *Eudemus*.

The fragment from Cicero, *De Divinatione ad Brutum* I. 25. 53, also furnishes some clues as to the main thesis and the particular philosophic content of the *Eudemus*. One major topic seems to be the problem concerning the reliability of dreams or apparitions. Aristotle apparently indicated here his belief that the messages or revelations which Eudemus had received in his dreams or while on the very threshold of death are bound to be fulfilled in the future— a theme which Aristotle also discusses, though in a different context and for an entirely different purpose, in a fragment usually attributed to the Aristotelian *On Philosophy*.[17] This view, which decisively touches upon the nature of the soul and its relation to the body, proclaims that whenever the body is asleep or approaching death, that is, finds itself close to a 'separation' or (as in the case of sleep) in a state of 'semi-separation,' the soul may at times foresee future events or visualize the 'world beyond.' It goes without saying that this position is but a specific version of the widely held Greek belief in *metempsychosis*—a position which, for instance, was advocated by Pythagoras[18] and Plato.[19] This, in turn, implies that in the *Eudemus* (and in the *On Philosophy*) Aristotle adheres to an essentially Platonic doctrine of the soul as it had been expounded, for instance, in the *Phaedo*—a doctrine which differs radically from that advanced in the Aristotelian *De Anima*. To put it more succinctly: in the *Eudemus* (and in the *On Philosophy*) Aristotle suggests or implies not only the 'substantiality' of the individual soul, but also maintains its personal immortality.

The other topic in Cicero's *De Divinatione ad Brutum*, which sheds some light on the main thesis of the *Eudemus*, is the implied message that death is the soul's 'going home' to the place whence it originally came (and where again it will be infinitely happy). But if this is so, then Aristotle propagates here a basically Platonic view: life on earth is at best a miserable exile, a temporary and unhappy absence from man's true ('heavenly') home. Since the *Eudemus* probably is also intended as a *consolatio mortis*, it is not surprising that Aristotle should have extolled death as a desirable incident, comparable to the exile's joyous return, or to a happy escape from an unwanted imprisonment.[20] Provided Cicero's testimony contains reliable information, the basic purpose or theme of the *Eudemus* should be fairly clear: dedicated to the honored memory of a dear friend who died while performing a noble deed, this dialogue searches out the ultimate meaning of life and death. For, if the ultimate and true meaning of death can be ascertained and the joyful significance of this event be established, the grief and sorrow that always accompanies the death of a person near and dear can be borne more serenely.[21] More than that: this particular topic in Cicero's *De Divinatione ad Brutum* also implies or, better, simply presupposes the immortality of the soul—the personal afterlife. For it would be meaningless to compare death to the happy return to one's true home unless it is also conceded that the individual soul survives the death of the body and forever retains its individuality and identity.

The assumption that the *Eudemus* also contains elements of a *consolatio mortis* receives additional support from Plutarch's *Consolatio ad Apollonium*.[22] Here we are told that earthly life is but a prolonged meaningless torture, and that to be born marks but the beginning of an almost uninterrupted chain of calamities. Plutarch's excursions, which are generally believed to be based on Aristotle's *Eudemus*, however, have a different scope than has the *Eudemus*. In somber words reminiscent of Plato's *Republic* 617D ff., Plutarch insists:[23]

Many wise men, Crantor relates, not only recently but long ago
have bewailed the fate of man, holding that life is a punishment
and that merely to be born a human being is the greatest of
misfortunes. Aristotle states that even Silenus revealed this to
Midas when caught by the latter. But it would be better to cite
the philosopher's own words which he utters in a work entitled
*Eudemus or On the Soul*: '. . . not to be born is the best thing of
all, and death is better than life. . . .' This, they say, is what
happened to the famous Midas when he had caught Silenus and
asked him what is the best thing for men and the thing most
desirable of all. Silenus at first would not say anything maintaining
an unbroken silence. But when at last by using every device
Midas, with great difficulty, had induced him to say something,
Silenus admitted under duress: 'Most wretched offspring of a sad
creature, product of a merciless fate, why do you compel me to
divulge things that would better remain unknown to you?
As long as we do not know the ills that are inherent in life, our
life is at least to some extent devoid of pain. It is as impossible
for men to know the best of all things, as it is impossible for
them to take part in the nature of the good. The best thing of all,
for all men and for everything, indeed, is not to have been born
or come about; and the second best thing—and this is attainable
for men—is that those who are born die as soon as possible.' It is
obvious, therefore, that in this manner Silenus demonstrated that
being dead is preferable to being alive.

The fragment preserved in Plutarch's *Consolatio ad Apollonium*
indicates that in the *Eudemus* Aristotle attempts to persuade himself as
well as his readers that to be dead is better than to be alive.[24] Since
Eudemus had died gloriously, fighting for a good cause—for the cause
of the Academy and for the principles for which it stood—he is actually
better off than if he were alive. Hence, there is no real reason why
people should grieve or be dejected over his death. In this sense, the
*Eudemus* may always be called a *consolatio mortis*, and it is likely, as for
instance the example of Cicero indicates,[25] that this dialogue became
one of the renowned literary prototypes on which many subsequent
Hellenistic *consolationes* were modeled. It would be erroneous to assume,
however, that the Aristotelian *Eudemus* was exclusively a *consolatio
mortis*. For in order to prove the immortality of the human soul—
obviously a decisive aspect of any *consolatio*—Aristotle had to discuss
the particular aspects or the unique constitution of the soul which

would guarantee this immortality.[26] The fragments so far discussed, however, suggest that the young Aristotle, whenever dealing with the nature of the soul or with its ultimate destiny, was definitely and decisively under the influence of Plato (*pace* Düring), especially, under that of Plato's *Phaedo* and the 'mythological proof' as well as the dramatic presentation of this subject employed in the *Phaedo*.

A fair number of ancient commentators, including the prolific Proclus,[27] report that in his exoteric dialogues, Aristotle propagates the immortality of the (substantial) soul. It is only reasonable to surmise that these commentators have in mind primarily the *Eudemus* which, after all, is concerned with life and death and the soul, as well as with the survival of the soul after death. Elias, for instance, forthrightly insists that 'in his dialogues [Aristotle] states that the soul is deathless (or immortal), because all people, following a natural impulse (αὐτοφυῶς), offer libations to the dead as well as swear in the name of the dead. But no one would offer libations to something that does not exist at all or in no way, or swear in its name.'[28] However, since after the time of Alexander of Aphrodisias probably few, if any, Aristotelian commentators had seen the original dialogues of Aristotle, it may be assumed that Elias and others derived their information about Aristotle's insistence on the immortality of the soul from second-hand sources.[29] It has even been suggested, though not always in an entirely convincing manner, that Elias arbitrarily injects here purely Neo-Platonic notions into his remarks which, as a consequence, may not be accepted at face value.[30] Elias[31] and Olympiodorus,[32] to be sure, concede that the early dialogues of Aristotle do not always proclaim Aristotle's true (late?) philosophic teachings. These commentators base their opinions on the fact that the dialogues advocate the (personal) immortality of the soul, while the later doctrinal works which, according to the same commentators, allegedly contain Aristotle's true or final philosophy, explicitly deny the immortality of the soul, including that of the 'rational soul' or νοῦς.[33] Incidentally, the thesis proposed by Elias and Olympiodorus, namely, that because of their 'Platonizing' content the early Aristotelian dialogues do not really convey Aristotle's true (mature?) philosophic thought, was revived in modern times by J. Bernays,[34] who flatly denies any and all 'Platonic elements' in Aristotle's earliest compositions. V. Rose who recognizes the many 'Platonisms' in the works credited to the young Aristotle, simply declares the early dialogues spurious because of these 'Platonisms'[35]—an interesting variation on the thesis advanced by Elias, Olympiodorus and Bernays.

If one were to concede, as some commentators and scholars have done, that in the *De Anima* Aristotle at least considers the imperishability of the rational soul or νοῦς,[36] and that the immortality of the soul advocated in the *Eudemus* only refers to the rational soul rather than to the 'whole soul,' then there would exist no serious doctrinal conflict between these two works. The only significant difference, according to Elias, is the method of demonstrating this immortality: the dialogues, Elias insists, use 'persuasive arguments,' while the doctrinal works rely on 'compelling arguments.'[37] But since the libations offered to the dead as well as the swearing in the name of the dead is, according to Elias, 'according to nature (and reason)'—αὐτοφυῶς—and, hence, 'compelling,' even this difference in argumentation or in the mode of demonstration loses much of its significance.[38]

W. Jaeger insists that 'in the *Eudemus* Aristotle follows the view of the [Platonic] *Phaedo* even in holding that "the whole soul" is immortal.'[39] For, Jaeger continues, if the *Eudemus* is indeed a *consolatio mortis*, then only the belief in the 'survival of the whole soul' can give 'religious comfort to the heart of man, which cares nothing for the eternity of the impersonal reason, without love and without memory of this life.'[40] F. Nuyens, in turn, points out that in the *Eudemus*, as in the other early dialogues of Aristotle (and in the works of Plato), there is no real distinction between νοῦς and ψυχή.[41] This being so, D. A. Rees suggests that whenever Aristotle refers to the ψυχή in the dialogues, he could very well have had in mind the νοῦς.[42] Hence, the νοῦς of the doctrinal writings and the ψυχή of the dialogues could very well be one and the same thing.[43] It might be contended, therefore, that there exists no good reason why the soul's immortality advocated in the *Eudemus* should be restricted to the rational soul or νοῦς.[44] If Nuyens' and Rees' views can be accepted, and there exist no particular reasons why they should be rejected, then a further obstacle to reconciling the *Eudemus* with the *De Anima* may have been removed, unless we insist that the basic tenor of the *Eudemus* differs so radically from the scope of the *De Anima* as to make any reconciliation of these two works simply impossible and unthinkable.

On the basis of what has been said so far, it seems to be fairly safe to assume that the Aristotelian *Eudemus* pointedly asserts the immortality of the soul. However, it is not always fully clear whether this immortality applies to the 'whole soul' or merely to the rational soul (*pace* Jaeger). Moreover, at least in the opinion of some scholars, especially those who read the doctrinal treatises of Aristotle through the eyes of either St. Thomas Aquinas or the mediaeval (and modern) scholastics or the Christian teachings in general, there exists no irreconcilable opposition between the concept of the soul advanced in the *Eudemus* and that advocated in the later doctrinal treatises. In his *Commentary to Plato's Timaeus*,[45] Proclus insists, however, that in the *Eudemus* Aristotle uses arguments in favor of the soul's immortality which are akin to the 'mythological discussions' of the same subject in Plato's *Phaedo*, *Gorgias* and *Republic*, but are quite different from the manner in which the soul is discussed in the *De Anima* of Aristotle. For in the *De Anima*, Proclus contends, Aristotle deals with the 'physical' aspects or characteristics of the soul and, hence, is not concerned with the soul's egress from the body or with its condition after death.[46] But if the *Eudemus* discusses the condition or fate of the soul after death rather than the 'physical' nature of the soul, then this fact would be an additional argument in support of the thesis that the *Eudemus* is primarily a *consolatio mortis* rather than a philosophic or scientific discussion of the nature of the soul. However, in the *Eudemus*, Aristotle seems also to have dealt with an analysis of the nature of the soul.[47] In its *Grundmotiv*, therefore, the *Eudemus* radically and substantially differs from the *De Anima*. The term 'myth,' as it is used here by Proclus, in its ultimate significance has always a 'meta-rational,' 'meta-logical' or 'meta-noetic' meaning, but never signifies something 'irrational' or 'illogical.' It refers to something 'intuitively suggestive' —to an intuitive immediate certainty or awareness which transcends science and scientific method. 'Myth' then is the ultimate but in a way undefinable expression of an essentially indifferentiated ('pre-philosophic') thought or experience which, in contrast to structured, articulated or conceptual thinking, intuitively formulates and comprehends something within and through itself. The truth of 'myth' lies on the level of the inner experience it expresses, while the 'myth' itself is the loving search of reason for something which actually transcends reason—for something in which the ever questing intellect participates and to which this intellect seeks to attune itself in the perennially reciprocal and wholly intimate relationship of knower and known. The Platonic Academy, especially during the last years of Plato's philosophic endeavors, by its ability to construct and by its determination to work with symbols and 'myths,' created a new and affirmative piety. This piety, through the intermediary of symbols and 'myths,' produced an innermost certainty and an ultimate justification of certain truths transcending discursive reasoning or logical consideration. Accordingly, possible doctrinal conflicts between the *Eudemus* and the *De Anima* must really be evaluated in light of their different intent as well as in light of the disproportionate significance of the philosophic message which they try to convey. The mere fact that in the *Eudemus* Aristotle admittedly makes use of 'myths'—and the term 'myth' frequently signifies some 'revealed (or religious) truth,' something of which reason becomes immediately and intuitively aware—only strengthens our conviction that when composing the *Eudemus* he was still strongly under the influence of Plato. And the use of 'myths' is fully in keeping with the nature of a *consolatio mortis*.

In his *Commentary to Plato's Republic*, Proclus observes that Aristotle had also insisted that the reason why the soul, when coming from a 'higher world,' forgets what it had visualized in this 'higher world,' and when leaving our world, remembers in the 'higher world' the experiences it had in our world, is a good reason and must be accepted together with the arguments made in its support. Aristotle, however, does not seem to disclose what this reason or these arguments are, but, according to the testimony of Proclus, merely illustrates his point by using the following analogy which, incidentally, is likewise Platonic: some people, when they fall ill, sometimes lose their memories, even to the extent of forgetting how to read or write, while those who are restored to health recollect what they had suffered while being sick. By the same token the soul that has descended into the body (which in itself is a kind of 'sickness') forgets what it had visualized during its former or 'pre-corporeal' existence.[48] But when in death the soul returns to its original home in the higher world, which incidentally is its proper home and hence is really a kind of 'recovery of health,' it fully remembers the experiences it has had while dwelling on this earth.[49] In this, the soul acts like a person who has recovered from a serious illness in that he remembers what he had suffered while being sick. Hence, according to Aristotle, the immortality of the soul is also related to the continuity of consciousness or, better, the continuity of (earthly) memory—an interesting variation on Plato's doctrine of the *anamnesis*. Such a recollection, it will be noted, also fits well the nature and purpose of a *consolatio mortis*: the departed is not only remembered by his friends, but he, too, forever remembers his friends here on earth—without doubt a comforting thought.

W. Jaeger accepts Proclus' remarks without hesitation or reservation as being wholly (early) Aristotelian (and, indirectly, wholly Platonic). He infers from these remarks that in the *Eudemus* Aristotle somewhat modified Plato's theory of the *anamnesis* or 'recollection' to mean a 'continuity of rational awareness.' This rational awareness actually 'stretches' from the soul's temporary 'incarceration in the body' to its 'liberated existence' after death. It is temporarily interrupted during the soul's 'incarceration in the body'[50]—which, after all, is but an abnormal condition of the soul akin to an illness accompanied by a 'loss of memory'—only to be resumed after death (or, temporarily, during a severe illness and, in some occasions, during sleep). Jaeger concludes that the whole purpose of this theory of a 'continuous awareness' or 'continuous consciousness' is to establish, in terms of a *consolatio*, the personal immortality of the whole substantial soul.[51] In consequence, Jaeger also finds himself compelled to surmise that in the *Eudemus* Aristotle accepts, at least by implication and with certain modifications, Plato's *anamnesis*: all true human knowledge is ultimately recollection of what the soul once had visualized before it started on its 'earthly journey.'[52] For reasons of his own, however, Aristotle insists that after its return to its heavenly home, the soul remembers what it has experienced on earth—an impossible notion for Plato, who would never admit that the soul could ever carry the recollection of imperfect experiences into the perfect world. The only plausible explanation for Aristotle's peculiar position, as has already been shown, is the following: for a *consolatio mortis* it is probably more significant and more important to know that the departed soul remembers what it had experienced and whom it had loved and cherished in this world.

Jaeger's thesis has been rejected by some scholars, among them I. Düring who, it appears, objects in principle to the assumption that there ever was a significant 'Platonic period' in Aristotle's philosophic development. In particular, Düring not only denies that the fragment from Proclus' *Commentary to Plato's Republic* has any direct reference to Aristotle or Aristotle's *Eudemus*, but he also maintains that this *Commentary* is exclusively concerned with Plato's concept of the *anamnesis* as it affects the Platonic *Republic*.[53] Düring insists (i) that this fragment has been given an importance or significance which it does not really deserve, and (ii) that this fragment actually does not at all refer to Aristotle, but rather to a particular passage on the *anamnesis* found in Plato's *Republic*.[54] Düring concedes, however, though somewhat reluctantly, that part of the passage from Proclus might originally have been part of the *Eudemus*, namely, the statement 'that on their journey from health to sickness some people forget even the letters they once had learned, but that no one ever had this experience when passing from sickness to health.'[55]

The problems raised by the two conflicting interpretations given to Proclus' fragment by either W. Jaeger or I. Düring may be reduced to the following: Jaeger insists that the notion of the 'continuity of rational awareness' simply implies the principle of *anamnesis*.[56] But then again, Aristotle expressly denies such an *anamnesis* in his later works. The pre-existence of the soul, no less than the personal immortality of a substantial soul, is likewise implied in this 'continuity of rational awareness.' It could be injected here, however, that neither the pre-existence, nor the personal immortality, nor the substantiality of the soul are due to, or dependent on, the *anamnesis*. They are attributes of the special nature of the soul as, thanks to the dominant influence of Plato, it has been defined or at least used in the *Eudemus*. The pre-existence of the soul, which also proclaims or implies the deathlessness of the soul, in a way parallels the eternity of the world which Aristotle advocates in his early dialogues.[57] Moreover, like Plato in the *Phaedo* before him, Aristotle seems to have accepted, at least in the *Eudemus*, the complete unity of the soul.[58] And since the soul is not a 'composite entity,' it has, as we know from Plato's *Phaedo*, no beginning and, by the same token, no end.

A last and undoubtedly a most difficult question connected with the Aristotelian *Eudemus* is the following: how is it possible that about the year 352–51 B.C. Aristotle should have adhered to, and propagated, a relatively early Platonic doctrine of the soul—the doctrine expressed in the *Phaedo* which was composed about thirty or thirty-five years previously—especially since in the meantime Plato himself had altered substantially some of his views on this subject in a number of later, more mature and, one must assume, more authoritative dialogues?[59] The only intelligent answer to this involved question, it seems, can probably be found in the ultimate purpose or motivation behind the *Eudemus*: the *Eudemus* is to a large extent, and perhaps primarily (though certainly not exclusively), a *consolatio mortis*. As such it is modeled on, and inspired by, Plato's *Phaedo* which without the least bit of exaggeration could likewise be called a *consolatio*. Wishing to erect a noble literary monument to his dead friend, Aristotle could find no nobler model than the *Phaedo* of Plato, the deathless monument to a deathless Socrates.[60] In this sense, the Aristotelian *Eudemus* is always Platonic. The somewhat unusual dependence of the *Eudemus* on the Platonic *Phaedo* might in itself be cited in support of the contention that the *Eudemus* is primarily a *consolatio mortis*.

Viewed in this manner, the fact that some of the notions expressed in the *Eudemus* conflict (or seem to conflict) with the views advanced in the later doctrinal works as well as in the later dialogues of Aristotle becomes irrelevant. Perhaps it would not be too far-fetched to conclude that under the special circumstances which prompted and surrounded the composition of the *Eudemus*, the obvious Platonism of this work does not convincingly establish or sustain Jaeger's general thesis of the 'Platonizing' early Aristotle, no matter how meritorious this thesis may be for a better understanding of Aristotle's intellectual evolution or progression in general.[61] Düring's efforts to deny the 'Platonism' of the *Eudemus* and, by implication, that of all of the earliest compositions of Aristotle (by disputing the relevance of Proclus' comments), under the circumstances likewise seem to be somewhat irrelevant, not to say a case of misplaced scholarly acumen and erudition. A 'memorial' such as the Aristotelian *Eudemus*, like any eulogy of a person near and dear or, perhaps, a *consolatio mortis*, is hardly the proper document for reliable inferences as to the author's true and ultimate philosophic convictions or teachings. Neither may it be considered a trustworthy 'stepping stone' in Aristotle's alleged intellectual development from an early Platonism to a later 'Aristotelianism.' Conversely, Plato's earlier teachings concerning the soul and its ultimate destiny, especially the Platonic *Phaedo*, without doubt supply the ideal topic for a *consolatio mortis* composed by a member of the Platonic Academy.[62] In the face of the tragic death of a close friend, 'the heart has its reasons which reason does not know' (Pascal). The ultimate theme of the *Eudemus* seems to be summarized in the following lines:

> 'O thou that from thy mansion
>     Through time and place to roam
> Dost send abroad thy children
>     And then dost call them home.'[63]

# Chapter V

# The Psychology in Aristotle's
## *Eudemus or On the Soul**

In the preceding chapter, an attempt was made to show that the views on the nature of the soul expressed by Aristotle in his lost dialogue *Eudemus or On the Soul* seem to conflict with some of the doctrines he advocated in his later doctrinal treatises (and probably in his later dialogues). Since the *Eudemus* is primarily a *consolatio mortis*, it was alleged that this conflict is somewhat irrelevant. A eulogy of a departed person 'near and dear' is hardly the proper document from which to draw reliable inferences as to Aristotle's true and ultimate philosophic convictions regarding the nature of the human soul.[1] Nevertheless, Aristotle's emphatic assertion in the *Eudemus* about the soul's immortality, which seems to be essential to any effective *consolatio mortis*, apparently compelled him to embark upon a lengthy theoretic discussion on the nature of the soul in order to justify philosophically this claim of immortality. After all, in their 'catalogues' of Aristotelian writings, Diogenes Laertius and the author of the *Vita Aristotelis Hesychii* refer only to an *On the Soul* (in one book), significantly omitting the sub-title, *Eudemus*[2] (which might be a later addition). This alone might indicate that in the *Eudemus* Aristotle discussed at some length and in some depth the nature of the soul, as well as the reason or reasons for its (personal) immortality.

In the *De Anima* 407 b 27–30, Aristotle insists that 'there is yet another theory about the soul which has recommended itself to many people as no less probable than any of those we have heretofore mentioned. This theory has given a good account of itself in the arena of public discussion. The advocates of this theory proclaim that the soul is a kind of attunement (harmony). . . .' Commenting in detail on this Aristotelian passage, Philoponus,[3] Simplicius,[4] Themistius,[5] Olympiodorus[6] and Sophonias[7] took issue with the statement that 'the soul is a kind of attunement or harmony.' In so doing, they apparently also referred to what Aristotle had said in the *Eudemus* about the nature of the soul. These references, therefore, may be considered surviving fragments reporting Aristotle's views concerning the nature of the soul as he expressed them in the *Eudemus*. These few fragments, though at times conflicting and confusing, enable us to gain a reasonably clear insight into the Stagirite's early doctrinal position concerning the soul.

Before discussing in detail the several fragments dealing with the question of whether the soul is only 'a kind of attunement or harmony,' it might be appropriate to look for a moment at Plato's *Phaedo* which, after all, seems to have had a determining influence on the psychology developed in the Aristotelian *Eudemus*. In the *Phaedo* (91E–94E), Plato enumerates no less than six arguments against the allegation that the soul is the attunement or harmony of the body. These are (i) the argument arising from the doctrine of the *anamnesis*, which implies that the soul exists prior to the body, while attunement cannot exist prior to its component elements, that is, to the several tunes (the elements of attunement are prior to attunement, but the body is not prior to the soul);[8] (ii) the argument from the pre-eminence of the soul, which implies that the soul commands or leads the body, while attunement does not command or lead by these elements but rather 'follows' them and is dependent on them;[9] (iii) attunement admits of degrees, that is, of a 'more or less,' while the soul never admits of degrees or of a 'more or less';[10] (iv) while there are good or virtuous souls and evil or vicious souls (in the case of attunement this would be tantamount to harmony and disharmony), one cannot maintain that attunement may at one and the same time be harmony or attunement and disharmony or non-attunement (for otherwise there would be a soul within a soul or an attunement within an attunement);[11] (v) if the soul is attunement, it cannot have any vice, because a harmony, as harmony, has no part in disharmony (and, concomitantly, a soul, which is absolutely soul, being identified with attunement, cannot have vice or have part in vice, and all souls, being identified with attunement, will be equally good);[12] and (vi) the soul, as soul, is often at variance with the body which it commands and restrains, while as the attunement of the body it cannot possibly be at variance with the body, nor can it command the body.[13] Some of these arguments, it will be noted, appear in the *Eudemus*.

Philoponus relates that[14]

Aristotle, after having criticized alike all those who had discussed the soul, for having said nothing about the body which was to receive it ... as might be expected, goes on to connect this

criticism to his own opinion about the soul. Some thinkers
tackled the same issue, namely, that the soul is not a body
resulting from a mere accidental constitution that shares in the
soul, but that it requires a definite constitution, just as attunement
is not produced by any accidental state of the strings, but requires
a definite degree of tension in these strings. These thinkers
thought, therefore, that the soul too is an attunement of the body,
and that the different kinds of soul correspond to the different
attunements of the body. Aristotle states, as well as rejects, this
opinion. At first he merely records the opinion itself, but
presently he sets forth the arguments that led these thinkers to
this opinion. He had already opposed this opinion elsewhere,
namely, in the dialogue *Eudemus*. Before him Plato, in the *Phaedo*
[91E–94E], had used some five [actually six, *note by the author*]
arguments against this view.... Aristotle himself ... has used in
the dialogue *Eudemus* the following two objections. One goes like
this: 'Attunement ... has a contrary, namely, lack of attunement,
but the soul has no contrary. Hence, the soul is not attunement.'
One might object to this statement by pointing out that there is
strictly no contrary to attunement, but rather an indefinite privation, and the soul, being a kind of form, has an indefinite opposite. Or, as we say in the case of music, a certain lack of
attunement changes into attunement. By the same token, a
certain kind of privation changes into soul. Aristotle's second
objection is this: 'The contrary of the attunement of the body is
the lack of attunement of the body, and the lack of the attunement of the living body is disease, weakness and ugliness.... If,
then, lack of attunement is disease, weakness and ugliness,
attunement is health, strength and beauty. For even Thersites, the
ugliest of men, had a soul. Therefore the soul is not an attunement.' This is what Aristotle says in the *Eudemus*. But here [*scil.*,
in the *De Anima*] he has used four objections to refute this opinion,
of which the third is the second of the objections made in the
*Eudemus*.... When Aristotle maintains that he said this in his
'public discussions,' he must refer either to his unwritten discussions
with his associates [in the Academy] or to the exoteric writings
(among which are the dialogues, e.g., the *Eudemus*), which are
called exoteric because they were not written for his real or
intimate disciples, but for the general advantage of the many....
'It is more appropriate to call health (or, generally, the good state
of the body) an attunement than to assert this of the soul.' This is

the third objection (the second in the *Eudemus*). That health is attunement he has shown in the *Eudemus*, reasoning from its being the contrary of disease. We have stated above the course of the syllogism.

It appears from Philoponus' comment, therefore, that in the *Eudemus* Aristotle made two major objections to the thesis that the soul is nothing other than the attunement or harmony of the physical body. The first objection runs as follows: while attunement has obviously its contrary, the soul has no such contrary.[15] Admittedly, this particular objection could be defeated by the counter-argument, not necessarily but possibly advanced by Aristotle, that to everything there might be opposed its contrary.[16] The second objection is this: attunement of the physical body is its health, strength or beauty, but the soul is neither physical health nor physical strength nor physical beauty.[17] As Plato had done before him in the *Phaedo*, so also Aristotle denounces and rejects here a predominantly 'materialistic' or corporeal conception of the soul which, on account of its compositeness (Plato), obviously would defeat the immortality of the soul. It is possible, and as a matter of fact quite likely, that Aristotle derives his two objections from Plato's *Phaedo*,[18] although in keeping with his peculiar mode of presentation and argumentation, he reformulates these objections. In so doing, he manifests his independence of and progression beyond Plato in matters of methodology and logic. In other words, Aristotle apparently reduces Plato's pre-eminently dialectical or eristic arguments, so characteristic of the 'obstetric method,' to their syllogistic or logical elements.

In the *De Anima* 407 b 30–408 a 18, Aristotle enumerates four objections to the thesis that the soul is a kind of attunement, that attunement is a blending or composition of opposites, and that the body is made up of contraries. Aristotle's third objection reads as follows: 'It would be more appropriate to call health (or generally one of the good states of the body) an attunement than to assert this about the soul.'[19] According to the testimony of Philoponus, this is but a restatement of the second objection made by Aristotle in the *Eudemus*,[20] where the Stagirite apparently added the further remark that physical 'health is an attunement' and 'the contrary of disease.'[21] Philoponus also relates that Aristotle proposes all this in the form of a concise syllogism.[22] This syllogism, it appears, operates with the non-identity of two substances or concepts demonstrated by the non-identity of their respective attributes—a theme which Aristotle further elaborates in the *Categories*.[23] This, in turn, implies that Aristotle, although still dependent on Plato in matters of general philosophic doctrine, is independent of and technically superior to Plato as regards mere methodology. For what Aristotle apparently produces here is a technique which in its subtleness and effectiveness surpasses Plato's somewhat primitive method.[24]

Commenting on Aristotle, *De Anima* 407 b 30–408 a 18, Simplicius reports that 'by the arguments used in public discussions [the "exoteric" works] Aristotle means those arguments which are adapted to the intelligence of most people, hinting perhaps at those made in the [Platonic] *Phaedo*, but meaning also those used by himself in the dialogue *Eudemus* in order to refute the theory that the soul is attunement (or harmony).'[25] In short, Simplicius claims outright (i) that in the *Eudemus* Aristotle objects to the theory that the soul is an attunement; (ii) that in the *De Anima* Aristotle again takes up these objections; (iii) that in his refutations Aristotle also took account of the arguments made in Plato's *Phaedo*; and (iv) that these refutations, or some of them, were part of certain public discussions, or to be more exact, were the topic of some of his 'exoteric' writings, and of the *Eudemus* in particular. Plato's arguments, of which Aristotle takes account in the *Eudemus* are as follows: if the soul is nothing other than attunement, and if there is a 'more or less' as regards this attunement, then the soul itself can be 'more or less soul.'[26]

Themistius relates that[27]

another opinion about the soul has been handed down . . . and has been examined both in public and private discussions. Some maintain that the soul is attunement. Attunement is a mixture and combination of contraries, and the body is composed of contraries, so that that which brings these contraries into concord and harmonizes them . . . is nothing other than the soul, just as the attunement of (different) notes blends low notes with high notes. This argument is plausible, but it has been refuted in many instances both by Aristotle [in the *Eudemus*] and Plato [in the *Phaedo*]. The soul, they both insist, is prior to the body, but attunement (or harmony) is posterior; the soul rules and oversees the body and frequently antagonizes it, but attunement (or harmony) does not antagonize the things that have been harmonized; attunement (or harmony) admits of a 'more' and of a 'less,' but the soul does not; attunement (or harmony), so long as it is preserved, does not admit non-attunement or disharmony, but the soul admits wickedness; if non-attunement or disharmony of the body is illness, ugliness or weakness, the attunement or harmony of the body must be beauty, health and strength, but never the soul. All these things have been said by the philosophers [*scil.*, Aristotle and Plato] elsewhere. . . . [But] from what Aristotle has said now [*scil.*, in the *De Anima*] and from what he has said elsewhere [*scil.*, in the *Eudemus*], it is clear that those people who maintain that the soul is attunement (or harmony) seem to be neither very near nor very far from the truth.

Themistius, it will be noted, fails to mention expressly the *Eudemus*, referring only in a general manner to what Aristotle says in the *De Anima* as well as 'elsewhere,' that is, 'in public discussions' (exoteric writings). A comparison of Themistius' argument with that of Philoponus or Olympiodorus, for instance, should make it sufficiently clear, however, that Themistius has the *Eudemus* in mind. When commenting on the thesis that the soul is 'a kind of attunement (or harmony),' Themistius merely restates or paraphrases Aristotle's arguments in the *De Anima*. Moreover, he briefly recites the five arguments against this thesis, four of which are actually objections made by Plato in the *Phaedo*. The fifth argument listed by Themistius is the second objection of the *Eudemus*:

'If non-attunement (or disharmony) of the body is illness, ugliness or weakness, attunement (or harmony) of the body must be beauty, health and strength (δύναμις, not ἰσχύς), but never the soul.' [28]
For some unknown reason, Themistius does not record, however, what, according to Philoponus, is the first objection, namely, that 'attunement (harmony) has a contrary, that is, the lack of attunement (non-attunement, disharmony), but the soul has no contrary.' [29]

The differences between the comments of Themistius and those of Philoponus raise some interesting problems. It is entirely possible that Themistius, whose account is certainly more succinct and probably less accurate than that of Philoponus, derived his information from Alexander of Aphrodisias rather than directly from Aristotle's original text. This, however, is by no means certain. The specific tradition on which Themistius relies did not, in all likelihood, report the first objection made by Aristotle in the *Eudemus*, to wit, that 'the soul has no contrary.' Neither does Themistius refer to the 'rebuttal' or 'counter-argument' (found in the commentary of Philoponus) to the effect that 'one might object to this argument [that the soul has no contrary] that there is strictly speaking no contrary to attunement (or harmony), but rather an indefinite opposite.'[30] These textual differences would suggest that Philoponus probably relied on a different tradition than did Themistius—that Philoponus probably consulted the Aristotelian *Eudemus* directly (*pace* Jaeger), while Themistius seems to rely on an (abridged?) intermediary source. They may also imply, though not necessarily, that, after all, the *Eudemus* might have contained this particular 'rebuttal' (or 'counter-argument') to the first objection. Hence, this 'rebuttal' might not simply be a later interpolation by some commentator (as certain scholars have suggested), but probably constitutes a thought of Aristotle originally expounded in the *Eudemus*. It is also interesting to observe that the first argument of the *Eudemus* is not restated in Aristotle's *De Anima*, while the second argument of the *Eudemus*, broadly speaking, is again taken up in the *De Anima*.[31]

Olympiodorus relates that 'in the *Eudemus* Aristotle makes the following objection: "Disharmony (non-attunement) is contrary to harmony (attunement), but since the soul is a substance (οὐσία γάρ), it has no contrary." This conclusion is obvious. Moreover, if the disharmony of the elements in an animal is disease, the harmony must be health, but not the soul. . . . The third argument [in Aristotle's *De Anima*] is the same as the second argument in the *Eudemus*.'[32] The only new information conveyed by Olympiodorus is the important, not to say startling, statement that the soul 'is a substance' or, better, that in the *Eudemus* Aristotle might have called the soul a substance.[33] Presumably, this statement was part of the first objection or argument originally contained in the *Eudemus*. But we cannot escape the impression that Olympiodorus' (or Aristotle's?) argumentation contains a *petitio principii* in that it simply presupposes the substantiality of the soul, which it is supposed to prove, in order to disprove the contention that the soul is mere attunement or harmony, and nothing more.[34]

Sophonias, finally, maintains that 'there has been handed down yet another opinion about the soul, which many people find plausible, as much as any of those opinions that have been recorded. This opinion, however, has already been dealt with and refuted by appropriate arguments which have been published—both by our arguments directed at the *Eudemus* and by those contained in Plato's *Phaedo*. Nevertheless, these arguments will be criticized now as well. Some say that the soul is attunement (or harmony).'[35] Obviously, Sophonias refers here to the objections to the thesis that 'the soul is attunement or harmony'—objections which had been listed in Plato's *Phaedo*, in Aristotle's *De Anima* and in Aristotle's *Eudemus*.

It should be borne in mind that any interpretation of the several fragments attributed to the *Eudemus* must always take into account the doctrinal foundation as well as the didactic range of the Platonic *Phaedo*. In the *Phaedo* Plato deals with the many problems connected with the soul from a variety of approaches: the soul constitutes the 'principle' of life; it is that substance or being which accounts for its own perfection or imperfection; and it may be called the '*locus* of knowledge' of the Ideas. Sometimes Plato speaks—in a manner reminiscent of a solemn 'exhortation to philosophy'—of the value and ultimate meaning inherent in a rational apprehension and comprehension of things eternal (the Separate Ideas), and of the proper means of achieving such apprehension and comprehension. The dramatic setting of the *Phaedo* undoubtedly elevates this dialogue to a deeply moving *consolatio mortis*. All this raises the complex problem of whether, and to what extent, the *Eudemus*, which likewise is a *consolatio mortis*, simply imitates the *Phaedo*—whether the *Eudemus* touches on the wide range of issues discussed in the Platonic *Phaedo*, and whether it does so in the same, or in a similar, manner as the *Phaedo*.[36] It must also be remembered that by the year 352 B.C., the likely year in which Aristotle composed the *Eudemus*, it was not probable that he should have been content with merely writing an exact imitation or, perhaps, a slightly revised (and in his opinion improved) version of the Platonic *Phaedo*; neither is it probable that at this time he should have discussed the question of whether the soul is attunement (or harmony) in exactly the same, or perhaps only slightly modified, dialectical context and in the same terms as Plato had done some thirty or thirty-five years previously.[37]

When discussing in detail the two objections (or proofs) of the *Eudemus*, namely, that the soul is not merely attunement or harmony of the body, and that the soul is not the health, strength or the beauty of the body, W. Jaeger insists that the very nature of the *Eudemus*— the fact that it is really a *consolatio mortis*—furnishes the starting point for a theoretic-speculative discussion of the immortality of the soul.[38] In a spirit reminiscent of the 'other-world-directed' eschatology so eloquently expounded not only in the Platonic *Phaedo*, but also in other Platonic dialogues as well, Aristotle attacks in the *Eudemus* any and every position that is opposed to, or may threaten, the doctrine of the immortality of the soul. For a *consolatio mortis* such as the Aristotelian *Eudemus* or the Platonic *Phaedo*, the immortality of the whole and substantial soul simply constitutes an absolute prerequisite. Hence, any attempt, directly or indirectly, to deny or even to question this immortality has to be defeated without compromise or concession. Aristotle's arguments, it will be noted, are essentially identical with those advanced in the Platonic *Phaedo*. His basic premise, like that of Plato, cannot possibly admit that the soul is merely the attunement or harmony of the bodily elements—that the soul, while certainly different from the body, is merely the harmonious arrangement (or the product of the proper arrangement) of the bodily elements. Aristotle rejects outright this notion by using the following argument: since attunements or harmony 'dies' whenever its component elements die, the soul, as attunement, would likewise die whenever the body dies. To refute the allegation that the soul is merely attunement, Aristotle uses two main arguments, the first of which reads as follows: 'Attunement has a contrary—non-attunement—but the soul has no contrary. Hence, the soul cannot possibly be attunement.' In short, the non-identity of attunement and the soul is demonstrated with the help of the non-identity of their respective 'characteristics' or contraries. This, in turn, implies that Aristotle grounds the identity of two objects on the identity of their respective attributes or contraries. This is, at least by implication, the main line of argumentation which Aristotle uses in the *Categories*: 'Another characteristic of a substance is that it has no contraries. For what could be the contrary of any primary substance, such as individual man or animal? It has no contrary.'[39] Moreover, Aristotle's argumentation in the *Eudemus* apparently is presented in the form of a tight syllogism. This syllogism, however, does not merely demonstrate that the soul is not, and cannot be, identified with attunement. It is also supposed to prove, at least by implication, that the soul is a substance.[40] It has already been pointed out that this demonstration or proof of the substantiality of the soul, at least in the manner in which it is presented by the reporters, contains a distinct *petitio principii*.[41] Whether or not Aristotle himself originally used this *petitio principii* in the *Eudemus*, or whether it is the 'contribution' of some later reporter or commentator, cannot be determined, however.

It will also be remembered that in the *Phaedo* Plato had insisted that attunement or harmony is an attribute of the soul, but never the soul itself.[42] Here Plato's argument is based on a logical argument which in a more abstract form is restated by Aristotle (?) in the *Categories*: 'One particular substance ... cannot be "more or less". ... The same quality is said to subsist in a thing in varying degrees. ... But a substance is not said to be "more or less" that which it is. ... Substance, then, does not admit of variation of degree.'[43] Hence, if the soul indeed is a substance, there cannot be different degrees of soul. Neither can the soul have contraries or, perhaps, be a 'more or less soul.'[44] In other words, according to Plato, the soul is either good or evil, depending on whether it is in a state of order (harmony) or in a state of disorder (or disharmony). And there can be various degrees—a 'more or less'—of order or disorder in the soul. But this order or disorder, it will be noted, cannot possibly be the soul itself, but merely a particular state or quality or characteristic of the soul. Thus, if the soul were indeed nothing other than the order or attunement of the various states (or attributes) of the soul, then there would also have to be a 'more or less soul,' as there is a more or less attunement.[45]

Aristotle's second argument runs as follows: 'The opposite of attunement (or harmony) of the body is non-attunement (disharmony) of the body. But this non-attunement (disharmony) of the living body is disease, weakness and ugliness. . . . If non-attunement (disharmony) is disease, weakness and ugliness, then attunement (harmony) constitutes health, strength and beauty. . . . Hence, the soul is not attunement (harmony).'[46] If, therefore, the soul should be nothing more than attunement (harmony), then sickness or vice, being non-attunement (disharmony), would be in fact 'non-soul.' As is commonly known, Plato frequently speaks of the virtues of the soul (wisdom, fortitude, temperance and justice) as well as of the virtues of the body (health, strength and beauty).[47] Each of these sets of virtues has a set of opposites, namely, the vices of the soul (lack of wisdom, cowardice, intemperance and injustice) as well as the 'defects' of the body (sickness, weakness and ugliness). With Plato, the virtues of the soul or the health of the body ultimately depend on a state of harmony (or symmetry), the vices of the soul or the sickness of the body on a state of disharmony (or lack of symmetry) within either the soul or the body.[48]

Closer analysis of Aristotle's two arguments against any identification of the soul with attunement, harmony or symmetry should make it amply clear that Aristotle's earliest psychology, as he expounded it in the *Eudemus*, is to a large extent grounded in Plato's metaphysics. Although differently formulated—in Aristotle they are presented in the technical form and language of a syllogism, while in Plato they are advanced with the apodictic directness characteristic of *mythos*—these Aristotelian arguments, or rather, these proofs for the immortality of the soul, are largely dependent on Plato's doctrine of the immortality of the soul. They are influenced, to say the least, by Plato's conception of substance (and, hence, by Plato's doctrine of the Separate Ideas) as well as by Plato's peculiar conception of the soul.[49] It cannot be disputed, however, that the assertion that attunement (harmony), being a quality or characteristic, 'has a contrary, but the soul, being a substance, has no contrary,' as has already been shown,[50] contains an implied *petitio principii*. This holds true not only as regards Aristotle's argumentation or proof in the *Eudemus* but also as regards Plato's reasoning or dialectics in the *Phaedo*, where we encounter the same dogmatic presupposition that the soul is an independent substance.[51] Such a presupposition, however, is in keeping with Plato's fundamental philosophic outlook which in this instance is also fully accepted by Aristotle. Here, as elsewhere in the early Aristotelian dialogues, we encounter an example of Aristotle's essential adherence to Platonism.[52]

Further analysis of the *Eudemus* and of Philoponus' (as well as Olympiodorus') *Commentary* also indicates that Aristotle not only asserts the substantiality of the soul but also endows his conception of the soul with certain attributes or 'qualities' characteristic of Plato's Separate Ideas. These characteristics or 'qualities' become manifest when the soul is being compared with the physical body.[53] This seems to follow from Philoponus' observation: 'One might object to the statement that strictly speaking there is no contrary to attunement (or harmony), but rather an indefinite privation. And the soul, being a kind of form (εἶδός τι), has an indefinite opposite . . . [and] a certain kind of privation changes into soul.'[54] In other words, even the soul, if conceived as a kind of form (εἶδός τι), in a certain sense has something like a contrary, namely, privation. This can mean but one thing: the soul, in so far as it is conceived as the 'form (εἶδος) of animation,' that is, as the 'principle' of animation which converts any body into a living body, can have a sort of 'contrary,' namely, the inanimate body. This does not preclude, however, that the soul, conceived as the 'Idea of Animation' and hence as a Separate Idea, is a substance.[55] An autonomous substance such as the soul can be both an independent substance and the principle of animation of the living body. In this sense it might also be called the 'form of a living body'—obviously a Platonic twist.

In the *De Anima* Aristotle points out that:[56]

we are in the habit of recognizing substance as one determinate kind of what is, and this in several senses, namely, in the sense of matter or that which in itself is not 'a this'; and, again, in the sense of form or essence, which is that precisely in virtue of which a thing is called 'a this'; and, finally, in the sense of that which is

compounded of both matter and form. Now matter is potentially
(potency), form actuality. Of the latter, there are two degrees
which are related to one another as, for instance, knowledge is
related to the exercise of knowledge. Among substances are by
general consensus reckoned bodies, and especially natural bodies.
For they are the principles of all other bodies. Of natural bodies
some have life in them, others do not. . . . Every natural body
which has life in it is a substance in the sense of a composite.
But since it is also a body of such and such a kind, *viz.* having
life, the body cannot be a soul. The body is the subject or matter,
not what is attributed to it. Hence, the soul must be a substance
in the sense of the form of a natural body having life potentially
within it.

Thus, Aristotle insists that the substantial nature of the soul is not
incompatible but essentially connected with the fact that it is also a
'form,' an εἶδός τι[57] or, perhaps, 'form in itself.' It is not, and this is
of paramount importance, merely an εἶδός τινος, that is, 'the form
of something.' It will be noted that Aristotle contends that substance is
'act' or 'actualization' or 'actuality.' Hence, he defines the soul as the
act or actualization of the body potentially endowed with life. In
other words, the soul, as substance, is not the act or actualization of any
physical body, but rather that of a *living* body, or at least potentially
living body. It is the actualization of a potentially living body or of a
body which has the 'potency of living'—the principle or form by
virtue of which a body becomes a living body, that is, an 'animated
body.'[58] This being so, the soul is inseparably connected with the living
body. For as long as the body lives, the latter cannot be separated
from the soul, at least not for a protracted period of time. In this sense,
and only in this, the soul is also to some extent an εἶδός τι—the εἶδος
τοῦ σώματος—without, however, losing its original and persevering
substantiality or εἶδός τι. Whenever the body ceases to live, the soul
becomes separated from the body. But since the soul is also a substance, an εἶδός τι, it lives on and persists even after this separation.
Hence, as an εἶδός τι, the soul is wholly independent of the body. It is
εἶδός τι, irrespective of whether it is connected with, or separated
from, the body. As an εἶδός τινος or εἶδος τοῦ σώματος, however,
it is also the 'quickening' principle of the body and, hence, in some
way connected with the body—or, as Plato would have it, 'temporarily
imprisoned' in the body.

In his *Commentary* to Aristotle's *De Anima*, Simplicius maintains:[59]

Plato is in every case accustomed to call by the same name the forms and the corporeal things which are formed according to these forms. Aristotle, however, when the thing thus formed is divisible, avoids using the same term, because of the great differences between the divisible corporeal thing and the indivisible form. The reasoning soul he describes not only as limited, but also as a limit (a measure ?). For as the soul is between the indivisible and the divisible, being in a sense both, so too the soul is between the limit and the limited, exhibiting both characteristics—the latter as moving discursively, the former because it always moves in obedience to limits, and because all that has been unfolded is gathered into one. In this respect, it is likened to the limiting reason. And because of this he says in his dialogue on the soul entitled *Eudemus* that the soul is a kind of form (εἶδός τι), and praises those who describe the soul as being receptive of forms— not the whole soul, but only the rational soul, as knowing the forms that have the second degree of truth. For it is to reason, which is greater than the soul, that the really true forms correspond.

These remarks of Simplicius are directed at the passages in the *De Anima*, where Aristotle discusses the rational or intellectual soul.[60] Here Aristotle insists that 'if thinking is like perceiving, thinking must be either a process in which the soul is acted upon by what can be thought, or a process different though analogous to that.' Accordingly, the rational soul is 'capable of receiving the form (εἴδη) of an object. Hence it must be potentially identical in character with its object without being this object itself. For the mind must be related to what is thinkable. . . .'[61] And:[62]

> since everything is potentially an object of thought, the intellect . . . must be free from all admixture. For the presence of what is alien to the intellect's nature is a hindrance and an obstacle. It follows, therefore, that the intellect too, like the sensitive part [of the soul], can have no nature of its own other than that of having a certain potentiality. Hence, that in the soul which is called the intellect, is, before it thinks, not actually any real thing. For this reason it cannot reasonably be regarded as integrated with the body. For if it were integrated, it would acquire some quality of the body. . . . But as it is, it has none. It was a good idea to call the soul the 'domicile of forms,' although this description is true only for the intellectual soul, and the soul holds the forms only potentially, not actually.

Simplicius' comments point to the fact that in the *De Anima* Aristotle proclaims a certain affinity of the intellectual soul with the 'forms' (εἴδη). This 'certain affinity' seems to consist in the fact that the intellectual soul is 'receptive of the forms.' Aristotle, Simplicius continues, prefers to call the intellectual soul a 'certain kind of form' (εἶδός τι), and not simply a form (εἴδη). It will be remembered that in the *Phaedo* Plato refers to the form and to whatever possesses this form as εἶδος (such as the Idea of the Good or the Good). Aristotle, on the other hand, avoids this identification, probably because the Idea of the Good is indivisible, while something good is plainly divisible. Since the rational or intellectual soul is capable of knowing the forms (εἴδη), at least potentially, Aristotle chooses to call the soul εἶδος—a term which is common to all pure forms in general. Or, to put it differently: in the *Eudemus*, as has been shown, the soul is not perchance 'the form of something' (εἶδός τινος), but rather a 'form in itself' (εἶδός τι)—an Idea or something of the nature of an Idea.[63] Hence, it may be concluded that Simplicius' reference to the soul as εἶδός τι is primarily an attempt to give expression to the fact that the soul is something incorporeal or immaterial (or intellectual), capable of intuitively grasping and thus of potentially possessing the true forms (εἴδη)—the intelligible forms common to all objects of rational knowledge.[64] No special comment is required to point out that this particular notion definitely has a Platonic flavor.

All this raises a further problem, already touched upon, namely, whether in the *Eudemus* Aristotle considers the soul (the rational soul ?) a Separate Idea—a problem which has preoccupied many scholars. In any event, W. Jaeger insists that in the *Eudemus* the soul is not simply the 'form of something (εἶδός τινος),' but rather a 'form in itself (εἶδός τι).' Hence, Jaeger concludes, the soul is 'an Idea, or something of the nature of an Idea.'[65] This being so, Jaeger concludes, at the time Aristotle composed the *Eudemus* he still subscribed to Plato's doctrine of the Separate Ideas.[66] In retrospect, it appears that Jaeger's thesis, which undoubtedly is influenced by his overriding concern with the evolutionary aspects of Aristotle's intellectual development, hinges on the assumption that for (the early) Aristotle all immaterial substances—and the soul is, and on account of its immortality must be, an immaterial substance—are Separate Ideas. Moreover, according to the testimony of Simplicius, the soul is an εἶδος. Jaeger's argument, however, overlooks the fact that in *Metaphysics* 1077 a 32–3 ('But how can lines be a substance (οὐσία)? Neither as a form [εἶδος] . . . as the soul. . . .'), Aristotle apparently still considers the soul a substance as well as an εἶδος or form, without considering it a Separate Idea.[67] A further argument against Jaeger's position would be the fact that Plato himself never considered the soul a Separate Idea, but rather as something 'mediating' between the Separate Ideas and the corporeal world. Perhaps R. A. Gauthier comes closest to what seems to be a sensible solution to this involved problem: the expression εἶδός τι conveys the notion that the soul is 'similar' to, rather than identical with, the Separate Ideas or εἴδη;[68] and that because it is an εἶδός τι, that is, something 'similar' to the Separate Ideas, it is capable of intuitively grasping (or receiving) the εἴδη. For only 'like can grasp like.'[69] Be this as it may, this much seems to be fairly certain: in the *Eudemus*, Aristotle maintains and demonstrates, perhaps in a somewhat 'primitive' manner, that the (intellectual ?) soul must be immaterial as well as substantial if it is to be immortal.

In conclusion, the following might tentatively be said about the doctrinal content of the *Eudemus*: the soul is a substance, though an immaterial substance; it lives on after the body has died; the soul's life after the body's death is happier, more 'natural' and certainly far superior to its state of earthly 'incarceration'; it (or at least its intellectual aspect) is immortal, that is, indestructible; it probably existed before it became connected with the physical body; and it is the 'quickening' principle of the living body. All these characteristics or functions of the soul—to which we should add that the soul is also a 'form in itself' (εἶδός τι)[70] or something similar to the Idea, and that it possesses recollection (*anamnesis*), at least (for Aristotle) recollection of what it has experienced while incarcerated in the body— are undoubtedly under the influence of the Platonic *Phaedo*, although we may discern that Aristotle does evince a certain independence of Plato on the subject of the soul, especially in matters of argumentation, demonstration and proof, which in the case of Aristotle frequently assume the technical form of a syllogism.[71] All this suggests that the *Eudemus* is also a 'reminiscence' of the Platonic *Phaedo*: both dialogues commemorate the death of a beloved person. In itself, this would lend support to the assumption that the *Eudemus* and the *Phaedo* are fairly similar in content as well as aim. Hence, it might also be maintained that, in a general way, the *Eudemus* is modeled on a Platonic dialogue composed about thirty or more years earlier. One might interject here that these thirty years were a period of intensive re-thinking and re-writing, by Plato[72] as well as by other members of the Academy, of the many problems discussed in the *Phaedo*. In this special sense, the *Eudemus*, which was composed about 352 B.C. (or slightly later), might be called a 'regression' to a philosophic position held by Plato during the eighties. The *Eudemus*, then, might actually be called the literary expression of a sentiment which found its natural and proper outlet in a reversion to a stage in the philosophic (and literary) development of Plato that was already a thing of the past at the time the *Eudemus* was written. This 'older' philosophic position, however, provided an emotionally satisfying expression befitting an exalted *consolatio mortis*.[73] The realization that the Aristotelian *Eudemus* is essentially a *consolatio mortis*, it is contended here, remains a decisive factor in the understanding and evaluating the particular psychology expounded in this early dialogue.[74]

# Chapter VI

# Aristotle's
## *On Justice*★

The *On Justice* (Περὶ Δικαιοσύνης) was probably the most extensive and, it appears, one of the most popular compositions among the lost early dialogues of Aristotle. The ancient 'catalogues' of Aristotle's writings indicate that it consisted of four books.[1] It is also known, or at least presumed, that a number of ancient authors refer to the *On Justice*, in most instances by indirection. Moreover, it is widely believed that, like the majority of Aristotle's earliest works, this *On Justice* was composed in the form of a dialogue.[2] It was probably a 'dialogue of discussion'—that is, it consisted of lengthy and sober philosophic expositions, demonstrations and investigations carried on in accordance with a strict and presumably undramatic method of presentation. Although this particular literary form (which becomes noticeable also in Plato's latest works) was probably influenced by Isocrates and his literary style, the extent of this influence is difficult to assess.

Until fairly recently it was widely held that except for a few meager and not too informative 'fragments,' excerpts or doxographical references of rather doubtful value, this important, and without doubt, instructive composition had been lost beyond all hope of successful recovery and possible reconstruction. This lamentable loss, together with the loss of the Aristotelian *Politicus*, the *To Alexander or A Plea for Colonization* and the *On Kingship*, has deprived modern scholarship of a better understanding and appreciation of the political and ethical theories entertained by the young Aristotle.[3] Notwithstanding this calamity, the *On Justice* seems to offer at least a chance of implementing our deficient knowledge of Aristotle's earliest views on ethics and politics, and this because we possess a number of what appear to be reliable fragments of this work, something not realized until quite recently.

In 1863, J. Bernays made the somewhat revolutionary but certainly correct suggestion that the lost or 'exoteric' writings (dialogues) of Aristotle, including the *On Justice*, are occasionally referred to or 'cited' in the preserved 'esoteric' or doctrinal treatises of the Stagirite. Bernays did not indicate or specify, however, to which particular lost work any one of these citations referred. Moreover, Bernays advanced the pioneering hypothesis that in the *On Justice* Aristotle probably approached his subject from a political, ethical, psychological and systematic point of view.[4] Bernays based his conjecture on three passages which he considered to be excerpts from or 'fragments' of this lost dialogue. First, Demetrius, in his *De Elocutione* 28 (frag. 82, Rose; frag. 1, Ross),[5] reports that in the *On Justice* Aristotle had remarked: 'What city or enemy have they [*scil.*, the Athenians] conquered that is worth their own city which they have lost?'[6] In the opinion of Bernays, this statement (which implies that the expansionist foreign policy of Athens during the fifth century B.C. was detrimental to Athenian domestic policy—to the democratic system as well as to social justice) would indicate that the *On Justice* dealt primarily with 'political justice.' Secondly, Chrysippus, according to the testimony of Plutarch, *De Repugnantiis Stoicis* 15 (fragment 86, Rose),[7] credits Aristotle with having maintained in the *On Justice* that if pleasure were to be considered the ultimate end as well as the final criterion of all human actions or, for that matter, the supreme moral good, justice in the moral sense of the term would most certainly be destroyed and with it all other virtues. This statement, Bernays surmised, seems to imply that the *On Justice* also discussed such ethical problems as the ultimate moral end, the highest ethical standard, the nature of pleasure, the relation of pleasure to moral virtue, and the relationship of justice to the other cardinal virtues.[8] Thirdly, Porphyry, according to Boethius, *Commentarii in Librum Aristotelis Περὶ Ἑρμηνείας* (frag. 87, Rose),[9] relates that in his *On Justice* Aristotle had insisted that 'thoughts' (νοήματα) are by nature (ψύσει) distinct from 'sensations' (αἰσθήματα). This, Bernays concluded, would indicate that in the *On Justice* Aristotle also discussed certain logical, epistemological, psychological and systematic-speculative topics. So broad an approach to the philosophic problem of justice, which includes political, ethical and general philosophic issues of an almost universal scope, Bernays conjectured, calls to mind a similarly all-encompassing treatment of essentially the same topics, using an equally broad basis: Plato's *Republic* which had, interestingly enough, in antiquity the subtitle, *On Justice.*[10] Bernays' thesis, which compared the Aristotelian *On Justice* and the Platonic *Republic*, at the same time implies that in his *On Justice* Aristotle also took issue with, as well as rejected, some of the notions advanced in Plato's *Republic*. This thesis is by no means an entirely novel idea. For already Carneades, according to the testimony of Lactantius (Cicero),[11] had insisted that the *On Justice* of Aristotle was a critique (?) of Plato's *Republic*. Finally, Bernays also observed that the remark found in Aristotle, *Metaphysics* 1076 a 28–9, that 'the majority of these points [*scil.*, the subject of the Separate Ideas] have been discussed frequently in the exoteric works,' undoubtedly refers to the *On Justice* or, to be more exact, to the systematic or logical treatment of justice in the *On Justice*.[12]

Likewise in the year 1863 Valentin Rose, in his unusual but fascinating work entitled *Aristoteles Pseudepigraphus* (Leipzig, 1863), took up the problem of Aristotle's *On Justice*. In keeping with his somewhat extravagant general thesis that there never existed any 'lost works' of Aristotle, Rose rejected as completely spurious each and every fragment assigned or credited to Aristotle's 'exoteric works' and, for that matter, all his 'exoteric works.' He did so on the grounds that these fragments were 'too Platonic' in tenor and doctrinal content to be considered trustworthy remnants of authentic Aristotelian compositions.[13] Like J. Bernays, Rose never conceded that there ever existed a 'Platonic period' in Aristotle's early intellectual development. He also alleged that the fragment from Demetrius, *De Elocutione* 28, contained a serious and indeed fatal anachronism in that it apparently referred to political events which, according to Rose, must have taken place after the death of Aristotle.[14] This is not the place, however, to discuss in detail the peculiar methods and views of Rose, which, as has already been noted, for some time exercised a controlling and almost fateful influence on all subsequent Aristotelian scholarship. Without abandoning his basic attitude that all fragments credited to the early Aristotle are wholly spurious, in 1886 Rose included in his *Aristotelis Qui Ferebantur Librorum Fragmenta* (Leipzig, 1886) a number of fragments which he believed to be in some ways related to the *On Justice* (which he still considered spurious): Cicero, *De Republica* III. 8. 12 (frag. 82); Demetrius, Περὶ Ἑρμηνείας (*De Elocutione*) 28 (frag. 82); Athenaeus, *Epitome* I. 6B (frag. 83); Suetonius, Περὶ Βλασφημιῶν (ed. Miller), p. 416 (frag. 84); Gregory of Corinth, *Ad Hermogenem* 19 (frag. 84); Suda, *Eurybatus* (frag. 84); Lactantius, *Insitutiones Divinae* V. 15; Lactantius, *Epitome Institutionum Divinarum ad Pentadium Fratrem* 55 (frag. 85); Plutarch, *De Repugnantiis Stoicis* 15 (frag. 86); Porphyry, *Comment. in Arist.* Περὶ Ἑρμηνείας, as he is quoted in Boethius, *Commentarii in Librum Aristotelis* Περὶ Ἑρμηνείας, vol. II (ed. C. Meiser, Leipzig, 1880), p. 27, line 13 (frag. 87); Themistius, *Oratio* II, p. 41, ed. L. Dindorf (frag. 88); Cicero, *De Officiis* II. 16. 56–7 (frag. 89); Athenaeus, *Deipnosophistae* VIII. 335F (fragment 90); Cicero, *Tusculanae Disputa-*

*tiones* V. 35. 101 (Strabo XIV. 5. 9—fragment 90); and Cicero, *De Finibus* II. 32. 106 (frag. 90). This list, which most certainly constitutes a very inadequate collection, in fact contains some rather doubtful fragments.[15]

E. Heitz, who made his own compilation of Aristotelian fragments,[16] on general grounds upheld the authenticity of the *On Justice* and, for that matter, that of most so-called 'exoteric' works of Aristotle. Because of the alleged anachronism contained in Demetrius' report (frag. 82, Rose; frag. 1, Ross)—Heitz assumes, as Rose had done before him, that Demetrius alludes here to the Lamian War which occurred in 322 B.C., the year in which Aristotle died—he denied, however, that this particular passage constitutes a fragment of the *On Justice* and, hence, ever was part of the original Aristotelian dialogue, or that it referred at all to this work.[17] Heitz concurred with J. Bernays that Aristotle, *Metaphysics* 1076 a 28–9, contains an allusion to the *On Justice* (which, therefore, must have been highly critical of Plato's doctrine of the Separate Ideas). Heitz, however, based his view primarily on the testimony of Proclus, *In Platonis Alcibiadem Comment.*, p. 45, lines 13 ff. (ed. L. G. Westerink).[18] Moreover, Heitz maintained that Carneades' simultaneous attacks upon the concept of political justice, as it had been devised by Plato and Aristotle (frag. 85, Rose), indicate substantial doctrinal similarities rather than philosophic disagreements[19] between the ethical and political teachings of Plato and those of Aristotle.[20] As a matter of fact, he insisted that certain early dialogues of Aristotle, including the *On Justice*, assume a philosophic position quite similar to that of Plato, and that, therefore, these dialogues to some extent also conflict with Aristotle's later doctrinal or 'esoteric' treatises. Thus, as early as 1865, Heitz believed to have detected in the early writings of Aristotle the beginning of a progressive evolution from an early, though not altogether convincing, 'Platonism' to a later 'Aristotelianism.'[21] In Heitz's opinion, this evolutionary trend is fully confirmed by a passage from Plutarch, *De Virtute Morali* 3 (*Moralia* 441F ff.), which Heitz, and no other scholar, related to the Aristotelian *On Justice*. According to this particular passage, Aristotle at one time must have adhered to Plato's theory of the tripartite soul, while at a later period he apparently combined the $\vartheta\upsilon\mu o\epsilon\iota\delta\grave{\epsilon}\varsigma$ and the $\grave{\epsilon}\pi\iota\vartheta\upsilon\mu\eta\tau\iota\kappa\grave{o}\nu$ into a single 'irrational part' or 'irrational function' of the soul which he then confronted with the 'rational function' or 'rational part.'[22] Finally, Heitz also believed that the following two passages were originally derived from the *On Justice*: Stobaeus, *Florilegium* III. 20. 55[23] (where we are told that whenever the $\vartheta\upsilon\mu\grave{o}\varsigma$ gains the upper hand over the rational part, it wholly confuses man and disables him to foresee the consequences of his action); and Stobaeus, *Florilegium* III. 20. 46[24] (where it is maintained that whenever blind passion gains full control, the rational part simply withdraws, avoiding the ϑυμὸς as one would avoid a despicable tyrant).[25]

On the strength of Demetrius, *De Elocutione* 28 (frag. 82, Rose; frag. 1, Ross), which until fairly recently was considered the only important and perhaps the only reliable (*pace* Heitz) excerpt from the *On Justice*, it could be argued with a reasonable degree of success that this dialogue discussed a concept of justice which had ethical as well as political (socio-ethical) implications. This fragment seems to denounce on moral grounds (and in ironical terms) any form of aggressive imperialism or expansionism which, as historical experience has shown, only too often leads to a restriction or complete loss of domestic political freedom and to a progressive deterioration of 'government by law.' In this sense the *On Justice* may also contain (as does, for instance, the Pseudo-Xenophontic *Old Oligarch*, Plato's *Gorgias* and *Republic*, or Aristotle's *Constitution of Athens*) a vicious attack upon certain aspects of Athenian foreign policy or upon certain Athenian statesmen (and perhaps on Athenian democracy in general). It also alludes to the tragic repercussions this policy was having, and had had, not only for the proper administration of justice at home, but also for the whole of Athenian domestic affairs. At the same time, the *On Justice* also condemns any and all efforts to make pleasure or some material gain ('compare the profit they have reaped with the loss they have sustained') the supreme principle as well as the ultimate end or criterion of all politics and ethics—to consider utilitarian or pragmatic considerations the final guide for all political actions. Moreover, the *On Justice* calls justice, or the practice of justice, the foundation or synthesis of all virtues, thus establishing a sort of ethical value hierarchy akin to that propagated in the Platonic *Republic*.

Aside from this rather meager information, which in its general aspects is much too broad and, again, much too restricted to afford a workable insight into the specific philosophic message of the *On Justice*, practically nothing was known about this dialogue. Thus it appeared that for the time being the search for the missing *On Justice*, on the whole, had been quite unsuccessful. Unless a novel approach to this problem could be devised, the general doctrinal content of the *On Justice* would forever remain unknown or at least become a matter of mere conjecture based upon the assumption that the main theme of the *On Justice* was fashioned after Plato's *Republic*.

In 1923, W. Jaeger made the proposal already suggested by J. Bernays in 1863, that the *On Justice* was modeled on the *Republic* of Plato. Jaeger believed that this could be inferred not only from the 'existence of so many corresponding dialogues,' but also from the fact that in his *De Republica* Cicero makes use of both Plato's *Republic* and Aristotle's *On Justice*. In Plato's *Republic*, Jaeger continued, 'the political philosophy develops out of the problem of justice, just as it must have done in the . . . [Aristotelian] *On Justice* . . . .[26] The [Platonic] *Republic* must already have obtained the subtitle of *On Justice* by the time of Aristotle.'[27] In keeping with his evolutionary thesis of the intellectual development of Aristotle's early philosophic thought, Jaeger, however, rejected J. Bernays' theory that the Aristotelian *On Justice* was a critique or, perhaps, even an outright rejection of the main ideas championed by Plato in his *Republic*. That the Aristotelian *On Justice* in some ways is related to the Platonic *Republic*, as we have already seen, may also be gathered from Lactantius, *Institutiones Divinae* V. 15 (Cicero, *De Republica* III. 6. 9), where we are informed that Carneades, a prominent member of the Middle Academy (*c.* 214–13 or 213/12–129/28 B.C.), jointly refuted 'Aristotle's and Plato's praise of justice.'[28] This joint refutation is interpreted by some scholars as an indication that Plato's *Republic* and Aristotle's *On Justice* advanced essentially similar (or identical?) political and philosophic views.

Jaeger's opinions have received the full support of E. Bignone.[29] Bignone also suggested that there exists a strong and perhaps compelling similarity between fragment 84 (Rose) of the *On Justice*—the account of the thief Eurybatus (or Eurybates) who remained unpunished by simply 'vanishing'—and Plato, *Republic* 359C ff. (and 612B),[30] which narrates the unusual story of Gyges and his wondrous ring that made its bearer invisible.[31] According to fragment 84 (Rose), in his *On Justice* Aristotle spoke about a thief called Eurybatus who, 'when he was caught and put in chains, was encouraged by his guards to show how he managed to get over walls and into houses. On being set free . . . he climbed very easily, escaped from the roof and got away.' The story of Gyges, as narrated by Plato in the *Republic*, relates that by making himself invisible with the help of his magic ring, Gyges committed a series of villainous crimes. Possessing such a ring, when used by evil people, Plato implies, 'no man would keep his hands off what is not his own, when he could safely take what he liked . . . or get into houses . . . or kill or release from prison whom he pleased, and in all respects would be like a god among men. Then the action of the just man would be like the action of the unjust man.

They would, in the final analysis, come to the same point.'[32] In re-counting the story of Eurybatus, Aristotle, as Plato had previously done in his reference to the fantastic deeds of Gyges, apparently wishes to demonstrate and illustrate the effects of a situation where crimes go unpunished and wickedness prevails.[33] Bignone also insisted, though probably without much success, that Aelian (*De Natura Animalium* IV. 49) and Stobaeus (*Florilegium* II. 7. 13), who maintain that all living creatures, including animals, have a sort of 'natural law' or 'natural justice,' take issue with something Aristotle supposedly had said in his *On Justice*.[34]

An entirely novel and, it seems, decisive as well as fruitful approach to Aristotle's *On Justice* and its possible recovery was inaugurated in 1957 by P. Moraux.[35] Instead of limiting himself to the traditional (and unpromising) attempts of seeking out likely quotations or excerpts from, or references to, this dialogue in a variety of ancient and Patristic authors, critics or doxographers, Moraux asserted two major and, it appears, essentially correct theses. First, certain definite stages in the doctrinal evolution of Aristotelian philosophy, including his ethical and political philosophy, in some ways must be reflected in the *On Justice*—a view that had already been held by H. Heitz,[36] J. Bernays[37] and W. Jaeger.[38] Secondly, the numerous references to the lost 'exoteric' compositions contained in the preserved 'esoteric' or doc-trinal treatises of Aristotle must, among others, also refer to the *On Justice*. As regards the subject matter, Moraux continued, it is only reasonable to assume that Aristotle's preserved works on ethics and politics would above all refer back to or reflect the *On Justice*.[39] After all, the *On Justice* was probably one of the most important and certainly the most extensive ethico-political composition belonging to the 'exoteric period' of Aristotle's literary activity. In short, according to Moraux, in his doctrinal treatises Aristotle at times (and for a variety of reasons) resorts to the expedient of citing or referring to some of his earlier writings.[40] Unfortunately, barring a few exceptions, Aristotle does not name the specific title of the particular work to which he refers, but rather limits himself to general allusions to the λόγοι ἐξωτερικοί, or to τὰ ἐξωτερικά. Since the *On Justice* treats of such subjects as ethics and politics, Moraux conjectured, it is only reasonable to surmise that whenever in his doctrinal treatises on ethics and politics Aristotle refers to the 'exoteric works,' he has foremost in mind the *On Justice*.

Like some of his predecessors, Moraux also insisted that the *On Justice* was composed in imitation (and at times in opposition to)

Plato's *Republic*.[41] Moreover, he contended that valuable and reliable traces of the *On Justice* ought to be contained[42] in the *De Republica* of Cicero, in the writings of Plutarch, as well as in those of Stobaeus (as already suggested by H. Heitz), Callicratidas the Neo-Pythagorean,[43] Pseudo-Archytas,[44] Ocellus Lucanus[45] and in the Platonic (?) *First Alcibiades*.[46] Moraux also called on the *On Justice* in order to explain a discernible lack of 'systematic integration' to be found in Book V of the *Nicomachean Ethics*,[47]—a most original and brilliant insight, which implies that Book V of the *Nicomachean Ethics* constitutes a valuable and unique fountainhead of many 'fragments' of or references to the *On Justice*. Finally, Moraux attempted to solve the vexing and involved problem of the alleged 'Platonism' propagated in the *On Justice*.[48] He conceded that indisputable similarities exist between the *On Justice* and certain basic doctrines as they have been advanced in Plato's *Republic* as well as in other Platonic dialogues. Nevertheless, he maintained that the *On Justice* also manifests substantial and far-reaching deviations from Plato. Specifically, Moraux stressed Aristotle's more realistic 'political pluralism' which justifies a variety of governmental forms and, in consequence, a variety of forms of (political) justice— notions which are radically opposed to the 'political monism' of the 'monolithic *politeia*' proposed by Plato. Moreover, the psychology advocated in the *On Justice*, Moraux maintained, differs considerably from that projected in the Platonic *Republic*. And, finally, while Plato taught an irreconcilable opposition between soul and body, Aristotle, in the *On Justice*, holds that the two co-operate in a certain way, thus making the body the useful and desirable handmaid or tool of the soul.[49]

The nature of the several fragments, excerpts or references— authentic as well as spurious—that are usually cited as remnants of the Aristotelian *On Justice* makes it impossible at this time even to think of reconstructing with any degree of success the details of this dialogue. G. Verbeke, who quite recently made an attempt to do so by relying on and co-ordinating the several fragments and references as well as the suggestions made by a number of scholars, has come to the distressing conclusion that the philosophic, ethical and political topics assigned to the *On Justice* might very well belong to some other 'exoteric' works of Aristotle.[50]

On the basis of certain similarities he believed to have detected between the psychology discussed in the Aristotelian *Protrepticus* (which has been dated fairly definitely about 352–50 B.C.), and the psychology advocated in the *On Justice*, P. Moraux has tried to date this dialogue shortly after the year 352 B.C.,[51] that is, about the same time as or slightly later than the *Protrepticus*. I. Düring, on the other hand, tentatively dates it about 355, that is, some time prior to the *Protrepticus*.[52] The present author, in turn, has attempted to date it slightly anterior to the *Protrepticus*, that is, between 358–57 and 352 B.C., and probably closer to the latter date.[53]

What appears to be an extremely important fragment of the *On Justice* (which, with the exception of Moraux, seems to have escaped the notice of scholars) can be found in Aristotle's *Politics* 1278 b 30–1279 a 21, where Aristotle explicitly refers to the distinction of the several kinds of authority already made in the λόγοι ἐξωτερικοί. It is contended here that this particular reference to the λόγοι ἐξωτερικοί definitely points to the *On Justice*. The topic would be in harmony with the basic tenor of the *On Justice* which, according to Moraux, justified a variety of constitutional forms within the body politic, thus refuting Plato's 'monolithic polity':

There is no difficulty in distinguishing the several types of authority. They often have been defined already in the λόγοι ἐξωτερικοί [*scil.*, in the *On Justice*]. Although the 'slave by nature' and the 'master by nature' have in fact the same interests, the rule of a master is nevertheless exercised primarily with a view to the interest of the master, but accidentally considers also that of the slave, since, if the slave should perish, the rule of the master terminates with him. The 'government' of a wife and children as well as that of a household, which we have called household management, on the other hand, is exercised above all for the good of the governed or for the common good of the governed, as we can see it to be the case in medicine, gymnastics and in the arts or crafts in general, which are only accidentally concerned with the good of the artists or craftsmen themselves.[54] For there exists no reason why the trainer may not sometimes practice gymnastics, and the helmsman is always a member of the ship's crew. The trainer or the helmsman considers the good of those committed to his care. But when he is one of the persons cared for, he accidentally participates in the advantage, for the helmsman is also a sailor, and the trainer becomes one of those who are in training. And the same also holds true in politics. When the city is constituted on the principle of equality and likeness, the citizens think that they ought to hold office by turns. Formerly, as might be expected, everyone would take his turn rendering public service. But then, again, someone would look after his private interests, just as he, while holding public office, had looked after their interests.[55] But now, for the sake of the advantage which is to be gained from public revenues and from public office, men want to be always in public office. One might imagine that the rulers, being sickly persons, were kept in health only while they continued in public office.[56] In such cases we may be sure that they would be hunting after public positions. The conclusion is evident. Governments which have a regard for the common interest are constituted in accordance with strict principles of justice and are therefore true (political) forms. But those governments which regard only the interest of the rulers are all defective and perverted forms, for they are despotic, whereas a city is a community of free men.

Aristotle might possibly recapitulate here some of the notions he had originally (and in greater detail) advanced in the *On Justice*.

In the light of the few and not always very enlightening fragments and excerpts, as well as on the basis of competent investigations, educated hypotheses and informed conjectures advanced by a number of scholars, no less than on the strength of some 'references' or what seem to be 'references' to the 'exoteric' works (the *On Justice*)[57] found in Aristotle's *Eudemian Ethics, Nicomachean Ethics, Politics* and in the *Magna Moralia*,[58] a few vague statements may tentatively be made here concerning the likely doctrines and views advanced in the *On Justice*. We cannot possibly know the exact wording of these doctrines, the particular sequence in which they were originally presented, or in what part or 'book' of this dialogue they appeared, provided they were at all contained in the *On Justice* and not, as some scholars would have it, in some other early composition or compositions of Aristotle, such as the *Politicus*, the *On Kingship* or the *To Alexander or A Plea for Colonization*. We cannot even be certain whether these passages are in fact 'references.'

The subsequent remarks, needless to say, are only generalized by statements or abstracts of certain basic ideas that might, or might not, have been contained in the *On Justice*. They are certainly not quotations, nor are they fragments in the traditional sense of the term, but should be regarded merely as a kind of tentative (and disorderly and probably incomplete) 'table of likely contents.'[59] They are culled, with varying degrees of success, from the extant Aristotelian writings on ethics and politics, especially from those passages where Aristotle

refs, or seems to refer, to what he had previously said in his λόγοι
ἐξωτερικοί[60]—where, judging from the general context, content,
phrasing or referential nature of the statement, it seems to be permissible
to assume that he had in mind something he had previously stated in an
earlier work, that is, in the *On Justice*. Moreover, these remarks are in
part reinforced by citations from ancient authors—the 'fragments' in
the traditional sense of the term—which refer, or appear to refer, to
this dialogue.[61]

(1) There are three fundamental forms or principles (ἀρχαί) of
authority: domestic authority, despotic (arbitrary) authority and
political authority.[62] (2) Certain undeniable analogies or similarities
exist between domestic authority (household authority) and political
authority.[63] (3) Justice is the basis of all proper authority.[64] (4) The
proper interaction of justice and authority brings about the right
relationship within any social or political organization and grouping.[65]
(5) Political justice[66] recognizes as well as determines the rights and
duties of the governed and the governing.[67] [(6) Political justice consists
of or is based upon what is just by nature as well as what is just according to (positive) law.][68] (7) Despotic (arbitrary) authority is exercised
primarily in the interest or for the benefit of the ruler.[69] (8) Despotic
authority, being devoid of justice (and friendship), is no authority at
all (at least, not in a moral sense)[70] [except perhaps in the relation of
master and slave or in the narrow confines of the household or
family (?)].[71]

(9) There are three forms of justice corresponding to the three forms
of authority: domestic justice, which is the relationship of husband and
wife, parent and child, and master and slave;[72] despotic justice, which
is in fact no justice at all; and political justice.[73] (10) [Political] justice in
general is a form of proportionate equality among (equal?) citizens of
one and the same city.[74] (11) This equality is based on the equality of all
citizens (natural equality or equality before the law?); and the equal,
equitable or just distribution of power, liability, rights, duties and
privileges is proportionate to the citizens' merits and abilities.[75]
(12) Equality among citizens within one and the same city consists in
the equality of rights and duties.[76]

[(13) Justice is (selfless?) obedience to the laws.][77] [(14) Justice
conceived as obedience to the laws guarantees a certain equality among
the citizens of one and the same city.][78] [(15) Justice is that which serves
the greatest number (and hence is also an 'altruistic virtue').][79]
(16) Social relationships are based not merely on justice (or laws), but
also on friendship.[80] (17) The several forms of friendship—friendship

founded on merit (or affection), friendship resting on mutual utility or advantage, and friendship based on mutual agreement[81]—are analogous to the several forms of justice.[82] (18) Like political justice, friendship has its foundation in the notion of equality (among equals?).[83] [(19) Friendship is superior to law and, hence, constitutes the basis of a superior kind of community, in the family (household) no less than in the body politic (city).][84]

(20) There is such a thing as 'love of oneself,' which implies that man is a friend unto himself.[85] (21) This 'love of oneself' is also a sort of standard or measure which enables man to determine and evaluate his love (or friendship) for others.[86] (22) Only by understanding the meaning of self-love can man have a true and unselfish love and friendship for others.[87] (23) 'Love of oneself' is the foundation of 'justice towards oneself';[88] love of the other, or friendship, is the basis of 'justice towards the other.'[89] (24) 'Love of oneself,' which requires a distinction between the lover and the loved, presupposes a 'bifurcation' of the soul[90]—a division of the soul into a rational and irrational (or appetitive) part.[91]

(25) The principles of justice, authority and friendship also apply to the soul.[92] (26) The soul consists of a governing (rational) and a governed (irrational or appetitive) part.[93] (27) Injustice is the discord between these two parts of the soul—a sort of self-hate that manifests itself in the several vices.[94] [(28) This implies that man can be an 'enemy to himself.'][95] (29) Justice is the harmony between the two parts of the soul in which the rational part controls (and restrains) the irrational part.[96] (30) The governance or authority of the rational part of the soul over the irrational part is virtue.[97] (31) Justice is the most excellent and most exalted of all virtues.[98]

(32) 'Rational concepts' or 'rational thoughts' ($\nu o \acute{\eta} \mu \alpha \tau \alpha$), being related to theoretic reason, are distinct from and superior to mere sensations ($\alpha \grave{\iota} \sigma \vartheta \acute{\eta} \mu \alpha \tau \alpha$) which are related to the irrational part of the soul.[99] (33) A distinction must also be made between 'theoretic reason' and 'practical reason.'[100] (34) 'Theoretic (or 'scientific') reason' is concerned with heaven and earth as they are; 'practical reason' ('deliberative reason') deals with things that are what they are in virtue of the fact that they are related to us in a certain (practical) way.[101] (35) The 'virtue' of theoretic reason is $\sigma o \varphi \acute{\iota} \alpha$, that of practical reason $\varphi \rho \acute{o} \nu \eta \sigma \iota \varsigma$.[102]

(36) According to the principle of justice, the body is the handmaid (or slave) of the rational soul, enabling the latter to carry out certain tasks within the corporeal world.[103] (37) Reason rules (or is supposed

to rule) the irrational (part of the) soul as well as the body with justice and affection (friendship), just as the good ruler rules his subjects and the good head of a household rules his family with justice and affection.[104] (38) The irrational part of the soul (and the body) 'in justice' defers and submits to the rational part of the soul and its commands or counsels.[105] (39) The submission of the irrational part of the soul (and of the body) to the rational part is also based on friendship: the irrational part (and the body) loves the rational part which, in turn, is solicitous about (and loves) the irrational part (and the body).[106] [(40) This, then, is part of man's 'justice towards himself' —his 'love of himself' or 'self-love.'][107] Whenever the irrational part of the soul (or the body) gains ascendancy or control over the rational part, the former (or the body) usurps a tyrannical authority to which it is not entitled and which, therefore, is 'injustice.'[108] [(42) Injustice is the rule of the irrational over the rational, of the 'wrong' over the 'right,' of the body (passion) over the soul (reason).][109] (43) Whenever passion gains control or dominates, reason takes to flight, avoiding the outbursts of irrational and blind passion, just as the just man avoids a despicable tyrant.[110] (44) When passion, like a rebellious and unjust subject, rises against reason, it blinds man and prevents him from foreseeing by way of reasoning the absurd consequences resulting from his uncontrolled passions.[111] (45) The 'composite' (and virtuous) soul, where the rational part rules, is like a 'virtuous' family (or household) where the head of the household (or father) benignly governs; and like the 'just' (harmonious and orderly) body politic, where the just ruler (or just laws) justly governs his subjects (or where the 'right political authority' and, hence, 'justice' rules).[112]

(46) Virtue is the particular (or peculiar) happiness of the individual; justice the peculiar happiness of the body politic.[113] [(47) Justice, being a 'total virtue,' is based on equality (among equals).][114] (48) Injustice (including the failure properly to punish criminals, or foreign conquests that result in the loss of true political justice at home) is the unhappiness (and perdition) of the individual as well as of the body politic.[115] (49) Justice, conceived either as political (social) justice or as individual justice, is the highest of all virtues.[116] [(50) Without justice, all other virtues disappear or, at least, are prevented from being practiced properly.][117] (51) If pleasure were to be the supreme moral end or norm, justice would be wholly destroyed and with it all other virtues.[118]

This seems to be about all that might tentatively be said concerning the essential doctrinal content of the Aristotelian *On Justice*. The admittedly conjectural and undoubtedly disorderly 'table of the likely contents' of the *On Justice* suggested here in all likelihood also contains elements which originally were not to be found in this dialogue. Conversely, it is probably incomplete and deficient in its presentation. To a large extent this 'table of likely contents' is based on the debatable assumption that the preserved doctrinal treatises dealing with ethical and political issues contain, in one way or another, direct or indirect references to the *On Justice*. It is, in short, only optimistic conjecture or, at best, mere approximation lacking in precision as well as sound confirmation. In light of the present status of available sources or materials, such a confirmation, however, is simply impossible or, at least, highly improbable. But any intelligent and disciplined effort to rediscover and reconstruct some of the likely contents of the Aristotelian *On Justice*, no matter how tentative, conjectural and perhaps faulty it may be, appears to be preferable to an overly cautious viewpoint. It seems fruitless to maintain that until we shall have uncovered beyond all reasonable doubt the specific details of this dialogue or, possibly, some additional and major fragments, or perhaps the whole original work itself, we should prudently abstain from reconstructing some of its probable contents or some of its likely doctrinal views.

A final and, it appears, most difficult question remains to be answered: Did the *On Justice* propagate essentially Platonic notions? It has already been noted that this dialogue was composed in imitation of Plato's *Republic*, although it may also have taken issue with some views expounded by Plato in the *Republic*. What strikes us first of all is the fact that both Plato and Aristotle, provided the 'reconstruction' attempted here is moderately correct, stress certain far-reaching congruities between the well-ordered (just) city and the well-ordered (virtuous) individual. Both Plato and Aristotle call justice the most exalted virtue; both speak of the several parts of the soul (although Aristotle seems to fuse into one the courageous and appetitive parts); and both emphasize the necessity that in the body politic as well as in the individual the rational part or element should dominate—a domination which both call 'justice.'

But then, again, Aristotle seems to have abandoned, at least in part, Plato's purely theoretic and in a way unrealistic treatment of political justice[119] in favor of a more 'realistic' and practical attitude, which takes into consideration also the *de facto* human condition. This realistic attitude of Aristotle's, which also comes to the fore in his work *On Kingship*,[120] rejects certain impracticabilities such as Plato had advocated in the *Republic*. In their place, he recommends a 'political knowledge' and a political behavior which are closer to the historical realities rather than to a philosophic ideal befitting an essentially 'inhuman Utopia.'[121] Moreover, Aristotle also seems to have advocated a sort of political pluralism, while Plato insisted on a rather unimaginative 'monolithic polity.' At the same time, Aristotle calls best that city or body politic where political justice is based on the equality of rights and duties for all citizens, thus raising the old issue of the ἰσονομία or equality before a law common to all, something which Plato complete-ly ignored and even ridiculed.[122] It will be noticed that Plato, although he admitted that true justice implies friendship,[123] did not elaborate on this subject, which with Aristotle assumes an important function within a well-ordered body politic.[124] And while Plato, true to the main tenor of his basic philosophy, saw in the human body primarily a prison and, hence, the antagonist of the soul, Aristotle seems to emphasize that the soul can and does use the body as its 'friend' and efficient instrument.[125] Such a view, however, makes the body the beloved tool of the soul. Applied to the city, this implies that for Aristotle every member of the political community, no matter what his work or social contribution may be, is a cherished and beloved part of the whole—a notion totally alien to Plato's 'political elitism' which grants the guardians a preferred status in the city at the expense of the two other classes.

But these differences, the number of which could probably be augmented, do not entitle us to assume that in the *On Justice* Aristotle had completely and irretrievably abandoned his early Platonism. The *On Justice*, it must be borne in mind, had for its model (and at times for its target) the *Republic* of Plato, not only as to its literary form but also as to much of its philosophic content. Like Plato before him, Aristotle develops his basic political philosophy in conjunction with and on the basis of the problem of justice, thus integrating ethics and politics—a typically Platonic characteristic. In light of the available evidence, no matter how scanty and conjectural it may be, it is fairly safe to surmise that Aristotle's lost dialogue *On Justice* was basically Platonic, something which V. Rose, J. Bernays, E. Heitz and W. Jaeger had already recog-nized.[126] Because of his penchant for sober conciseness and logical persuasiveness, it is possible and indeed probable that Aristotle presented his notions or arguments in a more 'expository' and hence less 'dramatic' form than Plato had employed in the *Republic*.

# Chapter VII

# A Brief Account of the Reconstruction of Aristotle's *Protrepticus**

Ioannes Stobaeus,[1] Alexander of Aphrodisias,[2] Olympiodorus,[3] Elias,[4] David,[5] Diogenes Laertius,[6] the author of the *Vita Aristotelis Hesychii*,[7] and Ptolemy (-el-Garib)[8] attest to the fact that the young Aristotle composed a work entitled *Protrepticus* (in one 'book'). This composition was lost in the course of time. We do not know, and probably never will know, the particular circumstances that caused the loss of the *Protrepticus* or the exact period in which it disappeared. It is reasonable to assume, however, that the recovery and edition of the doctrinal treatises of Aristotle during the first century B.C.,[9] and the ensuing concern with these treatises, at the expense of the 'exoteric' writings of Aristotle, gradually brought about the fatal neglect and subsequent loss of these 'exoteric' compositions, including the *Protrepticus*. It may be surmised, however, that some (earlier?) commentators of Aristotle's doctrinal treatises still had first-hand knowledge of the original *Protrepticus*.

Judging from the lasting and widespread impact it had on the 'protreptic literature' of the Hellenistic (and Patristic) era, the Aristotelian *Protrepticus* must have enjoyed a great reputation, an astonishing popularity and a considerable influence. The large number of authoritative *testimonia* attesting to the former existence of the *Protrepticus*, no less than its obvious and lasting literary importance as well as the discernible effect it had upon subsequent authors, needless to say, sooner or later would tempt some venturesome scholar not only to go in search of the surviving fragments of this work but also to undertake its recovery and reconstruction, provided such a recovery and reconstruction should be at all possible.

Anyone undertaking the arduous task of retrieving, much less reconstructing, the lost *Protrepticus* of Aristotle is faced with three major problems, each of which is sufficiently difficult and involved as to discourage even the most stouthearted scholar: first, he must locate, identify and delimit the authentic fragments, excerpts, reliable references, doxographical reports as well as the general allusions to the *Protrepticus*, which are dispersed and hidden throughout ancient and Patristic literature. Second, he must establish the proper order or sequence in which these fragments, once they have been recovered, should be arranged. And third, he must interpret the philosophic content or doctrine of these fragments, once they have been located and arranged. That there would be, and always will be, wide disagreements among scholars as to the correct selection, arrangement and interpretation of these fragments was to be anticipated and must be anticipated for all future efforts to resolve the problem of the Aristotelian *Protrepticus*. To complicate matters still further, philosophers, historians and philologists were never in agreement and still disagree as to what procedure should be applied in this complex venture, and as to who would be best qualified to carry out such an undertaking. The prime reason for these disagreements seems to be this: much of the work that has so far been seen, and remains to be done, of necessity is based, and probably always will be based, on conjectures and hypotheses. And conjectures, no matter how well informed they may be, still are 'guesses' and, at best, 'educated guesses,' the more so, since the relatively scanty and at time questionable evidence admits of more than just one identification or interpretation. Accordingly, it is not surprising that there exists nothing even remotely resembling consensus among the experts as regards the retrieval, reconstruction or philosophic message of the *Protrepticus*, nor as regards the manner in which all this may successfully be achieved. In some isolated instances it was even held, and is still being held, that the retrieval of the fragments of the *Protrepticus*, provided they actually exist and can be identified as such with any degree of certainty, is an extremely hazardous and, in all probability, impossible enterprise, as is the envisioned reconstruction of this composition.[10]

As early as 1863, J. Bernays,[11] who flatly denied any and all substantial or meaningful 'Platonic elements' in Aristotle's 'exoteric' writings, advanced the theory that the Aristotelian *Protrepticus* must have been a hortatory essay advocating the necessity (or priority) of theoretic philosophy, and stressing the advisability of studying and practicing philosophy. Moreover, Bernays conjectured that the *Protrepticus* was probably a polemic work, attacking in a sustained argument not only such pronounced opponents of purely theoretic philosophy (and the Platonic Academy in general) as, for instance, Isocrates and his followers, but also denouncing their professed cultural, intellectual and educational ideals or *paideia*. He surmised that it was

addressed to Themison of Cyprus and that it pleaded with the latter
to dedicate himself and perhaps his whole *régime* to the practice of true
philosophy. Bernays believed that Cicero's *Hortensius* in all likelihood
was an imitation of the Aristotelian *Protrepticus*.[12] Accordingly, he
proposed that any attempt to recover and reconstruct the *Protrepticus*
would have to be based on, or begin with, the surviving fragments of
the Ciceronian *Hortensius*.[13] Bernays was also the first scholar to
suggest that *Oxyrrhynchus Papyri* IV. 666 (Grenfell-Hunt) probably
constitutes a vital part of the original *Protrepticus*[14] or perhaps of some
other early work of Aristotle.[15] Bernays, it will be observed, correctly
analyzed certain important aspects of the original *Protrepticus*. His
suggestion, however, that a successful retrieval of this work would
have to rely on and start with Cicero's *Hortensius* not only proved to be
unworkable and abortive, but also came to be the source of many
subsequent failures to deal successfully with the Aristotelian *Protrepticus*.

I. Bywater, who, as Bernays and V. Rose had done before him,
refused in principle to recognize a distinct 'Platonic period' in the
early or earliest compositions of Aristotle, in 1869 made two momen-
tous and, it appears, essentially correct suggestions: first, Iamblichus'
*Protrepticus*, which Bywater appropriately considered a sort of 'text-
book' or 'reader' compiled from a variety of sources, contains many
references, excerpts and 'quotations' from several Platonic dialogues
(which can easily be identified); and, second, chapters V–XII (p. 34,
line 5 to p. 61, line 4, ed. H. Pistelli, Leipzig, 1888) of this work, in
particular, are replete with 'quotations' and excerpts from the
Aristotelian *Protrepticus*.[16] Bywater insisted that these particular
'quotations' definitely have an Aristotelian 'flair' or 'flavor.' He also
demonstrated that there exist many suggestive, not to say compelling,
similarities between some of these 'quotations' and certain other
'references' or excerpts recorded by different authors and expressly
credited to Aristotle or Aristotle's *Protrepticus*, such as, for instance,
Boethius, *De Consolatione Philosophiae* III. 8, which is very similar to
and almost identical with Iamblichus, *Protrepticus*, chapter VIII (p. 47,
lines 5–21, Pistelli). Bywater failed, however, to circumscribe accurately
the several individual fragments or groups of fragments. Neither did he
define or determine the particular philosophic background of these
fragments, that is, investigate in detail whether these excerpts from the
Aristotelian *Protrepticus* were 'Platonic' or 'Aristotelian' in their
philosophic message. Bywater also believed he had detected in the
'quotations' contained in Iamblichus' *Protrepticus* many significant
passages which fully coincide with the basic doctrinal views expressed

by Aristotle in his preserved treatises, especially in the *Magna Moralia, Eudemian Ethics, Nicomachean Ethics, Politics, Rhetoric, Poetics, Topics, Posterior Analytics, De Partibus Animalium, Historia Animalium, De Generatione et Corruptione, De Caelo, Meteorologica, Physics, Metaphysics* and in the *De Anima*. In so doing, Bywater suggested or at least implied that the philosophic standpoint advocated in the Aristotelian *Protrepticus* is essentially 'Aristotelian' (and not 'Platonic,' as W. Jaeger maintains),[17] a position subsequently also adopted by I. Düring.[18]

It will also be noted that Bywater's suggestion to seek in Iamblichus' *Protrepticus* substantial remnants of Aristotle's *Protrepticus* was stimulated, to a large extent, by J. Bernays' pioneering discovery that the Neo-Platonic authors and commentators, including Iamblichus, had a pronounced predilection for the early compositions of Aristotle. This unusually vigorous interest, Bernays rightly observed, was due to the 'syncretism' of the philosophic thought expounded in these early dialogues, which as an amalgam of Platonic and Aristotelian notions would naturally appeal to the syncretist Neo-Platonists and, hence, receive their special attention. This fact, the ultimate significance of which has never been fully explored, in itself would lend considerable support to W. Jaeger's thesis that the philosophic or doctrinal views expressed in the early Aristotelian compositions were essentially 'Platonic.' But it must always be borne in mind that it was Bywater who, by his ingenious insight, initiated a novel and extremely fruitful phase in what appears to be the only promising approach to the successful recovery and reconstruction of the Aristotelian *Protrepticus*. Bywater, however, never fully realized the basic importance and far-reaching consequences of his own discovery. Neither did he exploit it in order that he might gain a better understanding and more thorough evaluation of the particular philosophic content and orientation of Aristotle's lost works. This omission was probably caused by the fact that Bywater never suspected a 'Platonic phase' in Aristotle's early literary activities. Hence, he failed not only to conceive of an intellectual evolution of Aristotle from an initial 'Platonism' to a subsequent 'Aristotelianism,' but also to appreciate the particular position the *Protrepticus* held in this intellectual progression.

The theses advanced by Bywater, which subsequently became the solid foundations of all scholarly efforts to retrieve and reconstruct the lost *Protrepticus* of Aristotle,[19] in the beginning encountered determined opposition. In some instances they were modified or were simply ignored. R. Hirzel,[20] for instance, concurred with Bywater's theory that certain passages from the *Protrepticus* of Iamblichus might possibly be traced back to the authorship of Aristotle. He insisted, however, that the passages from Iamblichus' *Protrepticus* assigned by Bywater to Aristotle's *Protrepticus* were frequently devoid of all internal consistency, literary coherence and doctrinal continuity. Accordingly, Hirzel argued, these references in all likelihood refer not to just one single 'exoteric' composition of Aristotle, to wit, the Aristotelian *Protrepticus*, but probably to several of the lost or 'exoteric' works of the Stagirite, the identity of which can no longer be ascertained.[21] Relying on Bywater's discovery, Hirzel, however, recognized the many possibilities inherent in this line of approach. Moreover, unlike Bywater, Hirzel made the first sustained attempt to 'pin-point' within Iamblichus' text the several quotations from, or references to, Aristotle's *Protrepticus*. Hirzel concluded his observations with the remark, subsequently found to be erroneous, that only chapters VI–VIII (p. 36, line 27–p. 48, line 28, Pistelli) of Iamblichus' *Protrepticus*, and not, as Bywater would have it, the whole of chapters V–XII, contain references to, or excerpts from, Aristotle's *Protrepticus* or from some other early Aristotelian compositions. Hirzel was also the first scholar to emphasize that the doctrinal contents or philosophic teachings of these fragments or excerpts were unmistakably 'Platonic.' In this, Hirzel not only went beyond Bywater, but also anticipated Jaeger's thesis by almost fifty years.

In his *Aristoteles Pseudepigraphus* of 1863, and especially, in his *Aristotelis Qui Ferebantur Librorum Fragmenta* of 1870 (in volume V of I. Bekker's edition of the *Corpus Aristotelicum*), V. Rose somewhat reluctantly included certain suggestions made by J. Bernays.[22] In his final and separate edition of Aristotle's fragments, which appeared in 1886 under the old title of *Aristotelis Qui Ferebantur Librorum Fragmenta*,[23] he actually took up some of Bywater's findings. In any event, in this last edition of 1886 (pp. 56–73; frags. 50–61) he quoted a few lengthy passages from Iamblichus' *Protrepticus* (and from Iamblichus' *De Communi Mathematica Scientia Liber*): part of chapter VI (page 37, line 26 to page 41, line 5, Pistelli), as fragment 52;[24] part of chapter VIII (page 45, line 4 to page 47, line 4), as fragment 55; part of chapter IX (page 52, line 16 to page 54, line 5), as fragment 58; part of chapter VIII (page 47, lines 5–20), as fragment 59; part of chapter VIII (page 47, line 21 to page 48, line 9), as fragment 60; and part of chapter VIII (page 48, lines 9–21), as fragment 61. Rose, it will be remembered, labored under a particularly severe handicap or prejudice: he categorically denied any and all 'Platonisms' in Aristotle and, hence, flatly refused to admit a transition from Platonism to 'Aristotelianism' in the intellectual development of the young Stagirite. Since the fragments which were presented as remnants of Aristotle's early works definitely had a Platonic flair, Rose, in order to 'exorcize' this Platonism in Aristotle, resorted to the overly simple device of declaring them outright spurious. Nevertheless, despite this wholly antagonistic attitude, he laid the foundation, presumably against his own will, of all future scholarship concerned with the lost works of the young Aristotle, including the *Protrepticus*.

P. Hartlich, on the whole, subscribed to Bywater's general suggestion that Iamblichus' *Protrepticus* furnishes the most promising starting point for a successful recovery of the Aristotelian *Protrepticus*. He was somewhat reluctant, however, to accept Bywater's essentially correct but rather sweeping insistence that the whole of chapters V–XII of Iamblichus' *Protrepticus* should be consulted by anyone attempting to reconstruct the lost Aristotelian *Protrepticus*. Hartlich's painstaking investigations, it must be conceded, contributed much to the efforts of subsequent German scholars to recover Aristotle's *Protrepticus* with the help of Iamblichus' *Protrepticus*. Moreover, he also considered the possible influence of Plato on Aristotle and on Aristotle's *Protrepticus* in particular. He maintained, among other matters, that chapter V, parts of chapter IX, and chapter XII of Iamblichus' *Protrepticus* contain some references, excerpts or 'quotations' from Aristotle's original *Protrepticus*.[25] In so doing, he not only contradicted R. Hirzel, who had only accepted chapters VI–VIII, but he also disagreed in part with V. Rose, who without admitting the authenticity of the Aristotelian *Protrepticus*, recognized only parts of chapters VI and IX, and the whole of chapter VIII. It might be observed that the early reluctance to adopt Bywater's theses may be explained largely by the widely-held belief and seemingly fateful insistence that Cicero's *Hortensius* furnishes the only promising starting point for any promising attempt to recover the Aristotelian *Protrepticus*. This reluctance may also be due to the fact that during the nineteenth and early twentieth century continental scholars did not always familiarize themselves with the scholarly investigations carried on in other countries or in a language other than their own.

During approximately the same period, a number of scholars made some interesting and constructive contributions to the 'source problem' underlying the Aristotelian *Protrepticus*, among them such renowned men as E. Heitz,[26] C. G. Cobet[27] and H. Diels.[28] Heitz correctly observed that the *Protrepticus* was addressed to Themison of Cyprus with whom, Heitz theorized, Aristotle might have been personally acquainted through Eudemus of Cyprus.[29] Diels, who flatly contradicted R. Hirzel, denied that chapter X of Iamblichus' *Protrepticus* contained Platonic doctrines. Hence, he insisted that the expression, τὰ πρῶτα, simply meant 'universal' in the traditional Aristotelian sense of the term. (Hirzel, it will be remembered, discovered distinct 'Platonisms' in chapter X and, in consequence, refused to assign it to the Aristotelian *Protrepticus*, maintaining that it was based on some other early work or works of Aristotle, or more likely, referred to Plato himself.) Indeed, Diels maintained that there exists no evidence whatever for the alleged 'Platonism' in the Aristotelian *Protrepticus* and, for that matter, in any of Aristotle's early writings. But in the light of incontestable evidence, Diels conceded that, since the earliest compositions of Aristotle, including the *Protrepticus*, were addressed to a general audience which was accustomed to Plato's philosophic language and thought, Aristotle had to adopt, at least externally and superficially, the language and philosophy with which this general audience was familiar: the philosophic language and notions of Plato. Diels also contended that this would explain the alleged Platonism of the Aristotelian *Protrepticus*—a Platonism which, in the opinion of Diels, is plainly superficial and, hence, completely meaningless. It was only pedagogical considerations as well as rhetorical effects, rather than a genuine commitment to Plato's philosophy, that induced Aristotle to employ a form, method and philosophic orientation somewhat akin to that of Plato [30]—a peculiar method of 'spiriting away' the Platonism of the early Aristotle.

E. Zeller, who originally had maintained that the *Protrepticus* was primarily a kind of 'Introduction to Philosophy,' [31] in the third and revised edition of his monumental *Die Philosophie der Griechen*, published in 1879, once more tackled the many puzzling problems connected with the lost works of the young Aristotle.[32] After reviewing the conflicting suggestions and theories proposed by different scholars, Zeller reached the essentially correct conclusion that during his association with Plato and the Platonic Academy (367–48 B.C.), Aristotle, at least for a while, faithfully adhered to Plato and his philosophic teachings.[33] Zeller also suggested that at a relatively early time during his stay at the Academy, Aristotle authored some works of his own, among them the *Protrepticus*, which, in their literary form and doctrinal content, were basically Platonic.

The period between 1869 (the year I. Bywater announced his epoch-making thesis that we ought to seek the remnants of Aristotle's *Protrepticus* mainly in certain passages of Iamblichus' *Protrepticus*) [34] and

1923 (the year W. Jaeger, on the whole, confirmed the findings of Bywater)[35] was, generally speaking, an era in which two major theories concerning the Aristotelian *Protrepticus* were carefully and sometimes reluctantly examined and tested, in part rejected and in part accepted, often with considerable modifications, reservations and alterations: I. Bywater's epochal findings that Iamblichus' *Protrepticus* contains extensive as well as reliable fragments of the lost Aristotelian *Protrepticus*; and R. Hirzel's equally significant insistence that the philosophy expounded in Aristotle's *Protrepticus* was essentially Platonic in tenor.[36] During the same period, the view that Cicero's *Hortensius* should be consulted in all matters relating to the Aristotelian *Protrepticus*, was gradually abandoned, although a few isolated scholars still clung to this theory which apparently never completely lost its determined advocates.

In his *Aristoteles: Grundlegung einer Geschichte seiner Entwicklung*, first published in 1923,[37] W. Jaeger basically confirmed the main suggestion made by I. Bywater some fifty-four years earlier: the *Protrepticus* of Iamblichus contains lengthy and, on the whole, fairly accurate as well as reliable quotations, excerpts or reports from, or references to, Aristotle's *Protrepticus*. It must be borne in mind, however, that Jaeger's principal interest in the Aristotelian *Protrepticus* lay in his broader efforts to establish and verify his general thesis of Aristotle's intellectual progression from Platonism to Aristotelianism, rather than in an acribic and detailed investigation of the *Protrepticus* as such, or in an analysis of the sources of its interpretation and reconstruction. In discussing the *Protrepticus* of Aristotle (and that of Iamblichus), Jaeger succeeded not only in shedding a great deal of light on the literary form, background and philosophic or doctrinal content and orientation of this composition, but also in making lasting contributions to its ultimate recovery and reconstruction.[38] Despite some divergent opinions which were voiced subsequently, these contributions constitute one of the decisive turning points, if not the decisive turning point, in the history of the many efforts to solve the problems underlying the *Protrepticus*.

Jaeger disagreed with, and at some points corrected, Bywater on three important issues: he rejected the whole of chapter V of Iamblichus' *Protrepticus*[39] which Bywater had included among his 'sources'; he included chapters IX–XII, but rejected the last part of chapter XII (p. 60, line 10 to p. 61, line 4, Pistelli); and he repeatedly stressed the basic Platonism of the Aristotelian *Protrepticus*. As Bywater had done before him, Jaeger based his position on the following three major arguments: first, there exist significant and compelling similarities between certain passages found in Iamblichus' *Protrepticus*, chapters VI–XII, and other texts or fragments which are definitely Aristotelian. Second, the general style, language, expressions and philosophic nomenclature (but not always the philosophic doctrine) of these passages are essentially Aristotelian, provided we make certain allowances for Iamblichus' peculiarities and deficiencies as a reporter. Only the connecting phrases or structures relating the several Aristotelian quotations or concepts are by Iamblichus himself, who in presenting Aristotelian materials often proceeded in a most confusing and disorganized fashion.[40] Third, there exist compelling similarities between the doctrinal content of these passages or excerpts and the philosophic teachings expounded in the preserved doctrinal ('esoteric') treatises of Aristotle.[41]

Jaeger also observed that some of the passages or excerpts from Aristotle's *Protrepticus* which are found in Iamblichus' *Protrepticus* are frequently cast in the distinct language of Iamblichus. It is an indisputable fact, ascertainable from his other philosophic or literary works, that many of the ideas and notions expressed by Iamblichus in his *Protrepticus* go far beyond the somewhat limited and modest intellectual range of his own philosophic achievements. This fact in itself suggests that in his *Protrepticus* he is using or reporting the ideas advanced by other and certainly more talented thinkers—in our case those originally advocated by Aristotle in the Aristotelian *Protrepticus*. This does not imply, however, that the several references to Aristotle's *Protrepticus* contained in Iamblichus' *Protrepticus* are literal quotations from Aristotle's original work.[42] On the contrary, a great many of these references are most likely abbreviated, condensed and not infrequently severely mutilated renditions of Aristotle's original ideas or texts. To make matters worse, Iamblichus as a rule is a fairly poor stylist as well as a distressingly disorganized and muddled thinker who could hardly do justice to Aristotle's literary, stylistic and philosophic achievements, or to his systematic method of presentation—qualities that were characteristic of Aristotle's earliest compositions. Hence, the obvious inadequacies of style and expression, the frequent awkwardness in the formulation of philosophic ideas and the confusing over-all organization of the materials presented in the *Protrepticus* of Iamblichus should not be attributed to Aristotle who, in the considered judgment of competent ancient authors and literary critics, expressed himself with great elegance and admirable clarity in his exoteric compositions.[43] Jaeger's contributions to the reconstruction of the *Protrepticus* also include the discovery of many references to the *Protrepticus* in the later or 'esoteric' writings of Aristotle, in particular, in the *Metaphysics*, in the *Eudemian Ethics*, in the *Nicomachean Ethics* and in other works.

Moreover, Jaeger pointed out convincingly that the Aristotelian *Protrepticus* is more than a mere hortatory essay, or perhaps, a kind of 'mirror for princes,' addressed to Themison of Cyprus.[44] It is, in the opinion of Jaeger, a solemn proclamation of a new ideal of the philosophic life, a fervent appeal to the whole of mankind to embrace the truly theoretic life, and an eloquent call for a new aim of life and culture. In short, it is a plea for a total conversion to a cultural and pedagogical ideal as it had been advocated by Plato himself, and as it was practiced in the Academy. Jaeger further maintained that in the *Protrepticus* Aristotle, in his characteristically systematic manner, frequently transforms the conventional hortatory appeal into an argumentation or examination which at times assumes syllogistic forms. Jaeger is convinced that the Aristotelian *Protrepticus* constitutes a most successful combination of the hortatory content of Plato's *Gorgias*, *Phaedo* and *Euthydemus*, the rhetorical prose of Isocrates and Aristotle's penchant for 'scientific' or methodical argumentation.[45] At the same time, Jaeger insisted that the *Protrepticus* was also a rejoinder to Isocrates' utilitarian views on education and intellectual culture. Jaeger's discovery that the *Protrepticus* was really a rebuttal of Isocrates' pretensions, constitutes a major contribution to the proper understanding and evaluation of this work and the philosophic message which it conveys. Jaeger's view that the Aristotelian *Protrepticus* also was a rejoinder to Isocrates, and especially to Isocrates' *Antidosis*, in itself is of far-reaching importance: it further permits us to penetrate the true spirit of the *Protrepticus* by suggesting that when discussing the Aristotelian *Protrepticus* we must also look at the (preserved) *Antidosis* of Isocrates. Much of what Aristotle did say in his rebuttal is probably determined by what Isocrates had proclaimed in the *Antidosis*. It is this particular insight which also enables us to date the Aristotelian *Protrepticus* with reasonable accuracy.

Some of the theses of Jaeger, and by implication those of I. Bywater, received additional confirmation from H. Gadamer[46] who, however, disagreed with Jaeger as to the proper philosophic interpretation of the *Protrepticus*. Analyzing the working methods employed by Iamblichus or, to be more exact, by comparing those parts of Iamblichus' *Protrepticus* which definitely were derived from Plato's dialogues, with the Platonic original, Gadamer came to the conclusion that Iamblichus most certainly was an unoriginal thinker and frequently a poor stylist, though undeniably an extremely faithful, if not reliable, 'reporter' or 'citator' who did not introduce any novel elements or ideas of his own. This being so, Gadamer argued, there exists no good reason why we should challenge Iamblichus' reliability or accuracy as a 'reporter' of what Aristotle originally had said in his *Protrepticus*. Aside from the likelihood that in his usually eclectic manner he probably cited only parts of the Aristotelian *Protrepticus*, and most certainly not the whole of this work, the only serious 'deviation' from the Aristotelian original of which Iamblichus is guilty is the peculiar and almost erratic arrangement he uses to present the several excerpts from Aristotle's original *Protrepticus*. It is this utterly arbitrary, capricious and at times almost unintelligible arrangement which creates the erroneous impression that these reports or 'quotations' cannot possibly have been derived from a single unitary source, and most certainly not from so disciplined and systematic a thinker and writer as Aristotle. Hence, it is easy to understand the reluctance of such renowned scholars as R. Hirzel, V. Rose, P. Hartlich and others in the past to consider these reports truly Aristotelian, and concomitantly, to accept the *Protrepticus* of Iamblichus as the prime source for the reconstruction of the lost Aristotelian *Protrepticus*. Gadamer concluded that the only major—and, in his opinion, probably unsolvable—problem confronting modern Aristotelian scholarship is the establishment of the sequence in which the quotations from Aristotle's *Protrepticus* contained in Iamblichus' *Protrepticus* should be arranged.[47] To establish the proper sequence on the basis of some acceptable criteria soon came to be the foremost task of a number of scholars concerned with the works of the early Aristotle.

With some reservations, the findings of H. Gadamer were adopted and confirmed by I. Düring.[48] Going further than any of his predecessors, Düring maintained, on what appear to be good grounds, that with a few isolated exceptions, the 'transitional' or 'connecting' sentences used by Iamblichus—sentences relating those quotations or excerpts which definitely had been identified as having been taken from Aristotle's *Protrepticus*—were also Aristotelian, if not in their style or language, at least in their spirit. Moreover, Düring insisted that the whole relevant text of Iamblichus gives the unmistakable impression that Iamblichus not only had direct access to Aristotle's *Protrepticus*, but that he simply had copied *verbatim*, or almost *verbatim*, whole passages directly from the Aristotelian original. Düring also reclaimed part of chapter V (page 34, line 5 to page 36, line 20, Pistelli)[49] of Iamblichus' *Protrepticus* (which had been accepted by I. Bywater, but had been rejected by W. Jaeger) for his 'list of authentic sources' (or fragments) that could safely be used for the retrieval and reconstruction of the Aristotelian *Protrepticus*. But Düring agreed with Jaeger in rejecting the last part of chapter XII (page 60, line 10 to page 61, line 4, Pistelli). Following some suggestions made by P. Merlan in 1953,[50] Düring also insisted that Iamblichus' *De Communi Mathematica Scientia Liber* (page 79, line 15 to page 80, line 1; page 81, lines 7–16; and page 83, line 5, ed. N. Festa, 1891) contains lengthy excerpts from Aristotle's *Protrepticus*.[51] In contrast to Jaeger and others, Düring denied, however, that the philosophic tenor of the *Protrepticus* was essentially Platonic, insisting as J. Bernays, I. Bywater and H. Diels had done previously, that there exist no significant doctrinal differences between this early work and the later treatises of Aristotle. This view of Düring, which seems to conflict with the available evidence as well as with the dominant scholarly opinions, did not find universal acceptance. Finally, by using such elusive and controversial criteria as the 'logical development of an argument' or the 'rhetorical structure of a discussion,' Düring, in a most original and persuasive manner, attempted to re-establish the original Aristotelian order of presentation.[52] In so doing, he not only altered radically the sequence observed by Iamblichus, but also incurred—undeservedly—the opposition and disapproval of many a scholar.[53]

As to the particular literary form of the Aristotelian *Protrepticus*, scholars were, and still are, in disagreement. E. Heitz, R. Hirzel, E. Zeller, O. Hamelin, W. Jaeger, E. Bignone, P. Moraux, I. Düring, A.-H. Chroust and others are of the opinion that this composition was a discourse and that its literary form had been influenced by contemporary political and forensic orations and particularly by Isocrates' hortatory essays (the *Cyprian Discourses*). In any event, it appears that between 360 and 350 B.C. the dialogue began to be replaced by the expository essay, a change of style which also becomes manifest in Aristotle's *Protrepticus*. I. Bywater, V. Rose, P. Hartlich, H. Diels, H. Usener, W. D. Ross, D. J. Allan, H. Langerbeck, and others, again, maintain that the original Aristotelian *Protrepticus* was a dialogue. These scholars base their opinion on the assumption that all of Aristotle's earliest writings were dialogues; that the first nineteen compositions listed in the ancient 'catalogues' of Aristotle's works were dialogues— in Diogenes Laertius 'list' the *Protrepticus* is no. 12, in the *Vita Aristotelis Hesychii*, no. 14—although some ancient reporters (whose references constitute the extant 'fragments') in some instances suppressed the dialogue form; and that Cicero's *Hortensius*, which allegedly is a close imitation of Aristotle's *Protrepticus*, was a dialogue.

With the exception of the vexing problem of the proper sequence in which the fragments or excerpts culled from Iamblichus' *Protrepticus* should be listed, it seemed that by the middle 1950's the authority of Iamblichus' *Protrepticus* as the authentic source for the successful retrieval of substantial parts or fragments of the Aristotelian *Protrepticus*, on the whole, had been firmly established. In brief, the 'lost' *Protrepticus* of Aristotle, it appeared, had been recovered as regards its main doctrinal content, if not as regards its detailed teachings and particular literary form. Then suddenly, in 1957, when almost everything seemed about to be settled and nearly everyone appeared to be in close agreement, W. G. Rabinowitz, to the dismay of practically every scholar concerned with the Aristotelian *Protrepticus*, upset this rather idyllic consensus.[54] In a spirit of fierce antagonism and negative criticism, not devoid of much scholarly acumen and a great deal of learning, Rabinowitz made two radical and, at the same time, basic proposals: first, Cicero's *Hortensius* may under no circumstance be used as a source for the retrieval and reconstruction of Aristotle's *Protrepticus*—a view already taken by I. Bywater and others. The *Hortensius*, Rabinowitz insisted, is not necessarily based on, or even related to, the Aristotelian *Protrepticus*, but in all likelihood is just one of the many and widely diffused ancient compositions or proselytizing Hellenistic 'sermons' which are part of a more general literary (hortatory) type then much in vogue.[55] The congruity between Alexander of Aphrodisias[56] and Cicero[57] concerning the necessity of philosophizing under all circumstances is insufficient evidence to support any claim that the *Hortensius* is dependent on the *Protrepticus*.[58] Second, Iamblichus' *Protrepticus*, especially chapter VI which Rabinowitz subjected to a most thorough scrutiny, is not the product of quotations from, or references to, the original Aristotelian *Protrepticus*, but rather a helter-skelter conglomeration of excerpts from several Platonic dialogues, and of Neo-Pythagorean and Neo-Platonic (syncretist) interpretations of certain doctrines advanced by Speusippus and other early Academicians.[59] Rabinowitz made five specific arguments against the advisability of using Iamblichus as a source for the reconstruction of the Aristotelian *Protrepticus*: first, the Aristotelian elements in Iamblichus' *Protrepticus* could very well have been derived from Aristotle's esoteric or doctrinal treatises; second, it cannot convincingly be shown that the Aristotelian excerpts in Iamblichus' *Protrepticus* were taken from only one work of Aristotle; third, 'the indisputably genuine fragments of the [Aristotelian] *Protrepticus* are not extensive enough to provide an adequate *comparandum* against which to assess the contents of the supposed excerpts'; fourth,

Iamblichus proposes in his *Protrepticus* to deal with the whole of Aristotle's philosophy and not merely with a single (and relatively insignificant) work;[60] and, fifth, Iamblichus is quite capable of 'using a variety of sources in a wide variety of ways.'[61] In brief, Rabinowitz attempted nothing less than to prove conclusively that it is impossible, and as a matter of fact, not permissible to reconstruct adequately the Aristotelian *Protrepticus* from the materials contained in either Cicero's *Hortensius* or Iamblichus' *Protrepticus*.

As might be expected, the theses of Rabinowitz met with a deluge of adverse criticism.[62] The major arguments against his contentions were the following: with a very few exceptions, the language,[63] style and mode of argumentation found in the relevant excerpts from Aristotle's *Protrepticus*, as recorded by Iamblichus, on the whole are Aristotelian. If the several excerpts in fact were quotations from Plato rather than [from Aristotle, then we will also have to concede that in these particular excerpts Iamblichus employs a method of reporting or citing which for some unknown reason radically differs from the method he uses when quoting from sources that are unquestionably Platonic.[64] Since Aristotle wrote only one single 'protreptic' work, namely the *Protrepticus*, while many of Plato's dialogues are of a definitely 'hortatory' nature, it is reasonable to surmise that in the case of Plato, Iamblichus could fall back on a fairly large number of sources and authoritative statements, while in the case of Aristotle he had but one single source: the *Protrepticus*. And, finally, the Platonic, Speusippian or Academic flavor of some of these excerpts in itself is not conclusive. Aristotle was for about twenty years an active and conspicuous member of the Platonic Academy and as such probably made much use of (late) Platonic and Academic notions, especially in his earliest works. So much for the different rebuttals of Rabinowitz's arguments—arguments, that is, which should not be taken lightly or simply glossed over. They are a constant reminder that whenever we deal with so involved and conjectural a problem as the lost works of Aristotle, we must always proceed with utmost caution.

Aside from the radical and uncompromising criticism of Rabinowitz there also existed some minor differences among scholars as to the inclusion or exclusion of certain materials that could safely be claimed for the Aristotelian *Protrepticus*. Thus, W. Theiler, for instance, insisted that the whole of chapter X of Iamblichus' *Protrepticus* in some vague way seemed to be related to Aristotle's *Protrepticus*, but that this connection is purely external or verbal, and certainly not doctrinal.[65] E. Kapp, again, maintained that the whole of chapter X reads like a fustian of indiscriminate citations from many Platonic dialogues, such as the *Phaedrus, Philebus, Republic, Cratylus* and especially the *Statesman*. Hence, Kapp concluded, it is not permissible to claim this chapter for the Aristotelian *Protrepticus*.[66] O. Gigon, on the strength of a searching analysis, reached what seems to be a reasonable conclusion: page 55, line 7 to page 56, line 2 (Pistelli), a passage from chapter X of Iamblichus' *Protrepticus* which is commonly credited to the Aristotelian *Protrepticus*, in fact constitutes an excerpt from Aristotle's *Politicus* which in all likelihood is a close imitation of Plato's *Statesman*.[67] The main theme of this passage, Gigon and others pointed out, is certainly not what one might expect of the Aristotelian *Protrepticus*, namely, a demonstration of the advantages attending the pursuit of theoretic philosophy. It is, rather, an insistence on the essentially Platonic position that the truly philosophic (Platonic) statesman must always look to absolute truth and absolute being for his ultimate standards or norms, without considering their immediate practical usefulness.[68]

G. Müller, again, noticed that in his *Protrepticus*, as well as in his other works, Iamblichus simply ignores or obfuscates 'the more subtle articulation of Aristotle's thought.' Hence, Müller concluded, Iamblichus' *Protrepticus* constitutes a wholly inadequate source for the reconstruction of the Aristotelian *Protrepticus*. This 'obscurantism' of Iamblichus, in the opinion of Müller, is not deliberate, but rather the result of the syncretist efforts so typical of the Neo-Platonists, to whom any doctrinal differences between Plato and Aristotle are completely irrelevant and even undesirable. Since in his *Protrepticus* Iamblichus wishes primarily to recommend philosophy as such rather than, perhaps, Platonism or Aristotelism, he feels justified, Müller alleged, in citing and indiscriminately intermingling Platonic and Aristotelian elements. Hence, in the opinion of Müller (and others), there exists also a strong possibility that Iamblichus, who is undoubtedly an awkward and frequently inaccurate reporter, simply misquotes or misunderstands the notions advanced by other philosophers, including the opinions of those philosophers whom he quotes in his *Protrepticus*.[69] F. Wehrli, in turn, insisted that at present we possess no reliable means by which we might establish the peculiar method used by Iamblichus when making his particular excerpts from Plato and Aristotle, especially from the Aristotelian *Protrepticus*, provided Iamblichus uses the Aristotelian *Protrepticus* at all. All we are able to say, Wehrli maintained, is that in his *Protrepticus* Iamblichus seems to have combined Platonic and Aristotelian notions in a most arbitrary manner.[70]

In a searching and persuasive paper, H. Flashar raised a number of crucial issues concerning the identification and reconstruction of the Aristotelian *Protrepticus* (as well as some other lost works of Aristotle).[71] Flashar, who suggested that we ought to scrutinize further Iamblichus' peculiar method of excerpting his sources in general and Aristotle's writings in particular, entertained some serious doubts as to whether Iamblichus, *Protrepticus*, p. 54, line 10–p. 56, line 12, Pistelli (frag. 13, Walzer; frag. 13, Ross; frags. 46–51. Düring; frags. 43–8, Chroust), which traditionally has been credited to Aristotle's *Protrepticus*, is indeed part of this lost Aristotelian composition. A.-H. Chroust, who in his *Aristotle: Protrepticus—A Reconstruction*[72] still assigned this particular passage to the Aristotelian *Protrepticus*, has become somewhat skeptical and now claims that it should probably be credited to the lost Aristotelian *Politicus*.[73] Chroust argues that the general tenor and doctrinal content of this passage practically eliminates it from among those fragments which may safely be assigned to the Aristotelian *Protrepticus*. O. Gigon, who at present is preoccupied with the retrieval and reconstruction of the Aristotelian *Eudemus*, tentatively maintains that Iamblichus, *Protrepticus*, p. 48, lines 2–9 (frag. 60, Rose; frag. 10b, Walzer; frag. 10b, Ross; frags. 106–7, Düring; frags. 102–3, Chroust), which is generally listed among the genuine fragments of the *Protrepticus*, should actually be credited to the Aristotelian *Eudemus*.[74] Gigon's thesis, which seems to have much merit, was accepted by A. Grilli,[75] J. Brunschwig,[76] H. Flashar[77] and, in part, by K. Gaiser.[78] Thus, the first sustained, though tentative, efforts to reconstruct the Aristotelian *Protrepticus* (Düring, Chroust) were immediately met by a series of weighty challenges, an indication that the problem of the Aristotelian *Protrepticus* still awaits its final solution, provided there is actually such a thing as a final solution.

Already H. Gadamer had pointed out in 1928 that perhaps the most difficult, if not unsolvable, problem connected with the reconstruction of Aristotle's *Protrepticus* is the proper order or sequence in which Iamblichus' excerpts should be arranged.[79] In 1954, and again in 1955, by relying on what he considered the compelling principles of logical coherence and rhetorical progress, I. Düring attempted to establish a definite and, in a way, original organization of the surviving fragments.[80] This novel sequence, it will be noticed, differed considerably from that observed by Iamblichus and, for that matter, from any organization previously suggested by modern scholars. Dissatisfied with the results of his first efforts, in 1961 Düring substantially amended his earlier suggestions, proposing, again on the basis of logical and rhetorical principles of argumentation, the following sequence[81] which seems to have much merit: page 36, line 27 to page 37, line 22 (Pistelli);[82] page 49, line 1 to page 51, line 6; page 51, line 16 to page 52, line 5; page 51, lines 6–15;[83] page 52, lines 6–16; page 34, line 5 to page 35, line 18;[84] page 36, lines 7–20; page 37, line 22 to page 40, line 1;[85] page 41, lines 6–15;[86] page 52, line 16 to page 56, line 12; page 40, line 1 to page 41, line 5;[87] page 41, line 15 to page 43, line 25; page 43, line 27 to page 44, line 9; page 43, lines 25–7; page 44, line 26 to page 45, line 3; page 44, lines 9–26; page 56, line 13 to page 60, line 10;[88] and page 45, line 4 to page 48, line 21.[89] Düring justified his unusual sequence by remarking that since Iamblichus had arranged his materials or excerpts according to the subject matter rather than according to the logical development of the argument, he could not possibly have followed the sequence observed by Aristotle. But Düring also admitted frankly that his own suggestions, which are merely an attempt to organize the several fragments or excerpts in a reasonable order, are pure conjecture.[90]

Düring did more, however, than merely rearrange the several fragments of the *Protrepticus*. In a bold and, it appears, most useful and original fashion, he subdivided the excessively large fragments, as they had been listed by R. Walzer, W. Nestle and W. D. Ross (and in part by V. Rose), into many smaller and certainly more manageable segments. To cite but one example: the lengthy passage (Iamblichus, *Protrepticus* 56, 13 to 60, 1, Pistelli), which Walzer and Ross call fragment no. 14 (Rose does not list this fragment), becomes with Düring fragments 78–94. In so doing, Düring also insisted that what previously had been considered but one single and coherent fragment actually contains several fragments or citations, and that these several citations do not necessarily belong together or are stated in the proper sequence within this single large fragment. Thus, Düring listed fragment no. 6 of Walzer and Ross (Iamblichus, *Protrepticus* 41, 6 to 43, 25, Pistelli) as fragments no. 41 (41, 6–15) and nos 59–70 (41, 15 to 43, 25).[91] Düring's revolutionary suggestion of subdividing the traditional fragments into smaller segments and of renumbering them accordingly certainly has much merit and could be used to great advantage in future scholarship. In part it was adopted by A.-H. Chroust.[92]

S. Mansion, on the other hand, had insisted somewhat earlier that we should adhere as closely as possible to the organization or sequence found in Iamblichus.[93] K. Gaiser, again, in 1959, thought he had discovered in the several excerpts three major groups or 'clusters' corresponding to chapter VI (page 36, line 7 to page 41, line 5, Pistelli); chapters VII and VIII (page 41, line 7 to page 54, line 9); and chapters

XI, X, XI, and part of chapter XII (page 54, line 9 to page 60, line 10 or page 61, line 5).[94] Gaiser based his theory on the belief that each of these three groups contains a distinct and structurally self-contained 'hortatory topic.'[95] If accepted, the theory of Gaiser would expose Aristotle to a well-deserved charge of 'circular argumentation.' For it is obvious that the sequence of the arguments as presented by Iamblichus is indeed circular in a certain way. It was this consideration which, among other factors, prompted I. Düring in 1961 to propose his somewhat 'unorthodox' though persuasive organization of the several fragments.[96]

The present status of the several attempts at reconstructing and interpreting Aristotle's *Protrepticus*[97] may be summarized as follows: at this very moment the findings of I. Düring in his outstanding, though by no means unchallenged, *Aristotle's Protrepticus: An Attempt at Reconstruction* (1961), on the whole must be regarded as the most satisfactory, most advanced, most persuasive and certainly as the most scholarly and most detailed contribution to this hazardous undertaking which for nearly one hundred years has preoccupied some of the greatest classical scholars. Naturally, not all informed people will agree or are even expected to agree with Düring and his method, with his organization, with his selections and with his interpretations. The objections raised by W. G. Rabinowitz and others—objections which ought not to be taken lightly—as well as the modifications suggested by O. Gigon, H. Flashar, A. Grilli, K. Gaiser, A.-H. Chroust and others should make it quite clear that complete agreement on this matter has not yet been reached and probably never will be reached. The problem of whether the philosophic doctrines discussed in Aristotle's *Protrepticus* are wholly 'Aristotelian' in spirit, as I. Düring and others would have it,[98] or whether they are essentially 'Platonic', as Jaeger and his followers insist,[99] is really outside the limited scope of this chapter, although it must be admitted that this hotly debated problem has some bearing on the reconstruction (and interpretation) of the *Protrepticus*. Without detracting in the least from Düring's scholarship, it may be maintained, however, that in light of the available evidence his somewhat one-sided insistence on the 'pure Aristotelianism' of the *Protrepticus* will not find uniform acceptance.[100]

In his latest work, to be exact, Düring still denies that there ever existed a substantial difference between the philosophic teachings of the *Protrepticus* and those of the so-called doctrinal or 'esoteric' works of Aristotle. But he admits that, like all the 'exoteric' compositions, the *Protrepticus* differs from the 'esoteric' or doctrinal treatises not only in its literary form and style, but also in the philosophic opinions it proclaims. It was written as an exhortation meant to appeal to the popular mind and, hence, cast in a popular form and language.[101] Nevertheless—and Düring recognizes this as well—the philosophic teachings advanced in the *Protrepticus* also contain Platonic elements.[102] Viewed in this manner, Düring, who had always stressed (and still stresses) the 'Aristotelianism in Aristotle's *Protrepticus*,' in an oblique manner admits that, in the final analysis, Aristotle was, and always remained, to some extent a 'Platonist'—in the *Protrepticus* as well as in his later dogmatic or *intramural* works. Düring himself concedes that, in the *Protrepticus*, Aristotle's ideal of the philosopher is still that of Plato as described in the Platonic *Theaetetus* (174B ff.). 'But as a whole,' Düring concludes, 'the philosophy [of the *Protrepticus*] is not Plato's, but Aristotle's own, and he proves his thesis in a way which differs considerably from Plato.'[103] Despite the objections of Rabinowitz and others, this much, however, may be said confidently: the ingenious thesis of I. Bywater, advanced in 1869,[104] that the 'lost' Aristotelian *Protrepticus* could substantially be recovered from Iamblichus' *Protrepticus*, in a way came to full fruition in the work of I. Düring. Hence, all future attempts to come to grips with Aristotle's *Protrepticus* will have to take into account Düring's monumental *Aristotle's Protrepticus: An Attempt at Reconstruction*. One may agree with Düring or disagree with him—in part or *in toto*—but no one can ignore him on the subject of the Aristotelian *Protrepticus*.[105]

# Chapter VIII

# An Emendation to Fragment 13
# (Walzer, Ross) of Aristotle's *Protrepticus**

Iamblichus, *Protrepticus*, chapter X (54,10–56, 12, Pistelli), which since the days of I. Bywater (1869) has been regarded as an important fragment or 'cluster of excerpts' from Aristotle's *Protrepticus*,[1] contains the following lengthy argument:[2]

From a close study of the arts and crafts it can readily be ascertained that theoretic (philosophic) wisdom (φρόνησις) is of the greatest (practical) use in managing our lives (54,10–12). Just as the most skilled among the members of the medical profession and the majority of those who are experts in physical training agree that people who intend to be good physicians and good coaches (gymnasts) must have a general acquaintance with nature (φύσις), so too must good lawgivers have an encompassing knowledge and understanding of nature—and, as a matter of fact, an even better knowledge and understanding of nature than physicians and gymnasts (54,12–18). For the former use their skills exclusively for the well-being and strength of the human body, while the latter, being concerned not only with the well-being and virtues of the soul, but also with determining the salvation or perdition of the whole commonweal, need philosophy and philosophic knowledge to an even higher degree (54,18–22). Now, in the general and ordinary (mechanical) crafts and craftsmanlike operations, the most efficient tools or measures are derived directly from nature—for instance, the carpenter's ruler, the rod or compass in the house-builder's trade—the more so, since some of our tools were suggested by observing the behavior of water, others by observing the behavior of light and of the sun's rays. And it is through our reliance on these tools or measures that we determine what, according to our senses, is sufficiently straight and smooth (54,22–55,1). Similarly, the statesman must derive from nature as well as from objective reality some definite standards

105

with reference to which he determines what is just, what is good (honorable) and what is expedient (advantageous, 55,1–3). For just as in the general and ordinary crafts the above-mentioned tools are superior to all other tools, so too the most excellent standards (laws) or basic norms are those which are in the greatest possible conformity with nature or objective reality (55,4–6). But no one who has not practiced philosophy and is not capable of practicing philosophy and who does not possess objective truth, will be capable of doing this (55,6–7). But in the general or ordinary arts and crafts, men do not, perchance, derive their tools and their most accurate reckoning from 'first principles' (from 'originals') themselves and thus achieve something close to scientific (philosophic, theoretic) knowledge; rather, they borrow them at second or third or even more remote hand, and base their reasonings on experience and empirical observations (55,7–12). The philosopher, and he alone, imitates directly that which among all things (or measures) is the most exact (55,12–13). For what he gazes at is originality and exactness itself, not merely imitation (55,13–14). This being so, we may assert that just as a house-builder who borrows his measurements from other buildings instead of using the rod and other technical instruments is not a good architect, similarly, one who either enacts laws for cities or administers public affairs by observing and imitating the public administrations or constitutions devised by other men, whether those of the Lacedaemonians, Cretans or some other commonwealth, is most certainly not a good lawgiver or a conscientious statesman (55,14–21). For the imitation of that which is not good in itself cannot possibly be good, nor can the imitation of that which in its very nature is not divine (imperishable) and enduring, be imperishable and stable (55,21–3). It is obvious, however, that among all craftsmen the philosopher, and he alone, is familiar not only with laws that are truly stable, but also with practices that are truly right and proper (55,23–5). For the philosopher, and he alone, lives with his gaze fixed on nature (true reality) and on the divine (imperishable); and like a good helmsman [who takes his bearings from the unchanging stars] he will tie his life to what is eternal and unchanging, moor it to 'first principles' and live as the master of his own soul (55,26–56,2). Admittedly, this kind of knowledge is purely theoretic (56,2–3). Nevertheless, it enables us to determine our whole practical conduct and all our practical actions in conformity with this theoretic knowledge (56,3–4). For,

just as sight in itself produces or creates nothing—its only assignment is to distinguish and to reveal to us all that can physically
be seen—yet it not only enables us to act as it directs but also
assists us greatly in all our actions—for without sight we would be
almost completely immobilized—so it is also evident that, although
rational knowledge is purely theoretic, yet we still perform
thousands of things in full conformity with rational (theoretic)
knowledge, and, in fact, decide upon certain actions and forgo
others (56,4–12). Thus, on account of reason (and theoretic
knowledge), we achieve everything that deserves to be called
good (56,12).'

Closer analysis of this complex passage [3] exhibits an initial congruity
between the competent (practical) craftsman, physician or gymnast [4]
on the one hand, and the good (theoretic) philosopher (philosophic
lawgiver or statesman) on the other hand. Both the artisan and the
philosophic lawgiver, we are told, 'must have a general acquaintance
with nature' (54,16), and both will have to derive their proper tools
as well as their standards or norms 'from nature' (54,22–55,3). [5] But the
good (philosophic) lawgiver, we are informed, must have a knowledge
and understanding of nature (or reality) superior to that of the mere
physician or gymnast (54,17–18), because he is concerned with the
well-being or virtues of the soul as well as with determining the
salvation or perdition of the whole commonweal (54,19–20). This
being so, the good craftsman derives his specific tools from 'nature' [6]—
that is, as the illustrations seem to indicate (water, light, sun rays), from
scientifically observed or observable natural phenomena or 'accurate
reflections of objective reality.' [7] The philosophic lawgiver or statesman,
on the other hand, borrows his norms or standards (his 'tools') directly
from objective reality itself (55,1–2), [8] that is, from 'absolutes,' 'firsts'
or 'originals,' rather than from 'derivatives' or 'reflections,' as does
the craftsman. Thus, with the exception of the statement that the
philosophic lawgiver derives his standards from 'absolutes,' while the
general craftsman, including the physician and gymnast, imitates
'derivatives' found in (physical) nature and, hence, are part of 'nature,'
the parallel between the philosophic lawgiver or statesman and the
good general craftsman seems to be fairly complete.

Beginning with 55,7, that is, beginning with 'but in the general and
ordinary arts or crafts,' however, the philosophic lawgiver or statesman
suddenly is sharply contrasted with the good and competent craftsman.
Here the basic and, it appears, insurmountable differences in their

respective 'models,' tools or norms are emphasized: the models or tools proper to the general and ordinary crafts or skills, we are told, are not derived directly from 'originals' or, better, are not these 'originals' themselves, but are borrowed rather 'at second, third and even more remote hand' (55,9–10),[9] something the true philosopher or philosophic statesman could not do, and never would do. More than that: they are taken from, and based upon, our immediate experience of physical nature—from natural or physical phenomena as well as from empirical observations (55,10–12) which, in this instance, are looked upon as something decidedly inferior and, concomitantly, highly unreliable. 'Only the philosopher, and he alone,' we are reminded, '[knows and, hence,] imitates directly that which among all things [among all measures, standards or norms?] is the most exact' (55,12–13). For he, and he alone, is the 'spectator' of absolute and abiding truth—of what in its absoluteness and objectivity is most exact and most abiding. Hence, the true philosopher is not merely an (empirical) observer of some remote and less exact 'imitation' of, or 'derivative' from, this absolute and immutable truth.[10] It will be remembered that 54,22–55,7 referred to a 'technical' difference *within* the otherwise perfect analogy between the general arts or crafts properly exercised and the 'craft' of the true philosopher or philosophic lawgiver and statesman. There we are told that the general craftsman, including the physician and gymnast, takes his norms, standards or tools from certain natural phenomena or, to be more exact, from precise manifestations of objective nature. These phenomena are manifestations of 'first principles of nature' or of objective reality itself (54,22–24). The philosophic lawgiver and statesman, on the other hand, goes directly to 'first principles or nature itself,' to what (in Plato's terminology) constitutes 'objective reality itself' (55,2).[11]

In other words, beginning with 55,7 ff., we are suddenly, and without any transitional explanation, informed that the philosophic lawgiver and statesman no longer 'derives from "nature" some definite standards with reference to which he determines what is just, good and becoming' (55,1–3), by the same means as does, for instance, the good craftsman who derives his particular tools from (physical) 'nature.' In *contrast* to the craftsman, who at best goes to physical 'nature' for his most exact tools, the philosophic statesman *always* turns to what is 'beyond (corporeal) nature' and ordinary experience, and he *always* 'imitates that which among all things is the most exact' (55,12–13). For he, and he alone, as we have seen, 'gazes at originality and exactness itself, and not at mere imitation' (55,13–14; 55,23–5). He does not, and never will, take for his model what is only 'imitation' ('nature') and, hence, in Platonic terms, cannot possibly be perfect, abiding and most exact. Thus, the meaning of the term 'nature' (φύσις), as it had been used in 54,12–55,7, has also undergone a substantial change in that it is now the equivalent of something inferior (derived) and, therefore, 'evil.' In brief, the two terms 'nature' and 'objective truth (or, reality),' it must be admitted, are no longer synonymous, but rather express two opposite and somewhat irreconcilable 'principles'—an unmistakably Platonic position. To the philosopher alone, but never to the general craftsman, therefore, belongs what is perfect, true, most exact and most enduring. Hence, unlike the ordinary crafts and skills, philosophy is in principle purely theoretic and, hence, nonempirical. This purely theoretic standpoint, as the repeated references to the philosophic law-giver and statesman indicate, enables man to live his whole life in accordance with the dictates of the highest, purest, most exact and most immutable principles.[12] The general and always practical crafts-man, on the other hand, must constantly turn to physical 'nature', to mere 'manifestations' or inferior 'imitations' of the 'originals' for guidance, norms or measurements (55,7–12; 55,14–16). He borrows his standards and measurements 'at second, third and even more remote hand,' basing his reasoning on 'natural' experience and em-pirical observation, and frequently deriving his measurements or models from other human artifacts rather than from 'philosophic norms' directly and immediately copied from true 'originals,' that is, from objective reality and absolute as well as abiding truth, such as the Platonic Separate Ideas or Plato's notion of the Good (the One). Because the general craftsman 'imitates imitations'—because he copies what, by its very definition, must be infinitely inferior—he too is infinitely inferior to the philosophic lawgiver and statesman, who follows only 'originals.' In this fashion, the general craftsman and the philosophic lawgiver or statesman, who initially (54,10–55,7) were considered mutually compatible, are suddenly sharply contrasted and even opposed to one another as regards their respective working methods (and objects): they can no longer be compared with one another. They are contrasted as in Plato's philosophy the Separate Ideas are contrasted with the corporeal appearances, or as Being is contrasted with Becoming. Like in the Platonic 'cave analogy,' the general craftsman, even the most competent craftsman, mistakes mere shadows for reality and truth, believing that these shadows contain all the truth we may ever grasp intellectually. Hence, as a 'captive of the cave' he lives and works in a 'world of shadows.' Only the philosopher ascends to the pure vision of the world of abiding truth and true reality and thus escapes the realm of mere shadows.

At the same time, the meaning of the term 'imitation' seems suddenly to have suffered a drastic change. Earlier we had been told that the good craftsman employs tools, measurements and methods derived directly from 'nature' (54,22–4). These tools, measurements and methods, to be sure, are 'imitations'—and, according to Plato, everything in the world of corporeal existence or becoming is but an 'imitation.' However, since they are derived from 'nature' directly and without inter-mediaries, they are 'scientific (good) standards' within their own limitations, such as, for instance, the ruler, the rod, the compass or some other 'technically precise' or 'scientific' instrument. As such, these 'scientific' tools are still 'imitations,' but not just ordinary, everyday 'imitations'; rather, they are exact (or almost exact) copies of absolute standards, norms or measurements within the visible or physical world (54,24–5; 55,15–16) and, hence, to a high degree participate in the exactness and 'stability' of these absolutes. They are most certainly not crude or inept imitations of some infinitely remote original in the ordinary (and derogatory) sense of the term.[13] But beginning with 55,7 we are told of 'imitations at second, third and even more remote hand' (55,10–12). These 'remote imitations'—and this sounds very much like Plato—are badly corrupted and, hence, wholly unacceptable 'derivatives' which can no longer be used as 'scientific' norms, standards or measurements (55,16–17). They cannot possibly be employed as the 'norms' for the vital tasks confronting the philoso-pher or philosophic statesman, although they might be adequate for the banausic practical craftsman. Hence, the particular 'imitations' mentioned in this context are in fact 'imitations of imitations' or 'imitations of imitations of imitations,' such as certain human artifacts (55,16–17): they are, in other words, 'man made' instruments or tools or, as in the case of the poor lawgiver and statesman, 'man made' laws or institutions. They may be adequate for the humdrum activities of the non-philosophic artisan, but they must be roundly rejected by the true (theoretic) philosopher and by the philosophic lawgiver or statesman (the 'philosopher king').

With 55,14, it will be noted, the analogy between the good crafts-man and the philosophic (good) lawgiver and statesman is resumed: the good house-builder, we are told, is a craftsman who does not simply copy the buildings erected by some other house-builder, and the philosophic (good) lawgiver and statesman is not one who simply copies or imitates the laws, constitutions or institutions of other cities or peoples. It must be borne in mind, however, that in this context even the good craftsman 'imitates imitation,' that is, 'nature,' which, at least to Plato, is always an imitation of something more original. In other words, the good craftsman is always guided by the most 'perfect imitation' of the original—'nature'—while the good lawgiver and statesman looks only at the original, but never at an imitation, no matter how close it may be to the original. Thus the good craftsman never 'imitates imitations of imitations,' and the good lawgiver and statesman never 'imitates imitations,' thus compounding the deficiencies and inaccuracies inherent in all imitations. In this sense, the analogy between the good craftsman and the good lawgiver of necessity is always incomplete or imperfect—a characteristic feature of 55,7–56,2. 'The buildings erected by other house-builders' or the 'laws or institutions of other cities or peoples,' are always 'remote imitations,' inferior 'derivatives' (55,21–3) and, hence, are unacceptable standards. The imitation of poor imitations, that is, the use of poor and necessarily deficient standards, norms or measurements in itself must be poorer yet—obviously a Platonic notion.

Further analysis of 54,10–56,12 suggests that this particular chapter definitely contains two distinct trains of thought or two sets of arguments which seem to conflict with one another: first, the confrontation between the philosophic lawgiver or stateman who relies on 'absolute nature,' that is, on the vision of absolute truth or objective reality (in the Platonic sense) for devising the norms and standards of his thought and action, and the general craftsman who falls back on experience and the empirical observation of 'imitations,' 'derivatives,' or images; and, second, the analogy between the good philosophic lawgiver or statesman who takes for his norms or standards the most exact and most enduring of all standards, namely, objective reality ('absolute nature'), and the good craftsman who derives his tools (and measurements) from 'nature' itself—as well as the analogy between the bad (unphilosophic) lawgiver or statesman who takes for his model existing laws and existing institutions or constitutions found in other cities, and the poor house-builder who simply copies the buildings erected by others.

The relative incompatibility of these two trains of thought might possibly indicate that 54,10–55,7 and 56,2–12 could very well be somewhat garbled and condensed excerpts from Aristotle's *Protrepticus*[14] (which as an exhortation addressed to a ruling prince could not be entirely without some 'practical' or 'concrete' meaning), while 55,7–56,2 might possibly be an excerpt from some other lost work of

Aristotle. This latter passage, which Iamblichus in his usual eclectic, syncretist, but generally uncritical manner might very well have 'sandwiched' between two passages apparently taken from the Aristotelian *Protrepticus*, in its original form and context probably argued along the following lines: good craftsmen, including good physicians and gymnasts, no less than good (philosophic) lawgivers and statesmen, must derive their tools or standards from objective and absolute reality (as Plato saw it). Bad and incompetent craftsmen as well as bad (unphilosophic) lawgivers and statesmen, in contrast, use as their models and guides other human artifacts, that is, poor, inferior and hence bad imitations or 'remote derivatives.' Although the good craftsman superficially resembles the good (philosophic) lawgiver and statesman in that he, too, derives his tools and measurements from actual 'nature,' he still substantially differs from the latter in that by their very nature his particular tools and measurements do not come directly from first (purely theoretic) principles, that is, from pure contemplative reason. Instead, they come from natural (not artificial) phenomena, such as the natural behavior of water, light or sun rays, determined by disciplined (scientific) experience and copied in exact tools. For 'nature'—the totality of corporeal phenomena—is, in Plato's terms, always something infinitely inferior to objective reality represented by the Separate Ideas. In this sense, the method employed by the good 'scientific' (practical) craftsman and the method used by the purely theoretic (Platonic) philosopher, statesman and lawgiver, who never looks at imitations or 'derivatives' (and, hence, ignores 'nature'), but always goes directly to the first principles of truth, goodness and beauty, and who always looks to objective and unchanging reality, are essentially different. Their guiding principles are different (and, hence, their methods are different), not only in regard to their 'originality,' but also in regard to their 'exactness,' stability and degree of perfection.

The obvious incompatibility of 55,7–56,2 and 54,10–55,7 (as well as 56,2–12) suggests that Iamblichus might be quoting here from two different works: either from two different compositions of Aristotle, namely, from the Aristotelian *Protrepticus* (54,10–55,7 and 56,2–12), and from some other early Aristotelian composition (55,7–56,2) which is as yet to be identified; or from the Aristotelian *Protrepticus* and, perhaps, from Plato's *Statesman* or *Philebus*. The hypothesis that is being offered here, tentative though it may be, is that Iamblichus' other source is another lost work of the early Aristotle. Hence, we are faced with the task of identifying this 'other' Aristotelian composition. For those who are familiar with the surviving fragments of Aristotle's lost works, the reference to 'what among all things is the most exact' (55,12–13) has a familiar ring. It calls to mind a fragmentary statement, commonly ascribed to the *Politicus*, a lost Aristotelian dialogue: 'The good is the most precise (most exact) measure (or standard) among all things,'[15] that is, among all possible measures or standards. This fragment from the Aristotelian *Politicus*, it appears, is the only fragment of any real significance which has been credited to this lost dialogue with any degree of certainty.[16] Also, it might be conjectured here that the *Politicus* was composed shortly after the Aristotelian *Protrepticus* and, in all likelihood, slightly prior to the Aristotelian *On Philosophy*,[17] which is commonly dated in the vicinity of Plato's death in 348–47 B.C.[18] Finally, it cannot be denied that this fragment of the *Politicus*, provided it is in fact from this dialogue, restates some of the notions which Plato had advanced in his *Statesman* and *Philebus*.

It is quite likely, therefore, that 55,7–56,2 is actually a fragment or excerpt of Aristotle's *Politicus* rather than of the Aristotelian *Protrepticus*.[19] The main theme of this particular passage is not, as might be expected from the *Protrepticus*, a recommendation of the advantages attending the pursuit of theoretic philosophy above all other pursuits, but rather the bland and uncompromising insistence that the true lawgiver or philosophic statesman must always look to absolute truth and absolute being for his standards, guides and norms, without considering their immediate practicability or practical usefulness.[20] In other words, 55,7–56,2 emphatically and uncompromisingly establishes and discusses the qualifications of the ideal (Platonic) lawgiver and statesman. Although 54,10–55,7 also deals with the standards or tools applied either by the craftsman (physician and gymnast) or the true lawgiver and statesman, it still insists that theoretic wisdom (φρόνησις) is of the greatest practical use in living the good life; that physicians and gymnasts employ their skills for the sake of other men's physical well-being; and that good lawgivers and statesmen always act in the interest of the moral well-being and virtues of the soul as well as for the salvation of the true commonwealth. But beginning with 55,7, we hear only of absolute and most exact norms, standards and measurements which determine proper thought and proper action—of the purely theoretic foundations of right action. Then, beginning with 56,2, the text resumes the topic that theoretic knowledge of the philosophic type has indeed its practical uses, and that it vitally assists us in the correct performance of whatever we may undertake—a theme befitting the general scope of the Aristotelian *Protrepticus*.[21] Being an exhortation to philosophy, and at the same time extolling the practical usefulness of philosophy in general, the Aristotelian *Protrepticus* most likely played down as much as possible the differences between the practical general craftsman and the purely theoretic philosopher or philosophic statesman.[22] The Aristotelian *Politicus*, on the other hand, might very well have considered the work of the true statesman or the philosopher king as the 'craft of all crafts'—as the craft which is exclusively concerned with the 'measure of all measures,' that is, with 'absolute originals.' Hence, the *Politicus* might also have contrasted as much as possible the purely theoretic statesman (who always looks upon the abiding and perfect exemplars) and the practical general craftsman (who looks upon the affairs of this world). By contrasting the two, Aristotle actually destroys the analogy between them, an analogy which he probably had developed in the *Protrepticus*.

Another piece of evidence in support of the thesis that 55,7–56,2 might be assigned to the Aristotelian *Politicus* rather than to Aristotle's *Protrepticus*, can be detected in the indisputable affinity of this passage with certain views advanced in Plato's *Statesman* and *Philebus*. It has been claimed on what seems to be good grounds that the Aristotelian *Politicus* is closely related to the Platonic *Statesman*, not only as regards its title, but also as regards some (and perhaps much) of its philosophic content as well as its method of reasoning or demonstration.[23] It may be surmised that in the *Politicus* Aristotle discussed the 'ideal statesman,' and that he presumably did so in a like manner, but not necessarily on the same philosophic foundation or by using the same methodological approach, Plato had employed when in his *Statesman* he extolled the 'ideal statesman.' Assuming this, we might also speculate that there exists a certain affinity of thought, method and argumentation between the Aristotelian *Politicus* and the Platonic *Statesman*.[24] More specifically, 55,7–56,2 might possibly have been written under the direct influence of Plato, *Statesman* 293A–301C. Here Plato does not refer merely to the physician who heals 'according to the rules of his art,' to the 'statesman who rules according to science,' to gymnasts and helmsmen and to cities which are but a poor imitation of the ideal model of the perfect city. But he speaks of the true laws which are close imitations of objective (true) reality and, hence, are themselves closest to perfect truth. The fragment of Aristotle's *Politicus*, which relates that 'the good is the most precise measure among all things' (or, with R. Stark, 'the good is the most precise measure for all things'), on the other hand, seems also to restate certain views expounded in the Platonic *Philebus*, which assigns to the 'most exact measure' the first and upper-most place in the hierarchy of values or measures, the second place to the measurable, and the third place to reason capable of apprehending measure.[25] This fragment of the *Politicus* apparently also coincides with what Plato had to say about the 'hierarchy of measuration' as a progressive truth-criterion—a hierarchy which, in the final analysis, is determined by the 'purity' as well as exactness of the original measure.[26]

To Plato, especially to the late Plato of the *Philebus*, knowledge (including ethics and politics) is measurement; and true or exact knowledge, whether speculative or practical, is always a knowledge which measures everything according to an abiding absolute and absolutely determinate measure or norm.[27] The indeterminate, that is, 'the many' or 'the manifold' of the corporeal world is never, and never can be, the object of strictly philosophic knowledge. Hence, experience—the indeterminate and fleeting—can never supply truly reliable and accurate scientific standards or measurements. By the same token, Plato attempted to turn ethics into an exact science or into a 'pure theory of norms' with the help of the principles of measure and measuration: all that is good is measurable and, hence, determinate, and all that is evil is immeasurable and, hence, indeterminate. In other words, for Plato the Highest Good is the most universal and most precise measure as well as the absolute Unity or absolute One which makes the world of Separate Ideas 'determinate' and, consequently, real, good, abiding and knowable.[28] Plato's insistence on absolute exactness and absolute purity constitutes also the basis for any distinction between pure (Platonic) science and applied science, or as Aristotle would have it in the *Protrepticus*, between pure mathematics and architecture, between pure geometry and surveying, and between astronomy and navigation.[29] On account of their exactness, the former, it goes without saying, are infinitely superior to the latter; and because of their superior truth as regards measure and exactitude, they are the main concern—the exclusive concern—of the true philosopher. But this is in essence the doctrine underlying 55,7–56,2.[30]

This raises the further question of why Iamblichus should combine and intertwine here excerpts from two different Aristotelian works. The answer seems to be astonishingly simple: both excerpts, at least on the surface, appear to be quite similar, at least to a man of Iamblichus' intellectual limitations; both deal with a confrontation of the craftsman and the statesman or lawgiver. That the excerpt from the Aristotelian *Protrepticus* stresses the compatibility of the (practical) craftsman and the (active) statesman, while that from the *Politicus* emphasizes the basic contrast between the practical craftsman who relies on 'applied science,' and the theoretic statesman who always resorts to 'pure science,'—all this seems to have escaped the attention of Iamblichus. Hence, in his usual uncritical manner, Iamblichus did not hestitate to combine these two different excerpts from two different works into one single report, thus creating the impression that the whole of chapter X (54,10–56,12) had been taken from one single work—presumably from the original Aristotelian *Protrepticus*.[31] As a matter of fact, Iamblichus does this so convincingly that until recently no one seems to have noticed the essential incompatibility of these two excerpts.[32]

The possibility that 55,7–56,2 of Iamblichus' *Protrepticus* might be based on Aristotle's *Politicus* rather than on the Aristotelian *Protrepticus* raises a fundamental and far-reaching problem. Since the days of I. Bywater,[33] it has widely and almost unanimously been held that, barring a few minor exceptions,[34] Iamblichus' *Protrepticus* 36,27 (or 34,5)–60,10 (or 61,4) contains the major extant fragments of Aristotle's *Protrepticus*.[35] But if Iamblichus, *Protrepticus*, chapter X (54,10–56,12) should actually include fragments or excerpts not only from the Aristotelian *Protrepticus*, but also from Aristotle's *Politicus* (and, perhaps, from Plato's *Statesman* or *Philebus*),[36] then one might wonder whether chapter VI (or V)–XII, that is, 36,27 (or 34,5)–60,10 (or 61,4) of Iamblichus' *Protrepticus*, which have been used and relied upon, for the retrieval and reconstruction of Aristotle's *Protrepticus*, may not also be replete with fragments or excerpts from some of the other lost works of Aristotle[37] and possibly from some of Plato's dialogues. W. G. Rabinowitz, despite the fact that his remarkable and undoubtedly scholarly views have, on the whole, been rejected,[38] may after all be correct when he emphatically denies that we could successfully reconstruct the Aristotelian *Protrepticus* with the help of Iamblichus' *Protrepticus*.[39]

We would most certainly find ourselves on more secure grounds if we were able to gain reliable insight into the method by which Iamblichus compiled his excerpts from the sources or materials he consulted when writing his *Protrepticus*; and, especially, if we knew something about the particular manner in which he excerpted the works of Aristotle. Such an insight, however, is rendered extremely difficult, if not impossible, not only by the fact that we do not possess the originals of the Aristotelian writings on which Iamblichus apparently relied, but also by the fact that throughout his *Protrepticus*, Iamblichus, in keeping with his syncretist tendencies, seems to have combined and intertwined Platonic and Aristotelian notions in a most arbitrary manner.[40] Accordingly, we must always suspect that he quotes Plato and Aristotle side by side, without identifying or distinguishing either.[41] Moreover, these excerpts, provided they are indeed from the Aristotelian *Protrepticus* or, perhaps, from the Aristotelian *Politicus* (and possibly from some other lost work or works of Aristotle), are cast in the peculiar language of Iamblichus. It is also an indisputable fact, ascertainable from his other writings, that Iamblichus himself is, as a rule, a muddled thinker and often an awkward and not always reliable reporter. He frequently abbreviates, condenses and, at times, mutilates almost beyond recognition the ideas and notions advanced by others, while at the same time he misunderstands or misquotes them.[42]

Such, then, are some of the almost insurmountable difficulties facing anyone attempting to recover and reconstruct Aristotle's lost *Protrepticus* with the help of Iamblichus' *Protrepticus*, the only 'source' which at present seems to hold any promise that such a recovery and reconstruction may ever be accomplished. It is no wonder, therefore, that the general attitude of scholars towards the possibility of retrieving and reconstructing Aristotle's *Protrepticus* should range all the way from an attitude of resigned pessimism bordering on a depressing 'give-it-all-up' policy, to an optimistic and, perhaps, even reckless belief that in the *Protrepticus* of Iamblichus we actually possess, though probably in a somewhat distorted form, the 'lost' *Protrepticus* of Aristotle.[43]

In conclusion, it might briefly be stated that, although Iamblichus' *Protrepticus*, Books V (or VI)–XII, for the time being constitutes the only promising source or basis for the possible reconstruction of Aristotle's *Protrepticus*, Iamblichus 55,7–56,2, in particular, most likely may not be credited to Aristotle's *Protrepticus*, but rather must be considered a fragment of the Aristotelian *Politicus*.[44] Hence, for the reconstruction of Aristotle's *Protrepticus* we may safely rely only on Iamblichus 34,5 (or 36,27)–55,7 and 56,2–60,10 (or 61,4), ignoring 55,7–56,2. This, then, might also vitiate the widely held thesis that in chapters V (or VI)–XII of his *Protrepticus* Iamblichus relies exclusively on Aristotle's *Protrepticus*. In this case we may raise the further and, indeed, disturbing question: if in this section of his *Protrepticus* Iamblichus 'quotes' from the Aristotelian *Protrepticus* as well as from the Aristotelian *Politicus*, why should he not also cite from some of the other lost works of Aristotle, such as the *Eudemus*,[45] and perhaps from works authored by other philosophers. If we pursue this thought to its ultimate consequences, then we might as well admit that Iamblichus' *Protrepticus* can no longer be considered a safe basis for the reconstruction of Aristotle's *Protrepticus*—a totally unacceptable position. But this does not prevent us from assuming that *Protrepticus* 55,7–56,2 is a fragment of the Aristotelian *Politicus*. To an uncritical or non-analytical thinker such as Iamblichus, *Protrepticus* 54,18–56,12 probably sounded like one single and wholly integrated argument or train of thought.

# Chapter IX

# What Prompted Aristotle to Address the *Protrepticus* to Themison of Cyprus?★

According to the testimony of Ioannes Stobaeus (Teles), Aristotle addressed the *Protrepticus* to Themison, presumably a petty 'prince' or 'king' on the island of Cyprus. Stobaeus (Teles) relates rather cryptically that 'no one had greater advantages for becoming a philosopher [than Themison]. For he not only possessed great wealth and, hence, could afford to spend a great deal of money on philosophy, but also had a reputation and "social status" as well.'[1] This report, the historicity of which we have no reason to doubt, raises a number of puzzling questions: who was this Themison; what were the connections, if any, between Aristotle (or the Academy) and this Cypriot 'king'; why did Aristotle see fit to address him in particular in what seems to be one of his most important early compositions; and why did Aristotle approach him in the urgent tenor of a hortatory essay?

From Stobaeus, who recounts Teles' *Epitome*, we learn that Themison apparently was a 'king on Cyprus.' There is, however, no mention of the city or territory over which he ruled, provided he was indeed a 'king' or 'ruler.' Neither do we know to which dynasty he belonged or when or how long he reigned. Diodorus Siculus XVI. 42. 2, records that around the year 350 B.C. there were no less than nine important cities on the island of Cyprus, each ruled by a 'king.' But he does not mention a Themison. Thus, it is well-nigh impossible to identify this Themison.[2] It is probable, however, that he was a person of some wealth, standing and influence on Cyprus,[3] since otherwise there would have been little inducement for Aristotle to address this man in so important a work as the *Protrepticus*. Be this as it may, there is not sufficient evidence to substantiate even these meager assumptions.

We also know that Aristotle was apparently a close personal friend of Eudemus of Cyprus,[4] the Cypriot exile (?), in whose honored memory he wrote the *Eudemus or On the Soul* around the year 352 B.C.[5] It may be that through this friendship with Eudemus, Aristotle (or the Academy) at one time had established contacts with some of the more prominent Cypriots, including Themison.[6] If this were so, then the composition of the *Protrepticus* might have been inspired not only by Aristotle's desire to denounce as well as embarrass Isocrates and Isocrates' philosophic *paideia*, but also by a personal relationship or contact which linked Aristotle (and the Academy) and Themison (through the mediation of Eudemus?):[7] Aristotle addressed the *Protrepticus* to Themison in order further to ingratiate himself with Themison who, on account of his wealth and social position, might possibly bestow great favors on Aristotle and the Academy.[8] To incur the favors of influential (and wealthy) people and thus gain influence with them was, as the example of the two Dionysii of Syracuse indicates, a rather common practice with the Academy, which was vitally concerned not only with purely theoretic philosophy or political theory, but also with effective political action. There exists also the possibility that this Themison, who might have been a philo-Macedonian seeking the political support of Macedonia in the protracted struggle of the Greek settlers on the island of Cyprus against their Persian (Phoenician) overlords, at one time had visited Athens and contacted the Academy, including Aristotle, the Macedonian, requesting the latter to intercede for him with King Philip of Macedonia.[9] It might also be conjectured that Themison hoped that, with the active support of Macedonia, he might win political independence from Persian domination. These political schemes might have brought him into personal contact with the Platonic Academy as well as with some prominent Macedonians, especially with Aristotle who not only seems to have had considerable influence at the court of King Philip, but who also might have been personally interested in, and perhaps actively connected with, certain vital phases in the meteoric political ascendancy and expansion of Macedonia during the reign of King Philip.[10]

It has been suggested that by addressing the *Protrepticus* to Themison Aristotle attempted to encourage the latter to embrace and practice Platonic philosophy, as Plato himself had tried to turn Dionysius I and Dionysius II of Syracuse (and Dion of Syracuse) into practicing (Platonic) philosophers. The fact that Themison was apparently a person of wealth and standing probably made such an effort even more attractive and more promising.[11] In keeping with a practice observed by many ancient poets, artists, literati and philosophers—Socrates and the Cynics excepted—some schools of philosophy or philosophers tried to establish personal connections with some dynasties, tyrants and personages of wealth and influence in order to enhance their prestige, extend their influence, or merely to enjoy the advantages of wealth and luxury.[12] It has also been insinuated that the allusion to Themison's wealth and social status was mere flattery intended to ingratiate the author with the 'king' and thus make the exhortation to philosophy even more effective.[13] Others, again, insist that in the *Protrepticus* Aristotle did not really exhort Themison personally to embrace philosophy but tried rather to persuade him to initiate in his city a political program conforming to the political ideals propagated by Plato and the Academy—in brief, to inaugurate in his domain the Platonic 'ideal state.'[14] A final possibility which has been mentioned is that by flattering Themison Aristotle may have attempted to induce Themison to establish in his city a school of philosophy modeled upon the Athenian Academy—a kind of 'foreign branch' of the Platonic Academy—and to 'patronize' this venture.[15]

The *Protrepticus*, however, is apparently intended to be more than a personal, and hence limited, address or exhortation directed at a relatively insignificant and little known Cypriot. In a sense it is also a hortatory 'manifesto' appealing to the youth of Greece to choose the path of dispassionate reason—the theoretic life—in a confused and turbulent age when many of the traditional religious, political and social values of the past had become lost. This is clearly indicated by Elias and David, who maintain that Aristotle composed the *Protrepticus* 'to encourage young people to turn to philosophy.'[16] There is indeed no reason why a personal appeal to Themison should not also be coupled with a general appeal to mankind—why a single concrete person should not be the more immediate addressee, while the whole of humanity is meant to be the ultimate audience. Thus, if the statements of Elias and David supply reliable evidence, Aristotle is appealing not only to Themison but also to his contemporaries, exhorting them to espouse the true *paideia*—the right philosophy and the right way of life—by accepting and practicing the high philosophic ideals of the Platonic Academy, and by dedicating their lives to those intellectual and moral pursuits which stand in sharp contrast to the vulgar 'philosophy of the market place' propagated by such men as Isocrates and his disciples. As its title reflects, the *Protrepticus* is both a personal address and a general appeal or exhortation, encouraging future generations to choose wisely when committing themselves to a definite way of life. The experiences of St. Augustine attest the efficacy of this appeal.[17]

It is also widely held that aside from being a hortatory essay in praise of a life dedicated to philosophy the *Protrepticus* is a deliberate rejoinder to Isocrates' *Antidosis* (Einarson), as well as a 'rival' of Isocrates' *To Nicocles*, *To Evagoras* and *Nicocles or the Cypriots*.[18] The

*Protrepticus* was designed, we may surmise, to compete with, and if possible to counteract, Isocrates' influence in Athens as well as in other parts of the Hellenic world, including the island of Cyprus. It may also be considered an effort on the part of Aristotle and the Academy to invade Isocrates' field of patronage on Cyprus, and to terminate or curtail the intellectual and political influence he had gained there.[19] Judging from the evidence, Isocrates' influence in Cyprus and the prestige he enjoyed there must have been considerable. We know, for instance, that Isocrates was a personal friend of Conon and of Timotheus, the son of Conon. With Conon as an intermediary, Isocrates had probably succeeded in establishing close connections with the powerful Evagorids, the rulers or 'kings' of Cypriot Salamis, the most important city on the island. These contacts seem to be indicated by the aforementioned *Cyprian Addresses*, all of which were written after 373 B.C., the year Evagoras I died and was succeeded by Nicocles. Since the school of Isocrates was for a time well-known and highly regarded throughout the Hellenic world, it is possible that for a while Nicocles might also have been a pupil of Isocrates in Athens, although this is by no means certain.[20]

It appears that in 351–50 B.C. or thereabouts Isocrates found himself in a most embarrassing situation as regards his connections with the Cypriot Evagorids. For some time the Greek settlers on the island of Cyprus had been threatened by the constant encroachments of the Persians and especially of the Phoenicians, who were determined to take over the island and suppress or reduce all Greek influence there. This tense situation, the details of which do not interest us here, culminated in a general anti-Persian uprising by the Greek settlers which became particularly violent in 351–50 B.C. While the Greek settlers did seek the political and military support of the motherland, the Evagorids (Evagoras II) openly sided with the Persians.[21] The medizing policy of the Evagorids must have been a scandal to the Greeks and a crushing blow to Isocrates' prestige in Athens as well as throughout the whole of Greece. There was probably some speculation as to whether or not his educational philosophy, which had a strong pragmatic or utilitarian cast, might have been the ultimate cause behind the treacherous conduct of the calculating Evagorids who were, after all, the disciples and friends of Isocrates. Hence, this was obviously a most opportune moment for Aristotle and the Academy to deal Isocrates, their most serious rival as well as their most dangerous antagonist, a crushing blow from which he might never recover. At the same time, it afforded them a unique opportunity to gain an 'intellectual foothold' on the island of Cyprus (something to which the Academy apparently had aspired for a long time),[22] thereby enhancing the prestige and influence of the Academy throughout the Hellenic world.[23] The *Protrepticus*, however, does not seem to concern itself directly or explicitly with the political events which transpired in Cyprus during the middle of the fourth century B.C.; it merely uses these events to discredit Isocrates more effectively, and advance more tellingly the Academy's position in this part of the Mediterranean.

We know that the Platonic Academy was not merely concerned with philosophic or scientific studies, including political theory, or with the cult of the Muses, but also with effective political action.[24] It not only encouraged its members to take an active part in the political events which transpired throughout the Hellenic world but expected them to play a decisive (and allegedly messianic) role in these events.[25] There can be little doubt that the Academy intended to translate into concrete action Plato's teachings concerning the training and formation of future statesmen and rulers[26]—that it meant to produce future political leaders and 'philosopher kings,' steeped in the spirit of Plato's philosophic and political ideals, who one day would save the world (at least the Hellenic world) from its follies and evils.[27] As a matter of fact, a cursory survey of Greek history during the fourth and third centuries B.C. should make it amply clear that the political activities and political schemings of the Platonic Academy were manifold and persistent (and not always creditable), reaching into almost every corner of the Mediterranean world.[28] The several attempts of Plato and his pupils to make their political influence felt in Syracuse and Sicily, in Macedonia[29] and in the domain of Hermias of Atarneus[30] are too well known to require detailed elaboration. Ancient literature also indicates that the Academy had a great many political contacts and diplomatic dealings with a number of cities, peoples, dynasties and prominent personages; and that it was connected with certain political events which transpired throughout the Hellenic world.[31] Naturally, it is also possible that Aristotle, who seems to have had an active hand in certain political events related to the rise of Macedonia under King Philip, contacted Themison for political reasons, and that he did so at the instigation of Philip, who might have wished to extend Macedonian influence to the island of Cyprus, which at that time was in serious trouble with its Persian (and Phoenician) overlords.[32]

The keen and often bitter rivalry between the Platonic Academy and the school of Isocrates is a matter of record. Once before, in the

*Gryllus*, Aristotle had struck a blow for the Academy by attacking the kind of rhetoric which Isocrates and his school were advocating.[33] In his *Antidosis*, published in 353–52 B.C., as well as in other works, Isocrates had replied in a rather condescending manner to these attacks by denouncing as impractical, useless and even foolish the purely theoretic philosophy expounded by Plato and the Academy. Aristotle's rejoinder to these denunciations was the *Protrepticus*,[34] which was apparently meant to pursue several aims. It would disprove the contentions of the *Antidosis* and thus discredit Isocrates, thereby diminishing whatever influence the latter had in Cyprus and, perhaps, with Themison, the Cypriot. At the same time, being addressed to Themison, the Cypriot, the *Protrepticus* would effectively 'invade' what hitherto had been Isocrates' intellectual preserve: the island of Cyprus. By addressing the *Protrepticus* to Themison, Aristotle, as a representative of the Academy, serves notice that he is determined to encounter the formidable Isocrates in an arena where for some time Isocrates apparently had the exclusive and uncontested monopoly of speaking for the intellectual and cultural life of Athens and the whole of Greece.[35] This might be one explanation as to why the *Protrepticus* is addressed to the Cypriot Themison.

That the *Protrepticus* is addressed to a relatively insignificant and obscure ruler on the island of Cyprus is in itself significant. Plato and the members of the Academy, who, as has been shown, were taking an evergrowing interest in the political events which transpired throughout the Eastern Mediterranean, were undoubtedly aware of the political developments on Cyprus. It could not escape them that Isocrates had a considerable and perhaps dominant influence among certain important Cypriots. The anti-Persian revolt and the events of 351–50 B.C., as well as the ensuing medizing attitude of Isocrates' friends, created a situation in which the Academy could irreparably damage Isocrates' reputation and, at the same time, extend its own influence into Cyprus. The Academy required a Cypriot to serve as a convenient 'bridgehead' for this planned 'intellectual invasion.' Even someone of Themison's relative obscurity would suffice. Themison, however, apparently was not a mere 'nobody.' He seems to have been wealthy, and he was a 'king' of sorts. Hence, it is not surprising that the *Protrepticus* should be addressed to Themison. He was, after all, the most prominent Cypriot that the Academy, which stood in need of an addressee, could muster at the time.

The *Protrepticus*, although explicitly addressed to Themison, was certainly motivated not simply by Aristotle's solicitation of a minor

Cypriot ruler. It was a hortatory manifesto encouraging the entire younger generation of Hellenes to embrace the philosophic way of life outlined by Plato and, through the *vita contemplativa*, find a new and vital purpose. Moreover, as its close connection with Isocrates' *Antidosis* indicates, it was most assuredly a vehicle or manifestation of that heated controversy which raged between the Academy and Isocrates' school over the ultimate questions as to what constitutes the 'life according to reason,' the right *paideia* and the proper and meaningful life. Finally, the *Protrepticus* was also a 'political manoeuvre' aimed at extending the influence of the Academy to a part of the Mediterranean world which had theretofore been monopolized by Isocrates, the most formidable antagonist and rival of the Academy. If in this contest Isocrates should be the loser, such a consequence could only be welcomed by the Academy. The 'intellectual invasion' of Cyprus and the concomitant 'expulsion' of Isocrates seem to be at the heart of Aristotle's motivation in addressing the *Protrepticus* to Themison, the Cypriot, although the general theme or appeal of this essay reaches far beyond this rather limited aim. We should not overlook the possibility, however, that Aristotle's action might also have been part of Macedonia's political and diplomatic schemes or aspirations throughout the eastern Mediterranean. This would also be in accord with the assumption that during his lifetime Aristotle frequently played an active as well as important role in Macedonia's political ascendancy to a cosmocracy under the leadership of King Philip.[36]

# The Term 'Philosopher' and the Panegyric Analogy in Aristotle's *Protrepticus*★

There exists a widespread and apparently firmly entrenched tradition which maintains that the term 'philosopher' was coined by Pythagoras. Pythagoras is said not only to have been the first man who called himself a 'philosopher,' that is, 'a lover of wisdom,' but also to have explained, by way of an analogy, the meaning of this novel and, it appears, startling term.[1] The tradition which declares Pythagoras to be the originator and interpreter of the term 'philosopher' is commonly traced to Heracleides of Pontus and his Περὶ τῆς ἄπνου ἢ περὶ νόσεων,[2] a work which unfortunately is completely lost. Luckily, in his *Tusculanae Disputationes* V. 3. 8–10, Cicero has preserved what seems to have been the essentials of Heracleides' account.[3] It may also be presumed that Cicero recorded this story fairly accurately.

According to Cicero's report, Pythagoras once visited Leon, the tyrant of Phlius. When asked by his host in what particular 'art' or skill he excelled, he is said to have replied that he was a 'philosopher' and, hence, did not possess any particular (practical) skill. Explaining further this unusual term, which apparently baffled his listeners, Pythagoras continued his account by using what is called the panegyric analogy:

> The life of man resembles a great festival celebrated . . . before a concourse from the whole of Greece. At this festival some people sought to win the glorious distinction of a crown; and others, again, were attracted by the prospect of material gain through buying and selling. But there was also a certain type of people, and that quite the best type of men, who were interested neither in competing, applauding nor seeking gain, but who came solely for the sake of the spectacle itself and, hence, closely watched what was done and how it was done. So also we, as though we had come from some city to a crowded festival, leaving in like fashion another life or another nature of being, entered upon this life, and

some were slaves of ambition, and some slaves of money. But there were a special few who, counting all else for nothing, closely scanned the nature of things. These men gave themselves the name of 'philosophers' (*sapientiae studiosi*)—and this is the meaning of the term 'philosophers.' And just as at these festivals the men of the most exalted education looked on without any self-seeking intent, so in life, too, the contemplation of things and their rational (theoretic) apprehension (*cognitio*) or understanding by far surpasses all other pursuits.[4]

In his *De Vita Pythagorae* (or, *De Vita Pythagorica*) XII. 58 ff., it will be noted, Iamblichus in essence repeats this unusual, though attractive account. As a matter of fact, he follows Cicero's text so closely that it has been surmised that he either made direct use of Cicero's account or, more likely, that he used a source very close to that relied upon by Cicero or possibly that he used Heracleides' original account.[5] The panegyric analogy, interesting enough, is also employed in Alexinus' *Tarentinoi*, where the Pythagoreans come in for quite a bit of ridicule;[6] and in Sosicrates' *Successions of Philosophers*,[7] which relates that Pythagoras 'compared life to the Great Festivals, where some people went to compete for the prize, and others attended to sell their wares, but the best came as spectators. Similarly, in life some grow up with servile natures, greedy for fame [*scil.*, the athletes] and gain [*scil.*, the merchants], but the philosophers seek for truth.'[8] It should be noted that the sequence athletes, merchants and spectator-philosophers in essence restates the Platonic doctrine of the tripartite soul (and its 'reflections' or manifestations) as it is expounded, for instance, in Plato's *Republic*, *Phaedrus* and *Timaeus*.

That Heracleides of Pontus was not the inventor[9] or perhaps the first reporter of this engaging story might be gathered from Aristotle's *Protrepticus* which, it is fairly safe to assume, was composed around 350 B.C., that is, some time before Heracleides wrote his Περὶ τῆς ἄπνου. In the *Protrepticus*, Aristotle maintains: 'It is by no means strange that philosophic wisdom (φρόνησις) should appear devoid of immediate practical usefulness and, at the same time, might not at all prove itself advantageous. For we call philosophic wisdom not advantageous, but good. It ought to be pursued, not for the sake of anything else, but solely for its own sake. For as we journey to the games at Olympia for the spectacle itself, even if we should derive from them nothing more tangible than the sight of the spectacle itself—for the spectacle as such is worth more than "much money"—

and as we watch the Dionysia not in order to derive some material profit from the actors—as a matter of fact, we spend money on them— and as there are many more spectacles we ought to prefer to great riches: so, too, the viewing and contemplation of the universe is to be valued above all other things commonly considered to be useful in a practical sense. For, most certainly, it would make little sense were we to take pains to watch men imitating women or slaves, or fighting or running, but not think it proper to view, free of all charges, the nature and the true reality of everything that exists.'[10]

This passage from Aristotle's *Protrepticus*—and it is assumed here that in his *Protrepticus* Iamblichus cites fairly accurately from Aristotle's lost *Protrepticus*—has apparently been completely overlooked or simply ignored. It should make it quite clear that the use of the panegyric analogy for the purpose of explaining the proper meaning of the term 'philosopher' or 'philosophic man,' and for extolling the unsurpassed excellence of philosophy and the philosophic (contemplative) life, is certainly older than Heracleides' Περὶ τῆς ἄπνου and, perhaps, even older than Aristotle's *Protrepticus*.[11] It might also be conjectured that the term 'philosopher' was already known, and already used, during the first part of the fourth century B.C.; and, as fragment 194 B (Diels-Kranz) of Democritus seems to indicate,[12] it was probably employed before that time. The further question whether this term or the panegyric analogy may in fact be traced back to Pythagoras him-self is really outside the limited scope of this investigation. It seems doubtful, however, that so 'technical' or 'sophisticated' a term as that of 'philosopher' should have been in use as early as the latter part of the sixth century B.C.,[13] or that Pythagoras could already have invented or used the analogy of the three basic ways of life in order to extoll and recommend the philosophic life. In any event, unlike Heracleides, Aristotle does not specifically credit the creation of the term 'philosopher' or the use of the panegyric analogy to Pythagoras.[14] This fact in itself is highly significant in that it seems to reveal that Aristotle apparently had not yet fully succumbed to the many apoc-ryphal stories about Pythagoras which, as shall be shown presently, were put into circulation around the middle of the fourth century B.C., presumably by some members of the Platonic Academy who about this time began to display strong Pythagorizing tendencies. Aristotle's refusal (or omission) to credit the invention of the term 'philosopher' or the panegyric analogy specifically to Pythagoras, apparently sets him apart from the majority within the Academy. His particular attitude towards this whole issue may possibly be explained as follows:

it has been alleged on what seem to be fairly good grounds that Aristotle, even while he was still an active member of the Platonic Academy, refused to accept the strongly 'Pythagorizing tendencies' which became manifest not only in the latest dialogues of Plato (and probably in Plato's 'unwritten doctrine') but also among the majority of Plato's disciples. Perhaps it was his determined opposition to this particular philosophic trend which prompted him to suppress or ignore any and all references to Pythagoras as the presumed author or inventor of the term 'philosopher' as well as of the panegyric analogy. Perhaps Aristotle, whose passion for truth is widely attested,[15] knew only too well that this whole story was merely a legend deliberately put into circulation by some members of the Academy in order to exalt Pythagoras.

Both Pythagoras and Aristotle, above, all, seem to stress that θεωρία is enjoyable *per se*, even though it does not offer us any immediate gain or tangible advantage—a distinctly Platonic notion which is also expounded (and advocated) at great length in the Aristotelian *Protrepticus*. In his account, Heracleides, it appears, attempts to point out that in human life we might be either passionate participants in everything that goes on around us, or dispassionate spectators.[16] For some unknown reason, Heracleides links this observation to the story that Pythagoras invented the term 'philosopher.'[17] In this he apparently follows a contemporary vogue, rather popular in the Academy, of attributing certain apocryphal stories and legendary accomplishments to Pythagoras. The panegyric analogy employed by Aristotle and traditionally credited to Heracleides, it will also be observed, aside from its undeniable ambiguity, does not really explain the term 'philosopher,' but merely proclaims or illustrates the belief that dispassionate contemplation—the purely 'theoretic life' or, perhaps, the 'beatific vision of true reality'—constitutes the main or at least preferred activity of the true (Platonic) philosopher. Hence, it might also be argued that the link between the term 'philosopher' and the main activity of the true philosopher is not an altogether successful arrangement: it simply presupposes the term 'philosopher' as an already well-established concept.

It would not be too farfetched to surmise that the above mentioned passage from Aristotle's *Protrepticus* contains a faint echo of Plato, *Republic* 475D: 'Who, then, are the true philosophers? Those ... who are the lovers of the vision of truth (τοὺς τῆς ἀληθείας φιλο-θεάμωνας).' One might also quote here the many Platonic references to the true nature and function of philosophy or to the chief characteristics of the true philosopher: 'Philosophical minds always have knowledge of a sort which shows them the eternal nature' (*Republic* 485B); 'the philosophers alone are capable of grasping that which is eternal and unchangeable' (*Republic* 484B); 'those who love the truth in each thing are to be called philosophers' (*Republic* 480A); 'only the philosopher is capable of knowing the truth in each thing' (*Republic* 484D) and 'of experiencing the delight which is to be found in the understanding of true being' (*Republic* 582D); the philosopher alone, being capable of visualizing and loving absolute beauty, 'recognizes the existence of absolute beauty' (*Republic* 476B); the true philosopher's 'eyes are forever directed towards things immutable and fixed' (*Republic* 500C); 'God invented and gave us the gift of sight to the end that we might behold the courses of the intelligences in the heavens ... and from this source we have derived philosophy' (*Timaeus* 47A ff.); the mind of the philosopher, 'disdaining the pettiness and nothingness of human affairs ... is flying about, measuring earth and the heavens' (*Theaetetus* 173E); and the philosopher's mind, 'being fixed on true being, has surely no time to look down on human affairs.... And holding conversation with the divine order, he himself becomes ... divine' (*Republic* 500C ff.).

All these statements, which could be augmented almost indefinitely, in turn bring us close to the problem, discussed at great length in Plato's *Symposium* (201C ff.), namely, that the good is also the beautiful and, hence, truth as Plato understood it; and that love is directed towards the beautiful and the true. The dispassionate viewing of the sublimely beautiful is the dispassionate love of the sublimely beautiful and of the ultimate truth which is also the ultimate beauty. With Plato, the intimate interrelation or correlation of τὸ καλὸν and τὸ φίλον permits us to call philosophy also φιλοκαλία, and the philosopher a φιλόκαλος: 'But who are the lovers of wisdom? ... They are those who are in a mean between the two. Love is one of them. For wisdom is a beautiful thing, and love is of the beautiful. And therefore love is also a philosopher.'[18] These explanations, references and excursions, however, still leave unanswered and unsolved the problem of the panegyric analogy.

It might be safe to assume that the ideal of the contemplative or theoretic life, as it is extolled in the story credited to Pythagoras and stated in Aristotle's *Protrepticus* and Heracleides' Περὶ τῆς ἄπνου, was originally advocated by Plato and the Academy. Such a reverential attitude towards contemplation is fully in keeping with the essentially religious and contemplative mood which characterized the ultimate *raison d'être* of the Academy—a religious brotherhood fashioned after the Pythagorean (Orphic?) brotherhoods and dedicated to the worship of the nine Muses. At one time, we may surmise, this ideal of the philosophic life was retroactively attributed to Pythagoras, presumably when late Platonism assumed a distinct Pythagorizing tendency. Undoubtedly, the panegyric analogy refers primarily to the three basic ways of life,[19] already implied in Plato's tri-partite soul: the life of bodily pleasure or material gain, represented by those who attend the festival for the sake of 'buying and selling'; the life of virtue and honor (the practical or political life), represented by those who 'seek a crown'; and the life of pure contemplation (or theoretic life—θεωρία), represented by the dispassionate (philosophic) spectator who enjoys the magnificent (beatific) vision.[20] The philosopher—and this seems to be a distinctly Platonic twist—is wholly committed to a life of intellectual contemplation and 'theory,' that is, to a life centered around θεωρία,[21] which is by far 'the best life.'

Hence, the accounts of Aristotle and Heracleides of Pontus actually combine two major themes: the three fundamental ways of life and the way of the true philosopher. W. Jaeger suggests that Heracleides took these two themes directly from Aristotle's *Protrepticus* (and more remotely, from Plato), and, at the same time, combined or tried to integrate them into a single account. In order to endow this story with greater authority and persuasiveness, Jaeger contends, Heracleides projected it into the remote past by crediting it to Pythagoras.[22] Its retroactive attribution to Pythagoras, as has been shown, is probably due to the high esteem in which the Academy held this ancient sage when it came to realize its indebtedness to the so-called Pythagoreans for the 'Pythagorizing trend' that became so typical of late Platonism. In Aristotle's account, it will be noted, the key term is θεωρία—and it is this θεωρία which he advocates and extols.[23] For the purpose of illustration and dramatization, Aristotle draws certain parallels between the contemplative life of the true philosopher and the celebrated spectacle at Olympia or the Great Dionysia, or to be more exact, the dispassionate viewer of these spectacles. However, it must be borne in mind that, in the final analysis, this panegyric analogy is based on what seems to be a deliberate ambiguity of the term θεωρία, which signifies here both the 'viewing a sublime spectacle' and the 'being engaged in philosophic contemplation' or philosophic (theoretic) investigation.

From Plato, *Republic* 581C, it may be gathered that the story of the three basic ways of life ultimately goes back to Plato himself. In

*Republic* 581C we are informed that there exist 'three classes or types of men: the lovers of philosophic wisdom, the lovers of honor (or virtue or fame), and the lovers of material gain.' In short, according to Plato (and Aristotle), there are three main purposes in human life.[24] Different people seek their happiness and fulfilment in these three pursuits, namely, either in φρόνησις (theoretic speculation), or in (practical) virtue (honor or fame), or in physical pleasure and material gain. This triadic notion, which is vitally related to Plato's fundamental philosophic outlook, can also be found in Aristotle's *Eudemian Ethics*, which is incidentally a fairly early work: 'Now to be happy, to live blissfully and beautifully, must consist mainly in three things which appear to be most desirable. For some maintain that φρόνησις is the greatest good, some say virtue (or honor), and some say physical pleasure.'[25] Hence we realize that 'there are three lives which all those choose who have the power to do so, to wit, the life of the political (practical) man, the life of the philosopher, and the life of the voluptuary. Of these, the philosopher is determined to dedicate himself to φρόνησις; the "political (practical) man" to noble deeds, that is, to acts which originate with virtue; and the voluptuary to bodily pleasures.'[26] The triad of φρόνησις, virtue (or noble deeds) and physical pleasure, it may be restated here, is without doubt closely related to Plato's doctrine of the tripartite soul, that is, to a doctrine from which Plato derives not only the three basic ways of life and the three basic kinds of happiness or pleasure, but also the three basic types of men.[27]

In conclusion, it might be observed that the panegyric analogy employed in Aristotle's *Protrepticus*, in the main, touches upon two fundamental philosophic problems: first, the three basic ways of life in general and, second, the unrivalled excellence of the 'theoretic life' in particular. The 'theoretic life,' which indisputably is the most exalted way of life and, hence, the way of life most befitting the rational and moral man, had been advocated most eloquently by Plato throughout his writings. It is extolled by Aristotle in the *Protrepticus* and recommended by him to Themison, the immediate addressee of this hortatory essay. The very tenor of the *Protrepticus* as well as the fact that this composition is essentially Platonic in spirit and intent simply make it imperative that in his 'exhortation to philosophy' Aristotle should also refer to the three basic ways of life and should demonstrate the unchallenged superiority of the 'theoretic life' over the two other ways of life. In this particular context, then, a reference to the panegyric analogy must be regarded as a most appropriate and most persuasive argument. It might even be maintained that the panegyric analogy constitutes the basic outline and, at the same time, the very culmination of the entire *Protrepticus*—that this particular work is essentially but an elaboration and justification of the panegyric analogy and the ultimate message it conveys. Seen in this larger context, the Aristotelian *Protrepticus* is primarily an eloquent and perhaps impassionate exhortation urging the reader to embrace the contemplative life by dedicating himself to the whole-hearted pursuit of theoretic philosophy.[28] Hence, in its ultimate message, the *Protrepticus* is certainly more than a hortatory piece or, perchance, simply a kind of 'mirror for princes.' It is the solemn proclamation of a new ideal of the philosophic life and as such an urgent appeal directed to the whole of civilized mankind, calling for a new aim of life and culture. It is, in its ultimate significance, a comprehensive plan for the total conversion of humanity to the pedagogical and philosophic ideals advocated by Plato and the Platonic Academy.

# Chapter XI

# Aristotle's *Politicus* ★

The 'catalogues' of the early Aristotelian writings listed in Diogenes Laertius[1] and in the *Vita Aristotelis Hesychii*[2] enumerate a *Politicus* or *Statesman*. Judging from Cicero's remark,[3] one would have to admit that this composition was written in the form of a dialogue, and that Aristotle apparently cast himself in the role of one of the interlocutors and perhaps in that of the main interlocutor.[4] The particular title of the *Politicus* is likewise explained by Cicero,[5] who records that in this work Aristotle points out who should be 'the ruler' (*princeps*) in a properly organized body politic. Hence, it must be assumed that the term 'statesman,' as it is used by Aristotle in the *Politicus*, refers to the person or persons qualified to govern the body politic. It may therefore also be surmised that in the *Politicus* Aristotle discusses the qualifications of the 'ideal statesman,' and that he does so in a similar manner but not necessarily on the same philosophic basis or by the same method of argumentation as Plato had expounded the 'ideal statesman' or ruler in his *Statesman* (or *Republic*). This being so, it may also be conjectured that there probably exists a certain, though perhaps remote, affinity of thought between the Platonic *Statesman* (and perhaps the Platonic *Republic*) and the Aristotelian *Politicus*. It could be argued that such an affinity might possibly follow from the observation, likewise made by Cicero, that Aristotle had composed a work in which he discusses the body politic (*res publica*) as well as the 'foremost man (*vir praestans*)' within the body politic.[6] Obviously, this 'foremost man' within the body politic is he who stands at its head, that is, the 'ideal statesman' or 'ideal lawgiver'—in Plato's words, the 'philosopher king.'

It has already been pointed out that the Aristotelian *Politicus* was a dialogue. For a pupil of Plato, it would be natural that he should imitate the literary form used by his teacher and foremost model. But he also realized that the old 'obstetric' type of dialogue, which Plato himself had abandoned in his later works, was a thing of the past.[7] It is also possible, though quite unlikely, that Aristotle composed the *Politicus*, which undoubtedly was suggested by the Platonic *Statesman*, to improve upon Plato's dialogue of the same name; that in so doing Aristotle attempted to show how the treatment of the several issues discussed in Plato's dialogue might be improved upon; or that Aristotle tried to disprove some of Plato's arguments and 'tear them apart.' It is safer to assume, however, that in his *Politicus* Aristotle wished to imitate Plato rather than combat him—that, in the words of Syrianus, he still understood (and still adhered to) Plato's fundamental philosophic position when he composed the *Politicus* [8]—although it is quite likely that he took exception to some of the notions advanced by Plato in the *Statesman* or, at least, to the manner in which these notions were presented in this Platonic dialogue.

The dating of the Aristotelian *Politicus* is exceptionally difficult.[9] Obviously, this composition is later than the Platonic *Statesman*, a *tempus post quod* which is quite useless. The only really important or significant fragment of the *Politicus*,[10] provided we accept R. Stark's translation and interpretation, contains the statement that 'the Good is the most exact measure or standard for all things.'[11] This, in turn, would indicate that by the time Aristotle wrote the *Politicus* he might have abandoned Plato's notion of the Separate Idea of the Good. It should also be borne in mind that in the *Protrepticus* Aristotle defends the general philosophic ideal of Plato against the pretensions of Isocrates. Since Isocrates had propagated a practical not to say pragmatic attitude towards politics and political thought and at the same time ridiculed the purely theoretic-ethical approach to political philosophy advocated by Plato and the Early Academy, it is quite likely that in his *Politicus* Aristotle attempted to reassert the philosophic or theoretic approach to politics and political science, as well as proclaim the incontestable superiority of philosophic political theory over pragmatic political science. Hence, it could be maintained that the *Politicus* is also a special though somewhat delayed reply to or rebuttal of Isocrates' *Antidosis*.[12] Since the *Politicus* seems to antedate the Aristotelian *On Philosophy* (which was composed probably between 350–49 and 348 B.C.),[13] it might be permissible to date the *Politicus* around 350 B.C.[14]

W. Jaeger insists that the above-mentioned passage from Cicero's *Epistola ad Quintum Fratrem* III. 5. 1, especially the expression, '*vir praestans*,' seems to refer to the Aristotelian *Politicus*, while the term '*res publica*' indicates that it may possibly allude to the Aristotelian *On Justice*.[15] R. Weil, who discusses the *Politicus* with great acumen and much insight, fully accepts Jaeger's thesis that Cicero had in mind both the *Politicus* and the *On Justice*.[16] Thus Jaeger and Weil imply that Cicero's remarks may in fact refer to two entirely different works of Aristotle. R. Stark, who likewise subjects the *Politicus* to a searching analysis, maintains, on the other hand, that Cicero quotes the two terms '*vir praestans*' and '*res publica*' not from two different compositions, such as the *Politicus* and the *On Justice*, but rather from the second and first books of the *Politicus* respectively.[17] In so doing, Stark implies that the first Book of the *Politicus* deals with a somewhat different subject than the second Book, although both subjects are related to one another. If we accept Stark's theory, then we would also have to admit that the first Book of the *Politicus* contained a discussion of the ideal body politic, and that the second Book was concerned with an analysis of the ideal statesman or lawgiver—the philosophic ruler or 'philosopher king.'

According to the testimony of Syrianus,[18] in the second Book of the *Politicus* Aristotle maintained that 'the Good is the most precise measure.' In connection with this citation, the Neo-Platonist Syrianus also demonstrates that when making this particular statement Aristotle still understood Plato and Platonic philosophy, and that he understood it better than he did on other (and later) occasions. From all this, it might be inferred that the Stagirite meant to say here that since the Idea of the Good is the most exalted (or the first) among all the Ideas, it must also be the most exact measure among all measures or standards. In other words, Syrianus' observation indicates that when composing the *Politicus*, Aristotle still manifested an essential adherence to Plato's basic philosophy—a fact which is brought out by the statement that 'the good is the most precise measure [among all measures]'—but that at some later time he abandoned this Platonic position, something which Syrianus seems to regret. Hence, Syrianus' interesting comment lends weighty support to Jaeger's contention that in the *Politicus* Aristotle still adhered to Plato's doctrine of the Separate Ideas. Moreover, it also seems to support Jaeger's contention that this fragment signifies that 'the Good is the most precise measure [among all measures],' rather than, as for instance R. Stark would have it, that 'for everything [which transpires in this world] the Good is the most precise measure.'[19]

The statement that 'the Good is the most precise measure [among all measures],' which seems to be a direct quotation from Aristotle's *Politicus*, has, as Jaeger recognizes,[20] far-reaching implications as regards the doctrinal content and philosophic background of the *Politicus*. As a matter of fact, with the possible exception of Iamblichus, *Pro-*

*trepticus*, p. 55, line 7 to p. 56, line 2 (Pistelli), this statement seems to be the only fragment or citation of any real significance which has been located and ascribed to the *Politicus* with any degree of certainty. Assuming that this fragment is in fact by Aristotle and is properly interpreted by Syrianus, then we must also concede that it simply restates in a most concentrated manner the following fundamental (late) Platonic doctrines: first (*Statesman* and, especially, *Philebus*), pure measure occupies the first and uppermost rank in the hierarchy of goods and values, the second going to the measurable, and the third to the intellect (or reason) capable of apprehending (pure) measure (φρόνησις);[21] furthermore (*Republic*), the Good, or better, the pure Form of the Good, is called the ground of the being as well as the cause of our intellectual capacity for knowing the real world;[22] and finally (*Laws*), 'to us, God [*scil.*, the Absolute Good] ought to be the measure of all things.'[23]

According to the later Plato, especially in the *Philebus*, true philosophic knowledge is always exact measuring—the measuring (or evaluation) of all things, including the several Separate Ideas, by the absolute, ultimate, most exact, most abiding and most determinate measure or standard. All that is truly good, Plato insists, is measurable and determinate, while all that is evil is immeasurable, indeterminate and indefinite. This basic principle applies not only to the visible or corporeal universe, the ideal body politic or the soul but also to the world of the Separate Ideas. In this sense, Plato's later ethics and politics turn into a purely theoretic science of measurement, measure and norm—into a sort of *Ethica Ordine Geometrico Demonstrata* (Spinoza). In short, the Idea of the Good constitutes the highest and most universal measure simply because it is the absolute and abiding unity, oneness and symmetry within the real world of the Separate Ideas—because it makes Plato's pluralistic world of the Separate Ideas determinate and symmetrical and, hence, good, real and knowable—because it makes it one and as such meaningful. Hence, Jaeger concludes, it could be maintained that according to the Aristotelian *Politicus*, the Good—the Idea of the Good—constitutes the supreme (normative) value precisely because it is the highest, the most universal, the most absolute and, accordingly, the ultimate reality as well as the ultimate 'measure of measures.'[24]

Since according to the *Politicus*, the Idea of the Good constitutes the most exact of all measures, measurements and standards for both ethics and politics, it is fair to assume that this early work of Aristotle is still under the influence of Plato's later theory of Ideas. This theory

(as has been shown), in its final phases, is chiefly concerned with exactitude in that it stresses the overriding importance of the pure norms of
measure and measuring. Seen from this point of view, it would follow
that in the *Politicus* Aristotle fully adheres to Plato's late doctrine of the
Separate Ideas or, to be more exact, to the Idea Numbers as well as to
the notion of the 'One'; and that he believes, as Plato did, that political
philosophy and, indeed, all of ethics, could simply be reduced to an
'exact philosophy of science' or to a kind of 'metaphysics of ethics'
based solely on measure and measurement.[25] In other words, the
'science of politics,' like the 'science of ethics,' is essentially a science
of pure norms, a philosophic position which recently has been revived
by Hans Kelsen in his 'pure theory of law.' This, then, is the extremist
Platonic position which, judging from the Aristotelian *Politicus*, that
is, from the statement that 'the Good is the most precise measure
[among all measures],' apparently was also accepted by the young
Aristotle. In its ultimate consequences, this position demands that
ethical and political knowledge above all must be exact (and, hence,
purely theoretic), even though this 'exactitude for exactitude's sake'
makes it utterly useless and unworkable from a practical point
of view—an interesting variation on Tertullian's famed *credo quia
absurdum*.

Jaeger also maintains that the passage preserved by Syrianus fully
confirms his major thesis that in his early compositions Aristotle still
adhered to the Platonic doctrine of the Separate Ideas and, hence, was a
Platonist. This view, which constitutes an essential aspect of Jaeger's
evolutionary thesis, has found wide acceptance among many Aristotelian scholars.[26] It has been challenged, however, by R. Stark who
proposes an entirely different and, in a way, revolutionary translation
and interpretation of this particular passage.[27] He suggests that it would
be perfectly legitimate and, indeed, preferable to translate it as 'for
everything the Good is the most exact measure.'[28] In so doing, Stark
insists that Aristotle is not really concerned here with the proposition
that its 'greatest exactness' makes a good the 'highest good' among all
goods and, accordingly, the 'most perfect (or exact) measure' among
several measures. What Aristotle wishes to express here, Stark contends,
is merely the notion that a (moral) good, which must not necessarily
be conceived as a Separate Idea or perhaps as the 'greatest exactitude,'
is a general 'value criterion' or value standard by which all things as
well as all actions can be judged and evaluated properly.[29] As shall be
shown presently, this interpretation to some extent might vitiate, or at
least threaten, the evolutionary thesis of W. Jaeger. The passage from

Syrianus quoted above,[30] however, seems to imply that Syrianus is of the opinion that when he composed the *Politicus*, Aristotle still understood, and adhered to, Plato's basic teachings, that is, to the concept or doctrine of the Separate Ideas. This, in turn, would defeat Stark's interpretation. Conversely, it is possible that Syrianus himself gave this passage a distinct Platonic twist, something which it may not have had originally. This, then, would support Stark's contention.

If Stark's translation and interpretation should prove to be the correct one—something which cannot possibly be decided here—its acceptance would have far-reaching consequences for the whole philosophic tenor of the *Politicus*. In a work such as the *Politicus* which, it must be presumed, is primarily dedicated to 'political philosophy' or to the 'true science of politics' to be practiced by the 'true statesman,' this interpretation would be tantamount to the ultimate identification of 'practical politics' and 'personal ethics.' Such an identification, however, would come rather close to 'goal-directed' social or political planning, where an empirically and rationally determined good constitutes the ultimate criterion as well as the ultimate aim. In light of Stark's translation, a 'true science of politics' would have to be based on the concept of a highest (moral, political or social) good, that is, on the general human understanding and formulation of this highest good or highest goal, and its realization through proper action. More than that, the 'true science of politics,' as it is proposed here according to Stark, would not necessarily imply or presuppose, as Jaeger suggests, a reference to or reliance upon Plato's particular Idea of the Good as it is expounded in the Platonic *Republic*, *Statesman* or *Philebus*, or perhaps to Plato's notion of the Separate Ideas or Idea Numbers advocated in the later Platonic dialogues. The good of which Aristotle speaks in the *Politicus*, Stark contends, is certainly not the Platonic 'One,' but rather the moral end or goal—the 'good' in a more realistic and more concrete sense—of human action, or, to be more exact, of each human action.[31] This 'good,' then, can be determined by human reason and human experience properly employed rather than by some 'mystical vision' of the 'Highest Good' in terms of an 'Absolute (transcendental) Measure' or the 'Absolute One.' It would be something which reason could define on the strength of tested experience. Accordingly, the ultimate criterion would actually be the empirically definable good or practical goal at which concrete human action aims, or which concrete goal-directed human action creates, rather than a purely transcendent, 'separate' Good or Idea of the Good, a single and immutable 'One,' which we ought to imitate. But if this is so, then there exists no real doctrinal conflict between the ethical views advocated in the *Politicus*, and the moral theories advanced in the later Aristotelian treatises on ethics, such as *Nicomachean Ethics* 1176 a 17 ff., where Aristotle states that 'if . . . virtue and the good man as such are the measure of everything, those also will be delights which appear so to him, and those things pleasant which he enjoys.'[32] Hence, in both the *Politicus*—provided we can accept Stark's interpretation—and in the later doctrinal treatises on ethics, virtue and the (moral) good (or the good man) are the measure or criterion for each individual thing as well as for each individual action.[33]

The problems raised by Syrianus' fragment[34] might possibly be resolved as follows: the passage in the *Politicus*, namely, that 'the Good is the most precise measure *among* all measures' or, as Stark would have it, 'the Good is the most exact measure *for* everything,' seems to be closely related to a remark found in Plato's *Laws*, where in opposition to Protagoras' *homo mensura* maxim, Plato announces that God is the ultimate measure of all things:[35] 'Now God ought to be to us the measure of all things, and not perchance man, as men commonly assert [*scil.*, Protagoras] . . . And he who would be dear to God must, as far as this is possible, be like Him and such as He is.'[36] But this is most certainly not the Idea of the Good as Plato had expounded it in the *Republic* or the *Philebus*. Hence, it might fairly be alleged that the Aristotelian remark preserved by Syrianus is to be placed somewhere 'between' the Idea of the Good advocated in the Platonic *Republic* or the *Philebus* and the Idea of God suggested in the Platonic *Laws*. It could even be claimed that this remark in the *Politicus* is perhaps an attempt on the part of Aristotle to reconcile these two notions. Perhaps the ambiguous wording of this remark, which, as the disagreement between Jaeger and Stark seems to indicate, admits of two entirely different interpretations, is wholly intentional: the Good is the measure *for* all things, and the most exact measure (God) is the ultimate measure *among* all measures. In light of the surviving evidence, this latter suggestion, needless to say, is at best reasonable conjecture. It is possible, however, that in the *Politicus* Aristotle is more under the influence of Plato's *Laws*—the *Laws* and the *Politicus*, it appears, were composed at approximately the same time—and especially under that of *Laws* 716C, than under the influence of either the *Philebus*, *Statesman* or *Republic*. But if this be so, then one might also conjecture that the *Politicus* is Aristotle's 'counterpart' to Plato's *Laws* rather than, as it is widely held, a kind of imitation of Plato's *Statesman*.

It should also be borne in mind that the *Politicus*, as has been noted, probably was composed about the same time as, or shortly before, the Aristotelian *On Philosophy*.[37] Assuming this to be the case, then the *Politicus* was written shortly before 350–49 or 348 B.C. (the *On Philosophy* was composed between 350–49 and 348 B.C.). Hence, it must be conceded that the *Politicus* was conceived a considerable time after the completion of the Platonic *Republic* (which most certainly will have to be dated prior to the year 367) and approximately at the same time as the Platonic *Laws* (which was composed after 355 and possibly as late as 350). One might also gain the impression that the God or 'the Good' referred to in the *Politicus* is somewhat akin to the God in Aristotle's *On Philosophy* which, after all, was composed about the same time as the *Politicus*.[38]

According to Cicero,[39] who in this instance relies on an Epicurean source distinctly hostile to Aristotle,[40] the Stagirite declares in the third book of the *On Philosophy* that God is pure mind or intellect, that He is the (visible) universe, that He is some other Being to Whom the universe is subordinated and Who guides the movement of the universe, and that He is 'ether.' And Sextus Empiricus,[41] probably on the authority of Posidonius,[42] relates that in the *On Philosophy* Aristotle declares God to be author of the whole cosmic order.[43] Essentially the same notion is also recorded by Cicero in his *De Natura Deorum*.[44] In a passage reminiscent of Plato's famous 'image of the cave,'[45] Cicero (Aristotle) points out that if men should suddenly ascend from the bowels of the earth and perceive for the first time 'the whole sky laid out and adorned with stars . . . and the risings and settings of them all, and their courses controlled and immutable for all eternity, they would immediately think that these are the mighty works of the gods.'[46] This passage, which J. Bernays considered a direct quotation from Aristotle's lost dialogue *On Philosophy*,[47] likewise stresses the notion of a supreme author and director of the cosmic order. And finally, according to the testimony of Simplicius,[48] Aristotle proclaims in the *On Philosophy* that God is 'the most perfect Being' and, hence, 'the most immutable Being,'[49] Who on account of His perfection not only governs everything but also constitutes the ultimate and most perfect measure or standard for everything.

The few summary remarks about the concept of God (or the 'Supreme Good') found in the third Book of the Aristotelian *On Philosophy*[50] might lend significant support to the contention that whenever in his *Politicus* (which was composed in close proximity to the *On Philosophy*) Aristotle speaks of an ultimate and most perfect measure which constitutes the final criterion of everything, he probably has in mind the concept of God which he later developed in great detail in his *On Philosophy*. By realizing this, we might, with some reservations, resolve in favor of R. Stark the differences that exist between W. Jaeger's and R. Stark's translations and interpretations of the fragment which has been transmitted and, apparently, accurately reported by Syrianus. Or to be more exact: on the level of the relation of the 'Supreme Good' or God to everything that exists and transpired in this world, R. Stark's 'formula' seems to make better sense. On another level, namely on the level of the relation and co-ordination of a plurality of possibly conflicting goods or standards, we might side with W. Jaeger's thesis. This too, however, is at best highly problematic. In order to better understand and appreciate the disagreement between W. Jaeger and R. Stark, we must always bear in mind that in his last dialogues (as well as in his unpublished lectures delivered before a small circle of more intimate pupils and followers), Plato had shifted from an 'idealistic metaphysics' to a 'mathematical (Pythagorizing) metaphysics.' In his 'idealistic metaphysics,' at least in its last phases, Plato no longer considered the Separate Ideas to be dogmatic realities domiciled in a world of their own, but rather as something akin to 'hypotheses' or 'general principles' for the establishment of true Being, of the Good and of the True. In his 'mathematical metaphysics,' however, Plato operated with the 'One,' the 'Twoness' and with the Idea Numbers, as well as with measure, measuration and with the concept of the intellect capable of apprehending measure and measuration. Aristotle, it will be noted, largely subscribed to Plato's 'idealistic metaphysics,' which also included Plato's essential theology.[51] Remaining loyal to this 'idealistic metaphysics,' he rejected the 'mathematical metaphysics' (as well as the Pythagorizing trend noticeable in the latest Platonic writings), which, however, were taken up by Speusippus and Xenocrates.[52] Jaeger, it appears, would also have Aristotle accept the 'mathematical metaphysics,' while Stark, at least by implication, seems to deny this. This, then would appear to be at the basis of the disagreement among these two scholars. In any event, it is fairly safe to assume that as to its philosophic or doctrinal content, the *Politicus* still is strongly, though not completely, under the influence of Plato's basic teachings, that is, of Plato's 'idealistic metaphysics.' Among other indications, this might be gathered from the fact that in the *Politicus* 'politics,' in the main, is still considered a sort of 'metaphysics of ethics,' provided Syrianus' report contains reliable information. At the same time, assuming that R. Stark's translation and interpretation should prove to be the correct one, Aristotle, although still under the

dominant spell of Plato, makes here an initial attempt at 'emanci-
pating' himself from his teacher. In other words, in the *Politicus* he is
starting to move away especially from Plato's theory of the Separate
Ideas or, more likely, from the 'Idea of the One,' by claiming that the
'Good' in general, that is, the 'Good' as it can be derived from experience through reason properly employed, is an acceptable or appropriate measure for everything that transpires in the experiential world.

An additional fragment of the *Politicus* might possibly be Iamblichus,
*Protrepticus*, p. 55, line 7 to p. 56, line 2 (Pistelli):[53]

> But in the general and ordinary arts or crafts, men do not,
> perchance, derive their tools and their most accurate reckoning
> from 'first principles' (from 'originals') themselves and thus
> achieve something close to scientific (philosophic or theoretic)
> knowledge. Rather, they borrow them at second or third or even
> more remote hand, and they base their reasoning on experience
> and empirical observations. The [true] philosopher, and he alone,
> imitates directly that which among all things is the most exact.
> For what he gazes at is originality and exactness itself, not merely
> imitation. This being so, we may assert that just as a house-builder
> who borrows his measurements from other buildings instead of
> using the rod or other technical instruments is not a good
> architect, similarly, one who either enacts laws for cities or
> administers public affairs by observing and imitating the public
> administrations or constitutions devised by some other men,
> whether those of the Lacedaemonians, Cretans[54] or of some other
> commonwealth, is most certainly not a good lawgiver or con-
> scientious statesman. For the imitation of that which is not good
> in itself cannot possibly be good, nor can the imitation of that
> which by its very nature is not divine (imperishable) and durable,
> be imperishable and stable. It is obvious, however, that among all
> craftsmen the philosopher—and he alone—is familiar not only with
> laws that are truly stable, but also with practices that are truly
> (objectively) right and proper. For the philosopher—and he alone
> —lives with his gaze fixed on nature (on true and objective reality)
> and on the divine (or imperishable); and like a good helmsman
> [who takes his bearings from the unchanging stars] he will tie
> his life to what is eternal and unchanging, moor it to 'first
> principles,' and live as the master of his own soul.

This lengthy statement, it appears, displays a remarkable affinity
with the statement that 'the Good is the most exact measure among all

measures (or, for all things).' Here, as in the fragment from Syrianus, we are able to discern the preponderant influence of Plato's *Republic*, *Statesman* and *Philebus*. Iamblichus, *Protrepticus* 55,7–56,2, insists that the true—philosophic—statesman must always look to absolute (objective) being for his model but never to mere 'imitations' or 'shadows.' [55] It would not be amiss, therefore, to presume that Iamblichus, *Protrepticus* 55,7–56,2, was decisively influenced by Plato, *Statesman* 293A–301C, something which also can be said about the Aristotelian *Politicus*. For in *Statesman* 293A–301C, Plato speaks of the true (good) laws which are close imitations of objective reality and, accordingly, are themselves closest to absolute truth. Since we have discussed elsewhere and at some length the several problems connected with Iamblichus, *Protrepticus* 55,7–56,2,[56] it will not be necessary to repeat here in detail all the arguments in support of our thesis that this passage is probably a fragment of the *Politicus* rather than of the Aristotelian *Protrepticus*. It goes without saying, however, that what has been maintained in connection with our interpretation of Syrianus' fragment is also applicable to Iamblichus, *Protrepticus* 55,7–56,2, and *vice versa*.

The remaining fragments which have been assigned to the *Politicus*[57] are of small interest to us. They contribute little if anything to our understanding of this early Aristotelian dialogue. As a matter of fact, some scholars have raised serious doubts as to whether these fragments are in any way related to the *Politicus*.[58]

# Chapter XII

# The Probable Date of Aristotle's
## *On Philosophy*★

In his recent book, *Aristotele: Della Filosofia*,[1] Mario Untersteiner apparently accepts, without further discussion, W. Jaeger's well-known thesis that the *On Philosophy*[2] of Aristotle must have been composed during his sojourn in Assos (348/47–345/44 B.C.), after the death of Plato.[3] Jaeger, who also insists that the *On Philosophy* was written shortly after the completion of Book A of the Aristotelian *Metaphysics*,[4] bases his thesis on the following argument or 'evidence': in the *On Philosophy*, Aristotle assumes an undeniably critical and even negative attitude towards Plato's basic views concerning the Separate Ideas or Idea Numbers, and especially towards the particular manner in which Plato presented and discussed the Ideas in his latest dialogues.[5] In Jaeger's opinion, this is something that Aristotle would not have dared to do during the lifetime of Plato, in other words, during his active association with Plato and the Academy. Jaeger's dating of the *On Philosophy*, then, in the final analysis, rests on a sort of *a priori* reasoning, akin to a syllogism: while associated with Plato and the Academy, Aristotle was a faithful Platonist; the *On Philosophy* shows definite traces of 'un-Platonic' thinking; hence, the *On Philosophy* must have been composed after Aristotle had left Plato and the Academy, that is, after Plato's death in 348–47 B.C.[6]

Moreover, Jaeger also claims that Pliny's testimony seems to indicate that Plato was already dead when Aristotle began to compose the *On Philosophy*. In his *Historia Naturalis* XXX. 3—a passage, incidentally, which is commonly considered a fragment of the Aristotelian *On Philosophy*—Pliny maintains that the philosophy of the Magi (Zoroastrians) 'originated in Persia due to the efforts of Zoroaster. . . . Eudoxus [of Cnidus], who claimed that of all of the schools of philosophy the most important and the most influential was that of the Magi, also relates that this man Zoroaster lived six thousand years prior to the death of Plato. So says also Aristotle [in the first (?) Book of his *On Philosophy*]. . . .'[7] Assuming, then, that Pliny is actually quoting from

Aristotle's *On Philosophy* (from Book A of the *On Philosophy*, to be exact)—something which is by no means certain—the remark that 'Zoroaster lived six thousand years prior to the death of Plato' would suggest, at least to Jaeger, that Plato must have been dead by the time Aristotle composed the *On Philosophy*. Jaeger's view, it will be noted, hinges on the assumption that Pliny's remark, 'Zoroaster lived six thousand years prior to the death of Plato,' was originally contained in Aristotle's *On Philosophy* and not, as has been surmised by some scholars, only in the Γῆς περίοδος of Eudoxus of Cnidus, a work which Pliny apparently consulted. If this is so, then we may surmise that in his *On Philosophy* Aristotle only related that the philosophy of the Magi 'originated in Persia due to the efforts of Zoroaster,' and that 'of all the schools of philosophy the most important and the most influential was that of the Magi.'

Jaeger's theory, as regards the dating of the *On Philosophy*, was accepted, modified, or rejected by a number of prominent scholars, among them H. von Arnim,[8] P. Wilpert,[9] A. J. Festugière,[10] C. de Vogel,[11] D. J. Allan,[12] H. D. Saffrey[13] and others.[14] If Jaeger's views should indeed prevail, the proper *tempus post quod* for the dating of the Aristotelian *On Philosophy* would be the year 348–47 B.C. However, his dating, at least in part, is open to challenge, as are the arguments or reasons which he advances in support of his thesis, as well as his method. For if Aristotle's critique (and rejection) of Plato's Separate Ideas or Idea Numbers were to supply a valid criterion for the dating of the *On Philosophy* after the death of Plato, then Aristotle's *On (the) Ideas* and *On the Good* would also have to be placed after 348–47—a rather unlikely possibility.[15] The report of Pliny and that of Diogenes Laertius, on the other hand, may very well go back to (or be influenced by) Eudoxus of Cnidus, Hermippus or Theopompus, rather than to Aristotle,[16] and hence may contain information not to be found in Aristotle's *On Philosophy*. It will be noted, however, that the date proposed by Jaeger and his somewhat unusual method of proving it come very close to what appear to be the actual facts as they may be construed with the help of the available literary and historical evidence.

Before Jaeger and prior to the beginning of modern or critical Aristotelian scholarship, the *On Philosophy* was generally dated anterior to the death of Plato. As early as 1863, V. Rose, who never believed that there ever existed any authentic 'lost works of Aristotle,' pointed out the distinctly Platonic tenor and doctrinal orientation of this composition.[17] E. Heitz, who firmly established Aristotle's authorship, maintained outright that this composition reflected Plato's basic teachings and hence must have been written during Aristotle's active association with Plato and with the Platonic Academy.[18] As a result of Heitz's findings, the following theses came to be generally accepted: (i) the *On Philosophy* is unquestionably an authentic work of Aristotle; (ii) it was composed during Aristotle's Academic period, that is, somewhere between 367 and 348-47 B.C.; (iii) it is essentially Platonic in its fundamental philosophic outlook as well as in its literary form; and (iv) it contains a partial critique and refutation of some of Plato's basic teachings, especially of Plato's doctrine of the Separate Ideas and Idea Numbers. In brief, according to Heitz, during Plato's lifetime Aristotle had already begun to take issue, and to disagree openly, with certain philosophic views advocated by his teacher.[19] Some of Heitz's arguments were subsequently adopted, at times with certain modifications, by E. Zeller,[20] A. Kail,[21] T. Case[22] and others. More recently, W. Theiler[23] advanced the theory that the *On Philosophy* was not only composed during the lifetime of Plato, but that it actually preceded the Aristotelian *Protrepticus*.[24] Theiler's thesis, in part, found the support of F. Nuyens,[25] P. Moraux[26] and I. Düring,[27] although his assertion that the *On Philosophy* antedates the *Protrepticus* probably will not stand in the face of all available evidence.[28]

Assuming, then, that the *On Philosophy* was composed prior to the year 348-47 B.C.—something which is by no means certain—a further question arises. If it was produced during Aristotle's active association with the Academy, we must not only determine the approximate date of this event, but also, if at all possible, designate the factors as well as the circumstances or the occasion that prompted Aristotle to write the *On Philosophy*. Since this work constitutes a distinct and certainly most significant break on the part of Aristotle with certain aspects of Plato's fundamental philosophic position and doctrine, the establishment of the correct date of the *On Philosophy* as well as the determination of the factors which occasioned this dialogue is of crucial importance. For there can be little doubt that the *On Philosophy* is such a break, although the paucity of the surviving fragments and the difficulties connected with their interpretation make it extremely difficult to assess accurately the full extent of Aristotle's severance from Plato and Platonic philosophy, provided such a severance actually took place.

For some time, certain scholars have indicated undeniable parallels and points of contact between certain parts of Aristotle's *On Philosophy*, especially Book III (which contains Aristotle's early 'theology'), and Plato's *Timaeus*.[29] It is commonly held that Plato wrote the *Timaeus* after 360 B.C., and perhaps as late as 358-57, or later. Hence, it would seem that the *On Philosophy* might be dated approximately between the year 357 and, perhaps, the year 350. We must bear in mind, however, that only around the year 357 B.C. did Aristotle complete his 'preparatory studies' (which primarily revolved around 'rhetoric') in order to concentrate on the more fundamental problems of Platonic philosophy. Moreover, a good many scholars are of the opinion that Aristotle wrote the *On the Good*[30] and the *On (the) Ideas*[31] about, or shortly after, the year 357 B.C., and that these two compositions definitely precede the *On Philosophy*.[32] As a matter of fact, Book II of the *On Philosophy* is said to presuppose both the *On the Good* and the *On (the) Ideas*.[33]

Thus, if the *On Philosophy* actually was written prior to the death of Plato, it must have been composed somewhere between 357–56 (or 355) and 348–47 B.C. Now, in view of the fact that there exist certain points of contact between the Platonic *Timaeus* and the Aristotelian *On Philosophy*, and in view of the fact that the *On Philosophy* is posterior but probably in close proximity to the *On the Good* and the *On (the) Ideas*, it has been conjectured that it should be dated around the year 355 or 354 B.C.[34] The argument has been made that after the conclusion of the 'preparatory studies' Aristotle's intellectual development probably proceeded along the following lines: beginning with rhetoric, a subject which Aristotle taught around (or before) 355 B.C.,[35] he advanced to dialectics, an interest which becomes manifest in the *On the Good* and the *On (the) Ideas*. Subsequently, in the *On Philosophy*, which W. Jaeger aptly calls a 'Manifesto on Philosophy,'[36] he tackled the fundamental problems connected with Plato's metaphysics. Thus, the *On Philosophy* might be styled Aristotle's 'manifesto,' proclaiming his own attitude towards, and critique of, Plato's (and the Academy's) basic philosophic position, especially the last or 'Pythagorizing' phase of Plato's philosophy. This 'manifesto' consisted of three major parts, each of which constituted a separate book of the *On Philosophy*. The first part or book dealt with philosophy in general or philosophic σοφία, as well as with its history or 'origin'; the second part contained a critique of the Platonic οὐσίαι and the Separate Ideas or Idea Numbers; and the third part was concerned with the problems of the transcendent God, as well as with Plato's theology in general as it had been expounded in the *Timaeus* and, especially, in the *Laws*.

It appears that some time after the year 356 or 355 B.C. Plato began to write his last and most extensive work, the *Laws*.[37] He failed, however, to complete this composition or, to be more exact, to ready it for 'publication' before death overtook him.[38] Hence, if the assumption that Aristotle wrote his *On Philosophy* about 355 B.C. is correct, then Plato's *Laws*, at least the later books, in all likelihood would be posterior to the *On Philosophy*. This, in turn, raises a number of involved and interesting problems.

There are, as a matter of fact, several points of contact or similarities between Aristotle's *On Philosophy* and Plato's *Laws*. These connections might be explained in three different ways: first, if the *On Philosophy* is to be dated prior to the year 355 B.C., then Plato's *Laws*, or certain passages in the *Laws* (especially Books X and XII), might possibly be a reply to, or rebuttal of, or perhaps an elaboration on, or a modification of, the *On Philosophy* or of certain statements contained in the *On Philosophy*. Second, if the *On Philosophy* were to be placed after the year 348–47 B.C., that is, after the death of Plato, then it could likewise be a reply to, rebuttal of, or perhaps an elaboration on, or modification of, the *Laws* or of certain passages or statements contained in the *Laws*, especially of the kind of theology which Plato expounds there (in Books X and XII). Third, the Platonic *Laws* and the Aristotelian *On Philosophy* are contemporary works and are to some extent under the influence of Plato's *Timaeus* (or certain statements found in the *Timaeus*). If the third possibility could be proven, then the *Laws* (Books X and XII) and the *On Philosophy* would have a common 'starting point,' 'source' or 'motivation,' namely, the *Timaeus*. One might even conjecture that the *Laws*, at least some of its (later) parts, were influenced or motivated by the *On Philosophy*. It is highly improbable, however, that a man of Plato's age, stature and maturity should have been decisively influenced by one of his own disciples, even an Aristotle,[39] for whose intelligence and knowledge Plato apparently had a high respect.[40]

In Book X of the *Laws*, Plato attempts to prove the existence and reality of the Divine. In so doing, he touches on what appears to be the main theme of Book III of Aristotle's *On Philosophy*. Here Plato endeavors to disprove the claims of certain 'atheistic' philosophers who insist that 'the gods exist not "by nature" but rather by art.' To these philosophers Plato replies:[41] 'The legislator . . . ought to leave nothing unsaid in support of the ancient belief that there are gods. . . . He ought to acknowledge that both [*scil.*, law and art] alike exist "by nature," and are no less than "nature," if they are the creations of a mind that is co-extensive with right reason.'[42] We remember here that in the *On Philosophy* Aristotle identifies the rational order created by God with whatever is 'according to nature.' This is stated in the following passage, commonly credited to the *On Philosophy*: 'There is either one single first principle, or many. If there is but one principle, we have what we are looking for. But if there are many, they are either ordered or disordered. Now, if they are disordered . . . the world would not be a world, but rather a chaos. . . . If, on the other hand, they are ordered, they were ordered either by themselves or by some [single] outside cause. . .'[43] In what is probably a fragment of the *On Philosophy*, Philo of Alexandria records that 'Aristotle was surely speaking piously and devoutly when he . . . charged with grave ungodliness those . . . who thought that the great visible God [*scil.*, the orderly universe] . . . is no better than the work of man's hands. . . .'[44] These statements, it seems, are echoes of Plato's *Laws*. It is probable, therefore, that the absolutely rational 'Legislator' in Plato's *Laws*, the 'Mind,' takes the place of the Divine in Aristotle's *On Philosophy*, where the Divine is likewise referred to as 'Mind' or 'pure Intellect.' Perhaps the God of the *On Philosophy*, the 'great Artificer' or 'supreme Commander' of the orderly universe,[45] is just another version of Plato's absolute and divine 'Legislator.'

There are still other points of contact between the Platonic *Laws* and the Aristotelian *On Philosophy*, such as Plato's insistence that the soul (the 'intellect' or 'reason') is anterior to everything else, and that, if 'nature is the first creative force' and the soul is the 'primeval element,' then the soul—really the infinite 'Mind'—is the true 'nature.'[46] This true 'nature' moves everything, including the heavens. It also moves itself in that it is the cause of itself, as well as the cause of everything else.[47] Hence, this soul can be compared to a god: it is the 'best soul.'[48]

It goes without saying that some of the notions advanced here by Plato approach the 'theology' advocated by Aristotle in Book III of his *On Philosophy*.[49] The most striking feature of this new theology is the fact that, in the *Laws*, Plato no longer mentions the Demiurge, but refers to the 'best soul' (or 'Mind'), which now assumed some of the functions formerly (in the *Timaeus*) ascribed to the Demiurge. This 'best soul' of the *Laws* is not only self-moving as well as the cause of all motion; it is also the embodiment of everything good and orderly (and knowable) and, as such, subordinate to nothing.[50] The 'best soul,' it may be repeated here, is practically identical with the God of the *On Philosophy*, with one significant difference: the Aristotelian God is definitely a transcendent God (and perhaps a personal God),[51] while in the case of the Platonic God there is no way of telling exactly whether this Divinity is transcendent or immanent.[52] Moreover, in the *On Philosophy*, Aristotle makes a clear distinction between the single supreme God and the other divinities or 'souls,'[53] while Plato, due to the fact that his Supreme Deity seems to be both transcendent and immanent, apparently makes no such distinction.[54] It is perhaps on these issues that Aristotle, in Book III of the *On Philosophy*, disagrees with Plato, especially with Plato's concept of the Supreme Deity as he expounded it in Books X and XII of the *Laws*.

Assuming that Aristotle's *On Philosophy* is actually anterior to Book X (and Book XII) of Plato's *Laws*, then it could also be argued that Aristotle converted, or tried to convert, Plato to his basic theological views—that he attempted to interest Plato in his notion that in its unsurpassed beauty and perfect harmony, the visible universe itself, if properly understood and correctly evaluated, reveals to the thoughtful observer the existence of a single Supreme Deity Who is the cause of this beauty and harmony. This, then, might be the decisive point at which Aristotle broke away from Plato: while Plato, in his total contempt for the visible corporeal universe, relegates the ultimate truth, including God, to a transcendental world of pure Ideas, Aristotle argues that the visible world, if viewed intelligently and properly, contains this truth or at least points unmistakably to this truth. Thus, the break between Plato and Aristotle, provided such a break actually occurred, was probably occasioned by their basic disagreement over man's capacity to know God through 'His handiwork.' But if W. Jaeger's thesis should prove to be correct—the thesis that the *On Philosophy* was composed only after the death of Plato—then it would be a reasonable assumption that Aristotle's theology, as it found expression in Book III of the *On Philosophy*, might have been molded by Plato's new theology, as he expounded it in Book X of the *Laws*. At the same time, it is also most likely an attempt on the part of Aristotle to improve on, and modify, Plato's theology.

There exists also a significant similarity between certain passages from Book XII of the Platonic *Laws* and a remark by Sextus Empiricus, commonly believed to be a fragment of Book III of Aristotle's *On Philosophy*. In the *Laws* Plato maintains that 'there are two things which lead men to believe in the gods. . . . One is the argument about the soul, which has already been discussed[55]—incidentally the oldest and most divine of all things, to which motion ending in generation gives perpetual existence. The other was an argument from the order of the motion of the stars, and of all things under the dominion of the "spirit" which ordered the universe.'[56] Sextus Empiricus, quoting what seems to be a passage from Book III of Aristotle's *On Philosophy*, relates: 'And Aristotle maintains [in Book III of his *On Philosophy*] that the conception of the gods arose amongst men from two sources, from events that concern the soul, and from celestial phenomena. . . . On the strength of their experiences, Aristotle insists, men intuitively agree among themselves that something divine exists which in itself is akin to the soul and which above all is "pure intellect". . . . For when men beheld the sun circling around in the daytime, and by night they observed the orderly motions of the other stars, they supposed some god to be the cause of such motion and such orderliness. This is what Aristotle says.'[57] The parallels of these two passages are too obvious to require further comment, and the only question that remains to be resolved is which of the two preceded and, hence, possibly determined or influenced the other. For there can be little doubt that such an influence exists.

It is impossible, we might state again, to determine whether Aristotle was influenced by Plato's *Laws*, or whether Plato's *Laws* were influenced by Aristotle's *On Philosophy*, although one might reasonably be inclined to hold that it was the *Laws* which influenced or, at least, stimulated Aristotle. Perhaps the ultimate common 'source' for both Plato and Aristotle is Plato's *Timaeus*, on which both tried to improve. The *Timaeus* had already referred to the 'orderly and ordering functions of the pure intellect.' Or, perhaps, the theological views expressed in Book X and Book XII of the *Laws* as well as in Book III of the *On Philosophy* had become generally accepted by the members of the Academy during the last years of Plato's scholarchate.[58] In other words, the points of coincidence between the Platonic *Laws* and the Aristotelian *On Philosophy* do not necessarily prove a dependence of Aristotle on Plato (or of Plato on Aristotle). It is possible that both compositions are the parallel but independent results of the theological discussions which, since the publication of the *Timaeus* (and in conjunction with some of Plato's oral teachings?), preoccupied the Academy and its more prominent members. This, then, would vitiate the presumption that the date of composition of the *Laws*, especially of Books X–XII, constitutes the *tempus post quod* for the dating of the *On Philosophy*.

In order to establish the probable date of the Aristotelian *On Philosophy* more conclusively, the parallels that exist between the *Epinomis*[59] and the *On Philosophy* need to be discussed in detail. For it cannot be disputed that such parallels may be established.[60] The *Epinomis* relates, for instance, that, because of their size and the symmetry and perfect orderliness of their motions, the stars must be divine;[61] that there exists a fifth element or substance which constitutes the substance of the stars;[62] that since the stars move in a perfect and unchangeable circuit, they must be possessed of 'Mind';[63] that the soul is made up of an element or substance which is not identical and has nothing in common with the other four (or five) elements;[64] and that in each of the four (or five) elements there exist living creatures.[65] Moreover, the *Epinomis* also contains the information that the perfect order observable within the universe is indicative of the fact that it is governed by 'Mind';[66] that heaven, 'in bespangling itself and turning the stars which it contains in all their courses . . . produces the seasons';[67] and that 'God made the stars and the circuits of the celestial bodies' so that men may know the truth.[68] The same, or almost the same, statements, which could be multiplied many times, are also to be found in Aristotle's *On Philosophy*, although at times with a different connotation.[69] But it is difficult to ascertain whether the *On Philosophy* is posterior, or anterior or perhaps contemporary with the *Epinomis*. Since Isocrates apparently refers to the *Epinomis* as early as 346 B.C.,[70] the latter must have been composed prior to that date. Conversely, it is commonly held that the *Epinomis* was written by Philip of Opus after the death of Plato, that is, after the year 348–47 B.C., and that it is a sort of postscript to, or implementation of, Plato's *Laws*. This leaves but the years between 348–47 and 346 as the likely date of its composition. On what appear to be sound and persuasive grounds, E. Berti suggests that the *Epinomis* was influenced by the Aristotelian *On Philosophy*,[71] a view which, at least by implication, is also shared by W. Jaeger.[72] Hence, the *Epinomis* would have to be dated later than the *On Philosophy*. This, in turn, compels us to assume that the *On Philosophy* was written prior to the year 347–46 and perhaps even prior to the period between 348 and 346.[73]

Finally, when establishing the probable date of the *On Philosophy*, we must also take into account the possible connections between the Γῆς περίοδος of Eudoxus of Cnidus and the *On Philosophy*. In his *Historia Naturalis* XXX. 3, Pliny, as has already been shown,[74] reports that the philosophy of the Magi 'originated in Persia due to the efforts of Zoroaster. . . . Eudoxus [of Cnidus] . . . also relates that this man Zoroaster lived six thousand years prior to the death of Plato. So says also Aristotle [in the first (?) book of the *On Philosophy*].' We know that it was Eudoxus of Cnidus who claimed that Zoroaster lived six thousand years prior to the death of Plato, and that he made this statement in his Γῆς περίοδος.[75] According to K. von Fritz, Eudoxus died late in 347 B.C. and not, as had previously been assumed, in 355 B.C.[76] He composed the Γῆς περίοδος (which also contained a detailed description of the Magi and their particular 'philosophy,' including references to

Zoroaster) shortly before his death, but definitely after the death of Plato which occurred either late in 348 or, more likely, early in 347 B.C. Hence, one may safely assume that he wrote the Γῆς περίοδος in 347 B.C. In the light of Pliny, *Historia Naturalis* XXX. 3, it is possible, however, that when discussing the Magi Eudoxus may also have referred to Book I of the *On Philosophy*, although such an assumption has been rejected by some scholars. If this be so, then the *On Philosophy* must have been composed about 348–47 B.C., the likely date of the Γῆς περίοδος (and probably prior to the death of Plato).[77] If, however, in Book I of the *On Philosophy* Aristotle quoted from Eudoxus' Γῆς περίοδος, then the *On Philosophy* definitely would have to be dated after 347 B.C.

When dating the *On Philosophy*, we are faced with an additional difficulty. Traditionally, it has been held that Plato died in 348–47 B.C. —more likely, early in 347—and that after, or primarily because of, Plato's death, Aristotle left the Academy (and Athens) and went to Assos. A more recent claim, however, is that the death of Plato had nothing to do with Aristotle's rather sudden departure from Athens in 348 B.C.[78] Relying on II *Vita Syriaca* 3, which relates that 'being frightened by the execution of Socrates, he [*scil.*, Aristotle] fled from Athens and stayed near the Hellespont [*scil.*, in Assos],' the following thesis has been advanced: when in the year 348 B.C. King Philip of Macedonia stormed and sacked the city of Olynthus, the ally of Athens, violent anti-Macedonian reactions (and persecutions?) rocked Athens. Frightened by these outbreaks of intense hostility, Aristotle, the 'Macedonian,' who did not wish to be treated as Socrates had been treated some fifty years earlier, simply departed from Athens in the summer or early fall of 348 B.C. This, then, would eliminate the second half of the year 348 as the possible date of the composition of the *On Philosophy*. Aristotle's upsetting experience in the summer or early fall of 348 most certainly was not conducive to the writing of so complex and lengthy a work as the *On Philosophy*.

Although the likely *tempus ante quod* of the composition of the *On Philosophy* has tentatively been established as prior to the year 347–46 B.C. (provided the theses that the *Epinomis*, published in 346 (?), was influenced by the *On Philosophy*, and that Eudoxus' Γῆς περίοδος in fact cites from the *On Philosophy* can be sustained), it is extremely difficult to determine the *tempus post quod* of this composition. Undoubtedly, this work is later than the Platonic *Timaeus*, which was probably written between 360 and 358–57 B.C. If, as W. Theiler suggests, the *On Philosophy* is anterior to Aristotle's *Protrepticus*—and there exists no compelling evidence in support of this assumption—then it must have been written prior to the years 352–50 B.C., the most likely date of the composition of the *Protrepticus*.[79] However, the *Protrepticus* appears to be quite 'Platonic' (*pace* Düring) in content and philosophic tenor,[80] a persuasive indication that it is probably earlier than the *On Philosophy*. Despite W. Theiler's suggestion, it would be reasonable, therefore, to date the *On Philosophy* after the *Protrepticus*, that is, after 351–50 B.C. This, then, would leave the years between *c.* 350 and 348–47 or 347–46 B.C. as the most likely date for the composition of the *On Philosophy*. But there is a further problem: according to ancient testimony, Plato died after having completed the 'first draft' of the *Laws*, but before he was able to edit this draft for 'publication.' This was subsequently done by Philip of Opus.[81] If, therefore, the *On Philosophy* in some ways is dependent on Books X and XII of the *Laws*, then the *On Philosophy* ought to be dated after the death of Plato, that is, after Philip of Opus had issued the final edition of the *Laws*, provided he made this edition after the death of Plato. Naturally, it is possible that Aristotle had direct access to the unedited copy of the *Laws* (to Plato's original draft), or had advance knowledge of its main contents (something which we cannot possibly ascertain). It may also be argued that Aristotle wrote the *On Philosophy* either as the result of, or as a contribution to, some of the philosophic or 'theological' discussions which, since the publications of the Platonic *Timaeus*, or perhaps in connection with some of Plato's oral teachings (or perhaps in connection with what Plato had said, or was about to say, in the *Laws*), apparently were carried on in the Academy during the last years of Plato's life. These latter possibilities would make the establishing of the *tempus post quod* of the *On Philosophy* extremely difficult. Moreover, in this context, we must always bear in mind that Aristotle probably left Athens and the Academy in the summer or early fall of 348 B.C. Hence, it might be advisable to fix the likely *tempus post quod* of the *On Philosophy* about the year 350–49 or, perhaps, during the first half of the year 348 B.C.[82]

To sum up: in view of the fact that the *On Philosophy* seems to be dependent on Plato's *Timaeus*, it can safely be dated after 360–358/57. However, Aristotle completed his 'preparatory' or 'pre-philosophic' studies only about 357. Hence, it might be advisable to lower this date, especially since around the middle of the fifties Aristotle seems to have been primarily concerned with rhetoric and with the teaching of rhetoric. There also exists persuasive evidence that both the *On the Good* and the *On (the) Ideas* were composed prior to the *On Philosophy*. The

*On the Good* and the *On (the) Ideas*, in turn, have tentatively been dated between 357 and 356/55. Even more important seems to be the fact that the *On Philosophy*, in all likelihood, was written after the *Protrepticus* (*pace* Theiler). Since the *Protrepticus* appears to have been a 'rebuttal' of Isocrates' *Antidosis*, and since the *Antidosis* was definitely published in 353–52, the *Protrepticus* can fairly be dated about 352–50. From all this, it would follow that the *On Philosophy*, being posterior to the *Protrepticus*, was not written prior to the year 350, and perhaps a year or two thereafter. Moreover, if the *On Philosophy* is in fact influenced by Books X and XII of Plato's *Laws*—and the *Laws* was allegedly 'copied out' by Philip of Opus after the death of Plato—then the *On Philosophy* was probably authored during the first part of 348 B.C. (?). This date is based on the conjecture that in his Γῆς περίοδος (written late in 347 B.C.) Eudoxus might have made use of the *On Philosophy*, and that Philip of Opus began his editorial work while Plato was still alive or, more likely, in or after 348–47 B.C. This latter date also takes into account that in all probability Aristotle did not have access to the 'unedited draft' of the *Laws*. Obviously, there always remains the possibility that the Stagirite knew of the essential content of Books X and XII of the *Laws* prior to their 'publication' by Philip of Opus through conversations with Plato. Perhaps, during the last two or three years of his life Plato gave some lectures to an intimate circle of friends and pupils on the subjects he discussed in the last books of the *Laws*, and Aristotle attended these lectures. However, we do not know this for sure. Hence, the year 350–49, 349–48 or 348–47 B.C. seems to be as close a *tempus post quod* as we may reasonably determine. This date is based on the fair assumption that the Platonic *Laws* preceded the Aristotelian *On Philosophy*. If, however, the last books of the *Laws* should be posterior to the *On Philosophy*—an unlikely assumption—then the proposed *tempus post quod* (348 or 348–47 B.C.) would have to be converted into the *tempus ante quod*, and the *On Philosophy* would probably have to be dated prior to the year 350–49 or 349–48 B.C. If, on the other hand, Aristotle used Eudoxus' Γῆς περίοδος for Book I of the *On Philosophy*, the latter would definitely have to be dated after 347 B.C.

Conversely, the *tempus ante quod* for the composition of the *On Philosophy* can be established fairly accurately with the help of Eudoxus' Γῆς περίοδος, which was composed late in 347 B.C. (provided Eudoxus made use of the *On Philosophy*), as well as with the help of the *Epinomis*, which seems to have been written in 347–46 B.C. Since the *Epinomis* (and perhaps the Γῆς περίοδος) appears to have been influenced also by the *On Philosophy*, it must be surmised that it followed the latter. It may be assumed, therefore, that the *tempus ante quod* for the composition of the *On Philosophy* is probably the year 347–46 B.C.,[83] an assumption which is based on the further surmise that the *Epinomis* was written in 347–46 B.C.[84] Hence, as has already been shown, the most likely date for the composition of the *On Philosophy* is somewhere between 350–49 or early 348 and 347–46 B.C. The possible dependence of Eudoxus' Γῆς περίοδος on the *On Philosophy* would actually suggest that it was written not later than the first part of 347 B.C. W. Jaeger's original dating, after all, might be approximately correct, although the particular reasons which he adduces in support of his dating are open to challenge, as is the method by which he attempts to prove his point.

The date which has been proposed here, namely the time between 350–49 or 348–47 and 347–46, however, does not take into account the possibility that Aristotle left Athens rather hurriedly in the summer or early fall of 348 B.C., that is, before the death of Plato.[85] If Aristotle actually left Athens under such distressing circumstances in 348 B.C., then we would have to date the *On Philosophy* either in 350–49 and probably during the latter part of 349, or during the early part of 348 (or perhaps in 347 and possibly later). The dating of the *On Philosophy* in 347 or later, however, would defeat the assumption that Eudoxus of Cnidus made use of this work. But it would lend support to the thesis that in Book I of the *On Philosophy*, Aristotle made use of Eudoxus. In any event, it is quite unlikely that Aristotle should be able to compose so lengthy, so involved and so complex a work as the *On Philosophy* immediately after so shocking and so disruptive an experience as that of his enforced, sudden flight from Athens in the summer or early fall of 348 B.C., or during the first months of his 'exile' from Athens. Moreover, it has been shown that Aristotle's sojourn in Assos or Atarneus was not a 'philosophic excursion' in the company of Coriscus and Erastus but rather a 'diplomatic or political mission' undertaken at the request of King Philip of Macedonia.[86] This sojourn was in fact connected with King Philip's efforts to win, in the person of Hermias of Atarneus, both an ally and a bridgehead in Asia Minor for the encirclement of Thrace and for a possible future invasion of Asia Minor or attack upon Persia. Such a mission, needless to say, must have been pregnant with excitements and dangers and hence could not possibly have created the proper climate or background for the production of a major philosophic treatise. Since, according to our opinion, the *Epinomis* followed the *On Philosophy*, Aristotle must have completed the *On Philosophy* not later than 347–46 B.C. and probably in 347 B.C., assuming the *Epinomis* was completed in 346. Hence, the year 347 (or the early part of 346) is the most likely *tempus ante quod* for the completion of the *On Philosophy*. If pressed for a more concise date, and remembering Aristotle's disconcerting experiences after the summer or early fall of 348 B.C., the present author would maintain that the *On Philosophy* was written (and 'published') between the fall of 349 and the spring of 348 B.C. All these suggested dates, however, are at best conjectural approximations based upon, or derived from, rather elusive and not always reliable evidence.

# A Cosmological (Teleological) Proof for the Existence of God in Aristotle's *On Philosophy**

In a lengthy and startling passage contained in his *De Natura Deorum* II. 37. 95–6, a passage which most scholars ultimately trace back to Book III of Aristotle's lost dialogue *On Philosophy*,[1] Cicero relates:[2]

Aristotle stated this problem [namely, the question of the existence of God or of the gods, *note by the present author*] most brilliantly: 'Let us assume there existed human creatures who had lived always beneath the earth, in comfortable and well-lit dwellings, decorated with statues and pictures, and furnished with all the luxuries enjoyed by human beings considered supremely happy. Although they never had come forth above ground, they had learned by report and hearsay of the existence of certain deities or divine powers. Suppose, then, at some time the jaws of of the earth would open, and they would be able to escape from their hidden abodes and come forth into the regions which we inhabit. When, thus, they suddenly gained sight of the earth and the sea and the sky, and when they came to know the grandeur of the vast clouds and the might of the winds, and when they beheld the sun and realized not only its size and beauty, but also its power to cause the day by shedding light over the sky, and when after night had darkened the earth, they beheld the whole sky spangled and adorned with stars, and when they saw the changing phases of the moon's light, now waxing now waning, and the risings and settings of these celestial bodies and their courses fixed and changeless throughout eternity—when they should behold all these things, most assuredly they would think that the gods exist and that all these marvels are the handiwork of these gods.' Thus far Aristotle.

Philo of Alexandria, in his *Legum Allegoriarum Libri Tres* III. 32. 97–9, likewise seems to refer to Book III of Aristotle's *On Philosophy* when he writes:[3]

The earliest philosophers investigated how we succeeded in recognizing the Divine. Later, the most highly esteemed philosophers asserted that it was from the universe and its different parts and the powers inherent in this universe that we came to understand their ultimate cause. To cite just one example: when one should behold a house [perfectly constructed] . . . one would arrive at the idea of the architect in that one would indeed come to the conclusion that without the art of a craftsman—without architecture and without an architect—the construction of this house could not have been carried out to its perfection. And the same holds true when we behold a city or a ship or any structure, small or large. By the same token, if one were to enter upon this world as one might enter a large house or a gigantic city, and if one were to contemplate the heavens which rotate in perfect spheres containing all things within them, including the planets and the fixed stars which move uniformly in an orderly and harmonious manner and in a way that is to the advantage of the whole; and if one were to contemplate the earth which occupies the center of the world, the running waters and the streams of air between heaven and earth; and furthermore, if one were to perceive the animated creatures, some mortal and some immortal, and the great variety of plants and crops—if one were to behold all this one would most assuredly come to the conclusion that all these things could not possibly have come into being without a perfect art or design, but that there existed, and still exists, an artificer of this whole universe, namely God. Those, then, who reason in this fashion actually conceive of or grasp God by way of His shadow [*scil.*, though His handiwork] in that they acquire a knowledge of the Craftsman or Artificer through His artifacts.

Essentially the same ideas are restated by Philo of Alexandria in his *De Praemiis et Poenis* VII. 41–3, a passage which also might have been influenced by Aristotle's *On Philosophy*:[4]

If some people, by means of their philosophic knowledge, have been enabled to gain a comprehension of the author and governor of the whole universe, they proceeded from the lowly to the most high as the popular saying goes. Indeed, when they enter this world as if they were entering a city ruled by good laws, and when they contemplate the earth so exquisitely girdled with its mountain ranges and far-flung plains, strewn with shrubs and trees and fruit-bearing plants and also animals of all sorts, beholding in different places the oceans and the lakes and the many quiet streams and rushing torrents as well as the gentleness of the air and of the winds and the orderly annual changes of the seasons, and above them all the sun and the moon, the planets and the fixed stars and the heavens in their orderly and disciplined array (a contained world in itself which gyrates within the universe)— when they behold all this they marvel greatly and are struck with awe, and they come to the conclusion which is fully consonant with these grandiose manifestations, namely, that such wondrous beauty and such a sublime order could not possibly be the result of a mere accident, but must be the deliberate handiwork of an artificer, the creator of this universe, and that of necessity there must be a providence. For it is a principle of nature that the creative power cares about what it has created.

The ultimate influence of Aristotle's *On Philosophy* might also be seen in Sextus Empiricus, *Adversus Mathematicos* (*Physicos*) IX. 20–3 (I. 20–3):[5]

And Aristotle maintained [in his *On Philosophy*?] that the conception of the gods arose amongst mankind from two sources, namely, from events that concern the soul and from celestial phenomena. . . . On the strength of their experiences, Aristotle maintains, men intuitively agree amongst themselves that something divine exists which in itself is akin to the [human] soul and which above all is an intellect. . . . But the heavenly bodies, too, contributed to this belief. For when men beheld the sun circling round in the day-time, and by night they observed the orderly motion of the other stars, they supposed some god to be the cause of such motion and orderliness. This is what Aristotle advances.

And in *Adversus Mathematicos* (*Physicos*) IX. 26–7 (I. 26–7), Sextus Empiricus states:[6]

Some people have recourse to the unalterable and orderly motion of the heavenly bodies, and they insist that the first beginnings of men's conceptions about the gods did arise from this. For just as if a man seated on the Trojan Mount Ida had been gazing at the host of the Greeks marching in the plain in splendid order and array, 'Riding first, in the van, were the knights with their chariots and horses. Next came the soldiers on foot' [Homer, *Iliad* IV. 297–8]—such a man would most certainly have arrived at the idea that there exists someone who arranges this array and gives commands to the soldiers marshalled under him, such as Nestor or some other hero who understood how 'Rightful to marshal the steeds and the warriors armed with bucklers' [Homer, *Iliad* II. 554]; and just as the man who is familiar with ships, as soon as he sees in the distance a ship with a favorable wind behind it and with all the sails well set, concludes that there is someone who directs its course and brings it into its appointed harbors; so, too, those who first looked up to the heavens and beheld the sun running its course from its rising to its setting, and the orderly procession of the stars, looked for an artificer of this most beautiful array, conjecturing that it had come about not arbitrarily or by mere accident, but by the agency of some superior and imperishable nature, which was God.

W. Jaeger maintains [7] that, in his *On Philosophy*, Aristotle thoroughly investigates and discusses the psychological or psycho-genetic, [8] as well as the 'cosmological' sources of man's belief in God and in the existence of God. [9] To be more exact: in this fairly early work Aristotle, by reaching beyond direct revelation, attempts what amounts to the first grandiose and, at the same time, the most persuasive synthesis of the two most compelling proofs for the existence of God in the history of Western philosophy and theology: the psychological and the cosmo-logical (teleological) proof. Tradition has credited Aristotle with having introduced the cosmological proof for the existence of God into Greek philosophy or, at least, with having been the first ancient thinker who articulated this proof in philosophical terms. [10] He did so, Jaeger insists, not perhaps from the standpoint of dispassionate or disinterested intellectual curiosity, or in a spirit of speculative adventure so characteristic of many scholars and philosophers, but rather in order to communicate and explain his personal experiences of that ultimate sublimeness which is God, and thus enable others to experience what he himself had experienced. Apparently Aristotle was fully aware of the fact that even the most advanced logic and the most sophisticated science 'can never attain to that irresistible force of inner conviction which arises from the inspired presentiments of the soul,' [11] or from the awe-inspiring contemplation of the universe. In a passage, which both for its beauty and for its insight merits repetition, Jaeger maintains:

> No one in the ancient world ever spoke more beautifully and more profoundly about the personal and emotional side of all religious life than Aristotle during the years when religion was the

central problem in his mind. In the dialogue *On Philosophy* . . . he
spoke of the feeling of awe in the presence of that which is higher
than man. He recognized that inner composure is the essence of all
religious devotion. . . .[12] Aristotle derives the subjective conviction
of God's existence from two sources: from man's experience of the
inspired might of the soul . . . and from the sight of the starry
heavens.[13] This derivation is not to be understood historically. . . .
It is a frequent juxtaposition of the two great wonders that all the
enlightenment of the enlightened cannot explain. . . . What
Aristotle compresses here into a formulae is simply the religious
attitude of Plato's circle towards the Universe.[14]

These are the exalted words of Jaeger, who more than anyone else
seems to have captured and understood Aristotle's basic attitude and
outlook in matters pertaining to religion, religious experience and to
a philosophic discussion of the existence of God.[15]

An echo of Aristotle's theological views may possibly be detected
in the *Epinomis* which, it is contended here, was influenced by the
Aristotelian *On Philosophy*. In the *Epinomis* we are informed that the
observable and deliberate (perfect) order within the universe is declaratory of the fact that this universe is, and must be, governed by 'Mind,'
that is, by a Supreme Being or Perfect Intelligence.[16] Perhaps even
more significant is the statement, also contained in the *Epinomis*, that
'God created the stars and the perfect circuits of the celestial bodies'
so that man may know the truth—that man may know God and of His
existence through His handiwork.[17] It appears, therefore, that the
author of the *Epinomis* (Philip of Opus), in imitation of what Aristotle
had said in the *On Philosophy*, insists, at least by implication, that God
created (or ordered) the universe primarily for the purpose of enabling
man to know Him and to know of His existence through His handiwork. Hence, the right understanding of this deliberate handiwork or
artifact is also the road to the Supreme Artificer—the road to God.
Now we may also understand why, according to some sources, Aristotle
referred to the harmonious and perfect universe as 'the visible God.'

J. Bernays, it appears, was fully justified when he maintained that in
his psycho-genetic proof for the existence of God Aristotle not only
pays the most exalted homage to God, but also honors man, including
himself. Because he refuses to inject 'lowly motives' into the vital
relationships of man to God, Bernays argued, Aristotle proclaims that
man's belief in God and in the existence of God does not originate, as
it did with most of the ancient religions, with an abject feeling of

dependence and fear, based on superstition and ignorance. It apparently did not escape Aristotle that a trembling fear of God, like any 'brimstone theology,' in its ultimate implications is simply blasphemous in that it conceives of God as a sort of monstrous creature whose destructive wrath must constantly be 'bought off' by 'pacifying offerings,' soothing incantations and degrading acts of abject prostration. To Aristotle, man's belief in God and in God's existence arises primarily from an innate spiritual and affirmative strength which in its spontaneous manifestations—in its complete independence from physical or psycho-physical factors—generates in man a spontaneous, free and joyous realization that there exists, and must exist, an invisible, intelligent and omniscient Being that knows everything to perfection. This particular concept of the deity is in no way related to some frightening natural event or to the naïve assumption that the offering of some earthly gift might buy the benevolence of certain 'supernatural' forces. It is based, Bernays concluded, solely on man's perception and understanding of the sublime beauty and orderliness of the heavens and the heavenly bodies which forever move in their pre-ordained courses. Such a concept of order and beauty, which is at the basis of man's realization that a Supreme Being, Artificer, Orderer and Creator exists, and must exist, ultimately leads to an unshakable belief in God and in God's existence:[18] 'The heavens declare the glory of God, and the firmament sheweth His handiwork.'[19]

Cicero's more immediate source for the passage in *De Natura Deorum* II. 37. 95–6, it is widely held, is probably the *Concerning the Gods* of Posidonius, who in turn was influenced by Cleanthes of the Early Stoa.[20] Cleanthes, again, in all likelihood derived some of his theological views directly from Aristotle's *On Philosophy*.[21] It is possible, however, that Cicero, being deeply impressed by Aristotle's 'cosmological argument' as to why men believe in God and in the existence of God, might have tried to enlarge and even 'improve' on the image created by the Stagirite. He did so, we may surmise, in order to 'bring it up to date' and make it more attractive to his Roman readers: the subterranean dwelling places decorated with statues and paintings, to mention just one instance, seem to be Roman villas rather than Greek houses.[22] Cicero's account of the 'cave people,'[23] not to be found in Philo of Alexandria or Sextus Empiricus, on the other hand clearly insists that they live in a well-ordered, comfortable and, indeed, resplendent environment. Such a high state of material comfort, in turn, suggests that even beneath the earth and deprived of the vision of 'heavenly orderliness,' these 'cave people' must have possessed a highly developed sense of order and orderliness.[24] It might be interesting to note here that in *Metaphysics* 982 b 12 ff., Aristotle points out that men began to philosophize about ultimate causes and first principles only after they had provided for the necessities of life and secured 'the things that are conducive to comfort and relaxation'—after they had attained a certain level of material culture. In other words, man turns to philosophy only after he has provided for the necessities of life or plain survival—when he has achieved a state of leisure which permits him to pursue a kind of knowledge that does not necessarily result in some practical and tangibly material advantage. Cicero's account also implies that the 'cave dwellers' have attained this level of material culture, and that they understand the meaning of order and beauty and, hence, are fully capable of judging as well as appreciating the orderliness and beauty of the universe. Moreover, they are also able to realize that this cosmic orderliness and beauty is not the result of mere accident, but rather the deliberate product of intentional and intelligent design.

I. Bywater observed that if for Aristotle philosophy 'begins in wonderment,'[25] the Stagirite could very well maintain that religion, the initial form of all philosophy, begins with the stunning impression which the heavens and their perfect motions make upon thoughtful men.[26] This might well be the original (and ultimate) meaning of Aristotle's justly famed statement that 'it is owing to their wonderment that men both now begin, and at first began, to philosophize. They wondered . . . about the phenomena of the moon and those of the sun and the stars, and about the genesis of the universe.' This passage from the *Metaphysics* (982 b 12 ff.), it must be borne in mind, apparently was composed at approximately the same time as the *On Philosophy*. Hence, it would be maintained that for Aristotle true religion and true philosophy both begin in wonder; and since both begin in wonder, there must also be a certain affinity between true religion and true philosophy.

W. Jaeger, it appears, has correctly pointed out that the first thing we notice in the passage from Cicero's *De Natura Deorum* II. 37. 95–6— a theme which recurs again and again in Stoic theological writings[27]— is the obvious dependence of Cicero (or of his immediate source) on the 'cave analogy' found in Plato, *Republic* 514A ff.[28] In his matchless understanding of the ultimate motivation behind Aristotle's thoughts, Jaeger insists that this analogy[29]

is a magnificent representation of the fundamental experience of Plato's philosophy, namely, the reduction of the visible world to a realm of mere shadows, and the vision of true being by which the philosopher is separated from his brethren and rendered lonely. Aristotle's simile also breathes a new attitude towards the world. Cicero's men, however, have not lived in caves. They are "modern," cultivated, satiated, mis-educated persons who bury themselves like moles in the sunless and comfortless splendor in which they seek their dubious happiness. He makes them ascend one day into the light, here to perceive the drama that he himself sees, the immeasurable marvel of reality, the divine structure and motion of the universe. He teaches them to contemplate, not a supernatural world, but the world that is visible to all, and yet seen by none. He is conscious of being the first Greek to see the world with the eyes of Plato, and his intentional alteration of Plato's simile is an indication of this view of his historical mission. What he gives us instead of the Ideas is the contemplation of the wonderful shapes and arrangements of the cosmos, a contemplation which, intensified until it becomes religion, leads to the intuition of the divine director of it all.

Jaeger's analysis, it may be contended, seems to recast what Plutarch had said in his *De Tranquillitate Animi* 20 (*Moralia* 477C), a passage which is commonly considered a fragment of the *On Philosophy*: 'The universe is a most holy temple and as such most worthy of God. Man is introduced into this temple by being born into it ... [by becoming] the spectator of a sublime reality which is declaratory of the Divine Intellect. . . . Life, then, because it is indeed the initiation into this sublime reality, is in itself a sort of living initiation into the mysteries and, hence, must be the highest form of serenity and joy.'

It is only natural, Jaeger argues, that Aristotle, the disciple of Plato, should imitate his great teacher and borrow from him the 'myth of the cave,'[30] which in post-Platonic and Hellenistic literature gained much prominence and popularity. But there exists a basic difference between the 'cave motif' of Plato and that of Aristotle. In Plato the men imprisoned in the cave rise to the mystical or mythological vision of the world of the transcendent Separate Ideas. In Aristotle, on the other hand, mole-like creatures, who are by no means prisoners, suddenly behold the physical world as it actually is.[31] The implication, therefore, is that for Aristotle the actual physical world, if viewed intelligently, contains all the truth, at least for men with eyes to see and ears to hear[32] —a truth which Plato for reasons of his own relegates to an ideal or transcendent world accessible only to the philosophic (Platonic) man.

In this respect Aristotle's borrowings from Plato are more than mere imitations: they are far-reaching and, indeed, most radical modifications of Plato's essential doctrines.[33] And while there undoubtedly exist certain superficial similarities between Aristotle's 'Artificer' of the harmonious and unitarian universe and Plato's Demiurge, it must always be borne in mind that in the *Timaeus* Plato does not perchance attempt to prove the existence of God (or that of the Demiurge), nor does he seek to demonstrate how the notion of a 'Creator' originated in the human mind.

'The testimony of the *Epinomis*,[34] which is equally emphatic in assigning to theology the central position in all philosophy,' Jaeger insists, 'tells us that these lofty speculations met with strong opposition on the part of the Greeks. According to the popular Greek view, the knowledge of the divine . . . is a thing that must be forever unattainable to mortals. . . . Theology became possible to the Greeks only when the discovery of laws in the motions of the heavens had led to the assumption of astral souls,'[35] as well as to the belief in the wise and deliberate governance of an orderly universe by a single Supreme Intellect, Architect and Governor. Hence, it may also be maintained that the earliest works of Aristotle and the very late works of Plato mark the beginning of what might properly be called an articulate, though still somewhat rudimentary, Greek theology, rising far above the confusing humdrum of vague and fanciful *mythos* or poetic inspiration. In the past, theological speculation, on the whole, had been considered an unrewarding task (tolerantly relegated to fanciful poetic utterances), if not a 'forbidden fruit.' Aristotle, on the other hand, proposed and asserts here, as does the late Plato, that a knowledge of the Divine, aside from being the most delightful and most rewarding among all intellectual undertakings, is surely attainable through reason and experience properly employed and intelligently interpreted. Such an assertion is not only alien to the earliest Hellenic mind, but also stands in sharp contrast to the traditional Greek views on religious matters.

Besides the Platonic cave analogy, Aristotle might also have been influenced here by the probably much older analogy employed by Empedocles. The latter insisted that, when viewed from the lofty heights of the divine world, the visible world is but a cave or a pit.[36] Be this as it may, it is safe to assume that the particular Aristotelian analogy, which is considered to have been a vital part of Aristotle's *On Philosophy*, is in one way Platonic or, better, a *sui generis* continuation of Plato's religious mysticism, while in another way it is also a significant, far-reaching and most meaningful step beyond classical Platonism. In the final analysis, Aristotle 'replaces' (and, by implication, rejects) Plato's transcendent world of Separate Ideas—the only true, meaningful and real world for Plato—with his own concept of a single and meaningful reality, namely, the world in which we live. Moreover, this real world of Aristotle in its magnificent order and resplendent beauty, is caused and controlled by a Supreme Being: it is, in a certain way, the 'visible aspect' of this Supreme Being. This perfect order, this unsurpassed beauty, proclaims the existence of a Supreme Deity [37] and, at the same time, divulges something about this Supreme Deity. The Supreme Deity, Aristotle believes, deliberately and tellingly reveals itself and its existence in this matchless order and beauty. Thus Aristotle succeeds in establishing the vital union not only of the human spirit with the Divine Spirit—a union and communion which is also stressed in the *Epinomis* [38]—but also the union and communion of God and man in general in and through the created world, that is, in and through His own handiwork—in and through the 'visible God' or 'divine universe.' With Plato the corporeal visible world and the transcendent world of the Ideas are forever separated and contrasted to the point of almost meaningless opposition. With Aristotle, on the other hand, God, man and world are most intimately and most tellingly related.

I. Bywater, who subjected Aristotle's *On Philosophy* to a thorough investigation, believes that Philo of Alexandria, *Legum Allegoriarum Libri Tres* III. 32. 97–9, is definitely under the immediate influence of Book III of the *On Philosophy* of Aristotle. [39] Bywater's thesis, which subsequently was adopted by the majority of scholars, is based on the assumption that the whole of the Philonian argument as well as the greater part of the key terms originally used in the Aristotelian model have, in the main, been faithfully preserved by Philo—much more faithfully than is the case with Cicero. [40] But Bywater also notices that Philo, as happens so often with an epitomizer, not only compresses the Aristotelian account, but also omits some of the detailed excursions into the 'way of life' of the subterranean people, or into the unsurpassed orderly beauty of the visible world—details which probably were contained in the Aristotelian original. [41] This, then, would suggest that in the *On Philosophy* Aristotle described the infinite beauty of the orderly universe in exalted words which actually amounted to a solemn hymn in praise of the author of this beauty and orderliness.

When, on the other hand, Philo maintains in the *Legum Allegoriarum* that 'without architecture (or art) and without an architect the construction of a building could not have been carried out,' he seems to imply that in the *On Philosophy* Aristotle adopts and makes use of the Platonic doctrine of the Demiurge. Other fragments from, or references to, the Aristotelian *On Philosophy* indicate that Aristotle had insisted that the universe is uncreated or, to be more exact, without beginning and without end.[42] This is emphasized by Philo when he states that 'Aristotle was surely speaking piously and devoutly when he insisted that the universe is uncreated and imperishable, and when he charged with serious ungodliness those people who maintained the opposite—who thought that the great visible God, Who contains in truth the sun and the moon and the remaining pantheon of planets and fixed stars, is no better than the work of man's hands. . . .'[43] It is also held that in the *On Philosophy* Aristotle expressly rejected the Platonic notion, found in the *Timaeus* (42D ff., *et passim*), that the Demiurge 'created' the world (out of uncreated prime matter).[44]

In the *De Praemiis et Poenis* VII. 41 ff.,[45] Philo observes that some people do not at all recognize God or the existence of God, while others do not know how to arrive at the realization of God's existence by the best possible way. Some people, Philo continues, completely deny the existence of God, others remain in doubt about God's existence, while still others merely cling to the traditional or popular beliefs in God or the gods.[46] In Philo's opinion those men, who like Aristotle in his *On Philosophy* find 'the way to God' through His handiwork, still proceed in what Philo considers to be an 'inferior way.' For they know of God only through His 'shadow,'[47] that is, through His creation[48]—an imperfect though acceptable method of realizing the existence of God.[49] With Philo, it will be observed, the Platonic notion of a divine Demiurge is still very strong. Apparently he wishes to stress the existence and the perfection, as well as the activity, of a Supreme Artificer of the universe: the universe is compared to a perfect abode which simply presupposes the existence of a perfect Architect. It is not surprising, therefore, that Philo, whose Platonic leanings are obvious, should refer to, or have in mind, something akin to Plato's Great Architect—the Demiurge. In other words, the 'best possible world' must have as its architect the most perfect Creator. But when Philo insists further that this Demiurge is also 'providence,'[50] he merely adds an observation of his own or, perhaps, a Stoic notion: the Architect (or Creator) has an abiding interest in what he has built or created.[51]

In *Adversus Mathematicos* IX. 22,[52] Sextus Empiricus implies that when inferring or proving the existence of God from the sublime orderliness and purposefulness of the universe, Aristotle in fact appeals to the 'consensus among men'[53]—an argument, incidentally, which can also be found in Plato's *Laws* and in the *Epinomis*. In brief, both Plato and Aristotle also base their argument in favor of the divinity of the universe on the consensus among all peoples. But, in the final analysis, this consensus is the manifestation of a 'demonic force' in the human soul,[54] common to all men and endowing them with an intuitive certainty about the Divine—a certainty which transcends all logical or philosophic arguments.[55]

Despite the fact that Sextus Empiricus in *Adversus Mathematicos* IX. 26-7,[56] does not expressly mention Aristotle, almost all scholars ascribe this significant passage to Aristotle's *On Philosophy*.[57] It could be argued that Sextus Empiricus himself was not aware of the fact that he was actually citing here the Stagirite—he vaguely refers to 'some people'— and that in all likelihood he had in mind some member (Cleanthes?) or members of the Early Stoa. Hence, it could fairly be argued that the preservation of this important passage from the Aristotelian *On Philosophy* is probably due to the fact that some Early Stoic (Cleanthes?) adopted and reproduced almost verbatim an argument which he originally found in Aristotle's *On Philosophy*:[58] the comparison of the orderly heavens with a well-disciplined army,[59] and the comparison of God, Who effects this orderliness, with the supreme army commander. These comparisons, which play a conspicuous role in *Adversus Mathematicos* IX. 26-7, can also be found in Aristotle, *Metaphysics* 1075 a 11-19.[60] It has also been pointed out that for Aristotle, at least for the early Aristotle, the absolute perfection of the Prime Mover cannot simply be identified with the perfect (impersonal) order which becomes manifest throughout the universe and for which the Prime Mover is responsible. For this cosmic order in itself does not constitute a being *per se*. It is the result or the deliberate work of some Higher or Highest Being.

Keeping this in mind, one might understand why the young Aristotle compares the ultimate cause of the cosmic order to a supreme army commander who, although he is responsible for the order and discipline in his army, is not identical with this order or discipline. Moreover, a supreme commander has a distinct existence (or personality) of his own wholly apart from, and independent of, the army he commands, or of the commands which he issues.[61] This being so, one might even suggest that, at least in the *On Philosophy*, Aristotle comes rather close to the notion of a Personal God.[62] This might be inferred from the fact, recorded by Sextus Empiricus, that Aristotle speaks here not simply of a 'commander' or 'architect of a battle order' in general, but pointedly compares the heavenly commander of the orderly cosmic array to Nestor. But to the ancient Greeks, Nestor was a distinct person, a meaningful and identifiable single individual: '. . . there was someone arranging such an array and commanding the soldiers marshalled under him . . . [namely,] Nestor.'[63] If our interpretation of Sextus Empiricus, *Adversus Mathematicos* IX. 26–7, should prove to be correct, then Aristotle's attempt would be the only known effort in Greek antiquity to prove or, at least, to proclaim, by way of an analogy, not only the existence of God, but also the existence of a Personal God.

It has been stated already that, according to Sextus Empiricus, *Adversus Mathematicos* IX. 20–3, Aristotle maintained in the *On Philosophy* 'that men's thought of the gods [or of God] originated from two sources: the [personal] experiences of the soul and the phenomena of the heavens. To the first one belonged the inspirations and prophetic powers of the soul . . . . But the heavenly bodies likewise contributed to this belief. . . .' In brief, Aristotle held that religious beliefs, especially the belief in God and in His existence, originated either from direct and personal 'mystical revelation'—from an immediate, intuitive and personal 'illumination' or 'inspiration' where man's soul is directly affected by a personal awareness that results in spontaneous certainty; or from a 'derivative' or 'inferential' realization or knowledge of the divine.

Closer analysis of this passage from Sextus Empiricus should also divulge that in his *On Philosophy* Aristotle distinguished between a knowledge of God and of His existence which is grounded upon $\pi \alpha \vartheta \epsilon \hat{\imath} \nu$, and a knowledge of God (and of His existence, His manifestations and His efficiency) which is based on $\mu \alpha \vartheta \epsilon \hat{\imath} \nu$.[64] In other words, he distinguished between immediate, intuitive 'inner illumination' or 'direct revelation' in which the soul receives or is affected by an 'intuitive certainty' ($\pi \alpha \vartheta \epsilon \hat{\imath} \nu$), and between a 'derivative,' 'inferential' or 'discursive' knowledge which rests on distinct powers of reasoning ($\mu \alpha \vartheta \epsilon \hat{\imath} \nu$). The latter processes, it will be noted, also imply a $\phi \acute{\upsilon} \sigma \iota \varsigma - \tau \acute{\epsilon} \chi \nu \eta$ opposition—the inferential realization that artifacts, from the most insignificant human accomplishment to the most resplendent divine creation, are not 'by nature' ($\phi \acute{\upsilon} \sigma \epsilon \iota$) but rather 'by art' ($\tau \acute{\epsilon} \chi \nu \eta$), that is, the work or deliberate product (and, hence, also the significant manifestation) of an artificer.[65]

It will be noted that the fragments of Aristotle's *On Philosophy* listed in note 64, *supra*, maintain that whenever thoughtful men stand face to face with the wondrous and orderly universe they invariably reach the rational conclusion ($\mu \alpha \vartheta \epsilon \hat{\imath} \nu$) that all this beauty and orderliness must be caused by an ultimate single 'principle,' 'orderer,' 'creator' or 'architect.'[66] Cicero, *De Natura Deorum* II. 37. 95–6 (but not Sextus Empiricus or Philo of Alexandria), stresses the fact that the 'cave people' or 'subterranean people' had 'always lived in well-constructed and well-lit dwellings, adorned with statues and pictures, and furnished with everything in which those who are considered happy abound.' This statement, which also calls to mind Aristotle, *Metaphysics* 982 b 12 ff., implies that man turns to philosophy (and philosophic theology) only after he has provided for the essential necessities of life—after he has attained a state of 'prosperity' and leisure which permits him to pursue a kind of knowledge that does not necessarily result in some material advantage in terms of physical survival. It will also be observed that Cicero's account of the material culture developed by the 'cave people' implies that they are familiar with architecture, sculpture and painting. Hence they are qualified to judge artifacts, that is, order and beauty and, accordingly, are capable of appreciating the orderliness and beauty of the universe. Moreover, they are also capable of realizing ($\mu\alpha\vartheta\epsilon\hat{\imath}\nu$) that this cosmic order and beauty is not perhaps the result of mere accident, but rather the intended product of intelligent and deliberate design ($\tau\epsilon\chi\nu\eta$) and hence the handiwork of a superior or supreme artificer.[67]

It may be surmised, therefore, that in his *On Philosophy* Aristotle ultimately based his 'cosmological argument' in support of the existence of God or the gods—an argument which is based in the principles of $\mu\alpha\vartheta\epsilon\hat{\imath}\nu$—not only on the opposition of $\pi\alpha\vartheta\epsilon\hat{\imath}\nu$ (which is the foundation of direct 'mystical illumination' or 'prophetic inspiration') and $\mu\alpha\vartheta\epsilon\hat{\imath}\nu$ (which underlies inductive reasoning and, hence, 'rational theology'), but also on the contrast between $\varphi\acute{\upsilon}\sigma\iota\varsigma$ and $\tau\epsilon\chi\nu\eta$. As regards the latter, Aristotle probably argued, perhaps by implication, along the following lines: If rational man is sufficiently conversant with the arts, and if he understands the fact that the products of the arts are the results of deliberate action, he will also have to admit that the most orderly artifact or artifacts, namely, the orderly universe itself must be the product of art or $\tau\epsilon\chi\nu\eta$, that is, the deliberate handiwork of an artificer, and in the case of the most beautiful and most orderly universe, of the most perfect artificer—God.

According to Aristotle's *On Philosophy*, 'mystical revelation' or the 'direct experiences of the inspired soul' are based on $\pi\alpha\vartheta\epsilon\hat{\imath}\nu$ and $\varphi\acute{\upsilon}\sigma\iota\varsigma$, while 'rational theology' is founded on $\mu\alpha\vartheta\epsilon\hat{\imath}\nu$ and $\tau\epsilon\chi\nu\eta$. Philo of Alexandria appears to have understood Aristotle's dual approach to the problem of the origin of man's thought about the divine and about the existence of God or the divine when he states: 'If some people [such as Aristotle], by means of their philosophic knowledge, have been enabled to gain a comprehension of the author and governor of the whole universe, they proceeded from the lowly to the most high. . . .When they behold . . . [the marvels of the wondrously beautiful and orderly universe] they marvel and are struck with awe, and they come to the conclusion . . . that this wondrous beauty and this sublime order could not possibly be the result of mere accident, but must be the deliberate handiwork of an artificer, the creator of this universe. . . .'[68] In doing so, Philo continues, these people have chosen only 'the second best road,' however. For they know God and are aware of His existence solely through μαθεῖν—through 'His shadow,' that is, through His creation or 'manifestations.' The best way of knowing God or God's existence, Philo insists, is through God Himself—through divine and direct revelation and personal (prophetic) inspiration which, according to Aristotle, is based on παθεῖν.

In conclusion it might be stated that during his early literary career, Aristotle became profoundly interested in theological issues. This was probably due to the influence not only of the aging Plato, but also to the many theological debates within the Academy.[69] He seriously discussed the existence of a Supreme Being as well as the feasibility of knowing of the existence of this Supreme Being. In the course of these discussions, he touched upon a number of questions and issues, including the problem of the cosmological (teleological) proof for the existence of God, which he apparently combined with the psycho-genetic cause of man's belief in God and in the existence of God, as well as with a proof of the existence of God *e gradibus* (and, one might assert, with the 'historical proof' of the existence of God). We might even conjecture on reasonable grounds that, when investigating the problem of the existence of God, he actually came to the intuitive conclusion that the Supreme Being, which he compared to the supreme commander of a perfectly arrayed army, must be a Personal God. No one in antiquity, to be sure, has expressed the intellectual necessity, the emotional-psychological requirement, the aesthetic need for, and the ontological reality of God's existence more eloquently and more convincingly than Aristotle. In this, Aristotle, the Aristotle of the 'lost works,' not only carried on and brought to a climax the essentially mystical and hazy theology of the late Plato and that of some other members of the Early Academy, but he also improved upon this mystical theology by making it more meaningful and more persuasive—by pronouncing it an eminently intelligent and wholly intelligible rational pursuit which calls upon both reason and experience.[70] Compared with certain passages from the *On Philosophy*, which in their deathless significance touch on the ultimate issue of all religions and of all philosophies, the later doctrinal treatises credited to Aristotle become almost insignificant— almost a monumental irrelevance of astute, but empty, quibbling.

# Chapter XIV

# The Concept of God in Aristotle's
# *On Philosophy*
# (Cicero, *De Natura Deorum* I. 13. 33)*

Cicero, *De Natura Deorum* I. 13. 33, is generally considered an important 'fragment' of Aristotle's *On Philosophy*.[1] Here Cicero relates that

in the third Book of the *On Philosophy*[2] (*in tertio de philosophia*) Aristotle, in disagreement with his teacher Plato, submits a disjointed jumble of theories. Now he alleges that only 'mind' (*mens*), and 'mind' only, is the divinity (*divinitas*);[3] now, that the universe (*mundus*) itself is God (*deus*);[4] now he puts some other ruler (or deity—*alium* [*deum*?]) over the universe to whom he ascribes the power of guiding and maintaining the movements of the universe (or world) by means of a kind of 'reverse motion' (or, 'backward rotation'—*replicatio quaedam*);[5] now he claims that the 'ether' (or heat) in the heavens (*caeli ardor*) is God (*deus*),[6] thus losing sight of the fact that the heavens themselves are part of that universe which, in another passage, he himself had proclaimed to be God (*deus*). But all this raises a further question, namely, how could the 'divine sense' (the divine mind?—*divinus ille sensus*), which is identified with the heavens, possibly endure and remain always the same in the unimaginable speed of the perpetually rotating heavens?[7] Moreover, what would become of the many [stellar?, popular?] gods (*dii*) if we were to call the heavens God? Again, when he asserts that God (*deus*) is without a [material] body and without corporeal elements,[8] he actually deprives God (*deus*) of all senses and sensations (or sense-perceptions—*sensus*), including wisdom (or foresight—*prudentia*). Moreover, how is it possible that the universe (*mundus*) should move, if it lacks a body (or corporeal elements—*carens corpore*); and how, if it is actually moving itself constantly,[9] can this [divine] universe [or God] ever attain to calm serenity and true happiness?[10]

So far Cicero.

This sustained and emphatic criticism of Aristotle's allegedly 'disjointed jumble of theories' about the 'divine' is made by a certain C. Velleius,[11] a brash representative of Epicurean philosophy. Since Epicurus and his school were totally out of sympathy with Aristotle and his teachings, they availed themselves of every opportunity to deprecate the man and his philosophy.[12] Thus, it is reasonable to assume that Velleius' account and his critique are highly prejudiced, and that they are based on some Epicurean (and anti-Aristotelian) source or sources[13] which were also used, for instance, by Philodemus.[14] Moreover, Cicero's text, which in this instance might very well cite from an Epicurean source, is probably a conglomeration of Latin paraphrases, résumés and perhaps clichés. Nevertheless, in the absence of sufficient evidence to the contrary, it must be assumed that the account of Velleius (or, Cicero, who once stated that in his opinion Aristotle exceeded all other philosophers, Plato always excepted)[15] is in essence fairly factual and accurate and conveys, although perhaps in a somewhat garbled and intentionally distorted form, some fundamental features of Aristotle's early theology as stated in the third Book of his *On Philosophy*.

The lengthy passage quoted from Cicero's *De Natura Deorum* I. 13. 33 has precipitated much speculation and much disagreement among scholars. Judging from the more recent scholarly literature dealing with this subject, it appears unlikely, however, that these disagreements will be resolved in a manner satisfactory to everyone. No matter how judiciously and carefully this is done, any attempt to come to grips with this particular fragment or report will meet with objections on the part of some scholars. These disagreements and controversies may in part be attributed to the fact that Cicero's text consists of prejudiced arguments and objections made by an Epicurean whose anti-Aristotelian bias calls into question his objectivity as a reporter and critic. In part, these arguments are probably the result of the highly condensed and, hence, not always unambiguous text of Cicero, whose efforts as an accurate translator from the Greek original may also be questioned. Moreover, it must be borne in mind that thanks to such intermediary sources as Cleanthes Posidonius, Antiochus of Ascalon and probably others, in all likelihood Cicero's report has been 'contaminated' by post-Aristotelian and, especially, by Stoic notions. Nevertheless, Cicero's *De Natura Deorum* I. 13. 33, will have to be accepted, though with some reservations, as a kind of fragmentary 'doxographical report' of what Aristotle probably had said on 'divine matters' in his *On Philosophy*.[16] Thus, it can reasonably be maintained that, despite its apparent shortcomings our text indicates that in the third Book of the *On Philosophy* Aristotle not only discussed certain problems touching on the traditional gods but also insisted that the transcendent world is divine or, rather, that the ultimate divinity is transcendent.[17] This seems to be incontrovertible, or almost incontrovertible, while every other statement contained in the Ciceronian passage apparently raises a number of conflicting and almost unanswerable issues.

The introductory statement that 'Aristotle, in disagreement with his teacher Plato, submits a disjointed jumble of theories' has been the occasion of some dispute among certain scholars who have proposed to revise or correct the extant text of Cicero.[18] Thus A. J. Festugière, for instance, would alter this text to read: 'Aristotle causes a disjointed jumble of theories by disagreeing with his teacher Plato on one point.'[19] Festugière justifies his 'correction' by pointing out, though not always convincingly, that the several conceptions of God which Velleius (or Cicero) ascribes to Aristotle are, with one single exception,[20] identical with the conceptions of God credited to Plato in the self-same *De Natura Deorum*.[21]

Velleius enumerates four Aristotelian definitions of God, all of which he subsequently cites and decries as being mutually contradictory: (i) 'only "mind," and "mind" only, is the divinity'; (ii) 'the universe itself is God'; (iii) 'Aristotle puts some other ruler (or deity) over the universe, to whom he attributes the power of guiding and maintaining the movements of this universe by means of a kind of "reverse motion"'; and (iv) 'the "ether" in the heavens is God.' Immediately after reciting these four definitions, Velleius proceeds with his first objection: (v) in defining God as 'ether,' Aristotle 'loses sight of the fact that the heavens (or, the "ether") themselves are part of that universe which in another passage [*scil.*, in (ii)] he himself had proclaimed to be God.' Thus, according to Velleius, the fourth definition, which identifies God with the 'ether' in the heavens, conflicts with the second definition, which declares the universe to be God.

In order to better understand some of the subsequent objections made by Velleius, we must bear in mind that Aristotle probably proposed, at least by implication, a fifth definition of God or of the Divine —a definition which these objections simply presuppose: the stars are deities or are divine.[22] Assuming, then, that the stars are deities, the following problems arise, at least in the opinion of Velleius: (vi) 'How could this divine sense (or, divine "mind"), which is identified with the heavens, possibly endure and remain always the same in the unimaginable speed of the perpetually rotating heavens?'; (vii) 'what becomes

of the many [stellar] gods if we were to call the [whole] heavens God?';
(viii) 'when Aristotle asserts that God is without a [material] body and
without corporeal elements, he actually deprives God of all senses and
sensations (or sense-preceptions), including wisdom'; (ix) 'how it is
possible that the universe should move if it lacks a body'; and (x) 'how,
if it actually moves itself (or, is moving) constantly, can this universe
[or God] ever attain to calm serenity and true happiness [which are the
hallmarks of divinity]?'

The first definition—that only 'mind' is the divinity or God (*mens
omnis divinitas*)—poses a number of problems, not the least of which is
whether Cicero's Latin rendition of the original Greek source is, indeed,
accurate. Clearly, *mens* signifies νοῦς or 'pure intellect' (or 'mind').
If this is so, then we may also conjecture that in the *On Philosophy* God,
or the divine, was identified with νοῦς. This assumption receives some
support from *Metaphysics* 1072 b 14–30, where Aristotle defines God
(or the divine) as *actus purus* or νόησις νοήσεως;[23] and from Aristotle's
*On Prayer*, where we are informed that 'God is either "pure mind"
(νοῦς) or something beyond and above "mind."'[24] A further and
perhaps more fundamental problem is the following: Velleius (or
Cicero) seems to speak somewhat indiscriminately of *deus* (θεός) and
*divinitas*. He might actually be employing the term *deus* where Aristotle
would have preferred to speak of τὸ θεῖον.[25] Thus, what is actually
implied in the statement, *menti attribuit omnem divinitatem*[26]—whether
Aristotle calls the νοῦς the θεός or merely τὸ θεῖον—is not wholly clear
from Cicero's text. We know from the Aristotelian *Protrepticus*, however, that Aristotle believes that 'mind alone is divine';[27] that because
man alone can share in this 'divine mind,' 'he appears to be a god in
comparison with all other creatures';[28] and that 'since mind is "the
divine dwelling in us"' . . . mortal life possesses a certain element of the
divine.'[29] In any event, from a variety of sources it may be inferred that
for Aristotle the Supreme Being or God is 'pure mind' or 'pure
intellect'—the 'Mind of minds.' As such, God is 'beyond' the divine
universe and, indeed, beyond the human mind. This becomes abundantly clear in Aristotle's statement that 'as in the universe, so also in
the soul, God moves everything. Hence, the starting point of reasoning
is really not reasoning itself, but something greater than [and far be-
yond] reasoning. What, then, could be greater than rational knowledge
or the intellect but God?'[30]

The second definition, 'that the universe (*mundus*) itself is God'
(*mundum ipsum deum . . . esse*), poses similar problems. Here, too, the
question arises as to whether or not *deus* should be translated as τὸ θεῖον

rather than ὁ θεός.[31] In the *De Aeternitate Mundi* III. 10–11, and *ibid.*, V. 20–4[32]—two passages which are commonly considered to be 'fragments' of Aristotle's *On Philosophy*[33]—Philo of Alexandria credits Aristotle with having called the universe the 'immense visible God Who includes the sun, the moon . . . and the pantheon of the planets and the fixed stars.'[34] Philo seems to imply, however, that the divinity of the universe, this 'visible God,' is not identical with, or on the same level of meaning as, the 'Supreme God';[35] and that the 'Supreme God' has the capacity of destroying the universe (the 'visible God') and of creating a new universe (a new 'visible God'). Thus, the 'visible God' must be contingent upon the 'Supreme God.' From Sextus Empiricus,[36] Cicero[37] and Philo,[38] it may also be inferred that for Aristotle there exists a 'Supreme God' Who is the Creator, Governor, Maintainer and Commander of the universe or of the 'visible God' and, hence, cannot be identical with the 'visible God.' Moreover, these three authors insist that Aristotle believes that the sight of the visible universe—the 'visible God'—leads men to acknowledge the existence of the 'Supreme God' Who is quite distinct from the visible universe.[39] The 'divine universe,' the visible cosmos or 'visible God,' is at best a manifestation —and the most perfect manifestation—of the invisible 'Supreme God,' as, for instance, the artifact is a 'manifestation' of the artificer (and of his art), but never in itself the 'Supreme God' or the Artificer. 'The heavens declare the glory of God, and the firmament sheweth His handiwork.'[40] Philo insists, however, that a knowledge of God through 'His shadow,' that is, through His 'handiwork,' is an inferior though acceptable way of knowing God and of His existence.[41]

The seeming contradiction implied in the second definition of God which declares that the visible (physical) universe is God (or divine), while the first definition had defined God as 'pure and transcendent mind,' can be satisfactorily resolved if we were to assume that Aristotle is actually referring here to two different kinds of 'divinity.'[42] One divinity, the 'lesser' divinity or the universe—the 'visible God'—would have to be 'derived' from the other or 'superior' divinity (the νοῦς) and would have to remain wholly dependent upon the latter. Nor would there be a real contradiction if we were to surmise that in the *On Philosophy* Aristotle distinguishes between a 'Supreme God'—the νοῦς —Who is the true θεός, and a 'divine universe,' that is, a deathless, everlasting, ever-moving and unitary universe which transcends the limitations and imperfections of mere human or earthly existence. In the general Greek tradition, such a universe would be θεῖον,[43] but not θεός. The whole problem of the second definition of God, then, may be

satisfactorily resolved as follows: Philo of Alexandria points out that
'Aristotle was surely speaking piously and reverently when he insisted
that the universe is uncreated and imperishable [*scil.*, "divine"], and
when he charged with serious ungodliness those people [*scil.*, the
Atomists] who maintained . . . that [the universe] is no better than
the work of man's hands. . . .'[44] In other words, the visible universe,
being the 'visible God' or the 'reflection' of the invisible God (the
νοῦς), must itself be perfect and, hence, divine—that is, infinitely superior to man-made, imperfect and perishable human artifacts. This seems
to be the most persuasive answer to the problems raised by the second
definition. Hence, it appears that only the deliberate ill-will displayed
by the Epicurean Velleius could, in this instance, charge Aristotle with
flagrant inconsistency.

The third definition, namely, that God or 'the divine' is really 'some
other ruler over the [divine] universe, to whom he [*scil.*, Aristotle]
attributes the power of guiding and maintaining the movements of
this [divine] universe by means of a kind of "reverse motion"'
(*alium quendam [deum] preficit mondo eique eas partes tribuit ut replicatione
quadam mundi motum regat atque tueatur*), has been the subject of many
learned discussions as well as the object of many conflicting interpretations. The concept of a 'reverse motion' (*replicatio*), in particular,
seems to have disturbed and confused several scholars. H. Cherniss[45] has
summarized the several possible interpretations of this *replicatio*: (i) it
might refer to the concept of ἀνείλιξις (reversal) mentioned in Plato's
*Statesman*;[46] (ii) it might, on the other hand, refer to the motion or
ecliptic of the stars or planets, that is, to the diurnal motion in which the
sphere of the fixed stars, identified with the 'Supreme God' or the
'ultimate controlling power,' carries along the planets and thus controls
the motion of the universe by a kind of 'reverse (or, inverse) motion';[47]
or (iii) it might refer to the 'reverse (or, retrograde) motion' of the
planets or of their ecliptic in their relation to the fixed stars.[48]

The first scholar to tackle the involved problem of the *replicatio* was
J. Bernays, who believes that there is an unmistakable allusion to a
'Supreme God' in this Aristotelian passage—a God Who is wholly de-
tached from the physical universe, but Whose task it is to maintain and
govern its orbital movements.[49] This 'Supreme God,' Bernays opines,
is in fact the Unmoved Mover of Aristotle's later doctrinal works.[50]
Similar views were entertained by W. Jaeger, who insists that 'the God
to Whom the world is subordinated is the transcendental Unmoved
Mover, who guides the world as its final cause, by reason of the
perfection of his pure thought.'[51] Jaeger's thesis was rejected by H. von

Arnim who, among others, maintains that one may speak of a 'reverse motion' only in connection with the orbits of the several planets. Von Arnim contends that viewed from the sphere of the fixed stars, these planets appear to move 'backward.' The mover, who is accountable for this 'reverse motion,' however, is merely the 'mover of the planets,' but never the 'mover of the sphere of the fixed stars,' and most certainly not the 'mover of the whole universe' or, as Jaeger would have it, the Unmoved Mover. This 'mover of the planets,' von Arnim continues, is the 'ether' (or something that consists of 'ether') and, hence, something that moves itself.[52] J. Bidez likewise disagrees with Jaeger when he maintains that the 'ether' is divine because of the stars and, especially, because of the 'first heaven' or the sphere of the fixed stars.[53] Finally, A. J. Festugière believes that Velleius is referring here only to the sphere of the fixed stars, which he identifies with the *cosmos* as well as with the 'ether.'[54] Festugière, then, on the whole seems to concur with the view held by J. Bidez.

In the opinion of the majority of scholars, Aristotle does not explicitly introduce the notion or concept of an Unmoved Mover into his *On Philosophy*. Nevertheless, it is conceded that this concept is not entirely alien to, or perhaps incompatible with, the *On Philosophy*,[55] something which J. Bernays and W. Jaeger had already observed. W. D. Ross plainly hesitates to decide whether Aristotle is speaking of a transcendent (Unmoved) Mover of the universe, or whether he is simply referring to a self-moving divine universe. Ross believes that Cicero's text indicates that in the *On Philosophy* Aristotle enumerates several possible hypotheses as to the nature of the cosmic deity without, however, advocating a single ultimate definition.[56] W. K. C. Guthrie, who seems to have likewise decided on an 'intermediary' course between the views held by Jaeger (and J. Bernays) and the position taken by von Arnim, is of the opinion that in the *On Philosophy* Aristotle does not commit himself to a final definition of the divine. Hence, Guthrie continues, Aristotle is forced to limit himself to several tentative suggestions, without, however, trying to give preference to any one of these suggestions, or to reconcile them mutually. Guthrie concludes that in the *On Philosophy* Aristotle does not—and in view of the 'animated stars' cannot—postulate an Unmoved Mover, although the ultimate necessity of postulating such an Unmoved Mover is already apparent or, in any event, would be quite compatible with the fundamental tenor of the *On Philosophy*.[57] If Guthrie's acute analysis and interpretation should prevail, namely, that in the *On Philosophy* Aristotle does not wish to commit himself, or give preference, to a single and final definition, then we might also appreciate Velleius' insistence that Aristotle is a confused and inconsistent author.

Those scholars who, like J. Bernays, W. Jaeger, H. Cherniss, W. Theiler,[58] E. Berti,[59] M. Untersteiner[60] and others, maintain that in the *On Philosophy* Aristotle hit upon the notion of an Unmoved Mover, seem to rely primarily upon the *Scholia in Prov. Salomonis*,[61] which refers to 'something common that unites [the many], and this is the first principle.' More recently, J. Pépin, who aligns himself with H. von Arnim, W. K. C. Guthrie, J. Moreau, J. Bidez and A. J. Festugière, has denied, however, that Aristotle introduced the concept of an Un- moved Mover into his *On Philosophy*.[62] Pépin points out that the expres- sion '*quietus et beatus*,' which has been used to prove that the *On Philosophy* refers to the Unmoved Mover, can also be found in Aris- totle, *Metaphysics* 1074 b 29, in the *De Caelo* 284 a 15-17, and in *Epinomis* 985A.[63] Hence, Pépin is of the opinion that this expression does not refer to an Unmoved Mover but is simply part of late Platon- ism. Pépin, it will be noted, bases his view on Cicero, *De Natura Deorum* II. 16. 44,[64] where we are told: 'Nor can it be said that some greater force makes the stars move contrary to nature. For what power could be greater? What remains, then, is that the movement of the stars is voluntary.'[65] This statement, Pépin believes, definitely excludes the assumption of an Unmoved Mover who would 'interfere' with the 'voluntary' or spontaneous movement of the divine stars. Moreover, according to *Epinomis* 982BC, no compulsion is greater than that of the stellar soul, which has no peer. Conversely, one may argue against Pépin, that Cicero, *De Natura Deorum* II. 16. 44, merely suggests that the divine stars cannot move 'contrary to their nature,'[66] and that the effect which an Unmoved Mover has upon the stars would not be contrary to 'their nature.' *Epinomis* 982BC—and it is held here that this work is later than the *On Philosophy*—insists that there is nothing 'above' the stellar souls and that there cannot be a necessity that is greater than that of these stellar souls. This statement might very well be a rebuke of Aristotle who in the *On Philosophy* claimed that there is an Unmoved Mover—a necessity or force that is 'above' that of the stellar souls.[67]

In a lengthy and searching analysis of our problem, H. Cherniss demonstrates that within the cosmology advanced in the *On Philos- sophy*, a 'primary movement' of the 'first heaven' (or, 'outer sphere') apparently parallels a 'secondary movement' of the planets.[68] Cherniss suggests that if the 'reverse motion' or *replicatio* is in fact this 'secondary movement,' then we might actually have here a thesis quite similar to that referred to in Book XII of the *Metaphysics*.[69] It might therefore be presumed, Cherniss concludes, that in the *On Philosophy* Aristotle calls 'divine' not only the universe (or, the heavens, the outer perisphere or the 'ether'), but also the five elements (or 'substances').[70] Cherniss furthermore conjectures that, although the νοῦς is certainly the 'supreme deity,' there exists at least one other deity which directs—or is responsible for—the 'reverse motion' of the planets.[71]

These scholarly discussions and disagreements, it seems, have contributed much to a better understanding of Aristotle's third definition of God as 'some other ruler over the [divine] universe, to whom he [*scil.*, Aristotle] attributes the power of guiding and maintaining the movements of this [divine] universe by means of a kind of "reverse motion".' As regards the *replicatio quaedam*—this 'sort of reverse motion'—it is by no means decided whether this particular motion is identical with, or related to, Plato's concept of the ἀνείλιξις.[72] E. Berti, who in this might be under the influence of H. Cherniss, offers what seems to be a reasonable though by no means final solution to this confusing problem.[73] He suggests that viewed from one particular rotation or orbit, any other rotation or orbit always appears to be a 'reverse (or contrary) motion.' Hence he concludes that there is something akin to an 'inverse relation' between the movements of the fixed stars, which is 'primary motion,' and the movements of the planets, which is actually 'secondary motion.' Only the movement of the planets may be called a 'kind of reverse motion,' provided the latter is viewed in its relation to the fixed stars and their movement.[74] This thesis raises the further question as to what causes this 'reverse motion.' Berti believes that this cause might be either the sphere of the fixed stars itself[75] or perhaps a 'separate (and lesser) deity.'[76] Since Cicero unmistakably speaks of 'some other "ruler"' [who governs the universe]' (*alium quendam [deum] preficit mundo*), Berti is of the opinion that this 'other ruler' or this 'other deity' cannot be the 'pure mind' (νοῦς) or the deity which is identical with the universe itself. This 'other ruler' is charged with 'guiding and maintaining the movements of the planetary system by a kind of reverse motion.' Hence, Berti observes, this particular deity must also be distinguished from the divine universe as well as from the heavens of the fixed stars.[77] Naturally, there always exists the possibility that the Latin term *replicatio*, as it is used by Velleius (Cicero), simply signifies 'circular motion.' For all circular motion, in a certain sense, always 'returns' or 'reverses itself.' Such an explanation, then, would resolve all or almost all of the difficulties inherent in the vexing problem of the *replicatio*. Perhaps a remote solution of our problem may also be found in Plato, *Laws* 896DE, where we are informed that 'we must not suppose that there are less than two [cosmic] souls, one being the author of the good, the other the author or principle of evil.' For, according to Plato, *Theaetetus* 176A, 'there must always be something antagonistic to the good.' It is perhaps here that we must look for the likely origin as well as for the possible solution of the puzzling problem of the *replicatio* and the 'dualism' it presupposes. The additional possibility that this particular 'dualism' may ultimately be traced back to Zoroastrian teachings, or that it may have been stimulated by Zoroastrian notions, has already been mentioned.

The fourth definition identifies God with 'ether' or 'fiery ether' (*caeli ardor*).[78] Aristotle believed that, in order to establish and maintain the proper balance among the several elements (or 'essences') as well as among the several stars, the heavens must be filled with an element which is fundamentally different from the four traditional basic elements.[79] This particular element, also called the 'primary body,' is seen as an unchangeable quality.[80] It is 'something else beyond earth, fire, air and water.' Men 'give the highest place a name of its own, namely, "ether," which term is derived from the fact that "it runs always" (ἀεὶ θεῖν).'[81] Hence, this 'ether' exists above all the changeable elements; it is divine or, better, the 'divine' (θεῖος) or 'immutable' within the corporeal world,[82] which is made up of changing elements.[83] It is not surprising, therefore, that Velleius should call the 'ether' divine, since 'ether' not only is that unchanging (θεῖος) element which constitutes the divine stars but also is the most sublime part of the physical universe itself[84]—that part of the universe which, in the final analysis, is the abode of the 'Supreme God' and as such reveals the existence of the 'Supreme God.'[85] Assuming that this definition in fact may be traced back to Aristotle's *On Philosophy*, then it must also be conceded that during his association with the Platonic Academy Aristotle had already advanced the theory of a fifth (divine) element. It would be safe to surmise, therefore, that this theory was discussed (and probably accepted) by some members of the Academy (and, perhaps, by Plato himself), as may be gathered from the *Epinomis*.[86]

From these four definitions of God or of the divine, we might infer that Aristotle actually advanced two major concepts: that of a 'cosmic God' (*deus-mundus*), who is the universe itself or, at least, that 'all-embracing, fiery substance or element which surrounds and enfolds the universe';[87] and that of a 'Supreme God,' Who transcends the universe and is Himself 'pure mind' (νοῦς, *deus-mens*) as well as perhaps the Unmoved Mover (or Self-Moving Mover?) of this universe. One might speculate here still further: the 'cosmic God' or *deus-mundus*, at least for Aristotle, might be 'God Incarnate' or the 'visible Supreme God.' This could be inferred from Philo of Alexandria, *De Aeternitate Mundi* III. 10–11, where Philo, apparently referring to the *On Philosophy*, insists that 'Aristotle was surely speaking piously and devoutly when he maintained that the universe is uncreated and imperishable, and when he charged with serious godlessness those people who ... thought that the great visible God, Who contains in truth the sun and the moon and the remaining pantheon of the planets and fixed stars, is no better than an artifact of men's hands. ...'[88] The Unmoved (or Self-Moving ?) Mover, Who might already have been alluded to in the *On Philosophy*, would be the single final cause of all motion—of all that transpires in this universe. It is identified with the 'Supreme God' or highest Entity. He is *sine corpore, quietus et beatus* and, hence, identical with the νοῦς: He is the νοῦς or 'pure Mind.' If this is so, then the 'Supreme God' also influences the universe, including the 'cosmic God' and any other god or gods, as their ultimate and objective final cause. The 'cosmic God' is mentioned in the second and fourth definitions, and the 'Supreme God' is referred to in the first and third definitions. Since the 'cosmic God' is always subordinate to the 'Supreme God,' Aristotle's four definitions of the deity do not necessarily pre-suppose the kind of 'divine dualism' or pluralism[89] with which the Epicurean Velleius (and some modern scholars) have tried to charge him.

The first objection made by Velleius is that in calling God 'ether' Aristotle 'loses sight of the fact that the heavens [or, the "ether"] themselves are part of that universe which, in another passage [to wit, in the second definition] he himself had proclaimed to be God.' This objection, however, is based on the false assumption that to assert the divinity of the whole universe and, at the same time, to call divine a mere part or element of this self-same universe, creates two distinct deities of apparently equal rank.[90] This is an assumption one might expect from an 'atomistic' Epicurean. The impasse might fully be resolved if we were to assume that Aristotle called the universe θεός (the 'visible God'), while he referred to the 'ether' as θεῖον, a basic distinction, the far-reaching import of which seems to have escaped Cicero (Velleius), who rendered both terms simply as *deus*. This impasse might also be resolved if one were to concede that Aristotle referred to the universe as well as to the 'ether' as θεῖον without, however, calling either of them θεός. The assertion of a plurality of 'things divine,' needless to say, would not itself result in a theological pluralism or conflict as Cicero (Velleius) alleges.

In order to appreciate the remaining five objections, we must bear in mind that, as has already been shown, Aristotle probably proposed a fifth definition of the deity (or the 'divine') which is not expressly mentioned among the definitions enumerated by Velleius. This fifth definition is the identification of the deity with the stars[91] or the stellar gods. According to Cicero, *De Natura Deorum* II. 15. 42–16. 44,[92] a passage generally considered a 'fragment' of Book III of the *On Philosophy*,[93] the Stagirite maintains that

it is nonsense to assume that no animate being should be born in that element [*scil.*, the 'ether'],[94] which of all other elements is the one most perfectly equipped (or qualified) for the production of animate beings.[95] But the heavenly bodies have their abode in the ethereal sphere (or, in the 'ether'), which, being of the subtlest texture, is always in a state of vigorous motion. Thus, any living being born in this sphere, will possess the most acute sensibilities, and will move with incredible swiftness.[96] Since the heavenly bodies are born in the ethereal sphere, we may reasonably assume that they are endowed with sensibility and with intelligence.[97] Hence they must be considered to be among the number of gods. ... It is also quite possible that an intelligence of the highest order is to be found in the heavenly bodies, the more so, since they dwell in that part of the universe where the ether reigns supreme,[98] and since they are nourished by the exhalations from sea and land, rarified (or, purified) by their long journey across the vast interspace. Moreover, the systematic and regular movement of the stars furnishes the most convincing proof that these stars are animate and intelligent beings.[99] Methodical and consistent motion presupposes a plan[100] wherein there is no element of chance, change or accident.[101] Now, the orderly and eternally consistent orbit of the heavenly bodies, being in the highest degree intelligent, suggests neither mere natural forces nor accident, which loves variety and abhors consistency. It follows, therefore, that those [heavenly] bodies move of their own will, and because they are endowed with sense and are divine.[102] And surely, Aristotle deserves our praise for his theory[103] that all things which move are impelled either by nature, by some extrinsic force or by their own will.[104] Now the sun, the moon and all the stars [Aristotle says] are in motion. But things which move by nature are carried downward by reason of their weight, or upward by reason of their lightness.[105] But he [*scil.*, Aristotle] reminds us that the

heavenly bodies do not move in either of these two ways, their
motion being circular and orbital. And it certainly cannot be
maintained that they are compelled by some mightier power to
follow a course which is against their nature.[106] For what power is
mightier than they? We must, therefore, concede that the motions
of the heavenly bodies are voluntary.[107] Any man who realizes
all this and still denies the existence of gods, lays himself open to
to the charge not only of ignorance, but also to that of blasphemy.

Thus far Cicero. The divine or imperishable stars, then, are a complex
of soul (mind) and body, their body being the fifth element or essence,
that is, 'ether.' They possess both intelligence and free will.

In the *On Philosophy* Aristotle probably also discussed at some length
the theory that living beings exist in each and every element,[108]
including in the 'ether.' Since it can be shown, according to Aristotle,
that living creatures are to be found in earth, water, air and fire,[109] there
must also exist living beings in the fifth element, the 'ether'—namely,
the stars. In other words, since all the other elements contain life, the
'ether,' too, must contain life. From this it follows, at least for Aristotle
(?), that the visible stars must be living beings. In keeping with the
fineness and mobility of the 'ether,' these living beings—the stars—
must be of the highest intelligence. This fact is confirmed by the inviolability of the orderliness and regularity that is characteristic of their
perpetual orbital motions. All this, in turn, indicates that they behave
like, or better, are, conscious, rational (or intelligent) beings endowed
with free will. Hence, they cannot simply be the product of 'physical
nature,' because 'physical nature' does not act like a rational being
endowed with free will. Neither can they be the result of mere chance,
because chance vitiates constancy and design and, hence, predictability.
But if the motions of the stars are constant, their movements must be the
result of conscious intent, of an inner purpose and of free will. In brief,
the order and constancy of the stars and their movements, Aristotle
argues, imply reason, purpose and free will. The circularity of these
motions at the same time presupposes free will, which overcomes, or
counteracts, the 'natural' forces compelling all inanimate bodies to
move upwards or downwards in a rectilinear path.[110]

The second objection made by Velleius reads as follows: 'How could
this "divine mind" (or divine "sense"—*sensus*), which is identified with
the heavens, possibly endure and always remain the same—and keep
its senses—in the unimaginable speed of the rotating heavens?' This
objection not only poses numerous involved problems, but also has

become the subject of many scholarly discussions and disagreements. Presumably, all these problems can be satisfactorily resolved with the help of Cicero, *De Natura Deorum* II. 15. 42–4.[111] Anticipating the fourth, fifth and sixth objections, Velleius surreptitiously identifies the transcendent God or *deus-mens*,[112] the νοῦς (or the God Who is 'pure Intellect'), with the 'cosmic God,' the 'divine universe' or *deus-mundus*. Moreover, Velleius' criticism, it will be noted, is directed not at the *deus-mens*, but rather at the god or deity which is the author of, or is responsible for, the 'reverse motion' (*replicatio*).[113] We might answer Velleius' objections by pointing out that, according to Aristotle, the belief in a God Who is pure intellect (*deus-mens*) does not necessarily exclude the belief in the existence of (lesser) stellar gods.[114] The Judeo-Christian belief in God and in the existence of God, for instance, does not exclude the belief in angels or in the existence of angels. And angels, in the parlance of Aristotle, are 'divine,' that is, not subject to death and the natural incidents of terrestrial life, although they are never 'gods.' As Cicero, *De Natura Deorum* II. 15. 42–4, has shown, these stellar gods, but not the *deus-mens*, aside from intelligence and free will, have senses and sensations,[115] as well as a body. Thus, Velleius' objection is invalid, provided we are willing to concede that the *deus-mens* is substantially different not only from the *deus-mundus* or from the 'stellar gods,' but also from the 'god' which is the heavens, from the 'god' which is the universe, from the 'god' which is identified with the 'ether,' and from the 'god' which causes the *replicatio*.[116] In the light of Aristotle's basic religious or theological convictions, such an admission is more than reasonable.[117]

The third objection of Velleius, namely, 'what becomes of the many [stellar ?] gods, if we were to call the heavens God,' likewise anticipates the fourth, fifth and sixth objections. In the fourth objection, as shall be shown presently, we are told that if 'God is without a [physical] body and without corporeal elements,' then God is also 'without all sense and sensations, including wisdom (*prudentia*).' The fifth objection queries: 'How is it possible that the universe moves, if it is without body and without corporeal elements?' And the sixth objection raises the issue of 'how, if it is actually moving itself, can this [divine] universe ever attain to calm serenity and true happiness?' Obviously, according to Aristotle, the *deus-mens* is never simply the heavens, the 'ether,' the stellar gods or the universe. Hence, the notion of a *deus-mens* does not, and cannot, conflict with the notion of stellar gods, of a divine universe, or that of the divine heavens. Perhaps the most satisfactory solution of our problem is the following: the hypothesis that the 'ether' is god (or divine) leads to the complementary hypothesis that the stars, too, are gods, or at least divine. In the astral theology of the late Plato and in that of the *Epinomis*, God—the *deus-mens* of Aristotle—is in fact the οὐσία of the heavens as well as that of the stars and the stellar gods. For Aristotle, the 'ether' is 'god' (or divine) and, at the same time, the 'substance' or element (or 'essence') of the stellar gods or divine stars.[118] In other words, since the stellar gods or divine stars are 'ether,' they 'participate' in the 'divinity' of the 'ether,' which is also god[119] or, perhaps better, the 'visible God'[120] or the manifestation of the *deus-mens*. But the *deus-mundus* is never the *deus-mens*. It is the *deus-mens* Who becomes visible in a variety of divine manifestations, collectively referred to as *deus-mundus*, without, however, abdicating from, or sharing with the *deus-mundus*, His preferred position as the 'Supreme God.' These multiple and varied manifestations of the *deus-mens*—the heavens, the 'ether,' the stars (or stellar gods) and the universe in general—do not necessarily conflict with one another, nor do they mutually exclude each other. For it is surely permissible to call the heavens divine (or the 'visible God') and, at the same time, refer to the stars or the 'ether' as divine (or as the 'visible God'). In other words, the whole visible universe no less than such parts of the universe as the heavens, the stars or the 'ether' are divine, that is, 'visible aspects' of one and the same invisible *deus-mens* or 'Supreme God.'

The fourth objection, that 'when Aristotle asserts that God is without body and corporeal elements, he actually deprives God of all senses and sensations, including wisdom (*prudentia*),' sees a conflict between the first definition—God is 'only "Mind," and "Mind" only'—and the fourth definition—God 'is the "ether" in the heavens,' that is, corporeal matter. Obviously, the ἀσώματος God is the *deus-mens*, the 'pure Intellect' or 'Mind' or νοῦς,[121] in short, the 'Supreme God.' As such, Aristotle believes, He is and must be devoid of all senses and sensations,[122] including *prudentia*, provided this *prudentia* is the later Aristotelian φρόνησις and not, perchance, the Platonic σοφία.[123] The stellar gods or divine stars, on the other hand, are endowed with senses and sensations:[124] they are visible and, hence, must be corporeal; and they have, according to Aristotle, conscious intent as well as an inner purpose.[125] Thus, Aristotle assumes, they are not ἀσώματος and, in consequence, cannot be pure νοῦς. Aristotle would involve himself in a most serious contradiction, however, if he were to identify or confuse the ἀσώματος 'invisible Supreme God' with His visible manifestations or with the 'visible God'—if he were to identify or confuse, as Velleius implies, the ἀσώματος *deus-mens* with the corporeal stellar gods or, perhaps, with the 'ether' or the equally corporeal (and visible) *deus-mundus*. Despite Velleius' assertion, which undoubtedly is prompted by an uncritical anti-Aristotelian animus, there is, however, no indication that Aristotle actually falls victim to such a confusion or contradiction.

The fifth and sixth objections read as follows: 'How is it possible that the universe moves, if it is without a body (ἀσώματος—*carens corpore*), and how, if it is actually moving itself constantly, can this universe ever attain to calm serenity and true happiness?' These two objections seem to 'juggle' those definitions which call God 'pure Mind' and, hence, ἀσώματος (first definition) or the First (Unmoved?) Mover (third definition), and those definitions which identify God with the universe (second definition) and with 'ether' (fourth definition), that is, which declare God to be 'corporeal' (*deus-mundus*) and, therefore, in perpetual though perfect motion. On the strength of certain (intentional?) equivocations, Velleius contrasts two basic alternatives, both of which seem to imply some irreconcilable contradictions.[126] First, if the (divine) universe is ἀσώματος, how is it possible that it moves; and secondly, if the (divine) universe is in constant motion, how can it possibly be serene and happy?[127] These apparent contradictions can be satisfactorily resolved if we bear in mind that Aristotle proposes two distinct notions or concepts of the divine: the *deus-mens*, Who is the incorporeal and completely serene and perfectly happy First (or Unmoved?) Mover, and the *deus-mundus*, who is the eternally moving (or, eternally moved?) corporeal universe.[128] The mere fact that Aristotle calls divine the eternally moving corporeal universe does not mean, however, that he also identifies or equivocates the *deus-mundus* and the *deus-mens*, as the Epicurean Velleius would have us believe.[129] Finally, we must always bear in mind that in Greek philosophy the term 'divine' often signifies merely something which is not subject to ordinary generation or corruption—something which is above the vicissitudes of ordinary life and ordinary existence. In short, Velleius' arguments and objections would suggest that in the *On Philosophy* Aristotle refers to at least two distinct concepts of God or of the divine, namely, the 'invisible God' and the 'visible God' or manifestation of the 'invisible God.' The fact is, however, that only one of these concepts signifies the 'pure Intellect' or νοῦς. This 'pure intellect,' which is perhaps the Unmoved Mover or the First Mover of Aristotle's later works,[130] in all likelihood is the God (the 'Supreme God') of Aristotle or, at least the God or 'Supreme God' of the Aristotelian *On Philosophy*.

The fifth and sixth objections, it has already been suggested, might imply that in the *On Philosophy* Aristotle alluded to a transcendent Unmoved Mover (Whom he calls 'pure Intellect' or νοῦς), or, at least, that he was very close to such a notion.[131] This may be gathered from Aristotle's *Physics*, where the Stagirite insists that the expression, 'that for the sake of which,' has two distinct meanings, 'and the distinction is made in our work entitled *On Philosophy*.'[132] If, then, the universe, including the divine 'ether' and the divine stars, in brief, the 'visible God' (*deus-mundus*), is and exists for the sake of the invisible Supreme God (νοῦς, or *deus-mens*)—something which might be inferred from the whole tenor of Book III of the *On Philosophy*—then this 'visible God' is definitely subordinate to the invisible Supreme God. More than that: the visible God has its final (and efficient) cause in the invisible Supreme God. It will also be remembered that in the *Metaphysics* Aristotle maintains that a 'final cause may exist among unchangeable things. This is shown by the distinction of its meanings. For a final cause is something for the good of which an action is done, or something at which the action aims. And of these two, the latter exists among unchangeable beings, though the former does not.'[133] The doctrine of the Unmoved Mover is here upheld by showing that an unmoved being, as a divine being, can be the final cause of action—for the movements of the divine (imperishable) stars, of the heavens and of the 'ether.' The concept of an ultimate cause, that is, of a 'teleological Unmoved Mover,' is, therefore, at least implied in the *On Philosophy*. In any event, it does seem to be compatible with the basic tenor and spirit of the *On Philosophy*. Hence, W. Jaeger's view, after all, seems to be the correct one,[134] especially since this ultimate cause can surely be identified with the 'Supreme Being' or 'Supreme God.'[135] This divine 'Supreme Being,' which is ἀσώματος, *quietus et beatus*, in brief, which is identified with νοῦς, moves the entire universe as the ultimate (final) cause of the latter,[136] without being itself moved and without moving. The argument that the *deus-mens* constitutes the true God of the *On Philosophy* receives additional support from Aristotle's *On Prayer*.[137] Here the Stagirite states unequivocally that 'God is Mind (νοῦς) as well as something beyond (the human?) mind.'[138] In this significant passage, Aristotle identifies God with 'mind,' that is, with the 'pure intellect' or *actus purus* (the 'Mind of minds'), which transcends sensibility, prudence or wisdom. In this manner, Aristotle not only stresses the 'pure spirituality' of God, but also emphasizes that in a certain way God already transcends the 'pure intellect' or 'mind' and, concomitantly, the 'divine universe' and the human intellect.[139]

191

Velleius' observations in his sixth objection that, if God is actually moving Himself, He cannot possibly attain serenity and perfect happiness, unquestionably refers to the Epicurean ideal of 'happiness through serenity.'[140] And serenity, according to Epicurus, presupposes 'rest.' Aristotle himself admits that the life of the deity, if subjected to eternal and enforced motion, would be an unhappy life, lacking serenity.[141] The reference to 'serenity' (*quietus*) in Cicero's report might, in fact, imply that Aristotle has in mind the perfectly serene and, hence, perfectly happy Unmoved Mover, Who moves everything else as its final cause without Himself moving (or being moved). We also know from the Aristotelian *Metaphysics* that if 'thought is not the act of thinking [that is, pure thought], but merely a potency, it would be reasonable to surmise that the continuity of its thinking must be wearisome to it.'[142]

The several contradictions which Velleius believes to have detected in the definitions of God or the divine proposed by Aristotle, we may inject here, refer not merely to certain doctrinal disagreement between Aristotle and the Epicureans, but might also point to an incompleteness or possible inconsistency within Aristotle's own thought as he tries to express it in the *On Philosophy*.[143] This inconsistency, provided it actually exists, probably has its root in Aristotle's attempt to enumerate and discuss several concepts and definitions of God or of the divine without, however, completely integrating them, or without committing himself to one single concept or definition. This might be inferred from Cicero's statement that in the *On Philosophy* Aristotle 'submits a disjointed jumble of theories.' It may also reflect the possibility that in the *On Philosophy*, which after all was a dialogue, several interlocutors vented their widely divergent and seriously conflicting views on theological issues, some of which Aristotle rejected outright. This fact might have escaped the uncritical Velleius, or Velleius might have maliciously imputed to Aristotle certain statements made by other interlocutors with whom Aristotle disagreed. Finally, this alleged inconsistency might also reflect the different and often conflicting views about the nature of God or of the divine which were entertained (and debated) within the Academy. Aristotle's procedure of stating the several concepts of God or of the divine discussed in the *On Philosophy* and debated in the Academy obviously made it rather easy for Velleius to criticize the Stagirite and charge him with flagrant inconsistencies. It may be taken for granted that an Epicurean such as Velleius, a persistent and embittered detractor of Aristotle, would not pass up such an opportunity. He would be further encouraged if he could suppress the fact that these divergent and apparently conflicting views originally had been stated in a purely tentative or hypothetical form; that they had been listed without any attempt mutually to reconcile or critically to evaluate them; that in all likelihood they contain the suggestions made by different discussants disagreeing with one another; and that they might well be a spectrum of certain theological debates among the members of the Academy.

In conclusion, it may be pointed out that in his *On Philosophy* Aristotle probably enumerated several definitions of God or of the divine. Needless to say, the fact that Aristotle calls something 'divine' ($\vartheta\epsilon\hat{\iota}o\nu$) does not necessarily make it 'God' ($\dot{o}\ \vartheta\epsilon\dot{o}s$) for Aristotle. It is quite possible, however, that in keeping with his habit of paraphrasing the ideas expressed by others Cicero (or his source) confuses 'divine' and 'God,' and that he translates $\vartheta\epsilon\hat{\iota}o\nu$ and $\dot{o}\ \vartheta\epsilon\dot{o}s$ simply as *deus*. The Greek term 'divine,' and frequently also the Greek word 'God,' as has been shown, originally meant something 'first and foremost,' something which 'is more than human, not subject to death, everlasting.'[144] Hence, the first major problem raised by Cicero's report is whether Aristotle defines God as the universe, the 'ether' or the stars, or whether he refers to them only as being 'divine,' that is, 'more than human, not subject to death, everlasting.' In the latter case, the *voῦs* alone would be the sole true God—the 'Supreme God,' while all other 'divine things,' through which this 'Supreme God' or *deus-mens* manifests Himself, are infinitely inferior and eternally subordinate to Him, although, measured by the inadequacies of the human condition, these 'things' are still 'divine.' The second major problem raised by the Ciceronian text is whether the *voῦs* of the *On Philosophy* is, or approximates, the Unmoved Mover or the First Mover of Aristotle's later doctrinal works. Although the surviving evidence in Cicero's *De Natura Deorum* I. 13. 33 is extremely scanty, the statement, *quo modo semper se movens [divinus mundus] esse quietus et beatus*, suggests the hypothesis of an Unmoved (*quietus*) Mover. In brief, the fact that Velleius (Cicero) specifically contrasts a moving universe with something unmoved (*quietus*) suggests that in the *On Philosophy* Aristotle already strikes upon the notion of an Unmoved Mover. In the light of our scanty and probably garbled evidence, however, this remains at best reasonable hypothesis.[145]

# Chapter XV

# The Doctrine of the Soul in Aristotle's *On Philosophy*★

The reconstruction and interpretation of the particular psychology advanced by Aristotle in his lost dialogue *On Philosophy*—a doctrine which in its method and aim differs somewhat from the psychology expounded in Aristotle's *Eudemus or On the Soul*[1] and most certainly from that advocated in his *De Anima*—relies on four extensive fragments, excerpts or doxographical reports found in Cicero,[2] a rather scanty and relatively uninformative fragment from (Pseudo- ?) Clement of Rome,[3] and a somewhat confused fragment from Psellus.[4] These fragments, which have been assigned to Aristotle's *On Philosophy* by the majority of scholars, present what seems to be a unique doctrine of the soul. According to this doctrine, it appears that the soul has a special nature which sets it apart from the four (or five) traditional (material) elements or substances: the soul possesses an 'intellectual' ('spiritual' ?) or, at least, a 'non-material' nature of its own which is similar to, if not identical with, the nature of the 'divine.' Hence, provided these fragments accurately relate Aristotle's early views on the nature of the soul as he expressed them in the *On Philosophy* (there exists no valid reason why we should reject these fragments as either spurious or as inadequately or faultily reported), then at one time in his philosophic development Aristotle apparently advocated (i) the 'pure intellectuality' ('spirituality'?) or 'non-material' ('spiritual'?) nature of the soul (or something close to a 'spiritual nature'); (ii) the substantiality of the soul; (iii) the individuality of the soul; (iv) the (personal) immortality of the individual soul; (v) the independence of the soul from the material world; (vi) the superiority of the soul over the material (corporeal) world; and (vii) the co-naturality (or co-substantiality) of man's soul with the divine (or with God). The views advanced here are so startling and, indeed, differ so much from what Aristotle says about the soul in the *De Anima* (and in the *Eudemus*), that they call for a detailed investigation and explanation.

In *Academica* I. 7. 26, Cicero observes that Aristotle had declared

air . . ., fire, water and earth to be the primary elements. From
these spring the forms of animals and of the fruits of the earth.
Therefore these are also called first principles and, to translate
from the Greek, 'elements' (*elementa*). Of them, air and fire have
the power of producing movement and causing change, while the
role of the others—water and earth—is to receive and, as it were,
to suffer. The fifth kind, from which were derived the stars and
souls (minds, intellects, *mentes*), Aristotle thought to be something
distinct (or unique) and unlike the four elements I have mentioned
above.

In *Tusculanae Disputationes* I. 10. 22, Cicero observes that Aristotle,

after taking account of the four well-known classes of first
principles (elements) from which all things are derived, considers
that there is a fifth kind of 'nature,' from which comes 'mind' or
'intellect' (*quintam quandam naturam . . . e qua sit mens*). For
thought, foresight, learning and teaching, discovery, the riches
of memory, love and hate, desire and fear, distress and joy, these
and their like, he believes, cannot be included in any of the four
classes. Hence he adds a fifth, nameless (*vacans nomine*) class, and so
calls the mind or soul (*animum*) itself by the new name of *endelecheia*, as being a continuous and endless movement.

In *Tusculanae Disputiones* I. 17. 41, Cicero reports that 'the mind or
soul (*animus*) . . . is a fifth nature, which is without name but well
understood'; and *ibid.*, I. 26. 65–27. 66, he tells the reader:

But if there is a certain fifth nature, first introduced by Aristotle,
then this is the nature of both gods and minds or souls (*animorum*).
By following this view we have expressed it in these very words in
our *Consolatio*: 'The origin of minds or souls (*animorum*) is not to
be found on earth. For in mind or souls there is nothing mixed or
composite, nothing that seems to be born or fashioned of earth,
nothing even resembling water, air or fire. For in these natures
[*scil.*, earth, water, air or fire] there is nothing which has the power
of memory, intellect (*mens*) and thought (*cognitio*), which retains the
past, foresees the future and can grasp the present—for these alone
are living (divine, *divina*) powers—nor will it ever be discovered
whence these can come to man, except from God.' There is, therefore, a singular nature and power of the mind or soul, wholly
separate from these traditional and well-known natures. Thus,
whatever it is that feels, knows, lives or thrives, it must be celestial

and divine and, hence, eternal. Nor can God, Whom we know, be otherwise understood than as mind, intellect or soul (*mens*) apart from, free of, and separated from all perishable admixture, maintaining and moving all things, and Himself endowed with perpetual motion. Of this kind [and of the same nature] is the human mind, intellect or soul (*mens*).

(Pseudo-?) Clement of Rome, *Recognitiones* VIII. 15, relates that 'Aristotle introduced a fifth element which he called ἀκατονόμαστον, i.e., unnameable, and in doing so, without doubt, pointed to the being who by uniting the four elements into one made the world.' Michael Psellus, on the other hand, reports that

> according to Plato, all fixed stars and planets have a single and identical substance, which is the most luminous among all substances or elements, while Aristotle speaks of a fifth substance or element. Aristotle does not give a special name to this fifth substance, but calls the whole of the heavens as well as the starry universe a fifth element, because in comparison with the other four elements, the heavens and the starry universe move in a different manner.

E. Bignone,[5] L. Alfonsi,[6] A. J. Festugière[7] and others are of the opinion that these six fragments or 'doxographical reports' definitely refer to Aristotle's *On Philosophy*. K. Reinhardt[8] and G. Luck,[9] on the other hand, deny that these passages—at least those from Cicero's *Academica* and *Tusculanae Disputationes* I. 10. 22—may confidently be credited to the Stagirite.[10] O. Gigon, again, is of the opinion that the fragments from Cicero's *Tusculanae Disputationes* in all likelihood are related to Aristotle's *Eudemus or On the Soul*, rather than to the *On Philosophy*. Gigon also suggests that these fragments might be part of the general Hellenistic tradition (Antiochus of Ascalon ?, or Posidonius of Apamea ?) as regards the earliest Aristotelian teachings concerning psychology as they have been advanced in the so-called 'exoteric' compositions.[11] Hence, this tradition may not accurately relate what Aristotle had in fact said about the soul or about the nature of the soul in the *On Philosophy* (or in the *Eudemus* ?).

What is of particular interest to us in these fragments is the statement that there exists 'a fifth kind of principle [or nature or element],[12] from which were derived the [divine] stars and the souls,' and that Aristotle apparently held the view that this fifth kind of principle or element 'is something unique and distinct from, and unlike, the four [traditional] elements [earth, water, air and fire]. . . .' This fifth element is not, as some scholars have surmised, perhaps the 'ether,'[13] but something analogous to the ϑειότατον ψυχῆς γένος of the *Epinomis* (981BC). Since, according to the Aristotelian *On Prayer*,[14] God is not 'ether' but νοῦς, and νοῦς only; and since we are also told that the human soul is of the same (or of a similar) nature (substance) as the gods or God,[15] it would follow that 'ether' cannot possibly be the substance of the human soul. Moreover, as it will be shown presently, this fifth element or substance is ἀκατονόμαστον (*vacans nomine*, that is, nameless),[16] something which cannot possibly be said about 'ether.' From this fifth element, nature or substance, we are also told, 'comes mind (soul),' inasmuch as 'the origin of mind is not to be found on earth,' that is, is not derived from the four material elements or substances. This is likewise brought out by Philo of Alexandria, who might be under the influence of the *On Philosophy* when he claims that[17]

the soul, whose nature is intellectual and celestial, will depart to a father in the ether, the purest of all substances. For we may suppose that, as the men of old declared, there is a fifth substance or nature, moving in a circle, differing by its superior quality from the four [other elements]. Out of this they thought the stars and the whole of heaven have been made, and they deduced as a natural consequence that the human soul also was a 'fragment' thereof.

From all this it also follows that according to Aristotle's *On Philosophy* the soul is not akin to any of the four basic (material) elements. Hence, it must be non-material and, it may be presumed, 'intellectual' ('spiritual'?, or something close to 'spiritual'). We are also informed that the soul has a nature (or substance) all its own, essentially different from that of all material things: it is neither fire (ether), air, water or earth, nor is it perchance a combination of these material elements. It does not in any way participate in these four material elements, nor does it contain any admixture of these four elements.[18] Moreover, it is not, as is the case in the *De Anima*, a mere 'form' or, perhaps, 'a substance in the sense of the form of a natural (material) body,' which as a form in the order of substance constitutes the first actuality of the matter which it informs.[19] Obviously, according to Cicero, Aristotle also endowed the stars and the (human) soul, the specific substance of which he does not name (ἀκατονόμαστον), with continuous and spontaneous motion (ἐνδελέχεια)—that is, circular and hence continuous as well as perfect motion without end.[20] This circular motion, which is deliberate, is also indicative of the soul's perfection or 'divinity.' Being perfect, this circular motion can never change or cease; and although the soul has free will, because of its perfection it cannot will its own deterioration or destruction through the abandonment of its circular and continuous motion. In this sense, as Plato had already pointed out, the motion of the soul as well as that of the stars (and ultimately, their respective substance) is identical: the continuity of the intellect in its perpetual activities, like that of the soul in general, it appears, is related to the continuity of the soul's circular motion. And the most perfect circular and continuous motion is exemplified by the stars.[21] In any event, due to the fact that the soul is akin to the divine stars, it is also co-substantial with the divine stars or the divine in general in that it shares in the divine as well as in the divine activities.[22] Accordingly, Cicero could rightfully maintain that 'if there is a fifth nature, introduced first by Aristotle, this is the nature of both gods and minds (souls, *animarum*).'[23]

Relying on Aristotle's *On Philosophy*, Cicero reiterates that there is 'a fifth kind of "nature," from which comes mind (soul) . . . a fifth, nameless (ἀκατονόμαστον) class,' that is, a class having nothing in common with the four traditional elements. Hence, Aristotle 'calls the mind or soul itself by the new name of ἐνδελέχεια, as being a continuous and endless motion.'[24] The particular use of the term ἐνδελέχεια is apparent here. Ἐνδελέχεια, which is wholly unrelated to, and must be carefully distinguished from, the term ἐντελέχεια as it is discussed, for instance, in Aristotle's *De Anima*, signifies continuance, constancy or perpetuity. It will also be remembered that in the *Phaedrus* (245CD), Plato had insisted that the soul is self-moving (αὐτοκινήτατος)[25] and, hence, immortal:

> Every soul [Plato maintains in the *Phaedrus* (245CD)] is immortal. For that which is self-moved is immortal. But that which moves another or is moved by another, in ceasing to move (or to be moved), also ceases to live. Only that which is self-moving—that which never relinquishes its hold upon itself—never ceases to be in motion; and only that which is self-moving is also the origin and first principle of movement for everything else that is in motion. But a first principle is unbegotten, for that which is begotten of necessity has a first principle. But a first principle is begotten of nothing. For if it were begotten of something, then it would cease to be a first principle.

In brief, Plato seems to realize that if he were to determine the ultimate cause of change (and motion), he must first determine that which originates, or can originate, movement in itself. And that which can move itself or is capable of originating its own (perfect) motion is the soul. This is also Plato's way of proving the immortality of the soul. In the *Laws*, again, Plato insists that the soul is an essence; that this soul is an 'essence which is defined as something self-moved'; that the soul is 'the first origin and moving force of all that is, or that has become, or that will be' and, therefore, is 'the source of change and motion in all things'; that as such the soul 'is prior to the body' as well as 'the cause of different characters and manners, of wishes and reasonings, of true opinions, rational reflections and recollections'; that the soul is 'the cause of good and evil'; and that the soul 'also orders the heavens.' Plato continues by pointing out that 'that which moves in one place must move about a center,' and is therefore 'most akin and similar to the circular movement of the mind (the rational soul)'; that 'both mind (soul) and the motion, which is in one place, move in the same or like manner, in and about the same, and in relation to the same, and according to one proportion and one order';[26] and that mind (soul) becomes knowable in and by the effects which it has on other things.[27]

It would seem, then, that for Aristotle the concept of continuity or imperishability, as it is expressed in the term ἐνδελέχεια, constitutes a significant and, in conjunction with the notion of rationality (which is implied in the term ἐνδελέχεια), perhaps the most significant attribute of the soul.[28] In other words, the soul lives after the death of the body. This personal immortality is one of the most telling characteristics of the individual soul. Now we may also understand and appreciate why in the *Tusculanae Disputationes* I. 26. 65, Cicero should have referred to his own *Consolatio*:[29] although grieving over the death of his beloved daughter Tullia, Cicero finds comfort and solace in the realization that because of the immortality of Tullia's soul she is not really dead but had merely entered upon a new and more perfect life. This implies, in turn, that the immortality—continuity and imperishability—of Tullia's soul is personal, and that Tullia has a personal or individual soul. It also suggests that Cicero derived from Aristotle's *On Philosophy* the notion of a personal soul and a concomitant personal immortality of this soul. This may be inferred from Cicero's express statement that 'following the views advanced by Aristotle [in the *On Philosophy*] we have expressed it in these words in our *Consolatio*.'[30] Hence, it may be assumed that in the *On Philosophy*, a work which, like the *Eudemus*, is probably also under the influence of Plato's *Phaedo*, Aristotle proclaims and expounds the individuality and personal immortality of the soul.[31] The soul, according to Aristotle, is personally immortal because of its ἐνδελέχεια, that is, because of its very essence which spells enduring (rational) continuity.

In *Tusculanae Disputiones* I. 26. 65, Cicero explicitly states that 'the fifth nature, first introduced by Aristotle, is the nature of gods and [human] minds (souls) alike.'[32] *Ibid.*, I. 27. 66, he reiterates that the human mind (soul) is of 'the same kind and the same nature' as the 'divine mind.'[33] This, then, would imply the 'co-naturality' of the divine (God) and the human soul. Cicero also insists (*ibid.*, I. 27. 66) that it will never be discovered 'whence these [*scil.*, the living powers of the soul—the power to retain the past, foresee the future, and grasp the present] can come to man, except from God.'[34] Thus Aristotle once more falls back on the 'fifth nature' characteristic of the soul, as well as on the co-naturality of God and the human soul, in order to explain these powers and their origin—powers which he expressly calls divine. This, then, would also imply the 'super-naturality' of the soul as well as its immortality:[35] the intellectual ('spiritual' ?) powers of the human soul are identical with, or at least similar to, the divine powers. In short, the peculiar intellectual ('spiritual' ?) faculties of the human soul are indicative of its co-naturality with God—a typically Aristotelian method of proof, which might have been stated as follows: whatever has the power of memory, intellect and thought, not only must come from God, but also must be akin to God. The human soul has this power. Hence, it must not only come from God, but it must also be akin to God, that is, it must be divine and, in consequence, eternal (imperishable) or immortal.

It should be obvious that Aristotle insisted that the activities proper to the human soul and to the human intellect cannot possibly be induced by, or have their origin and principle in, the four traditional material elements or substances.[36] But if this be so, Aristotle argued, these activities must be the product or effects of a different element which as to its true nature and essence is 'much more perfect and much more pure' than any of these four elements. *Tusculanae Disputationes* I. 26. 66 (provided this passage contains reliable information concerning Aristotle's views) goes so far as to proclaim that the soul and the activities of the intellect are in fact 'divine' or, perhaps, 'spiritual.'[37] On account of this 'divinity' or 'spirituality,' there must exist, as we have seen, an undeniable co-naturality of God (the 'divine') and the individual human soul—a position, it will be noted, which by no means conflicts with some basic notions held by the young Aristotle and expressed in his earliest works.[38] It certainly does not conflict with the notion that the soul is self-moving and that its motion is both continuous and endless.[39]

Because of their unusual and, at times, confusing content or doctrine, some scholars have refused to assign Cicero, *Academica* I. 7. 26; Cicero, *Tusculanae Disputationes* I. 10. 22, and *ibid.*, I. 17. 41, and I. 26. 65–27. 66; and Clement of Rome, *Recognitiones* VIII. 15, to Aristotle's *On Philosophy*. The whole discussion about these sources, which also touches upon the issue of whether or not the 'fifth nature' or 'fifth substance' or 'fifth element' that constitutes the soul is nothing other than the 'ether,' has recently been reopened with great acumen by P. Moraux[40] and J. Pépin.[41] It will be noted that such renowned scholars as E. Bignone,[42] S. Mariotti,[43] J. Bidez,[44] H. Cherniss,[45] F. J. Nuyens,[46] A. Mansion,[47] A. J. Festugière[48] and others deny that the 'fifth nature,' as it is discussed (according to the testimony of Cicero and Clement) in the Aristotelian *On Philosophy* (or *Eudemus*) in connection with the soul, is identical with 'ether.'[49] Other scholars, among them A. Barigazzi,[50] G. Soleri,[51] J. Moreau,[52] E. Berti,[53] L. Alfonsi,[54] D. A. Rees,[55] P. Moraux,[56] R. A. Gauthier[57] and A. D. Leeman,[58] insist in varying degrees that in the *Academica* as well as in the *Tusculanae Disputationes* Cicero cites fairly accurately and rather faithfully from Aristotle's *On Philosophy* (or from Aristotle in general).[59] Some scholars, again, maintain that Aristotle fully identified this 'fifth nature,' that is, the element which constitutes the soul, with 'ether.'

K. Reinhardt suggests that the immediate source of Cicero is Antiochus of Ascalon (and, possibly, Posidonius). Antiochus, in turn, Reinhardt opines, combined and integrated the Peripatetic (Aristotelian) doctrine of the 'fifth element' (endowed with intelligence and regular circular motion) with the Stoic notion of 'fire' or 'fiery ether' in a most uncritical and arbitrary manner. According to Reinhardt, this Stoic fire or 'fiery ether' is nothing other than a substitution for the Peripatetic or Aristotelian concept of the 'ether.' Reinhardt further maintains that the notion of a 'nameless (ἀκατονόμαστον) element,' in other words, the notion that neither the soul nor the heavens (or their true 'substance') can be known or defined, actually goes back to the pronounced skepticism characteristic of the so-called Middle Academy. Reinhardt concludes that the identification of the soul with 'ether,' that is, with something definitely 'material,' is incontestably Stoic and, hence, cannot possibly be what Aristotle had originally stated about the soul either in the *On Philosophy* or in the *Eudemus*.[60] Hence, according to Reinhardt, the distinct 'nature' of the soul, this particular 'fifth nature,' of which Aristotle speaks in the *On Philosophy*, is not necessarily the 'ether.' With some modifications, the essential views of Reinhardt were accepted by P. Moraux[61] (who is of the opinion that the Ciceronian fragments are, in the final analysis, but an uncritical 'combination' of Aristotelian and Stoic teachings), by E. Berti[62] and by H. J. Easterling.[63] The identification of the soul with the 'ether' is, according to these scholars, definitely post-Aristotelian, that is, Stoic, but most certainly not by Aristotle himself, who, in their opinion, clearly and emphatically distinguished between the specific 'nature' of the soul and the 'ether.'

The views advanced by Reinhardt, Moraux, Berti and others were roundly rejected by M. Untersteiner[64] and J. Pépin.[65] Pépin, in particular, insists that it is quite possible that in the course of time, and due to some inaccurate or confused intermediaries, Aristotle's original views, as they had been expressed in the *On Philosophy* (or in the *Eudemus*?), subsequently might have been contaminated with Stoic notions. However, Pépin maintains that whenever Cicero, our main source of information, speaks about a 'fifth nature,' he refers directly and accurately to Aristotle's original ideas, that is, to the *On Philosophy*. Moreover, Pépin also holds that, when referring to this 'fifth nature,' Cicero had in mind the 'ether,' and nothing else.[66] Pépin concedes, on the other hand, that the term 'ether,' as it is used in the *On Philosophy* (and by Cicero), is not simply some 'ordinary matter'[67]—a view which is also held by P. Moraux.[68] Pépin further observes that already during the lifetime of Plato, the Academy had discussed the problem of whether the soul was 'ether.'[69] And finally, by following P. Moraux to some extent, Pépin also suggests that this 'fifth element' or 'fifth nature' advocated by Aristotle—an element which Pépin identifies with 'ether'—is something of an 'intermediary' between the material (visible) world and the immaterial (invisible) or 'spiritual' world[70]— something which effectively mediates between, and also links together, the physical-material world and the intellectual ('spiritual') world, that is, the world of the νοῦς.[71]

These many and often divergent views, which are championed with much acumen and much vigor (and which are supported by profound scholarship and great learning), should make it amply clear that the numerous problems connected with the ultimate nature of the soul, as the latter appears to have been expounded in Aristotle's *On Philosophy* (or, perhaps, in the Aristotelian *Eudemus*), are far from being adequately resolved. In the light of the present status of this scholarly controversy, full agreement on all these issues may never be reached. Being conversant with the problems which arise from our particular source (Cicero), from the manner in which Cicero's sources might have modified or adulterated the original Aristotelian views by injecting Stoic notions, and from the way in which these sources or 'fragments' might be interpreted,[72] the present author still maintains, however, that whenever Aristotle speaks of the particular 'nature' or 'element' or 'substance' which constitutes the soul, or whenever he refers to a 'fifth nature' in connection with the soul, he does not have in mind the 'ether.'[73] For 'ether' seems to be an essentially 'material element,' while, according to Aristotle, the soul is something 'non-material' and as such has no admixture of any material elements. And finally, as has already been shown, the soul is akin to the divine, that is, to God or to the pure νοῦς, Who is never 'ether.' Hence, the soul cannot be 'ether.'[74] This view finds additional support in *Epinomis* 981B ff., where we are informed that there are two kinds of existence, namely, the soul on the one hand and the five 'bodily' (material) forms (or elements), on the other hand, *viz.*, earth, water, air, fire and 'ether.' This, then, would clearly eliminate 'ether' as the material or 'substance' of the soul.

Careful reading and what seems to be proper interpretation of the several fragments from the *On Philosophy* preserved by Cicero would indicate that in this fairly early composition Aristotle apparently argued in favor of an 'intellectual' ('spiritual'?) or non-material nature of the soul; that he maintained the substantiality of the soul; that he advocated the individuality of the soul; that he proclaimed the immortality of the soul or, to be more accurate, the personal immortality of the individual soul; that he insisted upon the complete independence of the soul from the material world; that he maintained the infinite superiority of the soul over the material (corporeal) world; and that he suggested the co-naturality (or co-substantiality) of the (human) soul and the divine or God. These arguments or assertions, it will be noted, are radically different from Aristotle's treatment of the soul in the preserved 'doctrinal' treatises of a later date. Everything considered, probably the most startling as well as most telling piece of evidence in support of these seven assertions about the soul is probably Cicero's reference to his own *Consolatio*, which he composed on the occasion of the death of his beloved daughter Tullia.[75] An effective *consolatio mortis*, it must be conceded, makes sense only if we believe in an after-life—if we are convinced that the departed person, in the words of Philo of Alexandria (who might be quoting here from Aristotle's *On Philosophy*), has departed 'to a father in the ether [in heaven],'[76] forever to live there a happier and more perfect life. This, in turn, implies the immortality of the individual soul, which in all eternity never loses its identity. A true and effective *consolatio mortis* also implies that this after-life is vastly superior to all earthly existence, and that some day all those who were near and dear to us on earth will be reunited in everlasting joy. Relying on the Aristotelian *On Philosophy*, as he himself admits, Cicero expresses these sentiments as follows: 'The origin of minds (souls) is not to be found on earth,' because the living powers of the soul come to man from God directly. In short, the soul comes from God and in death returns to God. It is then that 'like is reunited with like'—that the soul, which as to its nature is co-substantial with the divine, rejoins God, whence it originally came.[77] The adjective, which is attached both to the substance of the divine and to the nature of the human soul (and which Cicero translates as *vacans nomine* or *non nominata*),[78] in itself is highly significant: being 'beyond,' and wholly unrelated to, the four physical or material elements, substances, or natures, the fifth substance or nature has 'no name.' This implies, in turn, that only physical-material things, which are the objects of sense-perception, can be adequately named. In this sense the Aristotelian God (and with Him, the innermost nature of the human soul) is also the 'Ineffable One.'

One final question remains which is impossible to answer: where did Aristotle derive the notion that the soul is an immaterial ('spiritual') substance or nature, co-substantial with the divine? Was this particular insight the product of his own deliberations, or did he gather it from some other source? There exists the possibility that he received the unusual concept of a nameless, immaterial ('spiritual') soul, co-substantial with the divine—unusual for a Greek philosopher—from some Zoroastrian teachings about the soul. In any event, judging from the surviving evidence, that is, from certain fragments and doxographical reports which have justifiably been assigned to the Aristotelian *On Philosophy*, Aristotle had some acquaintance with Zoroastrianism.[79] This, then, might possibly be the ultimate source of Aristotle's unusual doctrine of the soul as he apparently expounded it in the *On Philosophy*.[80] Needless to say, in view of the fact that the extant evidence is rather scanty and frequently confusing, such an assumption is mere conjecture.

The interpretations offered here do not preclude the possibility, however, that the particular fragments, excerpts or references which have been discussed, after all may be assigned to the Aristotelian *Eudemus* rather than to the *On Philosophy*.[81] Assuming, however, that these fragments indeed relate to the *On Philosophy* rather than to the *Eudemus*, the further question arises: since the *On Philosophy* apparently consisted of three books, to which of these books should we assign the discussion on the nature of the soul? It is commonly held that Book I contained a kind of 'history of philosophy,' Book II a sustained critique of certain aspects of Plato's philosophy, and Book III a discussion of what may be called 'theological' questions. It seems reasonable to surmise that these 'theological' discussions also touched upon problems connected with the soul, that is, upon that aspect of man which, on account of its special nature and constitution, is capable of understanding and communicating with God. In a certain sense, Aristotle might have considered the soul a sort of 'individual counterpart' of God or, perhaps, something like a 'connecting link' between God and man.[82] It was probably in this fashion that Aristotle tried to resolve the inescapable confrontation between God and man— a confrontation which in its ultimate psychological, moral, religious and metaphysical implications always remains an essential aspect of any meaningful 'theology.' Accordingly, we might be justified in surmising that Aristotle discussed the nature of the soul in Book III of his *On Philosophy*. It might also be conjectured here that in the interval between the *Eudemus* and the *On Philosophy* Aristotle became acquainted with Zoroastrian teachings. This, then, would explain Aristotle's difference of attitude towards the soul as it becomes manifest in a comparison of the *Eudemus* with the *On Philosophy*.[83]

# Chapter XVI

# Aristotle's *On Philosophy* and the 'Philosophies of the East'*

According to Diogenes Laertius I (Prologue), 8–9,

> in the first Book of his [dialogue] *On Philosophy*,[1] Aristotle relates
> that the Magi are more ancient than the Egyptians. Moreover, he
> asserts here that the Magi believe in two principles, namely, a good
> demon and an evil demon, the one called Oromasdes [Ahura
> Mazda or Ormuzd], the other Hades or Areimanius [Ahriman].
> This is confirmed by Hermippus in the first Book of his *On the
> Magi*, by Eudoxus [of Cnidus] in his *Voyage Around* [or
> *Circumnavigation of*] *the World*, and by Theopompus in the eighth
> Book of his *Philippica*. . . . This is also confirmed by Eudemus of
> Rhodes.[2]

Plutarch, in his *De Iside et Osiride* 46 (*Moralia* 370C), writes as
follows:[3]

> The Chaldeans [Magi] call two of the planets, which they consider
> benign gods, the authors or sources of everything that is good;
> two, on the other hand, the authors or sources of everything that
> is evil; and the three remaining planets they regard as being 'in
> between' or 'neutral,' participating in the two opposite qualities. . . .
> It is worthwhile also to observe that the [Greek] philosophers
> are in accord with the Chaldeans. For this reason Heraclitus [of
> Ephesus] outright declared 'war the father of everything'. . . .
> After him Empedocles [of Acragas] designated the benign
> principle as 'love and friendship,' and at times as 'the harmony
> of the serene eye,' while at the same time he defined the evil
> principles as 'the cursed discord' and 'the bloody struggle.' The
> followers of Pythagoras include a variety of terms under these
> categories: under the good they enumerate Unity, the Determin-
> ate, the Permanent, the Straight, the Odd, the Square, the Equal,
> the Righthanded and the Bright; while under the bad they set

Duality, the Indeterminate, the Moving, the Curved, the Even, the Oblong, the Unequal, the Left-handed and the Dark. . . . For these, however, Anaxagoras postulates Mind and Infinitude. . . . Aristotle [by following this tradition?] proclaims the [principle of] form and the [principle of] privation [as the two basic principles]. . . .

Pliny, in his *Historia Naturalis* XXX. 3, it will be noted, maintains the following:

Undoubtedly, this [science of the Magi] originated in Persia due to efforts of Zoroaster. . . . Eudoxus [of Cnidus], who claimed that of all the schools of philosophy the most important and most influential was that of the Magi, also reports that this man Zoroaster lived six thousand years prior to the death of Plato. So says also Aristotle [in his *On Philosophy*?]. . . .[4]

These three important passages, which have been identified with varying success as fragments of Aristotle's *On Philosophy*, explicitly credit the Stagirite with having been familiar with, and apparently interested in, Zoroastrian (or Chaldean) teachings, that is, with the 'philosophy of the Magi.' It is fairly safe to assume that these passages refer to statements made by Aristotle in the first Book of his lost dialogue *On Philosophy*, which many scholars consider perhaps the most important composition from among his early lost works. Moreover, it is surmised that Book I of the *On Philosophy* contained a kind of 'historical introduction to philosophy.' But there were probably also a number of statements or references in the other lost works of Aristotle as well as in his preserved doctrinal treatises which, according to some scholars, likewise reflect, though in a very modified and often garbled or hidden (or indirect) form, certain basic elements of the traditional Zoroastrian teachings.

Hence, a brief analysis of the passages from either Diogenes Laertius, Plutarch or Pliny seems to be appropriate. Such an examination appears to indicate that in the *On Philosophy* Aristotle quoted some 'oriental teachings.' Presumably, he did so in order to demonstrate the dependence of certain aspects of Greek philosophy on the 'philosophy of the Magi.' More than that: these passages actually suggest a substantial connection between some phases of Greek philosophy and old Iranian religious or quasi-religious traditions. Barring a few exceptions, in the past this connection has either been simply ignored or, in some

instances, violently disputed.[5] Some of Aristotle's religious or theological views as they are expounded, for instance, in the *On Philosophy*,[6]
might also indicate that he was profoundly interested in, and seriously
concerned with, the 'philosophy of the Magi.' One might even conjecture that some of his views were, directly or indirectly, influenced
by the religious teachings of the Magi.

V. Rose,[7] it will be noted, is of the opinion that the account of
Diogenes Laertius (DL I. 8) goes back to Sotion[8] or, perhaps, to
Eudemus of Rhodes. He bases his view on the fact that in Diogenes
Laertius (DL I. 9) we are told that Eudemus confirmed Theopompus'
report that according to the Magi 'man will live in a future life and be
immortal.' W. Jaeger,[9] on the other hand, suggests that in all likelihood
Eudoxus of Cnidus, the friend of Plato, introduced these 'orientalizing
tendencies' into the Academy, presumably during the later years of
Plato's scholarchate. This Eudoxus, according to the testimony of
Strabo (I. 1, and IX. 390 ff.) and Polybius (in Strabo X. 465), was an
astronomer and mathematician, as well as the author of a work on
geography, entitled *Voyage Around the World* (Γῆς Περίοδος). He is
said to have become profoundly interested (and rather learned) in
Egyptian and Oriental wisdom while visiting these parts of the world.[10]
Since Eudoxus apparently spent considerable time in the East (Persia),
he must have come into direct contact with Zoroastrian teachings. It is
possible that he carried to Greece the learning of the East as well as
certain aspects of its religious *Weltanschauung* which, barring a few
isolated instances, until about the middle of the fourth century B.C.
were largely unknown or only superficially known (and mostly
misunderstood) among the Greeks. Tradition has it that Eudoxus
visited Athens probably in 378–77 B.C. and, again, around the year
368 B.C. (or before that time), and that he was on good terms with
Plato and the other members of the Academy.[11] According to some
biographers of Aristotle, Eudoxus became 'acting scholarch' of the
Academy during Plato's second sojourn in Syracuse (367–365/64
B.C.),[12] a further indication that he must have been held in high regard
by Plato and by the members of the Academy.

Presumably in Book I of his *On Philosophy*, Aristotle, perhaps in the
form of a general introduction, started out with an outline of the
'history of philosophy.' Aristotle seemed to have had a predilection for
'historical introductions' as well as a laudable reverence for the achievements of the remote past, something which can be ascertained from his
preserved doctrinal treatises.[13] Moreover, in the *On Philosophy*, he
apparently did not limit himself to the early Greeks, as he has done, for

instance, in the *Metaphysics*, where he begins his account with Thales of Miletus.[14] Here he reached far beyond the Hellenic orbit, mentioning among others the 'philosophers' or sages of the East. In brief, in the *On Philosophy* he groped beyond the Egyptians, going back to the Magi, whom he considered to be older than the Egyptians.[15] To what extent the 'philosophy of the Magi' captivated Aristotle's interest and imagination may be gathered from the fact that in *Metaphysics* 1091 b 8 ff., one of the earliest parts of the *Metaphysics*, he still maintains that some of the earliest thinkers combined good and evil and made 'the Best' the original generating agent (or principle), 'as did the Magi and some of the later sages, such as Empedocles ... and Anaxagoras. ...'[16]

The question may be raised here once more of how and through what particular channels or intermediaries the 'philosophy of the Magi' or Zoroastrianism came to the attention of Aristotle.[17] It has already been noted that it was probably Eudoxus of Cnidus who introduced 'Oriental' philosophic notions to Greece, and to Athens and the Academy in particular.[18] Tradition also has it that during the last years of Plato's scholarchate, a Chaldean or follower of Zoroaster, or perhaps several Chaldeans, were members of, or had been associated with, the Platonic Academy.[19] As a matter of fact, the so-called *Prolegomena to the Philosophy of Plato* contains the startling information that 'for the sake of Plato the Magi came to Athens eager to participate in the philosophic teachings which he was expounding.'[20] This story seems to imply that the news of Plato's philosophic teachings and the activities of the Academy, perhaps in an exaggerated form, had in some way reached the Magi in Persia who, curious about the 'new prophet' or sage, sent to Athens some messenger or messengers to learn more about this 'new teacher' in the West.[21] Also of interest to us is the account, related by Diogenes Laertius (III. 25), that a Persian (Zoroastrian?) dedicated a statue in the Academy honoring Plato.

To what extent Chaldeans or followers of Zoroaster—in Greek sources Chaldeans and Magi are often identified and confused—influenced and molded the teachings of the Academy during the last decades of Plato's scholarchate is difficult to assess. In any event, according to Plato (?), *I Alcibiades* (121E-122E), the four cardinal virtues in a way are related to Persian (Iranian) or Zoroastrian 'ethical maxims.' Iranian astral theology, which definitely goes back to Zoroastrian teachings, in the *Epinomis* (986E and 987B; 987D-988A) is called the highest and most perfect form of wisdom—obviously a

Zoroastrian position.[22] It is also worthwhile to note that in *I Alcibiades* 122A we are informed that Zarathustra is the son (actually the 'spiritual son') of Ahura Mazda or Ormuzd. In Plato's *Laws* (896DE), it is stated that 'we must not suppose that there are less than two [cosmic] souls, one being the author of the good, the other the principle of evil.' It might be conjectured here that the 'good cosmic soul' is nothing other than the Zoroastrian Ormudz, and the 'evil cosmic soul' the Zoroastrian Ahriman. In the *Theaetetus* (176A), Plato insists that 'evils . . . can never pass away. For there must always remain something which is antagonistic to the good.' And the last part of the *Epinomis* (987A ff.), it will be noted, seems to point to what appears to be a Zoroastrian or 'Chaldean' (Syrian) source. As a matter of fact, the whole of the *Epinomis*, and especially the astral theology advocated there, as has already been shown, seems to reflect Zoroastrian influences.

Plutarch apparently summarizes the position of Plato as regards the perpetual conflict between good and evil and, for that matter, Plato's indebtedness to Zoroastrianism, when he states:[23]

> Plato, in many passages, as though hiding and veiling his opinion, names the one of the two opposing principles 'Identity,' and the other 'Difference.' But in the *Laws*, after he had grown considerably older, he asserts, not by the use of circumlocution of symbolic or metaphoric speech, but in specific and direct words, that the movement of the Universe is actuated not just by one [cosmic] soul, but perhaps by several [cosmic] souls, and certainly by no less than two [cosmic] souls. Of these two souls the one is benign and the other antagonistic to the former and the originator of things opposed [to the good cosmic soul]. Between these two souls he concedes that there might be a certain third nature, not inanimate or without reason or without the power of moving itself, as some have suggested, but dependent on both of these two other [cosmic] souls, and desiring the better always and yearning after it and pursuing it. . . .

Plutarch refers here probably to Plato, *Timaeus* 35A,[24] and to Plato, *Laws* 896D ff.[25] Perhaps he also has in mind Plato, *Statesman* 270D: 'The universe is guided at one time by an external power which is divine . . . but when released [from this guidance] it moves on its own, being set free at such a time as to have, during infinite cycles of years, a "reverse movement."'

W. Jaeger is of the opinion that these Zoroastrian influences go back to the time when Eudoxus of Cnidus was actively associated with the

Platonic Academy. Judging from the works of certain members of the Academy (Philip of Opus), 'Chaldean astronomy' or 'astral theology,' which was probably introduced by Eudoxus, apparently found an interested and receptive audience. But more than that: the Zoroastrian dualism of good and evil ultimately might be reflected in Plato's dualistic metaphysics, especially in its later formulation. Plato's philosophy, then, would actually be a dialectical search for the ultimate premises of a truth which, in a totally assertive manner, was presented by Zoroastrianism. Or to put it into different words: Plato's later philosophy attempts to verify, with the help of an accepted rational method, that is, on the level of dialectics, what the Zoroastrians forthrightly asserted as revealed truth. Hence, Plato's later philosophy might very well be called an attempt to integrate reason and revelation. The latter view would imply, however, that Zoroastrian influences on Plato might date back to the eighties or, at least, to the seventies of the fourth century B.C., depending on the dating of Plato's so-called classical dialogues, an unlikely assumption. The peculiar dualistic trend in Plato's latest metaphysics, which is commonly credited to 'Pythagorean' teachings, on the other hand, might very well be Zoroastrian.[26] If this be so, then also the 'mathematico-Pythagorean' phase during the ultimate stage of Plato's philosophy, including the theory of the Idea Numbers (which, judging from the *Epinomis,* seems to indicate a certain affinity with Zoroastrian astral teachings), might well have been influenced by Zoroastrianism.

It is quite likely that Aristotle, who for about twenty years was closely associated with Plato and with the Platonic Academy, should have gathered there whatever information he had about the Magi or Chaldeans. It should also be noted that in the eighth Book of his *Philippica,* which contains a collection of reports on unusual events, Theopompus compiled a survey of Zoroastrian teachings and maxims.[27] This compilation, it is claimed, was quite accurate and rather detailed. It was based on bits of information which Theopompus had collected in Persia proper. Theopompus probably wrote his 'report' as a kind of *excursus* into the realm of the unusual and miraculous in order to entertain his readers. At the same time he must have believed that there existed among the educated Greeks of his day a real interest in, and perhaps even some knowledge of, the 'philosophies of the East.'[28] We have no evidence, however, that in his *On Philosophy* Aristotle made use of Theopompus. Book eight of the *Philippica* was probably not yet written when Aristotle composed his *On Philosophy,* which is commonly dated between 350–49 and 348–47 B.C.

It might be contended, however, that certain Zoroastrian influences on Greek philosophy may possibly be detected long before Plato and the Academy.[29] Perhaps Heraclitus of Ephesus' claim that 'strife is the father of everything'[30] is but a formalization and restatement of the Zoroastrian belief in the perpetual struggle between the forces of good and those of evil. In a way this struggle is to the Zoroastrian believer the essence of existential reality. As a matter of fact, Plutarch (see above) directly connects this πόλεμος πατὴρ πάντων with the 'Chaldeans'— a reasonable assumption. The same might be said about Heraclitus' conception of the 'flux' as the basis or essence of all events that transpire in history, as well as about many other assertive statements by him which have the unmistakable ring and the apodictic directness of 'religious revelations.' Some of the more renowned utterances of such men as Empedocles, Parmenides, the Pythagoreans, Anaxagoras, Plato and even Aristotle in some ways also seem to be related to 'Chaldean philosophy.'[31] That Heraclitus of Ephesus, the 'Obscure,' might have been influenced by Zoroastrian teachings, has long been suspected.[32] The very surname, the 'Obscure'—'obscure' to those not initiated into the teachings of Zoroaster—seems to point in that direction, as does the aphoristic and hieratic character of some of his utterances, which in their cryptic form as well as in their assertiveness call to mind the sayings of some eastern prophets or religious poets. When Empedocles defines the Divine as 'Mind, holy and ineffable and only Mind, Which darts through the Universe with Its swift thought [*scil.*, is omnipresent],'[33] or when he calls 'Love' and 'Hate' the two prime agents operating throughout the universe, each becoming successively predominant,[34] he seems to restate and paraphrase the Zoroastrian 'definition' of God as well as the Zoroastrian 'dualism' of good and evil, the perpetual conflict between the two, and the principle of 'eternal recurrence.'[35]

Aside from the direct influence of Plato and the Academy, it was probably also these developments within early Greek philosophy itself that were behind Aristotle's pronounced concern with the Magi—a concern which he seems to have expressed in greater detail in the first Book of his *On Philosophy*. If we were to assume that the *On Philosophy* was the direct result of protracted philosophic debates (and disagreements) within the inner circle of the Academy, then it should also be obvious that certain basic aspects of Zoroastrianism had become a much discussed topic with Plato and his disciples. This seems to be borne out, for instance, by some of Plato's latest dialogues, by the *Epinomis* and by Aristotle's *On Philosophy*. In some other works of

Aristotle we can likewise detect traces of Zoroastrian teachings. The doctrine of the 'eternal return' or 'eternal recurrence'—the theory that truth returns at certain cyclic intervals[36]—which is definitely an essential element of Zoroastrian tradition, seems to be reflected, for instance, in Aristotle's *Metaphysics* 1074 b 1–13:

> Our forefathers in the most remote ages have handed down to posterity a tradition, in the form of a myth, that these [celestial] bodies are gods, and that the divine encloses the whole of nature. The rest of the tradition has been added later in mythical form. . . . But if one were to separate the first position from these later additions and take it alone, namely, that they believed the first substances to be gods, one must regard this as an inspired utterance, and reflect that, while probably each art and each science has often been developed as far as this is possible and has again perished, these opinions, together with others, have been preserved until the present day like relics of an ancient treasure.

And again: 'The same ideas, one must believe, occur and re-occur in the minds of men, not just once, but again and again.'[37] Moreover, Aristotle avers that 'the same opinions appear in cycles among men, not once nor twice, but infinitely many times.'[38] Hence, Aristotle reaches the conclusion that 'these and many other things have been invented several times over in the course of the ages, or rather, times without number.'[39] For if there is a kind of analogy between recurrence of certain necessary inventions and the recurrence of certain fundamental ideas, then there also must be a kind of ultimate necessity or 'law' behind these fundamental ideas—a notion which outright smacks of Zoroastrian teachings.[40]

All these passages suggest that Aristotle was somewhat conversant with, and perhaps at some time even accepted, at least in part, the Zoroastrian doctrine of the 'great cycle,' the 'eternal return' or the 'eternal recurrence,' as well as the Zoroastrian notion of the 'cosmic drama' which unfolds in the perennial struggle between Ahura-Mazda (Ormuzd) and Ahriman. According to old Iranian tradition or, more precisely, according to a certain version of this tradition, Ahura-Mazda and Ahriman rule in turn, each for three thousand years. For another three thousand years they battle with each other, each attempting to overthrow the other and destroy what the other had accomplished.[41] It is certainly no mere accident that, according to Eudoxus of Cnidus (and Aristotle?), six thousand years separate Zoroaster and Plato:[42] Both men are connected with a decisive stage in the great cosmic drama.[43] Thus it might be contended that, at least in some of his earlier works, that is, in the *On Philosophy* and perhaps in the earliest parts of the *Metaphysics* which are approximately contemporary with the *On Philosophy* (?), Aristotle refers to, and perhaps has been influenced by, certain Zoroastrian cosmological or cosmogonic teachings as well as by Zoroastrian (astral) theology.[44] One might even speculate a little further: according to Eudoxus of Cnidus and perhaps Aristotle [45] (provided Aristotle actually stated that Zoroaster lived six thousand years prior to Plato's death),[46] Zoroaster apparently stands at the beginning of a distinct cosmic cycle of three thousand years—the cycle which witnesses the rule of Ahura-Mazda– while Plato marks the end of another and later cycle [47] of three thousand years in which Ahura-Mazda and Ahriman battle one another and which precedes the third (dismal) cycle during which Ahriman temporarily gains the upper hand. This might possibly be inferred from the famous passage found at the end of Aristotle's *Elegy* which he wrote in the honored memory of Plato (or that of Eudemus of Cyprus),

> '[W]ho alone or first among all mortals clearly revealed
> By his own life and by the methods of his teachings
> That a man becomes good and happy at the same time.
> Now no one can ever attain to these things again.' [48]

The last line may imply that with Plato's death, a distinct cosmic period or era (of three thousand years) had come to an end—a period in which Ahura Mazda and Ahriman battle one another to a standstill, but in which it was still possible to become good and happy at the same time—and that after Plato's death, the rule of Ahriman sets in. This, then, would make Plato the last of the true 'children of Ahura Mazda.' After him the 'night of evil' descends upon the world, when no one can be both good and happy. All this is, however, conjecture based upon rather scanty evidence.

The fragmentary information culled from a variety of sources and from what appears to be a plausible interpretation of these frequently cryptic sources would indicate that in the *On Philosophy* (and in some of his other early writings) Aristotle displayed a remarkable acquaintance with, and a puzzling interest in, some aspects of Zoroastrian teachings. This is borne out not only by certain features of Aristotle's theology as he expounded them in the *On Philosophy*, or by his adherence to the doctrine of the 'eternal recurrence,' but also by his historical references to Zoroastrianism in Book I of the *On Philosophy*, and by the prominent place he assigns to it in the history of philosophy.

This might also lend weighty support to the thesis that, at the time he composed the *On Philosophy*, he was vitally concerned with 'theological' problems, and that 'theological' questions might have been the central theme of his whole philosophy. Aristotle's familiarity with Zoroastrian teachings (unfortunately we are unable to determine the extent or the depth of his acquaintance) should also be an indication that by the middle of the fourth century B.C. these teachings had apparently captivated the philosophic curiosity and religious interest of certain Greek intellectuals.[49] In view of its particular concerns, religious orientation and mystical commitments, it is not altogether surprising that the Platonic Academy and its more prominent members should have occupied themselves with certain aspects of Zoroastrian teachings.

# Aristotle's Criticism of Plato's 'Philosopher King': Some Comments on Aristotle's *On Kingship**

In a passage which is commonly regarded as a fragment of Aristotle's lost work *On Kingship*,[1] Themistius relates:[2]

> Plato, even if in all other respects he was divine and deserving of our unlimited admiration,[3] was utterly reckless when he made the statement that evils would never cease for men until either philosophers became kings, or kings became philosophers.[4] This pronouncement of Plato's has been refuted[5] and has paid its debt to time. We should honor Aristotle, who slightly altered Plato's statement and made his advice truer. Aristotle said that it was not merely unnecessary for a king to be a philosopher, but that this was even a distinct disadvantage. What a king should do is to listen to, and take the advice of, true philosophers. In so doing, he would enrich his reign with good deeds and not merely with fine words.

In view of the fact that the several ancient 'catalogues' of Aristotle's writings mention an *On Kingship*, there is no valid reason why we should doubt the authenticity of this work, although it is well-nigh impossible to verify whether the passage or fragment from Themistius is properly assigned to the *On Kingship*. Somewhat more difficult is the proper dating of this composition. It may be surmised, however, that it was written at the time when Aristotle was about to complete the education of Alexander[6]—provided, of course, that Aristotle actually was the preceptor of Alexander.[7] It seems more reasonable to assume that it was composed about the time King Philip appointed his sixteen-year-old son Alexander regent of Macedonia, while he himself was waging war in Thrace and in the Balkans in the year 340 B.C.[8] Frustrated in his attempt to take Perinthus and Byzantium, Philip withdrew to Thrace. When the Scythians near the mouth of the Danube revolted against their Macedonian overlords, he crossed the Balkan mountains to crush this uprising. While returning to Macedonia through the country of the Triballi, he became involved in some dangerous mountain warfare in the course of which he was severely wounded in the leg.

It is also fairly safe to conjecture that the *On Kingship* was a hortatory essay rather than a dialogue, and that it was probably fashioned after the Aristotelian *Protrepticus* or, perhaps, the *Cyprian Orations* of Isocrates.[9] By the year 340 B.C., it may be presumed, Aristotle had abandoned the literary form of the dialogue which had been characteristic of the majority of his earliest compositions. It might also be maintained that the *On Kingship* was akin to a 'Mirror for Princes.'[10] In this it continued a tradition which can be traced back to Hesiod's *Works and Days*.

Aristotle's objections to, or 'corrections' of, Plato's 'philosopher king' is wholly consistent with his essentially realistic and sober outlook on political life in general, and on the practical exigencies of the political community in particular. Although during his association with Plato and the Platonic Academy (367–48 B.C.) he undoubtedly still adhered to Plato's purely theoretic views on 'politics,'[11] in his *Politics* 1277 a 16 ff., Aristotle stresses the fact that 'the good ruler must be a wise (practical) man.' And *ibid.*, 1287 b 26 ff., he insists that rulers should avail themselves of the advice of other people (not necessarily philosophers)—in Plato's opinion an utterly heretical suggestion. In the *Protrepticus*, likewise a sort of 'Mirror for Princes' (which was written about 350 B.C.), Aristotle had already pointed out the relation between purely theoretic (Platonic) politics and practical or workable politics, which takes into account the *de facto* human condition:[12]

> For just as sight in itself produces or creates nothing [this remark may be directed at Plato's injunction that first of all we must 'visualize' the pure Forms, *note by the present author*]—its only assignment is to distinguish or to reveal to us all that can physically be seen—yet it not only enables us to act as it directs, but also assists us greatly in all our actions (for without sight we would be almost completely immobilized)—so it is also evident that although purely rational knowledge is exclusively theoretic, we still perform thousands of actions in full conformity with rational (theoretic) knowledge and, in fact, decide upon certain actions and forego others [in keeping with the dictates of rational (theoretic) knowledge].

Perhaps even more significant is a passage likewise contained in the Aristotelian *Protrepticus*:[13]

In my opinion we do not require the same kind of philosophic knowledge or philosophic wisdom as regards plain life that we need for living the perfect (theoretic) life. The majority of men may be wholly excused from doing the latter—for being completely satisfied with that sort of knowledge which is sufficient to lead a normal and plain life. These people, to be sure, wish for a higher form of intellectual happiness, but on the whole they are quite content if they can simply live and survive.

Plato most assuredly would have violently disagreed with Aristotle's realistic proposition that to stay alive and live somewhat decently is about all that may reasonably be expected of most people.

Aristotle's criticism of Plato's theoretic proposition that only philosophers should be kings probably arose from his insight that a good ruler 'should avoid impossibilities'[14] and impracticalities, such as Plato had indeed advocated in his *Republic*.[15] As a matter of fact, in Book II of the *Politics*, Aristotle does, among other things, take issue with Plato's basic political philosophy, pointing out some of its unrealistic and unworkable features. The ideal and purely theoretic *polis* of Plato is for Aristotle no longer the absolute criterion of what is desirable or even acceptable in a well-functioning body politic. Determined to abandon the exclusively theoretic (contemplative) approach taken by Plato, Aristotle pursued political knowledge in the realm of historical fact and practical experience. This is clearly indicated in Aristotle's statement:[16]

Our philosophic predecessors [Plato ?] have handed down to us the subject of legislation unexamined. Hence, it would be best for us to study this subject ourselves, and in general inquire into the question of what constitutes a constitution, in order to complete, to the best of our abilities, our philosophy of human nature. First, if anything has been said well in detail by earlier thinkers, let us try to review it; then, in the light of the constitutions we have collected [Aristotle alludes here to his *Collection of 158 Constitutions* of which only the first book, *The Constitution of Athens*, has survived, *note by the present author*], let us investigate what influences or factors preserve or destroy cities, and what influences or factors preserve or destroy particular kinds of constitutions or institutions, and to what cause it is due that some cities are well-administered, while others are badly governed. After these have been studied we shall perhaps be in a better position to see with a

comprehensive view which constitution is best, and how each
constitution must be arranged, and what laws and customs it must
apply, if it is to be at its best.

Aristotle's main arguments, it should be quite obvious, aim at a
practical, that is, workable ideal that would realistically take into
account not only existing realities and the actual human conditions,
but also all reasonable and natural human interests, aspirations and
expectations. In so doing, he constantly seeks to reconcile a political
(or communal) ideal with existential reality—to mediate between
what is desirable and what is reasonably attainable.[17]

It will also be noted that in Books IV–VI of the Aristotelian *Politics*,
the emphasis is decidely on empirical inquiry. Thus, the ideal though
'arrested' city, the single and monolithic political construct envisioned
by Plato in the *Republic*, no longer constitutes the single model in
Aristotle's political thought. The 'new statesman' must, according to
Aristotle, look with sympathy and understanding at the many actual
and possible types of cities and constitutions, and draw upon them as an
unbiased observer of political and social reality.[18] He will even admit
and take into account the fact that different people may rightfully
disagree about the relative desirability or value of certain goods.[19] In
short, Aristotle not only intends to grasp and develop the fundamental
factual conditions on which a particular—working and workable—
politically organized society may be grounded,[20] but he also wishes to
establish or strengthen the basic natural conditions for, and foundations
of, the existence as well as for the healthy survival of political organiza-
tions in general. Hence, he rejects, for instance, Plato's notion (discussed in *Laws* 737E) that the warrior caste should number 5,000 men,
pointing out that it would 'require a territory as large as Babylon, or
some other huge country, if so many people were to be supported in
idleness,'[21] a pertinent and timely reminder for all those rulers,
peoples or nations who are intent upon spending the greater part of
their national income on 'national defense.' Aristotle also points out
that since no city exists in splendid isolation, 'the legislator . . . must
never lose sight of the neighboring countries' and, hence, must take
appropriate action to prevent hostile aggression.[22] And finally, he
stresses the practical, that is, economic and social aspects of the different
constitutions, playing down purely formal classifications.[23]

Probably the most significant and, at the same time, most arresting
aspect of Aristotle's political philosophy or theory consists in his
efforts to establish a broad empirical basis for the manifold forms of

actual political life, with its many variations, combinations and transitions. In *Politics* 1321 b 26 ff., he insists that the true statesman must always consider 'two things in which all well-being consists: one of them is the choice of the right end and proper aim of all [political] action, and the other is the devising of those actions which are a means to the achievement of this right end. But the means and the end may agree or disagree.'[24] In other words, the true statesman and the wise legislator must always bear in mind the proper (workable) relation between the right means and the right end. Unlike Plato, Aristotle also insists that within the well-ordered city the dilemma of conflicting aims and irreconcilable ends should never harass the community and the individual, and thus become the source of mutual antagonism.[25] In this manner, he not only touches upon the age-old issue of 'personal (or individual) interests' *versus* 'social (or political) interests'—of 'man *versus* the state'—but also envisions a workable and healthy balance as well as accommodation between these two sets of interests. In so doing, he raises one of the most crucial (and most involved) problems of jurisprudence and political or social theory, a problem which Plato, in his monolithic approach, simply ignores or, worse, one-sidedly and uncompromisingly resolves in favor of the state. Moreover, Aristotle apparently understood and took into account the well-known fact of general human vulnerability, the limitations of the average human intellect and the frequently encountered inadequacy of knowledge and understanding in general, as well as the limitations of human will power, the limitations of natural and human resources, and the observable wide-spread selfishness of men. All these shortcomings demand a realistic political, social and legal order which fully takes into account the at times distressing realities of existential life.

It is also most significant that in Book I of the *Politics*, Aristotle identifies the 'best life' of the city with the 'best life' of the individual. This implies that there never should be a real or, perhaps, irreconcilable conflict between the city and the individual, between 'social (or political) interests' and 'individual (or personal) interests.' More than this: it also declares that each city has its own irreducible and irreplaceable individuality, and its own 'social or political interests,' which arise from particular circumstances that vary from case to case—a fact of which he probably became conscious when compiling the *Collection of 158 Constitutions*. In principle, Aristotle recognizes only two kinds of (practical) life: a life of pleasure based on material goods, and a life of practical goodness (virtue).[26] But he does not mention here the purely theoretic or contemplative life so eloquently advocated and extolled by

Plato as well as in some of Aristotle's earliest writings. The new Aristotelian 'ideal city' is always closely affiliated with historical or existential reality and, hence, must forego Plato's extravagant notion of a 'city of philosophers.' Unquestionably, there is still ample room for philosophic contemplation in Aristotle's city, but no room for the exclusively contemplative, abstract-theoretic life of the Platonic 'philosopher king.' By assuming an extreme and uncompromising position, Plato in fact had denied the possibility that there could ever be an acceptable accommodation between purely philosophic knowledge and practical life, between theoretic construct and existential fact. It is not surprising, therefore, that Plato's political philosophy, although still extolled in certain circles as the most perfect expression of social thought, has been called outright inhuman and, as such, has been rejected and even denounced by thoughtful people, including Aristotle.

Book II of the *Politics*, as has already been stated, contains certain criticisms of the earlier authors of political Utopias and a particularly detailed criticism of Plato's Utopian thesis—incidentally, the most detailed and sustained criticism of Plato to be found anywhere in the preserved works of Aristotle.[27] These criticisms almost always originate with Aristotle's insistence that in its essence, Plato's political philosophy is unrealistic as well as devoid of all practical significance, and that Plato's 'ideal city'—the city of the 'philosopher king'—is domiciled in a historical vacuum.[28] Of particular interest to us here is Aristotle's observation that Plato constructs his ideal *polis* in a sort of 'never-never-land':[29]

> It is claimed [by Plato] that the lawgiver ought to have his eyes directed to only two points—the people and the country. But adjoining cities must not be forgotten by the lawgiver, primarily, because the city for which he frames the laws is to have a [realistic] political life and not an isolated existence. A city must have sufficient military forces as will be serviceable against her neighbors, and not merely at home. Although it is admitted that the life of action is not the best life, either for individuals or cities, still a city should be formidable to its enemies. . . . [and possess sufficient military strength to deter aggression].

Hence, 'the lawgiver should also consider the relation of the city to its neighboring cities. . . . The government must be organized with a view to military strength. But of this not a word is being said [in Plato's writings, *scil.*, in the *Laws* 704A ff., and 747D, or in the

*Republic*].'[30] As a realistic political thinker and a man of experience, Aristotle also rejects[31] Plato's unrealistic (Spartan) notion that towns should not be fortified, but should rely solely on the virtue and proven prowess of their citizens.[32]

It was probably Aristotle's protracted personal contact and experiences with such shrewd and successful practical politicians or statesmen as Philip of Macedonia or Hermias of Atarneus which gave him a deeper insight into the realities of political, strategic and diplomatic life.[33] Since Aristotle stayed with Hermias from about 348–47 B.C. to about 345–44 B.C.,[34] it would be fair to surmise that he began to develop his more realistic outlook on politics around the year 347 B.C. or perhaps a little later, that is, while he resided at or became connected with the royal court of Macedonia (from about 343–42 to about 336–35 B.C.), observing (and perhaps actively participating in) Philip's most successful *Realpolitik*.[35]

Assuming, then, that due to the influence of Hermias, Aristotle's 'conversion' from Plato's purely theoretic political thought (which he still manifested in the *Politicus*) to a more realistic political attitude began about the year 345 B.C., and that this conversion received additional impetus during his long and close association with the Macedonian royal house, then it might also be contended that the *On Kingship* was written not much later than 340 B.C., the year in which Alexander was made regent of Macedonia by his father Philip[36]— and perhaps before that date.[37] It is quite possible that Aristotle feared that the young Alexander, whose character and disposition he knew only too well, might one day regard himself the self-appointed, omniscient, omnipotent, and god-like king, emulating or even exceeding the Platonic 'philosopher king' who, in Plato's opinion, is truly 'god-like.'[38] Thus, Aristotle prudently reminded the ambitious (and emotionally unbalanced) young prince and regent 'that it was not merely unnecessary but a distinct disadvantage for a king to be a philospher. What a king should do was to listen and take the counsel of true philosophers [that is, of men, who like Aristotle, possess a balanced knowledge of the pertinent facts]. In so doing the monarch would enrich his reign with good deeds and not merely with fine words [as Plato had done].'[39] Although the *Vita Aristotelis Marciana* 21 and the *Vita Aristotelis Latina* 21 relate that the advice which Aristotle gave to Alexander in the *On Kingship* allegedly moved the latter to exclaim, 'since today I have not done a good deed I have not reigned,'[40] subsequent events seem to indicate that Aristotle's exhortations fell on deaf ears.[41] As a matter of fact, tradition has it that at some later time

Aristotle and Alexander became estranged. It is possible that this estrangement began when Aristotle tried to remind Alexander, who was an impulsive and temperamental young man, that he should use restraint and always act with deliberation. According to some (exaggerated?) reports, Aristotle allegedly attempted to poison Alexander (for having killed Callisthenes?) or played a role in the alleged poisoning of the latter, while Alexander is said to have toyed with the idea of killing Aristotle.[42] This is not the place, however, to discuss in detail the estrangement which, it appears, gradually developed between Aristotle and Alexander even before the latter ascended the throne of Macedonia in 336 B.C.

# Conclusion

Provided they relate reasonably accurate information, the surviving fragments of the lost early works of Aristotle seem to indicate that these compositions have a distinctly Platonic flavor. They are Platonic not only in their fundamental philosophic orientation, their general topics or in their specific titles, but also in their particular motivation or intent. The Platonic Academy, we know, was concerned both with philosophic theory and practical action, that is, with the effective propagation of this theory. Hence, it encouraged and expected its members to participate actively and aggressively in the great philosophic debates of the time. The *Gryllus*, for instance, defends and extolls Plato's theory of rhetoric in an undeniably Platonic fashion. Moreover, it denounces Isocrates and his brand of rhetoric as well as his philosophy in general in a most vehement manner, thus continuing, in the name of Platonic philosophy and in the spirit of the Academy, the long-standing intellectual feud between Plato and Isocrates. In so doing, the *Gryllus* also carries out one of the avowed maxims or aims of the Academy, namely, to take active steps in the deliberate propagation of Plato's philosophy, as well as in the 'intellectual conquest' of the Hellenic mind for Platonic thought.[1] The same might be said about the *Protrepticus*. Here, too, Aristotle extolls the essentially Platonic view of the unrivalled superiority of the intellectual (Platonic) life over all other forms of life. This eloquent exhortation, which is addressed to a Cypriot, is in its larger implications a fervent appeal to the whole of the Hellenic world. It is used by Aristotle (and by the Academy) as an intellectual 'invasion' and 'conquest' of the island of Cyprus, the philosophic stronghold of Isocrates. In this, Aristotle seems to imitate Plato, who himself had attempted intellectually to 'conquer' Syracuse and Eastern Sicily by converting the two Dionysii to his philosophy. Since the *Protrepticus* is also addressed to the whole of the Hellenic world, in its ultimate intent it aspired to the philosophic 'conquest'

of the Greek mind—to a conversion of the whole of civilized mankind
to the teachings of Plato.

The *Eudemus or On the Soul*, which is primarily, though by no means
exclusively, a *consolatio mortis*, not only betrays the dominant influence
of Plato's eschatological and utterly pessimistic outlook as regards this
wholly inadequate world of ours, but also makes direct use of some of
the arguments advanced in Plato's *Phaedo* in order to disprove the
contention that the soul is merely a kind of attunement of several
component parts and, hence, as such has no distinct existence of its
own. Aside from borrowing its title from the Platonic *Statesman*, the
*Politicus*, provided the only surviving significant fragment is correctly
translated to mean 'the Good is the most precise measure [among all
measures],' seems to be influenced decisively by Plato's *Statesman* and,
especially, by Plato's *Philebus*, where we are told that pure measure
occupies the first and uppermost rank within the hierarchy of goods
and values, the second going to the measurable, and the third to the
intellect capable of apprehending measure. The *On Justice*, again,
to a large extent seems to be under the influence of Plato's *Republic*,
from which it borrows not only its title but also the vast range of
philosophic (and other) topics upon which it touches. It must be
assumed, however, that in the *On Justice* Aristotle disagrees with and
modifies some of the extreme and essentially unrealistic views advocated by the Platonic *Republic*. This critical attitude becomes even
more pronounced in the *On Kingship*, where Aristotle takes issue with
some of Plato's Utopian postulates.

The *On Philosophy*, too, manifests the dominant influence of Plato
and Platonism in general. Admittedly, Plato had contrasted his conception of the transcendent world of the Ideas and the world of corporeal appearances—the world of true and abiding Being and the world
of fallacious Becoming—to the point of making the latter utterly
meaningless and essentially worthless. Aristotle likewise uses this
'contrast' or 'confrontation,' but in drastic disagreement with Plato,
he declares that the visible world of corporeal appearances and becoming in itself is highly significant and eminently meaningful, not to say
valuable. If properly and affirmatively understood, he maintains, this
visible world in its unsurpassed beauty and orderliness points unmistakably to the ultimate abiding truths which by their very nature
transcend the visible world and its obvious limitations. In this sense,
the visible world is always declaratory of these ultimate transcendent
truths—the meaningful and indispensable as well as most eloquent
witness of an abiding reality and of an absolute truth. This becomes

manifest, for instance, in the *On Philosophy*, where Aristotle discusses the possibility (and validity) of a cosmological (or teleological) proof for the existence of God by employing Plato's justly famed 'cave analogy' (*Republic* 514A ff.). Hence, Aristotle makes full use of Plato's dualistic outlook, but instead of contrasting the world of pure Being or pure Mind and the world of mere appearances or 'shadows' in a posture of irreconcilable opposition, he propagates the affirmative and optimistic thesis that these two worlds in fact 'collaborate' with one another, and that they are meaningful to each other: the visible world is the surest road to the transcendental world, and the transcendental world endows the visible world with positive meaning and profounder worth. In so doing, Aristotle inaugurates not only a novel —optimistic, affirmative and fruitful—world view in general, but he also lays the foundation for a new and positive theology (or natural theology) in particular. Thus it might be maintained that in the *On Philosophy* Aristotle still employs the basic doctrines underlying Plato's ultimate philosophic outlook or viewpoint, but that by 'rearranging' these Platonic 'elements' in a spirit of positive and joyous affirmation, he radically revises the mutual interrelations between these two 'elements.'

The discussions of some of Aristotle's lost works, in the final analysis, are restricted to attempts at recapturing certain limited though probably significant aspects of these lost works. In view of the fact that we possess only a relatively small number of reliable fragments, much of what has been asserted in this book about the lost works to a large extent is still hypothesis but, it is hoped, intelligent and well-informed hypothesis. To reconstruct these lost works in their entirety, however, remains a task yet to be resolved, provided it can at all be resolved in a satisfactory manner.

Viewed in a broader and more comprehensive context, the many problems and issues discussed or implied in this book may ultimately point to the following conclusions: the life of Aristotle at times seems to be closely interwoven with his intellectual work and, again, on occasion appears to run a course wholly unrelated and even opposed to this intellectual work which seems to have been centered around theoretic contemplation and speculation. One and the same man, at least in his early compositions, extolls and recommends the theoretic life of the true philosopher. Withdrawn from and oblivious of the noisy and exciting world of action and activist involvement, he lives the first twenty years of his adult life almost exlusively in the monastic surroundings of the Platonic Academy. At the same time, he apparently becomes actively and deeply involved in the many and exciting political events which transpired in, and convulsed, the Eastern Mediterranean world during the crucial years between 359 and 323 B.C.—events which not only shook the Western world to its very foundations but also shaped it for all time to come. More than that: the philosophic views of this man, provided the works credited to him by posterity and collected in the *Corpus Aristotelicum* are wholly authentic, decisively influenced and molded for many centuries to come the history of Western philosophy as well as the history of theological thought—an influence which is still strongly felt today.

Unfortunately, in the light of the available sources, we may gain only occasional and, on the whole, not always reliable glimpses of this amazing life lived by an equally amazing man. We do not know for certain whether he was and perhaps always remained (probably with some modifications) an essential Platonist. Provided we are able to reconstruct and recapture with some degree of accuracy his early works, the latter seem to indicate that he had strong Platonic leanings. We no longer know and, as a matter of fact, have become increasingly suspicious as to whether the so-called doctrinal treatises contained in the traditional *Corpus Aristotelicum* and ascribed to his later years in their totality are really by Aristotle, at least in the form in which they have been handed down to us, or whether this *Corpus* is in fact an uncritical *mélange* of early *Peripatetica* and some *Aristotelica*—a *mélange* which might, perhaps more appropriately, be re-named *Corpus Scriptorum Peripateticorum Veterum*.[2] Thus, his life, of which we know so very little, essentially remains a riddle to us, as does his philosophic work, which is equally problematic and enigmatic.

Judging from the lost works, which seem slowly to be emerging from a host of confusing, involved and not always reliable fragments, excerpts or doxographical reports, Aristotle must have been essentially an 'other-world-directed' person. Viewed from the turbulent life he apparently lived, however, he must have been an active and deeply involved participant in many an important historical event—an active as well as realistic and 'this-world-directed' man, firmly grounded in the historical reality which he apparently helped to shape. This puzzling picture—puzzling because it is somewhat contradictory, if not irreconcilable—might indicate to a superficial observer that he had a 'split personality.' Nothing could be further from the truth, unless we should subscribe to the shopworn view that Aristotle was an 'ivory tower philosopher' who occasionally (and probably against his own inclination) took a 'fling' at politics. A passing glance at some of Aristotle's writings and a general acquaintance with the life he lived should immediately dispel this ridiculous notion. As a truly great man, he was apparently a totally committed man—committed to both intellectual speculation and practical action. This would also accord with his ultimate philosophic, religious, moral and aesthetic outlook.

But then, again, we will have to concede that whatever we know or think we know about Aristotle is gleaned from the questionable *Corpus Aristotelicum* and from some highly problematic fragments implemented by some equally problematic bits of biographical information supplied by not always reliable authors or biographers. Admittedly, the general picture which has thus been gained is deficient and may remain so forever. Perhaps it is misleading and even erroneous. But reasonable conjecture and intelligent interpretation of the scanty and at times confusing evidence, using wisely and judiciously whatever information is available at present, might assist us in restoring at least some relevant facts. Be this as it may, well-informed, intelligent and optimistic preoccupation with all the available biographical reports and with whatever remains of the lost works of the Stagirite seems to have all but destroyed the somewhat simple, or perhaps oversimplified, notions (or prejudices) we have entertained as well as propagated for too long a time about the man called Aristotle. As is so often the case with prominent men of antiquity, we may, *mutatis mutandis*, also apply to the historical Aristotle the famous Socratic dictum, 'I know that I know nothing.' This might well be the appropriate starting point—the honest maxim with which we should approach the desperately difficult and almost hopelessly involved problem of the historical Aristotle.

Any intelligent approach to the problem of the historical Aristotle, it is submitted here, must proceed along two major lines of inquiry: we must know more about the salient biographical data of this man, and we must know more about his lost (early) works which, after all, might be his only truly authentic or 'uncontaminated' works. Unquestionably, these two involved and frightfully elusive issues are vitally interrelated. Hence, they ought to be treated in unison as two complementary topics. In so doing, we might resolve at least some major problems and circumstances that surround the works of Aristotle. To cite but one instance: the true nature, content and the likely significance of the Aristotelian *Gryllus*, incidentally Aristotle's first major literary effort, is probably related to the likelihood that Aristotle for a while studied rhetoric with Isocrates before he finally 'transferred' to the Platonic Academy. This example, to be sure, could be augmented many times.

Hence, future Aristotelian scholarship, unless it intends to degenerate into sterile, unhistorical and unrealistic scholiasm, in a way will have to be determined as well as guided by these two major problems and their mutual interactions and interrelations: the life of Aristotle and the lost (early) works of Aristotle. This far-reaching insight is of paramount importance, especially since these lost works are definitely authentic and perhaps more authentic than some of the doctrinal treatises (or certain parts of these doctrinal treatises). To carry out in detail such an ambitious program will be the next major task facing us, and it will be an undertaking of almost insurmountable difficulty and exhausting labor. Conversely, it will most certainly deepen our understanding of Aristotle and Aristotle's philosophy in particular, as well as our comprehension of ancient philosophy in general, in that it conceives of the history of philosophy not merely as a disjointed record of some abstract, technical or scientific statements about a number of frequently unrelated topics, but rather an integral part of a significant totality of meaningful intellectual events or achievements grounded in a historical-existential reality. This totality, however, can adequately be established, comprehended and evaluated only if we are willing to ascertain, with a high degree of precision, what can reasonably and judiciously be inferred from all extant sources, namely, the special circumstances and the salient events in the life of Aristotle, his intellectual background and development, and the intellectual forces and personal experiences which determined the overall direction of his philosophic outlook. From the intelligent (and occasionally hypothetical or conjectural) determination and precise identification of all these factors we might proceed, with a fair degree of accuracy, to the reconstruction and subsequent evaluation of the genetic processes and trends of Aristotle's major thoughts and concerns. In so doing, we may understand more adequately how and to what extent his dominant views depend or are based, at least in part, on those of his predecessors; in part on some specific ideas and factors prevailing in his particular time or in the particular society in which—and to which—he speaks; in part on his unique nature or personality, his personal experiences and on his individual inclinations and ultimate aspiration; in part of his creative genius; and in part on certain events which molded his life and thus left an indelible impression on his mind.[3]

But let the reader beware: such a program, needless to say, in a way will also be an extremely risky and perhaps thankless task; and it will most assuredly encounter the determined opposition of many a scholar and the ridicule of many a critic. There are two main reasons for such opposition. First, by their very preoccupation, classicists, philologists and historians of ancient philosophy are essentially 'conservative' and, hence, in principle quite averse to innovations.[4] They apparently prefer to cling to traditionalist views, no matter how antiquarian and inadequate they may be.[5] No wonder, then, that in our age the natural sciences, by relying on and constantly devising ever new hypotheses, should sweep everything before them, including the humanities. This is one of the reasons why, in other words, the humanities have often fallen into bad ways: the humanities, unfortunately, have come to be too timid and at times too unimaginative in an age where, in the domains of the natural sciences, intellectual courage and creative imagination have succeeded in achieving results which only a generation ago would have been called impossible, ridiculous and insane. Secondly, by its very nature and in view of the many problems it faces, such a program will have to operate liberally with conjectures, hypotheses and 'educated guesses.' The inherent danger of any conjecture, no matter how disciplined and well-informed it may be, is always that it might overreach itself and thus treat as fact what is at best mere hypothesis. Admittedly, this danger is very real, and we might easily succumb to it in our enthusiasm or in our ignorance. But this danger shall not, and cannot, deter the ever-questing human mind from attempting to widen the horizons of human knowledge and human understanding in the boundless domains of the humanities which, by their very subject-matter, are and always shall be nearest and dearest to man as long as he considers himself the foremost object of his unceasing quest for profounder knowledge and greater understanding. Any generation and any society which abandons the humanities abandons itself. In so doing, it commits the 'great betrayal.'

# Werner Jaeger and the Reconstruction of Aristotle's Lost Works*

It is said that modern Aristotelian scholarship begins with Werner Jaeger, especially with his *Aristoteles: Grundlegung einer Geschichte seiner Entwicklung*, first published in Berlin in 1923.[1] Jaeger's approach to the problem of the historical Aristotle is based upon the following assumptions: (i) the early or earliest compositions of Aristotle, often, but not always correctly, referred to as the 'exoteric works,' propagate a pronouncedly Platonic philosophy; (ii) this Platonism of the early works conflicts with the 'Aristotelianism' of the later doctrinal treatises; (iii) the early 'Platonic' compositions of Aristotle are indisputably authentic; (iv) the later 'Aristotelian' treatises of Aristotle are likewise authentic; and (v) the only possible way of reconciling the early 'Platonic' compositions of Aristotle and the later 'Aristotelian' treatises of Aristotle while at the same time preserving the authenticity of both is to assume that in the course of his intellectual evolution Aristotle developed from an initial Platonist into a final 'Aristotelian.' In this ingenious fashion, Jaeger, who never so much as suspected that the later 'Aristotelian' doctrinal treatises might be in part spurious or, at least, 'contaminated' by post-Aristotelian Peripatetic teachings,[2] attempts not only to preserve the authenticity of both the early work and the later doctrinal treatises, but also to reconcile the two in the best possible way. Needless to say, Jaeger's whole thesis, which did so much for the establishment of the authenticity of Aristotle's early 'Platonic' works but never investigated the authenticity of Aristotle's later 'Aristotelian' doctrinal treatises, in the final analysis hinges on the still unresolved problem of the authenticity of these later doctrinal treatises traditionally ascribed to Aristotle.

In the course of his searching and masterly investigations of Aristotle's intellectual or philosophic development from an early and pronounced Platonism to a later and distinct 'Aristotelianism,' Jaeger of necessity had to deal in a most thorough manner with Aristotle's early and earliest (lost) compositions. It must always be borne in mind, however, that Jaeger's interest in the lost early compositions of Aristotle is not primarily motivated by his hope of retrieving new fragments nor by an effort to reconstruct some specific texts. What he attempts to do is to unearth and outline the progressive intellectual or philosophic evolution of Aristotle from an early (and distinct) Platonism to a later 'Aristotelianism.' Hence, his concern with the lost works of Aristotle is in a way only incidental to his main thesis. Jaeger, it will be noted, distinguishes between three major phases or periods in the intellectual development of the Stagirite: (i) Aristotle's close association with Plato and the Early Academy (367–48 B.C.) [3] and his essential adherence to the teachings of Plato; (ii) his sojourn (*Wanderjahre*) in Assos (Atarneus), Mytilene and Macedonia (Stagira?, 348/47–335 B.C.); and (iii) his return to Athens and second Athenian sojourn (or philosophic *Meisterjahre*, 335/34–323 B.C.). These three phases, Jaeger holds, roughly correspond to the three major periods in the philosophic orientation of Aristotle, namely, the 'Platonic-Academic period,' the 'transitional period' and the 'Aristotelian period.'

In order to determine as well as delineate Aristotle's fundamental philosophic outlook during his 'Platonic-Academic period,' that is, the years between 367 and 348 B.C., as well as in order to establish Aristotle's first decisive break with Plato and Platonism, Jaeger had to investigate at great length and in minute detail some of the early compositions of the Stagirite. This, in turn, compels him to 'reconstruct' and analyze the essential meaning, the basic tenor and the general philosophic outlook of these early works; as well as to establish their overall doctrinal orientation. Jaeger uses and discusses the *Eudemus or On the Soul* and the *Protrepticus* in order to demonstrate and substantiate the Platonism of Aristotle's early writings. He hails the *On Philosophy*, which is subjected to a particularly thorough and thoughtful analysis, as a 'Manifesto'—as the pivotal point at which Aristotle broke away from Plato and Platonism.[4] In the course of his discussions, Jaeger also touches on some of the other lost works of the early Aristotle, but he does so in a more casual manner. Thus he mentioned the Aristotelian *Gryllus or On Rhetoric* as an example of Aristotle's earliest efforts to imitate and, perhaps, to improve upon certain aspects of Plato's early dialogues;[5] the Aristotelian *Sophist*, *Menexenus* and *Symposium* as having been suggested (and probably influenced) by Plato's dialogues of the same titles;[6] the Aristotelian *On Justice* and *Politicus* in connection with his analysis of the 'original *Politics*' (*Urpolitik*) of Aristotle;[7] and the Aristotelian *On Poets* and *Didascaliae* as examples of Aristotle's early interest in scholarly and archivist 'collections' of facts and dates.[8]

For the extremely difficult and sensitive task of unravelling Aristotle's intellectual evolution by ascertaining his early philosophic posture, Jaeger had at his disposal only the inadequate and arbitrarily compiled collection of Aristotelian fragments by Valentin Rose, *Aristotelis Qui Ferebantur Librorum Fragmenta* (Leipzig, 1886). In view of this serious disadvantage, not to mention the pre-1923 status of Aristotelian scholarship in general or the conditions of scholarly investigations into the lost works of Aristotle in particular prevailing prior to 1923, Jaeger's accomplishments and contributions, despite the efforts of some detractors, still remain unsurpassed.

Jaeger's first, and by no means least important concern, is with the form and style in which the earliest works of Aristotle were written. Since within the Platonic Academy the dialogue was apparently considered the only proper literary form in which weighty philosophic issues were to be presented or discussed, there can be no doubt, Jaeger maintains, that the *Gryllus*, the *Eudemus* and other early compositions were cast in the form and language of dialogues, similar to such Platonic dialogues as the *Gorgias* or the *Phaedo*.[9] In some dialogues, such as the *Politicus*, the *On Justice* and the *On Philosophy*, Aristotle might have cast himself into the role befitting the leader of the whole discussion.[10] In so doing, Jaeger points out, Aristotle gave the traditional dialogue a more didactic and, certainly, a more 'scientific' tone, as well as a more substantial appearance and continuity of philosophic argumentation which Jaeger aptly calls 'the dialogue of scientific discussion.' This new literary trend, the beginnings of which are already reflected in Plato's late dialogues, according to Jaeger, presages the later Aristotelian doctrinal treatises. It might have been influenced by Plato's oral teachings, by the precepts laid down in the Platonic *Phaedrus*, and possibly by the rhetorical or protreptic prose of Isocrates. Jaeger warns us, however, that we must not seek to standardize the external form of the early Aristotelian writings, or assume that Aristotle perhaps used a fixed literary pattern or strategy from which he never deviated. The literary development of the young Aristotle, Jaeger concludes, mirrors his intellectual evolution, progressing from the 'obstetric' dialogue so characteristic of the early Platonic compositions, to the 'dialogue of scientific discussion,' to the hortatory prose essay and, finally, to the doctrinal treatise.[11]

In short, Jaeger made the fundamental and far-reaching discovery that, contrary to certain traditional but apparently ill-informed assumptions, the early works of Aristotle were cast in a variety of literary forms, ranging all the way from the 'obstetric' dialogue and the 'dialogue of scientific discussion' to the 'didactic' (and hortatory) essay and the sober scientific treatise. Hence, the literary form as such does not supply a reliable criterion for the establishment of the authenticity of either a particular work credited to the young Aristotle or that of a certain fragment ascribed to an early composition of Aristotle. Neither does it furnish a positive clue for the determination of the proper dating of the work to which this fragment has been credited. This realization is Jaeger's first important contribution to the retrieval, interpretation and possible reconstruction of the lost early works of Aristotle. He correctly refuted the old theory that all or at least the first nineteen of Aristotle's early compositions as they have been listed in the 'catalogue' of Diogenes Laertius (DL V. 22) must have been 'Platonic dialogues.' At the same time, Jaeger points out that Aristotle probably soon developed his own literary prose-style and that his primary stylistic (and philosophic) aim was to be clear and concise and to avoid shallow rhetoric—something which evoked the admiration of ancient authors and literary critics.[12]

In keeping with his evolutionary thesis, Jaeger claims that the earliest works of Aristotle are modeled to a large extent on certain Platonic dialogues: the *Gryllus* on the *Gorgias*, the *Eudemus* on the *Phaedo*, the *On Justice* on the *Republic*, the *Politicus* on the *Statesman*, and the *Protrepticus* on the *Euthydemus* (278B–282D). The fact that these particular Aristotelian compositions are modeled on certain Platonic dialogues does not mean, however, that they are nothing more than crude imitations of Plato nor that they must be dialogues. What Jaeger wishes to convey is the notion that these Aristotelian works discuss the same subject or topic as the corresponding Platonic dialogues without, however, using in every instance Plato's method, approach, literary form or perhaps Plato's range of suggestions and ideas. That the Aristotelian *Sophist*, *Menexenus* and *Symposium* were suggested by the Platonic dialogues of the same titles,[13] Jaeger believes, needs no elaboration, although it is not certain whether by choosing these titles Aristotle wished to indicate that he was merely writing some lengthy 'addenda' or comments to Plato's compositions; or whether, in keeping with the ancient educational principle of association-observation-imitation, he sought simply to copy the master. Jaeger, however, flatly rejects the notion that in some of his earliest writings, especially in those which bear the same titles as certain Platonic dialogues, Aristotle might have intended to treat certain philosophic problems more fully and more systematically than his teacher had done, and that he really attempted to improve upon Plato.[14]

In pointing out the close similarities in form and content between the early writings of Aristotle and certain dialogues of Plato, Jaeger makes two major contributions to our understanding of, and to the whole process of retrieving, the lost works of the Stagirite: first, the earliest compositions of Aristotle are strongly, if not decisively, under the influence of Platonic teachings;[15] and, second, this early Platonism is a valuable and perhaps paramount criterion in the identification and dating of these earliest works. It was also this insight which led Jaeger to the realization that Aristotle prepared his intellectual break with Plato and with certain aspects of late Platonism while still actively associated with the Academy. Aristotle's intellectual development towards a more personal conception of philosophy in general and a more individual mode of expression in particular, therefore, not only begins during the period of his association with Plato, but is actually grounded in, and stimulated by, this Academic relationship. In other words, it was the particularly stimulating atmosphere within the Academy itself—a sort of 'academic freedom' which permeated the Academy—which must be held accountable for Aristotle's striking out in a new philosophic and literary direction. Contrary to the views propagated by V. Rose and others, the Platonism apparent in certain fragments and excerpts credited to Aristotle's earliest writings is in itself a strong if not decisive indication of their unquestionable authenticity.[16] Moreover, this Platonism is an indispensable consideration in dating and interpreting the work or works to which the several fragments are assigned.[17] Though not unanimously appreciated and accepted, this insight constitutes Jaeger's second important and pioneering contribution to the treatment and understanding of Aristotle's lost early compositions. Hence, in a general manner, it may be concluded that Jaeger's main achievements as regards the lost early works of Aristotle are the following: (i) the literary form in which the several early compositions are cast in itself does not supply a reliable criterion for establishing the authenticity or the 'chronology' of a fragment or of the work to which this particular fragment has been assigned; (ii) the early works of Aristotle are strikingly Platonic; and (iii) the Platonism of the early writings in itself is an indispensable criterion in the identification, interpretation, authentication and dating of these early works.

Before Jaeger could successfully establish and defend his evolutionary thesis, he had to 'reconstruct' in some detail the essential philosophic content, though not necessarily the exact original text, of some of Aristotle's first compositions. He discusses minutely only three of the early lost works, namely, the *Eudemus*, the *Protrepticus* and the *On Philosophy*. Dating the *Eudemus* (*On the Soul*)[18] about 354–53 B.C., he holds that this particular dialogue—and it was definitely a dialogue—was wholly Platonic both in form and philosophic content; that it was written in close imitation of Plato's *Phaedo*; and that it is essentially a *consolatio mortis* rather than a doctrinal or systematic discussion of the nature of the soul.[19] This last contention, which represents a discovery of far-reaching consequences, to a large extent determines the whole interpretation and, by implication, the possible reconstruction of the *Eudemus*.[20]

Admittedly, by its very intent and purpose, a *consolatio mortis* must touch upon the nature of the soul, especially upon the personal immortality of the soul, including the conditions and causes of this personal immortality. For it is of the essence of any genuine *consolatio mortis* that it proclaim the departed person as living on as a person; insist that he has finally reached the 'land of bliss and eternal peace'; emphasize that he has gone to his ultimate and true home where he really belonged (and whence he originally came); maintain that his many longings are stilled and his wanderings and sufferings ended; and assert the assurance that some day there will be a happy reunion with all those who loved him and whom he loved.[21] For 'the life spent in death is better than that spent in life.'[22] All this, however, simply presupposes the immortality of the individual soul—of the whole soul as Plato pointedly stresses in the *Phaedo*—because only the belief in personal immortality can give real comfort, hope and solace to the sorrowing heart of man, a heart which reaches out for love and undying remembrance. The dream of Eudemus that he would soon be released from his exile and be allowed to return home signifies[23] that the deity itself, which appears to Eudemus during his illness, confirms the truth of Plato's insistence that the soul originally came from 'heaven' only ultimately to return to 'heaven,' that is, to its real home. It also corroborates—and this is even more important—the immortality of the soul.[24]

In the *Eudemus*, Jaeger correctly observes, Aristotle is wholly and firmly committed to Plato's doctrine that the soul existed before it became incarnated (or incarcerated) in the body; that at one time it became incarnated; and that it yearns forever for its true, heavenly home—for its 'eternal return.'[25] Hence, Aristotle must at one time have believed not only in the personal immortality of the individual soul, but also in the infinite superiority of the afterlife, a theme which is also at the basis of the Platonic *Phaedo*. And like Plato in the *Phaedo*,[26]

Aristotle tries to demonstrate dialectically the immortality of the soul,[27] although in his particular demonstration he alters somewhat the Platonic argument in that he reduces it to what amounts to a simplified syllogism.[28] All this, Jaeger insists, indicates that in the *Eudemus* Aristotle is still wholly dependent on and basically commited to Plato's metaphysics and psychology, that is, committed to Plato's particular conception of substance, as well as to Plato's assertion, unique in the *Phaedo* but recanted in the *Republic*, that the soul is a single, simple substance and, accordingly, is incorruptible and immortal.

Plato's influence on the *Eudemus*, Jaeger contends, also becomes manifest in the apocalyptic 'revelation' of Silenus who informs King Midas of the irredeemable wretchedness of the human condition on earth.[29] In its oracular tenor, this relevation parallels the story of Lachesis in the Platonic myth of Er,[30] both as to its style and content. It has its climax in the somber pronouncement that since 'it is impossible for living man to attain to the best of all things, it is best for both men and women not to be born at all; and second best, and the best that can be achieved by men, since they have been born, is to die as soon as possible.'[31] The Platonism of this passage, Jaeger points out, is simply overwhelming. It reflects the basic Platonic eschatological conviction that to be cast into the imperfect world of Becoming, into this 'vale of tears,' is a cruel and tortuous and in a way 'unnatural' punishment—an unbearable banishment or incarceration; to return to the world of perfect Being, which is the soul's natural (heavenly) home, is glorious redemption, the ultimate triumph and the joyous relief from a dreary, painful and unnatural 'exile.'[32]

Not to be born, not ever to be flung into the world of Becoming, to remain forever in the world of perfect Being, is the best of all things; and to return to this perfect world as soon as possible is certainly the second best thing.[33] This particular tenet and its peculiar type, Jaeger points out, indicates that in the *Eudemus* Aristotle still adheres to Plato's essentially religious (Orphic or Pythagorean?) views, proclaimed in the *Phaedo*, that the whole soul, and not as in the *Republic* merely the rational part of the soul (the νοῦς), is immortal.[34] Such a position, it has been shown, is the only tenable one in a *consolatio mortis* such as the Platonic *Phaedo* and the Aristotelian *Eudemus*. It arises, Jaeger maintains, from an impassionate and unshakable belief in another and better life beyond the vicissitudes, fears and sufferings of earthly 'non-existence.' It is grounded in the religious and ethical conviction that the whole soul is indestructible—independent of the corporeal world into which it has been banished.[35] And it presupposes the unquestioned assumption that the 'natural' corporeal world in the final analysis is something 'unnatural' for the soul. The Platonism of this position is too obvious to require detailed discussion.[36]

Finally, Jaeger insists, according to the *Eudemus*, the soul possesses recollection or memory—a characteristically Platonic twist. In Aristotle, however, this recollection becomes a continuity of awareness. Unlike Plato, Aristotle denies that the soul, while connected with the body, remembers something of its pre-earthly existence. Instead, Aristotle holds that upon its return to its heavenly home, the soul recollects what it has experienced in this world,[37] a notion completely alien and even repugnant to Plato, but vital for any *consolatio mortis* such as the *Eudemus*: the departed remembers and still loves persons 'near and dear' to him, as he is remembered and still loved by those persons 'near and dear' he leaves behind. All this, Jaeger correctly insists, indicates that for Aristotle the life without the body is the soul's normal and healthy existence, while its fusion with or incarceration within the body is an unnatural state and, as it were, a sort of temporary illness.[38] During this illness, the soul temporarily forgets what it had beheld before 'falling ill.' But when at the very threshold of death or when it temporarily leaves the body in dreams or in some exalted state (and thus momentarily recovers its 'health'), the soul regains its 'lost vision' of the world beyond. This argument, Jaeger points out,[39] is directly derived from Plato's *Republic* and *Philebus* (as well as the *Laws*), where Plato, in order to define the virtues or vices of the body and soul respectively, speaks of the health or sickness of either the body or the soul, that is, of the harmony (justice) or disharmony (injustice) within either.[40] Thus it further appears that the immortality of the soul spoken of in the *Eudemus* is an altered but nevertheless close derivative of the doctrine of recollection (*anamnesis*) as it was expounded by Plato in the *Phaedo* and in the *Meno*.[41] Jaeger insists that in the *Eudemus* Aristotle not only accepts the Platonic doctrine of recollection but apparently also adheres to Plato's teachings concerning the Ideas or Separate Forms. This seems to follow, says Jaeger, not only from the references to 'the things the soul saw there' when during an illness it left the body temporarily for 'the other world' only to return to this world during convalescence, but also from the reference to 'the things there,' that is, in the 'world beyond' which contains the Ideas.[42] And these 'things' are most certainly the Separate Ideas which, according to Plato, are the only true and abiding 'things' to be visualized by the soul in the other world. Moreover, for Plato, recollection and the Separate Ideas no less than pre-existence and immortality are inseparably linked together.

Hence, according to Jaeger, it appears that for both Plato and Aristotle (at least in the *Eudemus*), the immortality of the soul also depends on, and presupposes, the existence of the Separate Ideas in a 'supernatural' sphere.

Jaeger concludes his analysis of the *Eudemus* by pointing out that at least down to the year 354–53 B.C., the year in which he dates this dialogue, Aristotle was thoroughly imbued with Plato's philosophy. He concedes, however, that although Aristotle is still completely dependent on Plato's metaphysics in this particular work, he already manifests a certain undeniable independence and originality in matters of presentation, that is, in his methodology and logical technique. Jaeger ascribes this metaphysical dependence primarily to the fact that, in a *consolatio mortis* such as the *Eudemus*, Aristotle tries to give expression to a religious and personal feeling which finds its most adequate expression in the Platonic 'other-world-orientation' and, concomitantly, in the essentially religious myths of Plato. It is this inner need for solace, this intense seeking for a comforting as well as persuasive answer to the riddle of death, which forces Aristotle in the *Eudemus* to be a committed Platonist. Conversely, by applying his own method and logical technique, as well as by slightly altering some of Plato's views, Aristotle, in the opinion of Jaeger, not only preserves his individuality as a thinker and, hence, avoids outright imitation and plain plagiarism, but he also displays his particular talent for 'scientific' or logical argument.[43]

Jaeger's main contribution to the retrieval and better understanding of the substance of the *Eudemus*, then, is his insistence that this Aristotelian dialogue is primarily a *consolatio mortis*, modeled on the Platonic *Phaedo* in its literary form, general argumentation and doctrinal content.[44] That the *Eudemus* is essentially a *consolatio mortis*, rather than a treatise on the nature of the soul in itself, determines the work's basic tenor and *motif*. This realization in itself constitutes not only a major step forward in the correct evaluation of the *Eudemus*, but also amounts to an important directive for any future attempt at reconstructing this dialogue. Thanks to Jaeger's penetrating and persuasive insights into the nature and purpose of the *Eudemus*, we know that with some minor modifications, the *Eudemus* is basically Platonic in scope, method and treatment; and that we must look first to the Platonic *Phaedo* if we are ever to understand the *Eudemus*. Jaeger is most emphatic in pointing out that Aristotle's early Platonism becomes most tellingly manifest in his doctrine of the immortality of the soul—the main theme of the *Eudemus*.[45] Once properly established and characterized, this Platonism enables us not only to verify the authenticity of those fragments which have been, or will be, ascribed to the *Eudemus*, but also to determine their ultimate philosophic meaning.[46] And finally, it will further assist us in establishing the approximate date of composition for this dialogue which is an eloquent testimonial of Aristotle's original adherence to the philosophy of his teacher. Naturally, the heroic death of Eudemus of Cyprus in 354–53 B.C. always supplies us with a reasonable *tempus post quod* for the composition of the *Eudemus*, a date which is confirmed by the findings of Jaeger.[47]

As in the case of the *Eudemus*, Jaeger's principal interest in the Aristotelian *Protrepticus* lies in his broader effort to establish and verify the intellectual progression of Aristotle, rather than in an acribic investigation of this early work of the Stagirite.[48] According to Jaeger, the *Protrepticus* constitutes the first important stage in the evolution of Aristotle's ethical thought—a development extending from the *Protrepticus*, through the *Eudemian Ethics*, to the *Nicomachean Ethics*.[49] The detailed verification of this major thesis, needless to say, compelled him to discuss the *Protrepticus* in a rather thorough fashion. Jaeger's general analysis of Aristotle's *Protrepticus*, it must be admitted, succeeds not only in throwing much light on the *Quellenlage* of this lost composition but also on its literary form and background and on its philosophic or doctrinal content and orientation. It also makes lasting and far-reaching contributions to the recovery and reconstruction of Aristotle's *Protrepticus*.[50]

Jaeger insists that for philosophic content, the *Protrepticus* draws heavily upon Platonic doctrine, especially upon Plato's *Euthydemus* 278E–282D.[51] Its literary form as well as its peculiar method or argumentation, however, owe more to Isocrates and his protreptic addresses, particularly to the so-called *Cyprian Orations*[52] in which Isocrates employed, and improved upon, the type of hortatory essay devised by the Sophists. Jaeger contends that the Aristotelian *Protrepticus* is something more than an ordinary hortatory piece or, perhaps, simply a kind of 'mirror for princes.'[53] In its broader aspects, it is the solemn proclamation of a new ideal of the philosophic life—an eloquent appeal directed at the whole of civilized mankind to embrace the theoretic (philosophic) life, that is, the contemplative life, and a fervent call for a new aim of life and culture[54]—a blatantly Platonic pronouncement. In other words, it is in fact a plan for the total conversion of humanity to the pedagogical ideals as they were advocated by Plato and by the Platonic Academy.[55] To have seen this clearly is one of Jaeger's major contributions to Aristotelian scholarship and to classical scholarship in general. This insight in itself enables us to understand better the ultimate *motif* as well as the basic spirit of the *Protrepticus* and, hence, provides us with a firm foundation for the correct treatment and the proper reconstruction of this essay. As a solemn appeal to reason—Platonic reason—the *Protrepticus* reaches far beyond the confines of traditional philosophic investigation and discussion; and as a manifestation of an abiding faith in this reason and in the redeeming aspects of reason, it cannot possibly limit itself to just one single purpose.[56]

Jaeger also notes that Aristotle, in his characteristically systematic or scientific manner, frequently transforms the conventional type of hortatory appeals, which had a long and distinguished history, into a tight argumentation which at times assumes syllogistic forms. This novel presentation of arguments and demonstrations in the form of scientific rhetoric within the *Protrepticus*, Jaeger concludes, represents a most successful combination of the 'hortatory content of the Platonic *Gorgias* and the *Phaedo* with the uniform prose of the Isocratean protreptic.'[57] At the same time, according to Jaeger, the *Protrepticus* is an eloquent and effective rejoinder to Isocrates's utilitarian views on education and intellectual culture,[58] and a counter to Isocrates' position that the significance of all human knowledge must ultimately be measured by its practical efficacy, that is, by worldly success.[59] In short, the *Protrepticus*, probably the first fully and deliberately theoretical exhortation of its kind (barring perhaps Plato, *Euthydemus* 278E–282D), is thoroughly Platonic in spirit and fundamental values: it extolls the unchallengeable superiority of living in accordance with a principled (Platonic) philosophy. Thus, the argument advanced in the *Protrepticus* denounces any educational program, such as that advocated by Isocrates and his school, which was designed primarily as a preparation for the 'successful life' in terms of wealth and power.[60] At the same time, and probably for greater effectiveness (and in order to reach a larger public), the *Protrepticus* is cast in the rhetorical style of Isocrates. To achieve greater persuasiveness, it relies upon a tight logical or syllogistic mode of argumentation. This latter characteristic is without doubt Aristotle's original contribution to the hortatory type of essay.

With some minor though by no means negligible exceptions, Jaeger confirms (and amends) the pioneering suggestions which I. Bywater had made some fifty-four years earlier,[61] namely, that the *Protrepticus* of Iamblichus (chaps V–XII) contains lengthy and, in the main, fairly accurate and reliable quotations from, or references to, the *Protrepticus* of Aristotle.[62] Jaeger rightly believes that for certain parts of his *Protrepticus*, Iamblichus relied heavily on Aristotle's

*Protrepticus*, and that he did so because during the days of Iamblichus the Aristotelian *Protrepticus* was probably considered the prototype of this kind of hortatory literature. Moreover, the undeniably ascetic character of Aristotle's *Protrepticus* appealed to the Neo-Platonist Iamblichus, while the unmistakable Platonism of the Aristotelian text furnished Iamblichus with a welcome opportunity for reconciling the doctrinal differences between Platonic doctrines and Peripatetic teachings—an extremely important resolution for the essentially syncretist Neo-Platonists.[63] The hortatory tenor of the Aristotelian *Protrepticus*, in the opinion of Iamblichus, also lent itself admirably to the kind of 'philosophic reader for beginners' he envisioned when writing his *Protrepticus*.

As I. Bywater, R. Hirzel[64] and P. Hartlich[65] did before him, Jaeger attempts to fix more accurately the specific passages in Iamblichus' *Protrepticus* which are based upon, or refer to, Aristotle's work of the same title.[66] He rejects Bywater's thesis, however, that the whole of chapter V, chapters VI–XI, and the whole of chapter XII contain recognizable fragments from Aristotle's original composition. He insists that because chapter V is also replete with citations from Plato and Porphyry, it would be more than hazardous to credit to Aristotle the whole of chapter V of Iamblichus' *Protrepticus*, including pp. 34,5–36,26 (ed. H. Pistelli),[67] as some scholars had done. He also maintains that the last part of chapter XII (pp. 60,10–61,4) of Iamblichus' *Protrepticus*, which degenerates into a rabid, unctuous and confused sermon calling upon the reader to choose the 'heavenly path,' is too emotional (and too Neo-Platonic) to be safely assigned to Aristotle.[68] Jaeger suggests, rather, that we must look for fragments of, and references to, the Aristotelian *Protrepticus* beginning at p. 36,27, and ending at page 60,10, Pistelli. But he does not concern himself with establishing the probable sequence in which the several fragments culled from Iamblichus' *Protrepticus* should be arranged.[69] Such an endeavor, it goes without saying, is outside the particular scope of Jaeger's investigation and discussion. Jaeger is aware of the fact, however, that Iamblichus did not observe the sequence in which Aristotle had originally presented his ideas and arguments, but rather listed them according to specific subjects or topics.[70] Jaeger's observation that Iamblichus did violence to Aristotle's original order of presentation stimulated subsequent efforts to rearrange the several fragments in their proper sequence.

Although Iamblichus, *Protrepticus* 36,27–60,10, Pistelli, does not quote Plato directly, but perhaps *via* an intermediary source, the Aristotelian *Protrepticus* would appear to model its doctrinal or philosophic views on

Plato's *Euthydemus*.[71] Indeed, Jaeger maintains that the primary source of several of the identifiable Aristotelian fragments is unmistakably *Euthydemus* 278B–282D.[72] This does not mean, however—and Jaeger is quite emphatic about this—that Iamblichus, *Protrepticus* 36,27–60,10 is a collection of excerpts from the Platonic *Euthydemus*. Iamblichus makes direct use of Aristotle's *Protrepticus*, and Aristotle, in the opinion of Jaeger, is to some extent influenced here by Plato's *Euthydemus*. Jaeger warns, of course, that it would be foolhardy to rely too heavily upon Iamblichus for either competent comprehension or precise recording of the structure, sequence or philosophic content of the original Aristotelian *Protrepticus*; to derive Aristotle's original mode of presentation and argumentation directly and uncritically from Iamblichus' essentially confused and confusing account. For Jaeger is well aware of the fact that Iamblichus is a man of rather modest intellectual endowments, prone to misunderstand and misquote the notions entertained by others—a muddled thinker and a poor stylist, who, as often as not, does grave injustice to the sources he cites.[73] When discussing Iamblichus' qualifications as a reporter, Jaeger also analyzes and evaluates Iamblichus' peculiar method of excerpting, rearranging and presenting the Aristotelian prototype. He concludes that the Aristotelian materials or 'fragments' not only are frequently cast in the diction of the reporter, but also reflect the intellectual limitations of the latter. Hence, these citations are not perchance literal quotations, but rather abridged and occasionally severely mutilated renditions of the Aristotelian original by an essentially inept reporter.[74] In so doing, Jaeger also disposes of the argument that such a humdrum *mélange* of disjointed and often platitudinous statements as Iamblichus' *Protrepticus* could not possibly be traced back to so disciplined and talented a thinker as Aristotle.

Jaeger's further demonstrable findings are briefly the following: (i) there exist persuasive, not to say compelling, similarities between certain passages found in Iamblichus' *Protrepticus*, chapters VI–XII (60,10), and certain other texts definitely identified as belonging or being related to the Aristotelian *Protrepticus*;[75] (ii) the general language, style, technical expressions, philosophical nomenclature and particular mode of argumentation in these passages, so far as they have not been mutilated by Iamblichus, are convincingly Aristotelian (although the overall structure—as well as certain linking phrases—of the presentation of these fragments or excerpts by Iamblichus is definitely the handiwork of the latter, something which may be inferred from the frequently disorganized and characteristically confusing manner in which the whole account is presented);[76] and (iii) there also exist certain undeniable parallels between the doctrinal content of these fragments or excerpts, and the philosophic teachings found in the preserved doctrinal treatises of Aristotle.[77]

Jaeger observes, as has been noted, that some of these passages from Iamblichus' *Protrepticus* are frequently cast in the distinctive, but frequently unambiguous, language of Iamblichus. Since many of the ideas expressed here by Iamblichus indisputably extend far beyond his own rather limited intellectual range, it is reasonable to assume that he is simply using or reporting the notions advanced by more talented and more original thinkers—in this case, those of Aristotle. Jaeger cautions, however, that this should not imply that the several references to Aristotle's *Protrepticus* in Iamblichus are literal or essentially unadulterated quotations. On the contrary, a great many of these references are abbreviated and not infrequently severely mutilated renditions.[78] The obvious inadequacy of intellect, the limited facility of expression, the frequently appalling awkwardness in the formulation of philosophic ideas and arguments, and the patchwork disorganization in presentation—all of which mar the *Protrepticus* of Iamblichus—therefore, must exclusively be attributed to the latter. The poverty of Iamblichus' intellectual qualifications certainly ill-suited him to report adequately, or to do justice to, the thought and presentation of Aristotle who, in the considered judgment of competent ancient authors and literary critics, expressed himself with great elegance and admirable clarity in his early compositions.[79] Jaeger's pioneering insights into the nature of Iamblichus' *Protrepticus* and into the peculiarities as well as defects of Iamblichus as a reporter or commentator, cannot be stressed often enough. They are of decisive importance for all future attempts to come to grips with, and resolve, the many vexing problems connected with the *Protrepticus* of Aristotle.

Jaeger's particular and detailed analysis of Iamblichus, *Protrepticus* 41,6–45,3,[80] issues in the following conclusions:[81] In 41,6–15, Iamblichus states three major propositions in his own peculiar sequence as well as in his own ill-phrased way: (i) rational thinking is in itself of inestimable value to man; (ii) it is useful to life in general; and (iii) theoretic philosophy is essential to the true happiness of man.[82] To these three propositions correspond: (i) chapters VII–IX (41,15–54,9) of Iamblichus' *Protrepticus*; (ii) chapter X (54,10–56,12); and (iii) chapter XI (56,13–59,18) as well as the first part of chapter XII (59,19–60,10). The content or subject matter of 41,15–45,3, Jaeger insists, undoubtedly is comprised of excerpts from the Aristotelian *Protrepticus*, although the particular sequential arrangement is uncritically governed by the 'outline' suggested by Iamblichus in 41,6–15, rather than by Aristotle's original order.[83] In other words, Iamblichus uses his 'outline' as his basic scheme, implementing it with select passages from Aristotle's original *Protrepticus*. However, since Iamblichus' choices from the Aristotelian *Protrepticus*, on the whole, are random selections, he frequently does violence to Aristotle's original text or, at least, to the sequence followed by Aristotle.[84] This disregard of the original sequence in some instances leads not only to a misrepresentation or distortion of the original Aristotelian ideas, but also to the suppression of the specific (and often enlightening) arguments made by Aristotle in support of these ideas. Moreover, there can be little doubt that in his own arrangement Iamblichus not only omits certain passages which might be essential to the further clarification or justification of these ideas. He also adds some arguments or connecting phrases of his own which are not always to the point.

The first major sustained passage from Aristotle is found in 41,15–43,25, which, in Jaeger's opinion, constitutes a single line of thought.[85] As to its main content and essential form of argument, Jaeger insists that this passage is typically Aristotelian: the comparison of the 'pleasures of seeing' with the delights of the dispassionate spectator; the importance given to the concepts of function and work; the clear distinction between functions performed *in* certain activities and the functions merely performed *through* them; the distinction between the productive, the practical and the theoretic activities; the identity of the subject and object in the active intellect; the implied doctrine of the several levels of value according to which the higher levels always include the lower levels; and the doctrine of the three ways of life and the corresponding three points of view about life (namely, the hedonistic-sensual, the ethico-practical, and the purely intellectual or theoretic)[86]—all these topics and their specific treatment are, in the opinion of Jaeger, markedly Aristotelian (and Platonic).[87] Furthermore, the doctrinal content of 43,20–45,3, is indisputably Aristotelian,[88] as any comparison with *Metaphysics* 980 a 21–980 b 1 (incidentally, a part of the *Urmetaphysik*) should clearly reveal.[89] Iamblichus, Jaeger observes, combines here several distinct passages taken from different parts of Aristotle's *Protrepticus*[90] simply because the contents of these passages are, or appear to be, quite similar or closely related. The result is, according to Jaeger, that this forced fusion of disparate citations from Aristotle in 43,20–45,3 strikes us as being pointlessly repetitious and, at times, rather confusing—a fustian of indiscriminately selected citations from Aristotle's *Protrepticus*.

Chapters VI and VII of Iamblichus' *Protrepticus*, Jaeger continues, place great emphasis not only on dialectical (or logical) reasoning (a typical trait in Aristotle's earliest works), but also on the unrivaled self-sufficiency of purely theoretic knowledge. These characteristics, Jaeger believes, are in themselves a persuasive indication that the content as well as the method of presentation in these two chapters are ultimately derived from the Aristotelian *Protrepticus*.[91] The statement that the 'theoretic man' must be rated above the 'practical man'; the assertion that mere empiricism is incapable of providing sure knowledge and exact understanding; the insistence that all precise knowledge of the rational type must rely not on perception, but rather on 'first principles'; and the statement that these 'first principles' constitute the proper subject matter of the highest theoretic or philosophical studies[92] —all these assertions are, Jaeger believes, distinctly Aristotelian (and, in the final analysis, Platonic).[93]

The first part of chapter IX (49,3–52,16),[94] where Iamblichus lists and evaluates the several causes of 'coming into being,' is, in Jaeger's opinion, predominantly Aristotelian,[95] as are (a) the notion that nature is more purposive than art (49,26–28); (b) the statement that 'nature does not imitate art, but art, rather, imitates nature';[96] and (c) the claim that 'art exists to assist nature and to complete the work nature leaves undone' (49,28–50,2).[97] Also probably Aristotelian are the several examples or illustrations offered by Iamblichus to substantiate the latter three assertions (50,2–51,7).[98] As regards the last part of chapter IX (52,16–54,5),[99] Jaeger insists that the entire argument used to refute the notion that philosophic knowledge is largely useless for practical life is most certainly by Aristotle,[100] although in all likelihood Iamblichus manages to pervert the force of the original discourse.[101]

Chapters X–XII (54,10–60,10),[102] Jaeger judges, rely heavily on Aristotle's *Protrepticus*. This is indicated by the use of, or at least the point of view involving, the following basic notions (54,10–56,12): (i) all proper science of politics must rest on, and take its point of departure from, theoretic philosophy; (ii) only philosophy can furnish the statesman with ultimate, that is, valid and immutable norms or standards; (iii) politics or political science can become a true science only if thoroughly imbued with the spirit of philosophy; and (iv) although rational (philosophic) knowledge is always purely theoretic, in their practical actions men are forced, if they intend to engage in right political action, to fall back on it.[103] The one-sided emphasis on the theoretic nature of normative politics, Jaeger concludes, compellingly suggests that these passages, which have an overwhelming Platonic flavor, were originally part of that general elevation of pure theory or pure philosophy over actual practice. This 'priority' of theory over practice, according to Jaeger, constitutes the main theme of the (Platonizing) Aristotelian *Protrepticus*.[104] In an appeal addressed to a practicing statesman (Themison) Aristotle points out that politics, if it is to be stable and fruitful, must be based on philosophic principles rather than on general analogies taken from practical experience.[105]

Jaeger further claims that the dominant issue of chapter XI (56,13–59,18),[106] namely the relation between philosophic wisdom (*phronesis* in the Platonic sense) and pleasure, is Aristotelian, that is, directly taken from Aristotle's *Protrepticus*.[107] Indeed, according to Jaeger, this problematic relation was a perennial topic for discussion within the Academy.[108] Hence, it is reasonable to surmise that this discussion would also occupy an important place in an essay such as the Aristotelian *Protrepticus*, which, in its thoroughly Platonic spirit, endeavored to demonstrate that theoretic knowledge in itself is supreme happiness; and that the life of purely intellectual contemplation affords the most perfect pleasures.[109] In Aristotle's *Protrepticus*, where the theoretic life is extolled and elevated infinitely above the practical life, one must also expect that its author would regard the purely theoretic life as the most pleasurable and, hence, most desirable life—as the only life befitting rational man.[110]

The first part of chapter XII (59,19–60,7 or 60,10),[111] Jaeger points out, merely continues the discussion of the relation between philosophic knowledge and happiness, and so—on the aforementioned grounds—may safely be ascribed to Aristotle's *Protrepticus*. With some hesitation, Jaeger concedes, however, that the last part of chapter XII (60,10–61,4), which describes the *vita beata* (based on purely theoretic knowledge or pure contemplation), might possibly contain echoes of the concluding sentences or culminating arguments of the original Aristotelian *Protrepticus*.[112] Unlike I. Bywater before him,[113] Jaeger does not think, however, that sufficient evidence has been marshalled to justify the inclusion of the remainder of chapter XII (60,10–61,4) among the authentic fragments of Aristotle's original text.[114] In Jaeger's opinion, these passages, which culminate in a passionate and at times unctuous sermon, are too enthusiastic and much too emotional to fit the disciplined and essentially sober approach of Aristotle. In part they smack of Neo-Platonic 'ecstasy,' something totally alien to Aristotle.[115]

Jaeger is fully aware of the fact that an essentially hortatory essay such as the *Protrepticus* must necessarily encompass many philosophic problems, including the ultimate meaning as well as final justification of philosophy, and the proper place of philosophy in man's total life.[116]

He asserts that the Aristotelian *Protrepticus* was written out of an abiding and exuberantly Platonic faith in the irresistible power of philosophic knowledge, in the matchless superiority of the theoretic-contemplative life over all other forms of life, no matter how 'successful' in terms of worldly man. Having once grasped the urgent necessity of philosophy, Aristotle presses this point with all the vigor his disciplined mind could muster within the framework of a hortatory essay addressed to a worldly man. Here he proclaims the beatitudes of intellectual contemplation to which only true philosophy can attain.[117] This ultimate philosophic ideal, Jaeger insists, culminates in the almost visionary concept of the *phronesis*—philosophic wisdom in the Platonic sense.[118] *Phronesis*, in the final analysis, has only itself for its object. Hence, it produces nothing but itself, that is, pure contemplation. In so doing, it welds being, action and production into one. As the highest form of activity, *phronesis*, then, is the contemplative vision of the pure intellect which is active and productive in the highest sense. The discussion and recommendation of the 'beatific life of pure contemplation' (*phronesis*), according to Jaeger, constitute the climax as well as the ultimate philosophic message of the whole Aristotelian *Protrepticus*.

The *phronesis*, which possesses a crucial importance in this work, is without doubt one of the central themes, if not *the* central theme, in the Aristotelian *Protrepticus*. It is concerned, Jaeger avers, 'with the possibility, subject-matter, use, growth and happiness of theoretical knowledge. It may be interpreted as the creative apprehension of pure goodness through the inner intuition of the soul and at the same time as an apprehension of pure being, and also as the derivation of valuable activity and true knowledge from one and the same fundamental power of the mind.'[119] The *Protrepticus*, then, is wholly based on Plato's ethical metaphysics, on the unity of being and value, and keynoted by this one-sided Platonic concept of *phronesis*. *Phronesis*, then, is also νοῦς—pure active intellect; it is 'metaphysical speculation' in its most exalted form and, hence, that which is really divine in man. This is brought out in the statement that 'reason (νοῦς) is "the divine dwelling in us"... and because of reason, mortal life possesses a certain element or aspect of the divine.'[120] The *Protrepticus*, Jaeger concludes, is solidly anchored in Plato's architectonic doctrine of the four virtues: 'Since by mere preference all men choose what accords most with their own nature or character (the just man choosing to live justly, the brave man to live bravely, and the temperate man to live temperately), by the same token the wise man will choose, above all, to use his wisdom and intellect wisely, the more so since this constitutes the proper exercise of his particular faculty or powers. It is obvious, therefore, that according to the most authoritative opinion [Plato?], philosophic wisdom (*phronesis*) is the greatest of all goods.' [121] At this stage of his intellectual career, there is as yet no suggestion of Aristotle's later efforts to implement this particular doctrine with psychological factors. *Phronesis* is still contemplation of eternal norms and immutable Being, by reference to which man must conduct his life. [122]

The distinctive Platonism of the Aristotelian *Protrepticus*, Jaeger believes, becomes even more manifest in Aristotle's comments on the proper relationship of theoretic ethics to true politics—that is, philo-sophic politics, which painstakingly avoids imitating mere empirical facts or historical data and, hence, always seeks absolute norms. [123] In contradistinction to philosophic politics, Aristotle places 'artful politics,' which makes use of secondhand or practical (empirical) knowledge and in which decisions and judgments are based upon certain (and not too accurate) analogies from experience. [124] Such 'artful politics,' he judges, cannot give rise to truly creative and philosophically sound action. [125] In short, Jaeger holds Aristotle's position to be that ethics and politics constitute the most exact, the most 'principled' or most 'geometric' and, at the same time, the most abstract science. [126] This ideal of 'principled' or 'geometric' politics, however, clearly reflects Plato's later (Pythagorizing?) theory of Ideas or Idea-Numbers as it was expressed, for instance, in the *Philebus*, where we are told that true knowledge is measurement of all things in accordance with an absolute and immutable standard. [127] Thus, Jaeger argues to the conclusion that the Platonic *Philebus* had a decisive in-fluence on certain philosophic views propagated in the *Protrepticus*. [128] This fact, Jaeger surmises, also becomes apparent in Aristotle's attempt at contrasting pure science (philosophy) and applied (empirical) science, or pure (theoretic) geometry and surveying [129]—a contrast already used by Plato in the *Philebus*. [130] But if this is so, Jaeger notes, then Aristotle must have advocated the Platonic proposition that, in the final analysis, all true knowledge, including true political science, must be above all exact science—pure measurement founded on the most exact measure (*Philebus*)—even at the expense of becoming useless within a practical-pragmatic world such as ours. Such a proposi-tion, which most certainly befits a visionary artist rather than a practical politician, a 'Platonist' rather than an 'Aristotelian,' seems to echo certain Utopian notions advocated in Plato's *Republic*. [131]

Thus, Jaeger believes that in the *Protrepticus* Aristotle still fully adheres to Plato's doctrine of the Separate Ideas or Forms, and that he still accepts their significance as the 'most exact of all measures.'[132] This he infers from the following statement:[133]

> In the general or ordinary crafts and craftsmanlike operations, the most efficient tools are derived from nature. . . . In like manner, the statesman must have some definite standards derived from nature (objective reality) as well as from (absolute) truth itself, by which he will determine what is just, what is good, and what is expedient. For just as in the general or ordinary crafts, the above-mentioned tools are superior to all other tools, so too, the most excellent standards or basic norms are those which are established in the greatest conformity with nature. But no one who has not practiced philosophy and has not learned objective truth will be capable of doing this. In the general or ordinary arts and crafts, however, men perhaps do not derive their tools and their minute reckoning from first principles, and thus gain something close to scientific (philosophic) knowledge: rather, they borrow them at second . . . hand, and base their reasoning on empirical observations. The philosopher alone, of all men, imitates that which among all things is the most exact. For what he looks at is originality and exactness itself, and not merely imitation. . . .
> And so, just as a house-builder who borrows his measurements from other buildings instead of using the rod or other technical instruments is not a good architect, thus, similarly, one who either enacts laws for cities or administers public affairs by observing and imitating the public administrations or constitutions devised by other men . . . is not a good lawgiver or a conscientious statesman. For an imitation of that which is not good in itself cannot possibly be good . . . It is obvious, however, that among all craftsmen the philosopher alone is familiar with laws that are truly stable. . . . For the philosopher, and he alone, lives with his gaze fixed on objective reality (truth) and on the divine (immutable). . . .

Jaeger argues that such terms as 'imitation,' 'conformity,' 'nature (reality) in itself,' or 'most exact standard (or measure),' for instance, are wholly Platonic,[134] as is the assertion that philosophy alone contemplates things in themselves, while the arts merely imitate them.[135] Also Platonic is the statement that the 'things in themselves' (actually Separate Ideas) are immutable, and that the true statesman acts only by the intellectual vision of these 'immutable things in themselves': 'The true philosopher, and he alone, . . . imitates that which among all things is the most exact.' The true philosopher looks only at 'originality and exactness itself, not merely at imitations.' 'The true philosopher, and he alone, is familiar with laws that are truly stable, and with practices that are both truly right and truly proper. For the philosopher, and he alone, lives with his gaze fixed on nature (objective reality) and on the divine (imperishable), and like a good helmsman [who takes his bearings from the abiding stars] he will tie his life to what is eternal and unchanging, and moor it to first principles and, hence, will live as the master of his own [soul, or as the truly kingly person].'[136] The Platonism in these statements is immediately apparent. It is, in essence, but a restatement of Plato, *Republic* 500BC: 'The philosopher's eye is forever directed towards things immutable and fixed. . . . These he imitates, and to these he will, as far as this is possible, conform.'[137]

Jaeger further notes the distinct Platonism which becomes apparent in the *Protrepticus*, namely, where Aristotle discusses the elements that constitute reality:[138]

> The prior is always more knowable than the posterior, and the 'better by nature' is more knowable than the worse. For rational (philosophic) knowledge is more concerned with what is defined (determined) and ordered than with its contraries, and more with causes than with effects. Now, good things are more defined (determined) and ordered than evil things, and since this holds true also for men, a good man is better defined (determined) and more ordered than an evil man. Moreover, things that are prior are causes, more so than things that are posterior. For, if the former are removed, the things that derive their being from them are also removed: lengths, if numbers are removed; planes, if length is removed; solids, if planes are removed; and syllables, if letters are removed. . . . This also holds true in regard to matters concerning nature (or objective reality). It is of greater necessity to have knowledge of causes and first elements, rather than, perhaps, of things dependent on them. For the latter do not belong to the highest order (or reality), nor do the first principles arise from them. It is only from and through these first principles that all other things demonstrably proceed and are constituted.

And again: 'Whether it be fire, or air, or number, or any of the other natures that constitute the causes or first principles of all other things, as long as we are ignorant of these causes and first principles, we cannot possibly know any of the other things.'[139] These notions, Jaeger insists, are wholly Platonic and are completely in accord with Plato's paramount demand that before we can know anything we must know the Ideas.[140] This demand is most eloquently stated in the Platonic *Parmenides* 135BC: 'By doing away with the Ideas of things' and by denying 'that every individual thing has its own determinate Idea which is always one and the same, [we] will have nothing on which the mind can rest.'

Jaeger maintains that the essentially pessimistic outlook on life and on worldly affairs in general—the 'apocalyptic despair of this world'— which becomes manifest in some passages ascribed to the Aristotelian *Protrepticus*, is distinctly Platonic.[141] 'From the beginning [from the moment we are born] all of us are constituted by nature as if destined for punishment. For the divinely inspired among the ancient sages tell us that the soul pays penalties, and that we live [in this world] because we are punished for certain great sins we have committed. And, indeed, the union of the soul with the body strikes us as being very much such a punishment.'[142] This abject pessimism is the proper *Leitmotif* of a philosophy which, like that of Plato, is radically and uncompromisingly 'other-world-directed.' It is akin to that expressed by the somber 'revelation' of Silenus in Aristotle's *Eudemus*.[143] The *Protrepticus*, Jaeger argues, in a thoroughly Platonic vein exhorts its readers to disregard this sorry world of ours and to seek a higher, purer and more satisfying life in theoretic (unworldly) philosophy—in the 'heaven' of pure philosophic contemplation and dispassionate vision of immutable truth.

In concluding his stirring discussion of the Aristotelian *Protrepticus*, Jaeger emphasizes once more that Aristotle unreservedly adopts Plato's basic *Weltanschauung*. There are, and must be, higher as well as imperishable values, and there is, and must be, a perfect world which is accessible only to philosophic (Platonic) knowledge and contemplation. All else, Aristotle contends, is but sham and deception:[144]

If one contemplates human life in the bright light [of pure reason] . . . one will discover that all the things ordinary men believe to be great are just 'shadows on the wall.' Hence, one may properly maintain that nothing human is really sound and stable. Strength, size and beauty are simply a laugh and worth nothing. . . . If one were able to see as clearly as Lynceus is said to have seen—Lynceus saw through walls and trees—would one ever consider it endurable to look at a human being . . .? Honors and reputation . . . are but an indescribable humbug. To him that gazes upon what is eternal and real, it seems quite idiotic to strive after such things. . . . Men as such possess nothing of worth and have no cause to consider themselves perhaps divine or blessed, except in so far as they possess reason and philosophic wisdom (*phronesis*). This alone of all our endowments seems to be deathless, this alone seems to be divine. . . . For reason is 'the divine dwelling in us' . . . and because of reason, mortal life possesses a certain element or aspect of the divine. This being so, we ought either to pursue philosophy or bid farewell to life and depart from this world, because all other things seem to be utter nothingness and folly.

The classical Platonism of these statements is certainly blatant:[145] earthly life is really the death of the soul or, at least, a sickness of the soul; true life begins and ends in the transcendent world. Hence, death is really the triumphant return to a higher life, the only true life worth living; and life properly lived is but a preparation for death—a notion most eloquently extolled in Plato's *Phaedo*.[146] Like Plato before him, Aristotle exorts his readers not to become mired in the mundane. It is this contemptuous attitude towards the corporeal world and its petty affairs which further confirms Jaeger's general conviction that the message contained in Aristotle's *Protrepticus* is overwhelmingly Platonic, though his opinion is not shared by all scholars.[147] Jaeger concedes, however, that Aristotle's method of arguing his 'case' and of proving his conclusions differs considerably from that employed by Plato.

Jaeger does not date the *Protrepticus* precisely. From its Platonism he draws the implication that it must have been composed while Aristotle was still a member of the Platonic Academy, that is, prior to Plato's death in 348–47 B.C. Hence, the death of Plato would constitute the general *tempus ante quod* of the *Protrepticus*.[148] At the same time, Jaeger recognizes that the *Protrepticus* is in some way related to the so-called *Cyprian Orations* of Isocrates, and that the *Ad Demonicum*, in all likelihood authored by a disciple of Isocrates, is probably a reply to the Aristotelian essay.[149] But Jaeger does not make a detailed effort to ascertain the likely *tempus post quod* of the *Protrepticus*.[150]

It may be stated in summation that Jaeger's contributions to the retrieval, understanding and to the possible reconstruction of Aristotle's *Protrepticus* are manifold and decisively significant. He confirms and substantiates the findings of I. Bywater that Iamblichus' *Protrepticus* contains many fragments of, and excerpts from, the original Aristotelian text—and perhaps all, or almost all, of the essential segments. He also establishes beyond all reasonable doubt that the Aristotelian *Protrepticus* relies most heavily upon Platonic doctrine in general, and that to some extent it is dependent on Plato's *Euthydemus* 278B–282D in particular. The form of argumentation and presentation in the Aristotelian *Protrepticus*, Jaeger realizes, is influenced both by the Platonic dialogue and the protreptic prose 'essays' of Isocrates, although Aristotle frequently changes the conventional type of hortatory appeal into a syllogistic mode of argument. In short, Jaeger is the first scholar to subject the *Protrepticus* as a whole to a searching and detailed analysis and philosophic interpretation—the first scholar to fully understand the dominant spirit, the main theme and also the basic literary form of this important work. Without belittling the significant achievements and contributions of earlier scholars (especially those of I. Bywater), it can safely be maintained that all subsequent investigations and discussions of Aristotle's *Protrepticus* will necessarily have to begin with Jaeger's analyses. This does not mean, however, that we must accept all detailed findings and specific interpretations proposed by Jaeger.

As we have seen, Jaeger contends that Aristotle, in the course of his intellectual evolution, gradually 'moved away' from Plato's fundamental philosophical standpoint or, at least, abandoned certain aspects of traditional Platonism;[151] and that he did so in order to achieve his own distinctive philosophy. Jaeger cites the *On Philosophy* as the first sustained manifestation of the Stagirite's 'partial break' with Platonism.[152] Seen thus as a 'Manifesto' by Jaeger, the *On Philosophy* occupies a unique place, a pivotal position, in Aristotle's literary and philosophic development:[153] It stands like a monumental landmark between the early—Platonic—stage of Aristotle's philosophic thought and the final form of his intellectual outlook as it is revealed in the doctrinal treatises. Hence, the *On Philosophy* constitutes a signal part of a distinct period of intellectual transition when Aristotle was criticizing, rearranging and detaching himself in order to strike out in a novel philosophic direction.[154] This fact would also explain why Jaeger deals with the *On Philosophy* in a most thorough fashion and at great length. Probably nowhere, not even in his remarkable discussion of the *Protrepticus*, are Jaeger's insights, analyses and ideas more penetrating, more scintillating and, on the whole, more persuasive than here. It could rightly be argued that his treatment of the *On Philosophy* in all likelihood constitutes the climax, the most brilliant episode, in his renowned investigations into the historical Aristotle—into the genesis of Aristotle's work and thought.

Syrianus records Aristotle's mocking remark in Book II of the *On Philosophy* that 'if the [Platonic] Ideas [or Idea Numbers] are a different sort of number, we can have no understanding of them. For who can comprehend another kind of number, at any rate among the majority of us?'[155] Jaeger, who sees in this remark Aristotle's deliberate rejection of certain aspects of late Platonism if not of Platonism in general, notices that both Plutarch[156] and Proclus[157] relate that in his dialogues (the *On the Good*, the *On [the] Ideas* and the *On Philosophy*) Aristotle openly criticized Plato's theory of Ideas. Proclus also maintains that 'in his dialogues [e.g., the *On Philosophy*] as well as in his treatises,' Aristotle attacked Plato's theory of Separate Ideas, claiming that 'he could not agree with this doctrine, even if he lays himself open to the charge of opposing it from a love of polemics.' The concluding words of Proclus' remark, Jaeger contends, are a ringing appeal by Aristotle to intellectual honesty and the right to freely voice doctrinal dissent. At the same time, Aristotle emphatically attempts to forestall any charge that his disagreement with Plato was perhaps motivated by personal reasons.[158] All this would indicate that in Book II of the *On Philosophy*, Aristotle takes issue with certain aspects of (late?) Platonism, especially with Plato's belated doctrine of the Idea Numbers. Such a step, Jaeger holds, marks the point at which Aristotle intellectually 'broke away' from Plato and Platonism, at least in part.

Jaeger is also of the opinion that both the title and the many extant fragments credited to the *On Philosophy* (a work which remained the chief source of information about Aristotle's fundamental philosophic views throughout the third, second and the first half of the first century B.C.) are indicative of the fact that it must have been an unusual if not sensational composition as regards its philosophic approach and doctrinal content. In any event, it was cited, referred to, and even misquoted by a large number of authors, commentators and critics, among them Alexander of Aphrodisias, Asclepius, Boethius, Cicero, Clement of Alexandria, Clement of Rome, Diogenes Laertius, Lactantius, Nemesius of Emesa, Olympiodorus, Philo of Alexandria, Philodemus, Pliny, Plutarch, Porphyry, Priscinus Lydus, Proclus, Psellus, Seneca, Sextus Empiricus, Simplicius, Stobaeus, Synesius, Syrianus and others. Cicero's testimony suggests that, in view of the crucial nature of his undertaking, Aristotle himself appears in the *On Philosophy* as the leader of the discussion,[159] thereby turning it into a 'personal declaration' or 'profession.' Moreover, probably in order to avoid misunderstandings, he also prefaces each of the three books by a separate 'introduction' or 'introductory note.'[160] Jaeger maintains, therefore, that as to its particular literary form, the *On Philosophy* is midway between the earliest (Platonic) dialogues of Aristotle and the later doctrinal treatises, while as to its philosophic content and spirit it is closer to the latter. All this induces Jaeger to date the *On Philosophy* at approximately the same time as the critique of the Separate Ideas or Forms (or Ideas Numbers), launched in Book A of the Aristotelian *Metaphysics*,[161] or slightly later—that is, certainly later than the death of Plato in 348–47 B.C.[162]

According to Jaeger, Book I of the *On Philosophy* begins with an account of the historical development of philosophy or σοφία. Starting with a discussion of the Magi (Zoroastrians) and their contributions to philosophy,[163] Aristotle touches progressively on the earliest (pre-literary) representatives of Hellenic moral wisdom (the 'theologians'), the so-called Orphics,[164] and the 'proverbial wisdom' of the seven Wise Men preserved by the Delphic Oracle.[165] All these subjects and bits of information, Jaeger insists, were critically sifted and organized by Aristotle.[166] In so doing, Aristotle not only anticipates his later method of prefacing his systematic treatment of a certain philosophic subject by a historical discussion of the views and achievements of earlier thinkers[167] but also presages his later 'encyclopaedic collections' of facts and events, such as the *158 Constitutions*, the *List of Pythian Victors*, the *List of Olympic Victors*, the *Customs of the Barbarians* and others. In the process of sifting and organizing his materials in terms of an 'historical introduction to philosophy,'[168] Jaeger concludes, Aristotle probably also investigated and discussed the vital relationship between religion and philosophy,[169] a theme suggested by the very nature of such an 'introduction.'[170]

Jaeger points out that in the *On Philosophy* Aristotle displays a remarkable acquaintance with and grasp of the 'philosophy' of the Magi, that is, Zoroastrianism. This preoccupation with the Magi, Jaeger insists, was no novelty in the Academy, where (according to tradition) a 'Chaldean' or follower of Zoroaster was a regular member of the school during the last decade of Plato's life.[171] Philip of Opus, we know, was intensely concerned with Zoroastrian astral theology;[172] the dialogue *I Alcibiades*, although probably not a work of Plato, draws some striking parallels between Plato's theory of moral virtues and the ethics of Zarathustra (or Zoroaster);[173] and Eudoxus of Cnidus, who had spent some time in the East, seems to have stimulated much interest in 'Chaldean' (Zoroastrian) religion, 'philosophy' and astronomy among the members of the Academy[174] and perhaps in Plato himself.[175] Without doubt, this interest also extended to Aristotle who, judging from some of his other early works, including the *On Philosophy*, during the last years of his association with the Academy went through an intensely religious period.[176]

It was Jaeger who convincingly argued that Aristotle at one time seriously studied Zoroastrian teachings. This interest is implied by Diogenes Laertius, who reports that 'in the first Book of the *On Philosophy* Aristotle says that ... according to the Magi there are two principles, namely, a good spirit (*diamon*) and an evil spirit, the one called Zeus and Oromasdes, the other Hades or Areimanius.'[177] And Plutarch relates that 'Aristotle imitates the Chaldean dualism of good and evil forces by calling one [the principle of] form, the other [the principle of] privation.'[178] Relying on Plutarch's testimony, Jaeger believes that Aristotle at one time actually drew parallels not only between Zoroaster and Plato, but also between Zoroastrian doctrine and certain teachings advanced by some Pre-Socratics.[179] Moreover, Jaeger insists that Aristotle fully accepted the Zoroastrian dogma of the 'eternal return' or cyclic recurrence of certain events,[180] a doctrine which had also been proposed by Plato.[181] Jaeger's well-founded arguments in favor of certain vital intellectual contacts between Zoroastrianism and the Platonic Academy (and Aristotle in particular), it will be noted, are of far-reaching, if not revolutionary significance for the whole history of Western philosophy and its proper understanding and interpretation. Hence, they are certainly more than mere contributions to our understanding of Aristotle's *On Philosophy*: they amount, and this cannot be stressed enough, to a profound insight into the basic aspects of certain phases within Greek philosophic thought which, until very recently, has been considered as having arisen and always lived in 'splendid isolation' from all other philosophic and quasi-philosophic notions or beliefs.[182]

Book II of the *On Philosophy* is considered by Jaeger, among other matters, to contain a detailed and sustained criticism of Plato's Separate Ideas or Forms.[183] Jaeger, however, does not elaborate this criticism in detail, treating it only in a rather cursory manner in his discussion of the 'original *Metaphysics*' (*Urmetaphysik*) and the 'growth of the *Metaphysics*.'[184] The accounts of Syrianus,[185] Plutarch[186] and Proclus[187] state that Aristotle was critical of Plato's basic doctrines. Aristotle's judgment of their philosophic unacceptability is undoubtedly contained in Book II of the *On Philosophy*, as was his confession, already mentioned before, that his disagreements with Plato were based solely on philosophic considerations, never on personal differences or resentments.[188] Thus, in the opinion of Jaeger, despite his doctrinal disagreements with Plato, Aristotle speaks of his teacher in the *On Philosophy* with undiminished respect and reverence.[189] This, then, would imply that Aristotle's break with Plato and Platonism manifest in Book II of the *On Philosophy*, in the final analysis, was probably only a partial 'break-away,' restricted perhaps to certain aspects of late (Pythagorizing?) Platonism. What one misses in Jaeger's otherwise splendid treatment of the lost works of Aristotle is a thorough discussion and evaluation of Aristotle's *On (the) Ideas* and *On the Good.* Both compositions apparently precede the *On Philosophy.* Moreover, Aristotle in both works criticizes certain fundamental aspects of Plato's late philosophy. It is quite possible that some arguments made in the *On (the) Ideas* and *On the Good* were restated, perhaps in an improved form, in the *On Philosophy.*[190]

Jaeger maintains that Book III of the *On Philosophy* contains Aristotle's 'own view of the world; it was a cosmology and a theology; like the second [Book], it took the form throughout of a criticism of Plato, for the simple reason that it was dependent on him at every step.'[191] In all its essentials, Jaeger believes, Aristotle adopted the astral theology of Plato's later days—the notion that beyond the visible starry heavens lies the supersensible world of the Separate Ideas or Pure Forms, of which the visible universe is but a copy or 'shadow.'[192] But, unlike Plato, Aristotle is primarily concerned with the cosmological or visible side rather than with the transcendent and invisible aspect of this dual world. Analyzing the critical but somewhat confusing account of Cicero, *De Natura Deorum* I. 13. 33,[193] Jaeger reaches the conclusion that Aristotle proclaims in the *On Philosophy* that the supreme 'God to Whom the world is subordinated is the transcendental Unmoved Mover, who guides the world as its final cause, by reason of the perfection of his pure thought.'[194] This, Jaeger assumes, is the core of Aristotle's early theology—and Book III of the *On Philosophy* contains the basic elements of Aristotle's early theology.

According to Jaeger, even if Aristotle should also call the ether a 'divine' body, he certainly does not refer to it as God; and if below the transcendental Unmoved Mover there should also exist the star-gods whose matter is ethereal, or if God should also be identified with the universe as well as with ether, this does not constitute a real contradiction, provided we realize that Aristotle applies the term 'divine' first to the whole and subsequently to some of its component parts. This becomes even more apparent, Jaeger continues, if we bear in mind that by the term 'cosmos' Aristotle means primarily the heavens or the celestial perisphere.[195] In short, Jaeger tries here to explain and integrate, not always in a completely convincing manner, the confusing passage from Cicero, De Natura Deorum I. 13. 33, which is commonly considered an important fragment of the On Philosophy. This fragment contains the following statements: (a) 'pure mind' is the (supreme) deity; (b) the universe is God; (c) there is a God above and beyond the universe Who rules and preserves the movement of the universe by a sort of 'reverse motion'; (d) the 'ether' in the heavens is God; (e) the heavens are God; (f) the gods of popular belief also exist; (g) God is without a body and, hence, cannot move, while the universe moves; and (h) something in perpetual motion cannot be calm and serene and, hence, cannot be God.[196] Jaeger insists that the confusion seen in these conflicting statements is really in the mind of the critic (an Epicurean) rather than in that of Aristotle,[197] who in the On Philosophy definitely proclaims the existence of an Unmoved Mover[198]—the highest God— beneath Whom exist many separate 'things divine.'[199] This immaterial and purely intellectual Unmoved Mover or God, (or 'Mind') of the On Philosophy, Jaeger claims, is wholly separated from the visible universe. It is not only above and beyond everything, including other 'things divine' or gods, but also constitutes, or is responsible for, the ultimate unity within the total universe—a notion, incidentally, which may be traced back to Plato's Laws 898E.[200]

In the On Philosophy, Jaeger insists, Aristotle rejects the notion that the (divine) universe, the great 'visible god,' may have a beginning and an end.[201] In so doing, Aristotle not only refutes the views of the 'physicists' but also denies the creationist theory advanced by Plato in the Timaeus.[202] Moreover, Jaeger points out, Aristotle's assertion that the universe is uncreated and imperishable, in short, that it is eternal, constitutes his 'greatest innovation.'[203] Thus it appears that Aristotle transfers to the visible universe an attribute which Plato had reserved for his Ideas. Jaeger also holds that Aristotle's position in the On Philosophy regarding the divine universe amounts to nothing less than a complete fusion of theology and astronomy[204]—a fusion which ultimately goes back to Plato's insistence that the starry heavens are the visible image of the highest Idea or Form.[205] But since Aristotle rejects both the Platonic world of the Separate Forms and the Platonic Demiurge, Jaeger concludes that there remains only what Plato had called the 'image of the divine,' the visible universe. This visible universe becomes for Aristotle the divinity itself or, better, the 'visible

God' or 'God Incarnate.'[206] But this 'visible God' is not identical nor on an equal footing with the 'invisible God' or the pure 'Mind.'

Jaeger is also aware that Cicero, *De Natura Deorum* II. 15. 42–16. 44,[207] usually considered a fragment of the *On Philosophy*, is based on what appears to be a ready-made doxographical collection.[208] Here Cicero reports (and probably garbles) what was in all likelihood Aristotle's argument in favor of 'living stars' or star gods: since it can be demonstrated that living things occur in each of the four traditional elements, there also must exist living beings in the fifth element, the ether; and these living beings are the stars.[209] This argument, Jaeger contends, is not meant to demonstrate the existence of some mythically conceived gods, spirits or demons, as is the case with Plato's *Timaeus* or with the *Epinomis*. It is intended to be an empirical proof for the existence of stellar gods who are living in the ether, that is, in an element which because of its purity and power is most suited to produce or sustain beings of the highest intelligence, endowed with free will and with rapid as well as regular (and circular) motion.[210] From all this, it is further inferred that if all the living beings to be found in the four basic elements[211] were suddenly to disappear, these elements, too, would cease to exist. Hence, it would follow by way of analogy that the heavens, the sun, the moon and the stars (the living beings in the ether) would likewise suffer destruction if these living beings in the heavens (or in the ether) were to disappear. This, however, would conflict with the divine indestructibility of the heavens. In short, on the strength of Cicero's testimony (*De Natura Deorum* II. 15. 42–4), Jaeger surmises[212] that Aristotle infers the eternity or indestructibility of the heavens (and of the whole visible universe) from their durability (and perfection),[213] an inference which is automatically transferred or applied to all celestial bodies or beings—that is, to the whole visible universe.

Jaeger also attempts to show that the four fragments preserved by Philo of Alexandria,[214] and the two fragments recorded by Cicero[215]—if stripped of later Peripatetic, Stoic, Epicurean and Neo-Platonic additions or modifications (and perversions)—provide a fairly clear picture of Aristotle's theological views as they had been expounded in the *On Philosophy*. On the strength of this evidence, Jaeger insists that in the *On Philosophy* Aristotle already introduces: (i) the notion of an Unmoved Mover,[216] although in Jaeger's opinion it is not clear whether he actually originated the concept of an Unmoved Mover or whether he borrowed it from some other member of the Platonic Academy; (ii) that each of the four basic elements creates and contains its own particular living beings; (iii) that, like each of these four basic elements, the fifth element—'ether'—creates and contains the stars; (iv) that in keeping with their particular origin, these creatures of the ether must be endowed with the highest intelligence, as evidenced by the inviolability of their order and the regularity of their motion; (v) that since this perfect order and regular as well as circular motion cannot be the product of a mechanical nature, it must be the result of a conscious intent, a free will, a perfect (or superior) intelligence and an inner design;[217] (vi) that the universe itself is eternal and, hence, divine; and (vii) that the destruction of the visible universe would mean the 'obliteration' of the invisible and immaterial God (or at least deprive this invisible God of His meaning?), together with all the living beings in the ether, that is, the divine stars.[218]

The Aristotelian doctrine of the stellar gods as well as Aristotle's belief in the divinity of the heavenly spheres, Jaeger maintains, suggests Plato's[219] basic principle that all cosmic phenomena are controlled by 'mind' and determined by a rational order. Moreover, according to Jaeger, Aristotle's theory of the star-souls is the first grandiose effort to illustrate and prove, by way of analogy as well as on the basis of empirical fact and scientific observation, the cosmic 'rule of reason' ruling over matter—a distinct rebuke of the physicists.[220] This 'rule of reason,' Aristotle insists, can be ascertained and understood by anyone who uses his senses and reasoning powers properly. Accordingly, Jaeger argues, the major themes of Plato's and Aristotle's philosophy are really in fundamental agreement, although their respective methods and approaches differ sharply. Aristotle's argument in favor of a dominant cosmic 'rule of reason' is certainly more 'scientific' or philosophic in its quest for 'real proof' than is the predominantly mythological, inspirational or poetic approach of Plato.[221]

It will be noted that Jaeger does not discuss the peculiar psychology advanced in the *On Philosophy*. This psychology, which differs from that expounded in the *Eudemus* as well as in the *De Anima*, may be reconstructed with the help of four fragments from Cicero,[222] one fragment from (Pseudo-?) Clement of Rome,[223] and one fragment from Psellus.[224] According to these fragments, which are credited to the *On Philosophy*, it appears that in this dialogue Aristotle held (i) that the soul is a *sui generis* substance; (ii) that it has a nature which distinguishes it from the four material elements or substances; (iii) that it is completely independent of the material world; (iv) that it has a 'non-material' ('spiritual'?) nature which is similar to, if not identical with, the nature of the divine (the 'divine Mind'); (v) that it is co-natural or co-substantial with the divine (or the 'divine Mind'); (vi) that it is indestructible or immortal; and (vii) that this immortality is individual.[225] It might have been interesting and enlightening to know how Jaeger would have dealt with these rather startling statements concerning the soul. Needless to say, these views have a strong Platonic flavor (although they also differ from what Plato had to say about the soul), and they might possibly reflect the influence of Zoroastrian (?) teachings.[226] Perhaps the fact that these particular fragments were not listed by V. Rose and, hence, remained unknown, prevented Jaeger from discussing them.

Jaeger is of the opinion that in the *On Philosophy* Aristotle lays the real foundation of Hellenistic theology or 'philosophy of religion'[227] and, for that matter, of all future theology. He points out that Book III of this work, which evinces the influence of Plato's religious convictions,[228] contains the first telling and the first persuasive arguments for the existence of God. More than that, it constitutes the climax and probably the ultimate justification of the *On Philosophy*, and perhaps that of all of Aristotle's writings: 'It was [Aristotle] who, in the . . . *On Philosophy*, demonstrated the reality of a highest being with strict syllogistic arguments, and thus gave the problem the sharp, apodictic form which has continually goaded keen religious thinkers, in all later centuries, towards new attempts to make our experience of the ineffable visible even to the eye of understanding.'[229] No one in antiquity, Jaeger contends, ever spoke more beautifully or more profoundly and more persuasively about religion and the personal and emotional side of religious experience than Aristotle during these years when a craving to know something about God was apparently the central issue of his philosophic efforts.[230] In so doing, Aristotle, however, remained soundly grounded on reason and experience, avoiding the pitfalls of unrestrained emotion, boundless fantasy or mystical surrender.[231]

One of the methods used by Aristotle to demonstrate the existence of a Supreme Being is designated by Jaeger as the *argumentum e gradibus*[232]—an argument also used by scholastic thinkers—the argument contained in the *On Philosophy* that 'where there is a good there is a better, and where there is a better there is a best. And since, among existing things, one is better than another, there is also something that is best, which will be the divine.'[233] This argument, which touches the very roots of the ontological argument for the existence of God, Jaeger maintains, actually proceeds along the following lines: in the realm of existing things, there must be a perfect something which also must be most real. Such a perfect and most real something is identical with the divine. In stating the problem in this fashion, Aristotle in effect makes the first truly important attempt 'to render the problem of God amenable to scientific treatment, by basing dialectically cogent inferences on a consistent interpretation of nature. . . . Only the greatest logical architect of all time would have dared to compress the whole result of his immense efforts into these few simple-sounding sentences.'[234] It cannot escape the attentive reader, however, that this *argumentum e gradibus*, as might be expected of Aristotle, is closely interwoven with his teleological approach to theology.[235] It also contains an echo—and a radical methodological correction—of Plato's doctrine of the 'One' or of the Idea of the Good.

In keeping with its concern for the phenomena of the human spirit, the *On Philosophy*, according to Jaeger, also examined the psychological sources of man's belief in God and the existence of God. In so doing, the Stagirite indicates that even the most compelling and most refined logical arguments can never achieve that irresistible force of inner conviction which arises out of the inspired presentiments of the soul. Thus, Aristotle insists 'that we should nowhere be more modest than in matters of religion'[236]—that we must experience a feeling of awe in the presence of the all-high. Although Aristotle was the 'great architect of logic and scientific method,' he still understood the dichotomy of faith and reason, of feeling and understanding: 'Those who are initiated into the mysteries are not required to learn something rationally (*mathein*), but to have a certain inner experience (*pathein*) which comes "from the outside," to be put into a certain frame of mind. . . .'[237] It was the mysteries cultivated by Plato[238] and the Academy no less than the widespread Greek mystery religions and mystery cults in general, which taught Aristotle that true religion is possible only in the form of personal experience and personal awe in the face of the sublime, that is, in the form of, and through, personal devotion—that, in the final analysis, true religion is always a personal and most intimate experience. Jaeger rightly points out that this vital insight, formulated and expounded in the *On Philosophy*, ushered in a new era of religious understanding; and that the influence of this fundamental insight on the whole of Hellenistic religion and religious thought is beyond estimation.[239]

Aristotle notes, according to Jaeger, that man's personal and immediate conviction of God's existence actually stems from two major sources: the experiences of the inspired powers of the soul, and the contemplation of the starry universe.[240] In so doing, Jaeger maintains, Aristotle attempts the first synthesis of the two most compelling proofs for the existence of God: the psychological and the cosmological proof.

The inspired powers of the soul become manifest in the personal feeling of awe and reverence in the presence of the unfathomably sublime or ineffable.[241] They also become apparent whenever the soul, either in sleep or at the imminent approach of death, rids itself (so to speak) of the body and takes on its real nature.[242] In this state, the soul 'pierces the future' with a prophetic eye. Prophecy and the meta-rational faculties of the soul, two topics of many discussions within the Academy, are restated and analyzed at length by Aristotle in the *On Philosophy*. Here they are used to explain the psycho-genetic sources for man's awareness of God and His existence. The prophetic powers, which ordinarily slumber within the soul, awaken when the soul divests, or is about to divest, itself of the body and its confining effects—in Jaeger's opinion, a wholly Platonic position which Aristotle had already taken in the *Eudemus*.[243] It is from these inspired states of the soul that men derive their personal and innermost experiences of the existence and nature of God.[244]

Book III of the *On Philosophy*, Jaeger observes, also contains probably the first sustained and articulate cosmological (or teleological) proof for the existence of God.[245] This proof, which has survived in several later versions or fragments,[246] proceeds essentially as follows: if men were to come suddenly and unexpectedly face to face with the orderly universe and all it contains, they would have to admit, in view of its unsur-passed orderliness and sublime beauty, that it all is the handiwork of a supreme artificer, creator and director, namely, God.[247] Jaeger makes the further striking and correct observation that Aristotle must have been influenced in this argument by Plato's famous 'cave analogy'[248] (which reduces the whole visible universe to a mere shadow of true being). Jaeger's view is supported primarily by four quotations, all of which are considered to be fragments of, or references to, the *On Philosophy*: Cicero's statement in *De Natura Deorum* that 'if creatures who always lived beneath the earth . . . would be able to escape from their [subterranean] abode . . . and suddenly gain sight of the earth and the sky and the sea . . . they would most certainly have come to the conclusion that there are gods. . . .';[249] Sextus Empiricus' observation that 'the heavenly bodies also contributed to this belief [in the existence of the divine] . . . and [thus men] came to think that there is a God Who is the cause of such movement and order';[250] Sextus Empiricus' assertion that 'those who first looked up to the heavens . . . looked for a [divine] Craftsman of this beautiful design, and surmised that it came about . . . by the agency of . . . God';[251] and Philo of Alexan-dria's remark in the *Legum Allegiarum Libri Tres* that those who reason from creation to a Creator 'actually conceive of God through His shadow, apprehending the Craftsman through His handiwork.'[252]

In the opinion of Jaeger, Aristotle's espousal of a cosmological proof for the existence of God bespeaks a novel and affirmative attitude towards the visible world. Unlike Plato before him, Aristotle proclaims in the *On Philosophy* that we must contemplate, know and accept the indescribable wonders of the created universe; and that such contemplation, knowledge and acceptance must necessarily lead to the knowledge and acceptance of the Creator of all these wonders. Now also the famous Aristotelian statement that philosophy starts in wonder,[253] acquires a novel and more profound meaning.[254] Jaeger concludes that what Aristotle is saying here is simply this: the contemplation, knowledge and acceptance of the wondrous visible universe must be intensified and internalized until it becomes religion and religious conviction, that is, until it climaxes in the spontaneous awareness of the divine Creator and Maintainer of the cosmos[255]—in the unshakable conviction of God's existence. For Aristotle, then, Jaeger observes, the actual visible world, if understood and properly contemplated, contains all the truth any man may possibly want to know—a truth, which Plato for reasons of his own had relegated to the transcendent world of Ideas accessible only to the philosophic man. Seen thus, Aristotle's borrowings from Plato—and in his theology he certainly borrowed from his teacher—turn into fundamental modifications of Plato's theological views.[256]

Aristotle's enthusiastically affirmative attitude towards the visible universe, Jaeger concedes, conflicts with the basic position of Plato, who would never admit that the most sublime reality could be directly and validly inferred from the imperfect corporeal world. Plato's philosophy and theology, which ultimately become merged in Plato, teach us that we must contemplate the supernatural world exclusively, in complete independence (and rejection) of the visible world. Aristotle, on the other hand, considers the visible universe one of the surest roads to God.[257] Aristotle's theological position is also in conflict with certain traditional ideas espoused by Greek popular religions, which categorically deny that an adequate knowledge of the divine, aside from being dangerous, is empirically attainable by mortal man.[258] In the *On Philosophy*, Jaeger concludes, Aristotle lays the foundations not only of all future 'natural theology,' but also of theology in general. More than that, Aristotle's position implies, as may be gathered from *Metaphysics* 983 a 5-11 (incidentally, a section of the *Metaphysics* which might very well have been composed at approximately the same time as the *On*

*Philosophy*), that without a knowledge of God and God's existence, it is impossible for man to know anything else.[259] Hence, Aristotle's metaphysics is rooted in his basic theology, no matter how far this metaphysics may have been developed in later years along purely logical or systematic lines.[260]

In discussing Aristotle's basic attitude towards religion, Jaeger insists in words which always bear repetition, that the Stagirite delved into theological problems and issues

> not out of cold scientific curiosity, but in order that others might experience what he had experienced. He was . . . well aware that even the most gifted logic can never attain to that irresistible force of inner conviction which arises out of the inspired presentiments of the soul. Nobody in the ancient world ever spoke more beautifully or more profoundly about the personal and emotional side of all religious life than Aristotle during the years when religion was the central problem in his mind. In the dialogue *On Philosophy* . . . he spoke of the feeling of awe in the presence of that which is higher than man. He recognized that inner composure is the essence of all religious devotion. . . . The mysteries showed that to the philosopher religion is possible only as a personal awe and devotion, as a special kind of experience . . . as the soul's spiritual traffic with God. . . . It is impossible to estimate the influence of these ideas on the Hellenistic world, and on the spiritual religion that was in process of formation. Aristotle derives the subjective conviction of God's existence from two sources: from man's experience of the inspired might of the soul . . . and from the sight of the starry heavens. This derivation . . . is a pregnant juxtaposition of the two great wonders that all the enlightment of the enlightened cannot explain. . . . What Aristotle here compresses into a formula is simply the religious attitude of Plato's circle towards the universe. . . . No other formula could express so fitly the timeless truth of the religious element in Platonism. . . .[261] [Aristotle] teaches [man] to contemplate, not a supernatural world, but that which is visible to all and yet seen by none. . . . [When expounding his cosmological proof for the existence of God,] Aristotle is conscious of being the first Greek to see the real world with Plato's eyes. . . . What he gives us instead of the Ideas is the contemplation of the wonderful shapes and arrangements of the cosmos, a contemplation which, intensified until it becomes religion, leads up to the

intuition of the divine director of it all. . . .[262] In any event it is
impossible to understand Aristotle's influence on posterity unless
we realize that . . . his metaphysics is rooted [in his theology],
however far it might have developed beyond it on the logical
side. The establishment of the worship of . . . the transcendental
God Who is enthroned above . . . [all the peoples on earth—
infinitely above the miraculous universe itself], inaugurated the
era of religious and philosophic universalism. On the crest of this
last wave Attic culture streams out into the Hellenic sea of
peoples.[263]

These exalted and stirring words, which go to the very heart of
Aristotle's thought, are an everlasting monument to the Stagirite as
well as to Werner Jaeger.

Jaeger's contributions to a better and profounder understanding of
the Aristotelian *On Philosophy* are obviously many as well as significant.
He discusses the ultimate meaning of the several fragments ascribed to
this dialogue in a manner never before attempted, shedding much light
on their overt or implied meaning and importance. In so doing, he also
integrates these fragments into a single, coherent and persuasive narrative and argument which Jaeger aptly calls a monumental and monu-
mentally significant philosophic 'Manifesto.' The doctrinal starting-
point of many basic ideas advanced in the *On Philosophy*, Jaeger points
out, is still Plato's philosophy, but the specific treatment and detailed
exploitation of these ideas and notions is frequently critical of Plato's
philosophic position. (Jaeger also makes the interesting and far-reaching
observation that the basic disagreement underlying Aristotle's 'break'
with Plato may have been theological rather than philosophical.) What
is most striking in the *On Philosophy*, however, is not Aristotle's
disavowal of certain aspects of Platonic doctrine, but rather his
acquaintance with Zoroastrian religious teachings, his basic theological
convictions and his sustained efforts to prove the existence of God.
Jaeger is certainly correct when he claims that in the *On Philosophy*
Aristotle becomes the true founder of Hellenistic 'scientific' theology;
that here he exposes for the first time the personal and emotional side of
religious experience; that he devises the first scientifically formulated
cosmological proof for the existence of God; that he fully understands,
and uses, the dichotomy of faith and reason; and that it is his belief in
the existence of God which became the basis of his pronounced
affirmative attitude towards the world. The Scriptural 'the heavens
declare the glory of God, and the firmament showeth His handi-

work,'[264] was the *Leitmotif* of Aristotle's theology (or natural theology), as he proclaimed it in the *On Philosophy*. Perhaps nowhere in all his scholarly efforts is Jaeger more persuasive than in his brilliant discussion of the *On Philosophy*. It is here that he succeeds in recapturing the true spirit of this lost work in a manner which may never be equaled.[265] Measured by the depth of his insights and by the breadth of his understanding, the possibility that some of his detailed statements may not always be fully supported by the available evidence becomes wholly irrelevant.

These are, in summary, Jaeger's main and probably lasting contributions to the understanding, recovery and possible reconstruction of the *Eudemus*, the *Protrepticus* and the *On Philosophy*, three of the most important lost works of the young Aristotle. These contributions, essentially motivated by a desire to detail Aristotle's intellectual development, are geared into Jaeger's general theory of the Stagirite's evolution 'away' from Platonism. It is not surprising, therefore, that Jaeger should pay particular attention to the Platonic elements found in these works. Not all scholars are persuaded, however, that the young Aristotle of the Academy so thoroughly adhered to Plato's basic teachings; not all scholars are in agreement with Jaeger's particular treatment of these early writings;[266] and not all scholars are completely convinced that Aristotle ever abandoned Platonism.[267] It should be remembered, however, that the discovery and scholarly exploitation of the essential Platonism of the early works dates back to Valentin Rose, who in fact categorically denied the authenticity of these fragments precisely on the grounds of their Platonic content.[268]

It has already been stressed that Jaeger does not primarily concern himself with the detailed and acribic reconstruction of any of the lost Aristotelian compositions nor with the discovery of additional fragments. He relies, as we have seen, almost entirely on the inadequate collection of fragments compiled by V. Rose—a not altogether auspicious starting point. Being interested predominantly in establishing the intellectual development of Aristotle, Jaeger's evolutionary thesis begins in, and is founded upon, his unique, though essentially correct, interpretation of these early compositions and their surviving fragments. It is structured by his assumption that the later doctrinal treatises, which are 'Aristotelian' in tenor, are unquestionably authentic; that the lost early works, which in his opinion are essentially Platonic as to their philosophic standpoint, are likewise authentic; and that these two apparently conflicting doctrinal standpoints can be fully reconciled if we are willing to concede that in his intellectual evolution Aristotle changed from an early Platonism to a later 'Aristotelianism.' Jaeger's views and interpretations, in their far-reaching implications, were destined to become a powerful and lasting inducement to further investigations. Hence, regardless of whether succeeding scholars intend to substantiate further or, perhaps, to disprove (in part or *in toto*) Jaeger's theories, in order to support other theses or dissenting views these scholars will be required to produce more persuasive details about the lost Aristotelian writings. In this sense, Jaeger has come to be, directly or indirectly, not only the foremost stimulus for an intensified and sustained research into Aristotle's lost early works, but also the most powerful inducement to search for additional fragments and, if possible, to retrieve and reconstruct these lost works. More than that, he has become that one scholarly norm against which we must measure all that has been said and all that ever will be said about the lost early works of Aristotle.

During the past fifty years or so of scholarly investigations into the historical Aristotle and, especially, into the early Aristotle, Jaeger's insights and interpretations have invariably demonstrated their essential usefulness and fertility, even where minor modifications were warranted. So far, no single scholar has done as much to broaden and buttress our knowledge and understanding in this field. In spite of honest disagreements and dissents by serious and competent scholars, Jaeger's fundamental views are still the most important single guide, the most comprehensive statement, and the most secure foundation of all research in the domain of early *Aristotelica*. They represent the decisive turning point in modern Aristotelian scholarship, a directional indicator always to be reckoned with.[269] One student may accept Jaeger's theses, another may modify them to some degree, still another may reject them; but no one may rightfully ignore them.[270] *Mutatis mutandis* we may apply to Jaeger's Aristotelian scholarship Horace's famous lines: *Si quid novisti rectius istis, candidus imperti. Si non his utere mecum.*

# Notes

## INTRODUCTION

\* In a different form, part of this introduction appeared under the title of 'The problems of the *Aristotelis Librorum Fragmenta,*' *Classical Journal,* vol. 62, no. 2 (1966), pp. 71–4.

1 As early as 1581, to be sure, F. Patrizzi made a feeble and not altogether successful attempt to collate some of the fragments ascribed to Aristotle's lost works. F. Patrizzi, *Discursiones Peripateticae* (Basle, 1581), vol. I, part 7, pp. 74 ff. See also G. Mazonii Caesenatis, *In Universam Platonis et Aristotelis Philosophiam Praeludia, Sive de Comparatione Platonis et Aristotelis* (Venice, 1597), *passim.*

2 Diogenes Laertius V. 23 (DL V. 23), no. 51; *Vita Aristotelis Hesychii* 10 (*VH* 10), no. 48; Ptolemy (-el-Garib), no. 24.

3 V. Rose could not anticipate that of this *Collection of 158 Constitutions,* the *Constitution of Athens* would soon be discovered (in 1890).

4 V. Rose, *De Aristotelis Librorum Ordine et Auctoritate Commentatio* (Berlin, 1854), pp. 104–17. Rose also insists that Aristotle was never a true disciple of Plato, but merely a 'casual auditor' who from the very beginning rejected Plato's teachings without compromise. See A.-H. Chroust, 'The lost works of Aristotle in pre-Jaegerian scholarship,' *Classica et Mediaevalia,* vol. 25, fasc. 1–2 (1964–5), pp. 77–80.

5 Teubner edition, Leipzig, 1886. It should be noted that in this edition and, as a matter of fact, until the very end of his life, Rose maintained that all the fragments and excerpts credited to Aristotle are spurious. Hence, the title of *Aristoteles Pseudepigraphus* still applies to Rose's last and most authoritative collection.

6 Only in relatively few instances does an excerpt or fragment make specific reference to a specific work of Aristotle. See, for instance, frags 3, 6, 7, 9, 13 and 26 (Rose), to the *On Philosophy*; frags 37 and 44–5 (Rose), to the *Eudemus or On the Soul*; frag. 49 (Rose), to the *On Prayer*; frags 50–1 (Rose), to the *Protrepticus*; frag. 63 (Rose), to the *On Education*; frag. 65 (Rose), to the *Sophist*; frags 70 and 72 (Rose), to the *On Poets*; frags 75–6 (Rose), to the *On Poetry*; frag. 79 (Rose), to the *Politicus*; frags 82 and 87

(Rose), to the *On Justice*; frags 91 and 93–4 (Rose), to the *On Noble Birth*; and frag. 101 (Rose), to the *Symposium*; etc.

7 DL V. 22 (no. 13); *VH* 10 (no. 13).

8 In this Rose seems to follow the suggestions made by I. Bywater in his 'On a lost dialogue of Aristotle,' *Journal of Philology*, vol. 2 (1869), pp. 55–69.

9 One remarkable exception is O. Gigon, 'Prolegomena to an edition of the *Eudemus*,' *Aristotle and Plato in the Mid-Fourth Century* (Göteborg, 1960), pp. 19–33, who in a most scholarly manner takes issue with Rose's assignments and arrangements. Gigon's example has been followed by other scholars.

10 This is particularly true of certain Neo-Platonic authors who in their syncretist efforts wished to reconcile Plato and Aristotle and, accordingly, often did violence to both.

11 W. Jaeger, *Aristoteles: Grundlegung einer Geschichte seiner Entwicklung*, first published in Germany (Berlin) in 1923. An English translation was published in England under the title of *Aristotle: Fundamentals of the History of his Development* (Oxford, 1934 and 1948).

12 *Ibid.* (1948), pp. 39–166.

13 Thus Jaeger added to Rose's fragments or excerpts from the Aristotelian *Protrepticus* the following: Iamblichus, *Protrepticus* 34,5–35,8 (Pistelli); 36,7–38,22; 41,6–43,27; 44,9–45,3; 49,3–52,16; 54,13–60,10.

14 See A.-H. Chroust, 'Werner Jaeger and the reconstruction of Aristotle's lost works,' *Symbolae Osloenses*, fasc. 42 (1967), pp. 7–43, and Postscript, pp. 231 ff.

15 I. Düring, *Aristotle's Protrepticus: An Attempt at Reconstruction* (Studia Graeca et Latina Gothoburgensia, vol. XII, Göteborg, 1961). In his inimitable scholarship, Düring not only collected the fragments of the Aristotelian *Protrepticus* as well as many related texts or references, but in a most original and, it appears, most commendable manner, he also re-numbered the traditional fragments or materials. Moreover, he subdivided these fragments into more manageable and more sensible short 'units.' At the same time, Düring introduced a novel and, on the whole, most satisfactory sequence in which these 'reduced' fragments or 'units' should be arranged. A.-H. Chroust, *Aristotle: Protrepticus—A Reconstruction* (Notre Dame, 1964), although radically differing with Düring on the philosophic background and doctrine of the Aristotelian *Protrepticus*, to a large extent adopted Düring's novel subdivision, numbering and proposed sequence of the several fragments.

16 M. Untersteiner, *Aristotele: Della Filosofia* (Rome, 1963). Untersteiner not only restates and renumbers some of the fragments identified by V. Rose, R. Walzer, W. D. Ross and others, but also adds several new fragments. At the same time, he supplies most useful and most erudite commentaries to each fragment, as well as recites and comments on some of the recent scholarly discussions of the Aristotelian *On Philosophy*. Despite its many

scholarly merits, the book of Untersteiner has been subjected to an un-deservedly harsh and, in parts, unfair review by L. Tarán, in *American Journal of Philology*, vol. 87, no. 4 (1966), pp. 464–72. Tarán's review con-tains some highly questionable assertions of its own, as does probably every attempt to discuss the lost works of Aristotle, including the present book.

17 This becomes obvious not only in Jaeger's justly famous book of 1923 (see note 11), but also in those works which followed in its wake, including in A.-H. Chroust (see note 15), *passim*.

18 An outstanding example among many is E. Bignone, *L'Aristotele Perduto e la Formazione Filosofica di Epicuro*, 2 vols (Florence, 1936), *passim*.

19 W. G. Rabinowitz, concentrating on the *Protrepticus* of Aristotle, among other scholarly contributions, has made a critical beginning with a novel approach to the whole source problem and collection of fragments related to the lost works of Aristotle. See W. G. Rabinowitz, *Aristotle's Protrepticus and the Sources of Its Reconstruction* (University of California Publications in Classical Philology, vol. 16, no. 1, 1957), *passim*. A similarly critical approach has been taken by W. Haase, 'Ein vermeintliches Aristotelesfragment bei Johannes Philoponos,' *Synusia: Festschrift für Wolfgang Schadewaldt* (Pfullingen, Germany, 1965), pp. 323–54; and by H. Flashar, 'Platon und Aristoteles im Protreptikos des Jamblichos,' *Archiv für Geschichte der Philosophie*, vol. 47 (1965), pp. 53–79.

20 In the work mentioned in note 15, pp. 20–1, and 74–6 (frag. 13, Walzer; frag. 13, Ross; frags 48–50, Düring; frags 45–7, Chroust), the present author assigned a passage from Iamblichus, *Protrepticus*, chap. X (p. 55.7–56.2, Pistelli) to Aristotle's *Protrepticus*. In his 'An emendation to fragment 13 (Walzer, Ross) of Aristotle's *Protrepticus*,' *Tijdschrift voor Filosofie*, vol. 28, no. 2 (1966), pp. 366–77, he now assigns this passage to Aristotle's lost *Politicus*. See also Chapter VIII.

21 See A.-H. Chroust (see note 15), p. 377, note 32; and Chapter VIII, note 43.

22 A notable exception is P.-M. Schuhl (ed.), *Aristote: cinq Oeuvres perdues: De la Richesse—De la Prière—De la Noblesse—Du Plaisir—De L'Éducation*, Fragments et Témoignages, Édites, Traduites et Commentées sous la Direction et avec une Préface de Pierre-Maxime Schuhl, par Jean Aubonnet, Jannine Bertier, Jacques Brunschwig, Pierre Hadot, Jean Pépin, Pierre Thillet, Publications de la Faculté des Lettres et Sciences Humaines de Paris–Sorbonne, Série 'Textes et Documents,' vol. XVII (Paris, 1968). See also A.-H. Chroust, 'A note on some of the minor lost works of the young Aristotle,' *Tijdschrift voor Filosofie*, vol. 27, no. 2 (1965), pp. 310–19.

23 A thorough discussion and an attempt at reconstructing these two com-positions will be made in the near future by S. Mansion and É. de Strycker, *Aristote: 'Du Bien': Essai de Reconstruction*; and by G. E. L. Owen, *Aristotle's Essay 'On Ideas': An Attempt at Reconstruction*.

CHAPTER I · THE PROBABLE DATES OF SOME OF ARISTOTLE'S
LOST WORKS

\* In a different, shorter and probably less adequate as well as less annotated form, this chapter was first published in *Rivista Critica di Storia della Filosofia*, vol. 23, fasc. I (1967), pp. 3–23.

I Diogenes Laertius V. 22 (DL V. 22), no. 5; *Vita Aristotelis Hesychii* 10 (*VH* 10), no. 5; Ptolemy (-el-Garib), no. 3; Quintilian, *Institutio Oratoria* II. 17. 14. See also F. Solmsen, *Die Entwicklung der Aristotelischen Logik und Rhetorik* (Berlin, 1929), pp. 196–207; P. Thillet, 'Note sur le *Gryllos*: ouvrage de jeunesse d'Aristote,' *Revue Philosophique de la France et de l'Étranger*, vol. 82 (1959), pp. 152–4; P. Kucharski, 'La rhétorique dans le *Gorgias* et le *Phèdre*,' *Revue des Études Grecques*, vol. 74 (1961), pp. 371–406.

2 See, in general, A.-H. Chroust, 'Aristotle's first literary effort: the *Gryllus* —a lost dialogue on the nature of rhetoric,' *Revue des Études Grecques*, vol. 78, nos 371–3 (1966), pp. 576–91, and Chapter III.

3 DL II. 54; Pausanias I. 3. 4.

4 DL II. 55. Diogenes Laertius also relates that Xenophon, upon receiving the news of his son's heroic death, 'did not shed any tears, but exclaimed: "I know my son was mortal."' *Ibid.* The same story is told of Anaxagoras who, when informed of the death of his sons, commented: 'I knew that my children were born to die.' DL II. 13. *Ibid.*, we are informed that 'some people, however, tell this story of Solon, and others of Xenophon.'

5 See A.-H. Chroust, 'Aristotle's earliest course of lectures on rhetoric,' *Antiquité Classique*, vol. 33, fasc. i (1964), pp. 58–72, especially, pp. 69 ff., and Volume I, Chapter VIII.

6 F. Solmsen (note I), pp. 208–28.

7 I. Düring, *Aristotle in the Ancient Biographical Tradition* (Acta Universitatis Gothoburgensis, vol. LXIII, no. 2, Göteborg, 1957), pp. 258–9.

8 See Dionysius of Halicarnassus, *De Isocrate* 18; Dionysius of Halicarnassus, *Epistola ad Cn. Pompeium* I; Athenaeus, *Deipnosophistae* II. 60DE; III. 122B; VIII. 354B; Themistius, *Oratio* XXIII. 285AB (p. 345, ed. W. Dindorf); Eusebius, *Praeparatio Evangelica* XIV 6. 9–10.

9 I. Düring (see note 7). F. Blass, *Attische Beredsamkeit*, vol. II (Leipzig, 1892), pp. 451–3, on the other hand, maintains that the *Against Aristotle* was written after the death of Isocrates, that is, after 338 B.C.

10 It has been suggested, however, that the *Antidosis* of Isocrates might be a reply to Aristotle's *Protrepticus*, rather than *vice versa*. This thesis, however, has not found universal acceptance. See note 67.

11 For additional detail, see A.-H. Chroust (see note 2), *passim*, and Chapter III.

12 DL V. 23 (no. 31: Περὶ εἰδῶν); DL V. 23 (no. 54: Περὶ τῆς ἰδέας); VH 10 (no. 28: Περὶ εἰδῶν); *VH* 10 (no. 45: Περὶ ἰδέας); Alexander of Aphrodisias, *Commentaria in Aristotelis Metaphysica*, *Commentaria in Aristotelem Graeca* (hereinafter cited as *CIAG*), vol. I (ed. M. Hayduck,

Berlin, 1891), p. 79; line 7; p. 98, line 22; Syrianus, *Commentaria in Aristotelis Metaphysica, CIAG*, vol VI, part 1 (ed. W. Kroll, Berlin, 1902), p. 120, lines 33 ff.; etc. See also R. Cadiou, 'Le problème de la méthode dans la traité aristotélicien des idées,' *Revue Philosophique de la France et de l'Étranger*, vol. 81 (1956), pp. 94–100; S. Mansion, 'La critique de la theorie des idées dans le *Περὶ ἰδεῶν* d'Aristote,' *Revue Philosophique de Louvain*, vol. 47 (1949), pp. 169–202.

13 See, for instance, C. A. Brandis, *De Perditis Aristotelis Libris De Ideis et De Bono* (Bonn, 1823), p. 14; F. A. Trendelenburg, *Platonis De Ideis et Numeris Doctrina ex Aristotele Illustrata* (Leipzig, 1826), p. 3; E. Zeller, *Die Philosophie der Griechen*, vol. II, part 2 (Leipzig, 1879), p. 48; F. Ravaisson, *Éssai sur la Métaphysique d'Aristote* (Paris, 1837), vol. I, pp. 3–107; W. Bournot, *De Platonicis Aristotelis Operibus* (Potbus, 1853), pp. 4 ff. The relationship of the *On (the) Ideas* to the Platonic *Parmenides* becomes obvious in the following: Aristotle in the main restates the essential arguments against the Separate Ideas advanced in the Platonic *Parmenides* in *Metaphysics* 990 a 34 ff., and 1179 a 4–19, two passages which are part of the *Urmetaphysik* (Jaeger) and, hence, might very well be based on the *On (the) Ideas*. See W. Jaeger's review of P. Wilpert, *Zwei Aristotelische Frühschriften* (Regensburg, 1949), in *Gnomon*, vol. 23 (1951), pp. 247–52.

14 H. Karpp, 'Die Schrift des Aristoteles *Περὶ ἰδεῶν*,' *Hermes*, vol. 68 (1933), pp. 384–91. P. Wilpert, by analyzing Alexander of Aphrodisias' *Commentary to Aristotle's Metaphysics*, Book A, discovered additional elements or fragments of the *On (the) Ideas*. See P. Wilpert, 'Reste verlorener Aristotelesschriften bei Alexander von Aphrodisias,' *Hermes*, vol. 75 (1940), pp. 378 ff.

15 R. Philippson, 'Il *Περὶ ἰδεῶν* di Aristotele,' *Rivista di Filologia e d'Istruzione Classica*, vol. 64 (1936), pp. 113–25. Philippson's views were accepted by E. Frank, 'The fundamental opposition of Plato and Aristotle,' *American Journal of Philology*, vol. 61 (1940), p. 47, note 16.

16 It has been conjectured, though probably erroneously, that the Platonic *Parmenides* was written shortly after Plato's return from his third Sicilian voyage (361–60 B.C.). See A.-H. Chroust, 'The problem of Plato's *Parmenides*,' *New Scholasticism*, vol. 21 (1947), pp. 371 ff., especially, pp. 385 ff., 393 ff.

17 P. Wilpert (see note 13), pp. 97–118.

18 See pp. 8 ff.

19 See Chapter XII, pp. 145 ff.

20 W. Jaeger (see note 13).

21 P. Moraux, *Les Listes anciennes des ouvrages d'Aristote* (Louvain, 1951), pp. 328–37.

22 P. Moraux (see note 21) maintains that Eudoxus is referred to in the *On (the) Ideas*. But as a rule, Moraux insists, no living person would have been cited in a work such as the *On (the) Ideas*. Moraux is mistaken, however, when he places the death of Eudoxus in the year 355–54. K. von Fritz,

'Die Lebenszeit des Eudoxos von Knidos,' *Philologus*, vol. 85 (1929-30), pp. 478-81, firmly established the year 347 as the date of Eudoxus' death. This, then, would lend support to Wilpert's thesis (see note 13) that the *On (the) Ideas* was composed after the death of Plato. See also Chapter XII, note 7.

23 D. J. Allan, *The Philosophy of Aristotle* (London, 1952), pp. 16-21. Allan believes that behind the *On (the) Ideas* is the following situation: during his last years Plato became increasingly aware of the several difficulties connected with his doctrine of the Separate Ideas but did not succeed in resolving them to the complete satisfaction of some members of the Academy. Consequently, in his *On (the) Ideas*, Aristotle made a number of suggestions as to how certain of these difficulties might be resolved. A similar thesis was advanced by R. Stark, *Aristotelesstudien* (Munich, 1954), pp. 20-6. In *Metaphysics* 990 a 34-990 b 22, Aristotle criticizes at great length and with much acumen those 'who posit the Separate Ideas as causes.' Essentially the same criticisms can be found in *Metaphysics* 1079 a 4-19. In *Metaphysics* 1076 a 27-29, Aristotle refers to the fact that these criticisms had repeatedly been made in his 'exoteric discussions' (λόγοι ἐξωτερικοί). We may assume, therefore, that *Metaphysics* 990 a 34 ff., and 1079 a 4 ff. refer back to the *On (the) Ideas* and to the criticisms of the Separate Ideas made there originally. Hence, these two passages may be considered 'fragments' of the *On (the) Ideas*. See also P. Wilpert (see note 13), pp. 23-4.

24 I. Düring, 'Aristotle and Plato in the mid-fourth century,' *Eranos*, vol. 54 (1956), pp. 109-20.

25 This may be inferred from the following: in Book A of the *Metaphysics*, Aristotle refers to 'we' rather than to 'they.' This 'we' was probably transferred from the *On (the) Ideas* to Book A of the *Metaphysics*. Moreover, this 'we' indicates that the issues discussed here are 'purely internal matters,' solely concerning the inner circle of the Platonic Academy. Hence, the *On (the) Ideas* must be part of that 'internal discussion' over the nature and functions of the Ideas, a discussion which started soon after Plato's return from Sicily. Plato's absence might actually have encouraged certain criticisms of some of his basic teachings. See last part of note 23.

26 See pp. 41-2. The assumption that the year 357-56 is the likely *tempus post quod* for dating the *On (the) Ideas* does not coincide with Jaeger's basic view that throughout his stay at the Academy (367-348/47), Aristotle adhered faithfully to Plato's doctrine of the Ideas. In deference to Jaeger, it seems, P. Wilpert (see note 13), p. 10, dates the *On (the) Ideas* after the death of Plato. See also M. Gentile, 'La dottrina delle idee numeri e Aristotele,' *Annali della Reale Scuola Normale Superiore di Pisa*, Classe di Lettere e Filosofia, vol. 30, fasc. 3 (1930), pp. 85-105; M. Gentile, 'Nuovi studi intorno alla dottrina platonica delle idee numeri,' *ibid.*, series II, vol. 4, fasc. 1-2 (1937), pp. 111-27.

27 For details, see Chapter XII, pp. 145 ff.

28 See I. Düring (see note 24), pp. 109 ff. Düring dates the *On the Good*

about the year 355. If Düring's dating should prove to be correct, the date of the *On (the) Ideas* would probably have to be moved to the year 354 or, perhaps, 353.

29 That Aristotle wrote an *On the Good* is attested in DL V. 22 (no. 20); *VH* 10 (no. 20); Ptolemy (-el-Garib), no. 9. See also *VM* 32 and *VL* 33. Diogenes Laertius claims that this work consisted of three books, Hesychius that it was in one book, and Ptolemy (-el-Garib) that it contained five books. See also Alexander of Aphrodisias, *Comment. in Arist. Metaphysica, CIAG*, vol. I (ed. M. Hayduck, Berlin, 1891), p. 56, line 35; p. 59, lines 33–4; p. 85, lines 16–18; p. 250, line 20; p. 262, line 19; Philoponus, *Comment. in Arist. De Anima, CIAG*, vol. 15 (ed. M. Hayduck, Berlin, 1897), p. 75, line 34; Simplicius, *Comment. in Arist. De Anima, CIAG*, vol. 11 (ed. M. Hayduck, Berlin, 1882), p. 21, line 7; Simplicius, *Comment. in Arist. Physicorum Libros I–IV, CIAG*, vol. 9 (ed. H. Diels, Berlin, 1895), p. 151, line 8; p. 453, line 28; p. 454, line 20; Asclepius, *Comment. in Arist. Metaphysica, CIAG*, vol. VI, part 2 (ed. M. Hayduck, Berlin, 1888), p. 79, line 10; p. 237, line 14; p. 247, line 19. See also O. Kluge, *Darstellung und Beurteilung der Einwendungen des Aristoteles gegen die platonische Ideenlehre* (Diss. Greifswald, 1905), pp. 65–74; C. de Vogel, 'Problems concerning later Platonism,' *Mnemosyne* (series 4), vol. 2 (1949), pp. 197–216, and vol. 3, pp. 299–318; H. Cherniss, *Aristotle's Criticism of Plato and the Academy*, vol. I (Baltimore, 1944), *passim*; W. D. Ross, *Plato's Theory of Ideas* (Oxford, 1951), pp. 142–53.

30 This lecture is attested by Aristoxenus of Tarentum, *Harmonics* II (p. 30, lines 15 ff., ed. H. S. Macran, Oxford, 1903). Aristoxenus reports that many people, including 'outsiders,' attended this lecture expecting to learn something about such matters as wealth, health, strength and happiness in general. But when Plato spoke about mathematics and numbers and geometry and astronomy, and when he finally maintained that the Good was One, they were utterly baffled. Thereupon some among his audience were disappointed and despised the subject of Plato's discussions while others denounced it outright. No attempt will be made here to discuss the challenging and fascinating theories of H. J. Krämer, *Arete bei Platon und Aristoteles: Zum Wesen und zur Geschichte der platonischen Ontologie* (Heidelberg, 1959), which deal with the 'esoteric teachings' of Plato. Undoubtedly, the 'lecture' *On the Good* was part of these 'esoteric teachings.' Should Krämer's theories, which are by no means firmly established, prove to be correct, then much of the traditionalist (or commonplace) views about Plato's basic philosophy would have to be discarded.

31 See Philoponus (see note 29); Simplicius, *Comment. in Aristotelis De Anima* (see note 29); Simplicius, *Comment. in Aristotelis Physicorum Libros I–IV* (see note 29), p. 453, lines 28 ff.; p. 454, lines 20 ff. See, in general, H. Cherniss, *The Riddle of the Early Academy* (Berkeley-Los Angeles, 1945), pp. 2–4; pp. 12–13.

32 P. Wilpert (see note 14), pp. 376 ff., points out that Simplicius, *Comment.*

*in Aristotelis, Physicorum Libros I–IV* (see note 29), p. 247, line 30—p. 248, line 18—a passage which actually goes back to Hermodorus—reveals that there exists a connection between Plato's 'lecture' and Aristotle's *On the Good*. See also P. Wilpert, 'Neue Fragmente aus Περὶ τἀγαθοῦ,' *Hermes*, vol. 76 (1941), pp. 225–50; P. Wilpert (see note 13), pp. 121 ff.; W. Jaeger, in *Gnomon*, vol. 23 (1951), pp. 246–52; C. de Vogel (see note 29), *passim*. The theory that the composition of the Aristotelian *On the Good* had been stimulated by a lecture (or lectures) of Plato on this subject is refuted by H. J. Krämer (see note 30), *passim*.

33 J. Stenzel, *Zahl und Gestalt bei Platon und Aristoteles* (3rd ed., Darmstadt, 1959), pp. 67 ff., *et passim*. Stenzel's thesis has also been touched upon by A. Taylor, 'Forms and numbers: a study in metaphysics,' *Mind*, vol. 35 (1926), pp. 419 ff.; vol. 36 (1927), pp. 12 ff.; O. Toeplitz, *Das Verhältnis von Mathematik und Ideenlehre bei Platon*, in *Quellen und Studien zur Geschichte der Mathematik, Astronomie und Physik*, vol. I, part 1 (Berlin, 1929), pp. 18 ff. Already Porphyry had pointed out that there exist certain connections between Plato's *Philebus* and Aristotle's *On the Good*. See Simplicius (see note 29), p. 453, lines 25 ff.; p. 454, lines 17 ff.

34 W. D. Ross (see note 29), pp. 142–53.

35 P. Moraux (see note 21), p. 39; p. 325.

36 H. D. Saffrey, *Le Περὶ Φιλοσοφίας d'Aristote et la Théorie Platonicienne des Idées Nombres* (Leiden, 1955), *passim*.

37 Saffrey suggests the following chronological sequence: Plato's *Timaeus*, Aristotle's *On the Good* and Aristotle's *De Anima*.

38 See note 29, especially, Philoponus, *Comment. in Arist. De Anima*, *CIAG*, vol. XV, p. 75, lines 34 ff.; Simplicius, *Comment. in Arist. De Anima*, *CIAG*, vol. XI, p. 28, lines 7 ff. In recent times, this thesis has been accepted by C. de Vogel (see note 29), *Mnemosyne* (Series IV), vol. 2 (1949), pp. 203–5; G. S. Claghorn, *Aristotle's Criticism of Plato's Timaeus* (The Hague, 1954), pp. 5–19; H. D. Saffrey (see note 36), *passim*.

39 H. J. Krämer (see note 30), pp. 325 ff. and p. 332, however, disputes this.

40 Themistius, *Oratio* XXI. 245CD (vol. I, p. 299, ed. W. Dindorf), maintains that this 'lecture' was not delivered at the Academy, but rather in the Piraeus before a very large crowd. See also H. J. Krämer (see note 30), pp. 404–8.

41 It will be noted, however, that H. J. Krämer (see note 30), pp. 325 ff., suggests that the *On the Good* is not the 'product' of Plato's lecture, but rather the cause of it. See note 32. Should Krämer's thesis prevail—he himself seems to contradict it (see *ibid.*, p. 332)—then the *On the Good* might be anterior to the Platonic *Sophist*, the *Statesman*, the *Philebus* and the *Timaeus*—a very unlikely prospect.

42 See p. 13; Chapter XII.

43 See A.-H. Chroust, 'The probable date of Aristotle's lost dialogue *On Philosophy*,' *Journal of the History of Philosophy*, vol. 4, no. 4 (1966), pp. 283–91, and Chapter XII.

44 H. D. Saffrey (see note 36), p. X, for instance, argues that Aristotle, *De Anima* 404 b 16–24, refers back to Book II of the *On Philosophy*, and that Book II of the *On Philosophy* resumes issues which have been discussed in the *On the Good*.

45 See pp. 8 ff.

46 See, for instance, P. Wilpert (see note 13), pp. 148–51; H. J. Krämer (see note 30), p. 352.

47 I. Düring (see note 24), pp. 109 ff., dates the *On the Good* about 355.

48 See DL V. 22 (no. 1); *VH* 10 (no. 1); Ptolemy (-el-Garib) (no. 4); Cicero, *De Republica* III. 8. 12. The *On Justice* apparently consisted of four books. It is widely held that Diogenes Laertius lists the early compositions of Aristotle in the order of their length, starting with the longest work. Since the *On Justice* is listed in the first place, it has been surmised that it is the largest from among the earliest writings of the Stagirite. See, in general, P. Moraux, *A la Recherche de l'Aristote Perdu: Le Dialogue 'Sur la Justice'* (Paris-Louvain, 1957), *passim*; A.-H. Chroust, 'Aristotle's *On Justice*: a lost dialogue,' *Modern Schoolman*, vol. 43, no. 3 (166), pp. 249–63, and Chapter VI. See also Demetrius, *De Elocutione* 28; Boethius, *De Interpretatione* (ed. C. Meiser), p. 27; Suetonius, Περὶ βλασφημιῶν (ed. Miller), p. 416.

49 See J. Bernays, *Die Dialoge des Aristoteles in Ihrem Verhältnis zu Seinen Übrigen Werken* (Berlin, 1863), pp. 49–51; W. Jaeger, *Aristotle: Fundamentals of the History of his Development* (Oxford, 1948), p. 30, note 1; E. Bignone, *L'Aristotele Perduto e la Formazione Filosofica di Epicuro*, vol. I (Florence, 1936), p. 223; P. Moraux (see note 48), pp. 55 ff.

50 J. Bernays (see note 49). Bernays maintains that in the *On Justice* Aristotle rejects the doctrine of Ideas advanced in the Platonic *Republic*. He is also of the opinion that the reference to the 'exoteric discussions' in Aristotle, *Metaphysics* 1076 a 27–9, is related to the *On Justice*. See note 23. See, among others, Lactantius, *Institutiones Divinae* V. 15; Lactantius, *Epitome Divinarum Institutionum ad Pentadium Fratrem* 55; E. Heitz, *Die verlorenen Schriften des Aristoteles* (Leipzig, 1865), pp. 167–8. P. Moraux (see note 48), pp. 151 ff.

51 P. Moraux, 'From the *Protrepticus* to the dialogue *On Justice*,' *Aristotle and Plato in the Mid-Fourth Century* (Göteborg, 1960), pp. 113–32. Moraux's thesis, however, is not altogether convincing. See also P. Moraux (see note 48), pp. 124 ff. Moraux holds that the psychology advocated in the *On Justice*—the doctrine of the bipartite soul—is closely related to the bipartite psychology of the *Nicomachean Ethics* (1102 a 5 ff.). In *Nicomachean Ethics* 1102 a 26–7, Aristotle refers to what he had formerly said in the 'exoteric discussions.' Moraux believes that this is a reference to the *On Justice*. D. A. Rees, 'Bipartition of the soul in the early Academy,' *Journal of Hellenic Studies*, vol. 77 (1957), p. 118, on the other hand, holds that Aristotle refers here to the *Protrepticus*; and O. Gigon, 'Prolegomena to an edition of the *Eudemus*,' *Aristotle and Plato in the Mid-Fourth Century* (Göteborg, 1960), p. 29, insists that he refers to the *Eudemus*.

52 P. Moraux (see note 48), pp. 127–32. See also O. Gigon (see note 51).

53 I. Düring, *Aristotle's Protrepticus: An Attempt at Reconstruction* (Göteborg, 1961), pp. 287–8.

54 The fact that G. R. Morrow (in *Gnomon*, vol. 30, 1958, pp. 441–3), O. Kern (in *Scholastik*, vol. 35, 1960, pp. 117–18) and R. Weil (in *Revue Philosophique de la France et de l'Étranger*, vol. 87, 1962, pp. 401–12), in their respective reviews of P. Moraux (see note 48), point out that the Aristotelian *Politicus* (see pp. 11–12 and Chapter XI) 'implements' the Aristotelian *On Justice* is of no great help, except that it indicates that the *Politicus*, which has been tentatively dated around 350 or shortly thereafter, is posterior to the *On Justice*.

55 See notes 51 and 52.

56 See note 53.

57 DL V. 22 (no. 13); *VH* 10 (no. 13). Diogenes Laertius and Hesychius list an *On the Soul*, omitting the sub-title *Eudemus*. Ptolemy (-el-Garib) does not mention the *Eudemus*. See also Plutarch, *Consolatio ad Apollonium* 27 (*Moralia* 115B); Plutarch, *Dion* 22; Themistius, *Comment. in Arist. De Anima, CIAG*, vol. V, part 3 (ed. R. Heinze, Berlin, 1899), p. 106, lines 29 ff.; Philoponus, *Comment. in Arist. De Anima, CIAG*, vol. XV (ed. M. Hayduck, Berlin, 1897), p. 141, lines 30 ff.; p. 144, lines 24 ff.; p. 145, lines 2 ff.; p. 147, lines 6 ff.; Simplicius, *Comment. in Arist. De Anima, CIAG*, vol. XI (ed. M. Hayduck, Berlin, 1882), p. 53, lines 1 ff.; Elias (*olim* David), *Comment. in Porphyrii Isagogen et in Arist. Categorias, CIAG*, vol. XVIII, part 1 (ed. A. Busse, Berlin, 1900), p. 114, lines 22 ff.; p. 114, lines 32 ff.; p. 115, lines 11 ff.; Proclus, *Comment. in Platonis Timaeum* 338CD; Olympiodorus, *Comment. in Platonis Phaedonem*, p. 173, lines 20 ff. (ed. W. Norvin). See also J. Bernays, 'Aus dem aristotelischen Dialog *Eudemos*,' *Rheinisches Museum*, vol. 76 (1861), pp. 236–46; G. Méautis, 'L'Orphisme dans l'Eudème d'Aristote,' *Revue des Études Anciennes*, vol. 57 (1955), pp. 254–66; O. Gigon (see note 51), pp. 22 ff.; P. Gohlke, *Aristoteles: Fragmente* (Paderborn, 1960), pp. 8 ff.; D. A. Rees, 'Theories of the soul in the early Aristotle,' *Aristotle and Plato in the Mid-Fourth Century* (Göteborg, 1960), pp. 191 ff.

58 See A.-H. Chroust, '*Eudemus or On the Soul:* a lost Aristotelian dialogue on the immortality of the soul,' *Mnemosyne*, vol. 19 (series 4), fasc. 1 (1966), pp. 17–30, and Chapter IV; A.-H. Chroust, 'The psychology in Aristotle's lost dialogue *Eudemus or On the Soul*,' *Acta Classica*, vol. 9 (1966), pp. 49–62, and Chapter V.

59 Plutarch, *Dion* 18; Cicero, *De Divinatione ad Brutum* I. 25. 53; Diodorus Siculus XVI. 36. Plutarch's account seems to conflict with the historical facts. He reports that Eudemus was killed either in connection with the expulsion of Callippus in 353 (or perhaps early in 352), or in connection with Dion's seizure of power in 357. See also Plutarch, *Dion* 22. For a most detailed—and most convincing—discussion of the chronological problems connected with the death of Eudemus of Cyprus and, hence, with the dating of the *Eudemus*, see W. Spoerri, 'Prosographia,' *Museum Helveticum*, vol. 23, fasc. 1 (1966), pp. 44–57, and Chapter IV, note 14.

60 The fact that the Aristotelian *Eudemus* is strongly under the influence of Plato's *Phaedo* in itself should not be taken as proof of the allegation that around 353 B.C. Aristotle was still an 'orthodox Platonist.' A *consolatio mortis* such as the *Eudemus* would be a rather poor example of Aristotle's Platonism. The very nature of Plato's philosophy or fundamental philosophic outlook, it goes without saying, lends itself admirably to the belief, so vital for any *consolatio mortis*, that the departed person has gone (or has returned) to a better world where he will live on in a state of perfect bliss. It is also held that the news of Dion's death (in 353 B.C.) prompted Plato to compose his *Seventh Epistle* (provided this *Epistle* is actually by Plato), which is addressed to 'the friends of Dion.'

61 O. Gigon (see note 51), p. 24.

62 DL V. 22 (no. 12); *VH* 10 (no. 14); Ptolemy (-el-Garib), no. 1. Ptolemy's Syriac or Arabic translator probably combined and perhaps confused the Aristotelian *Protrepticus* and the Aristotelian *On Philosophy* when he lists 'a book in which he [*scil.*, Aristotle] exhorts to philosophy, in Greek entitled Προτρεπτικὸς Φιλοσοφίας.' See *Vita Aristotelis Arabica* of Ibn Abi Usaibia (*IV VA*). Naturally, the title recorded by Usaibia could refer either to the *Protrepticus* or to the *On Philosophy*, or to both. See also Stobaeus, *Florilegium* IV. 32. 21; Alexander of Aphrodisias, *Comment. in Arist. Topicorum Lib.*, *CIAG*, vol. II, part 2 (ed. M. Wallies, Berlin, 1891), p. 149, lines 9–17; Olympiodorus, *Comment. in Platonis Alcibiadem Priorem*, p. 144; Elias (*olim* David), *Comment. in Pophyrii Isagogen et in Arist. Categorias*, *CIAG*, vol. XVIII, part 1 (ed. A. Busse, Berlin, 1900), p. 3, lines 17–23; David, *Prolegomena et in Porphyrii Isagogen Comment.*, *CIAG*, vol. XVIII, part 2 (ed. A. Busse, Berlin, 1904), p. IX, lines 2–12. See, in general, I. Bywater, 'On a lost dialogue of Aristotle [*scil.*, the Protrepticus],' *Journal of Philology*, vol. 11 (1869), pp. 55–69; R. Hirzel, 'Über den *Protreptikos* des Aristoteles,' *Hermes*, vol. 10 (1876), pp. 61–100; H. Diels, 'Zu Aristoteles' *Protreptikos* und Ciceros *Hortensius*,' *Archiv für Geschichte der Philosophie*, vol. I (1888), pp. 477–97; P. Hartlich, *De Exhortationum a Graecis Romanisque Scriptarum Historia et Indole* (Leipziger Studien zur Klassischen Philologie, Leipzig, 1889), pp. 236–72; H. Gadamer, 'Der aristotelische *Protreptikos* und die entwicklungsgeschichtliche Betrachtung der aristotelischen Ethik,' *Hermes*, vol. 63 (1928), pp. 138–64; P. von der Mühll, 'Isokrates und der *Protreptikos* des Aristoteles,' *Philologus*, vol. 94 (1939–40), pp. 259–65; B. Einarson, 'Aristotle's *Protrepticus* and the structure of the *Epinomis*,' *Transactions and Proceedings of the American Philological Association*, vol. 67 (Ithaca, 1936), pp. 261–85; W. G. Rabinowitz, *Aristotle's Protrepticus and the Sources of Its Reconstruction* (University of California Publications in Classical Philology, vol. 16, no. 1, 1957), *passim*; I. Düring (see note 53); A.-H. Chroust, *Aristotle: Protrepticus—A Reconstruction* (Notre Dame, 1964); G. Schneeweisz, *Der Protreptikos des Aristoteles* (Doctoral Dissertation, Munich, 1966); E. Berti, *Aristotele, Esortazione alla Filosofia* (*Protrettico*), Classici della Filosofia (Padua, 1967); A.-H. Chroust, 'A brief account of

the reconstruction of Aristotle's *Protrepticus*,' *Classical Philology*, vol. 40 (1965), pp. 229–39, and Chapter VII.

63 W. Jaeger (see note 49), pp. 81–101.

64 W. Theiler, *Zur Geschichte der teleologischen Naturbetrachtung bis auf Aristoteles* (Zürich, 1924), pp. 80–7. Theiler maintains that in the *Protrepticus* Aristotle introduces a concept of 'nature' which assumes the place of Plato's Separate Ideas and Plato's 'Cosmic Soul.'

65 This should become obvious, for instance, from a comparison of *Antidosis* 258–9, and *Protrepticus* (Iamblichus, *Protrepticus*, p. 52, line 15 to p. 53, line 2, ed. H. Pistelli; frag. 58, Rose; frag. 12, Walzer; frag. 12, Ross; frag. 42, Düring; frag. 40, Chroust).

66 B. Einarson (see note 62), pp. 261–85. See also E. Berti, *La Filosofia del Primo Aristotele* (Università di Padova, Pubblicazioni della Facoltà di Lettere e Filosofia, vol. 38, Padua, 1962), p. 465; pp. 522–3; p. 543; I. Düring (see note 53), pp. 33 ff.

67 P. von der Mühll (see note 62), pp. 259–65. A. Lesky, *Geschichte der Griechischen Literatur* (Berne-Munich, 1962), p. 600, and R. Stark, in *Göttinger Gelehrter Anzeiger*, no. 217 (1965), p. 57, likewise maintain that the *Protrepticus* preceded the *Antidosis*. See also R. A. Gauthier, *L'Éthique à Nicomaque*, vol. I (Louvain-Paris, 1970), p. 13, note 28. The main arguments in support of the thesis that the *Protrepticus* preceded the *Antidosis* are as follows: *Antidosis* 84–6, repeatedly uses the term προτρέπειν (to exhort) as well as provides a fairly accurate account of the main content of the *Protrepticus*. Should the thesis of von der Mühll, Lesky, Stark and Gauthier prove to be correct, then the *tempus ante quod* of the *Protrepticus* would be the year 353–52.

68 F. Nuyens, *L'Évolution de la Psychologie d'Aristote* (Louvain, 1948), pp. 90–106. Nuyens' thesis was rejected by C. de Vogel, *Greek Philosophy*, vol. II (Leiden, 1953), pp. 24–8, who points out that this 'instrumentalist psychology' in the *Protrepticus* might very well be Platonic after all. Hence, de Vogel concludes, there is no reason why the *Protrepticus* should be dated after 348–47. A. J. Festugière, *La Révélation d'Hermès Trismégiste*, vol. II (Paris, 1949), pp. 90–6, claims that the *Protrepticus* generally displays a 'negative attitude' towards the empirical world. Nuyens distinguishes three phases in the development of Aristotle's psychology: the first phase is characterized by a (Platonic) dualism, where soul and body are conceived as two wholly independent and often mutually opposed entities or substances. To this phase, Nuyens believes, belongs, for instance, the Aristotelian *Eudemus*. The second phase, which Nuyens calls the period of 'mechanistic instrumentalism,' is characterized by a 'collaboration' between soul and body. Here the soul uses the body as its tool. This phase becomes manifest, Nuyens contends, in the *Protrepticus*, in the *Historia Animalium*, in books II and IV of the *De Partibus Animalium*, etc., as well as in the *Prior Analytics*, the *Posterior Analytics*, in Books A, B, M 9–10, K and N of the *Metaphysics*, in the *Eudemian Ethics*, in the *Nicomachean Ethics*,

and in books II, III, VII and VIII of the *Politics*. The third phase no longer conceives of the soul and body as two separate substances, but as 'related' to one another, analogous to the relationship of form and matter. This third and last phase finds its final expression in the *De Anima*.

69 J. Zürcher, *Aristoteles Werk und Geist* (Paderborn, 1952), pp. 23–4.

70 See W. Theiler, 'Bau und Zeit der Aristotelischen Politik,' *Museum Helveticum* vol. 9 (1952), pp. 66, note 6. See also note 64.

71 G. Müller, 'Probleme der aristotelischen Eudaimonielehre,' *Museum Helveticum* vol. 17 (1960), pp. 131–43.

72 G. Reale, 'Josef Zürcher e un tentativo di revoluzione nel campo degli studi aristotelici,' *Aristotele nella Critica e negli Studi Contemporanei, Scritti di Emanuele Severino . . . Giovanni Reale, etc.*, supplemento speciale al vol. 48, December 1956 (*Vita e Pensiero*, Milan, 1957), pp. 108–43.

73 I. Düring (see note 53), pp. 274–86, *et passim*; I. Düring, 'Aristotle in the *Protrepticus*,' *Autour d'Aristote* (Louvain, 1955), pp. 81–97; I. Düring, 'Aristotle on ultimate principles from "Nature and Reality": *Protrepticus*, Frag. 13,' *Aristotle and Plato in the Mid-Fourth Century* (Göteborg, 1960), pp. 35–55; R. Stark (see note 23), pp. 5–19.

74 Frag. 11, Walzer; frag. 11, Ross; frag. 11, Düring; frag. 10, Chroust (Iamblichus, *Protrepticus*, p. 49, lines 3–11, ed. H. Pistelli, 1888). This fragment reads as follows:

> Of all the things that come into being, some originate either from thought or from some art, such as, for instance, a house or a ship (for the cause of both of these is a certain art and a definite way of reasoning). Others, again, come into being not at all by way of art, but by nature. Nature is the cause of animals and plants, and all such things come into being according to nature. But some things, again, also come into being as the result of chance. And we say of most of the things that come into being neither by art, nature nor by necessity, that they come into being by chance.

> See Aristotle, *Physics* 196 b 22 ff.; 197 a 2 ff. Düring seems to overlook, however, that in *Laws* 889A, Plato states: 'They say that the greatest and fairest things are the work of nature as well as that of chance, the lesser that of art, which, receiving from nature the greater and truly original creations, moulds and fashions all those lesser works which are generally called "artificial."' See also Plato, *Laws* 709B: 'God governs all things, and chance and art co-operate with Him in the government of human affairs.'

75 I. Düring, 'Aristotle in the *Protrepticus*,' *Autour d'Aristote* (Louvain, 1955), pp. 81–97. Düring also insists that frag. 11, Walzer; frag. 11, Ross; frag. 12, Düring; frag. 11, Chroust (Iamblichus, *Protrepticus*, p. 49, lines 11–25, Pistelli), where Aristotle distinguishes between 'good things' and 'necessary things,' presupposes certain assumptions made in the *Metaphysics*, the *Physics* and the two *Analytics*. See, for instance, *Metaphysics* 1006 b 32;

1015 a 20 ff.; 1025 a 18; 1026 b 28; 1027 b 8; 1037 b 32; 1064 b 34; etc.; *Physics* 196 b 10 ff.; 198 b 11; 199 b 34 ff.; etc.; *Prior Analytics* 24 b 20; 25 a 6; 25 a 27 ff.; 26 a 3; 29 b 29 ff.; 30 a 15 ff.; 47 a 33; 53 b 18; 57 a 40; 62 a 11; etc.

76 I. Düring (see note 53), pp. 274–86.

77 A.-H. Chroust, *Aristotle: Protrepticus—A Reconstruction* (Notre Dame, 1964), pp. 44–110, on the other hand, attempts to show the many parallels that exist between certain passages from the *Protrepticus* and some of Plato's philosophic views.

78 F. Dirlmeier, *Aristoteles: Nikomachische Ethik* (Darmstadt, 1956), pp. 278 ff.; p. 449. Dirlmeier admits, however, that some of the ethical views advanced in the *Protrepticus* are fully identical with the ethical views held by the late Plato. Hence, Dirlmeier assumes, it is well-nigh impossible to call the *Protrepticus* 'a transition from Platonism to Aristotelianism,' or perhaps, an 'essentially "Aristotelian" work,' as I. Düring would have it.

79 See, for instance, É. de Strycker, 'On the first section of frag. 5 of the *Protrepticus*,' *Aristotle and Plato in the Mid-Fourth Century* (Göteborg, 1960), pp. 76–104; C. de Vogel, 'The legend of the Platonizing Aristotle,' *ibid.*, pp. 252–6; S. Mansion, 'Contemplation and action in Aristotle's *Protrepticus*,' *ibid.*, pp. 56–75. H. Gadamer (see note 62), pp. 142–5, insists that the *Protrepticus* is primarily a 'hortatory' rather than a 'philosophic' or 'systematic piece.' Hence, Gadamer maintains, it is illicit to draw any philosophic conclusions from this text. See also note 67.

80 See notes 66 and 67.

81 See Stobaeus, *Florilegium* IV. 32. 21 (frag. 50, Rose; frag. 1. Walzer; frag. 1, Ross; frag. 1, Düring; frag. 1, Chroust).

82 See A.-H. Chroust, 'What prompted Aristotle to address the *Protrepticus* to Themison?", *Hermes*, vol. 94, no. 2 (1966), pp. 202–7, and Chapter IX.

83 See DL V. 22 (no. 4: in two books); *VH* 10 (no. 4: in one book); Cicero, *Ad Quintum Fratrem* III. 5. 1; Cicero, *De Finibus* V. 4. 11; Syrianus, *Comment. in Aristotelis Metaphysica*, *CIAG*, vol. VI, part 1 (ed. W. Kroll, Berlin, 1902), p. 168, line 33. See also A.-H. Chroust, 'Aristotle's *Politicus*: A Lost Dialogue,' *Rheinisches Museum*, vol. 108, no. 4 (1965), pp. 346–53, and Chapter XI.

84 Syrianus (see note 83), p. 168, lines 33–5 (frag. 79, Rose; frag. 2, Ross). This is the translation and interpretation suggested by W. Jaeger. On the strength of his interpretation, Jaeger concludes that in the *Politicus* Aristotle still adheres to Plato's doctrine of the Ideas and, especially, to the Idea of the One (or the Good), which for Plato constitutes the ultimate measure among all measures as well as the highest Idea among Ideas.

85 This is the translation and interpretation proposed by R. Stark, a translation which was also adopted by W. D. Ross. See R. Stark (see note 23), pp. 26–7. Stark emphasizes that this fragment does not mean that 'the

Good is the most exact of all (possible) measures' (or, 'the highest value among all possible values'), but rather that 'the Good is the most exact measure of all things [which transpire in this world of ours].' See also frag. 2, Ross.

86 Aristotle, *Nicomachean Ethics* 1176 a 17 ff.

87 See, for instance, Plato, *Philebus* 64A ff.; Plato, *Statesman* 284A ff. See also Plato, *Laws* 716C.

88 Another possible fragment of the *Politicus* might be detected in Iamblichus, *Protrepticus*, p. 55, line 7–p. 56, line 2 (ed. H. Pistelli, 1888). This passage is traditionally, though not altogether convincingly, credited to Aristotle's *Protrepticus* (frag. 13, Walzer; frag. 13, Ross; frags 48–50, Düring; frags 45–7, Chroust). For a detailed discussion of the reasons why this passage should be credited to Aristotle's *Politicus* rather than to Aristotle's *Protrepticus*, see H. Flashar, 'Platon und Aristoteles im *Protreptikos* des Jamblichos,' *Archiv für Geschichte der Philosophie*, vol. 47 (1965), pp. 77–8; A.-H. Chroust, 'An emendation to fragment 13 (Walzer, Ross) of Aristotle's *Protrepticus*,' *Tijdschrift voor Filosofie*, vol. 28, fasc. 2 (1966), pp. 366–77, and Chapter VIII. See also O. Gigon, *Aristoteles: Einführungsschriften* (Zürich, 1961), p. 99. Should the passage just cited from Iamblichus' *Protrepticus* be in fact a fragment of the *Politicus* rather than of the Aristotelian *Protrepticus*, then the *Politicus* might have to be dated slightly prior to the Aristotelian *Protrepticus*, presumably close to the *On (the) Ideas* and the *On the Good*. This passage is rather Platonic (even though it refers to 'first principles' in the place of Separate Ideas—a characteristic twist of the *On (the) Ideas*)—and even more Platonic than the *Protrepticus*, which apparently makes some concessions to empirical reality. See, for instance, Iamblichus, *Protrepticus* 54,22–55,7 (frag. 13, Walzer; frag. 13, Ross; frag. 47, Düring; frag. 44, Chroust), where we are told that expert and competent craftsmen derive some of their tools from observing (physical or corporeal) nature as well as from the behavior of nature, and that tools devised in this manner are superior to all other tools because they conform to (physical or corporeal) nature. Obviously, the earlier dating of the *Politicus* would vitiate our hypothesis that this composition is in some ways related to the *Antidosis* of Isocrates. See Chapter XI.

89 See E. Bignone (note 49), vol. II, p. 100.

90 See note 88.

91 See Chapter XII, note 2.

92 See also A.-H. Chroust, 'The probable date of Aristotle's lost dialogue *On Philosophy*,' *Journal of the History of Philosophy*, vol. 4, no. 4 (1966), pp. 283–91.

93 The *Protrepticus*, it will be noted, is still quite Platonic (*pace* Düring). See A.-H. Chroust (note 77), *passim*.

94 See Vol. I. Chapter VII.

95 See Vol. I, Chapter XI.

CHAPTER II   A NOTE ON SOME OF THE 'MINOR LOST WORKS' OF
ARISTOTLE

* In a different and greatly abridged form, this chapter was first published in
  *Tijdschrift voor Filosofie*, vol. 27, no. 2 (1965), pp. 310–18.
1 See, for instance, P. Moraux, *A la Recherche de l'Aristote Perdu: Le Dialogue
  'Sur la Justice'* (Aristote, Traduction et Études, Collection Publiée par
  l'Institute Supérieur de Philosophie de l'Université de Louvain, Louvain,
  1957); I. Düring, *Aristotle's Protrepticus: An Attempt at Reconstruction* (Studia
  Graeca et Latina Gothoburgensia, vol. XII, Göteborg, 1961); A.-H.
  Chroust, *Aristotle: Protrepticus—A Reconstruction* (Notre Dame, 1964);
  G. E. L. Owen, *Aristotle's Essay 'On Ideas': An Attempt at Reconstruction*,
  to appear in the near future; S. Mansion and É. de Strycker, *Aristote,
  'Du Bien': Essai de Reconstruction*, to appear in the near future; O. Gigon,
  *Aristoteles Dialog Eudemos: ein Versuch der Wiederherstellung*, to appear in
  the near future; M. Untersteiner, *Aristotele: Della Filosofia* (Temi e Testi X,
  Rome, 1963); P. Wilpert, *Aristoteles Dialog 'Über die Philosophie': Ein
  Versuch der Wiederherstellung*, a work which was interrupted by the un-
  timely death of Professor Wilpert in 1967. Moreover, a great many papers
  have been published on these 'major' lost works. There are, however,
  some scholars who vigorously deny that even the 'more important' lost
  works of Aristotle may successfully be recovered or adequately reconstructed. See, for instance, W. G. Rabinowitz, *Aristotle's Protrepticus and
  the Sources of its Reconstruction* (Berkeley, 1957).
2 Such general collections were made by V. Rose, R. Walzer, W. D. Ross
  and H. G. Gadamer.
3 See, for instance, A.-H. Chroust, 'The problem of the *Aristotelis Librorum
  Fragmenta*,' *Classical Journal*, vol. 62, no. 2 (1966), pp. 71–3.
4 DL V. 22–7, no. 14 (*On Prayer*), no. 19 (*On Education*), no. 16 (*On Pleasure*),
  no. 11 (*On Wealth*), no. 17 (*To Alexander or On Colonization*), no. 15
  (*On Noble Birth*), no. 7 (*Sophist*) and no. 6 (*Nerinthus*). These titles also
  appear in the 'catalogue' found in *VH* 10, namely no. 9, no. 18 (and no.
  172), no. 15, no. 7 (and no. 151), no. 22 (and nos 176 and 196), no. 11
  (and no. 183), no. 8 and no. 6. The abbreviated 'catalogue' appended to
  the *Vita Aristotelis Arabica* of Ibn Abi Usaibia (which is based on Ptolemy-
  el-Garib and, ultimately, probably on Andronicus of Rhodes), contains the
  *Sophist* (no. 3), the *On Education* (no. 5), the *On Noble Birth* (no. 6) and the
  *On Pleasure* (no. 17). The later titles listed in the 'catalogue' of the *Vita
  Aristotelis Hesychii* (nos 159–97), it will be observed, are a scramble of
  repetitions and *pseudepigrapha*. This part of the 'catalogue' might reflect
  the inventory of a library or collection consulted by the source relied upon
  by the author of the *Vita Aristotelis Hesychii*. See, in general, *Aristote, cinq
  oeuvres perdues: De la Richesse—De la Prière—De la Noblesse—Du Plaisir—
  De l'Éducation*, Fragments et Témoignages Édités, Traduits et Commentés
  sous la Direction et avec une Préface de P.-M. Schuhl, par J. Aubonnet,

J. Bertier, J. Brunschwig, P. Hadot, J. Pépin, P. Thillet (Publications de la Faculté des Lettres et des Sciences Humaines de Paris-Sorbonne, Séries 'Textes et Documents,' vol. 17, Paris, 1968).

5 V. Rose, *Aristotelis Qui Ferebantur Librorum Fragmenta* (Leipzig, 1886). See also V. Rose, *De Aristotelis Librorum Ordine et Auctoritate Commentatio* (Berlin, 1854); V. Rose, *Aristoteles Pseudepigraphus* (Leipzig, 1863); V. Rose, *Corpus Aristotelicum* (ed. I. Bekker), vol. V (Berlin, 1870).

6 See also A.-H. Chroust (note 3).

7 DL V. 22 (no. 14); *VH* 10 (no. 9); Simplicius, *Comment. in Aristotelis De Caelo, Commentaria in Aristotelem Graeca (CIAG)*, vol. VII (ed. J. Heiberg, Berlin, 1894), p. 485, lines 19–22 (frag. 49, Rose; frag. 1, Ross). The *On Prayer*, which is presumed to have been a dialogue, apparently consisted of one book.

8 Simplicius, *loc. cit.* See also *Vita Aristotelis Latina* 52: '*Fecit autem Aristoteles librum de oratione, unde Simplicius: Quod enim intelligat aliquid et super intellectum et super substantiam, Aristoteles manifestus est apud finem libri de oratione plane dicens quod deus aut intellectus est aut aliquid ultra intellectum.*' This Latin passage, which cannot be found in the other extant *Vitae Aristotelis*, might possibly go back to William of Moerbeke's translation of Simplicius' *Commentary* to Aristotle's *De Caelo* (of A.D. 1271). See D. J. Allan, 'Mediaeval versions of Aristotle, *De Caelo*, and the commentary of Simplicius,' *Mediaeval and Renaissance Studies*, vol. II (1950), pp. 83–4: '*Quod enim intelligat aliquid et supra intellectum et supra substantiam Aristoteles manifestus est in calce libri De Oratore* [should read: *De Oratione*] *plane dicens quod Deus est intellectus aut et aliquid ultra intellectum.*' Cicero, *De Natura Deorum* I. 13. 33 (frag. 26, Rose; frag. 26, Walzer; frag. 26, Ross; frag. 38, Untersteiner), maintains that God is 'only "mind" (*mens, νοῦς*), and "mind" only.' It is interesting to note that Simplicius: (1) 'pinpoints' the place where this passage was to be found in the original Aristotelian *On Prayer*, namely, 'at the end of this work'; (2) that he expressly credits it to Aristotle; (3) that he mentions the title of this composition; and (4) that, by implication, he indicates that this work consisted of one book. All this speaks strongly in favor of the authenticity of this fragment.

9 See A.-H. Chroust, 'The concept of God in Aristotle's lost dialogue *On Philosophy* (Cicero, *De Natura Deorum* I. 13. 33),' *Emerita*, vol. 33, fasc. 1–2 (1965), pp. 205–28, especially, pp. 209 ff.; and Chapter XIV.

10 See, for instance, H. Cherniss, *Aristotle's Criticism of Plato and the Academy*, vol. I (Baltimore, 1944), Appendix X, p. 592, and Appendix XI, p. 609; É. des Places, 'La prière des philosophes grecs,' *Gregorianum*, vol. 41 (1960), p. 256; E. Berti, *La Filosofia del Primo Aristotele* (Padua, 1962), p. 286; E. Frank, 'The fundamental opposition of Plato and Aristotle,' *American Journal of Philology*, vol. 61 (1940), pp. 178 ff.

11 Similar notions are expressed by Proclus, *In Platonis Theologiam* I. 3 (p. 3, ed. E. D. Saffrey and L. G. Westerink, Paris, 1968). See also Plato, *Phaedrus* 246D. In Greek literature we may at times observe a pronounced incerti-

tude about the true nature of the Divine (see, for instance, Homer, *Odyssey* V. 445; Aeschylus, *Agamemnon* 160; Euripides, *Heracles* 1263), about the correct name of the Divine (see, for instance, Euripides, *Bacchae* 275–6; Plato, *Cratylus* 400E; Plato, *Philebus* 12C; 30D; Plato, *Phaedrus* 246D), about whether the Divine is 'this or that' (see, for instance, Euripides, *Heracles* 353–4), or about the Divine in general (see, for instance, Euripides, *Trojan Women* 884–7). See H. Kleinknecht, *Die Gebetsparodie in der Antike* (Tübinger Beiträge zur Altertumswissenschft, vol. 28, Stuttgart-Berlin, 1937), *passim*; J. Pépin, 'Aristote, "De la Prière,"' *Revue Philosophique de la France et de l'Étranger*, vol. 157 (1967), pp. 68–70; J. Pépin, in P.-M. Schuhl (ed.) (see note 4), pp. 45–77; W. Jaeger, *Paideia*, vol. II (New York, 1943), p. 285; p. 414, note 37.

12  See, for instance, Plato, *Republic* 509B; 517BC; Plato, *Phaedrus* 247CD; Plato, *Meno* 99CD.

13  See E. Frank (see note 11), pp. 178–80.

14  See, for instance, Plato, *Republic* 532C; 518C; 526E, where we are told that the divine or the Good is the best of all that exists.

15  See J. Pépin in P.-M. Schuhl (ed.) (see note 4), pp. 76–7.

16  In *De Partibus Animalium* 606 a 29, *Metaphysics* 1072 b 27; 1074 b 21–22 and in *Nicomachean Ethics* 1096 a 24–5, for instance, Aristotle closely associates God with νοῦς.

17  In Aristotle, *Eudemian Ethics* 1248 a 23 ff., it will be noted, God is one of the central issues: moral action is man's striving towards, and communion with, God. For 'there is a principle beyond which there is no further principle. As in the universe God moves everything, so it is with the human soul. In a certain sense it is the divine in us [*scil.*, the divine "pure intellect" dwelling in us] which moves everything. For the "principle of reason" is not reason (or "mind") itself, but something beyond reason (or, something higher than reason). And what could be higher than reason or rational knowledge unless it be God?' In the *Protrepticus* (Iamblichus, *Protrepticus*, p. 48, lines 13–21, ed. H. Pistelli; frag. 61, Rose; frag. 10c, Walzer; frag. 10c Ross; frags 109–10, Düring; frags 105–06, Chroust), Aristotle maintains that because of his affinity with the divine, man is 'a god when compared with all other creatures'; that 'reason is the divine dwelling in us'; and that 'because of reason mortal life possesses a certain element or aspect of the divine.' It will also be observed that Aristotle, *Eudemian Ethics* 1248 a 23 ff., cited above, contains what might be called a proof for the existence of God *e gradibus*. See Chapter XIII, note 9.

18  That only 'like can communicate with like' has already been stated by Empedocles (frag. 31 B, Diels-Kranz). See also Albinus, *Didascalicus* XIV. 2; Numenius, frag. 11 (Leemans); Iamblichus, *De Communi Mathematica Scientia Liber* 8 (p. 38, lines 6–8, ed. N. Festa); Proclus (see note 11); C. W. Müller, *Gleiches zu Gleichem* (Klassisch-Philologische Studien vol. XXXI, Wiesbaden, 1965), pp. 3–7; H. Levy, *Chaldean Oracles and Theurgy* (Cairo, 1965), p. 371, note 226.

19 See W. Jaeger, *Aristotle: Fundamentals of the History of His Development* (Oxford, 1948), p. 160; F. Nuyens, *L'Évolution de la Psychologie d'Aristote* (Louvain, 1948), p. 133; J. Pépin, 'Aristote, "De la Prière,"' *Revue Philosophique de la France et de l'Étranger*, vol. 157 (1967), pp. 59–70; J. Bernays, *Die Dialoge des Aristoteles in ihrem Verhältnis zu seinen übrigen Werken* (Berlin 1863), p. 122. Pépin musters persuasive evidence in support of the assertion that, everything considered, this fragment is Aristotelian rather than Neo-Platonic, as some scholars have maintained. The ancient discussions of the nature of prayer (and piety) in general as well as the ancient treatises *On Prayer* (see H. Schmidt, *Veteres Philosophi Quomodo Iudicaverint de Precibus, Religionsgeschichtliche Versuche und Vorarbeiten*, vol. IV, part 1, Giessen, 1907, pp. 15 ff.) raised the issue of the external efficacy of prayer *versus* the internal efficacy of prayer. They also asked the question which form of prayer was the most appropriate. Such discussions, it appears, would also have to touch upon the question of the particular manner in which God or the gods could, and should, be 'contacted' or prayed to—whether they may be reached 'in spirit,' that is, through the intellect or mind, or whether they may be reached through some other means. At the same time, and in keeping with these discussions, they also raised the issue of whether God or the gods were 'pure mind' accessible to the human mind (or human intellect), or whether God or the gods were beyond (above ?) mind (or beyond the human mind) and intellect and, hence, inaccessible to mind or intellect (or reason). See also E. Norden, *Agnostos Theos, Untersuchungen zur Formengeschichte religiöser Reden* (Leipzig-Berlin, 1913), pp. 143–7.

20 John 4:24.

21 See also A.-H. Chroust, 'Aristotle's religious convictions,' *Divus Thomas*, vol. 69, fasc. 1 (1966), pp. 91–7, and Vol. I, Chapter XVI.

22 To date the *On Prayer* is almost an impossibility, but it might be reasonable to place it in fairly close proximity to the *On Philosophy*, that is, close to the period between 350–49 and 348 B.C. For there seem to exist certain similarities between this work and Book III of the *On Philosophy*. It goes without saying that this suggestion is pure conjecture.

23 DL V. 22 (no. 19); *VH* 10 (no. 18 and no. 172); Ptolemy (-el-Garib), no. 5. All these 'catalogues' concur that this composition consisted of one book. *VH* 10 entitles it Περὶ παιδείας ἢ παιδευτικόν. See also J. Bernays, *Die Dialoge des Aristoteles in ihrem Verhältnis zu seinen übrigen Werken* (Berlin, 1863), p. 133.

24 Some scholars are of the opinion that the following additional passages are fragments of the *On Education*: Stobaeus (*Oxyrrh. Papyr.* IV. 666, Grenfell-Hunt), commonly assigned to the Aristotelian *Protrepticus*; Stobaeus, *Florilegium* II. 31. 50; II. 31. 35; II. 31. 47; II. 31. 46; DL V. 19; DL V. 21; DL V. 19; DL V. 20.

25 Plutarch, *Quaestiones Conviviales* VIII. 10.1 (*Moralia* 734D—frag. 62, Rose; frag. 1, Ross). E. L. Minar, *Plutarch's Moralia* (Loeb edition), vol. IX

(Cambridge, 1961), p. 205, translates the final sentence of this fragments as '[g]reat learning provides many starting points (ἀρχάς).' See also Eccles. I:18: 'For in too much wisdom is much grief; and he that increaseth knowledge, increaseth sorrow.'

26 Athenaeus, *Deipnosophistae* VIII. 354C.

27 DL IX. 53 (frag. 63, Rose; frag. 2, Ross). See also Gellius, *Attic Nights* V. 3.

28 Plato, *Theaetetus* 151C; 155D; 168A; Plato, *Republic* 485A; 486A.

29 This problem has also been discussed by Heraclitus of Ephesus (see DL IX. 1), and by Athenaeus, *op. cit.*, XIII. 610B. See also Plato, *Laws* 819A; Plato ( ?), *Erastes* 139A; Plato ( ?), *II Alcibiades* 147A.

30 Some scholars insist that the fragment from Plutarch, *Quaestiones Conviviales* VIII. 10. 1, should be translated as 'much learning provides many starting points (ἀρχάς),' rather than 'much learning (polymathy) causes many vexations and much confusion (ταραχάς).' If Aristotle indeed used the expression ἀρχάς, then polymathy is not a hindrance to philosophic reasoning, as the term ταραχὰς indicates, but rather the desirable product of proper philosophic reasoning as well as a proof of the ultimate effectiveness of philosophic reasoning. And the greater a man's factual knowledge, the more avenues are open to him to reach truth and true reality. See note 25.

31 See for instance R. Weil, *Aristote et l'Histoire: Éssai sur la Politique* (Paris, 1960), p. 148; J. Aubonnet, *Aristote: Politique, Livres I et II* (Paris, 1960), pp. xxiv–xxv; E. Berti, *La Filosofia del Primo Aristotele* (Padua, 1962), p. 452.

32 DL V. 22 (no. 16); *VH* 10 (no. 15); Ptolemy (-el-Garib), no. 17. These three 'catalogues' agree that the *On Pleasure* consisted of one book.

33 Athenaeus, *Epitome* I. 6D (frag. 83, Rose; frag. 1, Ross). V. Rose, *Aristotelis Qui Ferebantur Librorum Fragmenta* (Leipzig, 1886), p. 87 (frag. 83), however, believes that this fragment should be credited to Aristotle's lost work *On Justice*. This view is shared by P. Moraux, *A la Recherche de l'Aristote Perdu: Le Dialogue 'Sur la Justice'*, Publications Universitaires de Louvain (Louvain, 1957), p. 62. W. D. Ross, *The Works of Aristotle*, vol. XII: *Select Fragments* (Oxford, 1952), p. 63, on the other hand, denies that this fragment or passage has any connections with the Aristotelian *On Justice*. See here also Cicero, *Tusculanae Disputationes* V. 35. 101:

> How, then, can a life be pleasant—a life from which prudence and moderation have been removed? We see from this the error of Sardanapallus, the wealthy king of Syria, who ordered these words to be engraved on his tomb: 'What I ate and what sated lust drained to the dregs, that I have. Thus many a famous deed lies left behind.' 'What else,' Aristotle remarks, 'would you have inscribed on the tomb, not of a king, but of an ox? He says that he had in death the things which even in life he had no longer than for the moment of enjoyment.'

It is possible that this passage from Cicero, which is considered a fragment of the Aristotelian *Protrepticus* by some scholars (frag. 16, Walzer; frag. 16, Ross) or of the Aristotelian *On Justice* (frag. 90, Rose), actually constitutes a fragment of the *On Pleasure*. See also Athenaeus, *Deipnosophistae* IX. 395F; Strabo, XIV. 5. 9; Cicero, *De Finibus* II. 32. 106; Aristotle, *Eudemian Ethics* 1216 a 16 ff.

34 See, for instance, Thucydides III. 38. 5; Demosthenes, *Oratio* IV. 10.

35 Aristotle, *Eudemian Ethics* 1231 a 5–17.

36 See also Aristotle, *Nicomachean Ethics* 1118 a 32 ff., which might contain an allusion to Philoxenus.

37 P. Hadot, in P.-M. Schuhl (ed.) (see note 4), pp. 138–9, for instance, would credit this fragment to the Aristotelian *Symposium* or, like V. Rose (see note 33), perhaps to the Aristotelian *On Justice*. P. Moraux, *A la Recherche de l'Aristote Perdu: Le Dialogue 'Sur la Justice'* (Publications Universitaires de Louvain: Aristote, Traductions et Études, Louvain-Paris. 1957), p. 62, is also of the opinion that it should be assigned to the *On Justice*. It will be noted that of the seventeen 'fragments' of Aristotle's lost works found in Athenaeus' *Deipnosophistae*, twelve specifically relate to the Aristotelian *Symposium*, while two additional 'fragments' (335F and 564D) might very well be credited to the *Symposium* of Aristotle.

38 W. Jaeger (see note 19), p. 17.

39 An echo of this debate can still be detected in Aristotle, *Nicomachean Ethics* 1172 a 27 ff.

40 How profoundly Aristotle must have been impressed by the arguments advanced by Eudoxus of Cnidus on behalf of hedonism may be gathered from *Nicomachean Ethics* 1172 b 15 ff., where the Stagirite still speaks with great warmth and admiration about these arguments: 'His [*scil.* Eudoxus'] arguments carried much weight more because of the excellence of his [*scil.*, Eudoxus'] personal character than for their own sake.' See also *ibid.*, 1172 b 9.

41 The arguments advanced by Speusippus are referred to in Aristotle, *Nicomachean Ethics* 1172 a 28. See also *ibid.*, 1153 b 5.

42 See A. Diès, *Notice sur Platon, Oeuvres Complètes*, vol. IX, part 2: *Philebe* (Paris, 1949), pp. liii–lvii.

43 See DL IV. 4 (no. 3), in one book.

44 See *ibid.*, IV. 12 (no. 36), in two books.

45 If Jaeger's thesis should prove to be correct—and there exists no compelling reason why we should doubt it—then the Aristotelian *On Pleasure* was composed at approximately the same time, or slightly later, as the Platonic *Philebus*, that is, a short time after 358–55 B.C. In any event, if Eudoxus of Cnidus personally participated in this debate—and Aristotle, *Nicomachean Ethics* 1172 b 15 ff., seems to imply this—then it must have taken place before the latter part of the year 347 B.C., the time Eudoxus died. See K. von Fritz, 'Die Lebenszeit des Eudoxos von Knidos,' *Philologus*, vol. 85 (1929–30), pp. 478–81.

46 DL V. 22 (no. 11); *VH* 10 (nos 7 and 151). Both 'catalogues' agree that the *On Wealth* consisted of one book. See, in general, P. Thillet in P.-M. Schuhl (ed.) (see note 4), pp. 5–44.

47 Plutarch, *Pelopidas* 3 (frag. 56, Rose; frag. 1, Ross). V. Rose (see note 33), pp. 66–7, ascribes this as well as the following fragment to Aristotle's *Protrepticus*.

48 Frag. 56, Rose; frag. 1, Ross.

49 Frag. 89, Rose; frag. 2, Ross. Themistius, *Oratio* II. 26D ff., which is commonly credited to Aristotle's *On Justice* (frag. 88, Rose; frag. 6, Ross—see also Chapter VI), may possibly be a fragment of the Aristotelian *On Wealth*:

> Do I not remember the grounds on which Aristotle distinguishes vanity from true pride? In distinguishing them he says somewhere that with regard to great honors, as with regard to all other things that are called good, there is an immoderate care for them, but also a moderate and reasonable care. He adds that the man who is puffed up and raises his eyebrows at the noisy applause given him by the mob because he has spent much on theaters and horse-races for their entertainment, is a vain fellow afflicted with the vice to which Aristotle gives the name of vanity; while the man who despises the applause of the many and thinks it little better that the noise of the waves beating against the shore, but values more than anything else the approval without flattery which good men bestow on virtue, is truly noble and high-minded.

50 Philodemus, *Hercul. Papyr.* III. p. 3, col. 28 (frag. 3, Ross). See C. Jensen (ed.), *Philodemi Περὶ οἰκονομίας Qui Dicitur Libellus* (Leipzig, 1906), col. XXI, 28–35, pp. 59–60. Philodemus' statement might also contain a faint echo of Plato, *Republic* 379B: 'That which is good . . . is the cause of the good.' See also Plato (?), *Hipparchus* 230A and 232A, where a distinction is made between 'honest gains' and 'dishonest (or evil) gains.' Good men, we are told, refuse to consider every form of gain irrespective of whether it is honest or dishonest, accepting only an honest gain and refusing a dishonest gain. All this, in turn, might suggest that, when composing the *On Wealth*, Aristotle was still under the influence of Plato's notions concerning wealth. It is also possible, though rather unlikely, that Ioannes Lydus, *De Mensibus* IV. 7 and IV, 100, contains a fragment of Aristotle's *On Wealth. Ibid.*, IV. 7, we are told that 'Aristotle . . . stated: "If there is such a thing as virtue, there is no good fortune (or change). From bottom to top and from top to bottom, in fact, the incidents of good fortune make themselves felt in the affairs of man, in matters of wealth or earthly goods, in political power and, particularly, in the incidents of injustice . . . ."' *Ibid.*, IV. 100, we are told that 'Aristotle [says that] wherever there is virtue, there is no good fortune or change. Because . . . the incidents of

good fortune (or chance) make themselves felt in human affairs, in matter of wealth and earthly goods and, especially, in the incidents of injustice. Those who have a high regard for virtue, remember God and base their hopes on the truly blessed and immaterial realities, in no ways succeed in attaining the goods of this world . . . .' It is quite possible that Ioannes Lydus actually refers here to Theophrastus, Χαρακτῆρες.

51 See also Aristotle, *Nicomachean Ethics* 1122 a 16 ff. In the *On Wealth* and in the *Nicomachean Ethics* (1121 b 7 ff.; 1122 b 23 ff.; 1122 b 35 ff.; see also Aristotle, *Politics* 1321 a 37 ff.) Aristotle denounces vulgar and selfish display of wealth, but praises its social or humanitarian uses. In *Politics* 1257 a 21, he points out that circumstance and necessity may justify 'extravagant expenditures.' It will be noted that the term μικρολογία used by Plutarch, *Pelopidas* 3, can also be found in Aristotle, *Metaphysics* 995 a 10, but here it signifies 'pettifoggery' rather than 'pettiness.'

52 See, for instance, Plato, *Protagoras* 326C; Plato, *Laws* 661B; Plato (?), *Second Epistle* 310E. See, however, Plato, *Menexenus* 240D; Plato (?), *I Alciabiades* 134B.

53 See, for instance, Aristotle, *Nicomachean Ethics* 1172 b 7. It will be noted that in the two fragments preserved by Plutarch Aristotle actually suggests that wealth, on the whole, is something of a 'liability' or, to be more exact, as a rule, is used in a morally reprehensible manner.

54 See P.-M. Schuhl, 'Gains honorables et gains sordides,' *Revue Philosophique de la France et de l'Étranger*, vol. 82 (1957), pp. 355–7.

55 See here also Plato, *Republic* 379B, where we are told that God (the Good) is the cause of good things, but never the cause of evil things. Perhaps Aristotle paraphrases this Platonic statement. Similar notions were expressed by Aristophanes, *Thesmophoriae* 168–70; Pseudo-Plato, *Hipparchus* 230A ff. In Aristotle, *Nicomachean Ethics* 1175 b 27–28, we are informed that 'the pleasure derived from noble deeds is good, while the pleasure derived from ignoble deeds is evil.'

56 It is impossible to date the *On Wealth*. According to DL IV. 4 (no. 2), Speusippus likewise composed an *On Wealth* in one book. Perhaps Aristotle's work and that of Speusippus are contemporary, perhaps they were the literary results of a major discussion about the problem of wealth carried on within the Academy during the scholarchate of Plato.

57 DL V. 22 (no. 15); *HV* 10 (nos 11 and 183); Ptolemy (-el-Garib), no. 6. Diogenes Laertius and the *Vita Aristotelis Hesychii* concur that the *On Noble Birth* consists of one book. Ptolemy maintains, though probably erroneously, that it contains five books.

58 Stobaeus, *Florilegium* IV. 29 A 24; IV. 29 A 25; IV. 29 C 52; DL II. 26; Plutarch, *Aristides* 27; Athenaeus, *Deipnosophistae* XIII. 555D–556A (frags 91–4, Rose; frags 1–4, Ross). Some scholars are of the opinion that Philo of Alexandria, *On Noble Birth* (sections 187–227 of Philo's *De Virtutibus*, vol. V, pp. 224 ff., ed. Cohn-Wendland); Dio Chrysostom (of Prusa), *Oratio* XIV and *Oratio* XV. 28–32; Julian, *Oratio* II and *Oratio* III; and

Boethius, *De Consolatione Philosophiae*, contain fragments of the Aristotelian *On Noble Birth*. See P.-M. Schuhl (note 4), pp. 107–15 (J. Aubonnet). Philo's *On Noble Birth* manifests many suggestive parallels with certain passages from Aristotle's *Politics* (Books I and III), *Nicomachean Ethics*, *On Philosophy*, *On Justice* and the Aristotelian *On Noble Birth*. Dio's *Oratio* XV. 28–32, again, seems to be influenced by Aristotle's *Politics* 1255 a 32 ff. (O. Gigon, 'Die Sklaverei bei Aristoteles,' *La Politique d'Aristote*, Geneva, 1965, pp. 245 ff., considers this part of the *Politics* a 'reference' or 'fragment' of the Aristotelian *On Noble Birth*); Aristotle, *Rhetoric* 1360 b 31 ff. and 1390 b 16 ff. Julian's *Oratio* II. 198 c 3, seems to be dependent on Stobaeus, *Florilegium* IV. 29 C 52, while Julian, *Oratio* III. 25. 81 a–82 a and 26. 83, apparently is under the influence of Stobaeus, *Florilegium* IV. 29 A 24; IV 29 A 25; and IV. 29 C 52. Book III. 8 of Boethius' *Consolatio*, a passage which Rose (frag. 49), Walzer (frag. 10a) and Ross (frag. 10a) have credited to the Aristotelian *Protrepticus*, seems to restate some of Aristotle's notions about nobility. These notions might well go back to Aristotle's *On Noble Birth*.

59 Stobaeus, *op. cit.*, IV. 29 A 24–5. This passage from Stobaeus, which contains what seems to be a 'literal extract' or literal citation from Aristotle's work, is preserved in the original (Aristotelian) dialogue form. Its form and style remind us of Plato's dialogues.

60 Stobaeus, *op. cit.*, IV. 29 A 24. This is one of the few surviving references (or 'fragments') to the sophist Lycophron, probably a disciple of Gorgias of Leontini. Lycophron is mentioned by Aristotle in *De Sophisticis Elenchis* 174 b 32; *Physics* 185 b 25 ff.; *Metaphysics* 1045 b 8 ff.; *Politics* 1280 b 8 ff.; and *Rhetoric* 1405 a 34 ff. Lycophron was a representative of Greek 'enlightenment.' See, for instance, Aristotle, *Politics* 1275 b 26 ff.; Antiphon, frag. 44 B 2 (Diels-Kranz).

61 See M. Détienne, 'Simonide de Céos ou la sécularisation de la poésie,' *Review des Études Grecques*, vol. 78 (1964), pp. 405–19. Similar notions can be found in Euripides, *Aeolus*, frag. 22 (ed. A. Nauck); Julian, *Oratio* II. 81 a. See also Aristotle, *Politics* 1294 a 20.

62 Theognis' many caustic remarks about the decline of aristocracy or of aristocratic values, and about the rise of a new and socially powerful class of people who only honor money are too well known to require special comment.

63 This sentence refers to what Euripides had said. Euripides, it will be observed, frequently refers to the problem of noble birth.

64 In *Gorgias* 512C, Plato touches upon 'noble birth,' pointing out that virtue is a man's character rather than a 'hereditary quality.' See also *I Alcibiades* 120E. In *Theaetetus* 174E, Plato maintains that some people despise nobility of descent; and in *Menexenus* 247A ff., he insists that the honor and virtue of the ancestors are a noble legacy to their descendants. Finally, in *Laws* 690A and 714E, Plato proclaims that the 'noble' should rule over the ignoble. In his doctrinal works, Aristotle mentions noble birth in *Nico-*

*machean Ethics* 1136 b 22, etc.; *Eudemian Ethics* 1248 b 8 ff. and 1250 b 40, etc.; *Magna Moralia* 1207 b 19 ff.; *Rhetoric* 1360 b 31 ff. and 1390 b 16 ff.; 1394 a 17; *Politics* 1283 a 33 ff.; 1293 b 39; 1301 b 6, etc. It might be remembered that Plato was himself the descendant of most noble ancestors, and that Aristotle traced his ancestors back to the Homeric Asclepius. See Vol. I, Chapter V.

65 See here in particular Plato, *Theaetetus* 174E, where Plato ridicules the empty vanity of some nobles.

66 See E. Berti (note 31), pp. 451-52.

67 Stobaeus, *op. cit.*, IV. 29 A 25. The notion that 'good birth is excellence of stock' can also be found in Aristotle, *Rhetoric* 1390 b 22.

68 Stobaeus, *op. cit.* IV. 29 C 52, in essence repeats this argument:

> It is evident . . . why those born of a long line of wealthy or noble ancestors are considered to be better born than those whose possession of these advantages is rather recent. A man's own goodness is nearer to him than that of his grandfather, and on that basis it would be the good man that is nobly born. . . . Those are correct who give preference to ancestral (ancient) virtue. . . . Noble birth is 'excellence of stock' and excellence belongs to good men. Now this happens when the stock has had a good start. For an origin has the power of producing many products like itself. When, therefore, there has been a man of this kind in the stock—a man so good that many generations inherit his goodness—that particular stock is bound to be good. . . . Thus it is natural that not rich men nor good men, but those whose ancestors have long been rich or good, should be nobly born. . . . The origin counts more than anything else. Yet not even those born of good ancestors are in every instance nobly born, but only those who have among their ancestors originators [of a line or stock of virtuous men]. . . . People are nobly born if they come from such stock—not if their father is nobly born, but if the originator of the stock (or line) is so. For it is not by his own strength that a father begets virtuous men, but because he himself came of such a stock.

69 DL II. 26; Plutarch, *Aristides* 27; Athenaeus, *Deipnosophistae* XIII. 555D-556A. Plutarch and Athenaeus relate that Myrto was the granddaughter or great-granddaughter—not the daughter—of Aristides the Just (who died *c.* 467 B.C.). Plutarch (*loc. cit.*) also insists that she 'lived with Socrates the Wise, who was married to another woman [that is, to Xanthippe] but took Myrto under his protection because she was a widow, poor and lacking the necessities of life.' DL II. 26 states:

> Aristotle says [in his *On Noble Birth*] that he [*scil.*, Socrates] married two wives: his first wife was Xanthippe, by whom he had a son, Lamprocles; his second wife was Myrto, the daughter [*scil.*, the grand-daughter or great-granddaughter] of Aristides the Just, whom he

married without a dowry. By her he had Sophroniscus and
Menexenus. Others make Myrto his first wife and others, again,
including Satyrus and Hieronymous of Rhodes, affirm that they
[scil., Xanthippe and Myrto] were both his wives at the same time.
For they maintain that the Athenians were short of men and, wishing
to increase the population, passed a decree permitting a citizen to
marry one Athenian woman and have children by another; and that
Socrates accordingly did so.

Athenaeus, loc. cit., on the other hand, maintains that 'starting from these
facts, one must blame those authors who assign to Socrates two wedded
wives, Xanthippe and Myrto, the daughter of Aristides—not Aristides the
Just, for the dates do not permit this, but the third in descent from him . . .'
Aristotle apparently furnished these authors or reporters with part of their
information in his On Noble Birth. Plutarch, loc. cit., it will be noted,
questions the authenticity of the On Noble Birth ('if the work On Noble
Birth is to be reckoned among his [scil., Aristotle's] authentic works').
See also Pseudo-Plutarch, Pro Nobilitate 18.

70 See here also Porphyry, Historia Philosophiae, frag. XII (ed. A. Nauck),
frag. 133 (ed. Van Straaten); Seneca, De Matrimonio, frag. 62 (ed. F. Haase);
Cyrillus, Contra Julianum (P.G. LXXVI, pp. 784D–785A); Theodoretus,
Graecorum Affectionum Curatio XII. 61–4; Epistolographi Graeci: Epist.
Socrat. (ed. R. Hercher) XXIX. 3 (p. 629); Suda, 'article' Socrates. For a
detailed and critical discussion of all these involved and confusing reports,
see J. Pépin in P.-M. Schuhl (ed.) (see note 4), pp. 117–28; J. W. Fitton,
'That Was No Lady, That Was . . . ,' Classical Quarterly, vol. 20 (vol. 64,
continuous series, 1970), no. 1, pp. 56–66.

71 Stobaeus, op. cit. IV. 29 C 52. See also note 68.

72 Tradition also has it that Aristotle the Just was a poor though honorable
and virtuous man. See Demosthenes, Oratio XXIII. 209; Aeschines, Oratio
III. 258; Plutarch, Aristides 25. Socrates, too, is generally depicted as a
virtuous and honorable though poor man. The thesis that a poor man may
be a virtuous man (and that the rich man may be an evil man) was one of
the main themes discussed by Antisthenes (see DL VI. 11) and the Cynics
in general, as well as by some Stoics.

73 To date the On Noble Birth is simply impossible, unless one should draw
certain inferences from the fact that this composition was written in
dialogue form (see note 59) and, hence, in all likelihood belongs to the
early or Academic period of Aristotle's literary activities, that is, to a period
when he was still under the dominant influence of Plato's philosophic
teachings.

74 DL V. 22 (no. 7); VH 10 (no. 8); Ptolemy (-el-Garib) (no. 3). All these
'catalogues' agree that the Sophist consisted of one book. See also frags
65–7, Rose; frags 1–3, Ross. Plato's Sophist, among other topics, also
discusses the characteristic activities of the sophist. See ibid., 217A; 218C.

The sophist, not unlike an angler trying to catch a fish (218E ff.), attempts to snare wealthy young men (222B ff.). Sophistry is called an artful, but erroneous effort to produce shallow as well as unfounded opinions or misleading images. As such it arrives only at purely conjectural or apparent knowledge (233C ff.). Hence, sophistry is merely the art of superficial imitation (234B; 235A) or a deceptive technique of contriving images (236C), but most certainly not a serious attempt to establish objective truth.

75 DL VIII. 57 and IX. 25; Sextus Empiricus, *Adversus Dogmaticos* I. 6. It might be interesting to note that DL IX. 25 also states that in his *Sophist* (216A) and in his *Phaedrus* (261D), Plato mentions Zeno, calling him the 'Eleatic Palamedes.'

76 DL VIII. 63 (frag. 66, Rose; frag. 2, Ross).

77 DL IX. 54 (frag. 67, Rose; frag. 3, Ross). Aristotle alludes here to the fate of Protagoras, who on account of his allegedly atheistic or 'heretical' views as well as for his having composed a 'heretical' work *On the Gods*, in 411 B.C. was indicted for ἀσέβεια. To escape execution, he fled from Athens but on the way to Sicily was lost at sea.

78 DL VIII. 67.

79 See here also Aristotle, *Rhetoric* 1407 a 33-4, where Empedocles is cited as an example of those philosophers 'who although they have nothing to say, they nevertheless pretend to say something.' Throughout his later doctrinal treatises, Aristotle seems to have had little regard for Empedocles' philosophic views and for his ability to engage in 'principled' or systematic thought and philosophy.

80 See, for instance, Plato, *Sophist* 216A, where the Stranger from Elea, one of the interlocutors in this dialogue, is introduced as a disciple of Parmenides and Zeno. In Plato, *Sophist* 253CD, the particular dialectics of the sophists are strongly denounced. It is possible that there also exist some connections between the Platonic *Phaedrus* and the Aristotelian *Sophist*.

81 The *Gryllus* of Aristotle, incidentally, his first major composition, is commonly dated about 360 B.C., or shortly thereafter. See A.-H. Chroust, 'Aristotle's first literary effort: the *Gryllus*—a lost dialogue on the nature of rhetoric,' *Revue des Études Grecques*, vol. 178, nos 371-3 (1966), pp. 576-91, and Chapter III; A.-H. Chroust, 'The probable dates of some of Aristotle's lost works,' *Rivista Critica di Storia della Filosofia*, vol. 23, fasc. 1 (1967), pp. 3-23, and Chapter I, especially notes 1-11, and the corresponding texts. It is possible that Aristotle wrote the *Sophist* soon after the completion of the *Gryllus*. If this be the case, the *Sophist*, which probably discusses in a Platonic spirit the true nature and function of dialectics, might very well have been a kind of 'sequel' to the *Gryllus*.

82 DL V. 22 (no. 17); *VH* 10 (no. 22, and nos 176 and 196). It is possible, however, that the fragments usually assigned to the Aristotelian *On Kingship* (Περὶ βασιλείας, DL V. 22, no. 18; *VH* 10. nos 16 and 171; Ptolemy-el-Garib, no. 8), originally were part of the *To Alexander*. A further possibility is that these fragments originally came from a letter or letters

addressed by Aristotle to Alexander. In any event, DL V. 27 (no. 144), mentions *Letters to Alexander* (in four books), while *VH* 10 (no. 137) refers simply to *Letters* written by Aristotle.

83 Pseudo-Ammonius, *Comment. in Aristotelis Categorias* (Venice, 1546), fol. 5 b (frag. 646, Rose; frag. 1, Ross); Plutarch, *De Alexandri Fortuna aut Virtute* I. 6 (*Moralia* 329B—frag. 658, Rose; frag. 2, Ross); Strabo, I. 4. 9 (frag. 658, Rose; frag. 2, Ross).

84 If the fragments assigned to the *On Kingship* (see Chapter XVII) were to be credited to the *To Alexander* (see note 82), then we would have to add to the above list *VH* 10 (nos 16 and 176-7); *VV* 22 (frag. 646, Rose; frag. 1, Ross); *VM* 21 (frag. 646, Rose; frag. 1, Ross); *VL* 21; Themistius, *Oratio* VIII. 107CD (frag. 647, Rose; frag. 2, Ross).

85 Frag. 658, Rose; frag. 2, Ross. The fragment continues by pointing out that because Alexander did not play the part of a leader to the Greeks and that of a master to the barbarians, because he behaved alike to all, he did not 'fill his reign with wars, banishments and factions.'

86 Similar notions are advanced in Aristotle, *Politics* 1255 a 28 ff., where Aristotle maintains that barbarians are 'natural slaves.' See also 1252 b 7 ff.; 1254 a 20 ff.; 1285 a 20 ff., where we are informed that the barbarians are more servile than the Greeks.

87 See, for instance, Aristotle, *Politics* 1255 a 10 ff.; 'Even among the philosophers there exists a difference of opinion [on the question of whether there are any "slaves by nature"].' The Stoics most certainly condemned this view of Aristotle's.

88 Frag. 658, Rose; frag. 2, Ross. Eratosthenes, we are told here, also maintained that 'it was better to draw the division between virtue and vice,' rather than between Greeks and barbarians. As to how Alexander heeded these conflicting bits of advice, may be gathered from Strabo I. 4. 9 (frag. 648, Rose; frag. 2, Ross), who relates that 'Alexander did not ignore his advisers, but took their advice and acted accordingly, looking at the intention of those who had given him advice.' Judging from the subsequent deportment of Alexander, it must be conceded that, on the whole, he ignored the advice given by Aristotle. Whether this was due to 'political expediency' on the part of Alexander or due to the fact that in later years he distrusted Aristotle (see, for instance, the Callisthenes affair), cannot be determined.

89 See here also A.-H. Chroust, 'Aristotle's criticism of Plato's "philosopher king,"' *Rheinisches Museum*, vol. 111, no. 1 (1968), pp. 16-22, and Chapter XVII.

90 Philoponus, *Comment. in Aristotelis Categorias*, *CIAG*, vol. XIII, part 1 (ed. A. Busse, Berlin, 1896), p. 3, lines 22-4 (frag. 646, Rose; frag. 1, Ross).

91 *VM* 21 (frag. 646, Rose; frag. 2, Ross); *VV* 22; *VL* 21. This statement has also been credited to Emperor Titus. See Suetonius, *The Lives of the Caesars* VIII. 1.

92 Themistius (see note 84). This fragment, too, is usually assigned to the *On*

*Kingship* but could very well be credited to the *To Alexander*. There can be no doubt that this particular fragment also contains a criticism of Plato's 'philosopher king.' See A.-H. Chroust (see note 89).

93 DL V. 22 (no. 6); *VH* 10 (no. 6).

94 See also DL III. 46; IV. 2.

95 DL IV. 2, maintains that Zeno turned to philosophy after reading Book II of Xenophon's *Memorabilia*, while Themistius, *Oratio* XXIII. 295CD (p. 356, ed. L. Dindorf), insists that Zeno did so after reading Plato's *Apology*. It might be mentioned here that St Augustine was converted to the intellectual life after reading Cicero's *Hortensius*. See St Augustine, *Confessiones* III. 4. Cicero's *Hortensius*, through several intermediaries, was influenced by Aristotle's *Protrepticus*.

96 Themistius (see note 95) (frag. 64, Rose; frag. 1, Ross). None of the ancient 'catalogues' of Aristotle's writings mentions a *Corinthian Dialogue*. The identification of this *Corinthian Dialogue* with the *Nerinthus* is widely accepted, however. The confusion of Themistius might have been caused by Aristotle's reference to the 'Corinthian farmer.'

97 See A.-H. Chroust, 'Aristotle enters the Academy,' *Classical Folia*, vol. 19, no. 1 (1965), pp. 21–9, especially, p. 26; Vol. I, Chapter VII.

98 The argument in support of the thesis that Aristotle might first have attended the school of Isocrates runs as follows: *VM* 5, *VV* 4 and *VL* 5 relate that 'at the age of seventeen Aristotle kept company with [was a student of] Socrates in Athens, and stayed with him a short time.' *VL* 5 actually maintains that he stayed three years with Socrates. 'After that,' *VM* 5, *VV* 4 and *VL* 5 continue,' he did seek out Plato.' The epitomizer (or his source) either commits here a fatal anachronism—Socrates died in 399 B.C., while Aristotle was born in 384 B.C.—or he badly misspells the name of Isocrates, corrupting it to Socrates. It may be alleged that since the Platonic *Gorgias* also attacks Isocrates, the pupil of Gorgias, it is not impossible that this work 'opened' Aristotle's eyes to the shortcomings of Isocrates' philosophy and induced him to transfer to the Platonic Academy which, according to the *Gorgias*, propagated the only true philosophy as well as the only acceptable form of rhetoric.

99 See, for instance, W. Jaeger, *Aristotle: Fundamentals of the History of his Development* (Oxford, 1948), p. 23.

100 If this assumption should prove to be correct, then the *Nerinthus* and the *On Education* (see pp. 18–20) must have had certain topics in common.

CHAPTER III   ARISTOTLE'S FIRST LITERARY EFFORT: THE *Gryllus* —A WORK ON THE NATURE OF RHETORIC

* In a different and less detailed form, this chapter was first published in *Revue des Études Grecques*, vol. 78, nos 371–3 (1965–6), pp. 576–91.

1 DL V. 22 (no. 5) lists a Περὶ ῥητορικῆς ἢ Γρῦλος (also spelled Γρύλλος or

Γρύλλος) in one book. See P. Moraux, *Les Listes Anciennes des Ouvrages d'Aristote* (Louvain, 1951), *passim*.

2 *VH* 10 (no. 5) lists a Περὶ πολιτικῆς ἢ Γρῦλος in three books. See P. Moraux, *op. cit.*, pp. 195 ff.

3 The 'catalogue' of Ptolemy (-el-Garib), no. 3, lists a Περὶ ῥητορικῆς ἢ Γρῦλος in three books. See P. Moraux, *loc. cit.*

4 See J. Bernays, *Die Dialoge des Aristoteles* (Berlin, 1863), p. 62; V. Rose, *Aristoteles Pseudepigraphus* (Leipzig, 1863), pp. 76 ff.; E. Heitz, *Die verlorenen Schriften des Aristoteles* (Leipzig, 1865), pp. 189 ff. In keeping with his general though wholly erroneous thesis that all of the so-called 'exoteric' works credited to Aristotle are spurious, Rose denies that the Stagirite ever authored a *Gryllus*. He ascribes the *Gryllus* to Theophrastus. Rose's theses were refuted by E. Heitz.

5 Quintilian, *Institutio Oratoria* II. 17. 14 (frag. 69, Rose; frag. 2, Ross).

6 DL II. 55 (frag. 68, Rose; frag. 1, Ross).

7 It seems probable that in his earliest works Aristotle followed the Platonic model and, hence, used one-word titles, often naming these dialogues after some personage. See Diogenes Laertius V. 22 (*Nerinthus, Menexenus, Eudemus* and *Alexander*; or *Sophistes, Eroticus, Symposium* and *Protrepticus*). It might be conjectured that the 'sub-title,' *On Rhetoric*, is a later addition.

8 DL II. 54-5. See also Pausanias I. 3. 4.

9 While most scholars (see p. 30) are of the opinion that the *Gryllus* was composed shortly after the death of Gryllus in 362 B.C., F. Solmsen, *Die Entwicklung der aristotelischen Logik und Rhetorik* (Berlin, 1929), p. 200, insists that it must have been written several years after 362, because it apparently refers to many eulogies on Gryllus. See also P. Moraux, *op. cit.*, pp. 33, 323 ff.; P. Thillet, 'Note sur le *Gryllos*, ouvrage de jeunesse d'Aristote,' *Revue Philosophique de la France et de l'Étranger*, vol. 147 (1957), pp. 352 ff; O. Gigon, 'Interpretationen zu den antiken Aristoteles-Viten,' *Museum Helveticum*, vol. 15 (1958), pp. 169 ff., and note 42.

10 See A.-H. Chroust, 'The probable dates of some of Aristotle's lost works,' *Rivista Critica di Storia della Filosofia*, vol. 22, fasc. 1 (1967), pp. 3-23, especially pp. 3 ff., and Chapter I.

11 Aristotle was born in 384 B.C., and according to tradition, entered the Academy in 367 B.C.

12 See P. Thillet (note 9), pp. 353 ff.

13 The fact that Aristotle's earliest compositions were dialogues is attested to by Ammonius, *Commentarius in Aristotelis Categorias, CIAG*, vol. IV, part 4 (ed. A. Busse, Berlin, 1887), p. 6, lines 25 ff.; Simplicius, *Commentaria in Aristotelis de Caelo, CIAG*, vol. VII (ed. J. Heiberg, Berlin, 1894), p. 288, lines 31 ff.; Simplicius, *Commentaria in Aristotelis Physicorum Libros Quattuor Priores, CIAG*, vol. IX (ed. H. Diels, Berlin, 1882), p. 8, lines 16 ff.; Olympiodorus, *Prolegomena et in Aristotelis Categorias Commentarium, CIAG*, vol. XII, part 1 (ed. A. Busse, Berlin, 1902), p. 7, lines 5 ff.; Philoponus (*olim* Ammonius), *Commentarium in Aristotelis Categorias,*

*CIAG*, vol. XIII, part 1 (ed. A. Busse, Berlin, 1898), p. 3, lines 16 ff.; Elias (*olim* David), *Commentarii in Porphyrii Isagogen et in Aristotelis Categorias*, *CIAG*, vol. XVIII, part 1 (ed. A. Busse, Berlin, 1900), p. 114, lines 15 ff. and lines 22 ff.; p. 115, lines 3 ff.; p. 124, lines 3 ff. See also Plutarch, *Adversus Coloten* 14 (*Moralia* 1115BC); Dio Chrysostom, *Oratio* LIII. 1; St Basil, *Epistola* 135.

14 Plutarch, *Adversus Coloten* 14 (*Moralia* 1115BC) and 20 (1118C), calls the early writings of Aristotle 'Aristotle's Platonic works,' implying that in their literary form as well as in their philosophic content these writings were very similar to Plato's dialogues. See also Cicero, *Ad Atticum* IV. 16. 2 and XIII. 19. 4; Cicero, *De Oratore* III. 21. 80; Cicero, *Ad Familiares* I. 9. 23; Ammonius (see note 13), p. 6, lines 25 ff.; Elias (see note 13), p. 114, lines 15 ff.; p. 115, lines 3 ff.; p. 124, lines 3 ff.; Simplicius, *Commentarius in Aristotelis Categorias*, *CIAG*, vol. VIII (ed. C. Kalbfleisch, Berlin, 1907), p. 4, lines 20 ff. See Eusebius, *Praeparatio Evangelica* XIV. 6. 9: 'Cephisodorus . . . thought that Aristotle was a follower of Plato. Hence he denounced Aristotle, but he was really attacking Plato.'

15 See note 7. Cicero, who read some of Aristotle's earliest dialogues, attests that they were composed in a clear and incisive style; that they were remarkable for their literary form; and that they were replete with logical acumen. See Cicero, *De Oratore* I. 11. 49; Cicero, *Academica Priora* II. 38. 119; Cicero, *De Inventione* II. 2. 6; Cicero, *De Finibus Bonorum et Malorum* I. 5. 14; Cicero, *Topica* I. 3; Cicero, *Brutus* XXXI. 120–1; Cicero, *Lucullus* XXXVIII. 119; Cicero, *Ad Atticum* II. 1. 1. The Ciceronian testimony substantiates the remark of Quintilian, *Institutio Oratoria* II. 17. 14 (see note 5) and X. 1. 83. See also Themistius, *Oratio* XXIII. 319C.

16 See W. Jaeger, *Aristoteles: Grundlegung einer Geschichte seiner Entwicklung* (Berlin, 1923), pp. 29 ff. (*Aristotle: Fundamentals of the History of his Development*, Oxford, 1948, pp. 28 ff.). All subsequent references to Jaeger are from the translation of 1948. It will be noted that in his later dialogues, Plato changes from a 'dramatic' literary style to a more 'expository' treatment of his subject. W. Jaeger, *loc. cit.*, also credits Aristotle with having originated a type of dialogue which is tantamount to a 'scientific discussion.'

17 E. Heitz (see note 4), p. 167.

18 See A.-H. Chroust, '*Eudemus or On the Soul*: a lost Aristotelian dialogue on the immortality of the soul,' *Mnemosyne*, vol. 19 (series 4), fasc. 1 (1966), pp. 17–30, and Chapter IV.

19 See A.-H. Chroust (note 18), pp. 19 ff.; A.-H. Chroust (see note 10), pp. 3 ff. See also Chapter IV.

20 E. Heitz, *loc. cit.*

21 P. Thillet (see note 9), pp. 353 ff. Thillet argues that the *Gryllus* is a work on rhetoric, which might be referred to as *Gryllus*, but which should really be called *On Rhetoric*. He correctly assigns great importance to the fact that

the proper and full title of this dialogue is apparently *On Rhetoric or Gryllus* (and not merely *Gryllus*). To Thillet this particular order or sequence within the title is highly significant.

22 See note 5.

23 F. Solmsen (see note 9), pp. 196 ff.; P. Thillet, *op. cit.*, p. 353. See also E. Berti, *La Filosofia del Primo Aristotele* (Università di Padova, Pubblicazioni della Facoltà di Lettere e Filosofia, vol. 38, Padua, 1962), pp. 162 ff.

24 Quintilian, *op. cit.*, II. 17. 1. See frag. 69, Rose; frag. 2, Ross.

25 *Ibid.*, II. 17. 4.

26 *Ibid.*, II. 17. 5.

27 *Ibid.*, II. 17. 7.

28 *Ibid.*, II. 17. 11.

29 See, for instance, *ibid.*, II. 17. 14.

30 See note 5. Quintilian remarks that Aristotle displays 'his usual mental subtleness and acumen,' when he devised 'some tentative arguments of his own.' Quintilian, *op. cit.*, II. 17. 14.

31 Quintilian, *op. cit.*, II. 17. 14.

32 See note 6.

33 See Plato, *Gorgias* 462C; 463B; 502E; 513D. See also F. Solmsen, *op. cit.*, pp. 196 ff.

34 See F. Solmsen, *op. cit.*, pp. 196 ff.

35 That Xenophon was not exactly a friend of Plato is attested by DL II. 57: 'He [*scil.*, Xenophon] and Plato were jealous of each other. . . .' See also *ibid.*, III. 34: 'And it appears that Xenophon was not on good terms with him [*scil.*, with Plato]. At any rate, they have written similar accounts as if out of rivalry with each other. . . . And in the *Laws* [694C] Plato declares that the story of Cyrus' education [as reported in Xenophon's *Cyropaedia*] was a mere fiction. . . .' There can be little doubt that Aristotle, who was at the time a member of the Academy and a pupil of Plato, probably shared Plato's dislike of Xenophon.

36 It is entirely possible that Plato himself should have urged his pupil Aristotle to take these flatterers to task, especially since Isocrates, Plato's old rival, had also composed an epitaph or eulogy on Gryllus. Obsequious eulogies certainly violated the canons of rhetoric laid down by Plato in the *Gorgias* and more recently in the *Phaedrus*.

37 DL II. 55, on the authority of Hermippus, *The Life of Theophrastus*, reports that Isocrates, the most prominent and best known rhetorician of the mid-fourth century B.C., had likewise composed an encomium on Gryllus. It is quite possible that Isocrates (or perhaps Gorgias, the teacher of Isocrates) was the originator of this type of eulogy. This may be gathered from certain passages in Plato's *Gorgias*, which seem to be directed also against Isocrates. It will be noted that Plato, too, discusses the good man and father who 'had the misfortune of losing his son.' The good man, Plato insists, will bear the loss with greater equanimity than the bad man.

He . . . will be moderate in his sorrow. . . . For there is a principle
and dictate of reason in him, which commands him to resist [the
temptation to give vent to his emotions]. . . . This principle would
tell him to display patience in his sufferings and not to give way to
impatience, as there is no way of knowing whether such things are
good or evil. . . . He would take counsel about what has happened
. . . and . . . not like children . . . waste his time in setting up a howl,
but always accustom his soul forthwith to apply a remedy, raising
up that which is sickly and fallen, banishing the cry of sorrow by
the healing art [*scil.*, philosophy]. . . . This is the true way of meeting
the incidents of fate. (Plato, *Republic* 603E ff.)

38 See P. Thillet, *op. cit.*, p. 353. F. Solmsen, *op. cit.*, p. 198, note 1, suggests
that the *Gryllus* contained three distinct parts: (1) a critique of the traditional epitaphs and eulogies; (2) a critique of contemporary rhetoric in
general; and (3) a critique of Isocrates in particular. See also some of the
remarks in P. Merlan, 'Isocrates, Aristotle and Alexander the Great,'
*Historia*, vol. 3 (1954), pp. 60–81.

39 See, among others, A.-H. Chroust (note 10), especially pp. 13–17, and
Chapter I.

40 See A.-H. Chroust (note 10), pp. 17–18 and Chapter I.

41 See notes 72–5 and the corresponding text.

42 Undoubtedly, at that time Aristotle still adhered to Plato's doctrine of the
tri-partite soul. Hence, rhetoric, as exemplified in some of these eulogies,
would appeal exclusively to the appetitive—irrational—part of the
soul, which, in the Platonic system, constitutes the lowliest part of the
soul.

43 Plato, it will be remembered, entertained a purely intellectual notion of
τέχνη. To him τέχνη is that disciplined objective activity of the intellect
which gives account of the true facts and of true reality by relating these
facts to their ultimate cause or causes—the Ideas. See here É. des Places,
*Lexique de la Langue Philosophique . . . de Platon* (Paris, 1964), *s.v.*, and
p. xiii.

44 This is not the place to discuss in detail the extent to which the *Gryllus* was
influenced by Plato's *Phaedrus*. The *Phaedrus*, it will be noted, sheds new
light on Plato's later views about the nature of rhetoric (and also on his
relationship with Isocrates?). Modern scholarship insists that the main
theme of the *Phaedrus* is the connection between philosophy and rhetoric.
See A. Diès, *Autour de Platon* (Paris, 1927), vol. III, p. 418. In the *Phaedrus*,
Plato maintains that any form of rhetoric which merely attempts to
mislead the listeners is most certainly not a τέχνη. See Plato, *Phaedrus*
260E ff. But there exists another kind of rhetoric which is founded on an
understanding of truth and of the one true reality from which it derives
its arguments and methods. This kind of rhetoric may be called a τέχνη.
*Ibid.*, 263B ff. But if rhetoric is the art of persuading the soul in order to

make it virtuous, then the orator must know something about the nature of the soul. He

> must learn the differences of human souls, for there are so many souls . . . and from them come the differences between man and man. . . . [He] will next divide speeches into their different categories: 'Such and such persons,' he will say, 'are affected by this or that kind of speech in this or that way,' and he will tell you why. The pupil must have a good theoretical notion of them first, and then he must have experience of them in actual life and be able to follow them with all his senses about him, or he will never get beyond the precepts of his masters and teachers. But when he understands what persons are persuaded by what arguments, and sees the person about whom he was speaking in the abstract actually before him, and knows that it is he, and can say to himself, 'This is the man or this is the character who ought to have a certain argument applied to him in order to convince him of a certain opinion'—he who knows all this and knows also when he should speak and when he should keep silent, and when he should use pithy sayings, pathetic appeals, sensational effects and all the other modes of speech which he has learned— when, I repeat, he knows the times and seasons of all these things, then, and not till then, is he a perfect master of his art. . . .

*Ibid.*, 271E ff. Different scholars disagree as to whether Aristotle was acquainted with the Platonic *Phaedrus* at the time he composed the *Gryllus*. W. Jaeger, for instance, denies that about the year 360 B.C. Aristotle knew the *Phaedrus*. Jaeger's thesis, however, seems highly conjectural. The *Phaedrus*, it is widely held, was written about 370–69, or shortly thereafter, while the *Gryllus* is usually dated about 360 or shortly thereafter. It would have been rather unusual for Aristotle, 'the great reader,' not to have known the *Phaedrus* by 360 or, as seems even more unlikely, simply to have ignored it. But since the Platonic *Gorgias* which, judging from Aristotle's lost *Nerinthus*, made such an impression on Aristotle (see Themistius, *Oratio* XXIII. 295CD), denounces without exception the sophists and orators as well as their peculiar rhetoric, the *Gorgias* rather than the more conciliatory *Phaedrus* supplied Aristotle with the kind of materials and the form of argument he needed for his *Gryllus*. This might explain why Aristotle apparently did not make much use of the *Phaedrus* when composing his *Gryllus*. It must also be admitted that in the *Phaedrus* Plato discusses a type of rhetoric that is fundamentally different from the kind of rhetoric which he had condemned in the *Gorgias*. Hence, Plato could very well call rhetoric a τέχνη in the *Phaedrus*, whereas in the *Gorgias* he denies its categorization as a τέχνη. Finally, it should also be observed that in the *Gryllus* Aristotle attacks only obsequious rhetoric, that is, those orators who attempted to arouse emotions and passions. Here he denies that theirs is a τέχνη, but he does not denounce rhetoric in principle which can, after all, still be a τέχνη, provided it complies with certain rational principles. See also P. Kucharski, 'La rhétorique dans le *Gorgias* et le *Phèdre*,' *Revue des Études Grecques*, vol. 74 (1961), pp. 371 ff.

45 Plato, *Gorgias* 462B ff.

46 *Ibid.*, 465A.

47 See notes 5 and 30.

48 See also F. Solmsen, *op. cit.*, pp. 198 ff.

49 P. Thillet, *op. cit.*, pp. 353 ff. See also F. Solmsen, *op. cit.*, pp. 201 ff.

50 Quintilian, *op. cit.*, II. 17. 17.

51 *Ibid.*, II. 17. 18. It will be remembered that in the *Phaedrus, Theaetetus* and *Sophist* Plato warns us not to rely on deceptive opinions.

52 Quintilian, *op. cit.*, II. 17. 22.

53 *Ibid.*, II. 17. 26.

54 *Ibid.*

55 *Ibid.*, II. 17. 30. This could possibly be a reference to Isocrates, who in his younger days was a forensic orator or *logographer* taking on clients and arguing 'on both sides of a case' before the heliastic courts in Athens.

56 *Ibid.*

57 It is possible, however, that some of these arguments might also have been advanced by Athenodorus of Rhodes, Critolaus, Hagnon, Carneades, Diogenes of Babylonia, Clitomachus, Epicurus and others, all of whom were opposed to the rhetoricians and, hence, criticized their methods. See Quintilian, *op. cit.*, II. 17; Sextus Empiricus, *Adversus Rhetoricos, passim*; Cicero, *De Oratore, passim*; Philodemus, *Volumina Rhetorica, passim*; etc.

58 This fact alone would lend support to the contention that Quintilian, *Institutio Oratoria* II. 17. 14-30, contains fragments of the *Gryllus*.

59 DL II. 55. This information is apparently derived from Hermippus' *Life of Theophrastus. Ibid.*

60 See P. Thillet, *op. cit.*, pp. 353 ff.; P. Moraux (see note 1), p. 31; F. Solmsen, *op. cit.*, p. 204.

61 Quintilian, *op. cit.*, III. 1. 13. Quintilian continues: 'Our authorities are not in agreement as to who was his [*scil.*, Isocrates'] teacher. I, however, accept the statement of Aristotle on this subject [namely, that Gorgias was the teacher of Isocrates]. . . .' Frag. 139, Rose; frag. 3, Ross. V. Rose lists this passage from Quintilian among the fragments of the τεχνῶν συναγωγή, but W. D. Ross lists it among the fragments of the *Gryllus*. J. Bernays (see note 4), p. 157, already conjectured that this fragment belonged to the *Gryllus*. In any event, it is quite likely that Quintilian derived his information directly from Aristotle's *Gryllus*. Hence, it may also be assumed that in the *Gryllus*, Aristotle refers to Isocrates as the (most renowned?) disciple of Gorgias.

62 See also A.-H. Chroust, 'Aristotle's earliest course of lectures on rhetoric,' *Antiquité Classique*, vol. 33, fasc. 1 (1964), pp. 58-72, especially, pp. 69 ff.; vol. I, Chapter VIII.

63 Philodemus, *De Rhetorica*, in *Volumina Rhetorica*, col. XLVIII, 36-7 (vol. II, pp. 50-1, ed. S. Sudhaus, Leipzig, 1896).

64 *Ibid.*, col. LV, 43-4 (pp. 60-1, ed. S. Sudhaus), and col. LVI, 45-col. LVII, 46 (p. 62, ed. S. Sudhaus).

65 *Ibid.*, col. XLVIII, 37-col. XLIX, 37 (pp. 51-2, ed. S. Sudhaus).

66 *Ibid.*, col. LI, 40 (p. 55, ed. S. Sudhaus).

67 *Ibid.*, col. LII, 41 (pp. 56-7, ed. S. Sudhaus).

68 *Ibid.*, col. LIII, 42-col. LIV, 42 (p. 58, ed. S. Sudhaus).

69 *Ibid.*, col. LIV, 42 (p. 59, ed. S. Sudhaus).

70 *Ibid.*, col. LIV, 43-4 (pp. 60-1, ed. S. Sudhaus).

71 See A.-H. Chroust (see note 62), and Vol. I, Chapter VIII.

72 See, for instance, Athenaeus, *Deipnosophistae* II. 60DE; III. 122B; VIII. 354B; Dionysius of Halicarnassus, *De Isocrate* 18; Themistius, *Oratio* XXIII. 285AB (p. 345, ed. L. Dindorf); Eusebius, *Praeparatio Evangelica* XIV. 6. 9-10: Dionysius of Halicarnassus, *Epistola ad Cn. Pompeium* 1. The *Against Aristotle* consisted of four books.

73 F. Blass, *Attische Beredsamkeit*, vol. II (Leipzig, 1892), pp. 451 ff., holds that Cephisodorus' *Against Aristotle* was written after the death of Isocrates (338 B.C.); E. Bignone, *L'Aristotele Perduto e la Formazione Filosofica di Epicuro*, vol. II (Florence, 1936), pp. 58 ff., maintains that the *Against Aristotle* was a rejoinder to Aristotle's *Protrepticus* (written about 350 B.C.) which, in turn, was a rebuttal of Isocrates' *Antidosis*; and I. Düring, *Aristotle in the Ancient Biographical Tradition* (Göteborg, 1957), pp. 389 ff., on the strength of the evidence found in Dionysius of Halicarnassus, *Epistola ad Cn. Pompeium* 1, assumes that Cephisodorus' *Against Aristotle* was intended primarily to 'set the record straight.' Düring also insists that the *Against Aristotle* was composed about 360 B.C., or shortly thereafter. Should Düring's thesis prove to be correct, then the *Against Aristotle* could have been 'provoked' by the Aristotelian *Gryllus*. This would also lend support to the thesis that in the *Gryllus* Aristotle criticized Isocrates and his methods.

74 Eusebius, *op. cit.*, XIV. 6. 9.

75 Quintilian, *op. cit.*, II. 17. 14.

76 Aristotle, *Rhetoric* 1354 a 11 ff., it will be noted, contains a pointed attack on Isocrates, although in the main Aristotle's *Rhetoric* seems to take a more friendly attitude towards Isocrates.

77 See H. von Arnim, *Leben und Werke des Dion von Prusa* (Berlin, 1896), pp. 4 ff.; W. Jaeger, *Paideia*, vol. III (New York-Oxford, 1944), *passim*.

78 Isocrates, *Against the Sophists* 20 ff. The *Against the Sophists* seems also to be directed against the 'Socratics,' including Plato and his school.

79 It was probably this particular point of view which became the main target of Aristotle's (and Plato's) attacks: Isocrates' willingness to come to terms with existential reality, with the concrete human condition and with what is reasonably practical—a position which, in the eyes of Plato and the young Aristotle, was unforgivable 'heresy.'

80 See Isocrates, *Against the Sophists* 1; W. Jaeger (see note 77), pp. 83 ff. See also Isocrates, *Helen* 1 and 2–7; Isocrates, *Panegyricus* 47–9; Isocrates, *Nicocles* 8–9; Isocrates, *Ad Nicoclem* 35.

81 Plato, *Republic* 500B.

82 Judging from Quintilian, *op. cit.*, II. 17. 30, Aristotle's *Gryllus* also contained the information that in his earlier days Isocrates had been a *logographer* or forensic orator—not always a reputable profession—in order to make money. See note 55; Dionysius of Halicarnassus, *De Isocrate* 18; Cicero, *Brutus* 28. In later years Isocrates was most reluctant to mention this period of his life. In his *Gryllus* Aristotle probably brought to light these early activities of Isocrates, noting also that many of Isocrates' old forensic speeches could still be found in Athenian book shops. Dionysius of Halicarnassus, *loc. cit.*

83 The *Antidosis* of Isocrates, published in 353–52 B.C., might well be a 'rebuttal' of Aristotle's *Gryllus*. In the *Protrepticus*, published about 350 B.C., Aristotle also takes issue with the *Antidosis*. See A.-H. Chroust, *Aristotle: Protrepticus—A Reconstruction* (Notre Dame, 1964), p. xiv. Thus it appears that the Aristotle–Isocrates feud went on for some time. See notes 39–41 and the corresponding text.

84 In the light of all this, the report of Quintilian becomes comprehensible, namely, *op. cit.* III. 1. 14: '[Aristotle] ... [in the form of a travesty] quoted the well-known line from [Euripides'] *Philoctetes* as follows: "Isocrates still speaks, hence it would be a shameful thing should I remain silent."' The name of Isocrates is substituted for the original term 'barbarians' in the *Philoctetes*. See Euripides, *Philoctetes*, frag. 785, Dindorf; frag. 796, Nauck. See also DL V. 3, where Aristotle is credited with having remarked: 'It would be a base thing to keep silent and let Xenocrates speak out.' This, too, is a travesty of Euripides' line. Some scholars suggest that Xenocrates is but a corruption of Isocrates. See also Cicero, *De Oratore* III. 35. 141; Synesius, *Scholia in Hermogenem* II. 59. 21 ff. (ed. H. Rabe); Philodemus (see note 63), col. XLVIII, 36 (vol. II, p. 50, ed. S. Sudhaus).

85 A.-H. Chroust (see note 62), and Vol. I, Chapter VIII.

86 E. Berti (see note 23), pp. 115–16; pp. 159–66; pp. 174–5; p. 520; p. 522.

## CHAPTER IV *Eudemus or On the Soul:* AN ARISTOTELIAN DIALOGUE ON THE IMMORTALITY OF THE SOUL

\* In a different, shorter and less detailed form, this chapter was originally published in *Mnemosyne*, vol. 19 (series 4), fasc. 1 (1966), pp. 17–30.

1 DL V. 22 (no. 13); *VH* 10 (no. 13). Both 'catalogues' refer to an *On the Soul*, omitting the subtitle *Eudemus*, and both state that this work consisted of one book. The 'catalogue' of Ptolemy (-el-Garib) does not mention the *Eudemus*.

2 Plutarch, *Consolatio ad Apollonium* 27 (*Moralia* 115B–115E—frag. 44, Rose; frag. 6, Walzer; frag. 6, Ross).

3 In the course of Plato's literary activities, his dialogues underwent some considerable changes. In the *Theaetetus*, commonly dated about 369 B.C., the author's concern with philosophic issues begins to overshadow his interest in dramatic investigations, thus almost turning the *Theaetetus* into a treatise, although the somewhat outworn external form of the dialogue is still preserved. This general development of Plato becomes even more pronounced in the *Sophist* and in the *Statesman*, while in the *Timaeus* and in the *Philebus* the dialogue is but a 'stylistic peculiarity' or a purely formal 'carry over' that could easily have been omitted. Finally, in the *Laws*, the dialogue, for all practical purposes, is abandoned in favor of a 'lecture style' of presentation.

4 See W. Jaeger, *Aristotle: Fundamentals of the History of his Development* (Oxford, 1948), p. 28.

5 In this the *Eudemus* shared the fate of many of the other early ('exoteric') works of Aristotle. Some of the earlier Aristotelian commentators still made occasional use of the early dialogues, but on the whole, they did not know what to make of them. Taking notice of certain doctrinal differences that existed between the early 'exoteric' compositions and the later doctrinal treatises (Cicero, *De Finibus* V. 5. 12, for instance, was already aware of these differences), they devised a number of theories in order to explain the relation between these two types of writings. Some commentators insisted that the latter contained Aristotle's true philosophic views, while the former primarily reported on the 'erroneous opinions' of other philosophers, including the erroneous views held by Plato. See, for instance, Elias (*olim* David), *Commentarii in Porphyrii Isagogen et in Aristotelis Categorias* (*CIAG*), vol. XVIII, part 1 (ed. A. Busse, Berlin, 1900), p. 114, lines 15 ff. and p. 124, lines 3 ff. See Chapter III, note 13.

6 At this very moment, O. Gigon is preparing what promises to be the definitive reconstruction of Aristotle's *Eudemus*, under the title of *Aristoteles' Dialog Eudemus: ein Versuch der Wiederherstellung.*

7 See W. Jaeger, *op. cit.*, p. 39.

8 Eudemus had been exiled from his native country. This story contains a fine (Platonic) point: according to Plato (*Phaedo*), the human soul had been banished from 'heaven' or from its 'heavenly home' and original domicile, and had been incarcerated in, or exiled to, the body. In death, the soul returns from its exile to its original (heavenly) abode. Now we may also understand more clearly why the prophecy that Eudemus would return to his homeland in five years really signifies that he would die five years hence. See p. 46.

9 Cicero, *De Divinatione ad Brutum* I. 25. 53 (frag. 37, Rose; frag. 1, Walzer; frag. 1, Ross).

10 Plutarch, *Dion* 22. 3 (frag. 37, Rose; frag. 1, Walzer; frag. 1, Ross).

11 Plutarch, *loc. cit.*

12 See Plutarch, *op. cit.*, 58; Diodorus Siculus XVI. 36.

13 Xenophon, *Hellenica* V. 4; Diodorus Siculus XVI. 14; Plutarch, *Pelopidas* 35.

14 See G. Pasquali, *Le Lettere di Platone* (Florence, 1938), p. 38; W. Spoerri, 'Prosographia,' *Museum Helveticum*, vol. 23, fasc. 1 (1966), pp. 44–57. Spoerri, who questions the story that Eudemus was ever an exile from Cyprus (*ibid.*, p. 46), subjects the many and involved chronological problems connected with the death of Eudemus to a detailed and searching analysis. These, according to Spoerri, seem to be the ascertainable facts: Jason of Pherae was assassinated in August or September of 370 B.C. He was succeeded by his two brothers Polydorus and Polyphron. Polyphron soon murdered Polydorus and ruled singly for about one year when he was killed, probably in 369 B.C., by Alexander of Pherae, the son of Polydorus. In any event, at the time of the first Theban invasion of Thessaly in 369 B.C., under Pelopidas, Alexander of Pherae was already in power. Alexander of Pherae, in turn, was assassinated in 359–58 (or, perhaps, in 358–57 B.C.). Dion of Syracuse, we know, returned to Sicily in 357 B.C., and took Syracuse (the fortress Ortygia held out until 355 B.C.) by force of arms. In the summer of 354 B.C., Dion was slain by Callippus, who subsequently ruled Syracuse for a little over one year. The 'friends of Dion,' among them Eudemus of Cyprus, opposed Callippus, but were forced to retreat to Leontini. There they succeeded in winning over to their cause Hipparinus, the son of Dionysius the Elder and the nephew of Dion. While Callippus was engaged in Catana, 'the friends of Dion' and Hipparinus took Syracuse by surprise. This, Spoerri contends, probably happened during the latter part of 353 B.C. It is possible that Eudemus fell in battle in connection with the recapture of Syracuse by Hipparinus in 353 B.C. This also seems to be borne out by Cicero, *De Divinatione ad Brutum* I. 25. 53: '*Eudemum ad Syracusas occidisse.*' It is quite possible, however, that Eudemus had already died in 354 B.C., that is, during the first and unsuccessful uprising of 'the friends of Dion' against Callippus immediately after the assassination of Dion. It is fairly safe to assume, however, that Alexander of Pherae was murdered in 359–58 B.C., and that five years elapsed between this event and the death of Eudemus. Hence, we may accept the year 353 B.C. as the likely time of Eudemus' death. For the events which transpired in Sicily during the fifties, see also Plato (?). *Epistle VIII, passim*; Diodorus Siculus XVI. 36. 5; Plutarch, *Dion* 58; Polyaenus V. 4.

15 It has also been claimed that the news of Dion's death in 354 B.C. prompted Plato to compose the famous *Seventh Epistle*, provided the latter is indeed by Plato.

16 See A.-H. Chroust, 'The probable dates of some of Aristotle's lost works,' *Rivista Critica di Storia della Filosofia*, vol. 22, fasc. 1 (1967), pp. 3–23, especially, pp. 12–13, and Chapter I. O. Gigon, 'Prolegomena to an edition of the *Eudemus*,' *Aristotle and Plato in the Mid-Fourth Century* (Göteborg, 1960), p. 23, however, maintains that since the Platonic *Phaedo*,

written 'in memory' of Socrates, was composed several years after the death of Socrates, Aristotle's *Eudemus* might likewise have been written several years after the death of Eudemus. P. Moraux, 'From the *Protrepticus* to the Dialogue *Eudemus*,' *ibid.*, p. 120, note 1, refutes the thesis advanced by Gigon.

17 See Sextus Empiricus, *Adversus Mathematicos* IX. 20-3 (frag. 10, Rose; frag. 12a, Walzer; frag. 12a, Ross; frag. 14, Untersteiner); Cicero, *De Divinatione ad Brutum* I. 30. 63 (frag. 12a, Walzer; frag. 12a, Ross; frag. 14, Untersteiner). It will be noted that in the *On Philosophy*, Aristotle employs the prophetic powers of the soul to prove the existence of God. See A.-H. Chroust, 'A cosmological proof for the existence of God in Aristotle's lost dialogue *On Philosophy*,' *New Scholasticism*, vol. 40, no. 4 (1966), pp. 447-63, and Chapter XIII. O. Gigon (see note 16), *passim*, wishes to credit these two fragments and, for that matter, all fragments dealing with the soul, to the *Eudemus* rather than to the *On Philosophy*. See note 25.

18 See, for instance, DL VIII. 4-5; VIII. 14; VIII. 41. See also Empedocles, frag. B 129 (Diels-Kranz).

19 See, for instance, Plato, *Crito* 44A ff. See also P. Siwek, 'La clairvoyance parapsychique dans le système d'Aristote,' *Sophia*, vol. 29 (1961), pp. 296-311.

20 See also W. Jaeger, *op. cit.*, pp. 48-52. Plato, it will be remembered, had pointed out that the true philosopher is constantly concerned with death, and that philosophy may appropriately be defined as 'the meditation about death.' See Plato, *Phaedo* 67C; 61B; 64E ff.; Plato, *Republic* 486A. This Platonic definition of philosophy subsequently became one of the six basic definitions of philosophy listed in the Late Hellenistic *Isagogae* or *Prolegomena* to philosophy. See A.-H. Chroust, 'The Meaning of Philosophy in the Hellenistic-Roman World,' *Thomist*, vol. 17, no. 2 (1954), pp. 246 ff.

21 See, for instance, P. Moraux, *op. cit.*, p. 120; D. A. Rees, 'Theories of the soul in the early Aristotle,' *Aristotle and Plato in the Mid-Fourth Century* (Göteborg, 1960), p. 192; E. Berti, *La Filosofia del Primo Aristotele* (Università di Padova, Pubblicazioni della Facoltà di Lettere e Filosofia, vol. 38, Padua, 1962), p. 415; W. Jaeger, *op. cit.*, p. 40.

22 Plutarch, *Consolatio ad Apollonium* 27 (*Moralia* 115BE—frag. 44, Rose; frag. 6, Walzer; frag. 6, Ross). See also Cicero, *Tuscul. Disput.* I. 48. 114.

23 See preceding note. The statement that 'the second best thing . . . is . . . to die as soon as possible,' calls to mind Theognis 425 ff., where we are told that it is a good thing 'to pass with all speed through the gates of Hades.'

24 Now we may also understand and appreciate why O. Gigon (see note 16), p. 27; H. Flashar, 'Platon und Aristoteles im *Protreptikos* des Jamblichos,' *Archiv für Geschichte der Philosophie*, vol. 47 (1965), pp. 54-70; and K. Gaiser, 'Die Elegie des Aristoteles auf Eudemos,' *Museum Helveticum*, vol. 23, fasc. 2 (1966), pp. 84-106, wish to credit Iamblichus, *Protrepticus*, p. 47, line 21-p. 48, line 9, Pistelli (frag. 60, Rose; frag. 10b, Walzer; frag. 10b, Ross; frags 106-7, Düring; frags 102-3, Chroust) to the

Aristotelian *Eudemus* rather than to the Aristotelian *Protrepticus*, as is usually the case. This lengthy passage from Iamblichus, which might very well be an authentic fragment of the Aristotelian *Eudemus*, reads as follows:

> Who among us [living in this world] . . . would consider himself truly happy and blessed, especially since all of us . . . are from the beginning constituted by nature as if destined for punishment? For the divinely inspired among the ancient sages tell us that the soul pays penalties, and that we live [in this world] because we are punished [exiled?] for certain great sins we have committed. [This notion can also be found in Plato, *Cratylus* 400BC, *note by the author.*] And, indeed, the union of the soul with the body strikes us as being very much such a punishment. For, as the Etruscans are said often to torture prisoners of war by chaining human carcasses face to face with living men, matching part with part, so also the soul seems to be stretched throughout the body as well as tied to the sensitive parts of the body.

See here also St. Augustine, *Contra Julianum Pelagium* IV. 15. 78 (which St. Augustine probably derived from Cicero's *Hortensius*, frag. 95, Müller); J. Brunschwig, 'Aristote et les pirates Tyrrhéniens,' *Revue Philosophique de la France et de l'Étranger*, vol. 153 (1963), pp. 171–90; H. Flashar, 'Die Kritik der platonischen Ideenlehre in der Ethik des Aristoteles,' *Synusia: Festschrift für Wolfgang Schadewaldt* (Pfullingen, 1965), p. 240, and p. 245, notes; A. Grilli, 'Cicerone e l'Eudemo,' *La Parola del Passato*, fasc. 83 (1962), pp. 96–128. Part of the *Eudemus* rather than the Aristotelian *Protrepticus* might also be Iamblichus, *Protrepticus* p. 48, lines 9–21 (frag. 61, Rose; frag. 10c, Walzer; frag. 10c, Ross; frags 108–110, Düring; frags 104–6, Chroust), where we are told that the only thing worthwhile in man is his intellect (φρόνησις), and that this intellect is 'the divine dwelling in us.' Everything else is but 'utter nonsense and folly.'

25 Cicero, *Tuscul. Disput.* I. 26. 65–27. 66:

> But if there is a fifth nature introduced first by Aristotle, this is the nature both of gods and of souls (*animorum*). We, following this opinion, have expressed it in these very words in our *Consolatio*: 'The origin of souls is not to be found on earth; for in souls there is nothing mixed and composite, nothing that seems to be born and fashioned of earth, nothing even resembling water, air or fire. For in these physical natures there is nothing that has the power of memory, intellect and thought—that retains the past, foresees the future and can grasp the present—which alone are living powers; nor will it ever be discovered whence these can come to man, except from God.' There is, therefore, a singular nature and power of the soul, disjointed from these customary and well-known natures. Thus, whatever it is that feels, knows, lives and thrives, must be celestial and divine, and

therefore eternal. Nor can the God Whom we know be otherwise understood than as mind (soul) apart and free, separated from all mortal admixture, feeding and moving all things, and itself endowed with eternal motion. Of this kind and of the same nature is the human soul.

Although this fragment is commonly credited to the Aristotelian *On Philosophy* (see frag. 27, Walzer; frag. 27, Ross; frag. 30, Untersteiner), it is possible and, as O. Gigon would have it, probable that it is a fragment of the *Eudemus*. Cicero refers here to his *Consolatio*, which he composed in his grief over the death of his beloved daughter Tullia. The realization that Tullia's soul lives on—a realization which he admittedly derives from Aristotle—that she is not really dead but has merely departed for another and better world where he will meet her again, gives Cicero much comfort.

26 See A.-H. Chroust, 'The psychology in Aristotle's lost dialogue *Eudemus or On the Soul*,' *Acta Classica*, vol. 9 (1966), pp. 49–62, and Chapter V.

27 See, for instance, Proclus, *In Platonis Timaeum Commentaria* 338CD (ed. E. Diehl, Leipzig, 1903–6, Teubner; frag. 40, Rose; frag. 4, Walzer; frag. 4 Ross); Proclus, *In Platonis Rempublicam Commentarii* (ed. W. Kroll, Leipzig, 1899–1901), vol. II, p. 349, lines 13 ff. (frag. 41, Rose; frag. 5, Walzer; frag. 5, Ross).

28 Elias (*olim* David), *Commentarii in Prophyrii Isagogen et in Aristotelis Categorias*, CIAG, vol. XVIII, part 1 (ed. A. Busse, Berlin, 1900), p. 114, lines 25 ff. (frag. 39, Rose; frag. 3, Walzer; frag. 3, Ross).

29 W. Jaeger, *op. cit.*, p. 45, and R. Walzer, *Aristotelis Dialogorum Fragmenta in Usum Scholarum* (Florence, 1934), p. 15, claim that the immediate source of Philoponus' *Commentary* to Aristotle's *De Anima* is Alexander of Aphrodisias' lost *Commentary* to the Aristotelian *De Anima*. See also W. D. Ross, *The Works of Aristotle*, vol. XII (Oxford, 1952), p. 20. That some of the later commentators relied on Alexander of Aphrodisias (*floruit* A.D. 198–211) might also be inferred from Simplicius, *Comment. in Arist Categorias*, CIAG, vol. VIII (ed. C. Kalbfleisch, Berlin, 1907), p. 4, lines 19 ff.; Elias, *op. cit.* p. 115, lines 3 ff.

30 See, for instance, I. Düring, *Aristotle in the Ancient Biographical Tradition* (Acta Universitatis Gothoburgensis, vol. 63, no. 2. Göteborg, 1957), pp. 438–9.

31 Elias (see note 28), p. 115, lines 6–12.

32 Olympiodorus, *Prolegomena et in Categorias Commentarium*, CIAG, vol. XII, part 1 (ed. A. Busse, Berlin, 1902), p. 7, line 5.

33 Elias (see note 31). The commentators apparently did not take into consideration the possibility that at one time Aristotle may have accepted Plato's views on this subject. We know that in the *De Anima* 432 a 23, Aristotle denies the survival of the 'whole soul.' See note 36.

34 J. Bernays, *Die Dialoge des Aristoteles in ihrem Verhältnis zu seinen übrigen Werken* (Berlin, 1863), pp. 116 ff. See also H. Diels, 'Über die exoterischen

Reden des Aristoteles,' *Sitzungsberichte der Berliner Akademie der Wissen-schaften*, vol. 19, part 1 (Berlin, 1883), pp. 477–94.

35  V. Rose, *Aristoteles Pseudepigraphus* (Leipzig, 1863), *passim*. See also V. Rose, *De Aristotelis Librorum Ordine et Auctoritate* (Berlin, 1854), *passim*.

36  In *De Anima* 430 a 23, Aristotle states: 'When the soul is set free from its present conditions it appears as just what it is and nothing more: This alone is immortal and eternal. . . .' But, again, in *Nicomachean Ethics* 1111 b 22, he points out: 'But there may be a wish even for the impossible as, for instance, for immortality.' In the *Protrepticus*, which was composed shortly after the *Eudemus*, Aristotle maintains: 'Mankind as such possesses nothing of worth and has no reason to consider itself perchance divine (deathless), except in so far as it possesses reason. . . . This alone of all our endowments seems to be deathless. . . .' Iamblichus, *Protrepticus* (ed. H. Pistelli, 1888), p. 48, lines 9–13 (frag. 61, Rose; frag. 10c, Walzer; frag. 10c, Walzer; frag. 108, Düring; frag. 104, Chroust). See also Aristotle, *Protrepticus*: 'For reason is "the divine (deathless) dwelling in us" . . . and because of reason mortal life possesses a certain element or aspect of the divine (deathless). . . .' Iamblichus, *op. cit.*, p. 48, lines 16–21 (frag. 61, Rose; frag. 10c, Walzer; frag. 10c, Ross; frag. 110, Düring; frag. 106, Chroust). Some scholars (see note 21) are of the opinion that these two passages, which are commonly credited to the Aristotelian *Protrepticus*, are in truth fragments of the *Eudemus*. In *Nicomachean Ethics* 1177 a 15 ff., Aristotle calls reason 'divine' (deathless) as well as 'the most divine element in us.' See also *ibid.*, 1177 b 27 ff.; Aristotle, *De Generatione Animalium* 736 b 28: 'Reason is the only divine (deathless) element. . . .'

37  Elias, *op. cit.*, p. 114, lines 22 ff. See also Themistius, *Paraphrasis in Aristotelis Libros De Anima, CIAG*, vol. V, part 3 (ed. R. Heinze, Berlin, 1899), p. 106, lines 29 ff. (frag. 38, Rose; frag. 2, Walzer; frag. 2, Ross).

38  This view is advanced by Themistius (see note 37), when he insists that 'of the other arguments [about the immortality of the soul] those which are considered to be more persuasive could without difficulty be referred to reason. And this also holds true of the more persuasive arguments offered by Aristotle himself in the *Eudemus*.' Themistius also maintains here that in the *Phaedo* Plato teaches the immortality of the rational part of the soul.

39  W. Jaeger, *op. cit.*, pp. 50 ff. Jaeger insists that the passage from Themistius (see note 37), fully supports his position. *Ibid.*, p. 50, note 2. Jaeger's view has been contested by a number of scholars.

40  W. Jaeger, *op. cit.*, pp. 50–1.

41  F. Nuyens, *L'Évolution de la psychologie d'Aristote* (Publications de l'Univer-sité de Louvain, 1948), pp. 125–7. D. A. Rees (see note 21), pp. 191–3, maintains that whenever Aristotle speaks of the soul in the proper sense of the term, he always refers to the νοῦς. See also E. Berti (note 21), pp. 419–20.

42  D. A. Rees (see note 41).

43 This might also be gathered from some fragments traditionally assigned to the Aristotelian *Protrepticus*. See note 36.

44 W. Jaeger (see note 39), objects to this 'limitation' which has been suggested by a number of scholars.

45 Proclus, *In Platonis Timaeum Commentaria* 338CD (frag. 40, Rose; frag. 4, Walzer; frag. 4, Ross).

46 It should also be noted that Aristotle's discussion of the 'soul after death' in the *Eudemus* differs considerably from Plato's discussion of the soul in the *Timaeus*. Here Plato is primarily concerned with the 'physical' aspect of the soul. See also Proclus, *op. cit.* 338D, where we are informed that in the *Timaeus* Plato does not tell us

> what happens after the departure of the soul ... simply because he confined himself to what is in conformity with the specific purpose of the dialogue [*scil.*, the *Timaeus*], and admits here just as much of a theory of the soul as is 'physical,' describing the soul's relation to the body. In the *De Anima*, Aristotle, in imitation of Plato, discusses the soul in terms of 'physics' [*scil.*, in terms of the body-soul relations], saying nothing either of the origin or the ultimate fate of the soul. But in his dialogues [*scil.*, in the *Eudemus* and perhaps in the *On Philosophy*] he dealt separately with these topics [*scil.*, with the origin and ultimate fate of the soul]. ...

47 See Philoponus, *Comment. in Arist. De Anima*, CIAG, vol. XV (ed. M. Hayduck, Berlin, 1897), p. 141, line 22-p. 147, line 10 (frag. 45, Rose; frag. 7, Walzer; frag. 7, Ross); Simplicius, *Comment. in Arist. De Anima*, CIAG, vol. XI (ed. M. Hayduck, Berlin, 1892), p. 53, lines 1-4 (frag. 45, Rose; frag. 7, Walzer; frag. 7, Ross); Themistius, *Paraphrasis in Arist. Libros De Anima*, CIAG, vol. V, part 3 (ed. R. Heinze, Berlin, 1899), p. 24, line 13-p. 25, line 25 (frag. 45, Rose; frag. 7, Walzer; frag. 7, Ross); Olympiodorus, *Scholia in Platonis Phaedonem* (ed. W. Norvin, Leipzig, 1913), p. 173, lines 20 ff.; p. 173, line 30 (frag. 45, Rose; frag. 7, Walzer; frag. 7, Ross); Sophonias, *In Arist. De Anima Paraphrasis*, CIAG, vol. XXIII, part 1 (ed. M. Hayduck, Berlin, 1883), p. 25, lines 4-8 (frag. 7, Walzer; frag. 7, Ross). See also A.-H. Chroust (see note 26), and Chapter V.

48 The notion that the entry of the soul into the body is tantamount to becoming sick—that for the soul life without the body is its normal or 'natural' state—is definitely a Platonic or Pythagorean notion. From the works of Plato, we may gather that the latter considered the entry of the soul into the body a form of punishment, an exile from its heavenly home and a crushing misfortune. See also notes 8 and 24.

49 Proclus, *In Platonis Republicam Commentarii* (ed. W. Kroll, 2 vols, Leipzig, 1899-1901), vol. II, p. 349, lines 13-26 (frag. 41, Rose; frag. 5, Walzer; frag. 5, Ross). Aristotle apparently modifies or alters Plato's theory of the *anamnesis*. While Plato maintains that the soul in this world

remembers 'the higher world' from which it originally came, Aristotle insists that in 'the other world' the soul remembers what it has experienced in this world—for Plato a totally unacceptable surmise.

50 This is an interesting and, at the same time, radical modification of Plato's original doctrine of the *anamnesis*. On the threshold of death (or in a state of high fever) and, at times, during sleep, this recollection may temporarily return to living man.

51 W. Jaeger, *op. cit.*, p. 51.

52 *Ibid.* Jaeger's 'Platonic interpretation' of the 'continuity of rational awareness' was accepted by P. Moraux, *Les Listes Anciennes des Ouvrages d'Aristote* (Louvain, 1951), p. 35 and p. 324; Ph. Merlan, *From Platonism to Neo-Platonism* (The Hague, 1953), pp. 6–8; A. Mansion, 'La genèse de l'oeuvre d'Aristote après les travaux récents,' *Revue Néoscolastique de Philosophie*, vol. 29 (1927), pp. 318 ff.; E. Berti (see note 21), p. 421; C. de Vogel, *Greek Philosophy*, vol. II (Leiden, 1953), pp. 21–2; E. Bignone, *L'Aristotele Perduto e la Formazione Filosofica di Epicuro*, vol. I (Florence, 1936), pp. 70–7; F. J. Nuyens (see note 41), p. 84; D. J. Allan, *The Philosophy of Aristotle* (London, 1952), p. 65; and others.

53 This reference is obviously to the 'myth of Er.' Plato, *Republic* 614B ff. In the Platonic *Meno* 86A ff., it will be remembered, the *anamnesis* is also used in order to demonstrate the 'immortality' of the soul.

54 I. Düring, 'Aristotle and Plato in the Mid-Fourth Century,' *Eranos*, vol. 44 (1956), pp. 115–16. In this, Düring to some extent finds the support of O. Gigon (see note 16), p. 25.

55 Proclus (see note 49); I. Düring (see note 54).

56 The question whether the problem of the *anamnesis* also implies that in the *Eudemus* Aristotle accepted the Platonic theory of the Separate Ideas (as, for instance, W. Jaeger suggests) will not be discussed here.

57 This might be gathered, for instance, from Philo of Alexandria, *De Aeternitate Mundi* III. 10–11 (frag. 18, Rose; frag. 18, Walzer; frag. 18, Ross; frag. 21, Untersteiner). See also Philo of Alexandria, *op. cit.*, V. 20–4 (frag. 19, Rose; frag. 19a, Walzer; frag. 19a, Ross; frag. 29, Untersteiner); *ibid.*, VI. 28–VII. 34 (frag. 20, Rose; frag. 19b, Walzer; frag. 19b, Ross; frag. 28, Untersteiner); *ibid.*, VIII. 39–43 (frag. 21, Rose; frag. 19c, Walzer; frag. 19c, Ross; frag. 17, Untersteiner). See also A.-H. Chroust (note 17), and Chapter XIII.

58 See, for instance, frag. 45, Rose; frag. 7, Walzer; frag. 7, Ross (*Eudemus*); frag. 46, Rose; frag. 8, Walzer; frag. 8, Ross (*Eudemus*); frag. 43, Rose; frag. 9, Ross (*Eudemus*). See also Aristotle, *De Anima* 407 b 27: 'There is yet another theory about the soul, which has recommended itself to many as not less probable than any of those we have discussed so far. This theory has given public account of itself in the court of popular discussion. Its supporters maintain that the soul is a sort of harmony. . . .' See Chapter V, *passim*.

59 In the *Republic, Sophist, Statesman, Phaedrus, Philebus* and *Timaeus*—works

with which Aristotle must have been acquainted at the time he composed the *Eudemus*.

60 P. Moraux, for instance, insists that the *Eudemus* is 'an isolated instance' in Aristotle's literary activities which can be understood only in the light of his efforts to imitate Plato's *Phaedo*. P. Moraux, 'L'évolution d'Aristote,' *Aristote et Saint Thomas d'Aquin* (Journées d'Études Internationales, Chaire Cardinal Mercier, Louvain-Paris, 1957), p. 33.

61 Such prominent scholars as A. Mansion, A. J. Festugière, P. Moraux, Ph. Merlan, E. Bignone and others of like scholarly stature, on the whole, have accepted Jaeger's general 'evolutionary' thesis. In itself this is eloquent evidence of its unsurpassed merits. But in the particular case of the *Eudemus*, Jaeger possibly falls victim to a curious oversight: he seems to believe that in the year 352–51, or thereabouts, Aristotle still adhered *doctrinally* to the philosophic doctrines of the soul advanced in the *Phaedo*—doctrines which by that time were obviously 'antiquated' even for Plato.

62 Several fragments (see notes 47 and 58), which by common consensus are related to the *Eudemus*, deal with the particular nature of the soul. This problem, unfortunately, is beyond our limited scope. It will be discussed in Chapter V.

63 A. E. Housman, *For My Funeral* (1925). It has been suggested, though probably incorrectly, that Aristotle's *Elegy* preserved by Olympiodorus (*In Platonis Gorgiam*, ed. W. Norvin, p. 197), especially the famous passage, 'who alone or first among mortals revealed it clearly for everyone to see that man becomes happy [only] if he becomes good,' might have been dedicated to the memory of Eudemus rather than to that of Plato. See K. Gaiser, 'Die Elegie des Aristoteles auf Eudemos,' *Museum Helveticum*, vol. 23, fasc. 2 (1966), pp. 84–106. Gaiser, who denies that Aristotle ever erected an altar expressly in honor of Plato or dedicated this Elegy to his memory, suggests (p. 88) that with a view to Eudemus' sad fate, we trans-late the last line of this Elegy as follows: 'Now [in this sorry world of ours which no longer shelters Eudemus] it is impossible to be both virtuous and happy,' or perhaps: 'In this [sorry] world of ours it is impossible to comprehend the complete coincidence of virtue and happiness.' K. Gaiser, *op. cit.*, p. 91. See also *Laws* 660E, where Plato maintains that 'the good man, if he is both temperate and just, is fortunate and happy.' It is possible, but not likely, that in his Elegy Aristotle had in mind this passage from the *Laws*. But if this is so, then he could hardly have dedicated his *Elegy* to the memory of Eudemus who died in 354–53 B.C., that is, several years before the *Laws* were written, unless one would accept the suggestion of O. Gigon that the *Eudemus* was composed many years after Eudemus' death. Hence, it seems more reasonable to assume that Aristotle dedicated these famous lines (as well as the altar) to the memory of Plato, and that he did so perhaps on the occasion of his return to Athens in the years 335–34 B.C. See also Plato, *Meno* 85DE; Iamblichus, *Protrepticus* (ed. Pistelli), p. 60, lines 7–22. It will be noted that in their respective collections of Aristotelian fragments,

R. Walzer and W. D. Ross assign Iamblichus, *Protrepticus* 60, 7–15 to Aristotle's *Protrepticus*; W. Jaeger, *op. cit.*, p. 80, and *ibid.*, p. 101, note, credits the whole of 60, 7–22 to Aristotle's *Protrepticus* (or, perhaps, to the Aristotelian *Eudemus*), as does A. J. Festugière, *La Révélation d'Hermès Trismégiste*, vol. II (Paris, 1949), p. 173. In their respective attempts to reconstruct the Aristotelian *Protrepticus*, I. Düring and A.-H. Chroust assign only 60, 7–10 to Aristotle's *Protrepticus* (frag. 96, Düring; frag. 92, Chroust). H. Flashar (see note 24), pp. 54–79, especially, pp. 72 ff., wishes to credit the whole of 60, 7–22 to the Aristotelian *Eudemus*. Similar views have also been expressed by O. Gigon (see note 16), p. 27. This is not the place, however, to discuss the several theories which assign to the *Eudemus* certain fragments traditionally credited to the Aristotelian *Protrepticus* (see, for instance, K. Gaiser, *op. cit.*, this note, and O. Gigon, *loc. cit.*, this note, and note 24) or to Aristotle's *On Philosophy* (see O. Gigon, *op. cit.*, p. 23, and *ibid.*, p. 28 and 32; S. Mariotti, 'La *quinta essentia* nell' Aristotele perduto e nell' Academia,' *Rivista di Filologia e d'Istruzione Classica*, vol. 68, 1940, pp. 180–1; A. Grilli (see note 24), pp. 98–100).

## CHAPTER V   THE PSYCHOLOGY IN ARISTOTLE'S *Eudemus or On the Soul*

* In a slightly different form, this chapter was first published in *Acta Classica*, vol. 9 (1966), pp. 49–62.
1 A.-H. Chroust, '*Eudemus or On the Soul*: a lost dialogue of Aristotle on the immortality of the soul,' *Mnemosyne*, vol. 19 (series 4), fasc. 1 (1966), pp. 17–30, especially, pp. 29 ff., and Chapter IV.
2 DL V. 22 (no. 13); *VH* 10 (no. 13).
3 Ioannes Philoponus, *Comment. in Arist. De Anima*, CIAG, vol. XV (ed. M. Hayduck, Berlin, 1897), p. 141, line 21–p. 147, line 10 (frag. 45, Rose; frag. 7, Walzer; frag. 7, Ross).
4 Simplicius, *Comment. in Arist. De Anima*, CIAG, vol. XI (ed. M. Hayduck, Berlin, 1882), p. 53, lines 1–4 (frag. 45, Rose; frag. 7, Walzer; frag. 7, Ross).
5 Themistius, *Paraphrasis in Arist. Libros De Anima*, CIAG, vol. V, part 3 (ed. R. Heinze, Berlin, 1899), p. 24, line 13–p. 25, line 25 (frag. 45, Rose; frag. 7, Walzer; frag. 7, Ross).
6 Olympiodorus, *Scholia in Platonis Phaedonem* (ed. W. Norvin, Leipzig, 1913), p. 173, lines 20 ff.; p. 173, line 30 (frag. 45, Rose; frag. 7, Walzer; frag. 7, Ross).
7 Sophonias, *In Aristotelis De Anima Paraphrasis*, CIAG, vol. XXIII, part 1 (ed. M. Hayduck, Berlin, 1883), p. 25, lines 4–8 (frag. 7, Walzer; frag. 7, Ross).
8 Plato, *Phaedo* 91E–92E.
9 *Ibid.*, 92E–93B.
10 *Ibid.*, 93B.
11 *Ibid.*, 93B–93E.

12 *Ibid.*, 93E–94B.

13 *Ibid.*, 94BC.

14 See note 3.

15 Philoponus (see note 3), p. 144, lines 24–5 (frag. 45, Rose; frag. 7, Walzer; frag. 7, Ross).

16 *Ibid.*, p. 144, lines 25–30. W. Jaeger, *Aristotle: Fundamentals of the History of his Development* (Oxford, 1948), p. 45, believes that this particular 'rebuttal' or counter-argument is by Alexander of Aphrodisias rather than by Aristotle himself. Jaeger's assumption would imply that for his discussion or commentary Philoponus did not consult Aristotle directly, but rather relied on Alexander of Aphrodisias (*floruit* A.D. 198–211), who is said to have been one of the last commentators who still had read some of the early (lost) works or dialogues of Aristotle.

17 Philoponus, *op. cit.*, p. 144, lines 30–7.

18 See notes 8–13, especially note 11 and note 12.

19 Aristotle, *De Anima* 408 a 1–3.

20 Philoponus, *op. cit.*, p. 147, lines 6–7.

21 *Ibid.*, p. 147, lines 7–9. The other three arguments against the thesis that the soul is attunement—arguments or objections advanced in Aristotle, *De Anima* 407 b 30–408 a 18, but apparently not contained in the *Eudemus*—are the following: (i) attunement is a certain proportion or harmony of the constituents (or components) thus blended, but the soul is neither of these (to wit, proportion or harmony); (ii) the power of originating movement cannot belong to attunement; and (iii) the soul is neither the attunement (or harmony) of the several component parts of the body nor the ratio of these several elements.

22 *Ibid.*, p. 147, line 10.

23 Aristotle (?), *Categories* 3 b 24 ff. It will be noted that this syllogism not only proves that the soul is not an attunement, but it also implies that the soul is a substance. This particular syllogism, found in the *Eudemus*, may also assist us in dating the *Categories*, provided the latter is by Aristotle. See also note 40.

24 See also W. Jaeger (see note 16), p. 46.

25 Simplicius (see note 4), p. 53, lines 1–4 (frag. 45, Rose; frag. 7 Walzer; frag. 7, Ross). One particular issue seems to emerge from this passage: the arguments advanced in the *Eudemus*, that is, in the 'exoteric' works of Aristotle in general, are 'adapted to the intelligence of most [of the average] people.' They are devised for a non-philosophical audience. This, then, might imply that in the *Eudemus*, and in some of the other 'exoteric' writings, Aristotle advanced 'popular' views rather than philosophic problems, and that as a 'popular' work, the *Eudemus* does not really convey the true philosophic standpoint of Aristotle—a view which is held by some scholars. See also note 27.

26 Plato, *Phaedo* 93B ff., and note 10. For a more detailed discussion of this problem, see pp. 63–4.

27 Themistius (see note 5), p. 24, line 13–p. 25, line 25 (frag. 45, Rose; frag. 7, Walzer; frag. 7, Ross). It will be noted that just as Philoponus and Simplicius have done, Themistius refers to 'public discussions.' This could mean the so-called 'exoteric' works of Aristotle. See Philoponus (see note 3), p. 145, lines 21 ff. See note 14 and the corresponding text, and note 25. The involved and vexing problem of the so-called exoteric works of Aristotle, it has already been pointed out, has become the subject of many a learned discussion as well as the object of many disagreements among scholars.

28 See Philoponus, *op. cit.*, p. 144, lines 24–5. See also note 15 and the corresponding text. It should be noted that Themistius combines and integrates into one single objection what Philoponus considers to be two separate objections, namely, objections four and five.

29 Themistius, *op. cit.*, p. 24, lines 25–6. See also Philoponus, *op. cit.*, p. 144, lines 30–7, and *ibid.*, p. 147, lines 6–10.

30 Philoponus, *op. cit.*, p. 144, lines 25 ff.

31 Aristotle, *De Anima* 408 a 1–3. It will be observed that Themistius uses the term δύναμις, where Philoponus refers to ἰσχύς. See note 20.

32 Olympiodorus (see note 6), p. 173, lines 20–30 (frag. 45, Rose; frag. 7, Walzer; frag. 7, Ross).

33 W. Jaeger (see note 16), p. 42, points out that Plato 'infers the non-identity of soul and harmony from the impossibility of applying one and the same logical principle [*scil.*, the category of substance] to both conceptions [*scil.*, soul and harmony]; or, in Aristotelian terms, from their belonging to different categories.'

34 See J. Bernays, *Die Dialoge des Aristoteles in ihrem Verhältnis zu seinen übrigen Werken* (Berlin, 1863), p. 145, note 15. This *petitio principii* goes back to Plato's *Phaedo*. Philoponus, however, seems to avoid this *petitio principii*. Here the argument, at least by implication, proceeds from the absence of contraries to the fact that the soul is a substance. J. Bernays, *loc. cit.* See also W. Jaeger (see note 16), p. 44. It will be noted that the argument, 'the soul is not merely the attunement of the body,' likewise contains a *petitio principii* or, better, presupposes such a *petitio principii*. See note 51 and the corresponding text.

35 Sophonias (see note 7), p. 25, lines 4–8 (frag. 7, Walzer; frag. 7, Ross).

36 See O. Gigon, 'Prolegomena to an Edition of the *Eudemus*,' *Aristotle and Plato in the Mid-Fourth Century* (Göteborg, 1960), p. 30. Gigon (*ibid.*, pp. 31 ff.) suggests that many more fragments of the *Eudemus* might possibly be retrieved from Hellenistic, Patristic and Alexandrian literature. Gigon also maintains that certain fragments, which traditionally (*i.e.*, by V. Rose) have been assigned to Aristotle's *Protrepticus* or Aristotle's *On Philosophy*, or to some other early (lost) work of Aristotle, should be credited to the *Eudemus*, especially those fragments which refer to the soul. See also O. Gigon, *op. cit.*, pp. 23; 27; 28; 32; A. Flashar, 'Platon und Aristoteles im Protreptikos des Jamblichos,' *Archiv für Geschichte der*

*Philosophie*, vol. 47 (1965), pp. 54–70; A. Flashar, 'Die Kritik der platonischen Ideenlehre in der Ethik des Aristoteles,' *Synusia: Festschrift für Wolfgang Schadewaldt* (Pfullingen, 1965), p. 240 and p. 245, notes; K. Gaiser, 'Die Elegie des Aristoteles auf Eudemos,' *Museum Helveticum*, vol. 23, fasc. 2 (1966), pp. 81–106; A. Grilli, 'Cicerone e l'*Eudemo*,' *La Parola del Passato*, vol. 17, fasc. 83 (1962), pp. 98–100; S. Mariotti, 'La quinta essentia nell' Aristotele perduto e nell' Academia,' *Rivista di Filologia e d'Istruzione Classica*, vol. 68 (1940), pp. 180–1.

37 O. Gigon, *op. cit.*, p. 21 and p. 29. Gigon, *ibid.*, p. 30, also points out that the Platonic *Phaedo* differs from the *Eudemus* in that the former discusses the problem of immortality from the viewpoint of a man about to die (Socrates), while the latter discusses immortality from the standpoint of someone who grieves over the death of a recently deceased friend.

38 W. Jaeger (see note 16), pp. 40 ff.

39 Aristotle (?), *Categories* 3 b 24. W. Jaeger denies that the *Categories* are an authentic work of Aristotle. See, however, K. von Fritz, 'Der Ursprung der aristotelischen Kategorienlehre,' *Archiv für Geschichte der Philosophy*, vol. 40 (1931), pp. 439–96. Von Fritz believes that the greater part of the *Categories* is authentic. *Ibid.*, pp. 450–1, note.

40 See also W. Jaeger (note 16), pp. 40–1. K. von Fritz (see note 39), pp. 473–4, argues as follows: the *Eudemus* contains the argument that since harmony or attunement has a contrary, namely, disharmony or non-attunement, the soul cannot be harmony because it has no contrary. This argument implies that the soul must be a substance, because a substance has no contrary. The ultimate significance of this statement becomes fully clear only when it is related to the *Categories* of Aristotle (?), which demonstrates that categories and substances have no contraries. But the reasoning in the *Eudemus*, von Fritz insists, does not necessarily presuppose that at the time Aristotle composed the *Eudemus*, that is, about 352 B.C., he had already developed the basic principles of his doctrine of categories. Without doubt, prior to the final development of his integrated doctrine of categories as it can be found in the *Categories*, Aristotle did operate with certain isolated categories, such as the category of substance (which might have been discussed in the Academy and, it appears, in the Aristotelian *On (the) Ideas*, commonly dated between 357 and 355 B.C.). But Aristotle did so in a context in which these isolated categories were not yet integrated into a system of categories.

41 See notes 32 and 34. Olympiodorus, who claimed that, according to Aristotle's *Eudemus*, 'the soul is a substance (οὐσία γάρ),' had already pointed out that as a substance the soul cannot have 'a contrary.' See note 32.

42 Plato, *Phaedo* 92BD:

> My Theban friend [Simmias], you will have to think differently if you still maintain that harmony is a compound, and that the soul is

a harmony which is made out of strings set in the frame of the body. For you will surely never allow yourself to say that a harmony is prior to the elements which make up that harmony. . . . But do you not see that this is what you imply when you say that the soul existed before she took the form and body of man, and was composed of elements which as yet had no existence? For harmony is not like the soul, as you suppose. First the lyre, and the strings, and the sounds exist in a state of discord, and then harmony is produced last of all, and is the first to perish. And how can such a notion of the soul as this agree with the other? . . . And yet . . . there surely ought to be harmony in a discourse of which harmony is the theme. . . . But there is no harmony. . . . in the two propositions that knowledge is recollection, and that the soul is harmony. Which of them will you retain? I think, he replied, that I have a much stronger faith . . . in the first of the two, which has been fully demonstrated to me, than in the latter, which has not been demonstrated at all, but rests only on probable and plausible grounds and, therefore, is believed by the many. I know only too well that these arguments from mere probabilities are impostors, and unless much caution is used in the use of them, they are apt to be deceptive. . . . But the doctrine of knowledge and recollection has been proven to me on trustworthy grounds. This proof was that the soul must have existed before she came into the body, because to her belongs the essence of which the very name implies existence. Having, as I am convinced, rightly accepted this conclusion, and on sufficient grounds, I must, as I suppose, cease to argue, or allow others to argue, that the soul is harmony.

43 Aristotle (?), *Categories* 3 b 33–4 a 9.

44 *Ibid.*, 6 b 15 ff.: 'It is possible for relatives to have contraries. Thus virtue has a contrary, namely, vice, both of which are relatives. . . . It also appears that relatives can admit of variation of degrees. . . .' See also W. Jaeger (see note 16), pp. 41–2. Jaeger insists that in the *Phaedo* Plato infers the non-identity of soul and attunement (or harmony) from the impossibility of applying one and the same logical principle to both conceptions. Plato maintains that a 'more or less' or 'variation of degree' can take place only in the 'indeterminate,' but never in anything absolutely determined. The proposition, advanced in the *Phaedo*, that a substance does not admit a 'more or less,' is related (in the *Eudemus*) to the prior proposition on which the first proposition depends, namely, to the insistence that a substance admits of no contraries or opposites. See W. Jaeger, *loc. cit.*

45 See Plato, *Phaedo* 93BD:

I mean to say that harmony admits of degrees, and is more of a harmony, and more completely a harmony, when more truly and fully harmonized, to any extent which is possible; and less of a harmony, and less completely a harmony, when less truly and fully harmonized. . . . But does the soul itself admit of degrees, or is one soul in the very least degree more or less, or more or less completely, a soul than another? Most certainly not. Yet surely, of two souls one is said to have intelligence and virtue, and to be good, and the other to have folly and vice, and to be an evil soul. . . . But what will those who maintain that the soul is a harmony say of this presence of virtue and vice in the soul? Will they insist that there is another harmony, and another discord, and that the virtuous soul is perfectly attuned, and herself being a harmony has another harmony within her, and that the vicious soul is non-attuned and has no harmony within her? . . . And we have already admitted that no soul is more a soul than another. For this is equivalent to admitting that harmony is more or less harmony, or more or less completely a harmony. . . .

46 Philoponus (see note 3), p. 144, lines 30-7.
47 See, for instance, Plato, *Republic* 591B; Plato, *Philebus* 25D ff.; Plato, *Laws* 631C; *et passim*.
48 See, for instance, Plato, *Republic* 444A ff.; 609A ff.; Plato, *Sophist* 228A ff.; Plato, *Statesman* 296D; Plato, *Laws* 906D; 653A ff. See also W. Jaeger (note 16), p. 43. Jaeger maintains that Plato borrowed from contemporary medicine the definitions of disease, weakness and ugliness as a kind of disharmony or lack of symmetry. By analogy, Plato's ethics, especially his notions of a 'therapy of the soul,' are also modeled on contemporary medicine, for which he had much admiration. Plato's doctrine of virtues and vices is in fact a doctrine of the health or illness of the soul. It has as its underlying principle the concept of 'measure,' harmony or symmetry. But if harmony is the principle of bodily virtues, the soul cannot itself be the harmony of the body. In *Philebus* 55D ff., Plato maintains that the greatest or purest 'exactitude,' the 'most exact measure,' which also includes the 'perfect harmony,' constitutes the highest value. Similar notions are also to be found in the Platonic *Statesman*. See also note 59.
49 W. Jaeger, *op. cit.*, p. 44.
50 See notes 34 and 41, and the corresponding text. The argument is as follows: if the soul is a substance, then there cannot be any changes or variations of degree in the soul. But if the soul is attunement, then there can be changes or variations of degree in the soul (in the attunement). Conversely, since there are no, and cannot be any, changes or variations of degree in the soul, the latter is a substance.
51 See note 34.
52 We need not point out here that this Platonism in the early works of Aristotle has been demonstrated and emphasized not only by W. Jaeger, but also by a number of scholars preceding Jaeger. See A.-H. Chroust, 'The lost works of Aristotle in pre-Jaegerian scholarship,' *Classica et Mediaevalia*, vol. 25, fasc. 1-2 (1964-5), pp. 67-92. In Jaeger's justly famed

'theory of evolution,' the *Eudemus* constitutes a vital link in Aristotle's gradual progression from Platonism to Aristotelianism. The thesis of Jaeger, however, was emphatically though not altogether convincingly rejected by I. Düring and others, who disclaim that Aristotle was ever a Platonist.

53 This has been denied by Jaeger. See W. Jaeger, *op. cit.*, pp. 39 ff.

54 Philoponus (see note 3), p. 144, lines 25-30.

55 See E. Berti, *La Filosofia del Primo Aristotele* (Padua, 1962), p. 429.

56 Aristotle, *De Anima* 412 a 7-21.

57 See Simplicius (note 59).

58 See also W. Jaeger, *op. cit.*, p. 45.

59 Simplicius, *Comment. in Arist. De Anima*, CIAG, vol. 11 (ed. M. Hayduck, Berlin, 1882), p. 221, lines 20-33 (frag. 46, Rose; frag. 8, Walzer; frag. 8, Ross). In the *Philebus* 56A ff., Plato assigns to the 'most exact measure' (the 'highest Good') the first and uppermost place in the hierarchy of measures or values, the second place to the measurable, and third place to reason (intellect) capable of apprehending measure. This 'hierarchy of measuration,' which is determined by the purity as well as by the exactness of the measure, constitutes for Plato a progressive truth-criterion. See also note 48.

60 Aristotle, *De Anima* 429 a 10-29.

61 *Ibid.*, 429 a 13-17.

62 *Ibid.*, 429 a 17-29.

63 See also W. Jaeger, *op. cit.*, pp. 45-6.

64 See also E. Berti (note 55), pp. 432-4. As to Aristotle's notion of the 'intuitive' or 'mystic' vision of the 'primary, simple and immaterial object gaining true contact with the pure truth,' see Plutarch, *De Iside et Osiride 48* (*Moralia* 382DE), a passage which some scholars (J. Croissant, E. Bignone, O. Gigon, W. D. Ross and others) consider a fragment of the *Eudemus*. See frag. 10, Ross. Of no particular interest are frags 11 and 12, Ross. Frag. 11 contains a passage from Al-Kindi, *Cod. Taimuriyya, Falsafa 55*, which relates the story of a Greek king, 'whose soul, being caught up in ecstasy, for many days remained neither dead nor alive.' When the king regained full consciousness, he related what he had seen in 'the other world,' namely, 'souls, forms and angels.' He also began to prophesy future events. 'Aristotle asserts that the explanation for all this was that his soul had acquired this knowledge because it had been near the living body and had in a certain way been separated from it, and so had seen what it had seen. How much greater marvels of the upper world of the kingdom would it have seen, then, if it had really left its body completely.' See also J. H. Waszing, 'Traces of Aristotle's lost dialogues in Tertullian,' *Vigiliae Christianae*, vol. I (1947), pp. 137-49. Frag. 11, Ross, has also been credited to Aristotle's lost dialogue *On Philosophy* because of its affinity to Sextus Empiricus, *Adversus Mathematicos* IX. 20-3 (*Adversus Physicos* I. 20-3; frag. 10, Rose; frag. 12a, Walzer; frag. 12a, Ross; frag. 14, Untersteiner).

65 W. Jaeger, *op. cit.*, pp. 45–6. Jaeger's views were accepted, at least in part, by G. Soleri, *L'Immortalità dell'Anima in Aristotele* (Turin, 1952), p. 55; F. Nuyens, *L'Évolution de la Psychologie d'Aristote* (Louvain, 1948), p. 85; P. Merlan, *From Platonism to Neoplatonism* (The Hague, 1953), pp. 30 ff.

66 It may be argued here that the *Eudemus* is posterior to the Aristotelian *On (the) Ideas* and the *On the Good*, and that already in these two dialogues, which are usually dated between 357 and 355 (see Chapter I), Aristotle did take issue with Plato's Separate Ideas. But then, again, the very fact that the *Eudemus* is primarily a *consolatio mortis* might explain (and justify) why Aristotle should revert to a notion which, according to the *On (the) Ideas* and *On the Good*, he apparently had abandoned some years previously. The notion that the soul is an imperishable Idea is for any *consolatio mortis* an eminently satisfactory thought.

67 This is one of the early parts of the *Metaphysics*, almost contemporary with the Aristotelian *On Philosophy*.

68 R. A. Gauthier, *Aristote: L'Éthique à Nicomaque* (Louvain-Paris, 1970), vol. I, pp. 12–13.

69 The doctrine that 'only like can grasp like,' can already be found in Empedocles, frag. 31 B 109 (Diels-Kranz). See C. W. Müller, *Gleiches zu Gleichem* (Klassisch-Philologische Studien, Wiesbaden, 1965), pp. 3 ff.

70 See Simplicius (note 59).

71 Also distinctly Aristotelian is the notion that the soul recollects what it has experienced while incarcerated in the body. Plato would have rejected such a concept of the *anamnesis*.

72 The surviving fragments of the *Eudemus* do not necessarily indicate the influence of the philosophic standards or philosophic psychology advocated in Book IX of Plato's *Republic* or in the Platonic *Philebus*, although such an influence may actually have existed.

73 See here D. A. Rees, 'Theories of the soul in the early Aristotle,' *Aristotle and Plato in the Mid-Fourth Century* (Göteborg, 1960), pp. 191 ff.

74 See A.-H. Chroust (see note 1), pp. 17–30, and Chapter IV.

## CHAPTER VI   ARISTOTLE'S *On Justice*

\* With some modifications, this chapter was first published in *Modern Schoolman*, vol. 43, no. 3 (1966), pp. 249–63.

1 DL V. 22 (no. 1); *VH* 10 (no. 1); Ptolemy (-el-Garib), no. 3. See also Cicero, *De Republica* III. 8. 12, who likewise relates that the Aristotelian *On Justice* consisted of four books. J. Bernays, *Die Dialoge des Aristoteles in ihrem Verhältnis zu seinen übrigen Werken* (Berlin, 1863), pp. 131–2, maintained that the early dialogues or compositions of Aristotle were listed in the ancient 'catalogues' according to their length, starting with the longest, the *On Justice*.

2 Demetrius, *De Elocutione* 28 (frag. 82, Rose; frag. 1, Ross), should make it abundantly clear that the *On Justice* was a dialogue.

3 See W. Jaeger, *Aristotle: Fundamentals of the History of his Development* (Oxford, 1948), pp. 259 ff.

4 J. Bernays (see note 1), p. 49. Relying on the testimony of Plutarch, *Adversus Coloten* 14 (*Moralia* 1115BC), and Proclus (in Philoponus, *De Aeternitate Mundi* II. 2, p. 31, line 17, ed. H. Rabe), Bernays insisted that from the very beginning Aristotle was strongly opposed to Plato's fundamental philosophic doctrines. Bernays, indeed, never so much as admitted that there existed a 'Platonic period' in Aristotle's intellectual development. He did concede, however, that for some unknown reasons, Aristotle occasionally makes superficial and meaningless use of Platonic dialectics and Platonic philosophy in general. See J. Bernays, *op. cit.*, pp. 63 ff. and 95 ff. For a discussion of some of the earlier views concerning the lost works of Aristotle, see A.-H. Chroust, 'The lost works of Aristotle in pre-Jaegerian scholarship,' *Classica et Mediaevalia*, vol. 25, fasc. 1–2 (1965–6), pp. 67–92, especially, pp. 82–3.

5 V. Rose, *Aristotelis Qui Ferebantur Librorum Fragmenta* (Leipzig, 1886), pp. 86–7. See also note 2.

6 Frag. 1, Ross. J. Bernays, *op. cit.*, p. 49, believed he had detected here not only a reference to the ill-fated Sicilian expedition (415–13 B.C.), which ultimately led to the defeat and downfall of Athens in the Peloponnesian War and the subsequent perversion of the Athenian constitution, but also a vitriolic attack upon the internal political events in Athens after the death of Pericles (in 429 B.C.)—events which Aristotle probably considered violative of his concept of 'political justice.' See also Aristotle, *Constitution of Athens* XXVIII. 1–34 and XLI. 2.

7 Plutarch, *De Repugnantiis Stoicis* 15 (*Moralia* 1040E); V. Rose (see note 5), pp. 88–9. See also frag. 4, Ross; Cicero, *Hortensius*, frag. 81, Müller; St. Augustine, *Contra Julianum Pelagium* IV. 14. 72 (PL vol. XLIV, p. 774).

8 J. Bernays, *op. cit.*, pp. 49–50.

9 Vol. II, p. 27, line 13 (ed. C. Meiser, Leipzig, 1880). Boethius uses Porphyry's *Commentary* to Aristotle's Περὶ Ἑρμηνείας. V. Rose (see note 5), p. 89. See also frag. 5, Ross.

10 J. Bernays, *op. cit.*, p. 50.

11 Lactantius, *Institutiones Divinae* V. 15 (frag. 85, Rose; frag. 3, Ross); Lactantius, *Epitome Divinarum Institutionum ad Pentadium Fratrem* 55 (frag. 85, Rose; frag. 3, Ross). The evidence does not seem to support Bernays' assumption. See also Cicero, *De Republica* III. 6. 9.

12 J. Bernays, *op. cit.*, pp. 50–1. In this, Bernays seems to be in error. For Aristotle might refer here to the *On the Good, On (the) Ideas* or to the *On Philosophy*, rather than to the *On Justice*. Bernays also advanced the general, and unusual, thesis that already in his earliest writings, that is, during his close association with Plato and with the Platonic Academy, Aristotle roundly rejected certain vital aspects of Plato's philosophy. See note 4.

13 V. Rose, *Aristoteles Pseudepigraphus* (Leipzig, 1863), p. 26. Rose originally maintained that, perhaps with the possible exception of the *Problemata*,

*The Collection of the 158 Constitutions* and certain parts of the *Politics, Poetics* and of the *Metaphysics*, nothing of the authentic Aristotelian writings has ever been lost. He also insisted that the Alexandrian librarians, as well as other Hellenistic scholars, arbitrarily but erroneously attributed so-called 'exoteric works' to Aristotle. Moreover, Rose rather arbitrarily declared the following works to be spurious: the *Categories*, the *De Interpretatione*, the *Rhetoric*, Books K, Λ and M of the *Metaphysics*, Book H of the *Physics*, and all the works dealing with historical subjects, constitutional or political matters or archivist topics. *Ibid.*, pp. 4-7. Rose, who adamantly insisted that Aristotle never was a true disciple of Plato (*ibid.*, p. 3) and hence never a Platonist, used the undeniable Platonism of Aristotle's earliest dialogues to prove their apocryphal nature.

14 V. Rose, *op. cit.*, p. 89. Rose believed that the reference to 'the loss of political freedom' in Demetrius, *De Elocutione* 28 (frag. 82, Rose; frag. 1 Ross), relates to the political events after the Lamian War (322 B.C.), rather than to the Sicilian Expedition (415-13 B.C.), as J. Bernays had suggested.

15 Some of these fragments are to be found in W. D. Ross, *The Works of Aristotle*, vol. XII: *Select Fragments* (Oxford, 1952), pp. 100-2 (frags 1-6). Athenaeus, *Epitome* I. 68 (6D), frag. 83, Rose, for instance, has also been assigned to the Περὶ Ἡδονῆς of Aristotle (Ross). See here Cicero, *Tusculanae Disputationes* V. 35. 101 (frag. 90, Rose); Strabo XIV, 5. 9 (frag. 90, Rose); Cicero, *De Finibus* II. 32. 106 (frag. 90, Rose). Ross and Walzer assign the last three fragments to the *Protrepticus*.

16 E. Heitz, *Aristotelis Fragmenta: Aristotelis Opera Omnia Graece et Latine* (ed. Firmin, Didot, *et al.*), vol. IV (Paris, 1869). Heitz considered it unlikely that every composition which ancient tradition has ascribed to Aristotle could in truth be credited to the Stagirite. He did admit, however, that since these ancient authors claimed such a prodigious *oeuvre* for Aristotle, many of the early or 'exoteric' compositions must be authentic. For detail, see A.-H. Chroust (see note 4), pp. 83-4.

17 E. Heitz, *Die verlorenen Schriften des Aristoteles* (Leipzig, 1865), pp. 167-8. It will be observed that Heitz argued against V. Rose that the 'exoteric' writings of Aristotle were a '*sui generis* type of authentic works'; that they were composed prior to the preserved 'esoteric' works or doctrinal treatises; and that the *On Justice*, as did the other 'exoteric' works, propagated philosophic doctrines very much like those advocated by Plato, the teacher of Aristotle. Finally, Heitz also believed that Aristotle 'moved away' from Plato and Platonic philosophy only gradually, and that he fully disassociated himself from Plato only in his later 'esoteric' or doctrinal treatises. In this Heitz anticipated to some extent certain aspects of the 'evolutionary thesis' advocated by W. Jaeger in 1923.

18 See also Proclus, *In Platonis Alcibiadem Comment.*, p. 77, lines 7 ff. (ed. L. G. Westerink), and p. 73, line 14; p. 296, line 21.

19 See note 11; frag. 85, Rose; frag. 3, Ross.

20 E. Heitz (see note 17), pp. 169–73. See also note 28.

21 E. Heitz (see note 20).

22 E. Heitz, *op. cit.*, p. 171.

23 Pp. 550–1 (ed. O. Hense).

24 Pp. 548–9 (ed. O. Hense).

25 E. Heitz (see note 17), pp. 171–2. V. Rose first assigned these two fragments to the pseudo-Aristotelian Περὶ Παϑῶν (frags. 96 and 97 of the edition of 1870). In his *Aristotelis Qui Ferebantur Librorum Fragmenta* of 1886, he credits them to the (apocryphal?) correspondence of Aristotle with Alexander of Macedonia (frags. 660 and 661).

26 W. Jaeger (see note 3), p. 30, note 1.

27 *Ibid.* Jaeger also observed that this fact throws some light on the history of the origin of the subtitles to the Platonic dialogues.

28 Frag. 85, Rose; frag. 3, Ross. See also Lactantius, *Institutiones Divinae* V. 17. 4 ff.; Lactantius, *Epitome Institutionum Divinarum ad Pentadium Fratrem* 55; J. Bernays (see note 4), p. 152; notes 11, 19 and 20. In *Politics* 1253 a 15, Aristotle points out that man is the only animal which has a sense of justice. See also Cicero, *De Republica* III. 6. 9.

29 E. Bignone. *L'Aristotele Perduto e la Formazione Filosofica di Epicuro*, vol. I (Florence, 1936), p. 223.

30 *Ibid.* It should be noted, however, that this similarity had already been pointed out by R. Hirzel, *Der Dialog*, vol. I (Leipzig, 1895), p. 287. Gyges is also mentioned in Aristotle, *Rhetoric* 1418 b 31.

31 Frag. 84, Rose (frag. 2, Ross), which cites Suetonius, Περὶ Βλασφημιῶν p. 416 (ed. Miller); Gregory of Corinth, *Ad Hermogenem* 19; Suda, 'article' *Eurybatus.*

32 Plato, *Republic* 359C ff. See also *ibid.*, 612B, where Plato maintains: 'Let a man do what is just, irrespective of whether or not he possesses the ring of Gyges. . . .'

33 It is interesting to observe that Plato uses here a fantastic legend, while Aristotle mentions what was probably an actual incident. This 'realistic' attitude of Aristotle is in keeping with what he had to say in *Poetics* 1451 b 15 ff.: 'In tragedy, however, they still adhere to historic names, and this for the following reason: what convinces is the possible . . . and that which has actually happened is manifestly possible, else it would not have happened.' See also P. Moraux (note 35), p. 59.

34 E. Bignone (see note 29), vol. II, pp. 272–83. Bignone, whose view found the support of some scholars, insisted that this is also reflected in Epicurus, *Sovereign Maxims*, no. 32 (DL X. 150): 'Those animals which are incapable of making covenants with one another, to the end that they may not injure one another or be injured by the other [this is Epicurus' definition of law, *note by the present author*] are without either justice or injustice.' The implication is that since all law is based upon mutual agreement among rational creatures (see A.-H. Chroust, 'The philosophy of law of the Epicureans,' *Thomist*, vol. 16, no. 1, 1953, pp. 82–117, and vol. 16, no. 2,

pp. 217–67, especially, pp. 228 ff.), animals have friendship or, perhaps, 'natural law,' but never 'positive law' and, hence, have no 'justice' in the Epicurean sense of the term. For, according to Epicurus, all justice is based on positive law. Bignone saw in Epicurus' statement an attack upon Aristotle, who in his *On Justice* (Bignone surmised) had insisted that justice is not based on mutual agreement, but constitutes something more absolute.

35 P. Moraux, *A la Recherche de l'Aristote Perdu: Le Dialogue 'Sur la Justice'* (Aristote: Traductions et Études, Collection Publiée par l'Institut Supérieur de la Philosophie de l'Université de Louvain, Louvain-Paris, 1957). See also P. Moraux, 'From the *Protrepticus* to the dialogue *On Justice*,' *Aristotle and Plato in the Mid-Fourth Century* (ed. I. Düring and G. E. L. Owen, Göteborg, 1960), pp. 113–32; R. Cadiou, 'Aristote et la notion de justice,' *Revue des Études Grecques*, vol. 73 (1960), pp. 224–29; E. Berti, *La Filosofia del Primo Aristotele* (Università di Padova, Pubblicazioni della Facoltà di Lettere e Filosofia, vol. 38, Padua, 1962), pp. 437–46.

36 See note 17.

37 J. Bernays (see note 1), *passim*. It will be noted that in his *Index Aristotelicus* (Berlin, 1870), H. Bonitz, on the whole, concurs with Bernays.

38 See note 26.

39 P. Moraux (note 35), pp. 16 ff.; 53 ff.; 60 ff.; *et passim*. For critical reviews of Moraux's theses and suggestions, see G. Verbeke, 'Bulletin de littérature aristotélicienne,' *Revue Philosophique de Louvain*, vol. 56 (1958), pp. 608–14; G. R. Morrow, in *Gnomon*, vol. 30 (1958), pp. 441–3; O. Kern, in *Scholastik*, vol. 35 (1960), pp. 117–18; and R. Weil, in *Revue Philosophique de la France et de l'Étranger*, vol. 87 (1962), pp. 401–12. One of the main objections to Moraux's thesis was his insistence that whenever in the preserved treatises Aristotle refers back to what he had previously said about ethical or political δικαιοσύνη in his 'exoteric' writings, he has in mind the *On Justice*. Moraux's critics maintain that in so doing, Aristotle might very well allude also to such early compositions as the *Protrepticus*, the *Statesman* (*Politicus*), the *On Kingship*, the *On Education*, the *On Noble Birth*, the *To Alexander or A Plea for Colonization*, the *On the Good*, the *Of Household Management*, etc. (see DL V. 22), all of which are said to have discussed ethical and political topics. A. Jannone, 'I logoi essoterici di Aristotele,' *Atti dell' Istituto Veneto di Scienze, Lettere ed Arti*, Classe di Scienze Morali e Lettere, vol. 113 (1954–5), pp. 249–79, however, flatly denies the possibility of identifying the 'exoteric works' with the 'lost works' of Aristotle. See also A. Jannone, 'Les oeuvres de jeunesse d'Aristote et les Λόγοι 'Εξωτερικοί,' *Rivista di Cultura Classica e Medioevale*, vol. I (1959), pp. 197–207; W. Wieland, 'Aristoteles als Rhetoriker und die exoterischen Schriften,' *Hermes*, vol. 86 (1958), pp. 326–46. Should Jannone's thesis prove correct, something which is unlikely to happen, then Moraux's whole theory would collapse.

40 See also W. Jaeger, *op. cit.*, p. 265, note 2; Moraux, *op. cit.*, pp. 13 ff.

Moraux points out that Aristotle refers back to his 'exoteric works' at times in order to enlarge upon the topic under discussion, at other times in order to avoid repetition. R. Stark, *Aristotelesstudien: Philologische Untersuchungen zur Entwicklung der aristotelischen Ethik* (Zetemata: Monographien zur Klassischen Altertumswissenschaft, no. VIII, Munich, 1954), p. 95, insists, however, that Aristotle refers to his earlier compositions (the 'exoteric' works) in order to correct his previous views.

41 P. Moraux, *op. cit.*, pp. 55 ff.

42 *Ibid.*, pp. 65 ff.

43 Stobaeus, *Florilegium* IV. 22. 101 and IV. 28. 16–18. See also F. Wilhelm, 'Die Oiconomica der Pythagoreer Bryson, Kallikratidas, Periktione, Phintys,' *Rheinisches Museum*, vol. 70 (1915), pp. 167–85.

44 Stobaeus, *Florilegium* IV. 1. 137.

45 Stobaeus, *Florilegium* III. 9. 51. See here also E. Bignone (note 29), vol. II, pp. 530–1.

46 Provided the *First Alcibiades* is a spurious work (as most scholars will concede), composed about the year 340 B.C.

47 P. Moraux, *op. cit.*, pp. 109 ff.

48 *Ibid.*, pp. 141 ff.

49 *Ibid.*, pp. 151 ff.

50 G. Verbeke, 'Bulletin de littérature aristotélicienne,' *Revue Philosophique de Louvain*, vol. 56 (1958), pp. 608–14. See also note 39.

51 P. Moraux, 'From the *Protrepticus* to the dialogue *On Justice*,' *Aristotle and Plato in the Mid-Fourth Century* (Göteborg, 1960), pp. 112–123. Moraux's attempt to differentiate between the philosophic teachings of the *On Justice* and those of the *Protrepticus*, in the opinion of some scholars, was not altogether successful. See also P. Moraux (see note 35), pp. 124 ff.

52 I. Düring, *Aristotle's Protrepticus: An Attempt at Reconstruction*, Studia Graeca et Latina Gothoburgensia, vol. XII (Göteborg, 1961), pp. 287–8.

53 A.-H. Chroust, 'The probable dates of some of Aristotle's lost works,' *Rivista Critica di Storia della Filosofia*, vol. 22, fasc. 1 (1967), pp. 3–23, especially pp. 11–12 and Chapter I.

54 See also Plato, *Republic* 341D ff.

55 See Aristotle, *Politics* 1261 a 37 ff.

56 See here *Republic* 406C ff., where Plato discusses the 'political implications' of medicine and the right practice of medicine.

57 For these references to the 'exoteric works,' see, in general, H. Bonitz, *Index Aristotelicus* 104 b 44–105 a 48. It will be noted that this approach is similar to that suggested by P. Moraux. See note 35.

58 Some scholars insist that although the *Magna Moralia* in its preserved form definitely betrays post-Aristotelian influences and post-Aristotelian editorial work, its original version or 'nucleus' may well date back to the early period of Aristotle's literary activities, that is, to about 355–50 B.C. See, for instance, I. Düring (note 52), p. 287.

59 The bracketed statements and sentences in the following sections are of

highly doubtful authenticity, even more doubtful than the remaining statements.

60 See, in this connection, H. Bonitz, *Index Aristotelicus* (2nd ed., 1955), 104 b 44–105 a 48 and 433 b 30–47.

61 See the fragments collected by V. Rose and W. D. Ross.

62 See, in general, Aristotle, *Politics* 1278 b 30 ff. Plato, *Statesman* 258E–259C, it will be noted, discusses whether the terms 'statesman,' 'king,' 'master' and 'head of the household' are one and the same, or whether there is a special political or social theory corresponding to each of these terms. It is possible that in the *On Justice* Aristotle also criticized Plato's position, although he is probably under the influence of Plato's views.

63 Aristotle, *Politics* 1252 a 7–18 and 1278 b 37 ff.; Aristotle, *Nicomachean Ethics* 1160 b 22 ff.

64 Aristotle, *Politics* 1279 a 16 ff. and 1332 b 27 ff.

65 *Ibid.*, 1279 a 5 ff.

66 It is possible that Carneades' attacks upon Plato's and Aristotle's concepts of justice (frag. 85, Rose; frag. 3, Ross; Lactantius (see note 11); Cicero, *De Republica* III. 6. 9) are primarily directed against Plato's and Aristotle's attempts to overemphasize political justice. Carneades of Cyrene (214/12–129/28 B.C.), a prominent member of the (sceptic) Middle Academy and a tireless critic of Chrysippus the Stoic (see DL IV. 2; Sextus Empiricus, *Adversus Mathematicos* VII. 159), apparently had strong reservations concerning the Greek political systems in general and political methods or practices in particular. See Lactantius, *Institutiones Divinae* V. 14 ff. (frag. 85, Rose; frag. 3, Ross). He also insisted that the current philosophic views about political justice, which is always abstract or Utopian justice, were detrimental to the individual and to individuality, that is, to man's freedom of acting in accordance with his personal convictions as to what constitutes right and just action—an intolerable situation for a sceptic such as Carneades. As a matter of fact, Carneades is said to have enumerated all that had been said in favor of (political) justice, including Plato's and Aristotle's statements, and that he did so for the express purpose of disproving them. Perhaps in the *On Justice* Aristotle had already proclaimed that certain people are by nature destined to be slaves, and certain people are meant to be masters—an insufferable heresy in the eyes of a skeptic such as Carneades. Political justice, as probably expounded by Aristotle, then, would actually amount to an enforcement of this sort of 'natural predestination.' See here also St. Augustine, *De Civitate Dei* XIV. 23 and XIX. 21; Cicero, *De Republica* III. 24. 36 and III. 25. 37.

67 Aristotle, *Politics* 1279 a 5–21.

68 Aristotle, *Nicomachean Ethics* 1134 a 19–1135 a 5; Aristotle, *Magna Moralia* 1194 b 30 ff. This might possibly be Aristotle's reply to the arguments advanced by some sophists that, being based on convention, all laws change with time and place. Hence, justice founded solely on laws is

bound to be relative (and, in all probability, utilitarian). See here also Cicero, *De Republica* III. 8. 13; and note 33.

69 *Politics* 1278 b 30 ff. and 1279 a 19–21.

70 *Ibid.*, 1279 a 16–21; 1295 a 16–17; 1287 b 37–41; *Nicomachean Ethics* 1160 b 30–37 and 1161 a 30–1161 b 10.

71 *Politics* 1324 a 10–12 and 1324 a 35–1324 b 41.

72 *Nicomachean Ethics* 1160 b 24–27; Aristotle, *Eudemian Ethics* 1241 b 27–40; *Politics* 1253 b 3–12; 1259 a 37 ff.; 1259 b 10–17; 1278 b 30 ff.

73 *Politics* 1279 a 17 ff.; *Eudemian Ethics* 1241 b 27–40.

74 *Politics* 1279 a 8–10; *Nicomachean Ethics* 1134 a 23–34; *Eudemian Ethics* 1241 b 32–40 and 1242 a 11–13.

75 *Politics* 1279 a 7 ff.; *Nicomachean Ethics* 1130 b 30–1131 b 23; 1134 b 1–4; 1158 b 3. Aristotle might approach here the problem of 'distributive justice.'

76 *Politics* 1279 a 7 ff.; *Nicomachean Ethics* 1161 a 30 ff.

77 Cicero, *De Republica* III 8. 12 ff., especially III. 8. 18. See also Aristotle *Nicomachean Ethics* 1129 a 26 ff. E. Heitz (see note 17), pp. 169–74, pointed out that Carneades' refutation of Aristotle's views on justice were prompted by the Stagirite's insistence upon the altruistic nature of justice. See note 79 and the corresponding text, and Lactantius, *Institutiones Divinae* V. 14–15 (frag. 85, Rose; frag. 3, Ross). See also note 66.

78 *Politics* 1278 b 30 ff.; *Nicomachean Ethics* 1129 b 11 ff.; 1134 a 30 ff.; 1134 a 14–25.

79 Cicero, *De Republica* (Lactantius) III. 7. 10–11. See also Aristotle, *Nicomachean Ethics* 1129 b 14 ff. In *Politics* 1278 b 38, Aristotle states that the government of a household is 'exercised . . . for the good of the governed or for the good of both parties, but essentially for the good of the governed. . . .' In a certain sense, this statement reminds us of Bentham's social-utilitarian maxim of 'the greatest happiness for the greatest number.' It is not suggested here, however, that Bentham derived his maxim from Aristotle.

80 *Nicomachean Ethics* 1159 b 25–31 and 1155 a 22–28; *Eudemian Ethics* 1234 b 18 ff.; 1238 b 19–21; 1241 b 12–17; 1241 b 32–34; 1242 a 40 ff.

81 *Nicomachean Ethics* 1159 a 12 ff. and 1166 a 2–29; *Eudemian Ethics* 1234 b 18 ff. See also *Nicomachean Ethics* 1155 b 17 ff.; *Magna Moralia* 1209 a 3 ff. and 1210 b 34 ff.; *Eudemian Ethics* 1236 a 31 ff.; 1238 b 15 ff.; 1239 a 1; 1240 a 21–30; 1242 b 2 ff.

82 *Nicomachean Ethics* 1158 b 11 ff. and 1161 a 10 ff.; *Eudemian Ethics* 1238 b 15–30; 1241 b 12–24; 1242 a 35–40; 1242 b 21–31.

83 *Nicomachean Ethics* 1161 a 25–1161 b 16; *Eudemian Ethics* 1241 b 13–14; 1242 a 35 ff.; 1242 b 21–31. See also *Nicomachean Ethics* 1155 a 32 ff.; *Magna Moralia* 1208 b 7–20 and 1210 a 5–23; *Eudemian Ethics* 1235 a 4–31.

84 *Eudemian Ethics* 1242 a 40 ff. See also *Nicomachean Ethics* 1155 a 22–28 and 1159 b 25 ff.; *Magna Moralia* 1211 a 6–15; *Eudemian Ethics* 1234 b 31 ff.

85 *Nicomachean Ethics* 1166 a 10 ff.; *Magna Moralia* 1210 b 32 ff.; 1211 a 16 ff.;

1212 a 28 ff.; *Eudemian Ethics* 1240 a 8 ff. See also *Nicomachean Ethics* 1168 a 35 ff., and *Eudemian Ethics* 1240 a 9-13, where Aristotle refers to the λόγοι.

86 *Eudemian Ethics* 1240 a 8-1240 b 39; *Magna Moralia* 1210 a 32-1211 a 6 and 1212 a 28-1212 b 23; *Nicomachean Ethics* 1169 a 6 ff.

87 See notes 85 and 86.

88 *Eudemian Ethics* 1240 a 13-21 and 1240 b 11-30; *Nicomachean Ethics* 1166 a 29 ff.; *Magna Moralia* 1211 a 17 ff.

89 *Nicomachean Ethics* 1166 a 1 ff.; *Eudemian Ethics* 1240 a 21-23.

90 *Eudemian Ethics* 1240 a 16 ff.; *Nicomachean Ethics* 1102 a 23 ff.

91 See, in general, *Nicomachean Ethics* 1102 a 23 ff.; 1098 a 3-5; 1139 a 1-5; 1139 a 7-17; 1140 b 25-28; *Eudemian Ethics* 1219 b 27-31 and 1220 a 8 ff.; 1221 b 27-32; 1224 b 29-31; *Magna Moralia* 1185 b 3-12 and 1196 b 12-33; *Politics* 1254 b 2-9; 1260 a 4-7; 1277 a 5-7; 1327 b 23-38; 1333 a 16-24; 1334 b 17-22. The division of the soul into parts, which is an essential part of Plato's philosophy, is rejected in Aristotle's *De Anima* 432 a 15 ff.

92 *Nicomachean Ethics* 1132 b 2 ff. and 1138 b 5-13; *Politics* 1254 b 2-9 and 1254 a 28 ff.

93 *Politics* 1254 a 28 ff.

94 *Eudemian Ethics* 1223 a 36 ff. and 1240 a 16 ff.

95 *Ibid.*, 1240 a 13-21; *Nicomachean Ethics* 1166 a 33 ff. and 1168 a 28 ff.; *Magna Moralia* 1211 a 25-36.

96 *Nicomachean Ethics* 1102 b 13-1103 a 10.

97 *Ibid.*

98 Cicero, *De Republica* (Lactantius) III. 7. 11. See Plutarch, *De Repugnantiis Stoicis* 15 (*Moralia* 1040E—frag. 86, Rose; frag. 4, Ross). See also *Nicomachean Ethics* 1129 b 19 ff.; 1130 a 9-14; 1130 b 18-20.

99 See note 9.

100 Aristotle, *Nicomachean Ethics* 1140 a 2-3.

101 *Ibid.*, 1140 a 2-3; 1139 a 5-17; 1140 b 25-28; *Magna Moralia* 1196 b 12-33; *Politics* 1333 a 24-27.

102 This seems to follow from Plutarch, *De Virtute Morali* 5 (*Moralia* 443D ff.). See also Stobaeus, *Florilegium* II. 7. 13. It will be noted that in the early works of Aristotle, in the *Protrepticus* for instance, the term φρόνησις signifies 'theoretic reason' (Platonic), while in the later doctrinal treatises it has definitely 'practical' connotations.

103 Aristotle, *Politics* 1254 a 34 ff.; 1255 b 9-15; 1277 a 5-10; *Eudemian Ethics* 1242 a 28 ff.; *Nicomachean Ethics* 1161 a 10 ff.

104 *Politics* 1254 a 28 ff.; *Eudemian Ethics* 1241 b 27 ff.

105 *Nicomachean Ethics* 1102 b 13 ff.; 1138 b 4-14; 1134 b 9; *Eudemian Ethics* 1220 a 10-15.

106 *Eudemian Ethics* 1240 a 15 ff. See also note 11.

107 *Nicomachean Ethics* 1168 b 28 ff. See also note 85.

108 *Ibid.*, 1134 b 13; 1136 b 1; 1136 b 15-25; 1138 a 4-28; 1138 b 5-13; 1169 a 11 ff.

109 See note 108.

110 See note 25.

111 See note 23.

112 *Nicomachean Ethics* 1138 b 5–13.

113 *Politics* 1295 a 36 ff. See also *Nicomachean Ethics* 1098 a 15 ff.; 1153 b 10–12; 1177 a 12.

114 *Politics* 1280 a 7–22; 1282 b 14–1284 b 34; 1301 b 35–36; 1332 b 27.

115 See Suetonius, Περὶ Βλασφημιῶν (ed. Miller), p. 416 (frag. 84, Rose; frag. 2, Rose—see also notes 29–32); Demetrius, *De Elocutione* 28 (frag. 82, Rose; frag. 1, Ross). See also notes 6, 14, 16 and 17.

116 *Nicomachean Ethics* 1129 b 25–1130 a 13.

117 Lactantius, *Epitome Divinarum Institutionum ad Pentadium Fratrem* 55 (frag. 85, Rose; frag. 3, Ross). See also Aristotle, *Nicomachean Ethics* 1129 b 25 ff., and notes 11, 98 and 116.

118 Plutarch, *De Repugnantiis Stoicis* 15 (*Moralia* 1040E—frag. 86, Rose; frag. 4, Ross). See also note 7.

119 See, in general, A.-H. Chroust, 'A second (and closer) look at Plato's political philosophy,' *Archiv für Rechts- und Sozialphilosophie*, vol. 47, no. 4 (1962), pp. 449–86.

120 See A.-H. Chroust, 'Aristotle's criticism of Plato's "philosopher king,"' *Rheinisches Museum*, vol. 101, no. 1 (1968), pp. 16–22, and Chapter XVII.

121 In contrast to Plato, Aristotle maintains that reasonably just and well-ordered cities can and do exist while having nothing in common with Plato's Utopian political ideal.

122 Plato's well known aversion to 'equality before the law' becomes manifest, for instance, in *Republic* 557A; 558A; 560D ff.; 563A ff.; *et passim*.

123 Plato, *Republic* 351D and 463B ff.

124 See, for instance, Aristotle, *Nicomachean Ethics* 1155 a 22 ff.; *Eudemian Ethics* 1234 b 22 ff. See also notes 80–4.

125 This notion can also be found in Aristotle, *De Anima, passim*; *De Partibus Animalium, passim*.

126 P. Moraux, *op. cit.*, pp. 141 ff., on the other hand, does not readily accept the Platonism of the *On Justice*. See notes 48 and 49 and the corresponding texts.

CHAPTER VII   A BRIEF ACCOUNT OF THE RECONSTRUCTION OF
ARISTOTLE'S *Protrepticus*

* In a much shorter and less detailed form, this chapter was first published in *Classical Philology*, vol. 40, no. 4 (1966), pp. 229–39.

1 *Florilegium* IV. 32. 21 (p. 785, ed. C. Hense). Stobaeus quotes here from Teles. See *Teletis Reliquiae* (2nd ed., C. Hense, Tübingen, 1909), p. 45.

2 *Commentaria in Aristotelis Topicorum Libros*, CIAG, vol. II, part 2 (ed. M. Wallies, Berlin, 1891), p. 149, lines 9–17.

3 *Commentaria in Platonis Alcibiadem Prior.* (ed. G. F. Creuzer, Frankfurt, 1821), p. 144.

4 Elias (*olim* David), *Commentaria in Porphyrii Isagogen et in Aristotelis Categorias*, CIAG, vol. XVIII, part 1 (ed. A. Busse, Berlin, 1900), p. 3, lines 17-23.

5 *Prolegomena et in Porphyrii Isagogen Commentarii*, CIAG, vol. XVIII, part 2 (ed. A. Busse, Berlin, 1904), p. 9, lines 2-12.

6 DL V. 22 (no. 12).

7 *VH* 10 (no. 14). See P. Moraux, *Les Listes Anciennes des Ouvrages d'Aristote* (Louvain, 1951), pp. 195-271.

8 '*Catalogue of Aristotle's Writings*,' nos 1-2. This particular '*Catalogue*' probably goes back to Andronicus of Rhodes. Ptolemy (-el-Garib) states: 'His [*scil.*, Aristotle's] book in which he exhorts to philosophy, in three books. In Greek [it was] entitled Προτρεπτικὸς Φιλοσοφίας.' The fact that Ptolemy (-el-Garib) not only mentions here two titles, namely, the Προτρεπτικὸς and the [Περὶ] Φιλοσοφίας, but also insists that this work consisted of three books, suggests that he confounds or combines the Aristotelian *Protrepticus* (which consisted of one book, see DL V. 22, no. 14; *VH* 10, no. 14) and the Aristotelian *On Philosophy*, which, according to DL V. 22 (no. 3), contained three books, and, according to *VH* 10 (no. 3), four books. We could add to this list also Anonymous, *Scholia in Aristotelis Analytica Priora*, Cod. Paris. 2064, fol. 263a; and, perhaps, Cicero, *De Finibus* V. 4. 11. See also Nonius Marcellus, p. 394, lines 26-8 (ed. Lindsay); Martianus Capella, *De Nuptiis Mercurii et Philologiae* V. 44; *Scriptores Historiae August.* II. 97, lines 20-2 (ed. Hohl).

9 See A.-H. Chroust, 'The miraculous disappearance and recovery of the *Corpus Aristotelicum*,' *Classica et Mediaevalia*, vol. 23, fasc. 1-2 (1962), pp. 50-67.

10 See, for instance, W. G. Rabinowitz, *Aristotle's Protrepticus and the Sources of Its Reconstruction* (University of California Publications in Classical Philology, vol. 16, no. 1, Berkeley, 1957), *passim*; H. Flashar, 'Platon und Aristoteles im *Protreptikos* des Jamblichos,' *Archiv für Geschichte der Philosophie*, vol. 47 (1965), pp. 54-79; and others.

11 J. Bernays, *Die Dialoge des Aristoteles in ihrem Verhältnis zu seinen übrigen Werken* (Berlin, 1863), pp. 116 ff. See, in general, A.-H. Chroust, 'The lost works of Aristotle in pre-Jaegerian scholarship,' *Classica et Mediaevalia*, vol. 25, fasc. 1-2 (1964-5), pp. 67-92, *passim*, especially pp. 82-3.

12 Bernays based his theory on Alexander of Aphrodisias, *Commentaria in Aristotelis Topicorum Libros*, CIAG, vol. II, part 2, p. 149, lines 9 ff.: 'The expression "to philosophize" (or, "to pursue philosophy") implies two distinct things: first, whether or not we ought at all to seek [after philosophic truth]; and, secondly, our dedication to philosophic speculation.' Bernays assumed that this passage, which he attributed to the Aristotelian *Protrepticus*, had been restated in Cicero's *Hortensius*, namely, in frag. 4, Müller (Cicero, *Tuscul. Disput.* III. 3. 6); in frag. 7, Müller (Martianus Capella, *De Nuptiis Mercurii et Philologiae* V. 44); in frag. 8, Müller (*Scriptores Historiae August.*, ed. Hohl, vol. II, p. 97); in frag. 12, Müller (Lactantius,

*Institutiones Divinae* III. 16. 9); and in frag. 50, Müller (St Augustine, *De Trinitate* XIV. 9. 12). See also note 57. Other fragments of the Ciceronian *Hortensius* can be found in Nonius Marcellus (ed. Lindsay), p. 288; p. 521; p. 386 (frag. 23 and frag. 68, Müller); in St Augustine, *Contra Iulianum Pelagium* IV. 15. 78 (frag. 95, Müller); in St Augustine, *De Trinitate* XIV. 9. 26 (frag. 97, Müller); in St Augustine, *Contra Academicos* I. 3. 7 (frag. 101, Müller); in St Augustine, *Soliloquia* I. 17; Boethius, *De Differentiis Topicis* 2; Boethius, *De Consolatione Philosophiae* III. 8. As a literary type, the 'protreptic essay (or dialogue)' is fairly old. This is indicated by Theognis' '*Maxims*' addressed to Cyrnus, Hesiod's *Exhortations* addressed to Perses, and the didactic poem of Empedocles addressed to Pausanias (?). Antisthenes is credited with an *On Justice and Courage: A Hortatory Work* in three books (DL VI. 16), but we do not know whether this latter composition was a dialogue or a discourse. The 'protreptic essay,' which owes an everlasting literary and stylistic debt to Isocrates and his *Cyprian Orations*, came to be the model for the Hellenistic proselytizing sermon and, ultimately, the model for the sermons of the Christian Church. At times it was converted into a dialogue, as in the case of Plato's *Euthydemus* 278E ff. (which is definitely a protreptic passage) and Cicero's *Hortensius*.

13 J. Bernays, *op. cit.*, pp. 119 ff. See also H. Diels, 'Zu Aristoteles' *Protreptikos* und Ciceros *Hortensius*,' *Archiv für Geschichte der Philosophie*, vol. I (1888), pp. 477-97; H. Diels, 'Über die exoterischen Reden des Aristoteles,' *Sitzungsberichte der Berliner Akademie der Wissenschaften*, vol. 19 (Berlin, 1883), pp. 477-94; H. Usener, 'Vergessenes,' *Rheinisches Museum*, vol. 28 (1873), pp. 391-433, especially pp. 392 ff.

14 Stobaeus, *Florilegium* III. 3. 25 (200, Hense—frag. 57, Rose; frag. 3, Walzer; frag. 3, Ross; frags 2-5, Düring; frags 2-5, Chroust).

15 H. Diels (see note 13), pp. 477 ff., saw certain parallels between this papyrus and some fragments from Cicero's *Hortenius*; and I. Düring insisted that this papyrus contains the opening sentences of the original *Protrepticus*. I. Düring, *Aristotle's Protrepticus: An Attempt at Reconstruction*, Studia Graeca et Latina Gothoburgensia, vol. XII (Göteborg, 1961), pp. 176-7.

16 I. Bywater, 'On a lost dialogue of Aristotle,' *Journal of Philology*, vol. 2 (1869), pp. 55-69. See also A.-H. Chroust (see note 11), *passim*, especially p. 85.

17 See pp. 93 ff.

18 See pp. 103 ff.

19 Bywater's theses, it goes without saying, made obsolete Bernays' attempt at identifying the Aristotelian *Protrepticus* by way of the surviving fragments from Cicero's *Hortensius*, especially since the fragments from the *Hortensius* are extremely few, while Iamblichus' *Protrepticus* supplies what appears to be a host of valuable 'fragments.'

20 R. Hirzel, 'Über den *Protreptikos* des Aristoteles,' *Hermes*, vol. X (1876), pp. 61-100. See also A.-H. Chroust (note 11), *passim*, especially p. 85.

21  R. Hirzel pointed out that, since in his *Protrepticus* Iamblichus also quotes from *several* Platonic dialogues, there exists no good reason why we should assume that he would quote from only *one* Aristotelian composition. This argument was taken up later, for instance, by W. Rabinowitz (see notes 55-61 and the corresponding text), by H. Flashar (see note 10) and by other scholars.

22  See notes 11-13. Rose recognized the many 'Platonisms' in the compositions ascribed to the young Aristotle. On the strength of these 'Platonisms,' he simply declared them spurious (see text, pp. 90-1)—an interesting variation on J. Bernays' thesis. It is almost ironical to record that the first modern collection of Aristotelian fragments (by V. Rose) owes its origin to Rose's determined effort to prove these fragments spurious. See V. Rose, *Aristotles Pseudepigraphus* (Leipzig, 1863), *passim*; V. Rose, *De Aristotelis Librorum Ordine et Auctoritate Commentatio* (Berlin, 1854), *passim*. See also A.-H. Chroust (note 11), *passim*, especially pp. 77-80; A.-H. Chroust, 'The Problems of the Aristotelis Librorum Fragmenta,' *Classical Journal*, vol. 62, no. 2 (1966), pp. 71-4.

23  Published in Leipzig in 1886.

24  In frag. 52, Rose also quotes from Iamblichus, *De Communi Mathematica Scientia Liber*, chap. XXVI (p. 79, line 1-p. 81, line 7, ed. N. Festa 1891).

25  P. Hartlich, *De Exhortationum a Graecis Romanisque Scriptarum Historia et Indole* (Leipziger Studien zur klassischen Philologie, vol. XI, part 2, Leipzig, 1889), pp. 209-72, especially pp. 236 ff. See also A.-H. Chroust (note 11), *passim*, especially p. 85.

26  E. Heitz, *Die verlorenen Schriften des Aristoteles* (Leipzig, 1865), pp. 197-8. See also A.-H. Chroust (note 11), pp. 83-4.

27  C. G. Cobet, 'Platonica,' *Mnemosyne*, vol. 2 (1874), pp. 241-83, especially pp. 261 ff.

28  H. Diels (see note 15), pp. 477 ff. Somewhat later W. Gerhäusser advanced the hypothesis that the *Protrepticus* of Posidonius, especially his theory of the origin of civilization—that art imitates nature, and that all cultural advances are due to philosophy and philosophical discoveries—was influenced by Aristotle's *Protrepticus*. W. Gerhäusser, *Der Protreptikos des Poseidonios* (Doctoral thesis of the Univ. of Heidelberg, 1912). In 1920, E. Villa likewise took up the problem of the Aristotelian *Protrepticus* in his 'Il Προτρεπτικὸς di Aristotele,' *Rendiconti dell'Istituto Lombardo*, Classe di Lettere, Scienze e Storiche, vol. 53 (Milan, 1920), pp. 539-49.

29  E. Heitz (see note 26), pp. 166-7.

30  H. Diels (see note 13), pp. 477-97. It is interesting to observe that, like V. Rose, H. Diels would not concede a 'Platonic period' in Aristotle's writings. While Rose declared spurious all Platonizing compositions of Aristotle, Diels admitted that there were such Platonisms in Aristotle's early works and that these works were authentic, but denied these Platonisms any significance. It might be observed that this view of Diels' was

accepted by F. Susemihl, 'Die *Logoi Exoterikoi* bei Aristoteles und Eudemos,' *Jahrbuch für Philologie*, vol. 128 (1884), pp. 265–77, and even for a
short time by W. Jaeger, *Studien zur Entstehungsgeschichte der Metaphysik
des Aristoteles* (Berlin, 1912), pp. 134–7. See also A.-H. Chroust (note 11),
*passim*, especially p. 86.

31 E. Zeller, *Die Philosophie der Griechen in ihrer geschichtlichen Entwicklung*,
vol. II, part 2 (2nd ed., Leipzig, 1861), pp. 47–8 and p. 80. See also A.-H.
Chroust (see note 11), *passim*, especially pp. 80–2.

32 E. Zeller, *Die Philosophie der Griechen*, vol. II, part 2 (3rd ed., Leipzig,
1879), pp. 50–66 and pp. 109–26. See also A.-H. Chroust (note 11), *passim*,
especially pp. 86–8.

33 In support of this thesis, Zeller pointed out that when referring to the
'Platonists' Aristotle occasionally uses the first person plural (*Metaphysics*
989 b 18; 990 b 8; 992 a 25; 997 b 3; 1002 b 14), and that in his attacks on
Plato and the Platonists, Cephisodorus also denounced Aristotle. See E.
Zeller, *op. cit.*, vol. II, part 2 (3rd ed., Leipzig, 1879), pp. 9 ff.

34 See note 16.

35 W. Jaeger, *Aristoteles: Grundlegung einer Geschichte seiner Entwicklung*
(Berlin, 1923). We shall cite here from the English translation of 1948
(paperback, 1962), pp. 60 ff.

36 For a more detailed discussion of pre-Jaegerian scholarship in the field of
Aristotle's lost works, see A.-H. Chroust (see note 11), *passim*.

37 In 1955, a second German edition of this work was published.

38 For a more comprehensive and detailed discussion of Jaeger's contributions
to the retrieval and reconstruction of Aristotle's lost works, including the
*Protrepticus*, see A.-H. Chroust, 'Werner Jaeger and the reconstruction of
Aristotle's lost works,' *Symbolae Osloenses*, fasc. 13 (1967), pp. 7–43, and
Postscript.

39 Chapter V of Iamblichus' *Protrepticus*, Jaeger insisted, contained excerpts
from Plato, remarks by Iamblichus and perhaps some badly garbled
references to Aristotle.

40 It is this lack of proper or intelligent organization as well as the lack of an
adequate understanding of philosophic problems on the part of Iamblichus,
the 'reporter,' which, in Jaeger's opinion, creates the impression that the
passages in Iamblichus' *Protrepticus* which are credited to Aristotle, constitute a seriously contradictory and heterogeneous *mélange* unworthy of a
first-rate thinker such as Aristotle. These undeniable shortcomings must
be attributed solely to Iamblichus' ineptitude in arranging his excerpts
arbitrarily and according to the subject matter rather than according to
Aristotle's original narrative.

41 W. Jaeger (see note 35), p. 60.

42 Jaeger also pointed out that as to its philosophic content, the Aristotelian
*Protrepticus* is definitely under the influence of Plato, *Euthydemus* 278E–
282D, which in his opinion provided the protreptic archetype for Aristotle's *Protrepticus*. As to its form and method of argumentation as well as

literary style, Jaeger insisted, the *Protrepticus* owes a debt to Isocrates and his protreptic orations, especially to the so-called *Cyprian Orations*.

43 Cicero, *De Inventione* II. 2. 6; Cicero, *De Oratore* I. 11. 49; Cicero, *De Finibus* I. 5. 14; Cicero, *Acad. Prior.* II. 38. 119; Quintilian, *Institutio Oratoria* X. 1. 83; Dionysius of Halicarnassus, *De Verborum Compositione* 24; Dionysius of Halicarnassus, *De Cens. Vet. Scriptorum* 4. See also A.-H. Chroust, *Aristotle: Protrepticus, A Reconstruction* (Notre Dame, 1964), p. xi; A.-H. Chroust, 'The first thirty years of modern Aristotelian scholarship (1912–1942),' *Classica et Mediaevalia*, vol. 24, fasc. 1–2 (1964), p. 35, note 19.

44 See A.-H. Chroust, 'What prompted Aristotle to address the *Protrepticus* to Themison?,' *Hermes*, vol. 94, no. 2 (1966), pp. 202–7, and Chapter IX.

45 See W. Jaeger, *op. cit.*, p. 57.

46 H. Gadamer, 'Der aristotelische *Protreptikos* und die entwicklungsgeschichtliche Betrachtung der aristotelischen Ethik,' *Hermes*, vol. 63 (1928), pp. 138–64.

47 *Ibid.*, pp. 142–5. E. Bignone, in his monumental work, *L'Aristotle Perduto e la Formazione Filosofica di Epicuro* (Florence, 1936), unearthed quite a few references to Aristotle's *Protrepticus* in the writings of Epicurus and the Epicureans. Bignone's book, it will be noted, incorporates a number of articles which he had previously published on this subject. Subsequently, Bignone published some additional papers: 'Nuove testimonianze e frammenti del *Protrettico* di Aristotele,' *Rivista di Filologia e d'Istruzione Classica*, vol. 64 (1936), pp. 225–7; 'Chiaramenti e aggiunte all'Aristotele perduto,' *Atene e Roma*, series 3, no. 5 (1937), pp. 119–29; 'Conferme e aggiunte all'*Aristotele Perduto e la Formazione Filosofica di Epicuro* dall'epistola a Pitocle e dalla meteorologia epicurea,' *Annuaire de l'Institut de Philologie et d'Histoire Orientales et Slaves*, vol. 5 (1937), pp. 87–116; 'Importanti conferme all'Aristotele perduto,' *Atene e Roma*, series 3, no. 5 (1937), pp. 217–37; 'Seneca, Marco Aurelio e il *Protrettico* di Aristotele,' *Annali della Reale Scuola Normale Superiore di Pisa* (Classe di Lettere, Storia e Filosofia), series 2, no. 9 (1940), pp. 241–9.

48 I. Düring, 'Problems in Aristotle's *Protrepticus*,' *Eranos*, vol. 52 (1954), pp. 139–71. Düring's final and conclusive views, which modify some of his earlier theses, were stated in his *Aristotle's Protrepticus: An Attempt at Reconstruction*, Studia Graeca et Latina Gothoburgensia, vol. XII (Göteborg, 1961).

49 Later Düring rejected, however, the first part of Chapter V, namely, p. 24, line 24 to p. 34, line 4 (Pistelli).

50 P. Merlan, *From Platonism to Neoplatonism* (The Hague, 1953). We cite here from the second and enlarged edition of 1960, pp. 119–31. Merlan's suggestion was, in the main, accepted by A. J. Festugière, 'Un fragment nouveau du *Protreptique* d'Aristotle,' *Revue Philosophique de la France et de l'Étranger*, vol. 81 (1956), pp. 117–27, as well as by other scholars.

51 I. Düring (see note 15), *passim*, especially pp. 106–7.

52 For additional details see notes 80-9 and the corresponding text.

53 For additional contributions to the many problems connected with the *Protrepticus*, see, for instance, E. Bignone, *L'Aristotele Perduto a la Formazione Filosofica di Epicuro*, 2 vols (Florence, 1936), *passim*, and Bignone's several articles cited in note 47; L. Lazzati, 'L'Aristotle perduto e gli scrittori christiani,' *Vita e Pensiero* (Pubblicazioni dell'Università Cattolica del Sacro Cuore, series 4, vol. 26, Milan, 1938), who discovered traces of Aristotle's *Protrepticus* in the writings of Clement of Alexandria as well as in other early Christian authors; J. Bidez, *Un Singulier Naufrage Littéraire dans l'Antiquité: A la Recherche des Épaves de l'Aristote Perdu* (Brussels, 1943), pp. 28-32; J. Bidez, 'À propos d'un fragment retrouvé de l'Aristote perdu,' *Bulletin de la Classe des Lettres de l'Académie Royale de Belgique*, vol. 28 (1942), pp. 201-30; Q. Cataudella, 'Nuove ricerche sull'Anonimo di Giamblico e sulla composizione del *Protreptico*,' *Rendiconti della Reale Academia dei Lincei*, Classe di Scienze Morali, vol. 6, part 12 (1937-8), pp. 132-210; F. Nuyens, *L'Évolution de la Psychologie d'Aristote* (Louvain, 1948), p. 90 and pp. 128 ff.; P. Courcelle, *Les Lettres Grecques en Occident* (2nd edit., Paris, 1948), pp. 283-4; R. Cadiou, 'A travers le *Protreptique* de Jambliche,' *Revue des Études Grecques*, vol. 63 (1950), pp. 58-73.

54 W. G. Rabinowitz (see note 10).

55 *Ibid.*, pp. 23-7.

56 Alexander of Aphrodisias, *Commentaria in Aristotelis Topicorum Libros* (see note 2), p. 149, lines 9 ff.

57 Cicero, *Hortensius*, frag. 12, Müller (Lactantius, *Institutiones Divinae* III. 16. 9). See also note 12. Alexander of Aphrodisias, *loc. cit.* (see note 56), merely implies that something was said in Aristotle's *Protrepticus* concerning whether or not one must (or should) philosophize. This bit of meager evidence does not entitle us to assume that the Aristotelian *Protrepticus* actually contained a logical argument of the sort reported by the Neo-Platonic commentators which approximately runs as follows: 'You say that one should (or must) philosophize; ... then you should (or must) philosophize.... You say one should not philosophize ... then in order to prove your contention you must philosophize.... In any event, you must philosophize....' Frag. 51, Rose. See Olympiodorus (note 3), Elias (note 4), David (note 5), and an anonymous Neo-Platonic author (see note 8). These Neo-Platonic commentators, it will be noticed, not only made use of Alexander of Aphrodisias' remark, but they also make liberal additions of their own, distorting the original statement of Alexander. See note 12. J. Bernays (see note 11), pp. 118-19, held that this passage (frag. 51, Rose; frag. 2, Walzer; frag. 2, Ross; frag. 6, Düring; frag. 6, Chroust) was meant to refute Isocrates who ridiculed all preoccupation with purely speculative philosophy. W. Jaeger, *op. cit.*, pp. 72 ff., was of the erroneous opinion that this logical argument was part of the original *Protrepticus*. W. G. Rabinowitz, *op. cit.*, pp. 34-41; D. Furley, in his review of Rabinowitz's book, in *Journal of Hellenic Studies*, vol. 79 (1959), p. 178; as well as

I. Düring (see note 15), p. 178, insisted that this argument is a later (Neo-Platonic) paraphrase (and expansion) of the original Aristotelian passage which, according to Düring and others, read simply thus: 'The term "to philosophize" implies two distinct things: first, whether or not we ought to seek [after philosophic truth]; and second, our dedication to philosophic speculation.' P. Wilpert, in his review of Rabinowitz's book, in *Archiv für Geschichte der Philosophie*, vol. 42 (1960), pp. 101 ff., however, maintained that this particular argument was contained in the original *Protrepticus*. All these scholars overlook one salient fact, however: this logical argument is probably Stoic rather than Aristotelian in origin. See also A.-H. Chroust, *Aristotle: Protrepticus—A Reconstruction* (Notre Dame, 1964), p. 3 and pp. 48–9.

58 W. G. Rabinowitz, *op. cit.*, pp. 37–8. See also *ibid.*, pp. 23 ff. and pp. 34 ff.; note 57.

59 W. G. Rabinowitz, *op. cit.*, pp. 52–92.

60 This particular argument had already been made by R. Hirzel in 1876. See note 20.

61 W. G. Rabinowitz, *op. cit.*, pp. 94 ff. It might be observed here that Iamblichus, *Protrepticus*, p. 7, line 22 (Pistelli), actually refers to Chapter XXI of Iamblichus' *Protrepticus* and not, as Rabinowitz surmised, to the Aristotelian excerpts found in books VI–XI (or XII) of Iamblichus' *Protrepticus*.

62 See, for instance, the reviews by A. Mansion, in *Revue Philosophique de Louvain*, vol. 56 (1958), pp. 316–19; D. Furley (see note 57); L. Torraca, in *Sophia*, vol. 28 (1960), pp. 271–5; P. Wilpert (see note 57); W. Spoerri, in *Gnomon*, vol. 32 (1960), pp. 18–25. A fair and dispassionate discussion of Rabinowitz's theses can also be found in I. Düring (see note 15), pp. 11–14, and *ibid.*, pp. 27–9.

63 I. Düring (see note 15), p. 17, detected only twelve words that are not listed in Bonitz's *Index Aristotelicus* in those excerpts in Iamblichus' *Protrepticus* which are said to be 'reports' from the Aristotelian *Protrepticus*. But all these twelve words are terms which were fairly common during the middle of the fourth century B.C. They can be found in the dialogues of Plato as well as in the writings of contemporary Attic orators.

64 See, for instance, H. Flashar (see note 10), pp. 58 ff., especially pp. 77–8.

65 W. Theiler, *Zur Geschichte der Teleologischen Naturbetrachtung bis auf Aristoteles* (Zürich, 1924), pp. 86–8.

66 E. Kapp, 'Theorie und Praxis bei Aristoteles und Platon,' *Mnemosyne*, vol. 6 (series 3), fasc. 1 (1938), p. 184.

67 O. Gigon, *Aristoteles: Einführungsschriften* (Zürich, 1961), p. 99. Similar views were advanced by H. Flashar (see note 10), pp. 77–8; and by A.-H. Chroust, 'An emendation to fragment 13 (Walzer, Ross) of Aristotle's *Protrepticus*,' *Tijdschrift voor Filosofie*, vol. 28, no. 2 (1966), pp. 366–77, and Chapter VIII.

68 See, for instance, Plato, *Republic* 484B; 485C; 486E; 500BC; *et passim*.

69 G. Müller, 'Probleme der aristotelischen Eudaimonielehre,' *Museum Helveticum*, vol. 17 (1960), p. 138.

70 F. Wehrli, 'Aristoteles in der Sicht seiner Schule,' *Aristote et les Problèmes de la Méthode* (Louvain, 1961), pp. 321 ff. Also G. Müller (see note 69).

71 H. Flashar (see note 10), pp. 72 ff.

72 A.-H. Chroust (see note 57), pp. 19-22 and pp. 73-7.

73 A.-H. Chroust (see note 67), pp. 366-77, and Chapter VIII. See, however, K. Gaiser, 'Zwei Protreptikos-Zitate in der eudemischen Ethik des Aristoteles,' *Rheinisches Museum*, vol. 110, no. 4 (1967), pp. 314-45. In a most ingenious manner Gaiser attempts to prove that Iamblichus, *Protrepticus* 54,10-56,12, including the controversial passage in 55,7-56,2, is based on Aristotle's *Protrepticus*. Gaiser argues that Aristotle, *Eudemian Ethics* 1218 a 33-38, as well as *ibid.*, 1244 b 21-1245 a 10—two passages which deal with essentially the same involved topic as Iamblichus, *Protrepticus* 54,10-56,12— contain a direct and unmistakable reference to the Aristotelian *Protrepticus*. Gaiser's thesis rests upon the assumption that this reference, that is, the statement, ἐν τῷ λόγῳ γεγραμένον, or, ἐν τῷ λόγῳ γέγραπται, actually points to the Aristotelian *Protrepticus* (rather than, perhaps, to the *Politicus*).

74 O. Gigon, 'Prolegomena to an Edition of the Eudemus,' *Aristotle and Plato in the Mid-Fourth Century* (Göteborg, 1960), pp. 27 ff. Gigon's views were rejected by C. de Vogel, 'Did Aristotle ever accept Plato's theory of transcendental ideas? Problems around a new edition of the *Protrepticus*,' *Archiv für Geschichte der Philosophie*, vol. 42 (1965), pp. 261-98, especially p. 289.

75 A. Grilli, 'Cicerone e l'Eudemo,' *La Parola del Passato*, vol. 27, fasc. 83 (1962), pp. 96-121. See also S. Mariotti, 'La *quinta essentia* nell'Aristotele perduto e nell'Academia,' *Rivista di Filologia e d'Istruzione Classica*, vol. 68 (1940), pp. 180-1.

76 J. Brunschwig, 'Aristote et les Pirates Tyrrhéniens,' *Revue Philosophique de la France et de l'Étranger*, vol. 153 (1963), pp. 171-90.

77 H. Flashar, 'Die Kritik der platonischen Ideenlehre in der Ethik des Aristoteles,' *Synusia: Festschrift für Wolfgang Schadewaldt* (Pfullingen, 1963), p. 20 and p. 28.

78 K. Gaiser, 'Die Elegie des Aristoteles auf Eudemos,' *Museum Helveticum*, vol. 23, fasc. 2 (1966), pp. 84-106; K. Gaiser (see note 73), p. 320, note 14 and p. 342, note 53. R. Renehan, 'An Aristotelian mode of argumentation in Iamblichus' *Protrepticus*,' *Hermes*, vol. 92 (1964), pp. 507-8, points out that Iamblichus, *Protrepticus*, p. 53, lines 2-15 (Pistelli; frag. 58, Rose; frag. 12, Walzer; frag. 12, Ross; frag. 43, Düring; frag. 41, Chroust), makes use of a typical Aristotelian manner or technique of argumentation, as well as of Aristotle's characteristic language. This fact, Renehan argues, lends strong support to the assumption that this passage in Iamblichus' *Protrepticus* is an authentic fragment of Aristotle's *Protrepticus*.

79 See note 47 and the corresponding text. W. Nestle, *Aristoteles Hauptwerke* (Leipzig, 1934), *passim*, attempted to arrange the fragments in ten

'chapters.' The 'collection of fragments' compiled by V. Rose, R. Walzer and W. D. Ross, makes no effort to arrange the several fragments according to definite principle or plan.

80  I. Düring, 'Problems in Aristotle's *Protrepticus*,' *Eranos*, vol. 52 (1954), pp. 139–71; I. Düring, 'Aristotle in the *Protrepticus*,' *Autour d'Aristote* (Louvain, 1955), pp. 81–97.

81  I. Düring (see note 15), especially pp. 106–9.

82  Although it appears that p. 37, lines 3–22 (Pistelli), of chapter VI (frag. 4, Walzer; frag. 4, Ross; frags 8–9, Düring; frags 8–9, Chroust) constitute a sort of 'introduction' or 'introductory statement of purpose' to the *Protrepticus*, Düring, who in this partly agreed with I. Bywater, considered authentic p. 36, line 27 to p. 37, line 3, of chapter VI (frag. 7, Düring), a section which is usually rejected by scholars. About such an 'introductory statement' (κεφάλαιον), see H. Mutschmann, 'Inhaltsangabe und Kapitelüberschrift im Antiken Buch,' *Hermes*, vol. 46 (1911), pp. 93–107; R. Laqueur, 'Note,' *Hermes*, vol. 46 (1911), p. 184, note 2; R. Friderici, *De Librorum Antiquorum Capitum Divisione atque Summariis* (doctoral dissertation, Marburg, 1911). The first known 'introductory statements' can be found at the beginning of Book III of Polybius' *Histories*, in Diodorus Siculus, in Pliny's *Hist. Nat.*, and in Gellius' *Attic Nights*. The practice of prefacing a book or chapter with a κεφάλαιον was also adopted by such Neo-Platonic authors as Porphyry and Iamblichus.

83  To improve the continuity of argument, Düring (frags 18 and 19) changes the sequence suggested by R. Walzer (frag. 11) and W. D. Ross (frag. 11), who observe the order found in Iamblichus. Düring sequence is the following: frags 11–16, frags 18–19, frag. 17, and frags 20–1. See also G. Zuntz, 'In Aristotelis Protrepticum Conjecturae,' *Mnemosyne* (series 4), vol. 2 (1958), pp. 158–9.

84  I. Bywater included the whole of chapter V, as did later P. Hartlich, F. Nuyens, A. J. Festugière and V. Décarie. But R. Hirzel, V. Rose, W. Jaeger, R. Walzer, W. D. Ross and E. Berti have rejected it. I. Düring recognizes the last part of chapter V (frags 23–8). In this, he found support in S. Mansion, 'Contemplation and action in Aristotle's *Protrepticus*,' *Aristotle and Plato in the Mid-Fourth Century* (ed. Düring-Owen, Göteborg, 1960), p. 58, and in A.-H. Chroust (see note 57), frags 21–6. But Düring did not place frags 23–8, Düring, at the beginning of his proposed sequence.

85  With the exception of W. G. Rabinowitz (see note 10), pp. 77–84, this excerpt or fragment (p. 37, line 22 to p. 41, line 5) has been credited to Aristotle by I. Bywater, V. Rose (frag. 12), R. Walzer (frag. 5), W. D. Ross (frag. 5), I. Düring (frags 31–40 and 53–7) and A.-H. Chroust (frags 29–38 and 50–4), as well as by P. Hartlich and W. Jaeger. Düring, it will be observed, did not maintain the sequence found in Iamblichus and adopted by other scholars.

86  This excerpt or fragment (frag. 6, Walzer; frag. 6, Ross) was rejected by a number of scholars, but accepted by Düring (frag. 41) and A.-H. Chroust

(frag. 39) as a kind of 'introduction' to chapters VII–X (p. 52, line 16 to p. 56, line 12).

87 See note 85.

88 This part of chapter XII (p. 59, line 19 to p. 60, line 10) has been accepted by many scholars, among them R. Walzer (frag. 15) and D. W. Ross (frag. 15). The remainder of chapter XII has been accepted in part by W. Jaeger (to p. 60, line 15), R. Walzer and W. D. Ross, but was rejected by I. Düring and A.-H. Chroust on the grounds of both language and content, although previously Düring had accepted p. 60, lines 10–15. See I. Düring, 'Problems in Aristotle's *Protrepticus*,' *Eranos*, vol. 52 (1954), p. 168. P. Hartlich (see note 25), p. 254, on the other hand, would also include p. 60, line 10 to p. 61, line 4.

89 These excerpts (frags 59–61, Rose; frags 10a, 10b and 10c, Walzer; frags 10a, 10b and 10c, Ross; frags 97–110, Düring; frags 93–106, Chroust), which make up the last part of chapter VIII, do not necessarily constitute the concluding section of the original Aristotelian *Protrepticus*. But it might be argued that p. 48, lines 9–21 (frag. 61, Rose; frag. 10c, Walzer; frag. 10c, Ross; frags 108–10, Düring; frags 104–6, Chroust) is a concluding summary: 'Men as a whole possess nothing of worth and have no reason to consider themselves divine or blessed, except in so far as they possess reason and philosophic wisdom. This alone of all our endowments seems to be deathless, this alone seems to be divine. Since human life is capable of sharing this faculty [of reasoning and of acquiring philosophic wisdom], however wretched and difficult it may be otherwise, it is yet so wisely ordained that man appears to be a god when compared with all other creatures. For reason is "the divine dwelling in us" . . . and [because of reason] mortal life possesses a certain element or aspect of the divine. This being so, we ought either to pursue philosophy or bid farewell to life and depart from this world, because all other things seem to be but utter nonsense and folly.' A. Grilli (see note 75), pp. 96–121, insists that Iamblichus, *Protrepticus*, p. 47, line 21 to p. 48, line 21 (frags 60 and 61, Rose; frags 10b and 10c, Walzer; frags 10b and 10c, Ross; frags 106–10, Düring; frags 102–6, Chroust), is an excerpt from Aristotle's lost Dialogue *Eudemus* rather than from Aristotle's *Protrepticus*, a view with which O. Gigon concurred. See notes 74 and 75.

90 I. Düring (see note 15), p. 37. Düring admitted that 'since it is unlikely that we shall ever be able either to prove or disprove our case [*scil.*, his proposed new arrangement], I do not attach much importance to this aspect of our problem.' *Ibid.* With some slight modifications, the present author adopted the sequence proposed by I. Düring. See A.-H. Chroust (see note 57), *passim*. After some further reflection, he would omit or at least mark as doubtful frags 48–50, Düring; frags 45–6, Chroust. See note 67.

91 V. Rose did not include this fragment in his collection of fragments (of 1886).

92 See note 90.

93 S. Mansion (see note 84), pp. 56-75.

94 K. Gaiser, *Protreptik und Paränese bei Platon* (Tübinger Beiträge zur Altertumswissenschaft, vol. 40, Stuttgart, 1959), pp. 217-22. G. Schneeweisz,
*Der Protreptikos des Aristoteles* (doctoral dissertation, Munich, 1966), took
issue with the organization and sequence proposed by I. Düring and
K. Gaiser.

95 Gaiser (see note 94) was also of the opinion that each of these λόγοι
προτρεπτικοί in essence had already been devised by the sophists and
certainly by Plato.

96 For the several attempts at dating the *Protrepticus*, see A.-H. Chroust, 'The
probable dates of some of Aristotle's "lost works,"' *Rivista Critica di Storia
della Filosofia*, vol. 22, fasc. 1 (1967), pp. 3-23, especially pp. 13-17, and
Chapter I.

97 In his *Aristotle: Protrepticus—A Reconstruction* (Notre Dame, 1964), *passim*,
the present author, with certain exceptions, reservations and modifications,
in the main adheres to the major findings of I. Düring. But he does not
accept Düring's insistence that the Aristotelian *Protrepticus* is predominantly or primarily 'Aristotelian' in spirit and doctrinal content—that
there exist no serious doctrinal or philosophic differences between this
composition and the later doctrinal treatises. In brief, Chroust still believes
that the *Protrepticus* is essentially 'Platonic.'

98 See, for instance, W. Theiler (note 65), pp. 80 ff., who maintained that in
the *Protrepticus* Aristotle manifests a certain independence of Plato; H.
Gadamer (see note 46), pp. 138-64, who not only doubted the 'Platonism'
of the Aristotelian *Protrepticus*, but also pointed out emphatically that it is
not permissible to draw definite philosophic conclusions from a hortatory
essay such as the *Protrepticus*, and that it is well-nigh impossible to ascertain
with any degree of certainty whether or not in the *Protrepticus* Aristotle
still subscribes to the Separate Ideas; E. Kapp (see note 66), pp. 179-94, who
challenged the position that in the *Protrepticus* Aristotle accepted the
Separate Ideas; E. Frank, 'The fundamental opposition of Plato and
Aristotle,' *American Journal of Philology*, vol. 61 (1940), pp. 34-50 and pp.
166-85, who believed that there always existed basic doctrinal differences
between Plato and Aristotle; F. Nuyens (see note 53), pp. 168 ff., who
claimed that already in the *Protrepticus* Aristotle propagates an affirmative
'instrumentalist psychology'—the soul uses the body as its necessary and
useful tool—a position also found in the doctrinal works (and, concomitantly, radically opposed to Plato's views); R. Stark, *Aristotelesstudien* (Munich, 1954), pp. 5 ff., who insisted that the philosophy expounded in the *Protrepticus* is no longer Platonic, inasmuch as in the
*Protrepticus* he assigns, as he does in the doctrinal treatises, to philosophy a
distinctly practical significance, extols action and experience and sees in
philosophy a 'call to intelligent action.' Jaeger's views were rejected, at
least in part, also by F. Dirlmeier, *Aristoteles: Nikomachische Ethik* (Darmstadt, 1956), pp. 278 ff. and p. 449, who believed that the ethical doctrines

advanced in the *Protrepticus* are identical with those professed in the *Nicomachean Ethics* as well as with those of Plato, thus implying not only that there exists no real difference between Platonic ethics, the ethics proclaimed in the *Protrepticus* and the ethics discussed in the *Nicomachean Ethics*, but also that there never was, and never could have been, an 'evolution' of Aristotle's ethical thought from Platonism to Aristotelianism; and C. de Vogel, 'The legend of the Platonizing Aristotle,' *Aristotle and Plato in the Mid-Fourth Century* (Göteborg, 1960), pp. 252 ff. Previously de Vogel had agreed with certain views advanced by Jaeger. See note 99.

99 See, for instance, R. A. Gauthier and J. Y. Jolif, *Aristote: L'Éthique à Nicomaque* (Aristote, Traduction et Études, Collection Publiée par l'Institut Supérieur de Philosophie de l'Université de Louvain, Louvain-Paris, 1970), vol. I, pp. 10 ff. With some minor modifications, Gauthier subscribes to Jaeger's thesis that there is a distinct philosophic progression from the ethical viewpoint underlying the *Protrepticus* to that espoused in the *Nicomachean Ethics*; E. Bignone (see note 53), vol. I, pp. 112 ff. and pp. 371 ff., who believed that the essentially pessimistic tenor of, as well as the adherence to the Separate Ideas in, the *Protrepticus* are indicative of Aristotle's early commitment to Plato's philosophy, as is Aristotle's decidedly anti-hedonistic attitude manifest in the *Protrepticus*; A. J. Festugière, *La Révélation d'Hermès Trismégiste*, vol. II (Paris, 1949), pp. 168 ff., who maintained that the *Protrepticus* is declaratory of a somber pessimism as regards the corporeal world—a typically Platonic twist—and that, therefore, Aristotle must have believed in the Separate Ideas; C. de Vogel, *Greek Philosophy*, vol. II (Leiden, 1953), pp. 24 ff., who in direct contradiction to F. Nuyens (see note 98), insisted that the 'instrumentalist psychology' of the *Protrepticus* is eminently Platonic; S. Mansion (see note 84), pp. 56 ff., who was of the opinion that the basic tenor of the *Protrepticus* is still Platonic, although this work already manifests distinct Aristotelian features; É. de Stryker, 'On the first section of fragment 5a of the *Protrepticus*,' *Aristotle and Plato in the Mid-Fourth Century* (Göteborg, 1960), pp. 76 ff., who demonstrated that while some of the views discussed in the *Protrepticus* are undeniably Platonic, others are in full accord with the doctrines expounded in the later doctrinal treatises, and that Aristotle's allusions to an 'objective absolute reality' are in fact references to 'first principles' in general; and P. Merlan (see note 50), pp. 119 ff., who maintained that the *Protrepticus* manifests the influence of Plato's 'mathematical' or 'Pythagorizing' tendencies.

100 See, for instance, R. A. Gauthier and J. Y. Jolif (note 99), vol. I, *passim*. Düring believed not only to have discovered in the *Protrepticus* a teleology as well as a notion of an efficient cause which radically departs from that sponsored by Plato, but also to have found in this work arguments and notions which are typical of Aristotle's *Physics* and *Metaphysics*. Düring further insisted that whenever in the *Protrepticus* Aristotle refers, or seems to refer, to the Separate Ideas, he really has in mind the substances or,

perhaps, the 'essence' of things, and, possibly, 'first principles.' Moreover, Düring denied that the *Protrepticus* is pessimistic in outlook or anti-hedonistic in principle; that the term φρόνησις, as it is used in the *Protrepticus*, refers (as it does with Plato) to 'theoretic contemplation' rather than to 'practical wisdom'; and that in the *Protrepticus* the ultimate moral norm is the vision of the (Separate) Idea of the Good rather than human reason (and human experience) properly employed. In brief, according to Düring, the *Protrepticus* is declaratory of the fact that by the time Aristotle composed the *Protrepticus*, he had found and formulated his own philosophy, and that he had done so independently of Plato and Platonism in general.

101 This is in essence the thesis which J. Bernays (see note 11), pp. 63 ff. and pp. 95 ff.; and H. Diels (see note 15), pp. 477–97, had advanced many years ago. Bernays claimed that from the very beginning Aristotle was opposed to Plato's fundamental philosophic doctrines. But in order to be better understood (and in order to be more readily accepted), Aristotle occasionally (and superficially) made use of Platonic dialectics and Platonic doctrine. See note 30 and the corresponding text.

102 I. Düring (see note 15), pp. 274 ff.

103 *Ibid.*, p. 284. See also S. Mansion (see note 84), p. 70.

104 See note 16.

105 See, for instance, A.-H. Chroust, *Aristotle: Protrepticus—A Reconstruction* (Notre Dame, 1964); E. Berti, *Aristotele, Esortazione alla Filosofia* (*Protrettico*), Classici della Filosofia (Padua, 1967); G. Schneeweisz, *Der Protreptikos des Aristoteles* (doctoral dissertation, Munich, 1966).

CHAPTER VIII   AN EMENDATION TO FRAGMENT 13 (WALZER, ROSS) OF ARISTOTLE'S *Protrepticus*

* In a different and less detailed form, this chapter was first published in *Tijschrift voor Filosofie*, vol. 28, no. 2 (1966), pp. 366–77.

1 The first scholar to point out that the *Protrepticus* of Iamblichus contains fragments of the Aristotelian *Protrepticus* was I. Bywater, 'On a lost dialogue of Aristotle,' *Journal of Philology*, vol. 2 (1869), pp. 55–69. See Chapter VII, notes 16–19, and the corresponding text. V. Rose cites some sections, but not this particular passage, of Iamblichus' *Protrepticus*. W. Jaeger, who maintained that this passage constitutes an essential part of the original Aristotelian *Protrepticus*, relied on this section for his claim that when composing the *Protrepticus* Aristotle was still a Platonist. See W. Jaeger, *Aristotle: Fundamentals of the History of his Development* (Oxford, 1948), pp. 76–7, *et passim*. See also I. Düring, *Aristotle's Protrepticus: An Attempt at Reconstruction* (Göteborg, 1961), *passim*.

2 Frag. 13, Walzer; frag. 13, Ross; frags 46–51, Düring; frags 43–8, Chroust. Some of the views expressed in Iamblichus, *Protrepticus* 54,10–56,12, can also be found in Aristotle, *Eudemian Ethics* 1218 a 33–38. K. Gaiser, 'Zwei Protreptikos-Zitate in der Eudemischen Ethik des Aristoteles,' *Rheinisches*

*Museum für Philologie*, vol. 110 (1967), pp. 314-45, considers this passage from the *Eudemian Ethics* a fragment of the Aristotelian *Protrepticus*.

3 See also I. Düring, 'Aristotle's ultimate principles from "nature and reality,"' *Aristotle and Plato in the Mid-Fourth Century* (Göteborg, 1960), pp. 42-9.

4 Analogies between the good physician and the good philosopher are commonplace with Plato. See, for instance, Plato, *Statesman* 293B ff.; 295B ff.; 299BC; Plato, *Charmides* 156BC; Plato, *Laws* 902E and 903D; *Theaetetus* 167B; *Gorgias* 450A; 480A; 517E ff.; *Sophist* 230D; *et passim*. References to physicians and gymnasts can also be found in Plato, *Phaedo* 94D; *Republic* 404B and 405C; *Sophist* 226E ff.; *Laws* 889D; *et passim*.

5 It is impossible to ascertain, as I. Düring (see note 3), pp. 43-9, attempts to do, whether the term φύσις used in this connection refers to the 'principle of order and stability'—this would be its meaning in Aristotle's later didactic treatises—or whether it contains an allusion to Plato's notion of immutable being (Ideas). In any event, the general Platonic tenor of this passage seems to be rather obvious. This raises the further problem, not to be discussed in detail, of whether the Aristotelian *Protrepticus* is strongly 'Platonic,' as W. Jaeger has suggested, or whether it is 'Aristotelian,' as I. Düring maintains. In any event, Aristotle seems to be influenced here by Plato's famed expression (*Parmenides* 132A ff.; *Theaetetus* 176E) of 'patterns permanently fixed in nature.'

6 See Plato, *Philebus* 56B; *Cratylus* 389A. In *Philebus* 56B, which might have been Aristotle's model, Plato maintains: 'The art of the builder ... which uses a number of measures and instruments, attains through these measures and instruments to a greater degree of accuracy than all the other arts. ... In ship-building and house-building ... the builder has his ruler, lathe, compass, line. ...'

7 In *Sophist* 265A ff. Plato speaks of the 'imitative arts.'

8 See also Plato, *Republic* 500B ff.; *Laws* 962B ff. In *Republic*, *loc. cit.*, Plato refers to the philosopher statesman, 'whose mind is fixed upon true being.' This philosopher statesman 'surely has no time to look down upon the affairs of this earth. ... His eyes are forever directed towards things fixed and immutable. ... These he imitates. ...'

9 See also Plato, *Cratylus* 436A ff.; *Timaeus* 50C ff. and 51A.

10 See, for instance, Plato, *Republic* 475E: 'The philosophers ... are the lovers of the vision of truth.' *Ibid.*, 484B: 'The philosophers alone are capable of grasping that which is eternal and unchangeable.' *Ibid.*, 484D: 'Only the philosopher is capable of knowing the truth in each thing.' *Ibid.*, 485B: 'Philosophic minds always have a knowledge of a sort which shows them the eternal nature.' *Ibid.*, 500C: '[The true philosopher's] eyes are forever directed towards things immutable and fixed.' See also Plato, *Sophist* 249CD; etc., and note 8.

11 See p. 106. Plutarch, *De Genio Socratis* 7 (*Moralia* 579A ff.), relates the following interesting story: the inhabitants of the island of Delos turned to

the Academy for advice as to how they might increase the size of the altar of Apollo and, at the same time, retain its shape as a perfect cube. Plato assigned the solution of this problem to some of his disciples. But when he found out that they attempted to solve it through the use of technical instruments commonly used by builders and architects, he reproached them for degrading 'pure geometry' by having recourse to measurements 'taken from visible nature' rather than by relying on, or imitating directly, the eternal and immutable pure forms. See also Plutarch, *Quaestiones Conviviales* VIII. 2. 1 (*Moralia* 718E ff.); Plutarch, *Marcellus* 14; note 29.

12  The notion that theoretic knowledge guides our practical actions can also be found in Plato, *Statesman* 293A ff.; *Philebus* 56BC; *Republic, passim*. In *Republic* 352B ff., Plato stresses the fact that people devoid of justice (of the Idea of Justice) are incapable of committing just acts. See also Plato, *Charmides* 174C ff.; *Laws* 660E.

13  See note 6.

14  As a matter of fact, the vast majority of scholars who have dealt with the Aristotelian *Protrepticus* assign this passage to the latter work. This is also true with regard to 55,7–56,2. There are some scholars, however, who question this assignment. See note 19.

15  Syrianus, *Comment. in Arist. Metaphysica*, CIAG, vol. VI, part 1 (ed. W. Kroll, Berlin, 1902), p. 168, lines 33–5 (frag. 79, Rose; frag. 2, Ross).

16  See A.-H. Chroust, 'Aristotle's *Politicus*: a lost dialogue,' *Rheinisches Museum*, vol. 108, no. 4 (1965), pp. 346–53, especially pp. 347–49, and Chapter XI. R. Stark, *Aristotelesstudien: philologische Untersuchungen zur Entwicklung der aristotelischen Ethik* (Munich, 1954), pp. 27 ff., suggests that this passage should be translated as follows: 'The good is the most exact measure for (or, of) all things.' Thus, according to Stark, unlike Plato, Aristotle is not concerned here with the fact that its greatest 'exactness' makes a certain good 'the highest good' among all other goods and, hence, 'the most perfect measure (or standard)' among all measures. What Aristotle wishes to express here, Stark contends, is merely the fact that a (moral?) good is a value criterion by which all things or actions that transpire in our world may properly be judged and rightly evaluated. K. von Fritz and E. Kapp, *Aristotle's Constitution of Athens* (New York, 1950), pp. 214–15, who like R. Stark translate this fragment found in Syrianus as 'the most exact measure of all things in the good,' insist that Syrianus was

very much displeased with the unorthodox manner in which Aristotle deals here with the concept of 'the One' and 'measure,' and in order to show that Aristotle himself knew better than that, he quotes one sentence from the Aristotelian dialogue *Politicus*. Syrianus has no doubt that, in this sentence, 'the good' is the transcendent 'One' or God, Who, according to Plato (*Laws* 716C), is 'the measure of all things.' Probably Aristotle had not said anything in the *Politicus* that precluded this interpretation of the sentence. . . . To that extent, then, Aristotle may still have been an adherent of the 'doctrine of Ideas' when he wrote the lost dialogue [*scil.*, the *Politicus*].

17 See A.-H. Chroust, 'The probable dates of some of Aristotle's lost works,' *Rivista Critica di Storia della Filosofia*, vol. 22, fasc. 1 (1967), pp. 3–23, especially pp. 17–19, and Chapter I at the end.

18 See A.-H. Chroust, 'The probable date of Aristotle's lost dialogue *On Philosophy*,' *Journal of the History of Philosophy*, vol. 4, no. 4 (1966), pp. 283–91, and Chapter XII. See also A.-H. Chroust (note 17), pp. 19–22, and Chapter I at the end.

19 This has also been suggested, though without detailed discussion, by O. Gigon, *Aristoteles: Einführungsschriften* (Zürich, 1961), p. 99; and by H. Flashar, 'Platon und Aristoteles im *Protreptikos* des Jamblichos,' *Archiv für Geschichte der Philosophie*, vol. 47 (1965), pp. 77–8. In his *Aristotle: Protrepticus—A Reconstruction* (Notre Dame, 1964), pp. 20–1 (frags 45–7), the present author included 55,7–56,2 among the authentic fragments or excerpts from Aristotle's *Protrepticus*. After much reconsideration, he would now place frags 45–7 in brackets, indicating thereby that this particular passage is of doubtful authenticity; that, in all likelihood, it may not be traced back to the Aristotelian *Protrepticus*. This would not exclude, however, that it may have been taken from some other Aristotelian composition, to wit, from the *Politicus*.

20 See here Plato, *Republic* 500C ff., which suggests essentially the same views.

21 In Iamblichus, *Protrepticus* 39, 11–16 (frag. 52, Rose; frag. 5, Walzer; frag. 5, Ross; frag. 38, Düring; frag. 36, Chroust), we are told that 'philosophic wisdom . . . is the most useful of all things.' *Ibid.*, 54, 10–22 (frag. 13, Walzer; frag. 13, Ross; frag. 46, Düring; frag. 43, Chroust), it is stated that 'philosophic knowledge is of the greatest usefulness to us in the management of our practical lives.' It will also be noted that there exists no real connection between 55,26–56,2 and 56,2–3.

22 In this, 54,10–55,6 seems to pursue the general argument also to be found in 37,26–41,15 (frag. 52, Rose; frag. 5, Walzer; frag. 5, Ross; frags 32–41, Düring; frags 30–9, Chroust), as well as in Iamblichus, *De Communi Mathematica Scientia Liber* (ed. N. Festa, 1891), 79,1–81,7, provided this latter passage contains an excerpt from Aristotle's *Protrepticus*. For a discussion of some of the problems connected with the *De Communi Mathematica Scientia Liber*, see, for instance, K. Gaiser (see note 2), pp. 340–1, and notes 50 and 51.

23 See, for instance, W. Theiler, *Zur Geschichte der teleologischen Natur-betrachtung bis auf Aristoteles* (Zürich, 1924), pp. 86–8. Theiler, who believes that the whole of Iamblichus' *Protrepticus*, chap. X (54,10–56,12), is a series of excerpts from Aristotle's *Protrepticus*, insists, however, that this 'relation' is purely 'external' or 'verbal,' rather than 'substantial.' *Ibid.*, p. 88. E. Kapp, 'Theorie und Praxis bei Aristoteles und Platon,' *Mnemosyne*

(series 3), vol. 6, fasc. 1 (1938), p. 184, claims that chap. X of Iamblichus'
*Protrepticus* reads like a fustian of citations from many Platonic dialogues:
from the *Phaedrus* and the *Philebus*, from several passages of the *Republic*
and the *Cratylus*, and above all from the *Statesman*. See also G. Müller,
'Probleme der aristotelischen Eudaimonielehre,' *Museum Helveticum*, vol.
17 (1960), p. 138, who points out that Iamblichus' *Protrepticus* cannot be
taken at face value, and that Iamblichus himself is a thoroughly confused
and inaccurate reporter and epitomizer. Müller, *ibid.*, pp. 134–6, also
maintains that 54,10–56,12 is a late, that is, uncritical or syncretist Neo-
Platonic *mélange* of Platonic and Aristotelian elements. Müller, it will be
noted, is of the opinion that in his *Protrepticus* Aristotle sharply contrasted
the (Platonic) ideal of the theoretic life with the concept of the 'practical
life.' Similar views are also entertained by H. Flashar (see note 19), *passim*.
F. Wehrli, 'Aristoteles in der Sicht seiner Schule,' *Aristote et les Problèmes
de la Méthode* (Louvain, 1961), pp. 321 ff., insists that in his *Protrepticus*
Iamblichus indiscriminately combines not only Platonic and Aristotelian
notions, but also that he makes use of a variety of Aristotle's compositions,
both early and late, that is, the dialogues and the doctrinal treatises.

24 See A.-H. Chroust (see note 16), pp. 346 ff., and Chapter XI.

25 See Plato, *Philebus* 56A ff. and 66A ff. See also the following note.

26 *Ibid.*, 55D–58C. Plato refers here to a hierarchy of 'measurements,' norms
and 'exactitudes'—a hierarchy based on the purity of these 'measurements.'
With Plato, the craft of the house-builder (carpenter) ranks rather high in
exactitude, and the Platonic house-builder uses the same tools which are
enumerated in 54,24–25. But compared to the exactitude of the true
philosopher, the house-builder's craft is still vastly inferior in that the
former looks to 'eternal Being' and not, as does the house-builder, to 'the
things of this world,' that is, to 'things which are becoming.' *Philebus*
59AB. *Ibid.*, 56BC Plato speaks of the house-builder, and it is from this
passage that Aristotle (55,13–14) may well have borrowed his reference to
the house-builder. Naturally, there always exists the possibility that the
whole of 55,7–56,2, or at least some parts of it, was taken by Iamblichus
directly from Plato's *Philebus* (or *Statesman*) and, as is so often the case with
Iamblichus, was badly garbled by the latter. Another possibility is that in
his *Politicus* Aristotle himself used the passage from the Platonic *Philebus*,
combining it with what he had 'borrowed' from the *Statesman* (291D ff.)
of Plato. The fact that certain passages in the Platonic *Philebus* and *Statesman*
lend themselves to complete combination and integration needs no special
comment.

27 See, for instance, Plato, *Philebus* 56B ff.; 59C ff.; 64D ff.; 66A; *Republic*
479E; 500BC; 587A; 619CD; *Phaedrus* 256AB; *Phaedo* 79A; *Statesman*
305CD; *Timaeus* 30A and 47DE; *Laws* 780E; *Gorgias* 504A ff.

28 Essentially the same notions can be found in Plato, *Laws* 716C, where we
are informed that God—the Good in Itself and 'the Measure of all measures'
—ought to be for us the measure of all things.

29 Iamblichus, *Protrepticus* 55,7–56,2 (frag. 13, Walzer; frag. 13, Ross; frags

48–50, Düring; frags 45–7, Chroust). In the *Philebus* (56D and 57D), Plato had already distinguished between the 'pure mathematics' of the philosopher and the 'applied mathematics' of the empiricist (or artisan). As a matter of fact, Plato speaks here of the 'two ways' or the 'two arts' of measuration. See also note 11.

30 See also W. Jaeger (note 1), pp. 85–91.

31 G. Müller (see note 23), p. 134, insists that we may safely maintain the following axiom: during all periods of his intellectual activities, Aristotle, the greatest architect of logic and systematic thinking, is incapable of confusing or combining two essentially conflicting or irreconcilable notions. Iamblichus, on the other hand, is fully capable of doing this, as is evidenced by his *Protrepticus*. K. Gaiser (see note 2), pp. 341–2, holds that Iamblichus, *Protrepticus* 54,10–56,12, is an integral part or fragment of the Aristotelian *Protrepticus* in that it constitutes a typically Aristotelian attempt at harmonizing and integrating the several and apparently conflicting views or positions advanced in this fragment. Like W. Jaeger ((see note 1), p. 269) and I. Düring ((see note 1), pp. 242–4) before him, Gaiser bases his argument on the reasonable, though by no means proven, hypothesis that Aristotle, *Eudemian Ethics* 1218 a 33–38 and 1244 b 21–1245 a 10, seems to refer to Iamblichus, *Protrepticus* 54,10–56,12, or to be more exact, to the original Aristotelian model reported and relied upon here by Iamblichus. In *Eudemian Ethics* 1218 a 33–38, it will be noted, Aristotle states: 'Such *aporiae* clearly reveal that there is no such thing as a "good in itself." They also make it apparent that the Idea of the Good in itself would be of no use for practical politics. On the contrary, politics has its own particular good, as do all the other τέχναι, such as gymnastics and good physical condition or health. Moreover, that which we have written in our composition (ἐν τῷ λόγῳ) [*scil.*, in the *Protrepticus*?] certainly also applies here: either the Idea of the Good in itself is of no use to the several individual τέχναι, or it does so for all τέχναι alike. And finally, the Idea of the Good or the Good in Itself can never be the ultimate end of concrete (political) action.' Hence, Gaiser maintains that the whole of Iamblichus, *Protrepticus* 54,10–56,12, including the controversial passage in 55,7–56,2, is ultimately derived from Aristotle's *Protrepticus* rather than from the Aristotelian *Politicus*. It may be argued, however, that the statement, ἐν τῷ λόγῳ (*Eudemian Ethics* 1218 a 36 and 1244 b 30), might very well refer to the *Politicus*. F. Dirlmeier, *Aristoteles: Eudemische Ethik* (Berlin, 1962), pp. 460–1, and F. Dirlmeier, 'Merkwürdige Zitate in der Eudemischen Ethik des Aristoteles,' *Sitzungsberichte der Heidelberger Akademie der Wissenschaften*, Philos.-histor. Klasse, Abhandlung 2 (1962), p. 33, for instance, claims that this reference is to the Διαιρέσεις.

32 See note 19.

33 See A.-H. Chroust, 'A brief account of the reconstruction of Aristotle's *Protrepticus*,' *Classical Philology*, vol. 60, no. 4 (1965), pp. 229–39, and Chapter VII.

34 These exceptions are: Grenfell-Hunt, *Oxyrrhynchus Papyri* IV. 666 (frag. 57, Rose; frag. 3, Walzer; frag. 3, Ross; frags 2-5, Düring; frags 2-5, Chroust); Stobaeus, *Florilegium* III. 3. 25 (p. 200, ed. O. Hense—frag. 57, Rose; frag. 3, Walzer; frag. 3, Ross; frags 2-5, Düring; frags 2-5, Chroust); and *ibid.*, IV. 32. 21 (p. 785, ed. O. Hense—frag. 50, Rose; frag. 1, Walzer; frag. 1, Ross; frag. 1, Düring; frag. 1, Chroust); *Teletis Reliquiae*[2] (p. 45, ed. O. Hense—frag. 50, Rose; frag. 1, Walzer; frag. 1, Ross); Alexander of Aphrodisias, *Comment. In Aristotelis Topica Libri VIII*, *CIAG*, vol. II, part 2 (ed. M. Wallis, Berlin, 1891), 149,9-17 (frag. 51, Rose; frag. 2, Walzer; frag. 2, Ross; frag. 6, Düring; frag. 6, Chroust); and, perhaps, Iamblichus, *De Communi Mathematica Scientia Liber* (ed. N. Festa, 1891), 79,15-83,5 (frag. 52, Rose; frag. 5, Walzer; frag. 5, Ross).

35 I. Düring (see note 1) and A.-H. Chroust, *Aristotle: Protrepticus—A Reconstruction* (Notre Dame, 1964), have built their reconstructions of Aristotle's *Protrepticus* on this assumption. W. G. Rabinowitz, *Aristotle's Protrepticus and the Sources of its Reconstruction* (University of California Publications in Classical Philology, vol. XVI, no. 1, Berkeley, 1957), on the other hand, flatly denied that Iamblichus' *Protrepticus* constitutes a reliable basis for the recovery of the Aristotelian *Protrepticus*. See also A.-H. Chroust (see note 33), pp. 233-4, and Chapter VII.

36 We shall not investigate here the possibility that the passages from Iamblichus' *Protrepticus*, which have generally been assigned to Aristotle's *Protrepticus*, might also be excerpts from the dialogues of Plato. See G. Müller (see note 23), p. 138. I. Düring (see note 3), p. 45, emphatically denies that Aristotle borrowed here from the writings of Plato. E. Kapp (see note 23), p. 184, on the other hand, believes that large segments of the *Protrepticus* are a haphazard patchwork of passages and ideas taken from Plato's dialogues (as well as from Aristotle's early dialogue and late doctrinal treatises).

37 Thus Iamblichus, *Protrepticus* 47,5-48,21 (frags 59-61, Rose; frags 10a-10c, Walzer; frags 10a-10c, Ross; frags 104-10, Düring; frags 100-6, Chroust), which is reminiscent of Plato's *Phaedo*, has also been assigned to Aristotle's *Eudemus*. See J. Bernays, *Die Dialoge des Aristoteles in ihrem Verhältnis zu seinen übrigen Werken* (Berlin, 1863), p. 144; I. Düring, 'Problems in Aristotle's *Protrepticus*,' *Eranos*, vol. 52 (1954), p. 168; O. Gigon, 'Prolegomena to an Edition of the *Eudemus*,' *Aristotle and Plato in the Mid-Fourth Century* (Göteborg, 1960), pp. 27-8; H. Flashar (see note 19), p. 73. See also Chapter VII, notes 74-8. In his *Aristotle: Fundamentals of the History of his Development* (Oxford, 1948), p. 100, note, W. Jaeger concedes that Iamblichus, *Protrepticus* 47,5-48,21, calls to mind the Aristotelian *Eudemus*. In his *Aristotle's Protrepticus: An Attempt at Reconstruction* (Göteborg, 1961), p. 257, I. Düring, however, definitely assigns this passage to the Aristotelian *Protrepticus* (frags 104-10). Iamblichus, *Protrepticus* 35,18-22, which has been omitted from the authentic fragments of Aristotle's *Protrepticus* by Rose, Walzer, Ross, Düring and Chroust, might actually be an excerpt

from the Aristotelian *Eudemus*. See H. Flashar (note 19), p. 65. I. Düring, *op. cit.*, p. 193, however, denies this; and P. Hartlich, *De Exhortationum a Graecis Romanisque Scriptarum Historia et Indole* (Leipziger Studien zur Klassischen Philologie, vol. XI, Leipzig, 1889), p. 266, definitely assigns this passage to Aristotle's *Protrepticus*.

38 See, for instance, I. Düring (note 1), pp. 11–14 and pp. 30–1; and the reviews of Rabinowitz's book (see note 35) by P. Wilpert, in *Archiv für Geschichte der Philosophie*, vol. 42 (1960), pp. 101 ff.; by W. Spoerri, in *Gnomon*, vol. 32 (1960), pp. 18 ff.; and by F. Dirlmeier, in *Gymnasium*, vol. 70 (1963), p. 68. Previously, the same F. Dirlmeier, *Aristoteles: Eudemische Ethik* (Berlin, 1962), p. 152, had conceded, however, that 'the arguments advanced by Rabinowitz deserve serious consideration.' See also Chapter VII, note 62.

39 W. G. Rabinowitz (see note 35). A position somewhat similar to that held by Rabinowitz was recently taken by H. Flashar (see note 19), pp. 53–79.

40 See G. Müller (note 23), p. 138; E. Kapp (see note 23), p. 184; F. Wehrli (see note 23); A. Lesky, *Geschichte der griechischen Literatur* (2nd ed., Berne, 1963), p. 599.

41 Using the readily available originals of Plato's dialogues, we may be able to identify and trace Iamblichus' method of citing Plato and perhaps generalize these observations to the case of Iamblichus' more obscure sources. This, then, might supply us with something of a standard or criterion which would enable us to evaluate critically his citations from Aristotle's lost works. However, in view of Iamblichus' wholly arbitrary method of reporting, such an undertaking seems to be doomed to failure.

42 See, among others, W. Jaeger (note 37), pp. 64 ff.; K. von Fritz and E. Kapp (see note 16), p. 210; G. Müller (see note 23), p. 137 ff.; A.-H. Chroust (see note 35), pp. X–XI; H. Flashar (see note 19), pp. 58–62. G. Müller, *loc. cit.*, observes that Iamblichus simply ignored or obfuscated 'the more subtle articulation of Aristotle's thought.' Müller also explains Iamblichus' 'obscurantism' by pointing out that to a Neo-Platonic syncretist, any doctrinal differences between Plato and Aristotle were wholly irrelevant and even inconvenient. Iamblichus, Müller contends, wished to recommend philosophy as such to his readers rather than Platonism or Aristotelianism. Hence, according to Müller, Iamblichus indiscriminately cited both Plato and Aristotle—the two most prominent representatives of philosophy in general—without, however, naming them or making any distinction between the two men. As a matter of fact, Müller insists, Iamblichus intentionally intermingled Platonic and Aristotelian thought. I. Düring (see note 1), p. 24, on the other hand, is of the opinion that 'if we look at other passages excerpted from Plato [e.g., a passage from the *Phaedo* on p. 62, Pistelli, which is taken from *Phaedo* 64E–65D. It is clear that *Phaedo* 64A–69D suited Iamblichus' purpose well; the excerpts are found in p. 61,7–67,16, Pistelli.], we shall find that he follows the original pretty closely, suppressing the dialogue, cutting down

the original illustrative examples, and in general omitting the negative arguments. Most of the excerpts in chapters XIII–XIX have this character.' H. G. Gadamer, 'Der aristotelische *Protreptikos* und die entwicklungsgeschichtliche Betrachtung der aristotelischen Ethik,' *Hermes*, vol. 63 (1928), pp. 142 ff., likewise insists that with one single exception Iamblichus is a most accurate excerpter of Plato. H. Flashar (see note 19), pp. 58, on the other hand, emphatically states that 'the excerpts [from Plato's dialogues] digress in many instances from the Platonic original.' Flashar also distinguishes between 'technical digressions' and 'digressions as to philosophic content.' *Ibid.* A classic statement about Iamblichus' *Protrepticus* was made by I. Bywater (see note 1), pp. 55–6: 'It would perhaps be difficult to imagine a book more singularly devoid of any literary or philosophic merit of its own [than Iamblichus' *Protrepticus*]; it is the most shameless of centos, about one-third of it being a plagiarism from Plato, while for the other third the compiler is manifestly indebted to some Peripatetic archetype. . . . Iamblichus makes no secret of the composite origin of his book. . . .' *Ibid.*, pp. 65–6: 'To what "formative pressure" has Iamblichus subjected his borrowed materials? How far, that is, has he supplemented the original [Aristotelian text] by alien additions, and how much has he omitted to embody in his own work? That he has done this . . . is pretty evident. . . .'

43 Referring to the Aristotelian *Protrepticus* and the many problems confronting anyone attempting to recover and reconstruct this work, I. Bywater (see note 1), p. 68, who laid the foundation for the recovery of the *Protrepticus*, thoughtfully remarked: 'Negative criticism has its limits by transgressing which it degenerates into a senseless and unprofitable exercise in logic.' I. Düring (see note 1), p. 11, referring to W. G. Rabinowitz's scholarly but utterly negative criticism, emphatically denies that we should write off the whole problem of Aristotle's *Protrepticus* simply because some scholars are of the opinion that the present *Quellenlage* of the Aristotelian *Protrepticus* seems to vitiate any positive results. To which the present author, who counts himself among the 'reckless optimists,' wishes to add the following observation: it is preferable to have tried, in a spirit of disciplined and competent optimism, and with the aid of whatever relevant materials one may reasonably muster, to recover the lost Aristotelian *Protrepticus* and, for that matter, any and all of the lost works of the early Aristotle—no matter how far one may actually go astray—than not to try at all. Perhaps such a suggestion is too 'revolutionary' with some timid, 'conservative' or unimaginative souls who always shy away from novel conjectures and reasonable hypotheses. It should be borne in mind, however, that every bit of decent human progress throughout the ages has ultimately been the result of some 'revolutionary recklessness' proceeding along lines of valiant though educated and intelligent conjectures. Those who are perennially opposed to novel ideas and adventurous undertakings may not gloat whenever one of the 'reckless optimists' should stumble or

commit errors. Those who never 'get off the ground' and never even dream of taking the 'high road' of intellectual vistas cannot possibly take a fall. But neither will they ever experience the deep satisfaction of intellectual adventure which carries us beyond the confines of routinized knowledge. Hence, they should not belittle those who reach out for the seemingly unattainable.

44 See also Chapter XI.

45 See, for instance, Chapter IV, notes 17, 24, 36 and 63.

CHAPTER IX   WHAT PROMPTED ARISTOTLE TO ADDRESS THE *Protrepticus* TO THEMISON OF CYPRUS?

★ With some minor changes, this chapter originally appeared in *Hermes*, vol. 94, no. 2 (1966), pp. 202–7.

1 Stobaeus, *Florilegium* IV. 32. 21. (frag. 50, Rose; frag. 1, Walzer; frag. 1, Ross; frag. 1, Düring; frag. 1, Chroust). The *Protrepticus* was 'addressed' rather than 'dedicated' to Themison. The practice of dedicating literary works to some prominent personage is probably of a later date. See W. Jaeger, *Aristotle: Fundamentals of the History of his Development* (Oxford, 1948), p. 56.

2 It seems obvious that Themison was not an Evagorid. Hence he could not have ruled over Cypriot Salamis. W. H. Engel surmised that this Themison was the 'ruler' of Kyrenia on Cyprus. See W. H. Engel, *Kypros*, vol. I (Berlin, 1841), pp. 364–5. Engel also conjectured that Themison may have commanded the fleet of Antigonus Monophthalmus when the latter laid siege to the city of Tyre in 315–14 B.C. Should Engel's second conjecture prove to be correct, then Themison must have been a fairly young man at the time Aristotle addressed him in the *Protrepticus*; or our Themison was the father (?) of the Themison who took part in the siege of Tyre.

3 Plato already had pointed out that wealthy people have a greater opportunity of dedicating themselves to philosophy and the study of philosophy. Plato, *Protragoras* 326C. See also Plato (?), *Second Epistle* 310E: 'It is natural that wisdom and great wordly power attract one another. They are always pursuing and seeking after each other and are always coming together.' But wealth must always remain subservient to reason and, hence, to philosophy. Plato, *Laws* 661AB. This is also brought out in the *Protrepticus*. See frag. 57, Rose; frag. 3, Walzer; frag. 3, Ross; frags 2–4, Düring; frags 2–4, Chroust (*Oxyrrhynchus Papyri* IV. 666, Grenfell-Hunt).

4 See Cicero, *De Divinatione ad Brutum* I, 25. 53; frag. 37, Rose; frag. 1, Walzer; frag. 1, Ross.

5 Plutarch, *Dion* 22; frag. 37, Rose; frag. 1, Walzer; frag. 1, Ross. See also A.-H. Chroust, '*Eudemus or On the Soul:* a lost Aristotelian dialogue on the immortality of the soul,' *Mnemosyne* (series 4), vol. 19 (1966), pp. 17–30, and Chapter IV.

6 Some scholars are of the opinion that Eudemus played a role in some of the

negotiations between Macedonia and the Greek settlers on the island of Cyprus who during the fifties of the fourth century B.C. revolted against their Persian-Phoenician overlords and, hence, did seek Macedonian support. See also note 10.

7 This, in turn, might suggest that Aristotle wished to imitate Plato's efforts to establish close relations with Dionysius I and Dionysius II of Syracuse and that he did so by establishing contacts with Themison. According to Diogenes Laertius, *passim*, not a few prominent Greek philosophers of the fifth and fourth century B.C. sought connections with ruling dynasties. It is also a matter of common knowledge that the Platonic Academy had many contacts with kings, potentates and plain tyrants. Several of Plato's disciples subsequently became notorious as well as ruthless tyrants. Remembering the dismal records of some of these men, one might be justified in calling the Platonic Academy a 'seedbed of tyrants.' See A.-H. Chroust, 'A second (and closer) look at Plato's political philosophy,' *Archiv für Rechts—und Sozialphilosophie*, vol. 48, no. 4 (1962), p. 486, note 200; A.-H. Chroust, 'Plato's Academy: the first organized school of political science in antiquity,' *Review of Politics*, vol. 29, no. 1 (1967), pp. 25–40. See also note 12.

8 According to DL V. 3–4, Aristotle was on 'very friendly terms with Hermias,' the tyrant of Atarneus, and 'wrote a paean in honor of Hermias.' See also DL V. 5–7; *VH* 4; Athenaeus, *Deipnosophistae* XV. 696A ff.; Areius Didymus, *In Demosthenis Orationes Commenta* (ed. H. Diels and W. Schubart, Berlin, 1904), vol. I, p. 6, lines 18 ff. Aristotle's close connections with King Philip of Macedonia are well known. They are frequently referred to in the extant *Vitae Aristotelis*, which also relate that Aristotle had many personal as well as official contacts with kings, princes and cities; and that he was oftentimes honored by the last for his many services to them. For more detail, see, for instance, A.-H. Chroust, 'Aristotle and Athens: some comments on Aristotle's sojourns in Athens,' *Laval Théologique et Philosophique*, vol. 22, no. 2 (1966), pp. 186–96, and Vol. I, Chapter XIII.

9 A Cypriot named Themison, together with his brother Aristos, was a contemporary as well as a friend of King Antiochus II of Syria. See Athenaeus, *op. cit.*, VII. 289F and X. 438D. This particular Themison, who is called a 'Macedonian,' might have been a descendant of the Themison to whom Aristotle addressed his *Protrepticus*. All this might also indicate that our Themison was a 'philo-Macedonian.' See G. E. L. Owen, 'Logic and metaphysics in some earlier works of Aristotle,' *Aristotle and Plato in the Mid-Fourth Century* (Göteborg, 1960), p. 183, note 3. See also note 6 and J. Bernays, *Die Dialoge des Aristoteles in ihrem Verhältnis zu seinen übrigen Werken* (Berlin, 1863), p. 116. In 351–50 B.C., Cyprus became involved in open warfare with Persia (King Artaxerxes III, Ochus).

10 See, for instance, A.-H. Chroust (see note 8). It might be conjectured that Aristotle failed to interest King Philip in the affairs of Cyprus. In 352 B.C.

or thereabouts, Philip was in no position to undertake effective steps on behalf of the Greek settlers on Cyprus. It is possible that *in lieu* of such an active or military assistance, Aristotle might have addressed the *Protrepticus* to Themison.

11 See J. Bernays (see note 9), p. 117; I. Bywater, 'On a lost dialogue of Aristotle,' *Journal of Philology*, vol. 2 (1869), p. 68. From Stobaeus (Teles) IV. 32. 21, we may infer that Teles does not concur with the Aristotelian statement that 'Themison possessed great wealth and, thus, could afford to spend much money on philosophy.' Hence, Crates, the Cynic, observes: 'I think, Philiscus [a poor shoemaker], that I shall address a *Protrepticus* to you. For I realize that you [, a poor man,] have more advantages for the study of philosophy than were his [*scil.*, Themison's] for whom Aristotle wrote [his *Protrepticus*].' It will be noted that by indirection, Crates is recommending here the 'Cynic way of life.' To the Cynics as well as to the Stoics (who in this were under Cynic influence) wealth was a liability rather than an asset in the study of philosophy. Apparently, neither Crates nor Zeno (the Stoic) could understand or appreciate Aristotle's 'motivation' in addressing the *Protrepticus* to Themison.

12 See, for instance, DL I. 27; I. 72; I. 75; I. 77; I. 81; I. 83-4; II. 49-52; II. 61; II. 63; II. 67-9; II. 73; II. 77-82; II. 102; II. 110; II. 115-6; II. 127-30; II. 140-3; III. 9; III. 18-23; IV. 1; IV. 8-9; IV. 11; IV. 38-9; V. 1; V. 2; V. 3-4; V. 37; V. 58; V. 67-8; V. 78; VII. 6-9; VIII. 8; VIII. 79; IX. 12-14; IX. 21; IX. 60; etc. See also notes 7 and 28. This practice was vehemently denounced by the 'proletarian' Cynics and also scoffed at by some Stoics. See note 11. For the Cynic contempt for such practices, see DL VI. 25-6. Socrates, too, is said to have refused to seek favors from wealthy and influential people or to associate with tyrants. See DL II. 25; Seneca, *De Beneficiis* V. 6. 2 ff.; Aristotle, *Rhetoric* 1398 a 24 ff.; Stobeaus, *Eclogues* IV. 33. 28. See also Plato, *Crito* 53D; Libanius, *Apologia Socratis* 165-6; Plato, *Gorgias* 470D.

13 See H. Diels, 'Zu Arostoteles *Protreptikos* und Ciceros *Hortensius*,' *Archiv für Geschichte der Philosophie*, vol. I (1888), p. 482; P. Hartlich, *De Exhortationum a Graecis Romanisque Scriptarum Historia et Indole* (Leipziger Studien zur Klassischen Philologie), vol. 11, fasc. 2 (Leipzig, 1889), p. 238.

14 See R. Hirzel, 'Über den *Protreptikos* des Aristoteles,' *Hermes*, vol. 10 (1876), pp. 96-9; W. Jaeger (see note 1), p. 54.

15 See W. G. Rabinowitz, *Aristotle's Protrepticus and the Sources of its Reconstruction* (University of California Publications in Classical Philology, vol. XVI, no. 1, Berkeley, 1957), pp. 28-34. Plato's (?) *Sixth Epistle* seems to indicate that such a 'foreign branch' of the Academy, consisting of Erastus and Coriscus, apparently flourished in Assos under the patronage of Hermias of Atarneus. It is held that in 348-47 B.C., after his withdrawal from Athens, Aristotle joined this 'foreign branch.' See A.-H. Chroust, 'Aristotle leaves the Academy,' *Greece and Rome*, vol. 14, no. 1 (1967), pp. 39-43, and Vol. I, Chapter IX. But there might have been 'political' or

'diplomatic' reasons why Aristotle visited Hermias. See Vol. I, Chapter XIII.

16 See Elias, *Comment. in Porphyrii Isagogen et in Aristotelis Categorias*, CIAG, vol. XVIII, part 1 (ed. A. Busse, Berlin, 1900), p. 3, lines 17–23; David, *Prolegomena et in Porphyrii Isagogen Comment.*, *ibid.*, vol. XVIII, part 2, p. 109, lines 2–12. See also frag. 51, Rose; frag. 2, Walzer; frag. 2, Ross.

17 Tradition has it that the *Protrepticus* provided the foundation, through the intermediary of Cicero's *Hortensius*, for the conversion of the young St Augustine to the intellectual life and thus indirectly to his conversion to Christianity. See St Augustine, *Confessiones* III. 4. After reading Cicero's *Hortensius*, St Augustine admitted: 'Forthwith all my vain hopes became worthless to me, and with incredible ardor of heart I was craving for the immortality of wisdom.' It has long been surmised that Cicero's *Hortensius*, a composition which is likewise lost, was largely fashioned after Aristotle's *Protrepticus*. See, for instance, *Scriptores Historiae Augustae* II. 97. 20 ff. (ed. Hohl), where we are informed that in his *Hortensius* Cicero used arguments modeled on Aristotle's *Protrepticus*. Not all scholars, however, accept the thesis that the *Hortensius* was directly influenced by the *Protrepticus*.

18 See, for instance, W. Jaeger (see note 1), pp. 81 ff.; B. Einarson, 'Aristotle's *Protrepticus* and the structure of the *Epinomis*,' *Transactions and Proceedings of the American Philological Association*, vol. 67 (Ithaca, 1936), pp. 261–85. P. von der Mühll, 'Isokrates und der *Protreptikos* des Aristoteles,' *Philologus*, vol. 94 (1939–40), pp. 259–65; A. Lesky, *Geschichte der Griechischen Literatur* (2nd ed., Berne-Munich, 1963), p. 600; and R. Stark, in *Göttinger Gelehrter Anzeiger*, no. 217 (1965), p. 57, on the other hand, hold that the publication of the *Antidosis* was provoked by the publication of the *Protrepticus*. It is no mere accident that the Aristotelian *Protrepticus* was composed in the form of an exhortation, since exhortations, it will be noted, constituted an essential element of Isocrates' pedagogical method. Neither is it without significance that in the *Protrepticus* Aristotle should frequently use the expression, 'we must believe.' This expression appears no less than fifteen times in Isocrates' *To Nicocles*.

19 See G. E. L. Owen (note 9).

20 Nicocles is said to have been a *roué*. See Athenaeus, *Deipnosophistae* XII. 531DE.

21 Evagoras II soon was killed. He was succeeded by his son, Pnytagoras, who allied himself with the Athenians. But as far as Isocrates was concerned, the damage had been done by Evagoras II. See also Diodorus Siculus XVI. 42. 3–58, and K. J. Beloch, *Griechische Geschichte* (2nd ed.), vol. III, part 1 (Berlin-Leipzig, 1922), p. 526 and *ibid.*, vol. III, part 2 (Berlin-Leipzig, 1923), pp. 98–101.

22 The presence in the Academy of Eudemus of Cyprus, apparently a political exile from the island, might be indicative of these political aspirations. See note 6.

23 Contemporary Athenian comedy indicates that the average Athenian

probably regarded the members of the Academy and, for that matter, all philosophers and intellectuals, as 'eggheads,' 'cranks,' 'crackpots' or plain fools. This is also brought out by Plato, *Phaedo* 64A; Plato, *Euthydemus* 304D; Plato, *Republic* 489D ff.; 496B ff.; 498DE; 500A ff.; Plato, *Theaetetus* 173C ff. and 175B ff., as well as by many other ancient authors.

24 See Plutarch, *Adversus Coloten* 32-3 (*Moralia* 1126CE). See also P. M. Schuhl, 'Platon et l'activité politique de l'Académie,' *Revue des Études Grecques*, vols 59/60 (1946-7), pp. 46-52; P. M. Schuhl, 'Une école des sciences politiques,' *Revue Philosophique de la France et de l'Étranger*, vol. 84 (1959), pp. 101 ff.; M. Isnardi, 'Teoria e Prassi nel Pensiero dell'Academia Antica,' *La Parola del Passato*, vol. 11 (1956), pp. 401-33; M. Isnardi, 'Nomos e basileia nell'Academia antica,' *La Parola del Passato*, vol. 12 (1957), pp. 411-33; M. Isnardi, 'Studi recenti e problemi aperti sulla structura e la funzione della prima Academia platonica,' *Rivista Storica Italiana*, vol. 71 (1959), pp. 271-91; E. Berti, *La Filosofia del Primo Aristotele* (Padua, 1962), pp. 147-51.

25 See A.-H. Chroust, 'Plato's Academy: the first organized school of political science in antiquity,' *Review of Politics*, vol. 29, no. 1 (1967), pp. 25-40.

26 See, in general, Plato, *Republic* 519A and 534D ff.; *et passim.*

27 See, for instance, U. von Wilamowitz-Moellendorff, *Platon*, vol. I (Berlin, 1920), pp. 357 ff.; J. Stenzel, *Platon der Erzieher* (Berlin, 1928), *passim*; M. Gentile, *La Politica di Platone* (Padua, 1940), pp. 8-11; H. Marrou, *Histoire de l'Éducation dans l'Antiquité* (Paris, 1948), pp. 103-4; and note 24.

28 For detail, see A.-H. Chroust (note 25), *passim.*

29 See, for instance, Plato (?), *Fifth Epistle*, which is addressed to King Perdiccas III of Macedonia (365-59 B.C.), the son of King Amyntas III. Nicomachus, the father of Aristotle, was the personal physician as well as the close friend and adviser of King Amyntas III.

30 See Plato (?), *Fifth Epistle.*

31 See, for instance, Plutarch, *Adversus Coloten* 32-3 (*Moralia* 1126DE); Athenaeus, *Deipnosophistae* XI. 506E ff.; Plutarch, *Dion* 13 and 28; DL III. 23; Aelian, *Varia Historia* XI. 42 and XII. 30; Plutarch, *Ad Principem Ineruditum* 1 (*Moralia* 779D); Plato (?), *Sixth Epistle*; etc. For additional detail, see A.-H. Chroust (note 25), *passim.*

32 See here also A.-H. Chroust (see note 8), *passim*, and Vol. I, Chapter XIII. This view seems to receive some support from the story that Themison or, more likely, one of his descendants was called the 'Macedonian,' and that one of Themison's descendants played a role at the court of Antiochus II of Syria. See note 9. All this might imply that Themison (or his descendants) was a philo-Macedonian, and that he had some contacts with the Macedonian dynasty (or the Diodochi). See, however, note 10.

33 See A.-H. Chroust, 'Aristotle's first literary effort: the *Gryllus*—a lost dialogue on the nature of rhetoric,' *Revue des Études Grecques*, vol. 78, nos 371-3 (1966), pp. 576-91, and Chapter III. It is possible that Aristotle's

*Politicus* is likewise a rejoinder to Isocrates and the political and social philosophy he recommended.

34 See note 18.

35 I. Düring, *Aristotle's Protrepticus: An Attempt at Reconstruction* (Studia Graeca et Latina Gothoburgensia, Göteborg, 1961), p. 174.

36 See, in general, A.-H. Chroust (see note 8), *passim*, and Vol. I, Chapter XIII.

## CHAPTER X  THE TERM 'PHILOSOPHER' AND THE PANEGYRIC ANALOGY IN ARISTOTLE'S *Protrepticus*

\* In a different and much shorter form, this chapter was first published in *Apeiron*, vol. I, no. 1 (1966), pp. 14–17.

1 See A.-H. Chroust, 'Some observations on the origin of the term "philosopher,"' *New Scholasticism*, vol. 28, no. 4 (1964), pp. 423–34.

2 DL I. 12.

3 See also Iamblichus, *Protrepticus* (summaria), p. 4, lines 15 ff., Pistelli.

4 See also Iamblichus, *De Vita Pythagorica* XII. 58, p. 31, lines 20–p. 32, line 22 (ed. L. Deubner, Leipzig, 1937); Iamblichus, *Protrepticus*, p. 53, lines 15 ff.; Athenaeus, *Deipnosophistae* XI. 463DE; DL VIII. 8. Diogenes Laertius, *loc. cit.*, credits this story to Sosicrates, *Successions of Philosophers*, rather than to Heracleides of Pontus. The accounts of Cicero and Iamblichus, which contain a confrontation of the philosopher or philosophic man (Pythagoras, who by the fourth century had become the prototype of the philosopher or wise man) and the tyrant (Leon of Phlius), might be a variation on the popular theme, 'the wise and gentle man versus the ignorant and brutish tyrant.' The present author has suggested that this confrontation might be the precursor or perhaps part of a 'mirror for princes.' See A.-H. Chroust (see note 1), p. 426, note 6. See, in general, A. Alföldi, 'Der Philosoph als Zeuge der Wahrheit und sein Gegenspieler der Tyrann,' *Scientiis et Artibus*, vol. I (1958), pp. 7–19.

5 See also R. Joly, 'Le thème philosophique des genres de vie dans l'antiquité classique,' *Académie Royale de Belgique* (Classe des Lettres, Mémor. 51, sect. 3, Brussels, 1956), pp. 43 ff.

6 Athenaeus, *Deipnosophistae* XI. 463DE. See also DL II. 109.

7 DL VIII. 8. See also note 4.

8 For additional detail, see A.-H. Chroust (note 1), *passim*. DL I. 12 relates that Pythagoras was the first to use the term 'philosophy,' and the first to call himself a 'philosopher'; and that he did so because, as he said, 'no man is wise, but God alone.' This latter statement reminds us of Plato, *Phaedrus* 278D: 'Wise (σοφοί), I may not call them [*scil.*, those whose compositions are based on the knowledge of objective truth and who can defend or prove these compositions], for this is a great name which belongs to God alone. But "lovers of widsom" (φιλόσοφοι) is their modest and befitting title.' Neither Cicero, *Tuscul. Disput.* V. 3. 8–10, nor Iamblichus, *De Vita*

*Pythagorica* XII. 58 ff., contains the observation that 'no man is wise, but God alone.'

9 See note 13 and the corresponding text.

10 Iamblichus, *Protrepticus*, p. 53, line 15 to p. 54, line 5 (frag. 58, Rose; frag. 12, Walzer; frag. 12, Ross; frag. 44, Düring; frag. 42, Chroust). Already in Iamblichus, *Protrepticus*, p. 51, lines 7-10 (frag. 11, Walzer; frag. 11, Ross; frag. 18, Düring; frag. 16, Chroust), reference is made to the definition of philosophy as 'viewing reality': 'Pythagoras, when asked this question [*scil.*, to what particular purpose did nature and God bring us into being, *note by the author*], replied: "To view [or contemplate] the heavens." And he added that he was a viewer of nature [reality], and that he had come into life for this very purpose.' See here also note 14. This would indicate one of two things: either in the original Aristotelian text there were two references to this definition of the philosopher, and Iamblichus, *Protrepticus* 51,7-10 preceded Iamblichus, *Protrepticus* 53,15-54,5, in the original Aristotelian text; or Iamblichus, *Protrepticus* 51,7-10, is taken from another source.

11 It will be noted that Aristotle refers to the Olympic Games in *Nicomachean Ethics* 1099 a 9; and that St Paul, I Cor. 9:24, likewise uses the panegyric analogy when he alludes to the Isthmian Games. Since Pythagoras compares the philosopher to 'the fond (or dispassionate) viewer of the sublime spectacle (or vision),' he should have called himself a φιλοθεάμων (see Plato, *Republic* 475D and 476A) or, perhaps, a φιλοθέωρος (see Aristotle, *Nicomachean Ethics* 1100 b 19-20), rather than a φιλόσοφος. See note 17.

12 See note 14.

13 It is possible that the definition of the 'philosopher' as the 'lover of wisdom' originally goes back to Plato, *Phaedrus* 278D, quoted in note 8. See also Plato, *Republic* 480A, *et passim*; *Symposium* 204A ff.; etc.

14 According to Iamblichus, *Protrepticus*, p. 51, lines 7-10 (frag. 11, Walzer; frag. 11, Ross; frag. 18, Düring; frag. 16, Chroust), Aristotle mentions Pythagoras as having called himself a 'viewer of nature' without, however, referring to the panegyric analogy or to the three basic 'ways of life.' This might signify that *Protrepticus* 51,7-10 does not go back to Aristotle's *Protrepticus*, but to some other source which cannot be identified. See note 10. Iamblichus, *Protrepticus*, p. 51, lines 11-15 (frag. 11, Walzer; frag. 11, Ross; frag. 19, Düring; frag. 17, Chroust), also relates that Anaxagoras, when asked for what purpose one came into being and for what purpose one should live, replied: 'To view (or contemplate, εἰς θεωρίαν) whatever pertains to the heavens and to the stars and the moon and the sun in the heavens, everything else being of no importance.' The same story can also be found in DL II. 10. See Clement of Alexandria, *Stromateis* II. 130. According to DL II. 7, Anaxagoras declared the heavens to be his fatherland. Democritus is said to have stated that 'the great joys are derived from the vision (θεᾶσθαι) of beautiful and perfect works.' Frag. 194 B, Diels-Kranz. See also Menander, frag. 416; Aristotle, *Eudemian Ethics* 1216 a 1 ff.:

'... Anaxagoras answered a man ... asking why one would choose rather to be born than not: "For the sake of viewing the heavens and the whole order of the universe."'

15 See, for instance, *VL* 28 and 29; *VM* 33; *VV* 9.

16 When Cicero relates that Pythagoras had maintained that 'so also we, as though we had come from some city to a crowded festival, leaving in like fashion another life and another nature of being when entering upon this life,' then he definitely refers to the pre-existence and transmigration of the human soul—a doctrine taught by Pythagoras and the Pythagoreans, as well as by Plato.

17 It will be noted that neither Aristotle, nor Cicero (Heracleides), nor Iamblichus in this connection actually justify the use of the term 'philosopher.' This was done by Plato, *Phaedrus* 278D. Judging from what Pythagoras allegedly said, he would not have called himself a 'philosopher,' but, as has been shown, a 'viewer (or spectator) of the truth' ($\vartheta\epsilon\omega\rho\eta\tau\iota\kappa\grave{o}s$) or, perhaps, a 'fond viewer of the sublime vision' ($\varphi\iota\lambda o\vartheta\epsilon\acute{a}\mu\omega\nu$). See note 11.

18 Plato, *Symposium* 204A ff.

19 The sequence of athletes, merchants and philosophers is observed by Cicero and Sosicrates (DL VIII. 8). Iamblichus, on the other hand, mentions first the merchants. In so doing, Iamblichus apparently follows Plato's hierarchical structure of the tripartite soul: the appetitive part of the soul is represented by the merchants, the courageous part by the athletes, and the intellectual or rational part of the soul by the philosophers.

20 See also Plato, *Republic* 465C ff., where we are told that the guardians—the philosophers—are above the tribulations of daily life; they are not exposed to the drudgery of providing for their physical needs. But more than that, the life of the philosopher is to be ranked above that of a victor at Olympia. For the latter 'receives only a part of the blessedness' which is the share of the true philosopher. Here, too, the virtuous life of the active man is rated below the theoretic or contemplative life of the philosopher.

21 This notion is derived from Aristotle's *Protrepticus* and, ultimately, from Plato. See note 4. It need not be stressed here that for Plato the most perfect activity is the contemplation of the Separate Ideas or, better, of the Idea of the Good (or the One). This constitutes for Plato the 'beatific vision.'

22 W. Jaeger, *Aristotle: Fundamentals of the History of his Development* (Oxford, 1948), p. 98; W. Jaeger, 'On the origin and cycle of the philosophic ideal of life,' *ibid.*, pp. 432–3. Jaeger's suggestion that Heracleides of Pontus derived the panegyric analogy from Aristotle's *Protrepticus*, however, may be challenged. It might be more appropriate to surmise that Heracleides borrowed it from Plato or, perhaps, from a pre-Platonic source which, however, cannot be identified.

23 See also A.-H. Chroust, *Aristotle: Protrepticus—A Reconstruction* (Notre Dame, 1964), pp. 18–19, and the comments thereto at pp. 70–7.

24 See Plato, *Republic* 580D ff.; *Symposium* 204D.

25 Aristotle, *Eudemian Ethics* 1214 a 30 ff. See also Aristotle, *Protrepticus*, in: Iamblichus, *Protrepticus*, p. 41, lines 6–15 (frag. 6, Walzer; frag. 6, Ross; frag. 41, Düring; frag. 39, Chroust).

26 Aristotle, *Eudemian Ethics* 1215 a 35 ff.

27 See notes 8 and 19.

28 Aristotle, it appears, recommends here a sense of awe and reverence in the presence of the divine universe—in the presence of what is infinitely above and infinitely superior to man and his ever-questing mind. Accordingly, contemplative meditation and contemplation of the divine universe is also true worship and real piety. By becoming the dispassionate spectator of this ever-living reality, rational man achieves his highest calling. See Plutarch, *De Tranquillitate Animi* 20 (*Moralia* 477CF). Man is directed towards contemplation, towards what is eternal and divine—towards God Who dwells within as well as above the miraculous universe. See also Vol. I, Chapter XVI and Vol. II, Chapter II. A faint echo of this may still be felt in Aristotle, *Metaphysics* 982 b 12 ff., where we are told that 'philosophy starts in wonder and wonderment.' 'For it was owing to their wonder that men now begin and at first began to philosophize. They wondered . . . about the phenomena of the moon and those of the sun and the stars, and about the genesis of the universe. And a man who is puzzled and wonders thinks himself ignorant. . . . And since they philosophized in order to escape from ignorance, they were pursuing knowledge in order to know, and not for some utilitarian end.'

CHAPTER XI   ARISTOTLE's *Politicus*

\* With some considerable changes, this chapter was first published in *Rheinisches Museum für Philologie*, vol. 108, no. 4 (1965), pp. 346–53.

1 DL 22 (no. 4), which lists a Πολιτικός, in two books.

2 VH 10 (no. 4), which lists a Πολιτικόν, in one book. The 'catalogue' of Ptolemy (-el-Garib) apparently did not mention a *Politicus*.

3 Cicero, *Epistola ad Quintum Fratrem* III. 5. 1 (frag. 78, Rose; frag. 1, Ross).

4 See here J. Bernays, *Die Dialoge des Aristoteles in ihrem Verhältnis zu seinen übrigen Werken* (Berlin, 1863), p. 53; E. Heitz, *Die verlorenen Schriften des Aristoteles* (Leipzig, 1865), p. 189; P. Moraux, *Les Listes Anciennes des Ouvrages d'Aristote* (Louvain, 1951), p. 31. In his *Aristotle: Fundamentals of the History of his Development* (Oxford, 1948), p. 29, W. Jaeger points out that in such didactic dialogues as the *Politicus* or the *On Philosophy* Aristotle casts himself in the role of a leader of the philosophic discussion. Cicero, *Epistola ad Atticum* XIII. 19. 4, maintains that in his dialogues Aristotle is in the habit of leading the discussion. Obviously, this observation of Cicero does not apply to all of Aristotle's early dialogues, and certainly not to the *Gryllus or On Rhetoric* and to the *Eudemus or On the Soul*.

5 Cicero, *De Finibus* V. 4. 11 (*Testimonium*, Ross, p. 68).

6 Cicero, *Epistola ad Quintum Fratrem* III. 5. 1. See also note 3. Some scholars have suggested that Cicero's reference to Aristotle's 'discussion of the body politic (*res publica*)' relates to the (lost) Aristotelian *On Justice*, while the reference to 'the foremost man (*vir praestans*)' relates to the Aristotelian *Politicus*. See notes 14-15.

7 See W. Jaeger (note 4), pp. 26-31.

8 See note 18.

9 For detail, see A.-H. Chroust, 'The probable dates of some of Aristotle's lost works,' *Rivista Critica di Storia della Filosofia*, vol. 22, fasc. 1 (1967), pp. 3-23, especially pp. 17-19, and Chapter I, notes 83-90, and the corresponding texts.

10 See note 18. It will be shown later, however, that there might exist another important fragment of the *Politicus*—a fragment which in the past has generally been credited to the Aristotelian *Protrepticus*.

11 See note 26.

12 It could be argued that the *Protrepticus*, written between 352 and 350 B.C., is a general defense of the 'philosophic ideal of life' recommended by Plato, and that the *Politicus* is a kind of 'special plea' re-asserting the moral and philosophic implications of all political thought and action.

13 See A.-H. Chroust, 'The probable date of Aristotle's lost dialogue *On Philosophy*,' *Journal of the History of Philosophy*, vol. 4, no. 4 (1966), pp. 283-91, and Chapter XII.

14 If, on the other hand, we are to accept Jaeger's translation and interpretation, namely, that 'the good is the most exact measure among all measures,' then it should be obvious that when composing the *Politicus* Aristotle still subscribed to Plato's notion of the Separate Ideas and, perhaps, to Plato's 'mathematical (Pythagorizing) metaphysics' propagated in the latest Platonic dialogues. See text.

15 W. Jaeger (see note 4), p. 25, note 2. An *On Justice* in four books is listed in DL V. 22 (no. 1), *VH* 10 (no. 1), and Ptolemy (-el-Garib), no. 4. The whole passage from Cicero reads as follows: '. . . *Aristotelem denique quae de re publica et praestanti viro scribat ipsum loqui.*'

16 R. Weil, *Aristote et l'Histoire: Essai sur la 'Politique'* (Paris, 1960), p. 146.

17 R. Stark, *Aristotelesstudien: philologische Untersuchungen zur Entwicklung der aristotelischen Ethik* (Munich, 1954), p. 12. According to DL V. 22 (no. 4), the *Politicus* consisted of two books. See note 1.

18 Syrianus, *Commentaria in Aristotelis Metaphysica*, *CIAG*, vol. VI. part 1 (ed. W. Kroll, Berlin, 1902), p. 168, lines 33-35 (frag. 79, Rose; frag. 2, Ross).

19 R. Stark (see note 17), pp. 27 ff.

20 W. Jaeger (see note 4), p. 87.

21 Plato, *Philebus* 66A.

22 Plato, *Republic*, Books VI and VII, *passim*.

23 Plato, *Laws* 716C.

24 W. Jaeger (see note 19).

25  See here, for instance, Plato, *Philebus* 56BC; 57C-57D; 58C; *et passim*. See also A.-H. Chroust, 'An emendation to fragment 13 (Walzer, Ross) of Aristotle's *Protrepticus*,' *Tijdschrift voor Filosofie*, vol. 28, no. 2 (1966), pp. 366-77, and Chapter VIII. Here an attempt has been made to show that frag. 13, Walzer; frag. 13, Ross; frags 48-50, Düring; frags 45-7, Chroust (Iamblichus, *Protrepticus* 55,7-56,2, Pistelli), usually credited to Aristotle's *Protrepticus*, might indeed be a fragment of the Aristotelian *Politicus*. See text, pp. 143-4.

26  See, among others, M. Gentile, 'La dottrina platonica delle idee numeri e Aristotele,' *Annali della Reale Scuola Normale Superiore di Pisa* (Classe di Lettere e Filosofia), vol. 30, fasc. 3 (1930), p. 43; E. Bignone, *L'Aristotele Perduto e la Formazione Filosofica di Epicuro* (Florence, 1936), vol. II, p. 5 and vol. II, p. 102; P. Moraux (see note 4), p. 31; R. Weil (see note 16), p. 146; E. Berti, *La Filosofia del Primo Aristotele* (Università di Padova, Pubblicazione della Facoltà di Lettere e Filosofia, Padua, 1962), pp. 447 ff.

27  R. Stark (see note 17), pp. 27 ff.

28  Jaeger's translation and interpretation, it will be noted, make the Good the 'most exact measure [*among* all measures],' that is, *among* all measures or Ideas. Stark's translation, on the other hand, makes the Good 'the most exact measure *for* all things (in the world of experience).'

29  R. Stark (see note 27). Stark, it will be noted, wishes to demonstrate that the *Politicus* is not Platonic in doctrine but rather akin to Aristotle's later doctrinal treatises.

30  See note 18 and the corresponding text.

31  R. Stark (see note 17), p. 31.

32  See also Aristotle, *Nicomachean Ethics* 1113 a 29 ff. and 1128 a 31.

33  This is brought out in Aristotle's later ethics, which stand in contradiction to Platonic as well as early Aristotelian ethics. In the later Aristotelian ethics, the individual and autonomous ethical person becomes the ultimate moral standard. (This is also indicated by the radical change in the meaning of the term φρόνησις, which with Plato and the early Aristotle signifies purely theoretic knowledge or wisdom, while in the later works of Aristotle, it denotes a kind of practical knowledge concerned with the particular.) See, for instance, Aristotle, *Nichomachean Ethics* 1113 a 29 ff.: 'The good man judges each class of things rightly, and in each individual thing the truth as it appears to him. . . . The good man probably differs from other men mostly by seeing the truth in each individual class of things, being as it were himself the norm and standard of these things.' *Ibid.*, 1128 a 31 ff.: 'The refined and well-bred man . . . will be . . . a law unto himself.' R. Stark denies another of Jaeger's basic theses, namely, that in his later works Aristotle 'abandons' his original 'Platonic' position, which becomes manifest, among other early works, in the *Politicus*. But Stark goes still further: he propounds that Plato himself, at least in the *Philebus* and *Statesman*, actually reduces both ethics and politics to a 'science of measurement'—a science, that is, which turns into (Platonic) dialectics.

But such a situation most certainly does not require several 'measures' or 'standards' or 'values' among which the 'Supreme One' or the 'Ultimate Good' constitutes the most exact and, hence, the most appropriate measure. Rather, it presupposes the ability to judge or evaluate the worth of different things or different actions by that single and supreme and, at the same time, absolute criterion or measure which is the Good. See R. Stark, *op. cit.*, pp. 28–30.

34 See note 18.

35 Plato, *Laws* 716C. See also note 23.

36 See here also Plato, *Cratylus* 386A ff.; *Theaetetus* 152A.

37 For a detailed discussion of the likely date of Aristotle's *On Philosophy*, see Chapter XII.

38 For a discussion of the likely date of the *Politicus*, see notes 9–14, and the corresponding text; Chapter I, notes 83–90, and the corresponding texts.

39 Cicero, *De Natura Deorum* I. 13. 33 (frag. 26, Rose; frag. 26, Walzer; frag. 26, Ross; frag. 39, Untersteiner). See also M. Untersteiner, *Aristotele: Della Filosofia* (Rome, 1963), pp. 255–65; A.-H. Chroust, 'The concept of God in Aristotle's lost dialogue *On Philosophy* (Cicero, *De Natura Deorum* I. 13. 33),' *Emerita*, vol. 33, fasc. 2 (1965), pp. 205–28, and Chapter XIV.

40 This is probably the same source which has been used by Philodemus. Cicero, *De Natura Deorum* I. 13. 33 (frag. 235, Usener), reports that '*Epicurus Aristotelem vexarit contumeliosissime. . . .*'

41 Sextus Empiricus, *Adversus Mathematicos* IX. 26–7 (*Adversus Physicos* I. 26–7—frag. 11, Rose; frag. 12b, Walzer; frag. 12b, Ross; frag. 26, Untersteiner). See also M. Untersteiner (note 39), pp. 171–5.

42 Sextus Empiricus probably relies here on Posidonius, *De Divinatione*.

43 It should be noted that in *Metaphysics* 1075 a 11 ff., Aristotle likewise uses the analogy of a 'properly functioning and orderly army' to illustrate the notion of a universal and perfect order under a 'universal commander.' The excellence of an efficient army, we are told here, 'is to be found in the order and in its commander, and more in the latter. For he does not depend on the order, but the order depends on him.' This, in turn, calls to mind Plato, *Timaeus* 28A–29A, where the Demiurge is presented as the originator of the cosmic order.

44 Cicero, *De Natura Deorum* II. 37. 95–6 (frag. 12, Rose; frag. 13, Walzer; frag. 13, Ross; frag. 18, Untersteiner). See also M. Untersteiner (note 39), pp. 175–81. Cicero's more immediate source is probably Posidonius, *Concerning the Gods*. Posidonius, in turn, probably consulted Aristotle's *On Philosophy*.

45 Plato, *Republic* 514A ff. and 532A ff.

46 Cicero, *De Natura Deorum* II. 37. 95–6. See also Philo of Alexandria, *Legum Allegoriarum Libri Tres* III. 32. 97–9 (frag. 13, Walzer; frag. 13, Ross; frag. 15, Untersteiner); Philo of Alexandria, *De Praemiis et Poenis* VII. 41–3 (frag. 13, Rose; frag. 16, Untersteiner); Sextus Empiricus, *Adversus Mathematicos* IX. 20–3 (frag. 10, Rose; frag. 12a, Walzer; frag. 12a, Ross;

frag. 14, Untersteiner), and *ibid.*, IX. 26–7 (frag. 11, Rose; frag. 12b, Walzer; frag. 12b, Ross; frag. 26, Untersteiner). See also A.-H. Chroust, 'A cosmological proof for the existence of God in Aristotle's lost dialogue *On Philosophy*,' *New Scholasticism*, vol. 40, no. 4 (1966), pp. 447–63, and Chapter XIII.

47 J. Bernays (see note 4), p. 106.

48 Simplicius, *Commentaria in Aristotelis Quattuor Libros De Caelo, CIAG*, vol. VII (ed. J. L. Heiberg, Berlin, 1894), p. 288, line 28–p. 289, line 13.

49 See also Plato, *Republic* 380D ff., where Plato maintains that 'the things which are the best are also least liable to change. . . .'

50 See A.-H. Chroust (note 39) and Chapter XIV.

51 In his justly famous article, 'Aristotle,' *Encyclopaedia Britannica*, 11th ed., vol. II (Cambridge, 1910), pp. 501–22, especially pp. 502–3, T. Case discusses the significance of Aristotle's early adherence to Platonism. See also A.-H. Chroust, 'The lost works of Aristotle in pre-Jaegerian scholarship,' *Classica et Mediaevalia*, vol. 25, fasc. 1–2 (1964), pp. 67–92, especially pp. 89–91. Case maintains that during his long and fruitful association with the Platonic Academy (367–48 B.C.), Aristotle's interest in Plato's basic teachings underwent some significant changes. This is not surprising, Case points out, in view of the fact that during these twenty years Plato himself changed substantially his fundamental philosophic position by shifting from an 'idealistic metaphysics' to a 'Pythagorizing (mathematical) metaphysics,' which, it is maintained, became the main topic of Plato's unpublished lectures or discussions (and which also affected his latest dialogues). This final trend within Plato's philosophy, Case argues, was rejected by the young Aristotle who persisted in adhering to the 'idealistic metaphysics,' that is, to the doctrine of the Separate Ideas or Forms. Only in this sense, Case concludes, did Aristotle 'break away' from Plato.

52 In *Metaphysics* 1028 b 21–25 and 1069 a 35, *et passim*, for instance, Aristotle criticizes Speusippus and Xenocrates for their reliance on 'mathematical (Pythagorizing) metaphysics.'

53 Frag. 13, Walzer; frag. 13, Ross; frags 48–50, Düring; frags 45–7, Chroust. See also A.-H. Chroust (note 25), especially pp. 371–4, and Chapter VIII; H. Flashar, 'Platon und Aristoteles im *Protreptikos* des Jamblichos,' *Archiv für Geschichte der Philosophie*, vol. 47 (1965), pp. 77–8.

54 This might well be a slap at Plato, who greatly admired the constitutions of Sparta and Crete.

55 Similar notions are advanced in Plato, *Republic* 500C ff.

56 See A.-H. Chroust (note 25).

57 Seneca, *De Ira* I. 3. 3; I. 7. 1; I. 9. 2; I. 17. 1; III. 3. 1; Cicero, *Tuscul. Disput.* IV. 19. 43; Philodemus, *De Ira*, pp. 65, line 31–66, line 2 (ed. C. Wilke, Leipzig, 1914—frag. 80, Rose; frag. 3, Ross). See also Philodemus, *De Rhetorica; Volumina Rhetorica*, vol. II (ed. S. Sudhaus, 1896), p. 175 (frag. 4, Ross); *Hercul. Papyr.* 1020 (frag. 5, Ross).

58 Only one of the fragments credited to Aristotle's *Politicus*, namely, that

from Syrianus (see note 18), explicitly refers to the *Politicus*. Frag. 81, Rose, which Rose attributes to the *Politicus*, is credited to the lost Aristotelian *On Poets* by W. D. Ross. See frag. 5 (*On Poets*), Ross.

## CHAPTER XII   THE PROBABLE DATE OF ARISTOTLE'S *On Philosophy*

* In a different form, this chapter was first published in the *Journal of the History of Philosophy*, vol. IV, no. 4 (1966), pp. 283–91, copyrighted by the Regents of the University of California and reprinted with the permission of the Regents.

1 M. Untersteiner, *Aristotele: Della Filosofia* (Rome, 1963), pp. xvii ff. See also M. Untersteiner, 'Aristotle, *Phys.* I. 8–9: Frammenti del *Περὶ φιλοσοφίας*,' ¡*Rivisti di Filologia e d'Istruzione Classica*, vol. 87 (1959), pp. 1 ff.; M. Untersteiner, 'Il *Περὶ Φιλοσοφίας* di Aristotele,' *ibid.*, vol. 88 (1960), pp. 337 ff. and vol. 89 (1961), pp. 121 ff. In these earlier works, Untersteiner maintains that the *On Philosophy* manifests not only a marked independence of Plato, but also displays a remarkable agreement with the basic contents of Book N of the Aristotelian *Metaphysics*. Other scholars who discussed the proper dating of the *On Philosophy* are: M. Pohlenz, *Aus Platons Werdezeit* (Berlin, 1913), p. 401, note 1; F. Ueberweg, *Grundriss der Geschichte der Philosophie*, vol. I: *Philosophie des Altertums* (12th ed., ed. K. Praechter, Berlin, 1926), pp. 361–2; H. von Arnim, *Die Entwicklung der Gotteslehre des Aristoteles*, Sitzungsberichte der Akademie der Wissenschaften in Wien, Philosophisch-Historische Klasse, no. 212, vol. V (Vienna, 1931), p. 55, and *ibid.*, p. 8; U. von Wilamowitz-Moellendorff, *Aristoteles und Athen* (Berlin, 1931–2), vol. I, note 27; F. Nuyens, *L'Évolution de la Psychologie d'Aristote* (Louvain, 1948), pp. 99–106 and p. 172; P. Wilpert, *Zwei aristotelische Frühschriften über die Ideenlehre* (Regensburg, 1949), pp. 23–4 and p. 212, note 28; A. J. Festugière, *La Révélation d'Hermès Trismégiste* (Paris, 1950), vol. II, p. 220 and p. 227; E. Oggioni, *Aristotele: Metafisica* (Padua, 1950), p. 15 and p. 57; pp. 83–4; P. Moraux, *Les Listes Anciennes des Ouvrages d'Aristote* (Louvain, 1951), pp. 327–8; J. Tricot (ed.), *Aristotele: La Metaphysique* (Paris, 1953), vol. I, pp. xviii–xix; H. D. Saffrey, 'Le *Περὶ Φιλοσοφίας* d'Aristote et la théorie platonicienne des idées nombres,' *Philosophia Antiqua*, vol. 2 (Leiden, 1955), p. 13 and p. 50; I. Düring, 'Aristotle and Plato in the mid-fourth century,' *Eranos*, vol. 54 (1956), pp. 118–19; P. Wilpert, 'Die Stellung der Schrift *Über die Philosophie* in der Gedankenentwicklung des Aristoteles,' *Journal of Hellenic Studies*, vol. 77 (1957), p. 157 and p. 159; E. Berti, *La Filosofia del Primo Aristotele* (Padua, 1962), pp. 402–3.

2 That Aristotle wrote a work entitled *On Philosophy* is attested by several authors. See DL V. 22 (no. 33: in three books); *VH* 10 (no. 3: in four books); Ptolemy (-el-Garib), (no. 1: in three books). Ptolemy lists 'a book in which he [*scil.*, Aristotle] exhorts to philosophy, in Greek entitled *Προτρεπτικὸς Φιλοσοφίας*.' See also DL I. 8 (Prooemium), Syrianus, *Com-*

*ment. in Arist. Metaphysica, CIAG*, vol. VI, part 1 (ed. W. Kroll, Berlin, 1902), p. 159, line 35; Philodemus, *De Pietate* 7 b 4–8; Simplicius, *Comment. in Arist. De Caelo, CIAG*, vol. VII (ed. J. L. Heiberg, Berlin, 1894), p. 289, line 2; Philoponus, *Comment. in Arist. De Anima, CIAG*, vol. XV (ed. M. Hayduck, Berlin, 1897), p. 75, line 34 and p. 186, line 25; Alexander of Aphrodisias, *Comment. in Arist. Metaphysics, CIAG*, vol. I (ed. M. Hayduck, Berlin, 1891), p. 117, line 24; Simplicius, *Comment. in Arist. De Anima, CIAG*, vol. XI (ed. M. Hayduck, Berlin, 1892), p. 28, line 7; Asclepius, *Comment. in Arist. Metaphysica, CIAG*, vol. VI, part 2 (ed. M. Hayduck, Berlin, 1888), p. 112, line 19; Pseudo-Alexander of Aphrodisias, *Comment. in Arist. Metaphysica*, p. 777, lines 19–20; Philoponus, *Comment. in Nicomachi Math. Isagogen* (ed. R. Hoche, Leipzig, 1864) I. 1; *Prisciani Lydi Quae Extant, Supplementum Aristotelicum*, vol. I, part 2 (ed. I. Bywater, Berlin, 1886), p. 41, lines 16 ff.; Cicero, *De Natura Deorum* I. 13. 33; Philoponus, *On Happiness* (ed. Th. Gomperz), p. 72; Stobaeus, *Florilegium* III. 21. 26. Aristotle himself refers twice to his *On Philosophy*, namely, in the *De Anima* 404 b 19, and in the *Physics* 194 a 36. W. Haase, 'Ein vermeintliches Aristotelesfragment bei Johannes Philoponos,' *Synusia* (Pfullingen, 1965), pp. 323–54, has attempted to show that the first part of Philoponus' *Comment. in Nicomachi Math. Isagogen* I. 1 (frag. 13, Rose; frag. 8, Walzer; frag. 8, Ross; frag. 1, Untersteiner) is in no way related to Aristotle's *On Philosophy*, but must be considered primarily as an attempt on the part of Philoponus, in a characteristically Neo-Platonic (syncretist) fashion, to reconcile the teachings of Aristotle with those of Plato. The fragment from Philoponus, *Comment. in Nicomachi Math. Isagogen* I. 1, which some scholars have also credited to Aristotle's *Protrepticus*, has been ascribed to the *On Philosophy* by K. Gaiser, *Platons Ungeschriebene Lehre* (Stuttgart, 1963), pp. 236 ff.; M. Untersteiner, *Aristotele: Della Filosofia* (Rome, 1963), pp. 121 ff.; E. Berti, *La Filosofia del Primo Aristotele* (Padua, 1962), p. 327; R. Mondolfo, *La Comprensione del Soggetto Umano nell'Antichità Classica* (Florence, 1958), p. 675; P. Wilpert, 'Die aristotelische Schrift *Über die Philosophie*,' *Autour d'Aristote* (Louvain, 1955), pp. 59 ff. and 113 ff.; H. D. Saffrey, 'Le Περὶ φιλοσοφίας d'Aristote et la théorie platonicienne des idées-nombres,' *Philosophia Antiqua*, vol. 7 (Leiden, 1955), pp. 9–10; A. Grilli, 'La posizione di Aristotele, Epicuro, Posidonio nei confronti della storia della civiltà,' *Rendiconti di Class. Lettere* (Istituto Lombardo di Science e Lettere), vol. 86 (1953), p. 4; P. Moraux, *Les Listes Anciennes des Ouvrages d'Aristote* (Louvain, 1951), p. 30, note 12; A. J. Festugière, *La Révélation d'Hermès Trismégiste*, vol. II (Paris, 1949), p. 222, note 1 and pp. 587–91; E. Bignone, *L'Aristotele Perduto e la Formazione Filosofica di Epicuro*, vol. II (Florence, 1936), pp. 509 ff.; I. Düring, *Aristotle's Protrepticus: An Attempt at Reconstruction* (Göteborg, 1961), p. 131; W. Jaeger, *Aristotle: Fundamentals of the History of his Development* (Oxford, 1948), p. 137, note 1; I. Bywater, 'Aristotle's dialogue *On Philosophy*,' *Journal of Philology*, vol. 7 (1877), p. 65. Should Haase's thesis (see above, this note) prove to be correct—and there are indications that this might be the case—then Philoponus, *Comment. in*

*Nicomachi Math. Isagogen* I. 1, would have to be discounted as a reference to Aristotle's *On Philosophy*. This, in turn, might cast some doubt on the authenticity of other fragments credited to the *On Philosophy* and might ultimately compel us to subject the whole problem of the Aristotelian *On Philosophy* to a renewed critical investigation and cautious reappraisal. The present author, however, is not really concerned here with an acribic investigation of the likely source problem or specific content of the *On Philosophy*. Such an investigation, it was hoped, would be undertaken by P. Wilpert in his proposed major work, *Aristoteles, Über die Philosophie: ein Versuch der Wiederherstellung*, which was expected to appear in the near future. (Since Professor Wilpert died early in 1967, we may hope that this important undertaking will be carried on and brought to a successful conclusion by a competent successor.) The present author merely attempts to establish the likely date of composition of this important dialogue. He proceeds on the reasonable assumption that the majority, though perhaps not all, of the fragments commonly credited to the Aristotelian *On Philosophy* are authentic. Hence, his method might possibly be described as follows: assuming the majority of the fragments ascribed to the *On Philosophy* are authentic—an assumption which is by no means a certainty but rather a reasonable conjecture—then on the basis of certain indications it is also reasonable to surmise that this dialogue was composed approximately between 350–49 (or 349–48) and 348–47 B.C. Hence this chapter is neither an endorsement nor a refutation of the methods or materials which have previously been employed to retrieve and interpret the lost Aristotelian *On Philosophy*.

3 See also A.-H. Chroust, 'The probable dates of some of Aristotle's lost works,' *Rivista Critica di Storia della Filosofia*, vol. 22, fasc. 1 (1967), pp. 3–23, especially pp. 19–22, and Chapter I.

4 W. Jaeger, *Aristotle: Fundamentals of the History of his Development* (Oxford, 1948), p. 173.

5 *Ibid., et passim.*

6 W. Jaeger, whose views and arguments were accepted without much debate by many scholars, including M. Untersteiner (see note 1), also holds that Aristotle's departure from Athens in the year 348–47 B.C. was occasioned by the death of Plato. It is quite possible that Aristotle was compelled to leave Athens and the Academy in the summer or early fall of 348 (that is, some time before Plato died), because of the capture of Olynthus by King Philip of Macedonia, which triggered intensive anti-Macedonian sentiments among the Athenians. See A.-H. Chroust, 'Aristotle leaves the Academy,' *Greece and Rome*, vol. 14, no. 1 (1967), pp. 39–43, and Vol. I, Chapter IX. See also p. 157. Moreover, Jaeger does not pay much attention to the fact that already in the *On (the) Ideas* and in the *On the Good*, which were composed some time before Plato's death, Aristotle was rather critical of certain fundamental aspects of Plato's later philosophy.

7 See frag. 34, Rose; frag. 6, Walzer; frag. 6, Ross; frag. 3, Untersteiner.

V. Rose assigns this fragment to Aristotle's (?) *Magicus*, a work which is also mentioned in DL I. 1 and DL I. 8, but not in Diogenes Laertius' 'catalogue' of Aristotle's works. *VH* 10 (no. 192) mentions a Μαγικὸν among the spurious works of Aristotle. And spurious it probably is. W. Jaeger, M. Untersteiner and others are of the opinion that in his *On Philosophy*, Aristotle discusses the Magi (Zoroastrian teachings), a thesis which might well be accepted. See A.-H. Chroust, 'Aristotle and the philosophies of the east,' *Review of Metaphysics*, vol. 18, no. 3 (1965), pp. 573–80, and Chapter XVI. F. Gisinger, *Die Erdbeschreibung des Eudoxos von Knidos* (Leipzig-Berlin, 1921), p. 5, maintains that, according to Eudoxus' Γῆς περίοδος, frag. 58, the latter had calculated that Zoroaster lived 6,000 years before the death of Plato. Gisinger also demonstrates that Pliny derived his information about Zoroaster (and the time he lived) directly from Eudoxus. It has been claimed that Eudoxus outlived Plato, who probably died early in 347 B.C., by less than one year (see K. von Fritz, 'Die Lebenszeit des Eudoxos von Knidos,' *Philologus*, vol. 85, 1929–30, pp. 478–81); that he composed the Γῆς περίοδος shortly after Plato's death; and that he himself died late in 347 B.C. Hence, he must have written the Γῆς περίοδος in 347 B.C. This, then, would lend weighty support to Jaeger's thesis that the Aristotelian *On Philosophy*, provided the latter was dependent on Eudoxus, was composed after the death of Plato (and after Aristotle had left the Academy), unless we were to assume that Pliny derived his information that 'Zoroaster lived six thousand years prior to the death of Plato,' directly from Eudoxus' Γῆς περίοδος (perhaps through Hermippus?) rather than from Aristotle's *On Philosophy*. If this is so, then Aristotle's *On Philosophy* might well have been written before the death of Plato, although in this case it did not contain the statement that 'Zoroaster lived six thousand years prior to the death of Plato.' It is also possible that in his description of the Magi, Eudoxus quoted from or referred to, Aristotle's *On Philosophy*. This, then, would indicate that the *On Philosophy* was composed before 347 B.C. See also pp. 153–4; 156–7.

8 H. von Arnim (see note 1), p. 8 and p. 55. Von Arnim suggests that the *On Philosophy* was composed a short time before Plato's death. See also W. K. C. Guthrie, 'The development of Aristotle's theology,' *Classical Quarterly*, vol. 27 (1933), pp. 162 ff.; W. D. Ross, *Aristotle's Physics* (Oxford, 1955), pp. 94 ff.

9 P. Wilpert, 'Die Stellung der Schrift *Über die Philosophie* in der Gedanken-entwicklung des Aristoteles,' *Journal of Hellenic Studies*, vol. 77 (1957), pp. 155 f. See also P. Wilpert, 'Die aristotelische Schrift *Über die Philosophie*,' *Autour d'Aristote* (Louvain, 1955), pp. 99 ff. Wilpert argues that the main theme of the *On Philosophy* uses a notion of philosophy that is pre-eminently Platonic, that is, a 'science of the Divine.' Hence, Wilpert suggests that this dialogue should be dated not only prior to the death of Plato but even prior to the composition of the *On (the) Ideas* and Book A of the *Metaphysics*.

10 A. J. Festugière (see note 1), p. 220 and p. 227.

11 C. de Vogel, *Greek Philosophy*, vol. II (Leiden, 1953), pp. 29 ff. De Vogel holds that the *On Philosophy* clearly reveals that Aristotle had given up Platonism for some time.

12 D. J. Allan, *The Philosophy of Aristotle* (London, 1952), pp. 14 ff. and pp. 21 ff. Allan believes that the *On Philosophy* is indicative of the fact that Aristotle had rejected Plato's physics (as it is expressed in the *Timaeus*) as well as Plato's theology (as it is expressed in the *Timaeus* and in books X and XII of the *Laws*).

13 H. D. Saffrey (see note 1), p. 7; p. 13; p. 50.

14 Some of these scholars insist, however, that the *On Philosophy* is anterior to Book A of the *Metaphysics*. See, for instance, M. Gentile, 'La dottrina platonica delle idee numeri e Aristotele,' *Annali della Reale Scuola Normale Superiore di Pisa*, Classe di Lettere e Filosofia, vol. 30, fasc. 3 (1930), pp. 121 ff.; A. Mansion, 'La genèse de l'oeuvre d'Aristote d'après les travaux récents,' *Revue Néoscholastique de Philosophie*, vol. 29 (1927), p. 319; P. Wilpert (see note 9). F. Nuyens, *L'Évolution de la Psychologie d'Aristote* (Louvain, 1948), pp. 99 ff., however, rejects Jaeger's thesis that the *On Philosophy* is posterior to the death of Plato. He points out that the soul-body relation underlying the *On Philosophy* indicates that this dialogue must be contemporary with Aristotle's earlier writings. He concludes, therefore, that it must be dated several years before the death of Plato. This theory has won little acceptance. See note 1.

15 These two works are usually dated between 357–56 and 355. See A.-H. Chroust (note 3), especially pp. 5–11, and Chapter I.

16 See Pliny, *Hist. Natur.* XXX. 3, who relates that it was 'Eudoxus [of Cnidus] who claimed that . . . Zoroaster lived six thousand years before the death of Plato. . . .' DL I. 8, in turn, maintains that 'in the first book of his *On Philosophy* Aristotle states that the Magi are more ancient than the Egyptians. . . . This is confirmed by Hermippus . . . , Eudoxus . . . , and Theopompus. . . .' See also note 7.

17 V. Rose, *Aristoteles Pseudepigraphus* (Leipzig, 1863), pp. 27 ff.

18 E. Heitz, *Die verlorenen Schriften des Aristoteles* (Leipzig, 1865), pp. 184 ff.

19 Jaeger, it will be remembered, insisted that on the whole Aristotle remained an 'orthodox Platonist' (or, 'almost orthodox Platonist') until about the death of Plato. Like all great theses, Jaeger's, needless to say, solves a number of old problems and, at the same time, raises several new ones. To mention just a few of these new problems: if the *On Philosophy* indeed constitutes the pivotal point at which Aristotle broke away from Plato and Platonism, what, then, is the position of the Aristotelian *On (the) Ideas* or the Aristotelian *On the Good* in this progression (or regression?) from Platonism to Aristotelianism? Which particular fundamental views of Plato did Aristotle abandon first, and to what extent did he abandon them (or, perhaps, merely modify them) in his earliest attempts to emancipate himself from Plato's philosophy? To further complicate matters, some

scholars are no longer fully convinced that the whole of the extant *Corpus Aristotelicum* is indeed by Aristotle rather than by the Early Peripatus, although they are not certain which parts of the *Corpus*, if any, are authentically Aristotelian. Assuming that this somewhat unorthodox viewpoint can successfully be sustained, we may ask the question of whether the *Corpus* constitutes a reliable basis for sustaining the allegation that Aristotle progressively abandoned Platonism, or for assessing the degree to which he turned away from, or perhaps against, Plato. Is it possible that the historical Aristotle always remained essentially a Platonist but, like so many of his fellow members in the Academy, took issue with or dissociated himself from certain late views of Plato, such as, for instance, the 'Pythagorizing tendency' that became manifest in some of the latest Platonic dialogues and probably in Plato's oral teachings. These and many other questions related to our problem could probably be answered in a more satisfactory manner if we had some assurance that the doctrinal treatises collated in the *Corpus* are indeed by Aristotle. Jaeger never so much as questioned the authenticity of the *Corpus*. Hence, his sole task as well as his overriding concern was to reconcile the Platonizing early works of Aristotle and the later doctrinal treatises, something which he accomplished in a most brilliant manner by devising his justly famed 'evolutionary thesis.' To this thesis he subordinated every other consideration. Assuming, however, that the *Corpus* is at least in part spurious, then Jaeger's thesis might be in jeopardy.

20 E. Zeller, *Die Philosophie der Griechen*, vol. II, part 2 (Leipzig, 1879), pp. 58 ff.

21 A. Kail, *De Aristotelis Dialogis Qui Inscribuntur 'De Philosophia' et 'Eudemus'* (Vienna, 1913), *passim*.

22 T. Case, article 'Aristotle,' in *Encyclopaedia Britannica* (11th ed., Cambridge, 1910), pp. 501 ff. It will be noted that Case already anticipated certain aspects of Jaeger's famous thesis of Aristotle's intellectual evolution.

23 W. Theiler, *Zur Entstehung der teleologischen Naturbetrachtung bis auf Aristoteles* (Zürich, 1924), pp. 86 ff. More recently, Theiler proposes that the *On Philosophy* was composed in 354 B.C. See W. Theiler, 'Bau und Zeit der Aristotelischen Politik,' *Museum Helveticum*, vol. 9 (1952), p. 66, note 6.

24 The Aristotelian *Protrepticus* is usually dated around 352–50 B.C.

25 F. J. Nuyens (see note 14), pp. 99 ff.

26 P. Moraux (see note 1), pp. 323 ff.

27 I. Düring (see note 1), pp. 118–19, *et passim*.

28 See p. 156. See also A.-H. Chroust (note 3), at pp. 13–17, and Chapter I.

29 For a compilation of these scholarly views, see, for instance, E. Berti, *La Filosofia del Primo Aristotele* (Padua, 1962), pp. 258 ff. It has also been maintained that Book III of the *On Philosophy* contains, at least in part, a 'condensed summary' (as well as a sustained criticism) of the theological views which Plato advanced in the *Timaeus*.

30 The existence of an *On the Good* is attested by DL V. 22 (no. 20); *VH* 10
(no. 20); Ptolemy (-el-Garib), no. 9; *VM* 32, *VL* 33. See also Alexander of
Aphrodisias, *Comment. in Arist. Metaphysica, CIAG*, vol. I (ed. M. Hayduck,
Berlin, 1891), p. 56, line 35 and p. 59, lines 33 ff.; p. 85, lines 16 ff.; p. 250,
line 20; p. 262, line 19; Philoponus, *Comment. in Arist. De Anima, CIAG*,
vol. XV (ed. M. Hayduck, Berlin, 1897), p. 75, line 34; Simplicius,
*Comment. in Arist. De Anima, CIAG*, vol. II (ed. M. Hayduck, Berlin,
1882), p. 28, line 7; Asclepius, *Comment. in Arist. Metaphysica, CIAG*, vol.
VI, part 2 (ed. M. Hayduck, Berlin, 1888), p. 237, line 14 and p. 247, line
19; etc.

31 The existence of an *On (the) Ideas* is attested by DL V. 23 (no. 54: Περὶ τῆς
ἰδέας, in one book), and *ibid.* (no. 31: Περὶ εἰδῶν καὶ γενῶν, in one book);
*VH* 10 (no. 45: Περὶ ἰδέας, in one book), and *ibid.* (no. 28: Περὶ εἰδῶν, in
one book); Ptolemy (-el-Garib), no. 15. Ptolemy mentions here a work,
entitled *On (the) Ideas*, in three books. See also Alexander of Aphrodisias,
*Comment. in Arist. Metaphysica, CIAG*, vol. I (ed. M. Hayduck, Berlin,
1891), p. 79, lines 3 ff. and p. 85, lines 9 ff.; p. 98, lines 20 ff.; Syrianus,
*Comment. in Arist. Metaphysica, CIAG*, vol. VI, part 1 (ed. W. Kroll,
Berlin, 1902), p. 120, lines 33 ff.

32 See, for instance, H. Karpp, 'Die Schrift des Aristoteles Περὶ ἰδεῶν,'
*Hermes*, vol. 68 (1933), pp. 384–91; R. Philippson, 'Il Περὶ ἰδεῶν di
Aristotele,' *Rivista di Philologia e d'Istruzione Classica*, vol. 64 (1936), pp.
113–25; E. Frank, 'The fundamental opposition of Plato and Aristotle,'
*American Journal of Philology*, vol. 61 (1940), p. 47, note 16; P. Wilpert,
'Reste verlorener Aristotelesschriften bei Alexander von Aphrodosias,'
*Hermes*, vol. 75 (1940), pp. 378–85; H. Cherniss, *Aristotle's Criticism of Plato
and the Academy* (Baltimore, 1944), pp. 223–318 and pp. 488–505; P.
Moraux (see note 1), pp. 328–37; D. J. Allan (see note 12), pp. 16–22;
R. Stark, *Aristotelesstudien: philologische Untersuchungen zur Entwicklung der
aristotelischen Ethik* (Zetemata, Monographien zur Klassischen Altertumswissenschaft, Heft 8, Munich, 1954), pp. 20–6; I. Düring (see note 1), pp.
109–20. Philippson, Frank and Düring, it will be noted, date the *On (the)
Ideas* in the vicinity of the year 360 B.C., an unlikely early date. P. Wilpert,
*Zwei aristotelische Frühschriften über die Ideenlehre* (Regensburg, 1949), on
the other hand, maintains that the *On (the) Ideas* was composed after the
death of Plato (in 348–47 B.C.). See also W. Jaeger's review of Wilpert's
book in *Gnomon*, vol. 25 (1951), pp. 246–52.

33 See E. Berti (note 29), pp. 402 ff.

34 These are the views advanced by Theiler, Nuyens, Moraux and Düring.
See notes 23 and 25–7.

35 See, in general, A.-H. Chroust, 'Aristotle's earliest course of lectures on
rhetoric,' *Antiquité Classique*, vol. 33, fasc. 1 (1964), pp. 58–72, and Vol. I,
Chapter VIII.

36 See W. Jaeger (note 4), pp. 124 ff.

37 In *Laws* 638B, Plato mentions the fact that the Syracusans had conquered

the Locrians. Since this incident took place in the year 356 B.C., that is, during the Phocian or Sacred War, it must be assumed that Plato began to compose the *Laws* after 356–55 B.C.

38 See DL III. 37. After the death of Plato in 348–47 B.C., the *Laws* were 'published' by Philip of Opus, who is alleged to have been the author of the *Epinomis*. The latter may be called a kind of 'Postscript' to the Platonic *Laws*.

39 Books X and XII of the *Laws*, especially, have a certain affinity with Book III of the *On Philosophy*. But Books X and XII of the *Laws*, it must be remembered, were probably composed in close proximity to the year 348–47 B.C. Hence, if the *On Philosophy* were written around the year 355 B.C., almost seven years would have passed before Plato took issue with the *On Philosophy*.

40 According to *V M* 7, *VL* 7, *I VS* 5, *II VA* 12 and *IV VA* 29, Plato, referring to Aristotle's intelligence and industry, is said to have called him 'the Mind' (*νοῦς*).

41 Plato, *Laws* 888E ff.

42 *Ibid.*, 890C.

43 See *Scholia in Proverb. Salomonis*, Cod. Paris. Graec. 174, fol. 46a (frag. 17, Rose; frag. 17, Walzer; frag. 17, Ross; frag. 27, Untersteiner).

44 Philo of Alexandria, *De Aeternitate Mundi* III. 10–11 (frag. 18, Rose; frag. 18, Walzer; frag. 18, Ross; frag. 21, Untersteiner), and *ibid.*, V. 20–4 (frag. 19, Rose; frag. 19a, Walzer; frag. 19a, Ross; frag. 29, Untersteiner); VIII. 39–43 (frag. 21, Rose; frag. 19c, Walzer; frag. 19c, Ross; frag. 17, Untersteiner).

45 See Sextus Empiricus, *Adversus Mathematicos* IX. 26–7 (frag. 11, Rose; frag. 12b, Walzer; frag. 12b, Ross; frag. 26, Untersteiner); Cicero, *De Natura Deorum* II. 37. 95–6 (frag. 12, Rose; frag. 13, Walzer; frag. 13, Ross; frag. 18, Untersteiner); Philo of Alexandria, *Legum Allegoriarum Libri Tres* III. 32. 97–9 (frag. 13, Walzer; frag. 13, Ross; frag. 15, Untersteiner); Philo of Alexandria, *De Praemiis et Poenis* VII. 41–3 (frag. 13, Ross; frag. 16, Untersteiner). See also A.-H. Chroust, 'A cosmological proof for the existence of God in Aristotle's lost dialogue *On Philosophy*,' *New Scholasticism*, vol. 40, no. 4 (1966), pp. 447–63, and Chapter XIII.

46 Plato, *Laws* 891C ff.

47 *Ibid.*, 893B ff. The 'self-moving power' of the 'first' or 'best' soul is not something physical but rather something 'spiritual' or, better, 'Mind.' *Ibid.*, 896D ff., Plato asserts that there are at least two (cosmic) souls, 'the one the author of the good, the other the cause of evil.' The possibility that this passage as well as other passages in the late works of Plato have been influenced, at least in part, by Zoroastrian teachings, has been discussed in A.-H. Chroust (see note 7), pp. 572–80, especially p. 576, note 14, and in Chapter XVI.

48 Plato, *Laws* 898C.

49 For a summary of these problems, see A.-H. Chroust (note 45).

50 See Plato, *Laws* 898D–899B. The Platonic notion of a 'best soul' might have influenced Aristotle's proof for the existence of God *e gradibus*, which he expounded in the *On Philosophy*: 'Aristotle speaks of this in his work *On Philosophy*. In general, where there is a better, there is a best. Since, then, among existing things one is better than another, there is always something that is best, which will be the Divine.' See Simplicius, *Comment. in Arist. De Caelo, CIAG*, vol. VII (ed. J. H. Heiberg, Berlin, 1894), p. 289, lines 1 ff. (frag. 16, Rose; frag. 16, Walzer; frag. 16, Ross; frag. 25, Untersteiner).

51 This might possibly follow from Sextus Empiricus, *Adversus Mathematicos* IX. 26–7, where we are told that the perfect array of the Achaean army on the plains of Troy was the work of one man: Nestor. By the same token, the perfect order of the universe is ascribed to the efficiency of one (personal?) God. See also note 47 and Chapter XIII, notes 62–3, and the corresponding text.

52 See W. Jaeger, *Paideia*, vol. III (New York, 1944), pp. 258 ff. Jaeger is of the opinion that Plato's God is transcendent, a view which is not shared by A. J. Festugière, H. von Arnim, P. Moraux and others.

53 See Cicero, *De Natura Deorum* I. 13. 33 (frag. 26, Rose; frag. 26, Walzer; frag. 26, Ross; frag. 39, Untersteiner).

54 This seems to follow from Plato, *Laws* 898D ff. See here also F. Solmsen, *Plato's Theology* (Ithaca, 1942), p. 112.

55 This refers to Plato, *Laws* 893A ff., discussed in note 47, and the corresponding text.

56 Plato, *Laws* 966DE. The reference is to Plato, *Laws* 896C.

57 Sextus Empiricus, *Adversus Mathematicos* IX. 20 ff. (frag. 10, Rose; frag. 12a, Walzer; frag. 12a, Ross; frag. 14, Untersteiner). See also *ibid.*, IX. 26 ff.:

> Some people have recourse to the unalterable and orderly motions of the heavenly bodies, and they insist that the first beginnings of man's conceptions about the gods arise from this. . . . Those who first looked up to the heavens and beheld the sun running its course . . . and the orderly procession of the stars sought for an artificer of this beautiful array, conjecturing that it had not come about arbitrarily or by mere accident, but by the deliberate handiwork of some superior and imperishable nature which is God.

For additional *testimonia*, see A.-H. Chroust (note 45), *passim*.

58 There obviously exists a third possibility which cannot be discussed here: the views about the supreme Deity might be the result of Zoroastrian influences on the late Plato and the early Aristotle (and the Early Academy), for such influences did actually exist. For details, see A.-H. Chroust (note 7), and Chapter XVI.

59 DL III. 37 relates that Philip of Opus, the 'editor' of the *Laws*, composed the *Epinomis*. Most modern scholars accept this statement, although such

renowned scholars as A. E. Taylor, A. J. Festugière and H. Raeder insist that Plato authored the *Epinomis*. Philip of Opus, it is said, noticed that in the *Laws* (Book XII) Plato had neglected to propose a systematic education for the ruler. Hence, Philip of Opus attempted to implement the *Laws* by defining and describing in greater detail the special σοφία which the true ruler must possess. If the true ruler or lawgiver is in fact the 'Demiurge of the properly functioning human society' (as Plato insinuates in the latter passages of the *Laws*), in that this Demiurge shapes the true city after the model of the eternal order—as the Demiurge of the *Timaeus* reproduces the imperishable world of Ideas in the natural or corporeal world of phenomena—then this ruler or lawgiver must know something about the ultimate ruler or lawgiver of the orderly universe: God. In this sense, he must be a 'theologian,' as well as be trained in 'theology.' This is already hinted at in Plato, *Republic* 621A ff., and in the *Laws* 696A ff.

60 For further detail, see, for instance, E. Berti (note 29), pp. 408 ff.

61 Compare *Epinomis* 982C ff. (and *ibid.*, 983C), and Cicero, *De Natura Deorum* II. 16. 44 (frag. 24, Rose; frag. 21, Walzer; frag. 21, Ross; frag. 32, Untersteiner); Stobaeus, *Florilegium* I. 43 (Plutarch, *De Placitis Philosophorum*, V. 9.5–*Moralia* 908F); and Aetius V. 20. 1 (frag. 22, Walzer; frag. 22, Ross; frag. 33, Untersteiner).

62 Compare *Epinomis* 981B ff. (and 985AB), and Cicero, *Tuscul. Disput.* I. 10. 22 (frag. 27, Walzer; frag. 27, Ross; frag. 30, Untersteiner).

63 Compare *Epinomis* 982CD, and Cicero, *De Natura Deorum* I. 13. 33 (frag. 26, Rose; frag. 26, Walzer; frag. 26, Ross; frag. 39, Untersteiner).

64 Compare *Epinomis* 981BC, and Cicero, *Tuscul. Disput.* I. 17. 41 and I. 26. 65 ff. (frag. 27, Walzer; frag. 27, Ross; frag. 30, Untersteiner).

65 Compare *Epinomis* 981C ff., and Cicero, *De Natura Deorum* II. 15. 42 (frag. 23, Rose; frag. 21, Walzer; frag. 21, Ross; frag. 32, Untersteiner).

66 Compare *Epinomis* 982CD, and Cicero, *De Natura Deorum* II. 37. 95–6 (frag. 12, Rose; frag. 13, Walzer; frag. 13, Ross; frag. 18, Untersteiner); Philo of Alexandria, *Legum Allegoriarum Libri Tres* III. 32. 97–9 (frag. 12, Rose; frag. 13, Walzer; frag. 13, Ross; frag. 15, Untersteiner); Philo of Alexandria, *De Praemiis et Poenis* VII. 41–3 (frag. 13, Ross; frag. 16, Untersteiner); Sextus Empiricus, *Adversus Mathematicos* IX. 26–7 (frag. 11, Rose; frag. 12b, Walzer; frag. 12b, Ross; frag. 26, Untersteiner).

67 Compare *Epinomis* 977A, and the fragments of the *On Philosophy* cited in note 66. See also Chapter XIII.

68 Compare *Epinomis* 978D, and the fragments of the *On Philosophy* cited in note 66. See also Chapter XIII.

69 See A.-H. Chroust, 'The doctrine of the soul in Aristotle's lost dialogue *On Philosophy*,' *New Scholasticism*, vol. 42, no. 3 (1968), pp. 364–73, and Chapter XV; A.-H. Chroust, 'The concept of God in Aristotle's lost dialogue *On Philosophy* (Cicero, *De Natura Deorum* I. 13. 33),' *Emerita*, vol. 33, fasc. 2 (1965), pp. 205–28, and Chapter XIV; A.-H. Chroust (see note 45).

70 Isocrates, *To Philip* 12.

71 E. Berti (see note 29), p. 408.

72 W. Jaeger (see note 4), pp. 138 ff.

73 See also A.-H. Chroust (note 3), especially pp. 19-22.

74 See note 7.

75 See F. Gisinger (note 7), p. 5.

76 See K. von Fritz (note 7).

77 The remark that 'Zoroaster lived six thousand years prior to the death of Plato,' then, was contained only in Eudoxus' Γῆς περίοδος and not in Aristotle's *On Philosophy*. See note 7. Pliny XXX. 3 does not exclude this assumption. It is believed that Pliny derived his information from Hermippus who, in turn, consulted Eudoxus. See also DL I. 8-9.

78 See A.-H. Chroust (note 6).

79 See notes 21-5.

80 See, for instance, W. Jaeger (note 4), pp. 54 ff.; A.-H. Chroust, *Aristotle: Protrepticus—A Reconstruction* (Notre Dame, 1964), *passim*, especially the comments to the several fragments. These comments point out and discuss the close affinity between the views of Aristotle and those of Plato. On the other hand, in his many and very learned works on the Aristotelian *Protrepticus*, I. Düring consistently denies that such an affinity exists and states that wherever there are such affinities, they are wholly superficial. W. Jaeger, needless to say, considers the *Protrepticus* an eminently 'Platonic' work.

81 'Publication' of a work, at least by the members of the Academy, was frequently identified with the first 'official reading' (and discussion) of this work within the 'inner circle.'

82 See A.-H. Chroust (note 3). An additional method of dating the *On Philosophy* might be the following: in Book II of the *On Philosophy*, Aristotle takes issue with Plato's theory of Ideas. Because of this, some scholars, among them W. Jaeger, are of the opinion that the *On Philosophy* must be posterior to Book I, 9 of the *Metaphysics*. These scholars argue that in Book I, 9 of the *Metaphysics* Aristotle uses the first person plural, thus indicating that he still considers himself a Platonist. In the *On Philosophy*, on the other hand, he had already 'broken with Platonism.' Hence, Book I, 9 of the *Metaphysics* must be anterior to the *On Philosophy*. Other scholars, among them H. von Arnim, E. Frank, H. Cherniss and P. Moraux, however, deny that the use of the first person plural in Book I, 9 of the *Metaphysics* signifies that Aristotle considers himself a Platonist. Alexander of Aphrodisias, *Comment. in Arist. Metaphys.*, *CIAG*, vol. I (ed. M. Hayduck, Berlin, 1891), p. 117, line 24, when commenting on Aristotle, *Metaphysics* 992 a 10 ff., refers to the *On Philosophy*. This is not in itself an indication, however, that the *On Philosophy* is either posterior or anterior to Book I, 9 of the *Metaphysics*. Conversely, it may be observed that *Metaphysics* 983 a 33 ff.; 986 a 21 ff.; 986 b 16 ff.; 986 b 27 ff.; 989 a 24; 993 a 11 ff.; 998 a 21 ff (see also W. Jaeger at note 4, pp. 295-6), seem to presuppose the first two

Books of Aristotle's *Physics*. Moreover, the *On Philosophy* is referred to in *Physics* 194 a 35–6. This, then, would suggest that Books I and II of the *Physics* are posterior to the *On Philosophy*. Since Book I of the *Metaphysics* apparently presupposes Books I and II of the *Physics*, Book I, 9 of the *Metaphysics* would have to be posterior to Books I and II of the *Physics* and, concomitantly, posterior to the *On Philosophy*. It is impossible, however, to verify this sequence. In any event, since we are in no position to date either Book I, 9 of the *Metaphysics* or Books I and II of the *Physics*, the possible connections between these two works and the *On Philosophy* do not assist us in establishing the exact date of the latter.

83 If, on the other hand, the *On Philosophy* should be dependent on the *Epinomis*—if it should be a sort of 'competitor' of the *Epinomis* and only as such be dependent on Plato's *Laws*—then the year 347–46 would constitute the *tempus post quod* of the *On Philosophy*. In this unlikely case, it would be difficult to establish the *tempus ante quod*, unless one is willing to state in a general way that the *On Philosophy* was composed during Aristotle's stay in Assos, a view with which W. Jaeger would concur.

84 See note 70.

85 If Aristotle composed the *On Philosophy* during the first half of the year 348 (or, perhaps, even before that time)—something which is entirely possible—then the problem arises as to how he became acquainted with Books X and XII of the Platonic *Laws*, unless, as has already been mentioned, he had advance knowledge of the main philosophic content of these two books either through private conversations with Plato or through some public lectures or discussions which Plato held prior to his completing these two (late) books, which might have been completed early in 348 or perhaps a little before that time. It might also be possible that Philip of Opus had completed his 'edition' of the Platonic *Laws* prior to the death of Plato.

86 See Vol. I, Chapters XII and XIII.

CHAPTER XIII   A COSMOLOGICAL (TELEOLOGICAL) PROOF FOR THE EXISTENCE OF GOD IN ARISTOTLE'S *On Philosophy*

* In a different and abridged form, this chapter was first published in *New Scholasticism*, vol. 40, no. 4 (1966), pp. 447–63.

1 See Chapter XII, note 2. Some of the recent scholarly literature discussing the *On Philosophy* is cited in the notes to this Chapter, in the notes to Chapter XII and in the notes to Chapters XIV–XVI. For some interesting comments, see, among others, B. Effe. *Studien zur Kosmologie und Theologie der aristotelischen Schrift Über die Philosophie*, (Zetemata, Heft 50, Munich, 1970), *passim*.

2 Frag. 12, Rose; frag. 13, Walser; frag. 13, Ross; frag. 18, Untersteiner. In his *De Natura Deorum*, Cicero refers several times to Aristotle's *On Philosophy*. See, for instance, *ibid.*, I. 13. 33; I. 38. 107; *et passim*.

3 Frag. 12, Rose; frag. 13, Walzer; frag. 13, Ross; frag. 15, Untersteiner.
4 Frag. 13, Ross; frag. 16, Untersteiner. See also Philo of Alexandria, *De Specialibus Legibus* III. 34. 185–III. 36. 194 (frag. 13, Ross; frag. 16, Untersteiner).
5 Frag. 10, Rose; frag. 12a, Walzer; frag. 12a, Ross; frag. 14, Unsteiner. Similar views can be found in Lucretius, *De Rerum Natura* V. 1183 ff.
6 Frag. 11, Rose; frag. 12b, Walzer; frag. 12b, Ross; frag. 26, Untersteiner. In *Metaphysics* 982 b 12 ff., Aristole seems to 'restate' some of the notions he had expounded in the *On Philosophy*. See note 25.
7 W. Jaeger, *Aristotle: Fundamentals of the History of his Development* (Oxford, 1948), pp. 159–61.
8 These psycho-genetic sources of man's belief in the existence of God, which are not to be discussed here, are mentioned, for instance, in Sextus Empiricus, *Adversus Mathematicos* IX. 20–3 (*Adversus Physicos* I. 20–3—frag. 10, Rose; frag. 12a, Walzer; frag. 12a, Ross; frag. 14, Untersteiner):

> Aristotle used to say that man's thought of the gods originated from ... the experiences of the soul. ... To this ... belonged the inspiration or prophetic power of the soul in dreams. For when the soul is isolated in sleep, Aristotle states, it assumes its true nature and foresees and foretells the future. So, too, it is with the soul when at death it is separated from the body. In any event, Aristotle accepts even Homer as having observed this. For Homer has described Patroclus, in the moment of his death, as foretelling the death of Hector, and Hector as foretelling the death of Achilles. It was from such events, Aristotle insists, that men came to suspect the existence of something Divine, of that which in its nature is akin to the soul and of all things most full of knowledge. ... Such was also the belief of Aristotle.

See also Cicero, *De Divinatione ad Brutum* I. 30. 63–4 (frag. 12a, Walzer; frag. 12a, Ross; frag. 14, Untersteiner):

> When, therefore, sleep has freed the intellect (the mind, or the soul) from its association and contact with the body, it remembers the past, discerns the present and foresees the future. For the body of a sleeping man lies like that of a dead man, but his mind is active and alive. ... And when death approaches, it [*scil.*, the soul] is even more divine. ... That dying men have foreknowledge is confirmed by Posidonius through the examples which he adduces. ... Another instance of this is Homer's Hector, who when dying announces the approaching death of Achilles.

Similar notions can be found in Plato's *Timaeus* 71A ff., in Plato's *Phaedrus* 244D, and in the *Epinomis* 985C. In the *Epinomis* we are told that men have certain visions 'in sleep or in dreams,' and that 'messages have come to certain people among us in the form of voices or prophecies, in sickness or in health or, it may be, to men who come into contact with them in the hour of death. . . .' Conversely, in his *De Divinatione per Somnium* 462 b 20, Aristotle (?) denies that man receives 'revelations' in his dreams. In Cicero, *De Divinatione ad Brutum* I. 25. 53, a fragment which is commonly credited to Aristotle's lost dialogue *Eudemus or On the Soul* (frag. 37, Rose; frag. 1, Walzer; frag. 1, Ross), we are informed that Eudemus of Cyprus fell sick, and that in his feverish state he had a vision which foretold him certain future events. See, in general, P. Siwek, 'La clairvoyance dans le système d'Aristote,' *Sophia*, vol. 29 (1961), pp. 296–311. It is possible, though rather unlikely, that this fragment, which is usually credited to the Aristotelian *Eudemus*, originally was a part of Aristotle *On Philosophy*. O. Gigon, on the other hand, would include Cicero, *De Divinatione ad Brutum* I. 30. 63–4, and Sextus Empiricus, *Adversus Mathematicos* III. 20–3, which are commonly credited to the *On Philosophy*, among the fragments that should be assigned to the *Eudemus*. Philo of Alexandria maintains that the rational contemplation of the wondrous universe, the knowing of God through His handiwork, which leads man to the realization of God's existence, is only 'the second best way' (the 'indirect way') of knowing God and of realizing His existence. The best way of knowing God and of realizing God's existence, Philo contends, is through God Himself, that is, through direct revelation or divine pronouncement. See Philo of Alexandria, *De Praemiis et Poenis* VII. 40 ff. (frag. 13, Ross; frag. 16, Untersteiner). Assuming that Philo's statement in fact reports what Aristotle had said in the *On Philosophy*, then the Stagirite must also have insisted that we may know of God and of His existence through God himself, that is, through the 'inspired powers' of the soul—through 'personal revelation,' mystical experience and an innermost conviction. This, then, would also be an instance of the 'inspired powers' of the soul of which Aristotle speaks in the *On Philosophy*. It should be noted that in the *On Philosophy* Aristotle actually uses a third kind of proof for the existence of God, namely, the 'proof *e gradibus*,' which, however, will not be discussed here. See Simplicius, *Comment. in Arist. De Caelo, CIAG*, vol. VII (ed. J. H. Heiberg, Berlin, 1904), p. 289, lines 1 ff (frag. 16, Rose; frag. 16, Walzer; frag. 16, Ross; frag. 25, Untersteiner): 'Aristotle speaks of this in his work entitled *On Philosophy*. In general, where there is a better, there is a best. Since, then, among existing things one is better than another, there is also something that is best, which will be the Divine.' See also Philo of Alexandria, *De Praemiis et Poenis* VII. 41: 'If some people by means of their philosophic knowledge have been enabled to gain a comprehension of the author and governor of the whole universe, they proceed from the lowly to the most high.' Aristotle's *On Philosophy*, it has been pointed out, contains the first known instance of a proof for the existence of God *e gradibus*. For Aristotle's 'historical proof' for the existence of God, see note 9.

9 However, in *Metaphysics* 1074 b 1 ff. (one of the earliest passages in the *Metaphysics*), Aristotle makes a statement which seems to be rather close

to the astral theology discussed in the *Epinomis*. In *Metaphysics* 1074 b 1 ff., Aristotle states: 'Our forefathers in the most remote ages have handed down to posterity a tradition ... that these heavenly bodies are gods and that the Divine encloses the whole of nature.' This passage, which may be called an 'historical proof' for the existence of God or of the Divine, proclaims that the belief in God and in the existence of God is primarily a matter of timeless tradition. See also Plato, *Timaeus* 40D: 'To know or to tell the origin of the other deities is beyond us, and we must accept the traditions of the men of old times. . . .' Aristotle, *Nicomachean Ethics* 1098 b 27: 'It is impossible that the views held ... by the men of old are entirely mistaken.' In Cicero, *De Natura Deorum* II. 37. 95, we are informed that the subterranean people, 'although they have never come forth above ground, have learned by report and hearsay of the existence of certain deities or divine powers.' See also note 53.

10 See here also E. Berti, *La Filosofia del Primo Aristotle* (Padua, 1962), p. 347. Plato, too, mentions the psychological or psycho-genetic as well as the cosmological sources of man's belief in God and the existence of God. See, for instance, Plato, *Laws* 966DE, and note 14.

11 See Aristotle, *De Caelo* 284 b 3 ff.

12 Similar notions can also be found in Seneca, *Quaestiones Naturales* VII. 31. 1 (frag. 14, Rose; frag. 14, Walzer; frag. 14, Ross; frag. 19, Untersteiner), a passage which might possibly have been influenced by Aristotle's *On Philosophy* through the intermediary of Posidonius and Cicero. See also Plutarch, *De Tranquillitate Animi* 20 (*Moralia* 477C–frag. 14, Ross; frag. 19, Untersteiner). In Synesius, *Dion [of Prusa]* 10. 48A, and Psellus, *Schol. ad Joh. Climacum* 6. 171, two passages which have been credited to Aristotle's *On Philosophy* (frag. 15, Rose; frag. 15, Walzer; frag. 15, Ross; frag. 20, Untersteiner), we are told that true religion, in the final analysis, is really a matter of some 'inner experience,' something akin to the 'gift of faith.'

13 See also Sextus Empiricus, quoted in note 8, and the corresponding text.

14 Here Jaeger discusses Cicero, *De Natura Deorum* II. 37. 95-6. See note 2 and the corresponding text. Undoubtedly, this fragment (frag. 12, Rose; frag. 13, Walzer; frag. 13, Ross; frag. 18, Untersteiner) from Aristotle's *On Philosophy* (Book III) is under the influence of Plato's famous 'cave analogy.' Plato, *Republic* 514A ff. and 532A ff. See pp. 165 ff. In *Laws* 966DE, Plato insists that there are two things which lead man to believe in the gods. '. . . One is the argument about the soul . . . the other an argument from the order of the motion of the stars. . . . If a man should look upon the world not lightly or ignorantly, there was never any one so godless who did not experience that all things happen because of an intelligent will achieving the good .' See also *ibid.*, 896C. Essentially the same idea was restated by Immanuel Kant: 'Two things fill the human spirit with ever novel and increasing wonder and reverence, the more often and the more persistently

they are reflected upon: the starry heavens above me and the moral law within me.' I. Kant, *Critique of Practical Reason, Immanuel Kants Werke*, vol. V (ed. E. Cassirer, Berlin, 1922), p. 174.

15 See also A.-H. Chroust, 'Aristotle's religious convictions,' *Divus Thomas*, vol. 69, fasc. 1 (1966), pp. 91-7, and Vol. I, Chapter XVI. In passing, we might note here that in *De Caelo* 270 b 5 ff., Aristotle observes that 'all men have some conception of the nature of the gods; and all who believe in the existence of gods at all, whether barbarians or Greeks, agree in assigning the highest place to the deity, surely, because they suppose that immortal is linked with immortal, and regard any other supposition as plainly inconceivable.'

16 *Epinomis* 982CD.

17 *Epinomis* 978D.

18 J. Bernays, *Die Dialoge des Aristoteles in ihrem Verhältnis zu seinen übrigen Werken* (Berlin, 1863), pp. 106 ff. It is possible that Bernays' views influenced W. Jaeger.

19 Psalm XIX. 1.

20 See, for instance, I. Heinemann, *Poseidonios' Metaphysische Schriften*, vol. II (Breslau, 1928), p. 180; A. J. Festugière, *La Révélation d'Hermès Trismégiste*, vol. II (Paris, 1950), p. 418; E. Berti (see note 10), p. 348. In *De Natura Deorum* II. 5. 13, Cicero maintains that Cleanthes gave four reasons for the origin of the belief in God. The first (from the inspiration of the soul) and the fourth (from the grandeur of the starry heavens) are derived from Aristotle's *On Philosophy*, the two others probably from Democritus and Prodicus.

21 See W. Spoerri, *Späthellenistische Berichte über Welt, Kultur und Götter: Untersuchungen zu Diodor von Sizilien* (Basel, 1959), p. 168. I. Bywater, 'Aristotle's dialogue "On Philosophy,"' *Journal of Philology*, vol. 7 (1877), pp. 76-7, maintains that Cicero is wholly dependent on Aristotle without, however, being personally aware of this fact. He implies that Cicero never saw the *On Philosophy*, but used sources which were dependent on it. M. Pohlenz, *Die Stoa*, vol. I (Göttingen, 1948), p. 195, insists that Cicero relies here directly on Posidonius who, although on the whole he advances ideas held by the Early Stoics (Cleanthes?), also advocates notions propagated by Plato and Aristotle. O. Gigon, 'Cicero und Aristotles,' *Hermes* vol. 87 (1959), pp. 144 ff., points out that here Cicero transmits a tradition about Aristotle which subsequently was obscured and even eliminated by the new Hellenistic tradition concerning Aristotle and his work. In any event, Gigon concludes, Cicero's acquaintance with Aristotle and his writings is not based on the traditional *Corpus Aristotelicum* as it has allegedly been restored by Andronicus of Rhodes, but on much older texts and traditions which soon came to be lost and forgotten. A careful examination of Cicero's references to Aristotle divulges at once that his sources were the so-called 'exoteric' works of Aristotle rather than the 'doctrinal' treatises of the Stagirite. Similar views had already been voiced

by E. Heitz, *Die verlorenen Schriften des Aristoteles* (Leipzig, 1865), p. 184 and pp. 187 ff.

22 See M. Zepf, 'Der Mensch in der Höhle und das Pantheon,' *Gymnasium*, vol. 65 (1958), pp. 355-82, especially, pp. 361-2. Zepf believes that the version found in Philo of Alexandria, *Legum Allegoriarum Libri Tres* III. 32. 97-9, which compares the orderly universe to a well-built mansion (the dwelling place of God ?), is closer to the Aristotelian original than Cicero's account. For a comparison of Greek and Roman houses, see J. W. Graham, 'Origins and Interrelations of the Greek House and the Roman House,' *Phoenix*, vol. 20, no. 1 (1966), pp. 3-31.

23 For the post-Platonic history of the 'cave analogy,' see also P.-M. Schuhl, *La Fabulation Platonicienne* (Paris, 1947), pp. 60 ff.

24 See M. Zepf (note 22), p. 366, note 77. B. Effe (note 1), pp. 92 ff.

25 Aristotle, *Metaphysics* 982 b 12 ff. It should be noted that, already in the *Theaetetus* 155D, Plato had insisted that 'wonder is the feeling of a philosopher, and philosophy begins in wonder.' It is perhaps this passage from the *Theaetetus* which stimulated the young Aristotle to develop his particular cosmological proof for the existence of God, a proof which begins in wonder and awe.

26 I. Bywater (see note 21), pp. 78 ff.

27 See note 20.

28 W. Jaeger (see note 7), p. 163. See also V. Rose, *Aristotles Pseudepigraphus* (Leipzig, 1863), p. 40; A. S. Pease (ed.), *M. Tulli Ciceronis De Natura Deorum*, vol. II (Cambridge, Mass., 1958), p. 784. The similarity between the subterranean dwellers of Cicero, *De Natura Deorum* II. 37. 95-6, and the myth of the cave in Plato's *Republic* already was noticed by F. Fabricius, *Discussiones Peripateticae* (Basel, 1581), part I, p. 75. See also M. Zepf (note 22), *passim*; M. Untersteiner, *Aristotele: Della Filosofia* (Rome, 1963), p. 176. B. Effe (see note 1), pp. 92-4, on the other hand, interprets Cicero's reference to 'human creatures who had lived ... in comfortable and well-lit dwellings, decorated with statues and pictures, and furnished with all the luxuries enjoyed by human beings considered supremely happy,' as follows: judging from their 'style of life,' these cave-dwellers must know something about architecture, sculpture and painting. Hence, they cannot possibly fail to realize that these 'products of art' ($\tau \acute{\epsilon} \chi \nu \eta$) are the results of rational and deliberate activities. Realizing this, they reach the conclusion that the orderly universe, too, must be the product of a deliberate and rational $\tau \acute{\epsilon} \chi \nu \eta$ rather than the result of mere accident. This, Effe argues, suggests that Aristotle, on the basis of a $\varphi \acute{\upsilon} \sigma \iota \varsigma$-$\tau \acute{\epsilon} \chi \nu \eta$-analogy, attacks here the atomists and, hence, is not really concerned with a proof for the existence of a Supreme Being, Supreme Artificer or God. See also P. Aubenque, *Le Problème de l'Être chez Aristote* (Paris, 1962), pp. 344 ff.

29 W. Jaeger (see note 7), pp. 163-4 and pp. 333 ff.; pp. 387-8. Jaeger points out that in his later doctrinal treatises Aristotle completely breaks with the views he had advanced in the *On Philosophy* and in the *Eudemus*. Jaeger

also shows (*ibid.*, pp. 240-1) that in the *Eudemian Ethics*, God still consti-tutes the central problem. See *Eudemian Ethics* 1248 a 23 ff. The *Eudemian Ethics*, Jaeger insists, essentially belongs to the same intellectual period as the *On Philosophy* where Aristotle puts inspiration above discursive reasoning, because inspiration comes directly from God. In *Eudemian Ethics, loc. cit.*, Aristotle admits that 'the starting point of reasoning is not reasoning itself, but something greater. What, then, could be greater than rational knowl-edge and the intellect but God?.... For this reason those are called fortunate who, whatever they start on, succeed in it without being good at reasoning. And deliberation is of no advantage to them, for they have in them a principle which is better than intellect and deliberation.... [T]hey have inspiration, but they cannot deliberate. Though lacking reason, they attain the attribute of the prudent and wise, in that their divination is speedy. And we must mark off as included in it all but the judgment that comes from reasoning. In some cases it is due to (inner?) experience, in others to habituation in the use of reflection. And both (inner?) experience and habituation use God.... These are the men in whom the reasoning power is relaxed. Hence, we have the melancholic men, the dreamers of what is true.... It is clear, then, that there are two sorts of good luck: the one is divine, and thus the lucky ones seem to succeed owing to God. Men of this sort seem to succeed in following their aim or goal, while others seem to succeed contrary to their aim or goal. Both are irrational (meta-rational)....' See here also *Epinomis* 976E. It will be noted that, according to Jaeger, the evolution of Aristotle's ethical thought proceeds from the *Protrepticus* to the *Eudemian Ethics* (which is still a rather early work) and, finally, to the *Nicomachean Ethics*.

30 The 'cave analogy' can already be found in Empedocles, frag. 31 B 120, Diels-Kranz. See notes 36 and 23. *supra*.

31 See here also P. M. Schuhl (note 23), p. 57; W. Kranz, *Empedokles* (Zürich, 1949), p. 77. See p. 168.

32 Compare Mark VIII:18.

33 W. Jaeger (see note 7), p. 164. See, for instance, A.-J. Festugière, *La Révélation d'Hermès Trismégiste*, vol. II: *Le Dieu Cosmique* (Paris, 1949), pp. 172-3, who maintains that in the *On Philosophy*, Aristotle abandons the 'philosophic pessimism' characteristic of the *Eudemus* and of Plato's philosophy in general. In the *On Philosophy*, Festugière insists, Aristotle assumes a wholly 'optimistic' and 'affirmative' attitude towards the visible cosmos. Festugière also believes that, in the *Timaeus* as well as in the *Laws*, Plato somewhat modifies his original 'philosophic pessimism' or 'negativism' by assuming a more optimistic as well as more affirmative attitude. See also A. Manno, *Il Problema di Dio in Aristotele e nei Sui Maggiori Interpreti* (Naples, 1962), pp. 93 ff.

34 See, for instance, *Epinomis* 988E ff.: 'Let none of the Greeks fear that it is not right for mortal men ever to busy themselves with matters divine. They must hold entirely the opposite view.' In Plato, *Laws* 821A, the

Athenian Stranger, not Plato, states that we ought not inquire into the Supreme God, a statement which is refuted by Plato. See also *ibid.*, 866E. It is interesting to note that Aristotle, *Metaphysics* 982 b 28 ff., incidentally one of the earliest 'parts' of the *Metaphysics*, seems to echo some of these notions. See here also *Nicomachean Ethics* 1177 b 31 ff. This would also lend support to the thesis that the *On Philosophy* (and probably Book A of the *Metaphysics*) was composed in close proximity of, though in all likelihood slightly anterior to, the *Epinomis*.

35 W. Jaeger (see note 7), p. 164. See also M. P. Nilsson, 'The origin of the belief among the Greeks in the divinity of heavenly bodies,' *Harvard Theological Review*, vol. 33 (1940), pp. 1 ff.

36 Frag. 31 B 120, Diels-Kranz. See here P.-M. Schuhl (note 23), p. 57; W. Kranz (see note 31), p. 77; M. Zepf (see note 22), pp. 355 ff. See also note 31. It should be noted, however, that Empedocles, like Plato, visualizes a transcendent world, while Aristotle is concerned with the visible world.

37 W. Jaeger (see note 7), pp. 165–6, points out that in his earlier works Aristotle apparently held the view that we can know God (and of the existence of God) only 'if it is God Himself knowing Himself.' Aristotle conceives this activity of God 'as being something transcendent and beyond the merely human standard. The self is the *Nus*, which is said to "come in from without" and to be "the divine in us"; and it is through the *Nus* that the knowledge of God enters into us.' As a matter of fact, in *Metaphysics* 983 a 5 ff., Aristotle maintains that 'the most divine science is also the most exalted. And this science alone must be, in two ways, most divine. For the science which would be most adequate for God to possess is a divine science [*scil.*, the knowledge of Himself], and so is any science that deals with divine objects [and, hence, presupposes also the science of oneself]. And this [divine] science has both these characteristics. For God is thought to be among the causes of all things . . . and such a science either God alone can have, or God above all other beings.' Thus man's knowledge of God, which also presupposes man's knowledge of himself, is closely related to God's knowledge of Himself. It should never be overlooked that the whole of Aristotle's *Metaphysics* is ultimately based on this fundamental belief, regardless of how far on the systematic or theoretical (logical) side his metaphysical speculations may have been subsequently elaborated and developed beyond this basic position. See here also Aristotle, *Protrepticus* (Iamblichus, *Protrepticus*, p. 48, lines 16 ff., ed. H. Pistelli, Leipzig, 1888; frag. 61, Rose; frag. 10c, Walzer; frag. 10c, Ross; frag. 110, Düring; frag. 106, Chroust), where we are informed that 'reason is "the divine dwelling in us" . . . and [that] because of reason [because of God?] mortal life possesses a certain element of the divine.' This implies, however, that God dwells in man, and that man is a 'temple of the divine.' Hence, both individual man and the universe are a 'most holy temple and as such worthy of God.' See Plutarch, *De Tranquillitate Animi* 20 (*Moralia* 477C), cited p. 166 in the text.

38 *Epinomis* 986D and 976DE. *Ibid.*, 987D ff., we are told that, in the final
analysis, all ethical questions are vitally related to the knowledge of God.
In the *Greater Alcibiades* 132E ff., we find the statement that the Socratic
'know thyself' can be realized only in and through the self-contemplation
of the νοῦς—in the mirror of our knowledge of God. In his *Life of Socrates*,
Aristoxenus reports that an Indian (Zoroastrian ?—see also DL II. 45, who
speaks of a Syrian magician who came to Athens) informed Socrates that
man could not possibly know himself unless and until he knew God.
Aristoxenus, frag. 31 (Mueller).

39 I. Bywater (see note 21), p. 84.

40 Philo, for instance, refers to the Demiurge and to a single 'Artificer,' while
Cicero simply speaks of the '*opera deorum.*' It is safe to assume that, in
keeping with the prevailing Greek religious tradition, the cosmos is the
work of an artificer or 'orderer of the universe' who 'creates' the cosmos
not in terms of a *creatio ex nihilo*, but by establishing an 'orderly universe,'
by imposing 'form' upon prime matter. A repercussion of this thought can
still be seen in Aristotle, *De Caelo* 271 a 33. Hence, we may infer that Philo
is closer to the Aristotelian original. It is also interesting to note that in
Philo, *Legum Allegoriarum Libri Tres* III. 32. 97–9, we can discern a remote
echo of Aristotle's *Protrepticus* or *Politicus* (Iamblichus, *Protrepticus* 55.7–56,2;
frag. 13, Walzer; frag. 13, Ross; frags 48–50, Düring, frags 45–7, Chroust).

41 Philo of Alexandria (see note 40) III. 32. 97–9. The somewhat stilted,
awkward and at times garbled phrasing of Philo undoubtedly betrays the
work of an epitomizer who selects and condenses certain detailed excursions or 'illustrations' of his source material. Some of these details, although somewhat modified, are preserved by Cicero who tailors his report
to the taste of his Roman readers, and by Sextus Empiricus. These details
and detailed descriptions, it may be surmised, originally were contained in
Aristotle's *On Philosophy*. It is fair to assume that Cicero found these
details in the *Concerning the Gods* of Posidonius, his intermediary source.
See here H. A. Wolfson, *Philo: Foundations of Religious Philosophy in
Judaism, Christianity and Islam*, vol. II (Cambridge, Mass., 1948), pp. 75 ff.;
E. Berti (see note 10), pp. 351 ff. It will be noted that Berti, on the other
hand, voices some doubts as to whether the two passages from Philo are
actually related to the Aristotelian *On Philosophy*. This is not the proper
place to discuss in detail whether Philo refers to, or in part relies on, Plato's
*Timaeus*. It must be admitted, however, that Philo might have in mind here
also the Platonic *Timaeus*. See, for instance, B. Effe (note 1), pp. 17 ff.
Philo's use of the term 'Demiurge' or his omission of a detailed description
of the way of life of the subterranean people seems to indicate this. Hence,
Philo might have cited only indirectly the Aristotelian *On Philosophy*
which, it is widely held, is also influenced by Plato's *Timaeus*. See, for instance, Plato, *Timaeus* 42D; 69C; 77A ff.; *et passim*. See also note 44.

42 See, for instance, Cicero, *Lucullus* 38. 119 (frag. 22, Rose; frag. 20, Walzer;
frag. 20, Ross; frag. 22, Untersteiner).

43 Philo of Alexandria, *De Aeternitate Mundi* III. 10–11 (frag. 18, Rose; frag. 18, Walzer; frag. 18, Ross; frag. 21, Untersteiner). See also H. Leisegang, 'Philons Schrift über die Ewigkeit der Welt,' *Philologus*, vol. 92 (1937), pp. 156–76. Philo's observation that Aristotle had declared the universe 'uncreated and imperishable,' that he had called it 'the great visible God,' and that he had insisted that it may not be compared with the 'work of men's hands,' calls for some explanation. Obviously, the handiwork of the most perfect Artificer must itself be perfect and, hence, infinitely superior to any work done by mortal and imperfect man—a decidedly Platonic notion. Being the work of the most perfect Artificer, Who cannot produce anything imperfect, the universe must participate in the perfection of its Artificer. And being perfect, it must be without limitations, that is, without beginning or end or, as Aristotle puts it, 'uncreated and imperishable,' in other words, 'divine.' Moreover, since the universe is perfect, that is, 'uncreated and imperishable,' it is really the 'visible God' or 'God Incarnate.' For Aristotle, then, the universe is 'God' as far as God is, or may become, visible. This seems to be Philo's interpretation of what Aristotle had said about God in his *On Philosophy*. Judging from the general tenor of Book III of the *On Philosophy*, Philo's account might be accurate. See here also A.-H. Chroust, 'The concept of God in Aristotle's lost dialogue *On Philosophy* (Cicero, *De Natura Deorum* I. 13. 33),' *Emerita*, vol. 33, fasc. 2 (1965), pp. 205–28, and Chapter XIV. J. Pépin, 'L'interprétation du *De Philosophia* d'Aristote d'après quelques travaux récents,' *Revue des Études Grecques*, vol. 77, nos 366–8 (1964), pp. 464–5, suggests that the expression 'ungenerated' used here by Philo of Alexandria signifies 'without a definite or ascertainable beginning.' See also E. Berti (note 10), pp. 358–9 and p. 363. This, then, would resolve some of the problems raised by the Platonic creationist thesis (which is also discussed in the *On Philosophy*, see note 44), and by Aristotle's rejection of this thesis when he asserts that God is not the creator of the universe in the ordinary sense of the term, but merely the cause of the perfect cosmic order. 'Ungenerated,' then, would actually proclaim a *creatio ab aeterno* rather than the denial of a *creatio in tempore*. (The Neo-Platonic interpreters of Plato insist that Plato, too, had in mind a *creatio ab aeterno*.) Such a *creatio ab aeterno* seems to be suggested by Cicero, *De Natura Deorum* II. 37. 95–6, where the author speaks of the *opera deorum* as well as of the *in omni aeternitate ratos immutabilisque cursus*, as well as by Cicero, *Lucullus* 38. 119, where the author refers to *neque enim ortum esse unquam mundum*. This concept of a *creatio ab aeterno*, then, would reclaim for Aristotle those fragments which seem to advance a creationist thesis, and which for this very reason have been credited by some scholars to the Platonic interlocutor, in the *On Philosophy* (who might have advocated a *creatio in tempore*) rather than to Aristotle himself. See note 44. The creator, who is responsible for the creation of the universe *ab aeterno*, is never the Platonic Demiurge, but perhaps the Platonic cosmic soul (see Plato, *Laws* 897B and the *Epinomis*), which with Aristotle becomes the νοῦς.

44 It has been suggested (and also denied) that the Aristotelian *On Philosophy* is a dialogue. Hence, there must have been several interlocutors who presented their divergent views, among them probably Aristotle and Plato. See, for instance, M. Untersteiner, *Aristotele: Della Filosofia* (Rome, 1963), pp. xxi–xxii. If this is so, then there is no sure way of telling exactly whether a particular fragment credited to the *On Philosophy* relates what either Plato (or some other interlocutor) interjects, or whether it refers to what Aristotle proposes. See J. Pépin (note 43), pp. 458–9; P. Moraux, article 'Quinta Essentia,' in Pauly-Wissowa, *Realencyclopädie der classischen Altertumswissenschaft*, vol. 47 (Stuttgart, 1963), cols 1218–9; M. Untersteiner (see this note), pp. xxiv–xxv. This makes it also extremely difficult to distinguish between the 'Platonism' of Aristotle and the 'Platonism' of Plato. Some interlocutor, probably Plato himself (see Lactantius, *Institutiones Divinae* II. 10. 24), defends the particular creationist theory expounded in the Platonic *Timaeus*. Aristotle, the main discussant, on the other hand, rejects it. See, for instance, Cicero *De Natura Deorum* II. 15. 42 ff.; Cicero (see note 42); Lactantius (see this note). V. Rose, *Aristoteles Pseudepigraphus* (Leipzig, 1863), p. 33, had already claimed that Plato was one of the interlocutors in the *On Philosophy*. See also D. J. Allan, *The Philosophy of Aristotle* (London, 1952), pp. 22. ff. Some scholars hold that whenever a fragment refers to God as the author of the cosmic order, this fragment reflects what Aristotle himself had said. But when it speaks of the 'creator of the universe' or of a 'divine providence' (see note 50), such a fragment, which seems to be in accord with Plato's *Timaeus* (where we are told that the Demiurge or 'Creator' is independent of whatever he creates) or with Plato's *Laws*, Book X, 897B (where the Demiurge is replaced by a 'cosmic soul' immanent in the universe), might reflect what Plato or the Platonic interlocutor had suggested. See also E. Berti (note 10), p. 348 and p. 357; M. Untersteiner (see this note), p. XV; J. Pépin (see note 43), pp. 459–60. If this is so, then only Sextus Empiricus, *Adversus Mathematicos* IX. 20–3 (*Adversus Physicos* I. 20–3); Sextus Empiricus, *Adversus Mathematicos* IX. 26–7 (*Adversus Physicos* I. 26–7); and Cicero, *De Natura Deorum* II. 37. 95–6, would report what Aristotle had proposed (see M. Untersteiner, this note, p. 171, and *ibid.*, pp. 176–8; pp. 225–6; J. Pépin, see note 43, pp. 459–60), while most, though by no means all the fragments found in Philo of Alexandria would contain statements made by the Platonic interlocutor or by Plato himself. See M. Untersteiner (this note), p. 173; 181; 183; 185; 223; 280; M. Untersteiner, 'Il Περὶ Φιλοσοφίας di Aristotele,' *Rivista di Filologia e d'Istruzione Classica*, vol. 88 (1960), pp. 353–4 and 356. For a different view, see J. Pépin (note 43), pp. 461–2. If this is so, then Cicero, *De Natura Deorum* II. 37. 95–6, in essence might record Aristotle's 'rebuttal' of Plato or of the Platonic interlocutor. In brief, Plato and Aristotle seem to agree that the observable harmony and order throughout the visible universe furnish incontestable evidence for the existence of a 'divine being' responsible for this harmony and order—and this is of

primary interest to us. But they disagree among themselves as to how this harmony and order originally came about. See here also E. Bignone, *L'Aristotele Perduto e la Formazione Filosofica di Epicuro*, vol. II (Florence, 1936), p. 257; p. 380; pp. 525-9; H. A. Wolfson (see note 41), vol. II. p. 77; N. A. T. Reiche, *Empedocles' Mixture, Eudoxian Astronomy and Aristotle's Connate Pneuma* (Amsterdam, 1960), p. 120. From Philo, *De Aeternitate Mundi* III. 10, it becomes evident that in his *On Philosophy* Aristotle definitely rejects Plato's particular creationist theory. Perhaps Aristotle wishes to indicate that although he disagrees with some of Plato's doctrines, he nevertheless consistently carries on (and attempts to improve upon) the theological and cosmological tradition established by Plato in the *Timaeus*. See also E. Berti (note 10), p. 352. In view of the fact that in the *On Philosophy* to some extent Aristotle still adheres to certain Platonic doctrines, the distinction between the Platonic interlocutor and the Aristotelian interlocutor is difficult to maintain. This, then, is the crux of any attempt to reconstruct the essential philosophical views propagated by Aristotle in the *On Philosophy*.

45 Frag. 13, Walzer; frag. 13, Ross; frag. 16, Untersteiner.

46 Cicero, *De Natura Deorum* II. 37. 95, maintains that even the subterranean people somehow had heard about 'the existence of some deities or divine powers.' See also notes 9 and 53.

47 See here also A. J. Festugière (note 20), p. 231, note 1.

48 Philo's observation, that some people know of God and His existence only through His 'shadow,' is definitely a Platonic notion. Philo's Platonic and Stoic learning, and his frequent use of Stoic terminology, are too well known to warrant special discussion.

49 See here also Philo of Alexandria, *De Specialibus Legibus* III. 34. 185–III. 36. 194 (frag. 13, Ross; frag. 16, Untersteiner), where we are told that the teleological and aesthetic contemplation of the universe (to know God through His handiwork), which likewise leads to the realization of God's existence, is the 'second best' way of knowing God or of knowing the existence of God. It has already been stated that according to Philo, the best way of knowing God is through God Himself.

50 Philo of Alexandria, *De Praemiis et Poenis* VII. 43 (frag. 13, Ross; frag. 16, Untersteiner). W. J. Verdenius, *Platons Gottesbegriff* (Geneva, 1962), *passim*, has pointed out that the true position of the Demiurge in Plato's theology has never been adequately clarified.

51 In *Nicomachean Ethics* 1179 a 23 ff., Aristotle maintains: 'He who exercises his intellect and cultivates it seems to be most dear to the gods. For if the gods have a care for human affairs, as they are thought to have, it would be reasonable to assume that they should delight in what is best in man and most akin to them, and that they should reward those who love and honor this most, as caring for the things that are dear to them. ... And it should be manifest that ... the philosopher ... is most dear to the gods.' See also *ibid.* 1199 b 11 ff. It has been claimed that these passages from the *Nico-*

*machean Ethics* indicate that Aristotle believed in a divine providence. In *Timaeus* 30 B.C., Plato refers to the 'providence of God.' See also *Epinomis* 980D: 'The gods have a care for all things.' Philo's remark in *De Praemiis et Poenis* VII. 43 might substantiate the observation that in the *On Philosophy* Plato acts as one of the discussants (see note 44) defending his views about divine providence.

52 Or, *Adversus Physicos* I. 22 (frag. 10, Rose; frag. 12a, Walzer; frag. 12a, Ross; frag. 14, Untersteiner). *Epinomis* 983A ff. relates that the orderly movement of the Universe as well as its perfection is caused by God.

53 Aristotle refers to the 'consensus among men' in *De Caelo* 270 b 5 ff. and 284 a 2 ff. See also E. Bignone (note 44), vol. II, p. 427 and p. 451; W. J. Verdenius, 'Traditional and personal elements in Aristotle's religion,' *Phronesis*, vol. V. (1960), pp. 56 ff. Aristotle, *Metaphysics* 1074 b 1 ff., states that the belief in the existence of gods is a matter of timeless tradition. See note 9. See also Aristotle, *Politics* 1264 a 2 ff.; Aristotle, *Rhetoric* 1387 a 16 ff.

54 See *Epinomis* 976CE, where we are informed that God implanted in man the faculty of counting so as to enable him to comprehend. *Ibid.*, 978E we are also told that God bestowed upon us the gift of learning. All this seems to imply that the faculty of knowing God, no matter how this knowledge is being acquired, ultimately is a divine gift.

55 Hence, both Plato and Aristotle seem to hold that 'the will to believe,' especially 'the will to believe in God'—one might call this a 'commitment to faith'—is really an 'innate tendency' of the human soul and, hence, is common to all men. But if this is so, then Aristotle, in his *On Philosophy*, seems to have retained the Platonic doctrine of the soul, although he rejected Plato's doctrine of the Separate Ideas. See here Aristotle, *Eudemian Ethics* 1248 a 23 ff., and note 29. See also E. Berti (see note 10), p. 348.

56 Or, *Adversus Physicos* I. 26-7 (frag. 11, Rose; frag. 12b, Walzer; frag. 12b, Ross; frag. 26, Untersteiner).

57 The parallel between this passage and Aristotle, *Metaphysics* 1075 a 11 ff., is striking: 'We must also consider in which of two ways the nature of the universe contains the good as well as the highest good—whether as something separate and by itself, or as the order of the several parts. Probably in both ways, as an army does. For its excellence is to be found in its order and in its commander, and more so in the latter. For he does not depend on the order, but the latter depends on him.' This statement in the *Metaphysics* might well be an echo of the *On Philosophy*, especially, since Book XII of the *Metaphysics* is a fairly early work of Aristotle. See also E. Heitz (see note 21), p. 36.

58 See I. Bywater (see note 21), pp. 75-6. W. Spoerri (see note 21), p. 168, discusses the extent to which Cleanthes was influenced by the early Aristotle.

59 See here also P. Aubenque (see note 28), p. 343, note 1, and p. 347.

60 See note 57. In *Phaedrus* 246E, Plato writes: 'Zeus, the mighty lord, holding the reins of a winged chariot, leads the way in heaven, ordering all and

taking care of all. And there follows him the array of the gods and demi-gods, marshalled in eleven bands.'

61 See R. Mugnier, *La Théorie du Premier Moteur et l'Évolution de la Pensée Aristotélicienne* (Paris, 1930), pp. 126-7. The comparison of God (or the gods) with a supreme army commander, which might have been originated by Aristotle (in the *On Philosophy*), became fairly common during the Hellenistic period.

62 In this connection there also arises the problem, already discussed in Plato's *Parmenides* (134DE), of whether the supreme army commander, who is God, can know (or cares to know) the army he commands or the universe which he controls, especially since such knowledge in a way is actually beneath him. See here also Aristotle, *Metaphysics* 1074 b 15-35. If indeed the 'commander' has no knowledge of the universe, he cannot be conceived as the 'divine Demiurge' in the sense of Plato. Also, the comparison of the universe with a well-arrayed army which has God as its supreme commander does not shed any light on the specific problem nor explain the particular manner in which the world is actually controlled by this supreme commander, or the particular means he employs. For it is not permissible to infer from this analogy that God devises a particular plan for this world, or that He passes on certain commands to 'subordinates' (intermediary deities, demons or spirits), or that He creates and maintains the order within the universe by thinking about the universe or about any part of the universe. See here also Aristotle, *Metaphysics* 1074 b 15 ff. Conversely, *Nicomachean Ethics* 1179 a 23 ff., maintains that the gods may care for humans. See note 51.

63 Sextus Empiricus, *Adversus Mathematicos* IX. 26-7 (*Adversus Physicos* I. 26-7; frag. 11, Rose; frag. 12b, Walzer; frag. 12b, Ross; frag. 26, Untersteiner).

64 The 'μαθεῖν-thesis' can also be found in Sextus Empiricus, *Adversus Mathematicos* IX. 26-7 (frag. 11, Rose; frag. 12b, Walzer; frag. 12b, Ross; frag. 26, Untersteiner); Philo of Alexandria, *Legum Allegoriarum Libri Tres* III. 32. 97-9 (frag. 13, Walzer; frag. 13, Ross; frag. 15, Untersteiner); Philo of Alexandria, *De Praemiis et Poenis* VII. 41-3 (frag. 13, Ross; frag. 16, Untersteiner); Philo of Alexandria, *De Specialibus Legibus* III. 3. 185 ff (frag. 13; Ross; frag. 16, Untersteiner); Cicero, *De Natura Deorum* II. 37. 95-6 (frag. 12, Rose; frag. 13, Walzer; frag. 13, Ross; frag. 18, Untersteiner). See also A.-H. Chroust, '"Mystical revelation" and "Rational theology" in Aristotle's *On Philosophy*,' *Tijdschrift voor Filosofie*, vol. 34 (1972), pp. 500-12.

65 See also G. Lazzati, *L'Aristotele Perduto e gli Scrittori Cristiani* (Milan, 1938), pp. 59 ff.

66 In *Laws* 966D, Plato insists that of the two things which lead men to believe in the gods, 'one is the argument from the order and motion of the stars, and of all things under the dominion of the "Mind" which ordered the universe.'

67 In *Epinomis* 984A, we are informed that the stars are 'the ornaments of the heavens.' They are, it may be claimed, the 'statues and pictures' which, according to Cicero's account, adorn the well-constructed and well-lit dwellings of the 'subterranean people.'

68 Philo of Alexandria, *De Praemiis et Poenis* VII. 41–3. See also Philo of Alexandria, *De Specialibus Legibus* III. 34. 185 ff.; A. J. Festugière (see note 20), vol. II, p. 231, note 1. The notion that some people know God and are aware of His existence only through 'His shadow,' that is, through His creation, is definitely a Platonic notion. See Plato, *Republic* 514A ff., 532A ff.; 539F.

69 Plato seems to have indulged in some oral teachings or lecturing, although according to the *Seventh Epistle* (341CD) he apparently believed that his doctrine was orally incommunicable. The majority of scholars, though by no means all of them, are now of the opinion that there is such a thing as the 'oral—unwritten—teachings' of Plato. See, for instance, W. D. Ross, *Plato's Theory of Ideas* (Oxford, 1951), pp. 142–53; H. J. Krämer, *Arete bei Platon und Aristoteles* (Abhandlungen der Heidelberger Akademie der Wissenschaften, vol. VI, Heidelberg, 1959), *passim*. For additional literature, consult H. J. Krämer, 'Über den Zusammenhang von Prinzipienlehre und Dialektik bei Platon,' *Philologus*, vol. 110, nos 1–2 (1966), p. 35, note 2. These oral teachings or lectures, as a rule, were attended by the members of the Academy, who subsequently debated them and even wrote 'papers' on the subjects discussed by Plato. They stated their assent or disagreement, thus starting prolonged debates within the inner circle of the Academy. Some of Aristotle's earliest compositions are probably the result of these lectures and discussions. Moreover, it must always be borne in mind that Plato himself fully realized that some of his own basic notions were 'myths'—'myths' in the most exalted sense of the term—and that as such any 'myth' is but one of several possible hypotheses. See, for instance, Plato, *Laws* 898E. In admitting this, Plato, at least by implication, not only conceded to his disciples the right to question his hypotheses as well as his teachings, but also the right to propose entirely different hypotheses and, as a matter of fact, made it their intellectual and moral duty to seek more satisfactory solutions. In short, during his later years he granted them a sort of 'academic freedom.'

70 For a masterful understanding and matchless evaluation of Aristotle's contributions to future theology, see W. Jaeger (note 7), pp. 159 ff.

CHAPTER XIV   THE CONCEPT OF GOD IN ARISTOTLE'S *On Philosophy* (CICERO, *De Natura Deorum* I.13.33)

  ★ With some modifications, this chapter was first published in *Emerita*, vol. 33, no. 2 (1965), pp. 205–28.

1 Frag. 26, Rose; frag. 26, Walzer; frag. 26, Ross; frag. 39, Untersteiner.

2 See Chapter XII, note 2. Some of the recent scholarly literature discussing and analyzing the *On Philosophy* is cited in the notes to this Chapter, in the notes to Chapter XII and XIII, and in the notes to Chapters XV and XVI. See also A. Manno, *Il Problema di Dio in Aristotle e nei Sui Maggiori Interpreti* (Naples, 1962), *passim*; J. Pépin, 'L'interprétation de *De Philosophia* d'après quelques travaux récents,' *Revue des Études Grecques*, vol. 77 (1964), pp. 445-88; J. Pépin, *Théologie Cosmique et Théologie Chrétienne* (Paris, 1964), *passim*.

3 See, for instance, Aristotle, *Metaphysics* 1072 b 26-9 and 1074 b 33-5; Aristotle, *Eudemian Ethics*, 1248 a 24-7; etc.; notes 23-30 and the corresponding text.

4 See, for instance, Aristotle, *De Caelo* 284 a 2-8 and 286 a 9-12; Aristotle, *Metaphysics* 1074 a 34 ff.; etc. See also Plato, *Timaeus* 34B; 40D; 41A; 92C; Plato, *Laws* 821B; 821C; 899B; 950D; *Epinomis* 983C ff.; 986B ff.; 987B; etc.; notes 31-44 and the corresponding text.

5 This might possibly be a reference to Aristotle's First Mover or Unmoved Mover. The expression *replicatio* ('reverse motion'), ἀνείλεξις in Greek, might be traced back to Plato's *Statesman* 270D and 286B. It refers to the 'counter-rotation' of the planets (?). See also Aristotle, *Metaphysics* 1074 a 2. In *Laws* 987A ff., Plato points out that the soul—the 'cosmic soul' or 'mind'—'directs all things in the heavens and on earth ... and this soul disciplines all things to their happiness.' See also notes 46-77 and the corresponding text.

6 See Aristotle, *De Caelo* 269 a 30-32 and 270 b 22-25. Aristotle does not actually say, however, that the 'ether' itself is God. See Cicero, *De Natura Deorum* I. 14. 36; notes 78-86 and the corresponding text.

7 See Philodemus, *De Diis* 3, col. 10, lines 7-10 (p. 30, ed. H. Diels); notes 90-116 and the corresponding text.

8 *Sine corpore* is Cicero's translation of the Greek term ἀσώματος. See also Sextus Empiricus, *Pyrrh. Hypoth.* III. 218; notes 121-5, and the corresponding texts.

9 Aristotle speaks in general of an Unmoved Mover as well as of a Self-Moving Mover.

10 Calm serenity as the basis of true or perfect (intellectual) happiness is definitely an Epicurean ideal. See note 140; and notes 126-42 and the corresponding text.

11 See Cicero, *De Natura Deorum* I. 8. 18: 'And then Velleius began, in the habitually arrogant manner of the Epicureans, fearing nothing so much as that he might appear to be in doubt about something, and with the air of one who had just descended from the council of the gods in Epicurus' ethereal interspace.'

12 Instances of Epicurus' animosity towards Aristotle can be found in DL X. 8; Eusebius, *Praeparatio Evangelica* XV. 2. 1 (Aristocles); Athenaeus, *Deipnosophistae* VIII. 352D-354E; Aelian, *Varia Historia* V. 9; Sextus

Empiricus, *Adversus Mathematicos* I. 1; Cicero, *De Natura Deorum* I. 33. 93; Timaeus, in Polybius XII. 8; Suda, *Aristotle*; etc. See here also I. Düring, *Aristotle in the Ancient Biographical Tradition* (Acta Universitatis Gothoburgensis, vol. 41, no. 2. Göteborg, 1957), pp. 376 ff. and 384 ff., *et passim*. This hostile attitude of Epicurus towards Aristotle was maintained throughout by the Epicureans. E. Bignore, *L'Aristotele Perduto e la Formazione Filosofica di Epicuro*, 2 vols (Florence, 1936), has made use of Epicurus' attacks upon, and polemics against, Aristotle in order to ferret out some additional fragments of Aristotle's lost works. Since some of these polemics could not possibly have been directed against the preserved doctrinal treatises of the Stagirite, Bignone assumed that they must be aimed at the lost or 'exoteric' writings. From the tenor of these attacks, he reconstructed in a most ingenious manner the likely doctrinal content of these lost works.

13 See W. Jaeger, *Aristotle: Fundamentals of the History of his development* (Oxford, 1948), p. 138.

14 Philodemus, *De Pietate* 7 b 4–8. See also E. Bignone (note 12), vol. II, p. 365. Philodemus' antipathy towards Aristotle and Aristotelian philosophy as well as his anti-Aristotelian bias in general is too well known to warrant a detailed discussion.

15 Cicero, *Tuscul. Disput.* I. 10. 22.

16 See also O. Gigon, 'Cicero und Aristoteles,' *Hermes*, vol. 87 (1959), p. 153.

17 P. Wilpert, 'Die aristotelische Schrift *Über die Philosophie.*' *Autour d'Aristote* (Louvain, 1955), p. 106.

18 Some scholars substitute the word *uno* for *suo*, so as to make the passage read, 'Aristotle disagrees with Plato, his teacher, on one point.' See note 19. This 'one point' is the identification of God with 'ether.' See note 20. Others simply add the word *non* before *dissentiens*, so as to make the text read, 'Aristotle does not disagree with Plato, his teacher.' For a list of these divergent views, see E. Berti, *La Filosofia del Primo Aristotele* (Pubblicazioni della Facoltà di Lettere e Filosofia, Padua, 1962), p. 376.

19 A. J. Festugière, *La Révélation d'Hermès Trismégiste*, vol. II (Paris, 1949), p. 243. See also E. Bignone (see note 12), vol. II, p. 350.

20 Namely, that God is 'ether' (*caeli ardor*). According to Velleius, this would be Aristotle's fourth definition of God. See note 18. The other Aristotelian definitions of God recited by Cicero (Velleius) can be found, for instance, in Plato, *Republic*, *Timaeus*, *Sophist*, *Statesman* and *Laws*. See also note 21.

21 Cicero, *De Natura Deorum* I. 12. 30:

> It would take a long time, however, to point out all of Plato's inconsistencies [in his definitions of God]. In the *Timaeus* [28C] he maintains that no one can actually name the Creator of the universe, and in the *Laws* [821A] he relates that men must on no account investigate the nature of God. And yet he states that God is wholly without any corporeal elements [this is implied in *Republic* 381A ff.]

(or, as the Greeks say, ἀσώματος). But such a being cannot possibly be conceived, for such a being of necessity would have to be without sensations and, hence, also be totally devoid of wisdom which is born of experience, as well as devoid of pleasure and happiness. But such faculties have always had a place in our conceptions of the deity. And yet, both in the *Timaeus* [34B; 40D; 41A; 92C] and in the *Laws* [821B; 821C; 886D; 899B; 950D], Plato insists that the universe, the sky, the stars, the earth and our own souls are gods, as well as those gods that have been bequeathed to us in the lore of our ancestors. But these theories are manifestly unsound and mutually antagonistic in the highest degree.

In the *Timaeus*, Plato does not actually state that God is ἀσώματος, although DL III. 77, as well as other ancient authors who wrote on Plato, maintain this. See note 108. In *Laws* 897B, Plato calls the soul 'a god,' and in *Timaeus* 69E ff., he calls it 'divine.' In *Timaeus* 40D, Plato relates that 'to know ... the origin of the other deities is beyond us, and we must accept the traditions of the men of old times. ...' See also Aristotle, *Metaphysics* 1074 b 1 ff.; Aristotle, *Nicomachean Ethics* 1098 b 27 ff. Assuming, however, that Cicero's text, namely, that Aristotle in general disagreed with his teacher Plato, in the main is correct, then this particular passage constitutes a priceless piece of evidence in support of the thesis, advanced among others by W. Jaeger, that the *On Philosophy* marks the crucial point in the intellectual development of Aristotle, at which he moved away from Plato and Platonism. In some of his earlier works, such as the *On (the) Ideas* and the *On the Good* (which in time precede the *On Philosophy*), Aristotle had voiced limited criticisms of certain aspects of Plato's basic teachings. But in the *On Philosophy*, it is held by some scholars, Aristotle disagreed with Plato in a more determined fashion and on a much broader basis. Careful reading of the extant fragments assigned to the *On Philosophy* does not indicate, however, that Aristotle's breach with Plato and Platonism in this dialogue is as radical and as far-reaching as some scholars would have us believe. Perhaps it might be more appropriate to maintain that in the *On Philosophy* Aristotle modifies, or tries to improve upon, some of Plato's basic views, especially upon Plato's 'theological notions.' This does not mean, however, that he completely abandons Platonism. The thesis that the *On Philosophy* constitutes the decisive point at which Aristotle abandoned Platonism, in the final analysis, rests upon (and justifies) the hypothesis that Aristotle progressively evolved from an initial Platonist into an ultimate 'Aristotelian.' This far-reaching hypothesis, which among certain circles has come to be an almost sacred dogma, cannot be discussed here. Suffice it to point out that it is based on the assumption, by no means fully and satisfactorily ascertained, that the doctrinal treatises credited to Aristotle and included in the traditional *Corpus Aristotelicum* in their totality are indeed by Aristotle and not, perhaps, by the Early Peripatus. Since the early (lost but undoubtedly authentic) compositions of Aristotle are essentially Platonic in their fundamental philosophic orientation and outlook (*pace* Düring), while the later doctrinal treatises are obviously 'Aristotelian,' in order to reconcile these two conflicting philosophies a point had to be established at which Aristotle allegedly changed over from a Platonist into an 'Aristotelian.' As it happened, the *On Philosophy* was declared by W. Jaeger the crucial point at which this change took place. Obviously, the whole argument, which is as ingenious as it is fascinating, hinges on the assumption that the *Corpus Aristotelicum* in its totality contains the authentic works of Aristotle, an assumption, however, which has not yet been proven to the satisfaction of everyone.

22 Cicero, *De Natura Deorum* II. 15. 42-4. See also W. Jaeger (note 13), pp. 143 ff.; note 91. In this connection it might be rewarding to compare the *Epinomis*, which propagates astral theology. There might exist some connections between the astral theology of the *Epinomis* and what Aristotle had said about the divinity of the stars or the 'star gods' in the *On Philosophy*. See also Plato, *Timaeus* 41E ff.

23 See also Aristotle, *De Generatione Animalium* 736 b 27-8, 737 a 10. W. Jaeger (see note 13), p. 139, referring to this passage, states: 'The God to Whom the world is subordinated is the transcendental Unmoved Mover, Who guides the world as its final cause, by reason of the perfection of His pure thought.' See also Iamblichus, *Protrepticus* (ed. H. Pistelli, 1888), p. 48, lines 9-13 (frag. 61, Rose; frag. 10c, Walzer; frag. 10c, Ross; frag. 108, Düring; frag. 104, Chroust), a passage which Iamblichus derives from Aristotle's *Protrepticus* and which is probably a 'fragment' of the Aristotelian *Protrepticus*. For additional comments, see A.-H. Chroust, *Aristotle: Protrepticus—A Reconstruction* (Notre Dame, 1964), pp. 43, 108-9.

24 Simplicius, *Comment. in Arist. De Caelo, CIAG*, vol. VII (ed. J. Heiberg, Berlin, 1894), p. 485, lines 19-22 (frag. 49, Rose; frag. 1, Ross). See A.-H. Chroust, 'A note on some of the minor "lost works" of Aristotle,' *Tijdschrift voor Filosofie*, vol. 27, no. 2 (1965), pp. 310-19, especially, pp. 310-11, and Chapter II. See also notes 136-8. An *On Prayer* by Aristotle is mentioned in DL V. 22 (no. 14), *VH* 10 (no. 9) and in *VL* 52.

25 See H. Cherniss, *Aristotle's Criticism of Plato and the Academy*, vol. I (Baltimore, 1944), p. 592. W. Jaeger, *The Theology of the Early Greek Philosophers* (Oxford, 1947), p. 31, points out that τὸ θεῖον originally referred to some 'first' or 'highest' principle, or to a 'first cause.' See, for instance, Aristotle, *Metaphysics* 1074 b 1-3: 'Our forefathers in the most remote ages have handed down to their posterity a tradition . . . that the divine (τὸ θεῖον) encloses the whole of nature.' This τὸ θεῖον not only 'encloses the whole of nature,' but also 'nourishes and governs' the physical universe. See, for instance, Aristotle, *Physics* 203 b 11.

26 For some opposing views, see A. J. Festugière (see note 19), vol. II, pp. 248-55; P. Moraux, *Les Listes Anciennes des Ouvrages d'Aristote* (Louvain,

1951), pp. 120–1; W. Theiler, *Zur Geschichte der teleologischen Natur-betrachtung bis auf Aristoteles* (Zürich, 1924), pp. 83–4.

27 *Protrepticus*, frag. 61, Rose; frag. 10c, Walzer; frag. 10c, Ross; frag. 108, Düring; frag. 104, Chroust.

28 *Protrepticus*, frag. 61, Rose; frag. 10c, Walzer; frag. 10c, Ross; frag. 109, Düring; frag. 105, Chroust.

29 *Protrepticus*, frag. 61, Rose; frag. 10c, Walzer; frag. 10c, Ross; frag. 110, Düring; frag. 106, Chroust. Euclides of Megara is said to have called the supreme good 'God' or 'Mind.' See DL II. 106. See also Aristotle, *Nicomachean Ethics* 1153 b 32.

30 Aristotle, *Eudemian Ethics* 1248 a 23 ff. See also Aristotle, *Metaphysics* 1072 a 14–29 and 1074 b 15 ff. In *Republic* 509B, Plato states: 'The Good [*scil.*, God] is not only the author or cause of man's knowledge of all things known, but also the author or cause of the existence of these things. And yet this Good is no ordinary Being, but rather something that is far beyond Being....' Similar notions can be found in *Epinomis* 976DE. This is also brought out by Aristotle's *On Prayer*. See note 24. Some scholars have pointed out that the *deus-mens* or νοῦς referred to by Cicero and credited to the Aristotelian *On Philosophy*, is in fact the 'intellect of the universe' or, perhaps, the intellect which permeates the orderly cosmos. As such, the *deus-mens* actually moves everything in a most orderly fashion, although He Himself is wholly apart from what He moves. See Cicero, *Tuscul. Disput.* I. 26. 65–I. 27. 66 (frag. 27, Walzer; frag. 27, Ross; frag. 30, Untersteiner); J. Moreau, *L'Âme de Monde, De Platon aux Stoïciens* (Paris, 1939), p. 121. By 'integrating' the divine νοῦς and the cosmic reason, Aristotle in a way may have restated or modified some notions originally advanced by Plato. Thus, in *Timaeus* 30A (see also *ibid.*, 30C; 31B; 34A; 34C; 38C; etc.), the Demiurge is called ὁ θεός as well as νοῦς (*ibid.*, 39E), while the *Philebus* (22C) refers to the νοῦς θεῖος Who is the King of heaven and earth (Philebus 28C), or the 'sovereign νοῦς.' *Ibid.*, 30D. The νοῦς θεῖος is also mentioned in the *Laws* 897B ff., where we are told that this νοῦς θεῖος, by joining or co-operating with the cosmic soul, makes the latter divine as well as enabling it to guide everything in the proper manner. In brief, there exist a number of Platonic passages which refer, or imply, the existence of a *deus-mens* Who is 'beyond' and 'above' the orderly divine universe. In the *On Philosophy*, Aristotle, too, seems to imply that the *deus-mundus* or cosmic νοῦς is 'immanent' to the divine universe (and is perhaps the divine orderly universe itself), while the *deus-mens* is 'above' and 'beyond' the *deus-mundus* and, hence, superior to and independent of the divine universe or *deus-mundus*. See also (p. 189).

31 H. Cherniss (see note 25), p. 593, for instance, prefers τὸ θεῖον to ὁ θεός. This seems to follow from Aristotle, *De Caelo* 285 a 27–31. Θεῖος may also signify uncreated, incorruptible or perfect.

32 Frag. 18, Rose; frag. 18, Walzer; frag. 18, Ross; frag. 21, Untersteiner; and frag. 19, Rose; frag. 19a, Walzer; frag. 19a, Ross; frag. 29, Untersteiner.

33 See A.-H. Chroust, 'A cosmological proof for the existence of God in Aristotle's lost dialogue *On Philosophy*,' *New Scholasticism*, vol. 40, no. 4 (1966), pp. 447–63, and Chapter XIII.

34 Philo of Alexandria, *De Aeternitate Mundi* III. 10–11. See also *ibid.*, V. 20, and note 32. Plato, *Timaeus* 92C, might possibly be the original model for Aristotle's concept of a 'visible God.' Here we are told that 'the universe . . . [is] the visible . . . God . . . Who is the image of the purely "intellectual [God]" . . . the only-begotten universe.'

35 Philo of Alexandria (see note 34), VIII. 39–43 (frag. 21, Rose; frag. 19c, Walzer; frag. 19c, Ross; frag. 17, Untersteiner).

36 Sextus Empiricus, *Adversus Mathematicos* IX. 26–7 (frag. 11, Rose; frag. 12b, Walzer; frag. 12b, Ross; frag. 26, Untersteiner). See also Sextus Empiricus, *op. cit.*, IX. 20–3 (frag. 10, Rose; frag. 12a, Walzer; frag. 12a, Ross; frag. 14, Untersteiner).

37 Cicero, *De Natura Deorum* II. 37. 95–6 (frag. 12, Rose; frag. 13, Walzer; frag. 13, Ross; frag. 18, Untersteiner). The more immediate source of Cicero is probably Posidonius of Apamea who, in turn, was probably influenced by Cleanthes, the Stoic. Cleanthes, in turn, might have made use of Aristotle's *On Philosophy*. See also note 92.

38 Philo of Alexandria. *Legum Allegoriarum Libri Tres* III. 32. 97–9 (frag. 13, Walzer; frag. 13, Ross; frag. 15, Untersteiner). See Philo of Alexandria, *De Praemiis et Poenis* VII. 41–3 (frag. 13, Ross; frag. 16, Untersteiner); Philo of Alexandria, *De Aeternitate Mundi* V. 20–4 (frag. 19, Rose; frag. 19a, Walzer; frag. 19a, Ross; frag. 29, Untersteiner). See further Philo of Alexandria, *De Aeternitate Mundi* VI. 28–VII. 34 (frag. 20, Rose; frag. 19b, Walzer; frag. 19b, Ross; frag. 28, Untersteiner), and VIII. 39–43 (frag. 31, Rose; frag. 19c. Walzer; frag. 19c, Ross; frag. 17, Untersteiner).

39 See Sextus Empiricus, *Adversus Mathematicos* IX. 26–7 (frag. 11, Rose; frag. 12b, Walzer; frag. 12b, Ross; frag. 26, Untersteiner); Sextus Empiricus, *op. cit.*, IX. 23 (frag. 10, Rose; frag. 12a, Walzer; frag. 12a, Ross; frag. 14, Untersteiner); Cicero, *De Natura Deorum* II. 37. 95–6 (frag. 12, Rose; frag. 13, Walzer; frag. 13, Ross; frag. 18, Untersteiner); Philo of Alexandria, *Legum Allegoriarum Libri Tres* III. 32. 97–9 (frag. 13, Walzer; frag. 13, Ross; frag. 15, Untersteiner). For additional detail, see A.-H. Chroust (note 33).

40 Psalm XIX:1.

41 Philo of Alexandria, *De Praemiis et Poenis* VII. 40–6 (frag. 13, Ross; frag. 16, Untersteiner). See also Philo of Alexandria, *De Specialibus Legibus* III. 34. 185–III. 36. 194 (frag. 13, Ross; frag. 16, Untersteiner).

42 Such a 'contradiction' had already been noticed by J. Bernays, *Die Dialoge des Aristoteles in ihrem Verhältnis zu seinen übrigen Werken* (Berlin, 1863), pp. 99–101.

43 W. Jaeger (see note 13), p. 139, on the other hand, attempts to overcome this apparent contradiction by insisting that in this context, the term *mundus* (κόσμος) does not mean the physical universe encompassing all corporeal things, but rather the heavens or the perisphere.

44 Philo of Alexandria, *De Aeternitate Mundi* III. 10–11. See note 32. See also Cicero, *Lucullus* (ed. C. Plasberg) 38. 119 (frag. 22, Rose; frag. 20, Walzer; frag. 20, Ross; frag. 22, Untersteiner); Lactantius, *Institutiones Divinae* II. 10. 24 (frag. 20, Walzer; frag. 20, Ross; frag. 22, Untersteiner).

45 H. Cherniss (see note 25), pp. 591–2.

46 Plato, *Statesman* 270D. Here Plato states:

> But their motion is, as far as possible, single and in the same place, and of the same kind. It is, therefore, only subject to 'reversal,' which is the least change possible. For the lord of all moving things is alone capable of moving himself. But to think that he moves them at one time in one direction, and at another time in another, is blasphemy. Hence, we must not say that the universe is either self-moved, or in its entirety is made to go round by God in two opposite courses; or that two gods, having opposite courses, make it move around. But ... the universe is guided at one time by an external power which is divine and receives fresh life and immortality from the renewing hand of the Creator, and, again, when released, moves on its own, being set free at such a time as to have, during infinite cycles of years, a 'reverse movement'. ....

See also *ibid.*, 286B. E. Bignone (see note 12), vol. II, pp. 377–81, is of the opinion that Cicero's (Aristotle's) notion of the *replicatio* (ἀνείλιξις) ultimately goes back to, or is influenced by, Plato, *Statesman* 270D. Relying also on Plato, *Statesman* 269E ff. and 270D, Bignone further maintains that, according to Plato, at times God Himself directs the 'activities' of the universe, at times He leaves this universe to its own devices, and at times He actually reverses its course. These particular notions remind us of Zoroastrianism and the Zoroastrian teachings of the 'eternal recurrence' or 'eternal return.' That Plato was familiar with the Zoroastrian doctrine of the 'eternal return,' which is, indeed, a sort of 'reverse action,' has been shown, among others, by A.-H. Chroust, 'Aristotle and the philosophies of the east,' *Review of Metaphysics*, vol. 18, no. 3 (1965), pp. 572–80, and Chapter XVI. Bignone is also of the opinion that Plato's ἀνείλιξις was discussed in Aristotle's *On Philosophy*. In his commentary to Cicero, *De Natura Deorum* (Cambridge, 1880), pp. 120–21, J. B. Mayer points out that there might be a connection between the *replicatio* of the Aristotelian *On Philosophy* and Plato's ἀνείλιξις. See also W. Theiler (see note 26), pp. 83–4. Bignone's views were in part accepted by J. B. Skemp, *Plato's Statesman* (London, 1952), pp. 98–101, and by L. Elders, *Aristotle's Theory of the One* (Assen, 1961), p. 104, note 4. They were rejected by H. Cherniss (see note 25), v. 592, on the grounds that 'it is unintelligible that god should be said to maintain the motion of the universe by an ἀνείλιξις which ought to be the counter-rotation resulting from his temporary abandonment of the universe.' Cherniss seems to overlook the fact that already Plato (*Statesman* 270D) spoke of alternating 'guided' and 'unguided' movements within the universe, Perhaps Velleius' third definition points more at Plato than at Aristotle. We have no definite way of determining whether in the *On Philosophy* Aristotle subscribed to Plato's ἀνείλιξις. It has been held that, since the *On Philosophy* was a dialogue, several interlocutors presented their divergent views. Some interlocutor may have defended the Platonic doctrine of the ἀνείλιξις, while Aristotle, presumably the main interlocutor, may well have objected to this doctrine. If this be so, then Velleius' criticism would actually be directed against Plato or the 'Platonic interlocutor.'

47 This is the explanation offered by J. Moreau, *L'Âme du Monde de Platon aux Stoïciens* (Paris, 1939), v. 118. Moreau's explanation was accepted by J. Bidez, *Un Singulier Naufrage Littéraire dans l'Antiquité: A la Recherche des Épaves d'Aristote Perdu* (Brussels, 1943), v. 39; and by A. J. Festugière (see note 19), vol. II, pp. 245–6. It was rejected by H. Cherniss (see note 25), p. 592, on the grounds that it is impossible 'that Aristotle should have called the motion of the planets from east to west in the diurnal rotation a *retrograde* motion.'

48 This is the explanation submitted by H. von Arnim, 'Die Entstehung der Gotteslehre des Aristoteles, *Sitzungsberichte der Akademie der Wissenschaften in Wien*, Histor.-Philos. Klasse, vol. II, part 5 (1931), pp. 4–5. Similar views were entertained by E. Zeller, *Die Philosophie der Griechen*, vol. II, part 2 (Leipzig, 1879), pp. 374–84. Von Arnim's interpretation, which implies that there is a divinity which moves the heavens, and a divinity which moves the fixed stars or the firmament (see here also J. Bernays, see note 42, pp. 99–100), found the approval of H. Cherniss (see note 25), p. 592. In another sense the first part of the third definition, namely, that God is 'some ruler over the universe to whom he [*scil.*, Aristotle] attributes the power of guiding and maintaining the movements of this universe,' also lends substantial support to the assumption that in the *On Philosophy* Aristotle clearly distinguished between the Supreme God Who is pure νοῦς or *deus mens* (first definition) and the divine universe or *deus mundus* (second definition), and that the Supreme God or νοῦς controls, or rules over, the divine universe.

49 J. Bernays (see note 42), pp. 99–100.

50 See, for instance, Aristotle, *Metaphysics* 1072 a 9 ff. and *ibid.* 1073 a 26 ff.; Aristotle, *Physics* 260 a 13 ff.; etc.

51 W. Jaeger (see note 13), p. 139. Jaeger continues: 'This is the original nucleus of Aristotle's metaphysics.' But Jaeger does not explain exactly what the 'reverse motion' means in this connection. See also *ibid.*, p. 301. M. Gentile, 'La dottrina platonica delle idee numeri e Aristotele,' *Annali della Reale Scuola Normale Superiore di Pisa*, vol. 30, fasc. 3 (1930), pp. 131–4, essentially accepts the views advanced by Bernays and Jaeger. W. Theiler (see note 26), pp. 83–4, likewise believes that Aristotle refers here to the Unmoved Mover. W. Theiler, 'Ein vergessenes Aristoteleszeugnis,' *Journal of Hellenic Studies*, vol. 77 (1957), p. 127, maintains that Aristotle propagates a doctrine of two distinct gods—two gods which, however, are

not of equal rank—namely, the divine universe conceived as 'ether,' and the divine νοῦς conceived as the 'governor' of the divine universe. W. Jaeger also holds (pp. 140 ff.) that the notion of a transcendent Unmoved Mover is the third possibility mentioned in Plato's *Laws* 898E ff. and that Aristotle derived his concept of an Unmoved Mover from Plato's *Laws* 898E ff.: 'Either the soul ... moves the sun this way or that, residing within the circular and visible body, like the soul which carries us about every way; or the soul provides itself with an external body of fire or air ... and forcibly propels body by body; or, thirdly, the soul is without such a body, but guides the sun by some extraordinary and wonderful power.' Jaeger seems to overlook here that Plato's 'third possibility' identifies the mover with spontaneous self-motion.

52 H. von Arnim (see note 48), pp. 3–7. Disagreeing with Jaeger, von Arnim insists that in the *On Philosophy* Aristotle, acting in a thoroughly Platonic spirit, makes all motion dependent on a 'self-moving mover'—not on an Unmoved Mover—that is, on a 'soul' or 'mind' or something that is 'animated' (ἔμψυχον). Von Arnim, it will be noted, does not really explain the '*alium quendam [deum]*' of Velleius, that is, the deity which is accountable for the 'reverse motion' or *replicatio* of the planets. Von Arnim seems to believe that this particular 'mover' is just one of the general causes which move the heavenly sphere, and to which Aristotle alludes in *Metaphysics*, Book XII, chapter 8. By referring to Aristotle's *De Generatione et Corruptione* 336 a 15 ff., von Arnim stresses the importance in Aristotle's cosmology of a secondary motion along with the ecliptic (in addition to the primary motion of the first heaven). The *replicatio* might well be this 'secondary motion.' It would be fully consonant with Aristotle's general outlook, von Arnim believes, to place over the 'secondary motion' (or *replicatio* ?) another deity. See, for instance, Aristotle, *Metaphysics* 1073 a 26 ff.

53 J. Bidez (see note 47), p. 40.

54 A. J. Festugière (see note 19), vol. II, pp. 245–6.

55 From the Ciceronian passage, 'how, if it [*scil.*, the universe] is constantly moving itself, can this self-same universe ever attain to calm serenity and true (perfect) happiness' (*De Natura Deorum* I. 13. 33), one might infer that Aristotle had already considered, or had devised, the notion of an Unmoved Mover. For, according to Aristotle's own view, only an Unmoved Mover can be both perfectly serene and perfectly happy. See note 137.

56 W. D. Ross, *Aristotle's Physics* (Oxford, 1936), vv. 95–7.

57 W. K. C. Guthrie, 'The development of Aristotle's theology,' *Classical Quarterly*, vol. 27 (1933), pp. 164–5.

58 W. Theiler (see note 26), pp. 83–4.

59 E. Berti (see note 18), pp. 380–1 and 382–3, *et passim*.

60 M. Untersteiner, *Aristotele: Della Filosofia* (Rome, 1963), p. 207 and p. 260; pp. 291 ff., *et passim*; M. Untersteiner, 'Il Περὶ φιλοσοφίας di Aristotele,' *Rivista di Filosofia e d'Istruzione Classica*, vol. 89 (1960), pp. 133–5.

61 *Cod. Paris. Graec.* 174, fol. 46a (frag. 17, Rose; frag. 17, Walzer; frag. 17, Ross; frag. 27, Untersteiner).

62 J. Pépin, 'L'interprétation du *De Philosophia* d'Aristote d'après quelques travaux récents,' *Revue des Études Grecques*, vol. 77, nos. 366-8 (1964), pp. 466-73.

63 *Ibid.*, p. 468.

64 Frag. 24, Rose; frag. 21, Walzer; frag. 21, Ross; frag. 32, Untersteiner.

65 See also Cicero, *Tusculanae Disputationes* I. 27. 66 (frag. 27, Walzer; frag. 27, Ross; frag. 30, Untersteiner), who refers to a single 'mind' which is separate from everything else, and which is endowed with perpetual motion.

66 See, for instance, E. Berti (see note 18), pp. 370-1; W. D. Ross (see note 56), p. 96.

67 Philo of Alexandria, *De Aeternitate Mundi* V. 24 (frag. 19, Rose; frag. 19a, Walzer; frag. 19a, Ross; frag. 29, Untersteiner) claims that there is nothing outside the universe, and that nothing outside the universe can have any effect upon the universe. See here also Plato, *Timaeus* 32C.

68 H. Cherniss (see note 25), pp. 593-4. M. Untersteiner, 'Il Περὶ φιλοσοφίας di Aristotele,' *Rivista di Filologia e d'Istruzione Classica*, vol. 89 (1961), pp. 153-8, in essence accepts the views held by Cherniss, as does E. Berti (see note 18), pp. 380-1.

69 Aristotle, *Metaphysics* 1074 a 26-34:

> For if everything that moves is for the sake of that which is moved, and every movement belongs to something that is moved, no movement can be for the sake of itself or for the sake of another movement, but all the movements must be for the sake of the stars. For if there is to be a movement for the sake of movement, this latter movement also will have to be for the sake of something else. And since there cannot be an infinite regress, the end of every movement will be one of the divine bodies which move through the heavens.

It might be important to remember here that Book XII of the *Metaphysics* is part of what W. Jaeger calls the *Urmetaphysik* and, hence, was composed at approximately the same time as, or a few years later than, the *On Philosophy.*

70 In the *Epinomis* 981 C ff., it will be noted, the five substances, or at least some of them, are called 'divine.'

71 H. Cherniss (see note 25), pp. 593-4. See also W. Theiler (note 51), p. 127. Cherniss' thesis has the support of Aristotle, *De Generatione et Corruptione* 337 a 20-2: 'If the movement is to be continuous, that which initiates it must be single, unmoved, ungenerated and incapable of "alteration." And if the circular (or orbital) movements are more than one, their initiating causes must be, all of them, in spite of their plurality, in some way subordinated to a single "originative source."' In short, the relation of these several gods to one another is not explained, although according to the

*Scholia in Proverbia Salomonis*, God. Paris. Graec. 174, fol. 46a (frag. 17, Rose; frag. 17, Walzer; frag. 17, Ross; frag. 27, Untersteiner)—provided this fragment is correctly assigned to the *On Philosophy*—Aristotle apparently demanded a 'single first principle' as the prerequisite of an orderly universe. Other scholars, though holding sharply conflicting views as to how this Ciceronian passage about the *replicatio* should be interpreted, concur in part with Cherniss. See, for instance, A. J. Festugière (note 19), vol. II, p. 245; W. Theiler (see note 51), pp. 127-31; J. Moreau (see note 47), v. 118; E. Oggioni, *Aristotele: Metafisica* (Padua, 1950), pp. 24-5 and p. 32.

72 See notes 5 and 46. By identifying the Aristotelian *replicatio quaedam* with the Platonic ἀνείλιξις, we are faced with what seems to be an irreducible dualism in that we must assume that Aristotle postulates at least two deities: the deity which is 'pure mind' or νοῦς, and the diety which is responsible for the *replicatio*—a sort of Zoroastrian Ormuzd-Ahriman situation. See, for instance, H. Cherniss (note 25), pp. 593-4. W. Theiler (see note 51), pp. 127-31, likewise accepts the dualism of a deity that is 'pure mind' (*deus mens*) and a deity which is the universe (*deus mundus*). Theiler also identifies the former not only with the deity that causes the *replicatio*, but also with the Unmoved Mover, and the latter with the deity that is the 'ether' or the 'heavens.'

73 E. Berti (see note 18), pp. 381-2.

74 Since the movements of the fixed stars are 'primary,' they are also 'contrary' to or different from the movements of other celestial bodies (planets). See E. Berti (note 18), p. 382.

75 This is also the opinion of A. J. Festugière and J. Moreau. See notes 19 and 47.

76 This is the opinion held by H. von Arnim. See note 48. But according to Philo of Alexandria, *De Aeternitate Mundi* III. 10-11 (frag. 18, Rose; frag. 18, Walzer; frag. 18, Ross; frag. 21, Untersteiner), the heavens may be understood as the 'visible God' or, better, as the 'visible aspect' of the Invisible Supreme God Who is 'pure mind.' This 'visible aspect' of the invisible God may be the direct author of the *replicatio*. See also note 88.

77. E. Berti (see note 18), vv. 381-2.

78 See also Cicero, *De Natura Deorum* I. 14. 37: 'Cleanthes . . . concludes that the only true God is that infinitely remote, lofty, all-embracing, eternal and fiery substance, which unfolds and surrounds the universe, and which is called "ether" (*complexum ardorem, qui aether nominaretur*).' See *ibid.*, II. 15. 40; Aristotle, *De Caelo* 270 b 4-25; Plato, *Cratylus* 410B. See, in general, E. Sachs, *Die fünf platonischen Körper* (Berlin, 1917), *passim*; S. Mariotti, 'La Quinta Essentia nell' Aristotele perduto a nell' Academia,' *Rivista di Filologia e d'Istruzione Classica*, vol. 68 (1940), pp. 179-89; P. Moraux, article 'Quinta Essentia,' in Pauly-Wissowa, *Realencyclopädia der Classischen Altertumswissenschaft*, vol. 47, part 1 (Stuttgart, 1963), pp. 1171-266, especially, pp. 1210 ff.; pp. 1221 ff., 1231ff.; *et passim*; H. J. Easterling,

'Quinta Natura,' *Museum Helveticum*, vol. 21 (1964), pp. 73–85. The fact that under the circumstances Aristotle identifies God with 'ether' should also indicate that he considers 'ether' the fifth element or substance. See Cicero, *Tuscul. Disput.* I. 17. 41: 'If the mind is . . . a fifth nature (or element), which is unnamed . . . these beings are much more perfect and much more pure, so that they move very far away from the earth.' *Ibid.*, I. 26. 65: 'But there is a fifth nature (or element), introduced first by Aristotle, and this is the nature (or element) of gods and minds.' These two passages from Cicero's *Tusculanae Disputationes* are believed to be fragments of Aristotle's *On Philosophy*. See frag. 27, Walzer; frag. 27, Ross; frag. 30, Untersteiner. If, then, the (divine or imperishable) stars are a complex of mind (νοῦς) and body, this particular body is the 'ether,' that is, the fifth element or nature or essence. In *Academica* I. 7. 26, Cicero credits Aristotle with having maintained that the (divine) stars consist of a fifth element or nature, wholly different from the four other elements. See also *Epinomis* 981C ff. For a detailed and penetrating discussion of all these problems, see, among others, J. Pépin (note 62), pp. 466–88. It is possible, though unlikely, that this notion is actually Stoic rather than Aristotelian, and that Velleius (Cicero) mistakenly credits Aristotle with the Stoic definition of the divine (or God) as 'fiery ether' (*caeli ardor*). The Stoics proclaimed that the πῦρ or πνεῦμα ἔνθερμον or πῦρ τεχνικὸν is the deity. See, for instance, H. v. Arnim, *Stoic. Vet. Frag.* II. no. 300; no. 416; no. 1027; nos 1031 ff.; no. 1051; I. 171; etc.

79 Aristotle, *Meteorologica* 339 b 13 ff.; Aristotle, *De Caelo* 270 a 21 ff. In *Epinomis* 981D we are informed that in fire is born 'the divine race of the stars, endowed with the fairest bodies and with the happiest and best souls.' See also Plato, *Timaeus* 39E ff.; Plato, *Laws* 889B.

80 Aristotle, *De Caelo* 270 b 11 ff.

81 *Ibid.*, 270 b 21 ff. Aristotle holds that the natural movements of the stars or heavenly bodies are continuous and orbital, while the natural movements of the four terrestrial elements (fire, air, water and earth) are rectilinear and discontinuous. From this he concludes that the heavenly bodies or stars must be composed of a fifth element, namely, 'ether.' Unlike the four terrestrial elements, the 'ether' is not characterized by contrary qualities, such as dry or wet, hot or cold. It is this 'behavior' or these 'qualities' of the 'ether' which justifies, according to Aristotle, the belief in the divinity of the uppermost region or the stars. See, for instance, Aristotle, *De Caelo* 270 b 5 ff.; Aristotle, *Metaphysics* 1074 a 38 ff. In this sense the 'ether' is 'more divine' than the other four elements. See also Aristotle, *De Caelo* 268 b 12 ff. and 281 a 27 ff.

82 See also Aristotle, *Meteorologica* 339 b 25; Aristotle, *De Caelo* 270 b 11; 270 b 20; 284 a 4. See also E. Zeller (note 48), vol. II, part 2, pp. 434–9.

83 Similar notions can be found in *Epinomis* 981C ff.

84 See also *Epinomis* 981D.

85 In this sense, the fourth definition recited by Velleius is essentially identical

with the second definition which calls the universe 'God.' See also Philo of Alexandria, *Quis Rerum Divinarum Heres* 57. 283, where we are told that in death the soul 'will depart to a Father in the ether.' This passage, which might be a fragment of Aristotle's *On Philosophy* (see L. Alfieri, 'Un nuovo frammento del *Peri Philosophias* aristotelico,' *Hermes*, vol. 81 [1953], pp. 45-9), has not been included in the collections of Aristotelian fragments compiled by V. Rose, R. Walzer, W. D. Ross and M. Untersteiner. It indicates that the 'ether' is the abode of God, and, hence, cannot be the substance of God, or, perhaps, God Himself. The solution of this puzzling problem may possibly be found with the help of *Epinomis* 981B, where we are informed that there are two 'kinds of existences,' namely, on the one hand the soul and on the other hand the five 'bodily' (material) forms: earth, water, air, fire and 'ether.' See also *ibid.*, 983B; 984BC; Cicero, *Tuscul. Disput.* I. 10. 22. This, then, would clearly eliminate the 'ether' as the substance or 'element' of God, and incidentally, as that of the soul.

86 See *Epinomis* 981C and 984D ff. See also Plato, *Timaeus* 55C and 58D.

87 Cicero, *De Natura Deorum* I. 14. 37.

88 Frag. 18, Rose; frag. 18, Walzer; frag. 18, Ross; frag. 21, Untersteiner. See also note 76.

89 W. Theiler, 'Ein vergessenes Aristoteleszeugnis,' *Journal of Hellenic Studies*, vol. 77 (1957), pp. 127-31, insists, however, that Aristotle's views definitely result in a dualism. See also note 71. H. Cherniss (see note 25), pp. 592 ff., and M. Untersteiner (see note 68), pp. 153-8, on the other hand, attempt to avoid such a dualism by maintaining that only the first and the third definitions refer to ὁ θεός, while the second and the fourth definitions are concerned with τὸ θεῖον. It might be helpful to remember here that *Epinomis* 983B insists that 'no thing gets living spirit by any other means than by the act of God.' If we were to assume that the God of the *Epinomis*, Who bestows 'living spirit,' is the νοῦς or *deus-mens* of Aristotle, while the 'cosmic god' or *deus-mundus* and, for that matter, the divine universe, the 'ether' and the divine stars of Aristotle, on the other hand, are the 'things' referred to in the *Epinomis*, then any theological 'dualism' or 'pluralism' would be completely excluded. For there could be no 'cosmic god' or divine universe or divine stars or 'ether' but for the νοῦς.

90 See also the lengthy discussion of Velleius' fourth definition of God. For a detailed analysis of these problems, see P. Moraux (see note 78), *passim*.

91 This was also realized by A. J. Festugière (see note 19), vol. II, p. 244. In *Epinomis* 981C and 984D ff., 'ether' is called 'the fifth body.' See also note 22. The pronounced astral theology of the *Epinomis* in part might have been influenced by what Aristotle had said, or had not said, in the *On Philosophy*. During the last years of Plato's scholarchate, astral theology, which probably was brought to Athens from the East (Zoroastrian), was much discussed among the members of the Academy. This seems to be reflected in the late works of Plato, in the *On Philosophy* and in the *Epinomis*. See note 85, at the end. See also Chapter XVI.

92 According to W. Jaeger (see note 13), p. 143, Cicero derived his information as regards Aristotle's arguments concerning the existence of God or of
the gods 'not from his own reading, but from a ready-made collection. . . .
Even the collection itself did not derive everything from the originals, any
more than Sextus [Empiricus], who also made a collection of arguments for
the existence of gods, largely similar to this one in content.' See Sextus
Empiricus, *Adversus Physicos* I. 49. See also notes 36 and 37.

93 Frags. 23–4, Rose; frag. 21, Walzer; frag. 21, Ross; frag. 32, Untersteiner.

94 See also Plato, *Timaeus* 39E ff.; Plato, *Laws* 889B; *Epinomis* 981D.

95 See also Aristotle, *Historia Animalium* 552 b 10; Alexander of Aphrodisias,
*Comment. in Arist. Meteorologica*, *CIAG*, vol. III, part 2 (ed. M. Hayduck,
Berlin, 1899), p. 13, line 14; Cicero, *De Natura Deorum* II. 17. 45–7;
Athenaeus, *Deipnosophistae* VIII. 353F. See also note 93.

96 See *Epinomis* 984D; Plato, *Cratylus* 397D: 'I must suspect that the sun,
the moon, the earth, the stars and the heavens . . . were the only gods of the
earliest Greeks. And seeing that they were always moving and running,
from their "running nature" they were called gods or "runners" (θεοὺς
θέοντας). . . .'

97 See also Cicero, *De Natura Deorum* I. 43. 120 and II. 6. 17; Plato, *Republic*
435E and 563E; Plato, *Laws* 747D ff.; Aristotle, *Politics* 1327 b 19 ff.;
Herodotus IX. 122; Strabo II. 7. 102–3.

98 See also Plato, *Phaedo* 111A ff. This, as well as the following passage, is
probably not a part of Aristotle's *On Philosophy*. The notion that the stars,
which 'inhabit the region where the ether reigns supreme . . . are
nourished by the exhalations from sea and land,' is definitely Stoic, that is,
dependent on the Stoic doctrine of the fiery ether. This passage is also
incompatible with Cicero, *Academica* I. 7. 26 (frag. 27, Walzer; frag. 27,
Ross; frag. 30, Untersteiner), which has been called a fragment of the *On
Philosophy*. See H. Cherniss (see note 25), pp. 596–7.

99 See Plato, *Laws* 888E ff.; 891C; 892C; 896E ff.; *Epinomis* 981D ff.; 982A;
982E; Aristotle, *De Caelo* 270 b 13–16; Aristotle, *De Partibus Animalium* 641
b 18–19.

100 See Plato, *Timaeus* 37D; *Epinomis* 982E, where the movements of the stars
are compared to an orderly dance.

101 See Plato, *Laws* 888E ('all things become, or have become, or will become,
some by nature, some by art, and some by chance'), and 889C; Aristotle,
*Physics* 196 a 24 ff.; 196 b 10–17; 197 a 18–20; 198 a 9–13; Aristotle, *De
Caelo* 288 b 9–12 and 290 a 31; Aristotle, *De Partibus Animalium* 641 b 40
ff.; Aristotle, *Nicomachean Ethics* 1112 a 30–3.

102 Aristotle, *De Caelo* 284 a 28–35.

103 The notions expressed here are not in complete harmony with what
Aristotle states in Book I, part 2; Book II, part 1; and Book III, part 2, of
the *De Caelo*. Cicero, or his immediate source, is obviously not acquainted
with the *De Caelo*. See E. Bignone (note 12), vol. II, p. 366, note 1.

104 See note 101. See also Plato, *Laws* 898E ff.; Aristotle, *Metaphysics* 1015 a 30; Aristotle, *De Caelo* 301 b 17–22.

105 Of the four basic elements, earth and water are falling in a rectilinear motion, and air and fire are rising in a rectilinear motion. See Aristotle, *De Caelo* 268 b 17–19; 269 a 17–18; 269 a 23 ff.; 269 b 13–17; 311 b 13–15; Aristotle, *Physics* 212 b 2–3; 217 a 19–20; 248 a 18–22; 261 b 28–29; 265 a 13–15.

106 In *De Caelo* 269 a 1 ff., Aristotle insists that circular or orbital motion is 'unnatural' for earth, water, air and fire (see note 105), but 'natural' for other bodies, that is, heavenly bodies (endowed with intelligence and free will). See also note 110.

107 See also Plato, *Laws* 897C ff.; Aristotle, *De Caelo* 284 a 27 ff. This statement of Cicero's has been invoked by some scholars in order to deny that in the *On Philosophy* Aristotle refers to an Unmoved Mover. See p. 191.

108 In *Timaeus* 39E ff., Plato suggests that each of the four elements contains some living beings. See note 94; *Epinomis* 981C ff.

109 Aristotle apparently spoke also of 'fire-born' animals. This might be gathered from Apuleius, *De Deo Socratis* VIII. 137–8; Plutarch, *Placita Philosophorum* (*Moralia* 908A ff.); Aetius, *Placita* V. 20. 1; Stobaeus, *Florilegium* I. 43; Damascius (*olim* Olympiodorus), *Scholia in Platonis Phaedonem* (ed. W. Norvin, Leipzig, 1913), p. 180, lines 22–3. See also Philo of Alexandria, *De Somniis* I. 22. 135; Philo of Alexandria, *De Gigantibus* II. 7–8; Philo of Alexandria, *De Plantatione* III. 12; Sextus Empiricus, *Adversus Mathematicos* IX. 86 (*Adversus Physicos* I. 86); Philo of Alexandria, *De Aeternitate Mundi* XIV. 45. See also frag. 22, Walzer; frag. 22, Ross, frag. 33, Untersteiner. In the *Historia Animalium* 552 b 10 ff., Aristotle refers to fly-like creatures that live in fire.

110 See here also W. Jaeger (note 13), v. 149; P. Moraux (see note 78) *passim*; J. Pépin (see note 62), pp. 466 ff. It will be noted that *Epinomis* 982A ff. attempts to prove the existence of star-souls or stellar gods by referring to the observable regularity of the stars which proceed with the most perfect deliberation. It must be borne in mind that the circular motion of the stars or star-gods is indicative of their perfection. This circular and perfectly regular motion, which the stars contemplate and will, is the expression of their perfection and divinity. Being perfect, this circular motion can never change, because all perfection excludes change, and in the case of perfection, change implies deterioration. Although the stars or star-gods have free will, because of their perfection or divinity they cannot possibly contemplate their own deterioration, that is, their deviation from perfect circular motion. See also Plato, *Timaeus* 40C; *Laws* 822A ff.

111 See note 82.

112 Cicero might be alluding to the Unmoved Mover or 'transcendent God,' when in *De Natura Deorum* I. 13. 33, he speaks of the *deus quietus et beatus*. See also H. Cherniss (note 25), pp. 593–4. See notes 55 and 127.

113 See also Philodemus, *De Diis* 3, col. 10, lines 7–11 (p. 30, ed. H. Diels):

'Indeed, one must not assume that the celestial gods have no other activity except ... an orbital motion without interruption. Anyone who during his whole life moves constantly in this orbital vortex cannot possibly be happy.' Philodemus, the Epicurean, seems to take issue here with what Aristotle had said in the *On Philosophy*.

114 In *Epinomis* 984D ff., we are informed that the stellar gods move at a great speed, while the Supreme God is devoid of pain and pleasure (and, hence, does not move). See note 116.

115 See also note 110.

116 See also E. Bignone (note 12), vol. II, p. 360, note 3.

117 See, in general, A.-H. Chroust, 'Aristotle's religious convictions,' *Divus Thomas*, vol. 69, fasc. 1 (1966), pp. 91-7, and Chapter XVI, vol. I.

118 See L. Alfonsi, 'La dottrina dell' ἀκατονόμαστον del giovane Aristotele e un testo de Psello,' *Miscellanea Galbiati* (Milan, 1951), pp. 3-4.

119 See also P. Merlan, 'Aristotle's Unmoved Movers,' *Traditio*, vol. IV (1946), p. 17. Merlan points out that whenever Aristotle alternatively speaks of God and of gods, he actually means one and the same thing. See, for instance, Aristotle, *Nicomachean Ethics* 1176 b 10 ff., where Aristotle indiscriminately refers to the activities of the gods and the actions of God. Plato maintains that God is assisted in His work by subordinate and lesser deities. See Plato, *Timaeus* 41A. Cicero, *Tuscul. Disput.* I. 10. 22, relates that Aristotle 'introduces a fifth unnamed element, and in so doing he defines the soul by a new term, namely, ἐνδελέχεια, which signifies, so to speak, a certain regular and perpetual movement.' See also E. Bignone (note 12), vol. II, pp. 234-47. In Plato, *Laws* 896A ff., we are informed that the soul might be defined as the 'first origin and moving power of all that moves,' that is, as something which is self-moving as well as the source of motion in all other things and, hence, really 'beyond' ordinary motion. See also Plato, *Phaedrus* 245D.

120 See note 88 and the corresponding text.

121 Plato insists that God is ἀσώματος. See DL V. 32 and III. 77; Aristotle, *De Caelo* 278 b 14-15 and 288 b 4; Sextus Empiricus, *Pyrrh. Hypoth.* III. 218. See also note 21. M. Untersteiner (frag. 25) includes Albinus, *Isagoge* (*Didascalicus*) X. 7-8, among the fragments of the *On Philosophy*. Here Albinus maintains that God is ἀσώματος.

122 According to Plato, *Philebus* 33B, God knows neither pleasure nor pain. See also *Epinomis* 985A, and note 114.

123 In Aristotle, *Nicomachean Ethics* 1178 b 15, we are told that the gods have no desires and, hence, need no φρόνησις. It should be noted that in the *Protrepticus* Aristotle insists that on the Islands of the Blessed we too would not need practical φρόνησις (frag. 58, Rose; frag. 12, Walzer; frag. 12, Ross; frag. 43, Düring; frag. 41, Chroust), though we shall receive there 'theoretic (or contemplative) wisdom.' In *Metaphysics* 1072 b 15 ff., Aristotle claims, however, that the First Mover experiences pleasure. This might be the reason why the Epicureans could say—although until about

the latter half of the first century B.C. it is not likely that they could have read Aristotle's *Metaphysics*—that if the Aristotelian God is ἀσώματος, He cannot possibly experience pleasure, and if he experiences pleasure, He cannot possibly be ἀσώματος. See here also Plato, *Phaedrus* 278D: 'Wise . . . is a great name which belongs to God alone.' Hence, at least according to Plato, God possesses σοφία.

124 See also E. Bignone (see note 12), vol. I, pp. 195–6; A. J. Festugière (see note 19), vol. II, p. 244, note 2. See note 110.

125 This is also brought out in *Epinomis* 982E ff.

126 See A. J. Festugière (see note 19), vol. II, pp. 244 ff. It may be assumed that Velleius intentionally confounds and confuses the several points made by Aristotle. Thus Velleius claims: Aristotle suggests that the universe is moved, that it is God, that God is incorporeal, and that God is unmoved. Hence it appears that the universe is really incorporeal, and that although it is incorporeal, it is moved or moving—obviously a contradiction.

127 See also Aristotle *De Caelo* 284 a 27–35:

> 'Nor is it conceivable that [the universe] should persist by the necessitation of a soul. For such a soul could not live painlessly and happily under these conditions, since movement involves constraint, being imposed on the first body [the heavens] the natural motion of which is different and imposed continuously. The soul must therefore be uneasy and devoid of all rational satisfaction. For it could not even, like the soul of mortal animals, take recreation in the bodily relaxation of sleep. An Ixion's lot must needs be possess it, without end or respite.

W. Jaeger (see note 13), pp. 303 ff., insists that this passage from the *De Caelo* is a fragment of Book III of the *On Philosophy*. This view has found little acceptance. R. Walzer (frag. 29), W. D. Ross (frag. 30) and M. Untersteiner (frag. 23), however, include this passage among the fragments of the *On Philosophy*. *Epinomis* 985A, relates that 'God . . . is remote from all affection or pleasure and pain.' Conversely, Sextus Empiricus, *Adversus Mathematicos* IX. 45, a passage which might contain a fragment of the *On Philosophy*, maintains that since the ancients believed in the serene and happy human being, by way of analogy they also assumed the existence of a Supreme Being Who is supremely happy and serene. See also Plato, *Timaeus* 90A ff., especially 90C; Aristotle, *Metaphysics* 1072 b 28–30; Aetius, *Placita* I. 7. 9.

128 H. Cherniss (see note 25), pp. 593–4. See also note 89.

129 See E. Berti (see note 18), pp. 385–6.

130 See J. Pépin, 'Un nouveau fragment du *De Philosophia* d'Aristote?', Congrès de Lyon, Actes du Congrès (Paris, 1960), pp. 100–2. Pépin believes that St. Ambrose, *Hexameron* I. 1. 1–4, contains a fragment of Aristotle's *On Philosophy*. Here St. Ambrose speaks of an *operatorium*—

presumably the *deus-mens* or Unmoved Mover (?) or Prime Mover—as well as of the divinity of the universe, presumably the *deus-mundus*.

131 This is, as we have seen, the opinion of W. Jaeger (see note 13), pp. 141 ff. Jaeger's view was rejected, however, by H. von Arnim (see note 48), pp. 4–7; W. K. C. Guthrie (see note 57), p. 165; W. K. C. Guthrie, *Aristotle: On the Heavens* (London, 1939), p. xxvii; W. D. Ross, *Aristotle: Physics* (Oxford, 1936), pp. 95–6; and M. Wundt, *Untersuchungen zur Metaphysik des Aristoteles* (Stuttgart, 1953), p. 53, note 7. Some of these scholars insist that the concept of an Unmoved Mover cannot be found prior to *De Caelo* 292 a 22 ff. and 292 b 4 ff. See also J. Pépin (note 62), pp. 466–73; notes 50–67 and the corresponding text.

132 Aristotle, *Physics* 194 a 35–6. See also Aristotle, *De Anima* 415 b 2–3 and 415 b 20–1; Aristotle, *Eudemian Ethics* 1249 b 13–16.

133 Aristotle, *Metaphysics* 1072 b 1–3.

134 See note 131.

135 See also Aristotle, *De Caelo* 292 a 18 ff., where Aristotle explains the motion of the heavenly bodies as the deliberate effort on the part of these bodies to attain their ultimate and true end. See also note 110.

136 See H. Cherniss (see note 25), pp. 594–5. See also *Epinomis* 983B.

137 DL V. 22 (no. 14); *VH* (no. 9); Simplicius, *Comment. in Arist. De Caelo*, *CIAG*, vol. VII (ed. J. Heiberg, Berlin, 1894), p. 485, lines 19–22.

138 Simplicius (see note 137). See also note 23.

139 W. Jaeger (see note 13), p. 160, insists that in the *On Prayer* Aristotle maintains that 'God is *Nus*, or higher than all reason, and that only through *Nus* can a mortal approach Him.' Jaeger continues: 'The demand that we should pray in *Nus* and in truth arose in the Platonic community.' See John IV:24: 'God is a Spirit; and they that worship Him must worship Him in spirit and in truth.'

140 See, for instance, DL X. 131; X. 139; X. 144–5; etc. Epicurus probably derives the notion of 'happiness through serenity' from Democritus. See frags. 140; 209; 210; 215; 216; 246; and 257, Diels-Kranz. See also Plato, *Philebus* 33B.

141 Aristotle, *De Caelo* 284 a 35.

142 Aristotle, *Metaphysics* 1074 b 28–9.

143 H. von Arnim (see note 48), p. 6.

144 G. M. A. Grube, *Plato's Thought* (London, 1935), p. 150. See also U. von Wilamowitz-Moellendorff, *Platon*, vol. I (Berlin, 1909), p. 348; J. M. Rist, 'Theos and the one in some texts of Plotinus,' *Mediaeval Studies* (Toronto), vol. 24 (1962), p. 169.

145 One might speculate here about the following: as evidenced by the *Epinomis*, astral theology apparently had become a topic much discussed within the inner circle of the Academy. It is possible and, as a matter of fact it is quite likely, that Aristotle opposed this new theological trend or at least certain aspects of this trend which, in his opinion, would usher in a boundless religious mysticism (as well as an unwarranted disdain for the

visible universe) of which he did not approve. In the *On Philosophy*, among other matters, he gave vent to his disagreement. This, then, might possibly explain certain features of the *On Philosophy*, and it might shed some light on the ultimate meaning or background of Cicero, *De Natura Deorum* I. 13. 33. But if this is so, then any future attempt to reconstruct the Aristotelian *On Philosophy* would have to take a close look at the *Epinomis* for possible clues. In any event, there seem to exist certain undeniable 'points of contact' between the *On Philosophy* and the *Epinomis* which are yet to be fully clarified. This does not alter the fact, however, that in all likelihood the *Epinomis* is posterior to the *On Philosophy*.—A final remark: the fact that the Aristotelian *On Philosophy* in all probability was a dialogue which presumably included Aristotle and Plato among the several interlocutors creates a number of far-reaching problems. It must be assumed that in this dialogue Plato (or the Platonic interlocutor) advances Platonic views, while Aristotle advocates notions which are, in some way, opposed to what Plato maintains. Now it is quite possible that some surviving fragments assigned to the *On Philosophy* might contain what Plato (or the Platonic interlocutor) had interjected rather than what Aristotle had asserted. This, incidentally, may also be inferred from Cicero, *De Natura Deorum* I. 13. 33, where we are informed that Aristotle disagrees with his teacher Plato, and that Aristotle submits a 'disjointed jumble of theories.' Perhaps this reference to a 'disjointed jumble of theories' indicates the fact that when cited together, or put next to each other, the statements of Plato (or the Platonic interlocutor) and those of Aristotle are plainly irreconcilable and, hence, almost nonsensical. All this poses a problem which it is well-nigh impossible to resolve: it might be claimed—and this with some justification—that the recovery, reconstruction and interpretation of Aristotle's *On Philosophy* or, at least, of the philosophic position assumed by Aristotle in this composition, hinges on the question of whether a certain fragment relates to the Platonic interlocutor or to Aristotle. Assuredly, those scholars who have already made up their minds as to the particular philosophic standpoint Aristotle assumes in the *On Philosophy*, will credit the Platonic interlocutor (or, perhaps, some other interlocutor ) with those statements which do not fit, or do not seem to fit, their preconceived notions as to the philosophy which Aristotle propagated in the *On Philosophy*. Needless to say, through such an eclectic method, Aristotle may be converted into anything a preconceived fancy might suggest. But let the reader beware: all these remarks make sense only if we are willing to assume that the *On Philosophy* was a dialogue, and that this dialogue also contained a 'confrontation' of Plato's theology and that of Aristotle. See here Elias (*olim* David), *Comment. in Porphyrii Isagogen et in Aristotelis Categorias*, CIAG, vol. XVIII, part 1 (ed. A. Busse, Berlin, 1900), p. 115, lines 3–5: 'Alexander of Aphrodisias mentions another difference between the acroamatic compositions and the dialogues. In the former Aristotle states what he thinks to be true, while in the latter he cites the false opinions of others.' See also *ibid.*, p. 124, lines 3–6: 'In those of the general works which are dialogues, that is, in the exoteric works, . . . he [*scil.*, Aristotle] is versatile in his impersonations because he is arguing among dialecticians. . . .'

## CHAPTER XV   THE DOCTRINE OF THE SOUL IN ARISTOTLE'S *On Philosophy*

\* In a slightly different form, this chapter was first published in *New Scholasticism*, vol. 42, no. 3 (1968), pp. 364–73.

1 See A.-H. Chroust, '*Eudemus or On the Soul*: a lost Aristotelian dialogue on the immortality of the soul,' *Mnemosyne* (series 4), vol. 19, fasc. 1 (1966), pp. 17–30, and Chapter IV; A.-H. Chroust, 'The psychology in Aristotle's lost dialogue *Eudemus or On the Soul,' Acta Classica*, vol. 9 (1966), pp. 49–62, and Chapter V.

2 Cicero, *Academica* I. 7. 26; Cicero, *Tusculanae Disputationes* I. 10. 22; Cicero, *Tusculanae Disputationes* I. 17. 41; Cicero, *Tusculanae Disputationes* I. 26. 65– I. 27. 66 (frag. 27, Walzer; frag. 27, Ross; frag. 30, Untersteiner).

3 (Pseudo- ?) Clement of Rome, *Recognitiones* VIII. 15 (frag. 27, Walzer; frag. 27, Ross; frag. 30, Untersteiner).

4 Psellus, *De Omnifaria Doctrina* (ed. E. Westerink), p. 69, no. 131 (frag. 24, Untersteiner). Neither V. Rose, nor R. Walzer, nor W. D. Ross list this fragment. Other fragments of the *On Philosophy*, which bear on our subject, have more recently been unearthed by a number of scholars. See notes 11 and 71. The majority of these newly discovered fragments, which appear to be of no particular significance, essentially restate or paraphrase what Cicero (see note 2) said.

5 E. Bignone, *L'Aristotele Perduto e la Formazione Filosofica di Epicuro*, vol. I (Florence, 1936), pp. 195–6 and p. 288.

6 L. Alfonsi, 'La dottrina dell'ἀκατονόμαστον del giovane Aristotele ed un testo di Psello,' *Miscellanea Giovanni Galbiati* (Milan, 1961), pp. 71–8.

7 A. J. Festugière, *La Révélation d'Hermès Trismégiste*, vol. II (Paris, 1950), p. 228, note 1.

8 K. Reinhardt, *Poseidonios* (Munich, 1921), p. 472; K. Reinhardt, article 'Poseidonios,' in Pauly-Wissowa, *Realencyclopädie der Classischen Altertumswissenschaft*, vol. 22, part 1 (1953), pp. 576, 585.

9 G. Luck, *Der Akademiker Antiochos* (Berne and Stuttgart, 1953), pp. 33 ff. Reinhardt and Luck are of the opinion that these references go back to Antiochus of Ascalon and Posidonius of Apamea.

10 For a thorough and detailed discussion of the many problems connected with the sources used by Cicero, see M. Untersteiner, *Aristotele: Della Filosofia* (Rome, 1963), pp. 265–7. See also E. Berti, *La Filosofia del Primo Aristotele* (Padua, 1962), pp. 392–401; P. Moraux, article 'Quinta Essentia,' in Pauly-Wissowa, *Realencyclopädie der Classischen Altertumswissenschaft*,

vol. 47, part 1 (Stuttgart, 1963), pp. 1171–266, *passim*; J. Pépin, 'L'interprétation du *De Philosophia* d'Aristote d'après quelques travaux récents,'
*Revue des Études Grecques*, vol. 77, nos 366–8 (1964), pp. 468 ff.; B. Effe,
*Studien zur Kosmologie und Theologie der Aristotelischen Schrift Über die Phil-
osophie* (Zetemata, Heft 50, Munich, 1970), pp. 148–55; M. Untersteiner,
*op. cit.*, pp. 265–81.

11 O. Gigon, 'Cicero und Aristoteles,' *Hermes*, vol. 87 (1959), pp. 143–62;
O. Gigon, 'Prolegomena to an edition of the *Eudemus*,' *Aristotle and Plato
in the Mid-Fourth Century* (Göteborg, 1960), p. 23; p. 28; p. 32. Similar
views are held by S. Mariotti, 'La *quinta essentia* nell'Aristotele perduto
e nell'Academia,' *Rivista di Filologia e d'Istruzione Classica*, vol. 68 (1940),
pp. 180–1; and by A. Grilli, 'Cicerone e l'*Eudemo*,' *La Parola del Passato*,
vol. 83 (1962), pp. 98–100. This is not the place to subject these fragments
to an acribic investigation. For a further discussion of the problems
connected with these passages, see, among others, L. Alfonsi, 'Traces du
jeune Aristote dans la *Cohortatio ad Gentiles* faussement attribuée à Justin,'
*Vigiliae Christianae*, vol. 2 (1948), pp. 65–88; L. Alfonsi, 'L'assioco Pseudo-
platonico,' *Studi di Filosofia Greca* (ed. V. E. Alfieri and M. Untersteiner,
Bari, 1950), pp. 245–75; L. Alfonsi (see note 6), pp. 71–8; L. Alfonsi,
'Un Nuovo Frammento del Περὶ φιλοσοφίας,' *Hermes*, vol. 81 (1953),
pp. 45–9; D. J. Allan, 'The fragments of Aristotle,' *Classical Review*, vol. 70
(vol. 6, new series, 1956), pp. 225 ff.; A. Barigazzi, 'Sulle fonti del Libro I
delle Tusculane di Cicerone,' *Rivista di Filologia e d'Istruzione Classica*,
vol. 76 (vol. 26, new series, 1948), pp. 161–203 and vol. 78 (vol. 28, new
series, 1950), pp. 1–29; E. Berti (see note 10), pp. 392–401; J. Bidez, *Un
Singulier Naufrage Littéraire dans l'Antiquité: A la Recherche des Épaves de
l'Aristote Perdu* (Brussels, 1943), pp. 33 ff.; E. Bignone (see note 5), pp.
227 ff.; E. Bignone, *Studi sul Pensiero Antico* (Naples, 1938), pp. 296 ff.; E.
Bignone, 'Postilla Aristotelica sulla dottrina dell'*Endelecheia*,' *Atene e
Roma*, vol. 8 (1940), pp. 61–4; E. Bignone, 'La dottrina epicurea del
*Clinamen*: sua formazione e sua cronologia in rapporto con la polemica con
le scuole avversarie,' *Atene e Roma*, vol. 8 (1940), pp. 159–98; H. Cherniss,
*Aristotle's Criticism of Plato and the Academy*, vol. I (Baltimore, 1944), pp.
591–602; C. de Vogel, *Greek Philosophy*, vol. II (Leiden, 1953), pp. 35–6;
A. J. Festugière (see note 7), pp. 247–59; E. Garin, '*Endelecheia* e *Entelecheia*
nelle discussioni umanistiche,' *Atene e Roma*, vol. 39 (1937), pp. 234–47;
H. Hirzel, 'Über Entelechie und Endelechie,' *Rheinisches Museum*, vol. 39
(1884), pp. 169–208; A. Mansion, 'L'immortalité de l'âme et de l'intellec-
tuel d'après Aristote,' *Revue Philosophique de Louvain*, vol. 51 (1953), pp.
447–51; S. Mariotti, 'La *quinta essentia* nell'Aristotele perduto e nell'
Academia,' *Rivista di Filologia e d'Istruzione Classica*, vol. 68 (vol. 18, new
series, 1940), pp. 179–89; S. Mariotti, 'Nuove testimonianze ed echi dell'
Aristotele giovanile,' *Atene e Roma*, vol. 42 (vol. 8, new series, 1940), pp.
48–60; P. Moraux, 'Une nouvelle trace d'Aristote perdu,' *Les Études
Classiques*, vol. 16 (1948), pp. 89–91; J. Moreau, *L'Âme du Monde de*

*Platon aux Stoïciens* (Paris, 1939), pp. 106 ff.; P. Moraux (see note 10), *passim*; J. Pépin (see note 10); D. A. Rees, 'Theories of the soul in the early Aristotle,' *Aristotle and Plato in the Mid-Fourth Century* (Göteborg, 1960), pp. 199-200; G. Soleri, *L'Immortalità dell'Anima in Aristotele* (Turin, 1952), pp. 67-70; M. Untersteiner, 'Il Περὶ φιλοσοφίας di Aristotele,' *Rivista di Filologia e d'Istruzione Classica*, vol. 88 (1960), pp. 337-68, and vol. 89 (1961), pp. 121-59; M. Untersteiner (see note 10), pp. 54-5 and 265-81.

12 It appears that Cicero incorrectly identifies *initia* and *principia*, the Latin translations for ἀρχαὶ and στοιχεῖα.

13 See, for instance, W. Jaeger, *Aristotle: Fundamentals of the History of his Development* (Oxford, 1948), p. 144; E. Berti (see note 10), pp. 394 ff. S. Mariotti (see note 11), pp. 179 ff., especially p. 185, clearly distinguishes this 'fifth element' from the 'ether.' This is also brought out by *Epinomis* 981B, which insists that there are two kinds of 'existence': the soul on the one hand and the other five elements or forms (earth, water, air, fire and 'ether') on the other. It is now widely held that in his oral discussions Plato likewise spoke of five elements. This seems to follow from *Epinomis* 981C ff. See also notes 40-65; Aristotle, *Meteorologica* 339 b 21; 339 b 24; 339 b 27; Aristotle (?), *De Mundo* 392 b 5; Plato, *Cratylus* 410B.

14 Simplicius, *Comment. in Arist. De Caelo*, CIAG, vol. VII (ed. J. Heiberg, Berlin, 1894), p. 485, lines 19-22 (frag. 49, Rose; frag. 1, Ross).

15 Cicero, *Tuscul. Disput.* I. 26. 65 (frag. 27, Walzer; frag. 27, Ross; frag. 30, Untersteiner).

16 See Cicero, *Tuscul. Disput.* I. 10. 22: 'Aristotle ... adds a fifth nameless class....' *Ibid.*, I. 17. 41: '... a fifth nature which is without name....' (Pseudo- ?) Clement of Rome, *Recognitiones* VIII. 15: 'Aristotle introduces a fifth element, which he called ἀκατονόμαστον, that is, "which had no name"....' The term ἀκατονόμαστον, it has been suggested, does not refer to the whole soul, but merely to the 'rational soul' or to its 'intellectual (spiritual ?) powers.' See B. Effe, *Studien zur Kosmologie und Theologie der Aristotelischen Schrift 'Über die Philosophie'* (Zetemata, Heft 50, Munich, 1970), pp. 148 ff.

17 Philo of Alexandria, *Quis Rerum Divinarum Heres* 57. 283 (III. 64.7, ed. P. Wendland). See P. Moraux (see note 11); L. Alfonsi, 'Un nuovo frammento del Περὶ Φιλοσοφίας,' *Hermes*, vol. 81 (1953), pp. 45-9. The last sentence in Philo's statement is undoubtedly an addition by Philo himself, who in this particular case seems to have been under the influence of post-Aristotelian, that is, Stoic notions. See pp. 201-3. The idea that the individual soul is merely a 'fragment' of the divine universe (or of the divine heavens, or of the divine 'fire' or 'fiery ether') is clearly Stoic. Philo's predilection for Stoic philosophy is too well known to require detailed discussion. When Philo speaks here of 'a father in the ether,' he refers to the abode of God. But this abode—the 'ether'—does not constitute the 'substance' or 'nature' of God nor God Himself. This important fragment is not

included in the collections of V. Rose, R. Walzer, W. D. Ross or M. Untersteiner.

18 See also *Epinomis* 981D, where we are told that the soul 'has only one single form (has no admixture).' Neither is the soul a kind of 'attunement of the several elements.' See Chapter V, *passim*. Cicero, *Academica* I. 11. 39, relates that Zeno, the Stoic, objected to Aristotle's doctrine that the *quinta essentia*, which constitutes the 'nature' of the soul, is incorporeal or non-material. It will be noted that both Heracleides of Pontus (frags 98–9, Wehrli) and Critolaus (frags 16–18, Wehrli) advanced the thesis that the human soul and the heavenly bodies are of the same substance, a theory also advocated by the Stoics. In his *De Generatione Animalium* 736 b 29 ff., Aristotle insists that a certain analogy exists between the heavenly bodies and the soul. See P. Moraux, 'A propos du νοῦς θύρατεν chez Aristote,' *Autour d'Aristote* (Louvain, 1955), pp. 275 ff.

19 This implies that the soul and the matter which it 'informs' cannot be two different substances, each complete in its own order. Joined together, soul and matter constitute only one substance—the living body. See also *Epinomis* 981A.

20 Plato, *Timaeus* 39B; 40A ff.; 41E; 47B; Plato, *Laws* 898B; *Epinomis* 981BC; Aristotle, *De Generatione et Corruptione* 336 b 27; Aristotle, *De Anima* 407 a 7. See also E. Bignone, 'La dottrina epicurea del *Clinamen*: sua formazione e sua cronologia in rapporto con la polemica con le scuole avversarie,' *Atene e Roma*, vol. 8 (1940), pp. 161–4.

21 See here Cicero, *De Natura Deorum* II. 15. 42–16. 44, which is considered a fragment of the *On Philosophy* (frags 23–4, Rose; frag. 21, Walzer; frag. 21, Ross; frag. 32, Untersteiner). In this context see also Plato, *Laws* 888E ff.; 891C; 892C; 896B ff.; 897C ff.; Plato, *Timaeus* 37D; *Epinomis* 981D; 982A; 982E; Aristotle, *Physics* 212 b 2–3; 217 a 19–20; 248 a 18–22; 261 b 28–29; 265 a 13–15; Aristotle, *De Caelo* 268 b 17–19; 269 a 1 ff.; 269 a 17 ff.; 269 b 13–17; 270 b 13–16; 284 a 27 ff.; Aristotle, *De Partibus Animalium* 641 b 18–19. Plato had identified the perfect motion of the stars with the perfect motion (or acts) of the intellect or the intellectual part of the soul. See note 20. Similar notions can be found in the *Epinomis*. The circularity of stellar motion, which, according to Aristotle, pre-supposes intelligence and free will, clearly distinguishes the stars from all other material bodies composed of earth, water, air or fire. The latter always move upwards or downwards in a rectilinear path. See Chapter XIV, note 110, and the corresponding text.

22 In *Epinomis* 981E–982A we are told that the soul of each star is 'the happiest and best soul,' and that it is 'indestructible and immortal.'

23 Cicero, *Tusculanae Disputationes* I. 26. 65 (frag. 27, Walzer; frag. 27, Ross; frag. 30, Untersteiner). An echo of this might be detected in *Epinomis* 981BC, where a reference is made to the θειότατον ψυχῆς γένος. See also E. Bignone (note 20), p. 171, and note 14.

24 Cicero, *Tusculanae Disputationes* I. 10. 22. See also E. Bignone (note 5),

pp. 228 ff.; D. J. Allan, 'The fragments of Aristotle,' *Classical Review*, vol. 70 (vol. 6, new series, 1956), p. 225. For a detailed discussion of the term ἐνδελέχεια, see M. Untersteiner (note 10), pp. 269–75.

25 *Oxyrrh. Papyr.* VII. 1017, col. 5–6, has ἀεικινήτατος, that is, 'being in perpetual motion.' For additional detail and information, see G. Müller, *Studien zu den Platonischen Nomoi* (Munich, 1951), p. 85, note 2; C. Diano, 'Quod semper movetur aeternum est,' *La Parola del Passato*, vol. 21 (1947), pp. 189–92; W. D. Ross, *Plato's Theory of Ideas* (Oxford, 1951), p. 236, note 2; P. Shorey, *What Plato Said* (Chicago, 1933), p. 200.

26 Plato, *Laws* 898A ff. Similar notions can also be found in the *Epinomis*. See, for instance, *ibid.*, 980E ff.

27 Plato, *Laws* 898D ff. Compare also *Epinomis* 980E–988E, where we are informed that the soul is more venerable than the (material) body; that a 'living being' is a single combination of body and soul which produces a 'single form'; that the 'immaterial' (soul) is neither fire nor water nor air nor earth nor ether, but another kind of 'existence'; that the soul is the truly divine form of existence; that the soul is the only 'bodiless (invisible, immaterial) substance'; that the soul alone can create and fashion things; that the soul alone is possessed of knowledge, partakes of memory and the power of reasoning, and apprehends by reason; that the soul moves in an orderly and uniform fashion, thus proving its supreme intelligence; that the necessity which belongs to the soul is the greatest and most perfect of all necessities; that the soul, as the 'ruler,' commands and imposes rules; that the uniformity of motion characteristic of the stars is proof of the fact that they have a soul and that they possess intelligence; that the soul is infinitely superior to the body; that the soul is the cause of everything; that the soul creates all living beings; that the soul is the cause of the universe; that the soul is the cause of all change and movement; that the soul is the cause of all that is good as well as of all that is evil; and that the soul alone is capable of learning, remembering and reasoning. Some of these statements, it will be noted, can also be found in Plato. See, for instance, Plato, *Laws* 818A; 896A; 898E; 903D; 966E; Plato, *Timaeus* 40CD and 48B; Plato, *Philebus* 26D ff.; 29A; 33B; Plato, *Phaedrus* 246C; etc. Cicero, *Tusculanae Disputationes* I. 26. 65–27. 66, seems to repeat some of the statements found in *Epinomis* 980E ff.

28 See also *Epinomis* 982A.

29 Frag. 10, Müller.

30 Cicero, *Tusculanae Disputationes* I. 26 65–27. 66 (frag. 10, Müller; frag. 27, Walzer; frag. 27, Ross; frag. 30, Untersteiner). It has already been pointed out that O. Gigon is of the opinion that Cicero refers here to Aristotle's *Eudemus* rather than to the *On Philosophy*. See notes 11 and 31.

31 This is also the theme of Aristotle's *Eudemus*. See A.-H. Chroust, '*Eudemus or On the Soul:* a lost Aristotelian dialogue on the immortality of the soul,' *Mnemosyne*, vol. 10, fasc. 1 (1966), pp. 17–30, and Chapter IV. It is interesting to observe that O. Gigon (see note 11), in his proposed *Aristoteles'*

*Dialog Eudemos: Ein Versuch der Wiederherstellung*, intends to assign to the Aristotelian *Eudemus* certain fragments dealing with the nature of the soul and its immortality which are traditionally assigned to the *On Philosophy*. This was also proposed by S. Mariotti and by A. Grilli. See note 11 at the beginning.

32 See also *Epinomis* 981B.

33 See here also Aristotle, *On Prayer*, cited in note 14.

34 The power of memory, intellect and thought—*vis memoriae, mentis, cognitionis*, Cicero (see note 30)—cannot be derived from any material substances (or combination of material substances) or perhaps from 'ether.' The term ἀκατονόμαστον, which cannot be identified with the 'ether,' simply conveys the impossibility of accurately determining the ultimate 'nature' or 'essence' of the soul. Moreover, this term also indicates that for mortal man the ultimate 'nature' or 'essence' of the soul, like that of God, in the final analysis always remains a mystery. Hence, in the words of Seneca (*Quaestiones Naturales* VII. 30; frag. 14, Rose; frag. 14, Walzer; frag. 14, Ross; frag. 19, Untersteiner), we should be modest, not to say reluctant, whenever we discuss divine matters and admit our inability to define the divine, including the nature of the soul, and guard against saying something rashly or imprudently about the divine. This seems to be the ultimate meaning of the term ἀκατονόμαστον. In the *Protrepticus* (Iamblichus, *Protrepticus* p. 48, lines 16–21, ed. H. Pistelli; frag. 61, Rose; frag. 10c, Walzer; frag. 10c, Ross; frag. 110, Düring; frag. 106, Chroust), Aristotle calls reason (the intellect or the rational soul) 'the divine dwelling in us.' Moreover, he maintains that 'only because of reason mortal life possesses a certain element or aspect of the divine.' This, then, implies that reason—the rational soul—is a divine gift bestowed upon man by God. In *Epinomis* 976CD, we are informed that the faculty of knowing, including the faculty of knowing God, is a divine gift. See also Aristotle, *Metaphysics* 1072 b 14 ff.

35 The immortality of the soul is also shown by the fact that it is wholly 'separated from all material admixture.' For such an admixture with the material substances or elements would make the soul itself corruptible. See Cicero, *Tusculanae Disputationes* I. 27. 66. The same notion also appears in *Epinomis* 981BC.

36 Similar notions are found in *Epinomis* 980E ff.

37 In the *Theaetetus* 176AB, Plato insists that 'we ought to fly away from the earth to heaven and become like God, as far as this is possible; and to become like Him is to become holy, just and wise.' In the *Phaedrus* 252D, Plato points out that 'the followers of Zeus . . . have less difficulty in finding the nature of God in themselves, because they have been compelled to gaze intently upon Him. . . . They become possessed of Him, and receive from Him their character and disposition, so far as man may participate in God.' In the *Timaeus* 90BC, Plato maintains that 'he who has been earnest in the love of knowledge and true wisdom, and has

exercised his intellect more than any other part of him, must have thoughts immortal and divine. . . . He should attain the perfect life which the gods have held out to mankind both for the present and the future.' And in the *Republic* 613AB, Plato insists that 'for the just man all things will in the end work out for his good in life as well as in death. For the gods have a care of anyone whose desire it is to become just and to be like God . . . And if he is like God, he will surely not be neglected by Him.' An echo of these last two passages might be detected in Aristotle, *Nicomachean Ethics* 1179 a 22 ff.: 'He who exercises his intellect . . . is most dear to the gods. For if the gods have any care for human affairs . . . it would be reasonable to assume that they should delight in what is best and most akin to them [*scil.*, the intellect and its proper exercise], and that they should reward those who love and honor this [*scil.*, the intellect]. . . .' In *Nicomachean Ethics* 1177 a 15 ff., Aristotle calls the intellect 'divine' and 'the most divine element in us.' In the *Protrepticus*, as has been shown, Aristotle insists that reason (or the intellect) is 'the divine dwelling in us.' See Iamblichus, *Protrepticus*, p. 48, lines 16 ff. (ed. H. Pistelli—frag. 61, Rose; frag. 10c, Walzer; frag. 10c, Ross; frag. 110, Düring; frag. 106, Chroust).

38  See note 34.

39  See notes 24–7.

40  P. Moraux (see note 10), pp. 1171–266, especially, pp. 1196–231.

41  J. Pépin (see note 10), especially, pp. 473–88.

42  E. Bignone (see note 5), pp. 227–72.

43  S. Mariotti, 'La *quinta essentia* nell'Aristotele perduto e nell'Academia,' *Rivista di Philologia e d'Istruzione Classica*, vol. 68 (1940), pp. 179–89.

44  J. Bidez (see note 11), pp. 33–44.

45  H. Cherniss (see note 11), pp. 591–602.

46  F. J. Nuyens, *L'Évolution de la Psychologie d'Aristote* (Louvain-Paris, 1948), pp. 254–9.

47  A. Mansion (see note 11), pp. 447–51.

48  A. J. Festugière (see note 7), pp. 254–9.

49  S. Mariotti (see note 43), pp. 180–1, also insists that these passages from Cicero and Clement should be credited to the Aristotelian *Eudemus* rather than to the *On Philosophy*. See note 11 at the beginning. See also note 31.

50  A. Barigazzi (see note 11), pp. 161–203 and vol. 78, pp. 1–29.

51  G. Soleri (see note 11), pp. 67–70.

52  J. Moreau (see note 11), pp. 120–3.

53  E. Berti (see note 10), p. 400.

54  L. Alfonsi, 'Traces du jeune Aristote dans la *Cohortatio ad Gentiles* faussement attribuée à Justin,' *Vigiliae Christianae*, vol. II (1948), pp. 65–88; L. Alfonsi, 'Un nuovo frammento del Περὶ φιλοσοφίας,' *Hermes*, vol. 81 (1953), pp. 45–9.

55  D. A. Rees (see note 11), pp. 199–200.

56  P. Moraux (see note 11); P. Moraux, 'L'évolution d'Aristote,' *Aristote et Saint Thomas d'Aquin* (Louvain, 1957), p. 34.

57 R. A. Gauthier, *Aristote: L'Éthique à Nicomaque*, vol. I (Louvain-Paris, 1970), pp. 27-8.

58 A. D. Leeman, 'De Aristotelis Protreptico Somnii Scipionis Exemplo,' *Mnemosyne* (series 4) vol. 11 (1958), pp. 139-51. Leeman maintains that the fragments dealing with the soul should be assigned to the Aristotelian *Protrepticus* rather than to the *On Philosophy*—a thesis which is not likely to be accepted by many scholars, although the suggestion made by O. Gigon, S. Mariotti and A. Grilli (see note 11), that these fragments should be credited to the Aristotelian *Eudemus*, has some merit.

59 Some scholars insist, however, that Cicero (or his source) cites Aristotle inaccurately, while others are of the opinion that Cicero's immediate source had corrupted the original Aristotelian text.

60 K. Reinhardt, article 'Poseidonios,' in Pauly-Wissowa, *Realencyclopädie der Classischen Altertumswissenschaft*, vol. 22, part 1 (1953), pp. 576-86. It is quite possible that at some later time the doxographical tradition about Aristotle identified the Aristotelian ἀκατονόμαστον with the (Stoic) 'ether.'

61 P. Moraux, 'L'évolution d'Aristote,' *Aristote et Saint Thomas d'Aquin* (Louvain, 1957), p. 34; P. Moraux (see note 10), pp. 1171-266, especially, pp. 1218-226.

62 E. Berti (see note 10), pp. 398-401.

63 H. J. Easterling, 'Quinta Essentia,' *Museum Helveticum*, vol. 21 (1964), pp. 73-85.

64 M. Untersteiner (see note 10), pp. 267, *et passim*.

65 J. Pépin (see note 10), pp. 474-88.

66 Ibid., p. 481. See also W. Jaeger (see note 13), p. 144, note 2, who maintains that the 'ether' is the 'fifth body' or 'fifth element.' See also Plato, *Timaeus* 55C; *Epinomis* 981C.

67 J. Pépin, *op. cit.*, p. 482.

68 P. Moraux (see note 10), p. 1173 and p. 1249. *Ibid.*, p. 1212, Moraux maintains that the 'ether' is a 'favorable medium' in which the true substance of the soul can 'unfold' itself, but never the soul as such.

69 J. Pépin, *op. cit.*, p. 485. See also S. Mariotti (see note 43). In Plato, the 'ether,' which in part is made up of fire (*Timaeus* 40A), is but a 'special kind of air.' Plato, *Timaeus* 58D.

70 J. Pépin, *op. cit.*, pp. 487-8. See also P. Moraux (see note 10), p. 1173 and p. 1249.

71 The notion of a 'nature' which mediates between the physical world and the spiritual world—a notion which also underlies the Christian belief in angels—is discussed in detail by P. Moraux (see note 10), p. 1227 and p. 1249; pp. 1256-8. As to the Christian problem of 'mediators,' see, for instance, Gregory of Nazianzus, *Oratio* XXVIII 8 and 9; *Oratio* XLV 5. For additional sources and discussions bearing upon our problem, see S. Mariotti, 'Nuove testimonianze ed echi dell'Aristotele giovanile,' *Atene et Roma* (series 3), vol. 8 (1940), pp. 48-60; E. Bignone, 'Postilla aristotelica

sulla dottrina dell'endelecheia,' *Atene et Roma* (series 3), vol. 8 (1940), pp. 61-4; L. Alfonsi (see note 6), pp. 71-8; P. Moraux (see note 11); A. Mansion, Foreword to F. J. Nuyens, *L'Évolution de la Psychologie d'Aristote* (Louvain-Paris, 1948), pp. IX-XV; W. Theiler, 'Ein vergessenes Aristoteleszeugnis,' *Journal of Hellenic Studies*, vol. 77 (1957), pp. 127-31; and some of the other sources or authors mentioned in note 11.

72  To further aggravate these difficulties, it must always be borne in mind that the *On Philosophy* is a dialogue in which a Platonic interlocutor (or Plato himself ?) may have been cast in the role of a discussant opposing Aristotle. This being so, we can never be completely sure whether a particular fragment credited to the *On Philosophy* relates what the Aristotelian interlocutor asserts, or whether it reports what the Platonic interlocutor (or some other interlocutor) interjects. It is possible, therefore, that Cicero might be quoting, at least in part, Plato's objections or suggestions (or those of a third interlocutor) rather than Aristotle's assertions. See also Chapter XIV, note 145.

73  See here also P. Moraux (note 10), p. 1219 and p. 1221; E. Berti (see note 10), pp. 396 ff.

74  See notes 14-15 and the corresponding text.

75  Cicero, *Tusculanae Disputationes* I. 26. 65 ff. (frag. 27, Walzer; frag. 21, Ross; frag. 30, Untersteiner).

76  See Philo of Alexandria (note 17), and the corresponding text.

77  This is also the meaning of Philo of Alexandria (see note 17).

78  See note 16.

79  See A.-H. Chroust, 'Aristotle and the philosophies of the east,' *Review of Metaphysics*, vol. 18, no. 3 (1965), pp. 572-80, and Chapter XVI.

80  According to DL I. 9, Theopompus related that the Magi (Zoroastrians) maintained that 'man will live in a future life and be immortal.' It is possible that the Zoroastrian belief in the immortality of the soul and in an afterlife, a doctrine with which Aristotle was probably acquainted, molded his conception of the soul. In any event, at the time he composed the *On Philosophy*, Aristotle seems to have known something about Zoroastrian teachings. Conversely, when he wrote the *Eudemus* (c. 352 B.C.), he might not yet have come into contact with the teachings of the Magi.

81  See note 11 and the corresponding text.

82  This is a thoroughly Platonic notion. Plato also held that the (human) soul was a kind of 'connecting link' between the transcendental world of the Separate Ideas and the world of corporeal becoming and appearance.

83  This explanation, together with what was said in note 80, would defeat the thesis of O. Gigon and other scholars. See note 11. See also R. A. Gauthier (note 57). Gauthier maintains that the particular doctrine of the soul expounded in the *On Philosophy*, in the final analysis, is the result of Aristotle's determined effort to prove the immortality (or the 'divinity') of the soul and, at the same time, to deny the reality of Plato's Separate

Ideas. In the *Eudemus*, on the other hand, Aristotle still adheres to the doctrine of the Separate Ideas. This, then, is probably the main difference between the psychology of the *On Philosophy* and that proclaimed in the *Eudemus*—a difference which might also defeat the efforts of O. Gigon and others to ascribe to the *Eudemus* those fragments about the soul which traditionally have been credited to the *On Philosophy*.

CHAPTER XVI ARISTOTLE'S *On Philosophy* AND THE 'PHILOS-OPHIES OF THE EAST'

* In a different and much less detailed form, and under a different title, this chapter was first published in the *Review of Metaphysics*, vol. 18, no. 3 (1965), pp. 572–80.

1 This is not the place to discuss again the many vexing problems connected with Aristotle's *On Philosophy*. See, in general, M. Untersteiner, *Aristotele: Della Filosofia* (Rome 1963), *passim*; Chapter XII, note 2; and Chapters XII–XV.

2 Frag. 6, Rose; frag. 6, Walzer; frag. 6, Ross; frag. 11, Untersteiner.

3 Frag. 6, Rose; frag. 6, Walzer; frag. 6, Ross; frag. 11, Untersteiner. See also Plutarch, *De Procreatione Animae in Timaeo* 27 (*Moralia* 1026B):

> Thus having comprised the Same and the Other, by the similitudes and dissimilitudes of numbers which produce concord out of disagreement, it becomes the life of the world, sober and prudent, harmony itself, and reason overruling necessity mixed with persuasion. This necessity is by most men called fate or destiny, by Empedocles friend and discord, by Heraclitus of Ephesus the opposite straining harmony of the universe, as of a bow or harp, by Parmenides light and darkness, by Zoroaster God and Demon, naming one Oromasdes, the other Areimanius.

See Plutarch, *De Defectu Oraculorum* 10 (*Moralia* 415A). To avoid possible misunderstanding, it should be noted that Plutarch, *De Iside et Osiride* 46–7 (*Moralia* 370C ff.), in all likelihood is not an excerpt from, nor perhaps a fragment of, the *On Philosophy*. This might be inferred from the fact that Plutarch refers here to two good planets, two evil planets and three 'neutral' (or 'indifferent') planets, while Diogenes Laertius (I. 8), who probably quotes from the *On Philosophy* or from a source which had consulted the *On Philosophy*, speaks of the good demon or good god, and of the evil demon or evil god. In the *De Iside et Osiride* 46 (*Moralia* 369E), Plutarch also mentions Ormuzd and Ahriman. Moreover (*ibid.*) he maintains that Zoroaster lived five thousand years before the Trojan War, while Eudoxus of Cnidus relates that this happened six thousand years before the death of Plato. From all these bits of information it may be inferred that in the *De Iside et Osiride* 46–7 (*Moralia* 370C ff.), Plutarch does not quote from Aristotle and, hence, that this report is not a fragment of the *On Philosophy* in the traditional sense of the term 'fragment.' This becomes even more evident in the light of the following: in the *De Iside et Osiride* 46 (*Moralia* 370BC), Plutarch refers to a period of six thousand years, which is subdivided into two sub-periods of three thousand years each. During each of these two sub-periods one demon (or god) over-powers the other. See also note 20. But when stating this, Plutarch actually quotes Theopompus, that is, Theopompus' *Philippica*, but not Aristotle. What Plutarch reports here, and this alone is of interest to us, is that Aristotle was acquainted with certain aspects of Zoroastrian teachings. For the reference to the Pythagoreans, see, for instance, Aristotle, *Metaphysics* 985 b 22 ff.

4 Frag. 34, Rose; frag. 6, Walzer; frag. 6, Ross; frag. 11, Untersteiner. Rose assigns the fragment found in Pliny, *Hist. Natur.* XXX. 3, to the spurious *Magicus*, a work which is mentioned as well as credited to Aristotle in DL I. 1, and *ibid.*, I. 8, but which is not listed in Diogenes Laertius' 'catalogue' of Aristotelian compositions. *VH* 10 (no. 192), on the other hand, mentions a Μαγικὸν among the spurious writings of Aristotle. See W. Spoerri, 'Encore Platon et l'orient,' *Revue de Philologie*, vol. 83 (1957), pp. 209–23. M. Untersteiner (see note 1), pp. 81 ff., advances the theory that Aristotle refers to the Magi in his *On Philosophy*, a view which might well be accepted. See also W. Jaeger, *Aristotle: Fundamentals of the History of his Development* (Oxford, 1948), pp. 131 ff. According to DL I. 8, Aristotle also points out (in his apocryphal *Magicus*) that the Magi 'were wholly unacquainted with the art of magic.' Dinon, in his *History*, and Hermodorus, the disciple of Plato, maintain that the name Zoroaster signifies 'star-worshipper' (ἀστροθύτης)—a totally erroneous etymology. See DL I. 8; J. H. Moulton, *Early Zoroastrianism* (London, 1913), p. 426.

5 See, for instance, E. Zeller, *Die Philosophie der Griechen*, vol. I, part 1 (5th ed., Leipzig, 1892), pp. 19 ff. and p. 24, *et passim*. Zeller's views, which during the nineteenth century were contested by such scholars as A. Gladisch (see note 32) and E. Röth, have been uncritically accepted by the vast majority of historians of ancient philosophy. More recently, however, some scholars have paid increasing attention to the possibility that Zoroastrian-Iranian notions may have decisively influenced certain aspects of Greek (Pre-Hellenistic) philosophy. See p. 212.

6 See Chapters XIII–XV.

7 V. Rose, *Aristoteles Pseudepigraphus* (Leipzig, 1863), pp. 37 ff. *Ibid.*, p. 50, Rose, who assigns the passage from Pliny to the spurious *Magicus* (see note 4), claims that Pliny derived his information from Apion, *On the Magi*. It is now held, however, that Pliny probably consulted Hermippus, as might be gathered from Pliny, *Hist. Nat.* XXX. 3, where we are informed that 'Hermippus . . . wrote copiously about all that art [*scil.*, the art of the Magi] . . . and commented on two million lines written by Zoroaster. . . .' Hermippus, it may be surmised, in all likelihood consulted Eudoxus of Cnidus and Theopompus (and perhaps Aristotle's *On Philosophy*?). This seems to become evident from DL I. 8: 'This is confirmed

by Hermippus in the first book of his *On the Magi*, by Eudoxus [of Cnidus] in his *Voyage Around the World* (Γῆς Περίοδος), and by Theopompus in the eighth book of his *Philippica*.' It is also possible that Pliny made direct use of Eudoxus' Γῆς Περίοδος.

8 In this, Rose probably relies on DL I. 1, where we are told that 'there are some who maintain that the study of philosophy had its beginnings with . . . the Magi . . . for which they cite as authorities the *Magicus* of Aristotle, and Sotion in the twenty-third book of his *Succession of Philosophers*.' In his *Succession of Philosophers* (*Diadoche*), Sotion probably makes use of Hermodorus' *On Mathematics*, which is also concerned with 'astralism.' See DL I. 1, and *ibid.*, I. 8. That the beginnings of philosophy should be credited to the Magi and other 'barbarian philosophers' is also claimed by Clement of Alexandria, *Stromateis* I. 71. But Clement's source is unknown, unless it be Sotion. Recent scholarship has brought to light many and lasting influences which ancient Near-Eastern religious and quasi-religious thought or myths have had upon the beginnings of Greek philosophy. If these findings can be proven beyond reasonable doubt, then we would have to subject our traditional notions about Greek philosophy and its beginnings to a radical and far-reaching revision. One might even go so far as to maintain (*pace* Zeller, Burnet) that in many philosophic subject-matters the Greeks were avid borrowers from their eastern neighbors. What is truly original in early Greek thought is the disciplined and 'scientific' formulation and communication of what eastern myths had proclaimed in obscure, ambiguous or poetic language.

9 W. Jaeger (see note 4), pp. 132 ff. See here also J. Kerschensteiner, *Platon und der Orient* (Stuttgart, 1945), pp. 192 ff.; S. Pétremont, *Le Dualisme chez Platon, les Gnostiques et les Manichéens* (Paris, 1947), *passim*; W. Spoerri (see note 4), *passim*; B. L. van der Waerden, 'Das grosse Jahr und die ewige Wiederkehr,' *Hermes*, vol. 80 (1952), pp. 129–55; M. Untersteiner (see note 1), pp. 89 ff.; B. Effe, *Studien zur Kosmologie und Theologie der aristotelischen Schrift Über die Philosophie* (Zetemata, Heft 50, Munich, 1970), pp. 64 ff.; M. Untersteiner (see note 1), p. 89; P. Wilpert, 'Die Stellung der Schrift *Über die Philosophie* in der Gedankenentwicklung des Aristoteles,' *Journal of Hellenic Studies*, vol. 77 (1957), p. 157; and some of the authors cited in note 17.

10 See also J. Bidez, 'Platon, Eudoxe de Cnide et l'orient,' *Bulletin de l'Académie Belge* (Brussels, 1933), pp. 195–218 and pp. 273–319.

11 See DL VIII. 86–91; Strabo XIV. 656 and XVII. 806; Aelian, *Varia Historia* VII. 17. See also G. F. Unger, 'Eudoxos von Knidos und Eudoxos von Rhodos,' *Philologus*, vol. 50 (1891), pp. 191 ff.; F. Susemihl, 'Die Lebenszeit des Eudoxos von Knidos,' *Rheinisches Museum*, vol. 53 (1898), pp. 626 ff.; K. von Fritz, 'Die Lebenszeit des Eudoxos von Knidos,' *Philologus*, vol. 85 (1929–30), pp. 478 ff.; G. Gisinger, *Die Erdbeschreibung des Eudoxos von Knidos* (Leipzig-Berlin, 1921), p. 5; G. de Santillana, 'Eudoxus of Cnidos: a study in chronology,' *Isis* (1940–47), pp. 248 ff.

12 See *VM* 13; *VL* 11. In DL VIII. 90, we are told that 'Eudoxus flourished about the 103rd Olympiad (368–64 B.C.).'

13 See, for instance, Aristotle, *Metaphysics* 993 b 11 ff.; Aristotle, *De Anima* 403 b 20 ff.; Aristotle, *Politics* 1264 a 1 ff. and 1329 b 34 ff.

14 In Book A of the *Metaphysics* (981 b 23), Aristotle briefly remarks that 'mathematics was founded in Egypt by the priestly caste.'

15 DL I. 8. In *Meteorologica* 352 b 19 ff. and in *Politics* 1329 b 31 ff. Aristotle states, however, that the 'Egyptians appear to be of all people the most ancient.' See here also Plato, *Timaeus* 23E, where we are informed that Athens was founded one thousand years before Egypt (Sais), and that Egypt was founded eight thousand years before the time of Solon.

16 This particular passage, which sounds much like Plutarch, *De Iside et Osiride* 46–7 (*Moralia* 370C ff., see also p. 206 and note 3), could very well be a 'restatement' of what Aristotle previously had said in his *On Philosophy*. Hence, this passage might be included among the fragments of this lost dialogue. What is likewise of interest to us here is the fact that Book N of the *Metaphysics* (as W. Jaeger has pointed out rather convincingly) and the *On Philosophy* must be dated in close proximity. Equally striking (and probably correct) is Aristotle's realization that some basic notions of Empedocles and Anaxagoras had been shaped by Zoroastrian teachings or, to be more exact, by the Zoroastrian dualism (and antagonism) of good and evil. See p. 212.

17 See, in general, J. Croissant, *Aristote et les Mystères* (Paris, 1927); E. Dirlmeier, 'Peripatos und Orient,' *Die Antike*, vol. 28 (1928); É. Benveniste, *The Persian Religion According to the Chief Greek Texts* (Paris, 1929); P. Boyancé, *Le Culte des Muses chez les Philosophes Grecques* (Paris, 1937); J. Bidez and F. Cumont, *Les Mages Hélénisés* (Paris, 1938); É. Benveniste, *Les Mages dans l'Ancien Iran* (Paris, 1938); J. Kerschensteiner (see note 9); F. Cumont, *Lux Perpetua* (Paris, 1949), pp. 148 ff.; W. Brandenstein, 'Iranische Einflüsse bei Platon,' (Miscellanea Giovanni Galbiati III), *Fontes Ambrosiani*, vol. 27 (Milan, 1951), pp. 83–8; W. J. W. Koster, *Le Mythe de Platon, de Zarathoustra et des Chaldéens: Étude Critique sur les Relations Intellectuelles entre Platon et l'Orient* (Leiden, 1951); J. Duchesne-Guillemin, *Ormadz et Ahriman: L'Aventure Dualiste dans L'Antiquité* (Paris, 1953); G. P. Carratelli, 'Europa e Asia nella storia del mondo antico,' *La Parola del Passato*, fasc. 40 (1955); J. Duchesne-Guillemin, *La Religion de l'Iran Ancien* (Paris, 1962); J. Hani, 'Plutarque en face du dualisme iranien,' *Revue des Études Grecques*, vol. 77, nos 366–8 (1964), pp. 489–525; R. M. Afnan, *Zoroaster's Influence on Greek Thought* (New York, 1965); R. M. Afnan, *Zoroaster's Influence on Anaxagoras, the Greek Tragedians, and Socrates* (New York, 1969); M. L. West, *Early Greek Philosophy and the Orient* (London, 1971). This is not the place to discuss the many problems and issues which have been raised regarding the relationship that might exist between Zoroastrianism and other religions, including Christianity.

Such a discussion would have to be carried on within the framework of a comparative study of the history of religions.

18 It is outside the limited scope of this investigation to speculate on whether the 'arrival' and acceptance of Zoroastrian ideas in ancient Greece were perhaps the result of a reaction to the general religious and moral 'vacuum' which had become rather typical of fourth century Greece, and which Zoroastrianism was supposed to fill. This is the thesis of R. M. Afnan, *Zoroaster's Influence on Greek Thought* (see note 17), *passim*. It has also been claimed that certain aspects of Greek philosophic mysticism, including Orphic and Pythagorean mysticism, as well as certain aspects of Greek soteriology, have been decisively influenced by Zoroastrian teachings. See, for instance, E. Eisler, *Weltmantel und Himmelszelt* (Munich, 1910), *passim*; R. Reitzenstein, *Das Iranische Erlösungsmysterium* (Bonn, 1921), *passim*; R. Reitzenstein and H. H. Schrader, *Studien zum Antiken Synkretismus aus Iran und Griechenland* (Leipzig-Berlin, 1926), *passim*; R. Reitzenstein, *Die Hellenistischen Mysterien-religionen* (Leipzig, 1920), *passim*. Some of these views were rejected, at least in part, by J. Bidez, *Éos, ou Platon et l'Orient* (Brussels, 1945), *passim*; J. Kerschensteiner (see note 9), *passim*; W. J. W. Koster (see note 17), *passim*; J. Duchesne-Guillemin (see note 17), *passim*.

19 See *Index Philosophorum Academicorum Herculanensis* (ed. S. Mekler), col. III, 13.

20 P. 15, ed. E. Westerink. It is possible that the Magi mentioned here are identical with the Chaldean referred to in the *Index Philosophorum Academicorum Herculanensis*. See note 19. Josephus, *Contra Apionem* 176, relates the story of a Jew who came to Aristotle during the latter's sojourn in Assos in order to study philosophy with him and some of the other members of the school (Coriscus, Erastus and Xenocrates).

21 This story calls to mind the following incident. During the reign of Emperor Augustus, the historian Nicholas of Damascus met three Indian 'envoys' at Antioch in Syria. These envoys had heard of the 'new king of the West,' and were on their way to present gifts to the 'new ruler of the world.' Thus it seems that the rumor of Augustus' exploits had reached India, which promptly dispatched emissaries to find out more about this 'new king of the world.' Needless to say, these three Indian emissaries at a later time were identified with the three Wise Men of the East who were seeking 'the king of the Jews.' See Matt. 2:2.

22 See here also W. Jaeger (see note 4), p. 132.

23 Plutarch, *De Iside et Osiride* 46 (*Moralia* 370F ff.). Chapters 46-7 of this work, it will be observed, contain ancient reports concerning Zoroastrian teachings.

24 Plato, *Timaeus* 35A: 'Out of the Indivisible and Unchangeable and also out of that which is divisible and has to do with material bodies, he compounded a third and intermediary kind of essence, partaking of the nature of the one and of that of the other, and this compound he placed

accordingly in a mean between the Indivisible and the Divisible or Material.'

25 See, in general, R. Reitzenstein, 'Vom Dāmdād zu Platon,' in R. Reitzenstein and H. H. Schrader, *Studien zum Antiken Synkretinismus aus Iran und Griechenland* (Leipzig-Berlin, 1926); A. Götze, 'Persische Weisheit im griechischen Gewande,' *Zeitschrift für Indologie und Iranistik*, vol. II (1923), p. 60 and pp. 167 ff.; W. J. W. Koster (see note 17); W. Hinz, *Zarathustra* (Stuttgart, 1961). R. Reitzenstein (see this note) essays to demonstrate that Plato was influenced by the *Dāmdād-Nāsk*, an old-Iranian work of Avesta, and that Plato himself either had read this work or at least had heard of it through Eudoxus of Cnidus, who is said to have been acquainted with the *Dāmdād-Nāsk*. See also the literature cited in note 17.

26 See, for instance, Aristotle, *Metaphysics* 1091 b 11, where Aristotle mentions the Magi as the forerunners of Plato's philosophical dualism.

27 See, for instance, DL V. 8; J. Bidez and F. Cumont (see note 17), vol. I, p. 20; J. Hani (see note 17), pp. 520 ff.

28 See Plutarch, *De Iside et Osiride* 46 (*Moralia* 370BC). When referring to the several stages in the Zoroastrian story of the struggles between Ormuzd and Ahriman, Plutarch cites Theopompus: 'Theopompus states that, according to the wise men of old, one god is to overpower, and the other god to be overpowered, each in turn, for a space of 3,000 years. Afterward, for another 3,000 years, they will struggle and make war upon another, and the one shall undo the works of the other. Finally, Hades [*scil.*, Ahriman] shall pass away. Then shall the people be happy. . . . The god who has contrived to bring about all these things, shall then have quiet and shall repose for a time. . . .' See also note 31.

29 See, for instance, M. L. West (see note 17), *passim*.

30 Frag. B 53; frag. B 80, Diels-Kranz. One could cite here several fragments of Heraclitus which would bring out, frequently in a purely metaphoric manner, this 'struggle of opposites.' See, for instance, frags B 8; B 10; B 12; B 51; B 58; B 59; B 60; B 61; B 62; B 67; B 88; B 91; B 126, Diels-Kranz.

31 See Plutarch (see note 28), chap. 46 (*Moralia* 370D ff.), quoted in the text at the beginning of this chapter; Plutarch, *De Procreatione Animae in Timaeo* 27 (*Moralia* 1026B), cited in note 3; Plutarch, *De Defectu Oraculorum* 10 (*Moralia* 415A ff.). See also Aristoteles, *Metaphysics* 1091 b 8 ff., and notes 16 and 26. K. Joël, *Der Echte und der Xenophontische Sokrates*, vol. II, part 1 (Berlin, 1901), p. 168, claims that the moral teachings of Antisthenes show the influence of Zoroastrianism. It will be noted that Plutarch speaks of Zoroastrianism or Mazdaism not only in the *De Iside et Osiride*, but also in some of his other writings, including the *Parallel Lives*.

32 The story told in DL IX. 3 (see also Marcus Aurelius III. 3; Suda, 'Heraclitus'), namely, that Heraclitus left instructions to have his body covered with cow dung rather than be cremated, reflects Zoroastrian-Parsee burial rites. This was realized already by A. Gladisch, *Herakleitos und Zoroaster*

(Vienna, 1859), pp. 63–6. See also L. Mills, 'Zarathustra and Heraclitus,' *Journal of the Royal Asiatic Society* (1902), pp. 897–907; A. Stöhr, *Heraklit* (Vienna, 1920), pp. 7–8; F. M. Cleve, *The Giants of Pre-Socratic Greek Philosophy*, vol. I (The Hague, 1965), pp. 33–4. See also frag. B 96, Diels-Kranz: 'Corpses are worth throwing out rather than dung.' Strabo XVI. 26; Plutarch, *Symposium* IV. 4. 3 (*Moralia* 669A). Moreover, Heraclitus' insistence that he was no man's disciple (DL IX. 5) might point in the direction of Zoroastrianism: he was taught by the *logos* which still spoke through him. See also A.-H. Chroust, 'A Prolegomena to the Study of Heraclitus of Ephesus,' *Thomist*, vol. 22, no. 4 (1957), pp. 470–87. It should also be borne in mind that during the last decade of the sixth century B.C., King Darius (521–485 B.C.) made Zoroastrian religion the official creed throughout the Persian empire, including the Greek settlements in Asia Minor. See, for instance, E. Herzfeld, *Zoroaster and His World* (Princeton, 1947), *passim*. Under the circumstances, it would have been nothing short of a miracle if Heraclitus as well as some other early Greek philosophers who hailed from Asia Minor had not come into contact with some Zoroastrian teachings.

33 Frag. B 134, Diels-Kranz.

34 Frags B 17; B 20; B 21; B 22; B 26; B 30; B 35, Diels-Kranz. See also F. Altheim, *Porphyrios und Empedokles* (Tübingen, 1954), pp. 42 ff.; J. Bidez and F. Cumont (see note 17), vol. I, p. 239; F. M. Cleve (see note 32), p. 338, p. 347; p. 354.

35 It has been claimed that upon his accession to the throne of Persia in 485 B.C., Xerxes immediately set about crushing the many revolts which had flared up throughout the Persian empire against Darius' efforts to make Mazdaism or Zoroastrianism the official creed of the land (see note 32), and suppressing all forms of idolatry (a view which is also reflected in DL I. 9). Subsequently Xerxes undertook the conquest of the Western World in the name of Ahura Mazda in order to convert all men to Mazdaism. In this sense, Xerxes' invasion of Europe in 480 B.C. was a sort of holy crusade in the name of Ahura Mazda against the Greek idolators. This would also explain why during his advance Xerxes destroyed all pagan temples and shrines, including those of Attica and Athens. Empedocles, who had probably embraced Zoroastrianism at some earlier time, is said to have celebrated Xerxes' crossing of the Hellespont and invasion of Europe by composing a poem or hymn. According to Aristotle's lost work *On Poets* (frag. 70, Rose; frag. 1, Ross; see also DL V. 22, no. 7; *VH* 10, no. 7; Ptolemy, no. 7), 'Empedocles ... wrote a poem commemorating Xerxes' crossing of the Hellespont . . .. But a sister of his or, as Hieronymus states, a daughter of his, deliberately burned this Persian [Zoroastrian] poem because it was unfinished.' See also DL VIII. 57; J. Bidez and F. Cumont (see note 34); F. Altheim (see note 34).

36 This doctrine, which proclaims that mankind is incapable of maintaining permanently the same high level of truth, knowledge or civilization it had

once attained, is based on the assumption that at certain (preordained?) intervals truth, knowledge and civilization are destroyed or 'pushed back' by the forces of evil and darkness. This event often assumes the form of regular cycles. Traces of this theory (which, incidentally, seems to have been accepted by some modern philosophers of history) can also be detected in the writings of Heraclitus of Ephesus (see, for instance, frags B 30; B 31; B 103, Diels-Kranz), and in those of Empedocles (see, for instance, frags B 8; B 17; B 26; B 30; B 35; B 135, Diels-Kranz; see also note 35), as well as in Plato, *Republic* 546A ff.; Plato, *Timaeus* 22A–22C; Plato, *Critias* 109D; 111B; 112A; Plato, *Statesman* 268E; Plato, *Laws* 677A; 702A; and perhaps, Plato, *Statesman* 274DE; 273A; Aristotle, *Metaphysics* 1074 a 38 ff.; Synesius, *Calvitii Encomium* XXII. 85c (frag. 8, Rose; frag. 8, Walzer; frag. 8, Ross; frag. 1, Untersteiner).

37 Aristotle, *De Caelo* 270 b 19–21.

38 Aristotle, *Meteorologica* 339 b 28; 352 a 28 ff. See also Aristotle, *De Motu Animalium* 699 a 27 ff. In *Statesman* 270D, Plato maintains that at one time the universe is guided by the 'divine,' while at another time it moves 'on its own,' and that this goes on 'in the infinite cycles of the years' in the form of a 'reverse motion.' When the 'evil material universe' moves 'on its own,' we may surmise that it is guided by the 'forces of evil' (Ahriman) which, according to Plato, are identified with the material-corporeal world. There might exist a connection between the concept of an 'eternal recurrence' and the Platonic (or Aristotelian) notion of the ἀνείλιξις. See Plato, *Statesman* 286B. See also Chapter XIV, notes 6 and 46–77, and the corresponding text.

39 Aristotle, *Politics* 1329 b 25–7. See also Plato, *Laws* 676A ff.; W. Jaeger (see note 4), p. 137 and p. 389.

40 Aristotle, it will be noted (DL I. 8), already seems to have accepted what appears to be a later version of Zoroastrianism, namely, the 'parity' of Ahura Mazda and Ahriman. According to the earlier version, the High God, Ahura Mazda, created two 'spirits,' a good spirit, namely, Spenta Mainyu, the partisan of Truth, and an evil spirit, evil by his own choice, namely, Angra Mainyu, the partisan of the Lie. At some later time Ahura Mazda became identified with the Good Spirit or Spenta Mainyu. In this fashion what had originally been two opposed spirits subordinate to a single Supreme God were converted into two gods, Ormuzd and Ahriman. Eudoxus of Cnidus (and Eudemus of Rhodes), according to Damascius (*De Princ. Par.* 125b), on the other hand, refers to the older Iranian version which knows only of a conflict between Ahura Mazda and Ahriman, but not of an 'equality' or 'parity' between the two. According to the older version, Ahura Mazda is always the superior (and the ultimate conqueror) in this conflict ('the gates of hell shall not prevail,' Matt. 16:18). It also appears that Plato and the majority of his disciples accepted the later or 'parity' version. Plutarch seems to have been acquainted with the 'disparity' version. See, for instance, Plutarch, *De Iside et Osiride* 46 (*Moralia*

369DE ff.). For additional detail, see among others, J. Bidez and F. Cumont (note 17), p. 39; É. Benveniste, *The Persian Religion According to the Chief Greek Texts* (Paris, 1929), pp. 72–3; and some of the authors cited in note 17.

41 In the *Timaeus* 23E (the founding of Athens) and in the *Critias* 108E (the repulsion of the Atlantic invaders—see also *Timaeus* 25C), Plato seems to imply a cycle of nine thousand years, which is without doubt a Zoroastrian twist. Thus, nine thousand years before Plato, the gods divided the universe among themselves, making the world inhabitable. After that began a period of perfect bliss, both at Athens and on Atlantis. But gradually a process of degeneration or deterioration started to make itself felt until in a single night and day of calamity, Atlantis sank beneath the ocean (*Timaeus* 25D and 23A ff.), and cloudbursts, earthquakes and flashfloods laid waste to Attica (*Timaeus* 25D; *Critias* 112A and 109D ff.; *Laws* 677A ff.; *Statesman* 273A). See also Aristotle, *Meteorologica* 339 b 19 ff.; 352 a 28 ff.; Aristotle, *De Caelo* 270 b 16 ff.; Aristotle, *Metaphysics* 1074 a 38 ff.; 1074 b 10; Aristotle, *Politics* 1264 a 3 ff.; 1269 a 5 ff.; 1329 b 24 ff.; Censorinus, *De Die Natali* XVIII. 11; Seneca, *Quaestiones Naturales* III. 29. 1; Plutarch, *De Iside et Osiride* 46 (*Moralia* 370BC), who quotes Theopompus in support of the thesis that each of the several 'stages' or cycles of the 'cosmic drama' or 'cosmic conflict' lasts three thousand years. See F. Jacoby, *Frag. Hist. Graec.*, Theopompus, F. 64. Of interest also is Plutarch's account (*op. cit.*, 370B) that, according to the Magi, 'a pre-ordained time shall come when it is decreed that Ahriman, engaged in bringing on pestilence and famine, shall by these be utterly annihilated and shall vanish. And then shall the earth become a level plain, and there shall be a common manner of life and one form of government for a blessed people who shall speak one tongue.' See, among others, C. Mugler, *Deux Thèmes de la Cosmologie Grecque: Devenir Cyclique et Pluralité des Mondes* (Paris, 1953), pp. 104 ff.; F. M. Cornford. *Plato's Cosmology* (London, 1952), pp. 116 ff.; R. Weil, *Aristote et l'Histoire* (Paris, 1960), pp. 328 ff.; B. Effe (see note 9), pp. 62 ff.; J. Hani (see note 17), pp. 506 ff.

42 Pliny, *Hist. Nat.* XXX. 3. This information, which Pliny probably derived from Hermippus, ultimately goes back to Eudoxus of Cnidus, Γῆς Περίοδος (composed late in 347 B.C., see note 7; F. Gisinger, see note 11). In Pliny XXX. 3, we are also informed that, according to Hermippus, Agonazes (or Azonazes or Azanak, a name which signifies 'the Great Sage' or 'the Great Teacher'), the teacher of Zoroaster, lived 5,000 years before the Trojan War (which, according to Eratosthenes, is usually dated *c.* 1194–84 B.C.). See also DL I. 2: 'The date of the Magi, beginning with Zoroaster, the Persian, was five thousand years before the fall of Troy, as given by Hermodorus, the Platonist, in his work on mathematics. But Xanthus, the Lydian, reckons six thousand years from Zoroaster to the Persian invasion under Xerxes.' See also Plutarch, *De Iside et Osiride* 46 (*Moralia* 369E). Similar views were held by Sotion.

43 In passing it might be noted that by assigning to Plato such an important

or decisive place in the cycle of the great cosmic events, Aristotle, provided this bit of information actually was contained in Aristotle's *On Philosophy*, pays the highest tribute to his teacher. This, then, might also be cited as an additional piece of evidence in support of the contention that contrary to some ill-informed sources the relationship between these two men must have been excellent. For some different though interesting views, see, for instance, H. Leisegang, *Philologische Wochenschrift*, no. 48 (1928), pp. 1412 ff.; J. Kerschensteiner (see note 9), pp. 195 ff. and p. 207; W. Spoerri (see note 4), pp. 215 ff. These scholars reject the thesis that, according to Aristotle's *On Philosophy*, Plato marks a decisive turning-point in the cyclic events that result from the cosmic struggle between Ormuzd and Ahriman.

44 This influence might also be reflected, for instance, in Aristotle's concept of God or of the Divine, as it can be found in the *On Philosophy*, and as it is related by Cicero, *De Natura Deorum* I. 13. 33. See A.-H. Chroust, 'The concept of God in Aristotle's lost dialogue *On Philosophy* (Cicero, *De Natura Deorum* I. 13. 33),' *Emerita*, vol. 33, fasc. 2 (1965), pp. 205-28, and Chapter XIV.

45 See Pliny, *op. cit.* XXX. 3: '... This Zoroaster lived six thousand years before the death of Plato. So says also Aristotle.' In passing, it will be noted that W. Jaeger uses the statement that 'Zoroaster lived six thousand years before the death of Plato,' as proof that the *On Philosophy*, from which this statement supposedly is taken, was composed after the death of Plato in 348-47 B.C. Jaeger, however, seems to overlook that Eudoxus of Cnidus wrote his *Voyage Around the World* in 347 B.C., that is, after the death of Plato, and that Pliny in all likelihood derived his information from Eudoxus (perhaps through the intermediary of Hermippus). Although Pliny might also have consulted Aristotle's *On Philosophy* (or a source which made use of the *On Philosophy*), the statement, 'Zoroaster lived six thousand years before the death of Plato,' was not necessarily contained in the *On Philosophy*. Hence, Pliny's remark may not be relied upon for the proper dating of Aristotle's *On Philosophy*, or for the assertion that it was composed after the death of Plato. See notes 7, 11 and 42. See also Chapter XII.

46 In the *On Philosophy*, which might have been composed shortly before the death of Plato, Aristotle probably stated that 'Zoroaster lived six thousand years before Plato.' This suggestion, which permits us to date the *On Philosophy* prior to the death of Plato, does not conflict with the report found in Pliny, *op. cit.*, XXX. 3.

47 See here also R. Mondolfo, *La Composizione del Soggetto Umano nell' Antichità Classica* (Florence, 1958), pp. 686 ff.

48 Olympiodorus, *Comment. in Platonis Gorgiam* (ed. W. Norvin), p. 197. See also *VM* 26, *VV* 11 and *VL* 30, which contain a 'fragment' of this Elegy.

49 Plutarch, *Adversus Coloten* 14 (*Moralia* 1115A), relates that Heracleides of Pontus wrote a work on Zoroaster.

CHAPTER XVII ARISTOTLE'S CRITICISM OF PLATO'S 'PHILOS-
OPHER KING': SOME COMMENTS ON ARISTOTLE'S *On Kingship*

* In a much less elaborate form this chapter was first published in *Rheinisches Museum für Philologie*, vol. 101, no. 1 (1968), pp. 16–22.

1 DL V. 22 (no. 18); *VH* 10 (no. 16 and no. 171); Ptolemy (-el-Garib), no. 8. See also Cicero, *Ad Atticum* XII. 40. 2, and *ibid*., XIII. 28. 2; Philoponus, *Comment. in Aristotelis Categorias*, CIAG, vol. XIII, part 1 (ed. A. Busse, Berlin, 1898), p. 3, lines 22–24; *VM* 21; *VV* 22; *VL* 21. While DL, *VM*, *VV*, *VL* and Philoponus maintain or imply that this work consisted of one book, Ptolemy (-el-Garib) insists that it contained six books. See also frag. 647, Rose; frag. 2, Ross. For additional detail, see Chapter II notes 82–92, and the corresponding text. Cicero, *Ad Atticum* XII. 40. 2, informs Atticus that he had tried to write a letter of advice to Julius Caesar, but that he had found nothing to say to a man like Caesar. He also relates that he had consulted the books which Aristotle and Theopompus had addressed to Alexander, and that Alexander and Caesar had little in common. According to Cicero, in their books Aristotle and Theopompus 'wrote what reflected honor upon them and, at the same time, was acceptable to Alexander....' *Ibid*., XIII. 28. 2, Cicero repeats that he still finds himself unable to advise Caesar, and that men as eloquent and learned as Aristotle and Theopompus exhorted Alexander (a young man inspired by a desire for truest glory and the kind of advice which would secure his everlasting fame) to conduct himself honorably.

2 Themistius, *Oratio* VIII. 107D (p. 128, lines 14 ff., ed. W. Dindorf, Leipzig, 1832). In some of his other writings (see, for instance, *Oratio* II, p. 38, lines 20 ff., Dindorf; and *Oratio* XVII, p. 260, lines 18 ff., Dindorf), however, Themistius approves of Plato's concept of the 'philosopher king.' Hellenistic literature abounds with works 'On Kingship' or 'On the Nature of Kingship,' that is, with 'Mirrors for Princes' or Λόγοι Προτρεπτικοί. Xenocrates, Theophrastus and Straton of Lampsacus, for instance, wrote '*Exhortations Addressed to Kings*.' Beginning with the 'Pythagoreans' of the second century B.C., down to Themistius (*c.* A.D. 320–90), a good many Hellenistic authors discussed the duties and obligations of the enlightened and conscientious ruler. All these '*Exhortations*' may contain 'fragments' of the Aristotelian *On Kingship*.

3 Themistius himself is essentially an Aristotelian or Late Peripatetic, although in keeping with the major philosophic trends of his time, he frequently combines Aristotelian (Peripatetic) and Platonic teachings. As a matter of fact, at times he sides with Plato (whom he greatly admires and frequently cites) against Aristotle, whom he calls his intellectual guide and inspiration. See *Oratio* II, p. 31, lines 15 ff. (ed. W. Dindorf).

4 This is almost a literal citation from Plato, *Republic* 473CD: 'Until philosophers are kings, or the kings and princes of this world have the spirit and power of philosophy, and political greatness and philosophic

wisdom meet in one . . ., cities will never have rest from their evils, nor will the whole of mankind.' See also *ibid.*, 487E; 501E ff.; 540A ff.; etc.

5 Plato (*Republic* 497E) had already admitted that his call for a 'philosopher king' would meet with great difficulties, observing that 'all great efforts are attended with risks. Everything excellent is difficult.' It will be noted that Spinoza concludes his *Ethics* with the admission that 'everything excellent is both difficult and rare.'

6 See W. Jaeger, *Aristotle: Fundamentals of the History of his Development* (Oxford, 1948), p. 259; P. Moraux, *Les Listes Anciennes des Ouvrages d'Aristote* (Louvain, 1951), p. 38 and p. 341.

7 See A.-H. Chroust, 'Was Aristotle actually the preceptor of Alexander the Great?,' *Classical Folia*, vol. 18, no. 1 (1964), pp. 26–33, and Vol. I, Chapter X.

8 Diodorus Siculus XVI. 77; Plutarch, *Alexander* 9. See, however, E. Berti, *La Filosofia del Primo Aristotele* (Padua, 1962), p. 452; R. Weil, *Aristote et l'Histoire: Essai sur la Politique* (Paris, 1960), pp. 154–9.

9 See, for instance, E. Heitz, *Die verlorenen Schriften des Aristoteles* (Leipzig, 1865), p. 168; pp. 196–7; 204–8; R. Hirzel, 'Über den *Protreptikos* des Aristoteles,' *Hermes*, vol. 10 (1876), pp. 61 ff.; W. Jaeger (see note 6), pp. 259–60, note 2.

10 It will be noted that in his *On Kingship* (DL X. 28, no. 39), Epicurus chastises Aristotle for having given advice to kings and princes. See also note 2.

11 This becomes manifest, for instance, in Aristotle's lost dialogues dealing with 'political theory,' namely, the *On Justice* and the *Politicus*. See A.-H. Chroust, 'Aristotle's *On Justice*: a lost dialogue,' *Modern Schoolman*, vol. 43, no. 3 (1966), pp. 249–63, and Chapter VI; A.-H. Chroust, 'Aristotle's *Politicus*: a lost dialogue,' *Rheinisches Museum*, vol. 108 no. 4 (1965), pp. 346–53, and Chapter XI.

12 Iamblichus, *Protrepticus* (ed. H. Pistelli, Leipzig, 1888), p. 56, lines 2 ff. (frag. 13, Walzer; frag. 13, Ross; frag. 51, Düring; frag. 48, Chroust). An echo of this passage might be detected in *Nicomachean Ethics* 1144 b 11 ff., where we are told that 'a strong body, which moves without sight, stumbles badly.' In Aristotle, *Physics* 252 a 33 ff., we are informed that sense-perception (practical experience) often shows us that a theory or hypothesis is incorrect. See also Aristotle, *Posterior Analytics* 99 b 35 ff.; Aristotle, *De Partibus Animalium* 644 b 22 ff.

13 Iamblichus, *Protrepticus*, p. 46, lines 22–8, Pistelli (frag. 55, Rose; frag. 9, Walzer; frag. 9, Ross; frag. 103, Düring; frag. 99, Chroust). Being an understanding and tolerant man, Aristotle apparently grants that the majority of people are satisfied, and should be satisfied, with just doing an 'adequate job' and with staying alive decently. See here also *Nicomachean Ethics* 1109 b 34 and 1109 b 19 ff.; Aristotle, *Politics* 1252 b 30 ff. and 1342 a 19 ff.; *Magna Moralia* 1201 a 1 ff.

14 Aristotle, *Politics* 1265 a 17. See also *ibid.*, 1325 b 38.

15 Many, and perhaps the most important aspects of Plato's *Republic*, it will be observed, are befitting a monastic organization rather than a practical and workable body politic. In a most general manner, it might be argued that the Platonic *Republic* contains what may be called three 'levels of meaning,' namely, a 'political' level, a monastic level and an eschatological level. The 'political' level, it appears, in essence (though by no means exclusively) is but the outer shell, the conceptual vehicle or framework by means of which Plato, through the use of an analogy, advances his monastic and eschatological views. He could expect that his Athenian readers were familiar with the problems and intricacies of political life and corporate existence. It is held here that, contrary to the notions entertained by many political scientists, in the *Republic* Plato did not intend to write primarily a political tract in the ordinary sense of the term, nor did he discuss politics and political issues as such. The monastic level, like the eschatological level, on the other hand, touches upon the very foundation and the ultimate spirit of the *Republic* and, indeed, of Plato's whole philosophy. We know that, according to Plato, the human soul pre-existed the body, and that originally this soul lived in the presence of the Ideas, enjoying what may well be called 'beatific vision.' For some grave wrong which it committed the soul was exiled from this heaven of Ideas and, as a punishment, incarcerated in the body. Man's ultimate mission in this imperfect world of ours, therefore, is to return from this exile to his original or heavenly home. As the Pythagorean brotherhoods and the Platonic Academy seem to indicate, such a return is greatly facilitated and expedited if the exiles 'travel' together and encourage each other by discussing philosophy (and by revitalizing their recollection of the perfect Ideas once visualized) and by urging one another along the difficult road back to 'heaven'—if they are properly guided, inspired and constantly reminded of the ultimate meaning and goal of their pilgrimage. In this sense, the Platonic *Republic* is also a description as well as a fervent recommendation of the 'best road' and the most efficient way back whence man originally came—most assuredly a monastic notion. The eschatological level, again, is the visualization of the transcendent 'heavenly Athens' (the 'new Jerusalem'), of the perfect 'City of the Ideas,' which in the form of a pure or intellectual vision is held out to the pilgrims as the ultimate goal which they are bound to reach if they proceed properly and determinedly during their long and toilsome monastic journey.

16 Aristotle, *Nicomachean Ethics* 1181 b 12–23. This passage, which is the conclusion of the *Nicomachean Ethics*, not only contains the 'program' for the Aristotelian *Politics*, but also a 'manifesto' fusing ethics and politics into a single empirical science of man. It proclaims Aristotle's intention to devise an ideal political construct (Plato) with a positive, empirical, and workable foundation culled from historical experience. Plato's radically theoretic conception and construction of the ideal city becomes with Aristotle a 'scientific' undertaking based on a factual appreciation of the re-

433

alities of time, place and circumstance. This should also explain why Books IV–VI of the *Politics* are replete with historical examples and illustrations, in all likelihood drawn from Aristotle's *Collection of 158 Constitutions*. This *Collection*, it must be borne in mind, was really a comprehensive history of legal, constitutional and political institutions. See also note 18.

17 Aristotle insists that in projecting our ideal city, we may assume the best *possible* conditions, but never impossible or unrealistic conditions. See *Politics* 1265 a 17 ff. and 1325 b 38 ff.

18 Unlike Plato, Aristotle pays a great deal of attention to particular historical and political phenomena and situations. According to him there is no city so hopelessly evil or corrupt that it cannot be restored to some kind of good. This is the meaning of *Politics* 1290 b 25 ff. See also 1288 b 21 ff., where Aristotle rejects those one-sided political theorists who concern themselves exclusively with the 'ideal (Utopian) city,' ignoring the question of how to improve upon an existing city (which is in a bad condition) without completely 'cleaning the canvas.' Plato, *Republic* 500D, and *ibid.*, 541A; Plato, *Statesman* 293 C ff. In a truly scientific manner, the Aristotelian statesman studies the many and varied social and political phenomena of living political societies, and like a competent physician, he diagnoses the many kinds of political illness and prescribes the proper and sensible cure. See Book V of the *Politics*. Hence, he rejects the radical and at times unrealistic and even inhuman methods proposed by Plato to start or maintain the 'good city.' See A.-H. Chroust, 'A second (and closer) look at Plato's political philosophy,' *Archiv für Rechts-und Sozialphilosophie*, vol. 48, no. 4 (1962), pp. 449–86. While in the *Republic* Plato assumes an adamant theoretic position, in the *Laws* he moderates some of his earlier radical notions in order to bring his city closer to reality. It has been claimed that in his *Politics* Aristotle merely continues an evolution already initiated by Plato in his old age. This view is open to debate: Aristotle, it appears, does not merely carry on an already established tradition; he originates a novel approach to the many vexing problems of political philosophy. In his *Politicus*, however, an early work which reflects Aristotle's close association with Plato, the Stagirite still seems to subscribe to Plato's Utopian political philosophy. See A.-H. Chroust, 'Aristotle's *Politicus*: a lost dialogue,' *Rheinisches Museum*, vol. 108, no. 4 (1965), pp. 346–53, and Chapter XI; A.-H. Chroust, 'An emendation to fragment 13 (Walzer, Ross) of Aristotle's *Protrepticus*,' *Tijdschrift voor Filosofie*, vol. 28, no. 2 (1966), pp. 366–77, and Chapter VIII.

19 *Politics* 1323 a 35. Hence, it will also be the task of the Aristotelian 'new statesman' to balance the different (and conflicting) interests of citizens in a manner which will preserve the social peace within the city. This can be inferred from *Politics* 1323 b 7: 'External goods have a limit.'

20 Book VII of the *Politics*, which, according to W. Jaeger, is still very 'Platonic' in that it discusses the 'ideal city' by identifying the proper end of the city with the end of the individual. The ultimate end of the individual

is actually the city, towards which man is predisposed by nature. See *Nicomachean Ethics* 1097 b 11; 1162 a 17; 1169 b 18; *Eudemian Ethics* 1242 a 22-7, and 1245 a 11-27; *Politics* 1253 a 2; 1253 a 30; 1278 b 20. Aristotle's famous statement that man is a 'political animal' simply means that man is an animal that lives, or is supposed to live, in an orderly *polis*.

21 *Politics* 1265 a 13 ff.

22 *Ibid.*, 1265 a 18 ff. See also *ibid.*, 1267 a 19, and notes 29-30.

23 *Politics*, Book III.

24 See here also Aristotle, *Eudemian Ethics* 1227 b 19 ff.

25 See, for instance, *Politics*, Book II, chaps 1-6.

26 *Politics* 1323 b 1. A similar notion can be found in Aristotle's *Protrepticus* (*Oxyrrh. Papyr.* IV. 666, Grenfell-Hunt; Stobaeus, *Florilegium* III. 3. 25): 'Neither wealth nor strength nor beauty is of much use to those who have an evil and ill-disposed soul. The more lavishly a man is endowed with these gifts, the more serious and frequent harm they will cause him that possesses them and, at the same time, lacks true (philosophic) wisdom.' Frag. 57, Rose; frag. 3, Walzer; frag. 3, Ross; frag. 4, Düring; frag. 4, Chroust. This passage calls to mind Matthew 16:26: 'For what is a man profited if he shall gain the whole world, and lose his own soul.' See also Mark 8:38; Luke 9:25. See Aristotle, *Nicomachean Ethics* 1094 b 16 ff.: 'Earthly goods ... bring harm to many people. ... Men have been undone by their wealth.' Aristotle, *Politics* 1323 b 8 ff.; Aristotle, *Rhetoric* 1355 b 6: 'A man ... can inflict the greatest of injuries by the wrong use of earthly goods.' See also Aristotle's lost composition, *On Wealth*, discussed in Chapter II, notes 46-56, and the corresponding text.

27 That this part of the *Politics* was written shortly (?) after the year 345 B.C. seems to follow from Aristotle's reference (*Politics* 1272 b 20 ff.) to the invasion of Crete by mercenaries under the leadership of the Phocian Phalaecus in 345 B.C. This incident is mentioned by Aristotle as having occurred quite recently. See W. Jaeger (note 6), pp. 285-6.

28 See, for instance, *Politics* 1265 a 10 ff. In a spirit of personal reverence for his teacher Plato, Aristotle admits that 'the discourses of Socrates [in the Platonic *Republic*] are never commonplace: they always exhibit grace and originality of thought, but perfection in everything can hardly be expected.' In other words, they fly into the face of historical actuality and, hence, cannot be accepted as being correct, that is, realistic, although they most certainly contain interesting notions. In stating his position, Aristotle also seems to advocate and defend the freedom of thought and expression.

29 *Politics* 1265 a 18 ff. See also note 22.

30 *Politics* 1267 a 19 ff. See also *ibid.*, 1327 a 41 ff.: 'A city should be formidable not only to its citizens but also to its neighbors or, if necessary, be able to assist them. ... The proper number of its ships or the size of its naval forces is relative to the special circumstances of the city.' In other words, it should be determined by the 'strategic' or 'geo-political' location of the city.

31 *Politics* 1332 b 32 ff.

32 Plato, *Laws* 778D.

33 This is reflected, for instance, in *Politics* 1265 a 20 ff.; 1267 a 19 ff.; 1269 a 40 ff.; 1330 b 32 ff. It should be borne in mind that Aristotle not only lived for some time with Hermias and, hence, was able to observe him 'at work,' but also that strong ties of personal friendship united these two men. Hermias, a thoroughly realistic man—a *Realpolitiker* and presumably a banker or bank clerk at one time—started his political career by taking hold of some minor mountain villages near Mount Ida. Later he succeeded in securing the formal recognition of the Persians, who, in return for certain monetary considerations, permitted him to assert a degree of independence. Through clever manipulations and calculations, although in control of only a very small territory, Hermias skillfully managed to extend and consolidate his territorial possessions as well as his political influence. Being a political realist, Hermias fully realized his precarious position: on the European side of the Hellespont he was faced with a steadily advancing and expanding Macedonia under the leadership of King Philip, an ambitious and shrewd ruler, while on the Asiatic side he was confronted by the might of the Persian empire (where he was utterly distrusted), especially after the ascendency of Artaxerxes III Ochus to the throne of Persia in 358 B.C., who made every effort to restore full Persian control over Asia Minor. Sandwiched between these two major powers—Macedonia and Persia—which sooner or later were to engage in warfare, he succeeded in maintaining himself for some time. See Aristotle, *Politics* 1267 a 19–37. It was probably in Hermias' 'school of realistic politics' that Aristotle learned the 'facts of political life' which Plato was prone to ignore.

34 DL. (Apollodorus) V. 9; Dionysius of Halicarnassus, *I Epistola ad Ammaeum* 5.

35 *Ibid.* See also E. Barker, 'The life of Aristotle and the composition and structure of the *Politics*,' *Classical Review*, vol. 45 (1931), pp. 165–6; W. Jaeger (see note 6), pp. 259 ff. The extant *Vitae Aristotelis* are most emphatic about Aristotle's many contacts with kings and princes, as well as about the numerous political and diplomatic services he rendered rulers and cities, and Macedonia (Philip) in particular. See A.-H. Chroust, 'Aristotle and Athens: some observations on Aristotle's sojourns in Athens,' *Laval Théologique et Philosophique*, vol. 22, no. 2 (1966), pp. 186–96, and Vol. I, Chapter XIII. The present author attempts to show here that during the whole of his mature life and, especially, during his second sojourn in Athens (335/34–323 B.C.), Aristotle was actively and often successfully involved in the many political and diplomatic maneuvers connected with the meteoric rise of Macedonia to a world power within one generation—and that he might well have been a 'political agent' or emissary of Macedonia in Athens.

36 This seems to follow from Cicero, *Ad Atticum* XII. 40. 2, where we are informed that Aristotle addressed a book to Alexander, 'writing about what was honorable for the philosopher and acceptable to the king.'

37 See notes 6 and 8.

38 This might be inferred from the fact that subsequently Alexander had himself deified. See Arrian III. 3–4 and IV. 9–12; Plutarch, *Alexander* 26–28 and 50–5; Curtius Rufus IV. 7. 5–16; IV. 7. 25–32; VIII. 5. 5–24; Diodorus Siculus XVII. 49–51 and XVIII. 8.

39 See note 2.

40 See also Elias (*olim* David), *Comment. in Porphyrii Isagogen et in Arist. Categorias*, CIAG, vol. XVIII, part 1 (ed. A. Busse, Berlin, 1900), p. 112, lines 24–7. A similar statement has been credited to Emperor Titus. See Suetonius, *The Lives of the Caesars* VIII (Titus). 1: 'On another occasion, remembering . . . that [as the Emperor] he [*scil.*, Titus] had done nothing for anyone all that day, he uttered that memorable and praiseworthy statement: "Friends, I have lost a day."' It cannot be determined, however, whether Suetonius was influenced here by some unidentifiable Alexandrian source which ascribed this dictum to Alexander. Xenophon, *Memorabilia* III. 9. 10–13, points out that he is not the true king who merely bears the title, but only he who practices εὐεργεσία and ἐνέργεια. I. Düring, *Aristotle in the Ancient Biographical Tradition* (Acta Universitatis Gotheburgensis, vol. XLIII, no. 2, Göteborg, 1957), p. 111, maintains that he had 'not been able to find this dictum ascribed to Alexander in any source earlier than Ptolemy [-el-Garib],' who wrote his *Vita Aristotelis* (from which the *Vita Aristotelis Marciana* and the *Vita Aristotelis Latina* are ultimately derived) probably during the first half of the fourth century A.D.

41 This is borne out, for instance, by the sordid Callisthenes incident. See Plutarch, *Alexander* 53 ff.; Arrian, *Anabasis* IV. 10–14; DL V. 5; Valerius Maximus VII. 2. 11; Curtius Rufus VIII. 8. 22. See also A.-H. Chroust, 'Aristotle and Callisthenes,' *Classical Folia*, vol. 20, no. 1 (1966), pp. 32–41, and Vol. I, Chapter VI. And there are many other incidents in the life of Alexander where the latter acted more like a god-like 'philosopher king' rather than like the follower of the sound advice given by Aristotle.

42 See, for instance, Plutarch, *Alexander* 55 and 77; Pliny, *Hist. Nat.* XXX. 53. 149; Arrian, *Anabasis* VII. 28; Zonaras, *Annales* IV. 14; Curtius Rufus X. 10; Dio Cassius LXXVII. 3; Diodorus Siculus XVII. 118; Dio Chrysostom, *Oratio* XLIV. 20. See also R. Merkelbach, *Die Quellen des griechischen Alexander-Romans* (Zetemata, vol. IX, Munich, 1954), pp. 126 ff.; M. Plezia, 'Arystotcles trucicielem Aleksandra wielkiego (Aristotle as the poisoner of Alexander),' *Meander*, vol. III (1948), pp. 492–501; W. Tarn, *Alexander the Great*, vol. II (Cambridge, 1948), pp. 301 ff.

## CONCLUSION

1 In a way, the Platonic Academy anticipated Matt. 28:19: 'Go ye therefore, and teach all nations. . . .' See also Mark 16:15. Historians of ancient philosophy as well as classicists are prone to overlook the fact that the

Academy was concerned not only with philosophic or political theory, but also with effective and often aggressive political action or reformatory activism. See, for instance, Plutarch, *Adversus Coloten* 32 (*Moralia* 1126D); A.-H. Chroust, 'Plato's Academy: the first organized school of political science in antiquity,' *Review of Politics*, vol. 29, no. 1 (1967), pp. 25–40.

2 G. E. R. Lloyd, *Aristotle: The Growth and Structure of his Thought* (Cambridge, 1968), p. 16, for instance, admits that 'the Aristotelian Corpus undoubtedly contains works which were not written by Aristotle himself.'

3 See Vol. I, Preface, text at the beginning.

4 E. Havelock's remarks are still in point:

> It will, I think, be readily granted by an audience of classicists that our own discipline is not partial to the use of theory and distrusts an *a priori* approach to any problem. A self-restraint which in other fields of knowledge might be viewed as cramping the style of the investigator by limiting the methodological choices open to him is by ourselves felt to be a matter of pride. This accords with my own recollections of a Cambridge classical training which, so it seems to me in retrospect, actively discouraged the use of general concepts and working hypotheses lest they lead to imaginative reconstructions based on assumptions which are not amenable to strict proof or controlled by evidence which was specific and concrete.

E. Havelock, 'Pre-literacy and pre-Socratics,' *Institute of Classical Studies*, University of London, Bulletin n. 13 (1966), p. 44.

5 It appears that unimaginative scholars are, as a rule, conservative, although conservative scholars are not necessarily unimaginative. See Part I, Introduction, note 29.


## POSTSCRIPT: WERNER JAEGER AND THE RECONSTRUCTION OF ARISTOTLE'S LOST WORKS

\* With certain modifications and omissions, this Postscript was first published in *Symbolae Osloenses*, fasc. 42 (1967), pp. 7–43. It is dedicated to the memory of a great scholar, inspiring teacher and generous friend: to Professor Werner W. Jaeger, who died in 1961. His matchless contributions to modern Aristotelian scholarship will forever be remembered and cherished.

1 See A.-H. Chroust, 'The first thirty years of modern Aristotelian scholarship (1912–1942),' *Classica et Mediaevalia*, vol. 24, fasc. 1–2 (1963–4), pp. 27–57. A German translation (and considerable expansion) of this paper was published in *Wege der Forschung: Aristoteles in der neueren Forschung* (ed. P. Moraux, Darmstadt, 1968), vol. I, pp. 95–143, under the title of 'Die Ersten Dreissig Jahre Moderner Aristoteles-Forschung (1912–1942).' All citations from Jaeger are from the English translation, *Aristotle: Funda-*

*mentals of the History of his Development* (Oxford, 1948). Jaeger's first attempt to come to grips critically with some problems of Aristotle's philosophic development dates back to his *Studien zur Entstehungsgeschichte der Metaphysik des Aristoteles* (Berlin, 1912).

2 In view of the manner in which Aristotle's 'intra-mural' or doctrinal treatises were transmitted after the death of Theophrastus, it is more than likely that some compositions of Theophrastus, Eudemus of Rhodes, Aristoxenus, Dicaerchus, Demetrius of Phaleron and other Early Peripatetics came to be incorporated in what is now collectively referred to as the *Corpus Aristotelicum.* See A.-H. Chroust, 'The miraculous disappearance and recovery of the *Corpus Aristotelicum,*' *Classica et Mediaevalia,* vol. 23, fasc. 1–2 (1962), pp. 50–67.

3 Jaeger believes that Aristotle left Athens and the Academy because of Plato's death in 348–47 B.C. The present author has attempted to show that Aristotle's flight from Athens took place in the summer or early fall of 348 B.C., that is, prior to the death of Plato, and that he departed from Athens for 'political reasons.' See A.-H. Chroust, 'Aristotle leaves the Academy,' *Greece and Rome,* vol. 14, no. 1 (1967), pp. 39–43, and Vol. I, Chapter IX. Jaeger is also of the opinion that upon his return to Athens in the year 335–34 B.C. Aristotle founded his own independent school, the Peripatus (or 'Lyceum'), and that he became the first scholarch of this new school. It is very doubtful, however, whether Aristotle ever established or owned an independent school of his own that was on a par with the Academy, or that he was the first scholarch of this school. Although Aristotle may be called the founder of Peripatetic philosophy, it would be more correct to call Theophrastus the founder and first scholarch of the Peripatus. It should also be noted that in his last will and testament (Diogenes Laertius V. 11–16) Aristotle never so much as mentions the school, the school property, the library or his successor in the scholarchate. Theophrastus (*ibid.,* V. 51–57), Straton of Lampsacus (*ibid.,* V. 61–64) and Lycon (*ibid.,* V. 69–74), on the other hand, refer at great length to a school and school property.

4 Jaeger does not take into account that already in the *On (the) Ideas* and the *On the Good,* usually dated between 357 and 355 B.C., Aristotle apparently disagreed with some of Plato's fundamental philosophic views. See note 14. Some scholars hold, however, that the *On (the) Ideas* and the *On the Good* were composed after 348–47 B.C. This also seems to be the view of Jaeger.

5 W. Jaeger, *Aristotle: Fundamentals of the History of his Development* (Oxford, 1948), pp. 29–30.

6 *Ibid.,* p. 30.

7 *Ibid.,* pp. 259 ff.

8 *Ibid.,* p. 326.

9 The *Eudemus or On the Soul,* for instance, still employs the Socratic (obstetric) formula of question and answer. See Plutarch, *Consolatio ad Apollonium* 27 (*Moralia* 115BE—frag. 44, Rose; frag. 6, Walzer; frag. 6,

Ross). It is also interesting to observe, Jaeger notes, that in some early dialogues Aristotle uses images and myths directly derived from Plato, such as the famous cave analogy (in the *On Philosophy*) or the apocalyptic pronouncement of Silenus (in the *Eudemus*), which seems to be an echo of Plato, *Republic* 617D ff. See W. Jaeger, *op. cit.*, p. 30.

10 See, for instance, Cicero, *Ad Atticum* XIII. 19. 4; Cicero, *Ad Quintum Fratrem* III. 5. 1; Cicero, *Ad Familiares* I. 9. 23; Plutarch, *De Virtute Morali* 7 (*Moralia* 447F ff.).

11 W. Jaeger, *op. cit.*, pp. 29-30. Jaeger points out (p. 29) that the literary change-over from the eristic or obstetric dialogue to the 'dialogue of scientific discussion,' was not perchance the result of a 'literary decline' but rather the product of an inevitable transition: 'The dialogue of discussion is simply an expression of the fact that the scientific element in Plato finally burst its form and remoulded it to suit itself. It was not a mere matter of aesthetics; it was a development of the philosophic mind, which necessarily produced its own new form.' *Ibid.*, p. 29.

12 See note 79.

13 It has been suggested that Aristotle's first (short) dialogues were headed by one-word titles (some borrowed from Plato). Later, when he proceeded to lengthier (and weightier) compositions which outwardly were still dialogues, but already displayed some of the features of the later treatises, he used titles beginning with 'On.' This theory, which cannot be substantiated and to which Jaeger does not subscribe, may be questioned.

14 W. Jaeger, *op. cit.*, p. 31. Jaeger's refusal to admit this third possibility is not altogether convincing. In the *On the Good* and the *On (the) Ideas*, both written about 357 and 355 B.C. (see A.-H. Chroust, 'The probable dates of some of Aristotle's lost works,' *Rivista Critica di Storia della Filosofia*, vol. 77, fasc. 1, 1967, pp. 3-23, especially pp. 8-11, and Chapter I), Aristotle certainly disagrees with some of Plato's basic tenets. See note 4. Adhering to his unique evolutionary thesis, Jaeger at times proceeds on the basis of the following *a priori* hypothesis or method: (1) during his active association with Plato (367-48 B.C.), Aristotle was a loyal Platonist; (2) there exist some early (and undeniably authentic) works of Aristotle which are critical of certain views held by Plato, something which he would not have done, or have dared to do, while Plato was still alive; (3) hence, these works must be dated after the death of Plato in 348-47 B.C. This is, for instance, the method by which Jaeger attempts to date the *On Philosophy*—see A.-H. Chroust (this note), pp. 19-22; A.-H. Chroust, 'The probable date of Aristotle's lost dialogue *On Philosophy*,' *Journal of the History of Philosophy*, vol. 4, no. 4 (1966), pp. 283-91, and Chapter XII. This form of argument or 'proof' might satisfy the formal logician, but it occasionally encounters difficulties in the face of historical facts.

15 It was this Platonism in the early works of Aristotle which induced V. Rose to declare all of the so-called lost writings of the Stagirite spurious. See V. Rose, *De Aristotelis Librorum Ordine et Auctoritate Commentatio* (Berlin,

1854), *passim*; V. Rose, *Aristoteles Pseudepigraphus* (Leipzig, 1863), *passim*. J. Bernays, *Die Dialoge des Aristoteles in ihrem Verhältnis zu seinen übrigen Werken* (Berlin, 1863), *passim*, does not deny the authenticity of these early compositions of Aristotle. He insists, however, that because of this unmistakable Platonism we must not take them seriously. From this, Bernays infers that Aristotle never was a Platonist.

16 The 'Platonism' of the early works of Aristotle (see also note 15) was first pointed out by C. A. Brandis, *Handbuch der Geschichte der griechisch-römischen Philosophie* (Berlin, 1835), vol. I, part 2, sect. 1, *passim*; C. A. Brandis, *De Perditis Aristotelis Libris de Ideis et de Bono sive de Philosophia* (Bonn, 1823), *passim*; F. Ravaisson, *Essai sur la Métaphysique d'Aristote* (Paris, 1835-46), pp. 219 ff.; V. Rose, *De Aristotelis Librorum Ordine et Auctoritate Commentatio* (Berlin, 1854), pp. 104 ff.; V. Rose, *Aristoteles Pseudepigraphus* (Leipzig, 1863), *passim*; E. Zeller, *Die Philosophie der Griechen in ihrer geschichtlichen Entwicklung* (2nd ed., Leipzig, 1861), vol. II, part 2, pp. 44 ff.; E. Zeller, *Die Philosophie der Griechen* (3rd ed., Leipzig, 1879), vol. II, part 2, pp. 50 ff., and *ibid.*, pp. 109 ff.; E. Heitz, *Die verlorenen Schriften des Aristoteles* (Leipzig, 1865), *passim*; R. Hirzel, 'Über den Protreptikos des Aristoteles,' *Hermes*, vol. X (1876), pp. 61 ff.; P. Hartlich, *De Exhortationum a Graecis Romanisque Scriptarum Historia et Indole* (Leipziger Studien zur Klassischen Philologie, vol. XI, no. 2, Leipzig, 1889), pp. 236 ff.; A. Gercke, article 'Aristoteles,' in Pauly-Wissowa, *Realencyklopädie der Classichen Altertumswissenschaft*, vol. II (Stuttgart, 1896), pp. 1012 ff.; T. Case, article 'Aristotle,' in *Encyclopaedia Britannica* (11th ed., Cambridge, 1910), vol. II, pp. 501 ff. For a summary of these views, see also A.-H. Chroust, 'The lost works of Aristotle in pre-Jaegerian scholarship,' *Classica et Mediaevalia*, vol. 25, fasc. 1-2 (1964-65), pp. 67-92. As early as 1910, T. Case, in his article on Aristotle (see this note), developed the thesis that Aristotle 'progressed' from an early Platonism to a later 'Aristotelianism.' Whether W. Jaeger was influenced by Case's thesis cannot be determined.

17 See W. Jaeger, *op. cit.*, pp. 33-8.

18 W. Jaeger, *op. cit.*, pp. 39-53. See also A.-H. Chroust, '*Eudemus or On the Soul*: a lost Aristotelian dialogue on the immortality of the soul,' *Mnemosyne*, vol. 19 (series 4), fasc. 1 (1966), pp. 17-30, and Chapter IV; A.-H. Chroust, 'The psychology in Aristotle's lost dialogue *Eudemus or On the Soul*,' *Acta Classica*, vol. IX (1966), pp. 49-62, and Chapter V.

19 W. Jaeger, *op. cit.*, p. 40.

20 O. Gigon, 'Prolegomena to an edition of the *Eudemus*,' *Aristotle and Plato in the Mid-Fourth Century* (Göteborg, 1960), p. 28 and p. 32, credits to the *Eudemus* certain fragments (dealing with the problems of the soul) which are commonly ascribed to the *On Philosophy*. See also A. Grilli, 'Cicerone e l'Eudemo,' *La Parola del Passato*, vol. 17 (1962), pp. 96-121. For the fragments usually credited to the *On Philosophy* and dealing with the soul, see A.-H. Chroust, 'The doctrine of the soul in Aristotle's lost dialogue

*On Philosophy,*' *New Scholasticism*, vol. 42, no. 3 (1968), pp. 364–73 and Chapter XV. In his proposed *Aristoteles' Dialog Eudemos: ein Versuch der Wiederherstellung*, O. Gigon intends to clarify these vexing problems which originally were created by V. Rose's rather arbitrary assignment of different fragments to different works. See A.-H. Chroust, 'The problems of the *Aristotelis Librorum Fragmenta*,' *Classical Journal*, vol. 62, no. 2 (1966), pp. 71–4.

21 The many ancient *consolationes mortis*, some of which may be under the influence of Aristotle's *Eudemus*, bring out these points.

22 Plutarch, *Consolatio ad Apollonium* 27 (*Moralia* 115E—frag. 44, Rose; frag. 6, Walzer; frag. 6, Ross).

23 Cicero, *De Divinatione ad Brutum* I. 25. 53 (frag. 37, Rose; frag. 1, Walzer; frag. 1, Ross).

24 W. Jaeger, *op. cit.*, pp. 51–2.

25 This is echoed by Cicero, *De Divinatione ad Brutum* I. 25, 53: '. . . when Eudemus' soul had left his body, it had returned home.'

26 Plato, *Phaedo* 93BD.

27 See, for instance, Philoponus, *Comment. in Arist. De Anima* (*CIAG*), vol. XV (ed., M. Hayduck, Berlin, 1897), p. 141, lines 21 ff. and pp. 144 ff. For details, see A.-H. Chroust, 'The psychology in Aristotle's lost dialogue *Eudemus or On the Soul*,' *Acta Classica*, vol. 9 (1966), pp. 49–62, and Chapter V.

28 This syllogism goes as follows: harmony admits of a 'more or less' (of degrees); the soul does not admit of a 'more or less'; hence, the soul cannot be harmony. See also Aristotle (?), *Categories* 3 b 24 ff.; 3 b 33 ff.; 6 b 15 ff. See W. Jaeger, *op. cit.*, p. 46, note 3. Jaeger's view that the *Categories* might be spurious is not unanimously accepted. See, for instance, K. von Fritz, 'Der Ursprung der aristotelischen Kategorienlehre,' *Archiv für Geschichte der Philosophie*, vol. 40 (1931), pp. 439–96, especially, pp. 450–1, note. It will be noted that, according to Plato, a 'more or less' can occur only in the indeterminate, but never in the determinate (such as the Idea). But whenever or wherever we have contraries, we also have a 'more or less.' Thus the proposition that a substance cannot admit of contraries. Since Aristotle apparently saw this, he was able to reduce these two arguments to one single argument or syllogism. Jaeger's comment is worth recording: '. . . Aristotle was completely independent of Plato in the sphere of logic and methodology. Though dependent on him for his view of the world, here he is quite free, and perhaps even has a slight feeling of superiority. His reduction of Plato's proof to its elements, and the technical excellence of the two proofs that he constructs out of them, reveal long experience in these things; and the knowledge embodied in the doctrine of the categories forms the presupposition of his corrections [of Plato].'

29 W. Jaeger, *op. cit.*, p. 48; Plutarch, *Consolatio ad Apollonium* 27 (*Moralia* 115BE—frag. 44, Rose; frag. 6, Walzer; frag. 6, Ross).

30 Plato, *Republic* 617C ff.

31 Plutarch (see note 29), 27 (*Moralia* 115 E).

32 See, for instance, Plato, *Philebus* 53C ff. This is also brought out in Aristotle's *Protrepticus* (Iamblichus, *Protrepticus* 48, 2–9, ed. H. Pistelli, Leipzig, 1888; frag. 60, Rose; frag. 10b, Walzer; frag. 10b, Ross; frag. 107, Düring; frag. 103, Chroust): 'Indeed, the union of the soul with the body strikes us as being very much such a punishment [for certain sins we have committed. See Aristotle, *Protrepticus* (Iamblichus, *Protrepticus* 47, 21–48, 2; frag. 60, Rose; frag. 10b, Walzer; frag. 10b, Ross; frag. 106, Düring; frag. 102, Chroust)]. For, as the Etruscans are said often to torture prisoners of war by chaining human carcasses face to face with living men, matching part with part, so also the soul seems to be stretched throughout the body as well as tied to the sensitive parts of the body.' This passage, which according to O. Gigon (see note 20) and others should be credited to the *Eudemus* rather than the *Protrepticus*, indicates that in the *Protrepticus* Aristotle still adheres to some views he advocated in the *Eudemus*. See here also Plato, *Cratylus* 400BC, where Plato maintains that 'the body is the grave of the soul,' that 'the soul is buried in our present life,' that 'the soul is suffering the punishment for sin [by being incarcerated in the body],' and that 'the body is the stockade or prison in which the soul is incarcerated . . . until the penalty is paid.' Empedocles (frag. 118, Diels-Kranz) and Philolaus (frag. 14, Diels-Kranz) held similar views.

33 W. Jaeger, *op. cit.*, pp. 48–9.

34 This latter view is held by Aristotle not only in *Metaphysics* 1070 a 24 (incidentally, an early part of the *Metaphysics*), but apparently also in the *Protrepticus*. See Iamblichus, *Protrepticus* (Pistelli) 48, 9–21 (frag. 61, Rose; frag. 10c, Walzer; frag. 10c, Ross; frags 108–10, Düring; frags 104–6, Chroust).

35 A similar notion can be found in Cicero, *Tusculanae Disputationes* I. 26. 65–27. 66 (frag. 27, Walzer; frag. 27, Ross; frag. 30, Untersteiner), a fragment commonly ascribed to the *On Philosophy*, but, according to O. Gigon (see note 20), part of the *Eudemus*: 'We, following this opinion [of Aristotle], have expressed it in these very words in our *Consolatio* [written on the occasion of Tullia's death, *note by the author*]: "The origin of minds [souls] is not to be found on earth. . . ." Whatever it is that feels, knows, lives and thrives must be celestial and divine and, hence, eternal [immortal].'

36 W. Jaeger, *op. cit.*, pp. 48–9, points out that with Aristotle the apocalyptic pessimism voiced by Silenus (Plutarch, *Consolatio ad Apollonium* 27, 115BE) is not just a restatement of the general pessimistic *Weltanschauung* which permeated the Greek mind when it believed that there is no hope either in this world or in the other world. What Aristotle wishes to convey here is the Platonic notion that there is a perfect 'other world' and that it is best for the soul not to leave the perfect 'other world' and become incarcerated or entangled in this imperfect world—not to become part of 'Becoming.' Because 'Becoming' is opposed to 'Being' as imperfection is opposed to perfection. See Plato, *Philebus* 53C ff. Hence, the real meaning of Silenus'

utterance is that man, since he has left the world of perfect Being, should return to this world of perfect Being as soon as possible. This, however, implies the belief in the existence of a perfect world of Being, that is, a belief in the world of the Platonic Separate Ideas.

37 Proclus, *Comment. in Plat. Rempublicam* (ed. W. Kroll, Leipzig, 1901), vol. II, p. 349, lines 13–26 (frag. 41, Rose; frag. 5, Walzer; frag. 5, Ross): 'In their journey from health to disease some people forget even the letters they once have learned, but . . . no one ever has this experience when passing from disease to health. . . .'

38 *Ibid.*: 'Life without the body, being natural to souls, is like health, and . . . life in the body, being unnatural, is like disease. For there they live according to nature, but here contrary to nature. . . .'

39 W. Jaeger, *op. cit.*, pp. 43–4.

40 See, for instance, Plato, *Republic* 591B ff., *et passim*; Plato, *Philebus* 25D ff. and 26B, *et passim*; Plato, *Laws* 631C, *et passim*.

41 In Plato, *Phaedo* 73A ff., and in Plato, *Meno* 86A, recollection constitutes a proof for the immortality of the soul.

42 Proclus (see note 37); W. Jaeger, *op. cit.*, pp. 52–3.

43 W. Jaeger, *op. cit.*, pp. 52–3 and p. 46.

44 It is quite possible that aside from the *Phaedo*, the Aristotelian *Eudemus* was also influenced by Plato's *Meno*, *Phaedrus*, *Theaetetus* and *Philebus*.

45 W. Jaeger, *op. cit.*, p. 49.

46 The ultimate confirmation or refutation of Jaeger's analysis of the *Eudemus* will have to await publication of O. Gigon's *Aristoteles' Dialog Eudemos: ein Versuch der Wiederherstellung*. See note 20.

47 See W. Jaeger, *op. cit.*, p. 39.

48 W. Jaeger, *op. cit.*, pp. 54–101.

49 See W. Jaeger, 'On the origin and cycle of the philosophic ideal of life,' Appendix II, in W. Jaeger, *op. cit.*, pp. 426 ff., especially pp. 438 ff. For a discussion of this 'sequence,' see A.-H. Chroust, 'Some comments on Aristotle's major works on ethics,' *Laval Théologique et Philosophique*, vol. 21, no. 1 (1965), pp. 63–79. See also notes 86 and 117.

50 See A.-H. Chroust, 'A brief account of the reconstruction of Aristotle's *Protrepticus*,' *Classical Philology*, vol. 60, no. 4 (1965), pp. 229–39, especially, pp. 231–2, and Chapter VII. Attempts at reconstructing the Aristotelian *Protrepticus* have been made by I. Düring, *Aristotle: Protrepticus—An Attempt at Reconstruction* (Studia Graeca et Latina Gothoburgensia, vol. XII, Göteborg, 1961); and by A.-H. Chroust, *Aristotle's Protrepticus: A Reconstruction* (Notre Dame, 1964). W. D. Rabinowitz, *Aristotle's Protrepticus and the Sources of its Reconstruction* (Univ. of California Publications in Classical Philology, vol. 16, no. 1, Berkeley, 1957), *passim*, insists that in light of the present 'source situation' it is well-nigh impossible to reconstruct this work intelligently and convincingly. See also notes 66, 104 and 133.

51 W. Jaeger, *Aristotle: Fundamentals of the History of his Development* (Oxford, 1948), p. 30; p. 55; p. 60; p. 62.

52 The *Nicocles*, the *Ad Nicoclem* and the *Ad Evagoram*. We might mention here also Isocrates' *Antidosis*. In all likelihood, Aristotle's *Protrepticus* is a rebuttal of Isocrates' *Antidosis*. This view is held, for instance, by E. Einarson, 'Aristotle's *Protrepticus* and the structure of the *Epinomis*,' *Transactions and Proceedings of the American Philological Association*, vol. 67 (Ithaca, 1936), pp. 261-85. P. von der Mühll, 'Isocrates und der *Protreptikos des Aristoteles*,' *Philologus*, vol. 94 (1939/40), pp. 259-65, on the other hand, maintains that the *Antidosis* is a reply to the *Protrepticus*. The view of von der Mühll was accepted by A. Lesky, *Geschichte der Griechischen Literatur* (2nd ed., Berne-Munich, 1963), p. 600; and by R. Stark, in *Göttinger Gelehrter Anzeiger*, no. 217 (1965), p. 57. The *Antidosis* is usually dated about 353-52 B.C.

53 The *Protrepticus*, Jaeger points out, is addressed, not 'dedicated,' to Themison, a sort of 'king' or 'ruler' on the island of Cyprus. See Jaeger (note 51), p. 54 and pp. 56 ff.; A.-H. Chroust, 'What prompted Aristotle to address the *Protrepticus* to Themison?,' *Hermes*, vol. 94, no. 2 (1966), pp. 202-7, and Chapter IX.

54 See Elias, *Comment. in Porphyrii Isagogen et in Aristotelis Categorias*, CIAG, vol. XVIII, part 1 (ed. A. Busse, Berlin, 1900), p. 3, lines 17-23; David, *Prolegomena et in Porphyrii Isagogen*, CIAG, vol. XVIII, part 2 (ed. A. Busse, Berlin, 1904), p. 9, lines 2-12. See also frag. 51, Rose; frag. 2, Walzer; frag. 2, Ross.

55 It may be noted that the Platonic Academy by no means limited its activities to purely theoretic contemplation. See A.-H. Chroust, 'Plato's Academy: the first organized school of political science in antiquity,' *Review of Politics*, vol. 29, no. 1 (1967), pp. 25-40.

56 W. Jaeger, *op. cit.*, p. 79.

57 *Ibid.*, pp. 55-57.

58 Jaeger's insistence that the *Protrepticus* is also a rejoinder to Isocrates, specifically to the *Antidosis* (published about 353-52 B.C.), is a major contribution to the proper dating and interpretation of the *Protrepticus*. See also note 52.

59 This is brought out in W. Jaeger, *Paideia*, vol. II (Oxford and New York, 1943), *passim*, which discusses brilliantly the educational and cultural ideals of Isocrates.

60 Iamblichus, *Protrepticus* 40, 1-11 (frag. 52, Rose; frag. 5, Walzer; frag. 5, Ross; frag. 53, Düring; frag. 50, Chroust). The author of the *Ad Demonicum* 19, presumably a disciple of Isocrates, strongly objects to the educational policy advocated by the *Protrepticus*. Hence, W. Jaeger, *Aristotle: Fundamentals of the History of his Development*, pp. 58-60, correctly maintains that the *Ad Demonicum* is also a rejoinder to Aristotle's *Protrepticus*, written by a disciple of Isocrates.

61 I. Bywater, 'On a lost dialogue of Aristotle,' *Journal of Philology*, vol. II (1869), pp. 55-69. Bywater's important discovery, it will be noted, was made possible by J. Bernays' research which brought to light the interest

of the Neo-Platonists in the early and earliest works of Aristotle. See note 63. Bywater's thesis, on the other hand, made obsolete Bernays' suggestion that we must look to Cicero's *Hortensius* for the possible retrieval and reconstruction of the Aristotelian *Protrepticus*. J. Bernays (see note 15), pp. 116 ff. and pp. 119 ff. Bywater failed, however, to delimit accurately the several individual fragments or groups of fragments of the Aristotelian *Protrepticus* as they are believed to be contained in Iamblichus' *Protrepticus*. He also failed to note the pronounced Platonism of these fragments (*pace* Düring), the very quality which induced V. Rose to declare them spurious. See note 14; A.-H. Chroust, 'A brief account of the reconstruction of Aristotle's *Protrepticus*,' *Classical Philology*, vol. 60, no. 4 (1965), pp. 229-30, and Chapter VII.

62 W. Jaeger, *op. cit.*, pp. 60 ff.

63 *Ibid.* Already J. Bernays had called attention to the predilection of Neo-Platonic authors for the early works of Aristotle. This interest, noted Bernays, was owing to an amalgam of Platonic and Aristotelian notions—characteristic of these early works—which would appeal to the syncretist Neo-Platonists. See note 61.

64 R. Hirzel (see note 16), pp. 83 ff.

65 P. Hartlich (see note 16), pp. 209-72, especially, pp. 236 ff.

66 W. Jaeger, *op. cit.*, pp. 61 ff. Jaeger rejects the suggestion made by R. Hirzel that in addition to the Aristotelian *Protrepticus*, Iamblichus also made use of some other early writings of Aristotle. H. Flashar, 'Platon und Aristoteles im *Protreptikos* des Jamblichos,' *Archiv für Geschichte der Philosophie*, vol. 47 (1965), maintains, however, that in all likelihood Iamblichus quoted here from several Aristotelian works. See also A.-H. Chroust, 'An emendation to fragment 13 (Walzer, Ross) of Aristotle's *Protrepticus*,' *Tijdschrift voor Filosofie*, vol. 28, no. 2 (1966), pp. 366-77, and Chapter VIII, who claims that in his *Protrepticus* Iamblichus cites also from Aristotle's *Politicus*. See notes 104 and 133.

67 Jaeger admits, however, that chapter V, which contains elements from the writings of Plato and other authors, might also quote from Aristotle's *Protrepticus*. But these passages are too indefinite to credit them confidently to Aristotle.

68 W. Jaeger, *op. cit.*, pp. 62 ff. and p. 79.

69 With varying success, this was done by H. Gadamer, 'Der aristotelische *Protreptikos* und die entwicklungsgeschichtliche Betrachtung der aristotelischen Ethik,' *Hermes*, vol. 63 (1928), pp. 142-5; I. Düring, 'Problems in Aristotle's *Protrepticus*,' *Eranos*, vol. 52 (1954), pp. 139-71; I. Düring, 'Aristotle in the *Protrepticus*,' *Autour d'Aristote* (Louvain, 1955), pp. 81-97; I. Düring, *Aristotle: Protrepticus—An Attempt at Reconstruction* (Göteborg, 1961), p. 37 and pp. 106-9; S. Mansion, 'Contemplation and action in Aristotle's *Protrepticus*,' *Aristotle and Plato in the Mid-Fourth Century* (Göteborg, 1960), pp. 56-75; K. Gaiser, 'Protreptic and Paränese bei Platon,' *Tübinger Beiträge zur Altertumswissenschaft*, vol. 40 (Tübingen,

1959), pp. 217–22; A.-H. Chroust, *Aristotle: Protrepticus—A Reconstruction* (Notre Dame, 1964), pp. xvi–xvii, *et passim*. See also A.-H. Chroust (note 61), pp. 234–5, and Chapter VII.

70 See W. Jaeger, *op. cit.*, pp. 64 ff.:

> But the hope that he [*scil.*, Iamblichus] has preserved for us undamaged whole trains of arguments from Aristotle's *Protrepticus* unfortunately turns out to be illusory. . . . He has used Aristotle's ideas as building stones, and crudely forced them into his own miserable framework. No trace of the original architecture remains. . . . Iamblichus' arrangement of his material is superficial. . . . The chapters in which he has articulated this train of thought [*scil.*, a connected proof for the independent value of philosophy], though outwardly polished, are pretty crude and violent combinations of Aristotelian materials. Their outward conjunction does not allow us to infer that they are undamaged, or that they really belong together. . . . The 'chapters' are phantom buildings. They crumble as soon as one taps the brittle mortar that holds their members in place. Only the members themselves, falling out of their settings, will stand investigation. . . .

71 In view of the fact that throughout his *Protrepticus* Iamblichus quotes rather liberally from Plato—quotations which are readily identifiable—it is rather puzzling that in *Protrepticus* 36,27–60,10, Iamblichus' reliance on Plato's *Euthydemus* should be so indefinite, provided he relies at all on Plato's *Euthydemus*.

72 Jaeger is convinced that Plato, *Euthydemus* 278E–282D, provided the protreptic archetype for Aristotle's *Protrepticus*. See p. 254. This view is not shared by all scholars. See W. Jaeger, *op. cit.*, p. 30; p. 55; pp. 62 ff.

73 W. Jaeger, *op. cit.*, pp. 64 ff.; p. 73; 79.

74 W. Jaeger, *op. cit.*, p. 61, calls the *Protrepticus* of Iamblichus 'a sorry piece of work.'

75 These texts were collected by I. Düring, *Aristotle's Protrepticus: An Attempt at Reconstruction* (Göteborg, 1961), pp. 112–47.

76 It is this lack of intelligent organization and adequate understanding of philosophic problems by Iamblichus which, in Jaeger's opinion, accounts for the impression that the passages credited to Aristotle constitute a seriously contradictory and often heterogeneous *mélange* of confused notions, unworthy of a first-rate thinker. These undeniable shortcomings, which may be attributed solely to Iamblichus' ineptitude (he arranged his excerpts quite arbitrarily according to subject matter rather than according to Aristotle's original presentation), undoubtedly are responsible for the reluctance of R. Hirzel, V. Rose, P. Hartlich and others to accept these passages as originally Aristotelian.

77 See, for instance, W. Jaeger, *op. cit.*, pp. 67 ff.; p. 78; 86; 88; pp. 232 ff.; 261 ff.

78  W. Jaeger, *op. cit.*, pp. 63 ff.

79  See Cicero, *De Inventione* II. 2. 6; Cicero, *De Oratore* I. 11. 49; Cicero, *Topica* I. 3; Cicero, *De Finibus* I. 5. 14; Cicero, *Academica* II. 38. 119; Quintilian, *De Verborum Compositione* X. 1. 83; Dionysius of Halicarnassus, *De Cens. Vet. Scriptorum* 4. See also A.-H. Chroust, *Aristotle: Protrepticus— A Reconstruction* (Notre Dame, 1964), p. XI; A.-H. Chroust, 'The first thirty years of modern Aristotelian scholarship (1912–1942),' *Classica et Mediaevalia* vol. 24, fasc. 1–2 (1963–64), p. 35; A.-H. Chroust (see note 61), pp. 229–39, and Chapter VII. Jaeger's contributions to the recovery and reconstruction of the Aristotelian *Protrepticus*, it will be noted, also include the discovery of certain references to the *Protrepticus* in the later or doctrinal treatises of Aristotle as, for instance, in the *Metaphysics*, the *Eudemian Ethics* and in the *Nicomachean Ethics*.

80  Frags 6–7, Walzer; frags 6–7, Ross (41,6–15 omitted); frags 41, 59–70, 72, 71, 74–7, and 73, Düring; frags 39, 55–6; 68, 67, and 69–73, Chroust.

81  W. Jaeger, *op. cit.*, pp. 65 ff.

82  Frag. 6, Walzer; frag. 6, Ross; frag. 41, Düring; frag. 39, Chroust. The last part of this fragment might be spurious.

83  W. Jaeger, *op. cit.*, p. 66.

84  I. Düring, for instance, suggests the following sequence: 41,15–43,25; 43,27–44,9; 43,25–27; and 44,9–45,3. Thus Düring follows rather closely the sequence observed by Iamblichus.

85  Iamblichus, *Protrepticus* 43,25–27, is probably an addition or insertion by Iamblichus himself, a view not shared by I. Düring.

86  W. Jaeger, *op. cit.*, p. 67 and pp. 232 ff. It will be noted that, according to Jaeger, certain passages from the *Eudemian Ethics* fully correspond—in doctrinal content and idiom—to Iamblichus, *Protrepticus* 41,15–43,25. This fact, Jaeger believes, indicates that *Protrepticus* 41,15–43,25, is Aristotelian in origin. Further analysis suggests that Aristotle's *Protrepticus* to some extent constitutes the archetype for certain passages found in the *Eudemian Ethics*. This would also indicate, Jaeger surmises, that the *Eudemian Ethics* was composed in fairly close proximity to the Aristotelian *Protrepticus*. Moreover, it would also lend some support to Jaeger's thesis that the development of Aristotle's ethical writings progressed from the *Protrepticus* to the *Eudemian Ethics* and, finally, to the *Nicomachean Ethics*. See also notes 49 and 117.

87  Frag. 6, Walzer; frag. 6, Ross; frags 59–70, Düring; frags 55–66, Chroust.

88  Frag. 6, Walzer; frag. 6, Ross; frags 70, 72, 71, 74–7 and 73, Düring; frags 66, 68, 67, 69 and 70–3, Chroust.

89  W. Jaeger, *op. cit.*, pp. 69 ff.

90  *Ibid.*, p. 70, Jaeger maintains that since Iamblichus, *Protrepticus* 43,20–45,3, definitely goes beyond the scope and text of *Metaphysics* 980 a 21 ff., Iamblichus must have consulted the Aristotelian *Protrepticus* rather than the Aristotelian *Metaphysics*.

91  *Ibid.*, pp. 73–4.

92 Iamblichus, *Protrepticus* 37,22–41,5 (frag. 52, Rose; frag. 5, Walzer; frag. 5, Ross; frags 31–40 and 53–7, Düring; frags 29–38 and 50–4, Chroust).

93 The Platonism of this lengthy passage has been denied by I. Düring, but was re-affirmed by A.-H. Chroust, *Aristotle: Protrepticus—A Reconstruction* (Notre Dame, 1964), pp. 78–81.

94 Frag. 11, Walzer; frag. 11, Ross; frags 10–21, Düring; frags 10–20, Chroust.

95 W. Jaeger, *op. cit.*, p. 74. Jaeger also stresses the similarity of this particular passage with some of the views expressed in Book II of the Aristotelian *Physics* (incidentally, an early work). See, for instance, *Physics* 193 a 8 ff. It will be noted that essentially the same idea reappears in *Metaphysics* 1025 a 23; 1032 a 12 ff.; 1070 a 6; 1070 a 17.

96 Frag. 11, Walzer; frag. 11, Ross; frag. 13, Düring; frag. 12, Chroust. This notion contains *in nucleo* some of the ancient theories of the origin and evolution of human civilization. W. Jaeger, *op. cit.*, p. 76, holds that Posidonius, who developed the thesis that art imitates nature into a comprehensive theory of the origin of human civilization, and the thesis that all advances in civilization are due to philosophic discoveries, might have derived these notions from the Aristotelian *Protrepticus*.

97 *Ibid.* See here also Aristotle, *Physics* 199 b 8 ff.; Aristotle, *Politics* 1337 a 1 ff.

98 Frag. 11, Walzer; frag. 11, Ross; frags 13–16, Düring; frags 12–15, Chroust.

99 Frag. 58, Rose; frag. 12, Walzer; frag. 12, Ross; frags 42–4, Düring; frags 40–2, Chroust.

100 See, for instance, Aristotle, *Metaphysics* 982 b 24 ff.; Aristotle, *Nicomachean Ethics* 1147 a 23 and 1096 b 16 ff.; Aristotle, *Politics* 1338 b 2 ff.

101 W. Jaeger, *op. cit.*, p. 73, insists that Cicero's *Hortensius* (frag. 50, Müller) contains a rendition of this Aristotelian argument which is superior to that recorded by Iamblichus. This can be verified, according to Jaeger, by a comparison of frag. 50, Müller, and Aristotle's *Nicomachean Ethics* 1178 a 24 ff. Cicero points out that on the 'Islands of the Blessed' we would need neither practical skills nor virtues, but only rational knowledge and pure contemplation. In *Nicomachean Ethics* 1178 a 24 ff., Aristotle avers that the life of action requires many 'aids,' while the 'pure knower' needs no external 'aids' to exercise knowledge.

102 Frags 13–15, Walzer; frags 13–15, Ross; frags 46–51 and 78–96, Düring; frags 43–8 and 74–92, Chroust.

103 Frag. 13, Walzer; frag. 13, Ross; frags 46–51, Düring; frags 43–8, Chroust.

104 W. Jaeger, *op. cit.*, pp. 76–7. *Protrepticus* 55,7–56,2, however, has also been credited to Aristotle's *Politicus* rather than to the *Protrepticus*. See, for instance, H. Flashar (note 66), pp. 77–8; A.-H. Chroust (see note 66), especially pp. 371 ff., and Chapter VIII. See also notes 66 and 133.

105 W. Jaeger, *op. cit.*, p. 77. Jaeger believes that Aristotle's reference to the alleged 'model constitutions' of Crete and Sparta (55,20) contains an attack upon Isocrates and his pragmatic views about the nature and function of

the state. Book II of the Aristotelian *Politics*, which discusses the constitutions of Sparta, Crete and Carthage, might be related to the *Protrepticus*. See also W. Jaeger, *op. cit.*, pp. 261 ff.

106 Frag. 14, Walzer; frag. 14, Ross; frags 78–92, Düring; frags 74–88, Chroust.

107 W. Jaeger, *op. cit.*, pp. 77–8.

108 This may be gathered, for instance, from *Nicomachean Ethics* 1172 b 15 ff., where we are informed that Eudoxus of Cnidus had declared pleasure the highest good.

109 Frag. 14, Walzer; frag. 14, Ross; frags 87–92, Düring; frags 83–8, Chroust. Plato discusses the problem of intellectual pleasures in *Philebus* 52A ff. and 60A.

110 Similar views can be found in Aristotle, *Eudemian Ethics*, *passim*. Jaeger, *op. cit.*, pp. 232–58, holds that there exist close connections between the *Protrepticus* and the *Eudemian Ethics*.

111 Frag. 15, Walzer; frag. 15, Ross; frags 93–5, Düring; frags 89–91, Chroust. Both Düring (frag. 96) and Chroust (frag. 92) include 60, 7–10 among the authentic fragments.

112 W. Jaeger, *op. cit.*, p. 79. Jaeger apparently does not realize that chapter VII (48, 9–21) in all likelihood contains this concluding remark. See frag. 61, Rose; frag. 10c, Walzer; frag. 10c, Ross; frags 108–110, Düring; frags 104–6, Chroust. As O. Gigon (see note 20) and others have pointed out, this passage might originally have been part of the *Eudemus*.

113 I. Bywater (see note 61), pp. 55 ff.

114 Neither I. Düring (see note 75), nor A.-H. Chroust (see note 93), include Iamblichus, *Protrepticus* 60,10–61,4, among the authentic fragments of Aristotle's *Protrepticus*. R. Walzer (frag. 15) and W. D. Ross (frag. 15), on the other hand, include 60,10–15.

115 W. Jaeger, *op. cit.*, p. 79: 'But to suggest that he [*scil.*, Aristotle] is the author of the conclusion actually found in Iamblichus (p. 60,7–61,4) is to let desire stifle critical reflection. Enthusiastic the sentences may be, and even inspired; but it is not the controlled enthusiasm of Aristotle, who never forgoes the strict rhythm of his apodictic advance, and values form higher than the highest inspiration, often as his arguments perceptively overflow with the latter.'

116 W. Jaeger, *op. cit.*, pp. 72 ff. and pp. 79 ff.

117 This also becomes manifest in the 'panegyric analogy' referred to in 53,15–54,5 (frag. 58, Rose; frag. 12, Walzer; frag. 12, Ross; frag. 44, Düring; frag. 42, Chroust), which extolls pure intellectual contemplation above all other activities. It may be observed here that the three types of people who congregate at the Panhellenic Games—the 'vendors,' the athletes and the 'pure spectators'—correspond to the three basic ways of life: the pleasurable life, the virtuous (active) life and the contemplative life. See also Plato, *Republic* 580D ff. and 581C; Plato, *Symposium* 204D; Aristotle, *Eudemian Ethics* 1214 a 30 ff.; Iamblichus, *Protrepticus* 41,6–15

(frag. 6, Walzer; frag. 6, Ross; frag. 41, Düring; frag. 39, Chroust). For the 'panegyric analogy' see also Cicero, *Tusculanae Disputationes* V. 3. 8-10; Iamblichus, *Vita Pythagorae* (ed. A. Nauck, St. Petersburg, 1884), pp. 55 ff.; Diogenes Laertius I. 12, and *ibid.*, VIII. 8; Athenaeus, *Deipnosophistae* XI. 463DE. See also A.-H. Chroust, 'Some reflections on the origin of the term "philosopher,"' *New Scholasticism*, vol. 28, no. 4 (1964), pp. 423-34; A.-H. Chroust, 'The term "philosopher" and the panegyric analogy in Aristotle's *Protrepticus*,' *Apeiron*, vol. I, no. 1 (1966), pp. 14-17, and Chapter X.

118 The term *phronesis*, as it is used in the Aristotelian *Protrepticus*, has been translated in a great variety of ways: wisdom, philosophic wisdom (as distinguished from practical wisdom), philosophic knowledge, theoretic knowledge, intuitive wisdom, etc. To translate it as 'practical wisdom,' thus giving it the meaning this term has in Aristotle's later doctrinal works, is not permissible, however.

119 W. Jaeger, *op. cit.*, p. 81. As previously suggested (see note 118), the term *phronesis* undergoes a radical change of meaning and connotation in Aristotle's later works. See, for instance, Aristotle, *Nicomachean Ethics* 1140 a 25 ff.; 1141 a 25 ff.; 1141 b 4 ff., *et passim*. Here *phronesis* signifies a 'habit' or 'disposition' of the mind to deliberate in a thoroughgoing practical manner about everything concerning human affairs. This usage effectively recants the Platonic concept of *phronesis* as the theoretic speculation which Aristotle had advocated in the *Protrepticus*.

120 Iamblichus, *Protrepticus* 48,16-18 (frag. 61, Rose; frag. 10c, Walzer; frag. 10c, Ross; frag. 110, Düring; frag. 106, Chroust).

121 Iamblichus, *Protrepticus* 39,20-41,1 (frag. 52, Rose; frag. 5, Walzer; frag. 5, Ross; frag. 40, Düring; frag. 38, Chroust). The Platonic tenor of this passage is unmistakable. In this fragment, which is definitely a part of the Aristotelian *Protrepticus*, Aristotle mentions (or refers to) Plato's four cardinal virtues. See also W. Jaeger, *op. cit.*, p. 85; Iamblichus, *De Communi Mathematica Scientia Liber* (ed. N. Festa, Leipzig, 1891), p. 79, line 1 to p. 81, line 7.

122 W. Jaeger, *op. cit.*, p. 83. The *Protrepticus*, according to Jaeger, also reflects a general change of attitude towards philosophy—a change which took place within the Academy and which becomes manifest in Plato's later dialogues: the 'practical' Socrates is no longer the 'philosophic ideal of life.' He is replaced by the 'ideal of the purely theoretic life' based on *phronesis*. See W. Jaeger, 'On the origin and cycle of the philosophic ideal of life,' W. Jaeger, *op. cit.*, Appendix II, p. 431 and p. 437.

123 Iamblichus, *Protrepticus* 54,22-55,7 (frag. 13, Walzer; frag. 13, Ross; frag. 47, Düring; frag. 44, Chroust). See also notes 81-3.

124 Iamblichus, *Protrepticus* 55,7-25 (frag. 13, Walzer; frag. 13, Ross; frags 48-9, Düring; frags 45-6, Chroust). It has already been pointed out (see notes 66 and 104) that 55,7-56,2 might possibly be credited to Aristotle's *Politicus* rather than to the *Protrepticus*.

125 W. Jaeger, *op. cit.*, p. 85. It should be noted, however, that in *Nicomachean Ethics* 1098 a 26 ff. Aristotle identifies the true statesman with the practical carpenter, who inquires into the principles of geometry only as far as this might be necessary for the kind of practical work he performs.

126 This follows from Iamblichus, *Protrepticus* 54,22–55,25, quoted in the text, p. 250.

127 Plato, *Philebus* 56B ff.; 57C ff.; 58C; 59A; 66A. See also Plato, *Laws* 716C. For a more detailed discussion of these problems, see A.-H. Chroust (note 66), pp. 373–4 and Chapter VIII.

128 W. Jaeger, *op. cit.*, pp. 87–90.

129 Iamblichus, *De Communi Mathematica Scientia Liber* (ed. N. Festa), p. 80,1 ff. (frag. 52, Rose; frag. 5, Walzer; frag. 5, Ross). Jaeger's view, not universally accepted, is that the *De Communi Mathematica Scientia Liber* relies heavily on the Aristotelian *Protrepticus*.

130 Plato, *Philebus* 56D and 57D.

131 For a merciless critique of Plato's political philosophy, a critique of which Jaeger would never have approved, see A.-H. Chroust, 'A second (and closer) look at Plato's political philosophy,' *Archiv für Rechts- und Sozialphilosophie*, vol. 48, no. 4 (1962), pp. 449–86. But then it should always be borne in mind that Plato's *Republic* is also a sort of 'monastic program.' See Chapter XVII, note 15.

132 See also Aristotle, *Politicus* (DL V. 22, no. 4; *VH* 10, no. 4), where, according to Syrianus, *Comment. in Arist. Metaphysics*, CIAG, vol. VI, part 1 (ed. W. Kroll, Berlin, 1902), p. 168, lines 33–5 (frag. 79, Rose; frag. 2, Ross), Aristotle states that 'the good is the most accurate measure [of all measures?].' This fragment traditionally has been credited to the Aristotelian *Politicus*. See note 133; A.-H. Chroust, 'Aristotle's *Politicus*: a lost dialogue,' *Rheinisches Museum*, vol. 108, no. 4 (1965), pp. 346–53 and Chapter XI.

133 Iamblichus, *Protrepticus* 54,22–56,2 (frag. 13, Walzer; frag. 13, Ross; frags 47–50, Düring; frags 44–7, Chroust). It has been argued, however, that Iamblichus, *Protrepticus* 55,7–56,2 should be assigned to Aristotle's *Politicus* rather than to the Aristotelian *Protrepticus*. See notes 66, 104 and 124. If this be so, then Jaeger's argument would lose some of its force, but it would not seriously affect or defeat Jaeger's main thesis that the Aristotelian *Protrepticus* is essentially Platonic.

134 See, for instance, Plato, *Republic* 476C; 484B; 500BC; 501C ff.; 581B ff.; *et passim*. See also what Plato has to say about the 'philosopher king.' *Ibid.*, 473C; 499B ff.; 501E. In *Cratylus* 436A ff., Plato insists that reliance on second-hand knowledge rather than on first-hand knowledge (Ideas) leads to inaccuracy and error. See also Plato, *Timaeus* 50C ff. and 51A; *Parmenides* 135BC; *Statesman* 293A ff.; *Sophist* 249CD and 254A; etc.

135 See, for instance, Plato, *Republic* 599A; 600A; 602C; 603A; 605B; *et passim*.

136 Iamblichus, *Protrepticus* 55,7–56,2 (frag. 13, Walzer; frag. 13, Ross; frags

48–50, Düring; frags 45–7, Chroust). Plato, *Statesman* 296E ff. and *Republic* 488E, likewise compares the statesman to a helmsman. The observations made in notes 50, 66, 104, 124 and 133 also apply here.

137 In *Republic* 409B Plato admits, however, that a good judge should also have learned from experience and observation.

138 Iamblichus, *Protrepticus* 38,3–14 and 38,22–39,4 (frag. 62, Rose; frag. 5, Walzer; frag. 5, Ross; frags 33 and 35, Düring; frags 31 and 33, Chroust). The Platonic doctrine of the Separate Ideas implies: (a) that the Idea (the 'better') is more knowable than the corporeal thing (the 'lesser,' *Republic* 505A and 532A ff.); (b) that the Idea (the 'prior') is more knowable than the corporeal thing (the 'posterior,' *Republic* 475E ff.; *Symposium* 211BC); (c) that the 'determinate' and 'ordered' (the Idea) is more knowable than the 'indeterminate' (the corporeal thing, *Republic* 479E; 500BC; 587A; 619CD; *Philebus* 59C ff.; *Phaedrus* 256AB; *Phaedo* 79A; *Statesman* 305CD; *Timaeus* 47DE; *Laws* 780E); (d) that the better is more 'determinate' and more 'ordered' than the lesser (*Gorgias* 504A ff.; *Philebus* 64D ff. and 66A; *Timaeus* 30A); (e) that the Ideas as the 'causes' of corporeal things are more knowable than the corporeal things (the 'effects' of the Ideas, *Republic* 508E ff. and 509D); (f) that the 'prior' is 'more cause' than the 'posterior' (*ibid.*); and (g) that if we were to do away with the Ideas (or first principles) we would utterly destroy the power of reasoning and, hence, make true knowledge simply impossible (*Parmenides* 135BC). It might be interesting to note that in his later works Aristotle rejected some views which he had advocated in his *Protrepticus*. See, for instance, Aristotle, *Metaphysics* 1017 b 18 ff. and 1090 b 5 ff.; etc.

139 Iamblichus, *Protrepticus* 39,4–6 (frag. 52, Rose; frag. 5, Walzer; frag. 5, Ross; frag. 36, Düring; frag. 34, Chroust). Aristotle continues: 'For how could we possibly recognize speech if we did not know the syllables, or know syllables, if we knew none of the letters?'

140 W. Jaeger, *op. cit.*, pp. 94–9.

141 See, for instance, Iamblichus, *Protrepticus* 47,21–48,21 (frags 60 and 61, Rose; frags 10b and 10c, Walzer; frags 10b and 10c, Ross; frags 106–10, Düring; frags 102–6, Chroust). Plato's pessimistic outlook as regards this world is too well known to require special comment.

142 Iamblichus, *Protrepticus* 47,23–48,3 (frag. 60, Rose; frag. 10b, Walzer; frag. 10b, Ross; frags 106–7, Düring; frags 102–3, Chroust).

143 W. Jaeger, *op. cit.*, pp. 98–101. See also notes 29–32 and the corresponding text. It has already been shown that some scholars wish to credit these 'pessimistic' passages to the Aristotelian *Eudemus*. See, for instance, note 32.

144 Iamblichus, *Protrepticus* 47,5–48,21 (frags 59–61, Rose; frags 10a, 10b and 10c, Walzer; frags 10a, 10b and 10c, Ross; frags 104–5 and 108–10, Düring; frags 100–1 and 104–6, Chroust).

145 See, for instance, Plato, *Phaedo* 66B ff.; *Sophist* 216BC; *Phaedrus* 252D; *Theaetetus* 176AB; *Republic* 500D and 613AB; *Crito* 48B; *Laws* 661BD and 707D; *Gorgias* 512AB; *et passim*.

146 See, for instance, Plato, *Phaedo* 67C; 61B; 64E ff.; *Republic* 486A.

147 See, for instance, I. Düring (note 75), *passim*. Despite his superb scholarship, Düring's attempt to prove the 'Aristotelian' nature of the *Protrepticus* is not altogether convincing. A.-H. Chroust (see note 93), especially, in his 'brief comments' to the individual fragments, on the other hand, insists on the dominant Platonism of the *Protrepticus*. See also note 16.

148 See, however, note 3.

149 W. Jaeger, *op. cit.*, pp. 56–60. Jaeger is the first scholar to show the undeniable dependence of the *Ad Demonicum* on the Aristotelian *Protrepticus*. It is rather startling to realize that certain passages of the *Ad Demonicum* have not been used as 'fragments' of the Aristotelian *Protrepticus* or, at least, as corroborating evidence for the fact that Iamblichus' *Protrepticus* contains substantial (and reliable) fragments of the Aristotelian *Protrepticus*. See also P. Wendland, *Anaximenes of Lampsakos* (Berlin, 1905), pp. 92 ff.

150 See A.-H. Chroust, 'The probable dates of some of Aristotle's lost works,' *Rivista Critica di Storia della Filosofia*, vol. 22, fasc. 1 (1967), pp. 3–23, especially, pp. 13–17; and Chapter I. As regards the proper arrangement or sequence of the several fragments assigned to the Aristotelian *Protrepticus*, Jaeger does not make any detailed suggestions. He is aware of the fact, however, that Iamblichus' organization of the materials originally taken from Aristotle's *Protrepticus* is wholly arbitrary: Iamblichus re-arranges the Aristotelian materials according to certain topics and, hence, most likely does not follow the original Aristotelian order of presentation or sequence of argumentation. See text, p. 243.

151 It has already been noted that Jaeger's thesis concerning the 'break-away' of Aristotle from Plato and Platonism hinges on the authenticity of the later doctrinal treatises credited to Aristotle. Conversely, Aristotle's disagreements with certain aspects of Plato's philosophy as they become manifest, for instance, in the *On the Good*, the *On (the) Ideas* and the *On Philosophy*, might well be part of that general discussion about the ultimate nature of true reality which during the sixties and fifties enlivened the Academy. Plato's *Philebus* 15A and *Parmenides* 130B ff. seem to allude to these discussions and controversies. See also notes 4 and 14.

152 W. Jaeger, *op. cit.*, p. 125, attempts to explain this 'break-away' from Plato by pointing out that, after his departure from Athens and the Academy, Aristotle 'had to explain the Platonic philosophy on his own responsibility and according to his own conception of its nature.' This ingenious explanation overlooks, however, a number of pertinent facts: already during the fifties, Aristotle had disagreed with some of Plato's fundamental views. It is also known that during the lifetime of Plato, some members of the Academy took issue with certain teachings of the master. Perhaps A. Gercke's thesis is not entirely without merit. Aristotle, Gercke insists, fully accepted Plato's philosophy, at least for systematic reasons, although he modified some of its more detailed aspects. Concurrent with these efforts to systematize the metaphysical notions of Plato, Aristotle also

developed a penchant for collecting, investigating and classifying large amounts of empirical facts or data, something for which Plato had little interest. It was the confrontation of these two divergent tendencies and interests which, Gercke insists, ultimately induced Aristotle to go beyond the obvious limitations of Platonic philosophy—a philosophy which the Stagirite no longer considered adequate to cope successfully with empirical and historical facts. A. Gercke (see note 16), pp. 1012 ff., especially pp. 1034-9.

153 W. Jaeger, *op. cit.*, pp. 124 ff. Because the *On Philosophy* constitutes a 'break-away' from Plato's teachings, Jaeger, by employing a kind of *a priori* reasoning, dates this composition shortly after the death of Plato (348-47 B.C.). See here also A.-H. Chroust, 'The probable date of Aristotle's lost dialogue *On Philosophy*,' *Journal of the History of Philosophy*, vol. 4, no. 4 (1966), pp. 283-91 and Chapter XII. See also note 14.

154 W. Jaeger, *op. cit.*, p. 125.

155 Syrianus, *Comment. in Arist. Metaphys.*, CIAG, vol. VI, part 1 (ed. W. Kroll, Berlin, 1902), p. 159, lines 33 ff. (frag. 9, Rose; frag. 11, Walzer; frag. 11, Ross; frag. 13, Untersteiner). Syrianus quotes this passage from Book II of the *On Philosophy*.

156 Plutarch, *Adversus Coloten* 14 (*Moralia* 1115BC—frag. 8, Rose; frag. 10, Walzer; frag. 10, Ross; frag. 12, Untersteiner):

> With regard to the [Platonic] Ideas, about which Aristotle chides Plato, misrepresenting them completely and bringing every possible objection against them . . . in his popular dialogues [*scil.*, in the *On Philosophy*] he seemed to some to be polemic rather than philosophic in his attitude towards this doctrine, as though his object was to belittle Plato's philosophy. So far was he from accepting it.

157 Proclus, in Philoponus, *De Aeternitate Mundi* (ed. H. Rabe, Leipzig, 1899), p. 32, lines 5 ff. (frag. 8, Rose; frag. 10, Walzer; frag. 10, Ross; frag. 12, Untersteiner).

158 W. Jaeger, *op. cit.*, pp. 126-7. Jaeger also believes that it was possibly a member of the Academy who challenged Aristotle's motives in criticizing Plato and Plato's philosophy; that it was this charge which prompted Aristotle to publish his criticisms in the *On Philosophy*; and that by publishing these criticisms Aristotle tendered notice to a larger audience, including the other members of the Academy, of his disagreements with certain teachings prevailing in the Academy. This story calls to mind the report that Aristotle once allegedly remarked: '*Amicus quidam Socrates, sed magis amica veritas.*' See *VL* 28; *VV* 9; *VM* 28. The same idea is also brought out in Aristotle, *Nicomachean Ethics* 1096 a 12-17: 'It would perhaps be considered to be better and, indeed, to be our duty, for the sake of upholding the truth, even to deny what touches us most closely, especially since we are philosophers and lovers of wisdom (truth). For while both [friends and truth] are dear to us, piety requires us to honor truth above

our friends.' See also Plato, *Republic* 595B ff. Ancient authors, ostensibly hostile to Aristotle, claim that the latter had many unpleasant encounters with Plato, and that in his personal dealings with Plato he often acted from spite or jealousy. For a list as well as a discussion of the ancient authors who claimed that Aristotle opposed Plato's philosophy out of spite, see, I. Düring, *Aristotle in the Ancient Biographical Tradition* (Acta Universitatis Gothoburgensis, vol. 43, no. 2, Göteborg, 1957), pp. 318-32.

159 Cicero, *Ad Atticum* XIII. 19. 4. Jaeger, *op. cit.*, p. 127, holds that only in the *On Philosophy* and in the *Statesman* (*Politicus*), but in no other of the early dialogues, does Aristotle lead the discussion.

160 See Cicero, *Ad Atticum* IV. 16. 2.

161 *Metaphysics* 990 a 33 ff. See also *ibid.*, 1078 b 6 ff.

162 W. Jaeger, *op. cit.*, p. 128. It has already been pointed out that the *a priori* method employed by Jaeger to date the *On Philosophy* is open to challenge. See notes 3, 14 and 153. It should be borne in mind, however, that Jaeger's dating of the *On Philosophy*, after all, is approximately correct, although the particular reasons which he offers in support of his date may be questioned.

163 DL I. 8; Pliny, *Hist. Nat.* XXX. 3; Plutarch, *De Iside et Osiride* 46 (*Moralia* 370C—frags 6 and 34, Rose; frag. 6, Walzer; frag. 6, Ross; frags 3 and 11, Untersteiner). It will be noted that in Book A of the *Metaphysics* Aristotle limits himself to Greek philosophers, beginning with Thales. See Aristotle, *Metaphysics* 981 b 23. See also *Metaphysics* 1091 b 8 ff.; A.-H. Chroust, 'Aristotle and the philosophies of the east,' *Review of Metaphysics*, vol. 18, no. 3 (1965), pp. 572-80 and Chapter XVI.

164 Aristotle, for instance, inquires into the authenticity (and chronology) of the so-called Orphic poems, reaching the conclusion that the mystification of these Orphic poems dates back to Onomacritus (sixth century B.C.).

165 See frags 1-7, 13 and 34, Rose; frags 1-8, Walzer; frags 1-8, Ross; frags 1-11, Untersteiner.

166 W. Jaeger, *op. cit.*, p. 130, is also of the opinion that this sifting and organizing ultimately led Aristotle to believe that the same basic truths constantly reappear in human history. See, for instance, Aristotle, *De Caelo* 270 b 19 ff.: 'The same ideas, one must believe, occur and re-occur in the minds of men not just once, but again and again.' Aristotle, *Meteorologica* 339 b 28 ff.: 'The same opinions appear in cycles among men, not once nor twice, but infinitely many times.' Aristotle, *Metaphysics* 1074 b 10 ff.: 'Probably every art and every science has often been developed as far as this is possible, and again has disappeared.' See also Aristotle, *De Sophisticis Elenchis* 183 b 17 ff. Hence, Aristotle insists, 'it is necessary . . . that we consult the views . . . of our predecessors.' Aristotle, *De Anima* 403 b 20 ff. See also Aristotle, *Metaphysics* 993 b 11 ff.; Aristotle, *Rhetoric* 1355 a 18 ff. This belief, as well as his interest in 'proverbial wisdom,' prompted Aristotle to make a collection of Greek proverbs (DL V. 26, no. 138; *VH* 10, no. 129), on the ground that these proverbs are the survivals of a pre-

literary philosophy. See Synesius, *Calvit. Encom.* 22. 85C (frag. 13, Rose; frag. 8, Walzer; frag. 8, Ross; frag. 1, Untersteiner); Athenaeus, *Deipnosophistae* II. 60D.

167 Aristotle's *Physics, Metaphysics, Politics, Poetics,* compositions on *Ethics* and other later works or treatises are admittedly treasure troves of historical information.

168 W. Jaeger, *op. cit.,* p. 129, also observes that Aristotle mentions the philosophic achievements of the Sophists, and that he restores them to their proper place in the history of Western philosophy, thus reversing Plato's contemptuous attitude towards the Sophists.

169 For details, see W. Jaeger, *op. cit.,* pp. 130-1.

170 Aristotle also attempts to assign specific dates to the earliest philosophers, 'wise men' and mystics.

171 See *Index Philosophorum Academicorum Herculanensis* (ed. S. Mekler, 1902), col. III, 13. See also the so-called *Prolegomena to the Philosophy of Plato* (ed. E. Westerink), p. 15, where we are told that 'for the sake of Plato, the Magi came to Athens eager to participate in the philosophy which he was expounding.' Diogenes Laertius III. 25 relates that a Persian (Zoroastrian?) erected a statue in the Academy honoring Plato.

172 Philip of Opus, *Epinomis* 986E; 987B; 987D ff.; *et passim.*

173 Plato (?), *I Alcibiades* 121E-122A.

174 This interest might also be reflected in *Epinomis* 986E; 987B; 987D-988A; *et passim.*

175 See, for instance, Plato, *Laws* 896E, where Plato admits that 'we ought not to suppose that there are less than two cosmic souls, one the author of the good, the other the author of the opposite.' Traces of Zoroastrian teachings, especially of the view that at certain cyclic intervals truth or civilizations are destroyed or 'pushed back' by the forces of evil, might also be detected in Plato, *Timaeus* 22A ff.; 22C; 22D; 23A; *Republic* 546A ff.; *Critias* 109D; 111B; 112A; *Statesman* 268E ff.; *Laws* 677A; 702A. Plutarch, *De Iside et Osiride* 46-7 (*Moralia* 370C ff.), claims that Plato, in a veiled manner, had for some time advocated the Zoroastrian dualism of good and evil. Plutarch may also be alluding to Plato, *Theaetetus* 176A: 'Evils ... can never pass away. For there must always remain something which is antagonistic to the good.' He may also have in mind *Timaeus* 35A. Theopompus claims that Plato derived the 'myth of Er' (*Republic* 614B ff.) from Zoroaster. See *Frag. Hist. Graec.* (ed. F. Jacoby) 2B, p. 591. Proclus, *Comment. in Platonis Rempublicam* (ed. W. Kroll) II, p. 109, lines 7 ff. and p. 116, lines 19 ff., simply substitutes Zoroaster for Er, calling the latter the son of Areimenius (Ahriman). See A.-H. Chroust (note 163), *passim,* and Chapter XVI.

176 See, for instance, A.-H. Chroust, 'Aristotle's religious convictions,' *Divus Thomas,* vol. 69, fasc. 1 (1966), pp. 91-7, and Vol. I, Chapter XVI. It is entirely possible that the Aristotelian *Eudemus* and the Aristotelian *On Prayer* are likewise under the influence of Zoroastrian teachings. Of the

*On Prayer* only one significant fragment has been recovered so far: 'That Aristotle has the notion of something above reason and being is shown by his saying clearly, towards the end of his work *On Prayer*, that God is either "mind" (*νοῦς*) or something even beyond "mind."' Simplicius, *Comment. in Arist. De Caelo, CIAG*, vol. VII (ed. J. Heiberg, Berlin, 1894), p. 485, lines 19–22 (frag. 49, Rose; frag. 1, Walzer; frag. 1, Ross). See Chapter II.

177 DL I. 8. Oromasdes is the Zoroastrian Ormudz or Ahura-Mazda, Areiman-ius is Ahriman. See here also Pliny, *Hist. Nat.* XXX. 3. Pliny mentions that 'Zoroaster lived six thousand years prior to the death of Plato.' This remark is also used by Jaeger to date the *On Philosophy* after Plato's death. See W. Jaeger, *op. cit.*, p. 136. Aside from Aristotle, Pliny also consulted Hermippus who, in turn, relied on Eudoxus of Cnidus and his *Γῆς περίοδος*. This latter work was composed late in the year 347 B.C., that is, after the death of Plato. Pliny's remark that 'Zoroaster lived six thousand years prior to the death of Plato,' might not necessarily have been contained in Aristotle's *On Philosophy*. Hence, Jaeger's dating is open to challenge. See Chapter XVI.

178 Plutarch, *De Iside et Osiride* 46 (*Moralia* 370F). Plutarch might have found other vestiges of the Zoroastrian theory of the cyclic 'eternal return' or 'eternal recurrence' in Aristotle's writings. See note 166. See also Aristotle, *De Motu Animalium* 699 a 27 ff.; Aristotle, *Politics* 1329 b 25 ff.; and Aristotle, *Metaphysics* 1091 b 8 ff., where we are informed that 'Pherecides and some others made the original generating agent the best, and so do the Magi, and some of the later sages also, such as, for instance, Empedocles . . . Anaxagoras. . . .' Compare this statement with Plutarch, *De Iside et Osiride* 46 (*Moralia* 370D):

It is worthwhile also to observe that the [Greek] philosophers are in accord with the Chaldeans. For this reason, Heraclitus [of Ephesus] declares 'war the father of everything'. . . . After him Empedocles designated the benign principle as 'love and friendship,' and at times as 'the harmony of the serene eye,' while at the same time he defines the evil principle as the 'cursed discord' and 'the bloody struggle'. . . .

See also Chapter XVI, note 3.

179 W. Jaeger, *op. cit.*, p. 133, referring to Plutarch, *De Iside et Osiride* 46 (*Moralia* 370C ff.). See note 178. It is possible that Heraclitus' famous contention that 'strife is the father of everything' (frag. B53, Diels-Kranz) is but a formalization of the Zoroastrian perennial struggle between the forces of good and the forces of evil—a struggle, which for Heraclitus (and the Zoroastrians) is 'existential reality.' In any event, Plutarch (see this note) connects this statement of Heraclitus with the teachings of the 'Chaldeans.' And when Empedocles calls 'Love' and 'Hate' the two prime agents in the universe (frag. B17, Diels-Kranz), he seems to restate the Zoroastrian dualism of good and evil. It might be interesting to note that during the last decade of the sixth century B.C. King Darius of Persia

(521-486/85 B.C.) made Zoroastrianism the official creed throughout the Persian Empire, including the Greek settlements in Asia Minor. Under the circumstances, it is not surprising that Heraclitus and some early Greek philosophers who hailed from Asia Minor should have come in direct contact with Zoroastrian teachings. See Chapter XVI, note 31.

180 See notes 166 and 178. Jaeger (*op. cit.*, p. 137) observed that Aristotle probably did not derive the doctrine of the 'eternal return' or 'eternal recurrence' from Eudoxus of Cnidus.

181 See note 175.

182 The influence of Zoroastrian astronomy on early Greek astronomy is simply decisive, but the same might be said of certain aspects of Greek and Hellenistic philosophy in general. The latter is denied, for instance, by E. Zeller, *Die Philosophie der Griechen*, vol. I (5th ed., Leipzig, 1892), pp. 19-41. See Chapter XVI, note 31.

183 Some of these criticisms may actually go back to Aristotle's earlier work *On (the) Ideas*, a composition which Jaeger mentioned only in passing (pp. 93 and 172).

184 W. Jaeger, *op. cit.*, pp. 167-93 and 194-227.

185 See note 155.

186 See note 156.

187 See note 157. Jaeger might have added the following sources which attest to the fact that Aristotle was critical of certain aspects of Plato's teachings: Atticus, in Eusebius, *Praeparatio Evangelica* XV, *passim*; Plutarch, Adversus Coloten 14 (*Moralia* 1115A); Cicero, *Academica* I. 9. 33; Diogenes Laertius III. 37; Justin Martyr, *Cohortatio ad Graecos* 5; *Vita Platonis*, p. 198 (p. 396, ed. A. Westermann); Ammonius, *Comment. in Porphyrii Quinque Voces*, CIAG, vol. IV, part 3 (ed. A. Busse, Berlin, 1891), p. 42, lines 22 ff.

188 See note 158.

189 This fact, Jaeger alleges, is also brought out by Aristotle's effort to relate Zoroaster and Plato, conceding Plato a position in the intellectual and spiritual history of the world similar to that assigned to Zoroaster. See Pliny, *Hist. Nat.* XXX. 3, who claims that six thousand years separate Zoroaster and Plato. In view of the cycle of three thousand years advocated by the Zoroastrians, both Zoroaster and Plato are prominently connected with a decisive stage in the universal cosmic drama. In positioning Plato so importantly in the cycle of cosmic events, Aristotle pays the highest possible tribute to his teacher. See A.-H. Chroust (see note 163), pp. 579-80, and Chapter XVI. Another piece of evidence in support of Aristotle's respect and reverence for Plato might be seen in the hymn which he composed in honor of Plato (or, of Eudemus), and in the fact that he erected an altar commemorating Plato. See Chapter IV, note 62.

190 See note 183.

191 W. Jaeger, *op. cit.*, p. 138.

192 Plato's astral theology can be found in Books X and XII of the *Laws*. It was further elaborated by Philip of Opus, the disciple of Plato, in the *Epinomis*.

Probably due to the influence of Eudoxus of Cnidus, astral theology came to be a subject much discussed in the Academy. Eudoxus, on the other hand, in all likelihood derived his knowledge of astral theology directly from the Magi or Zoroastrians. See A.-H. Chroust (note 163), and Chapter XVI.

193 Frag. 26, Rose; frag. 26, Walzer; frag. 26, Ross; frag. 39, Untersteiner. See also A.-H. Chroust, 'The concept of God in Aristotle's lost dialogue *On Philosophy* (Cicero, *De Natura Deorum* I. 13. 33),' *Emerita*, vol. 33, fasc. 2 (1965), pp. 205-28, and Chapter XIV.

194 W. Jaeger, *op. cit.*, p. 139. Already J. Bernays (see note 15), pp. 99-100, had suggested this. Jaeger's views were rejected by H. von Arnim, 'Die Entstehung der Gotteslehre des Aristoteles,' *Sitzungsberichte der Akademie der Wissenschaften in Wien*, Histor.-Philos. Klasse, vol. II, part 5 (Vienna, 1931), pp. 4-5; and by H. Cherniss, *Aristotle's Criticism of Plato and the Academy* (Baltimore, 1944), pp. 592 ff. See also W. D. Ross, *Aristotle's Physics* (Oxford, 1936), pp. 95-7; W. K. C. Guthrie, 'The development of Aristotle's theology,' *Classical Quarterly*, vol. 27 (1933), pp. 164-6; M. Untersteiner, 'Il Περὶ Φιλοσοφίας di Aristotele,' *Rivista di Filologia e d'Istruzione Classica*, vol. 89 (1961), pp. 153-8; E. Berti, *La Filosofia del Primo Aristotele* (Padua, 1962), pp. 380 ff.

195 See *Epinomis* 977AB and 987B, where we are informed that it makes no difference whether we call the highest God Who dwells in the heavens Uranus or Olympus or Cosmos. The most appropriate name for the highest God is, indeed, Cosmos, that is, 'Universe.'

196 For a detailed discussion of all these problems, see A.-H. Chroust (see note 193), *passim*, and Chapter XIV.

197 Jaeger, *op. cit.*, p. 139, points out that for Aristotle the term 'universe' signifies here the perisphere, while for the Epicurean (materialistic) critic of Aristotle it means something which contains all animate and inanimate creatures or 'things.'

198 W. Jaeger, *op. cit.*, p. 139 and pp. 141 ff.

199 A number of scholars, among them H. von Arnim, J. Bidez and A. J. Festugière, deny that Aristotle had already conceived the notion of an Unmoved Mover when writing the *On Philosophy*. W. D. Ross and W. K. C. Guthrie, on the other hand, concede that the notion of an Unmoved Mover is perhaps compatible with the basic ideas or general tenor of the *On Philosophy*. See note 194. Jaeger apparently does not make much of Aristotle's statement (Cicero, *De Natura Deorum* I. 13. 33) that God is pure 'Mind,' although he mentions (p. 160) the reference to God as 'Mind' in Aristotle's lost work *On Prayer*. Frag. 49, Rose; frag. 1, Walzer; frag. 1, Ross. See note 176.

200 W. Jaeger, *op. cit.*, p. 142. In *Laws* 898E, Plato refers to three hypotheses concerning the causes of all heavenly motions: either the stars are bodies possessed of a soul; or the soul fashions for itself a body out of fire or air by means of which it moves the stars; or the soul has no body whatever, but guides the movements of the stars by some 'wonderful power.'

201 Philo of Alexandria, *De Aeternitate Mundi* III. 10-11 (frag. 18, Rose; frag. 18, Walzer; frag. 18, Ross; frag. 21, Untersteiner). See also *ibid.*, V. 20-4 (frag. 19, Rose; frag. 19a, Walzer; frag. 19a, Ross; frag. 29, Untersteiner); *ibid.*, VI. 28-VII. 34 (frag. 20, Rose; frag. 19b, Walzer; frag. 19b, Ross; frag. 28, Untersteiner); and *ibid.*, VIII. 39-43 (frag. 21, Rose; frag. 19c, Walzer; frag. 19c, Ross; frag. 17, Untersteiner). See also Lactantius, *Institutiones Divinae* II. 10. 24 (frag. 20, Walzer; frag. 20, Ross; frag. 22, Untersteiner); Cicero, *Lucullus* (*Acad. Prior.*) XXXVIII. 119 (frag. 22, Rose; frag. 20, Walzer; frag. 20, Ross; frag. 22, Untersteiner).

202 This seems to follow from Cicero, *De Natura Deorum* I. 13. 33 ('In the third Book of the *On Philosophy* Aristotle disagrees with his teacher Plato. . . .'), as well as from Philo of Alexandria, *De Aeternitate Mundi* III. 10 ('Aristotle . . . charged with godlessness those who thought that the great visible god [*scil.*, the Universe] . . . is no better than the work of man's hands. . . .'). Philo's (and Cicero's?) remark, Jaeger believes, refers to Plato's Demiurge.

203 W. Jaeger, *op. cit.*, p. 140. It appears, therefore, that the divine visible Universe, the 'visible God,' although 'created' and 'controlled' by the invisible Supreme God, is co-eternal with the invisible Supreme God. Hence, the 'creation' of the visible God by the invisible Supreme God must be a *creatio ab aeterno*.

204 This fusion can be detected already in Plato, *Laws* 821A ff.; 898C; 899A.

205 See Plato, *Timaeus* 30D: 'For God, intending to make this Universe like the fairest and most perfect of intelligible beings, devised one visible animal (living being) containing within itself all other animals (living beings) of a kindred nature.' See also *ibid.*, 40C.

206 W. Jaeger, *op. cit.*, p. 141. It will be noted that this interpretation of Jaeger's views, which has much merit, does not accord with the view that the universe is but the 'handiwork of God' (see p. 264), unless it is also admitted that God's 'handiwork' is likewise divine, though perhaps of a 'lesser divinity.' See note 203. But this still leaves unanswered the problem of the original 'Artificer' Who is pure 'Mind' and as such must be infinitely 'above' or 'beyond' His artifact—'beyond' the visible universe. This, however, would be Platonism pure and simple.

207 Frags 23-4, Rose; frag. 21, Walzer; frag. 21, Ross; frag. 32, Untersteiner. For a detailed discussion of this fragment, see W. Jaeger, *op. cit.*, pp. 143-54.

208 It cannot be determined whether this 'collection' is Posidonius' *On the Gods* or some other work on this subject. In any event, Cicero's account, which definitely contains Stoic elements, must be used with extreme caution.

209 It should be borne in mind that according to Plato, *Timaeus* 39E ff, the four basic elements are populated with as many divine beings. This view was also adopted in the *Epinomis* which, however, speaks of five (or six?) elements. See *Epinomis* 984D ff.

210 In *Laws* 747D, Plato maintains that climate and diet influence the human

body as well as the human mind. It is possible that this notion was adopted by Aristotle: since the stars dwell in the purest of atmospheres and are nourished by the finest of exhalations from the earth and from water, they must be perfect. See Cicero, *De Natura Deorum* II. 15. 42–16. 44 (frags 23–4, Rose; frag. 21, Walzer; frag. 21, Ross; frag. 32, Untersteiner). The Stoic influence on this particular passage from Cicero has already been noted. See note 208.

211 See also Stobaeus, *Florilegium* I. 43 (frag. 22, Walzer; frag. 22, Ross; frag. 33, Untersteiner): 'Plato and Aristotle state that there are four kinds of animals (living beings), namely, land-animals, water-animals, winged animals and heavenly animals. The stars, too, they insist, are said to be animals (living beings), and the universe is divine—a rational and immortal animal (living being).' See Aetius, *Placita* V. 20. 1; Plutarch, *Placita Philosophorum* V. 9. 5 (*Moralia* 908 F); Apuleius, *De Deo Socratis* VIII. 137 ff.; Philo of Alexandria, *De Gigantibus* II. 7 ff.; Philo of Alexandria, *De Plantatione* III. 12; Philo of Alexandria, *De Somniis* I. 22. 135; Sextus Empiricus, *Adversus Physicos* I. 86; Philo of Alexandria, *De Aeternitate Mundi* XIV. 45 (all in frag. 33, Untersteiner).

212 W. Jaeger, *op. cit.*, pp. 147–8. The divinity of the stars may also be inferred from their circular or orbital motion. See *ibid.*, pp. 151–3. All motion, Aristotle contends, is caused either by nature or by an external force or by free will. 'Natural motion' is always rectilinear—either straight upwards or straight downwards, but never circular or orbital. Neither is the orbital motion of the stars caused by some outside force. Hence, the only intelligent explanation of the perfectly circular or orbital motion of the stars is by endowing them with free will and with perfect intelligence.

213 This is also brought out by Philo of Alexandria, *De Aeternitate Mundi* III. 10–11 (frag. 18, Rose; frag. 18, Walzer; frag. 18, Ross; frag. 21, Untersteiner): 'Aristotle was surely speaking piously and devoutly when he insisted that the universe is uncreated and imperishable, and when he charged with serious blasphemy those people who maintained . . . that the great visible God, Who contains in truth the sun and the moon and the remaining pantheon of the planets and fixed stars, is no better than the work of man's hands. . . .' See also note 201; A.-H. Chroust (see note 193) and Chapter XIV.

214 Philo of Alexandria (see note 213). See also *ibid.*, V. 20–4 (frag. 19, Rose; frag. 19a, Walzer; frag. 19a, Ross; frag. 29, Untersteiner); *ibid.*, VI. 28–VII. 34 (frag. 20, Rose; frag. 19b, Walzer; frag. 19b, Ross; frag. 28, Untersteiner); and *ibid.*, VIII. 39–43 (frag. 21, Rose; frag. 19c, Walzer; frag. 19c, Ross; frag. 17, Untersteiner).

215 Cicero, *De Natura Deorum* I. 13. 33 (frag. 26, Rose; frag. 26, Walzer; frag. 26, Ross; frag. 39, Untersteiner); and *ibid.*, II. 15. 42–4 (frags 23–4, Rose; frag. 21, Walzer; frag. 21, Ross; frag. 32, Untersteiner).

216 See notes 194 and 198.

217 See also note 212.

218 W. Jaeger, *op. cit.*, pp. 141–54. It does not follow, however, that the destruction of the visible universe would bring in its wake the destruction of the 'invisible God.' See Philo of Alexandria, *De Aeternitate Mundi* VIII. 39–43 (frag. 21, Rose; frag. 19c, Walzer; frag. 19c, Ross; frag. 17, Untersteiner):

> The most conclusive argument [in support of the statement that the visible universe or visible God is ungenerated and imperishable is the following:]. . . . Why should God destroy the universe? Either to save Himself from continuing in creating, or in order to make another universe. The former of these two purposes is alien to God. For what befits Him is to turn disorder into order, not order into disorder. Furthermore, He would be admitting into Himself repentance, which is an affection or disease of the soul. For He should either not have made the universe at all, or else, if He judged the work as becoming to Him, He should have rejoiced in the product. . . . If instead of the present universe He is to make another universe, the universe which He makes will be in any case either worse or better than the present universe, or just like the present universe. Each of these possibilities is open to objection: (1) If it is worse, its artificer will be worse. But the works of God are blameless . . . incapable of improvement, fashioned as they are by the most perfect art and knowledge. . . . (2) If the new universe is like the old universe, its artificer will have labored in vain. . . . (3) If He is to make a better universe, the artificer himself must have become better, so that when He made the former universe He must have been more imperfect both in art and in knowledge— which is unlawful even to suspect. For God is equal and like Himself, admitting neither of slackening towards the worse or intensification towards the better.

This lengthy passage, if it is indeed a fragment of Aristotle's *On Philosophy*, would defeat Jaeger's statement that the destruction of the visible universe is tantamount to the destruction of the 'invisible God.'

219 See Plato, *Laws* 898E.

220 It might be interesting to note here that in the *Epinomis* 982BC it is suggested that the stars or star-souls act from perfect deliberation, and that since they impose their will on or 'legislate' to matter, they must have intelligence, free will and a conscious purpose.

221 W. Jaeger, *op. cit.*, p. 155. In this connection, Jaeger raises a problem all serious students of Aristotle must face. Plato was fully aware of the mythological background (and prophetic-poetic outlook) of his ultimate philosophic or metaphysical position. By admitting that these 'myths' are but one of several possible hypotheses (see *Laws* 898E), Plato, at least by implication, granted his disciples the right to go their own independent intellectual ways. Hence, whoever raises the age-old question of whether Aristotle really understood his teacher Plato cannot have sufficient knowl-

edge or understanding of either Plato or Aristotle. See W. Jaeger, *op. cit.*, pp. 155-6.

222 Cicero, *Academica* I. 7. 26; Cicero, *Tusculanae Disputationes* I. 10. 22; I. 17. 41; I. 26. 65-I. 27. 66 (frag. 27, Walzer; frag. 27, Ross; frag. 30, Untersteiner).

223 (Pseudo-) Clement of Rome, *Recognitiones* VIII. 15 (frag. 27, Walzer; frag. 27, Ross; frag. 30, Untersteiner).

224 Psellus, *De Omnifaria Doctrina* (ed. E. Westerink), p. 69, no. 131 (frag. 24, Untersteiner).

225 See A.-H. Chroust (note 20) and Chapter XV.

226 Since Book I of the *On Philosophy* discussed in a rather thorough manner the 'philosophy of the Magi' (Zoroastrianism), it may be surmised that this particular philosophy also influenced some of the views on theology and psychology expounded in Book III of the *On Philosophy*.

227 W. Jaeger, *op. cit.*, pp. 156-7.

228 Especially in Books X and XII of the *Laws*.

229 W. Jaeger, *op. cit.*, p. 158.

230 *Ibid.*, p. 159.

231 See also *ibid.*, p. 156:

> Aristotle founded not merely Hellenistic theology, but also that sympathetic but at the same time objective study of the inner religious life for which antiquity had no name and no independent discipline apart from metaphysics. . . . This is another aspect of the early Aristotle which, in spite of its inestimable importance for the history of the human mind, has been overlooked or ignored down to the present day—perhaps because the conventional picture of him (as a purely intellectualist metaphysician) might have been disturbed if it had appeared that his dialectical operations are inspired from within by a living religion, with which all the members of the logical organism of his philosophy were penetrated and informed.

232 *Ibid.*, pp. 158-9.

233 Simplicius, *Comment. in Arist. De Caelo*, CIAG, vol. VII (ed. J. L. Heiberg, Berlin, 1894), p. 289, lines 1 ff. (frag. 16, Rose; frag. 16, Walzer; frag. 16, Ross; frag. 25, Untersteiner). See also Philo of Alexandria, *De Praemiis et Poenis* VII. 40 ff. (frag. 12, Rose; frag. 13, Walzer; frag. 13, Ross; frag. 16, Untersteiner).

234 W. Jaeger, *op. cit.*, p. 159. The manner in which Jaeger re-formulates this *argumentum e gradibus* calls to mind Plato, *Philebus* 56B ff. See also note 127. It is possible that Aristotle derived this argument from the Platonic *Philebus* or, at least, was influenced by the *Philebus* when he devised (and recast) his argument. In *De Caelo* 284 b 3, Aristotle still speaks of the co-operation of scientific speculation and the 'inner sense (or awareness) of God.'

235 With Aristotle, nature has a form as well as a purpose which works and

creates from within. This teleological order is to Aristotle a 'law of nature' that can be demonstrated empirically.

236 Seneca, *Quaestiones Naturales* VII. 30 (frag. 14, Rose; frag. 14, Walzer; frag. 14, Ross; frag. 19, Untersteiner).

237 Synesius, *Dion [of Prusa]* 10. 48A (frag. 15, Rose; frag. 15, Walzer; frag. 15, Ross; frag. 20, Untersteiner). See also Psellus, *Scholia ad Ioh. Climacum* (Cat. des Manusc. Alchim. Grecs, ed. J. Bidez, Paris, 1928), 6, 171 (frag. 15, Walzer; frag. 15, Ross; frag. 20, Untersteiner): 'I undertook to teach you what I have learned, not what I have personally experienced [within myself].... One is a matter for teaching, the other for mystical experience.... The second comes when reason itself has experienced illumination, something which Aristotle described as mysterious....' A distant echo of this view can still be detected in Aristotle, *Eudemian Ethics* 1248 a 30 ff.

238 See here also Plato, *Seventh Epistle* 341CD.

239 W. Jaeger, *op. cit.*, pp. 160-1. See also A.-H. Chroust (note 176), and Vol. I, Chapter XVI.

240 In *Laws* 966D, Plato derives the belief in God from two distinct sources: the ever-flowing being of the inner life of the soul, and the sight of the eternal and immutable order of the stars and the heavens.

241 The mysteries, Jaeger points out (*op. cit.*, p. 161), had made it abundantly clear that true religion 'is possible only as personal awe and devotion, as a special kind of experience enjoyed by natures that are suitable for it, as the soul's spiritual traffic with God....'

242 Sextus Empiricus, *Adversus Mathematicos* IX. 20-3 (*Adversus Physicos* I. 20-3—frag. 10, Rose; frag. 12a, Walzer; frag. 12a, Ross; frag. 14, Untersteiner). See also Cicero, *De Divinatione ad Brutum* I. 30. 63-4 (frag. 12a, Walzer; frag. 12a Ross; frag. 14, Untersteiner). Cicero derived his information probably from Posidonius, *On Divination*. See also Plato, *Timaeus* 71E-72B; Plato, *Phaedrus* 244D; *Epinomis* 985C.

243 Cicero, *De Divinatione ad Brutum*, I. 25. 53 (frag. 37, Rose; frag. 1, Walzer; frag. 1, Ross). See also notes 29-32 and 37-42, and the corresponding text.

244 The Stoics (Cleanthes) likewise mention this Aristotelian argument for the origin of man's personal belief in God and in the existence of God. See Cicero, *De Natura Deorum* II. 5. 13.

245 See also A.-H. Chroust, 'A cosmological proof for the existence of God in Aristotle's lost dialogue *On Philosophy*,' *New Scholasticism*, vol. 40, no. 4 (1966), pp. 447-63, and Chapter XIII.

246 Cicero, *De Natura Deorum* II. 37. 95-6 (frag. 12, Rose; frag. 13, Walzer; frag. 13, Ross; frag. 18, Untersteiner); Philo of Alexandria, *Legum Allegoriarum Libri Tres* III. 32. 97-9 (frag. 12, Rose; frag. 13, Walzer; frag. 13, Ross; frag. 15, Untersteiner); Philo of Alexandria, *De Praemiis et Poenis* VII. 41-3 (frag. 13, Walzer; frag. 13, Ross; frag. 16, Untersteiner); Philo of Alexandria, *De Specialibus Legibus* III. 34. 185-III. 36, 194 (frag. 13, Walzer; frag. 13, Ross; frag. 16, Untersteiner); Sextus Empiricus, *Adversus*

*Mathematicos* IX. 26–7 (*Adversus Physicos* I. 26–7—frag. 11, Rose; frag. 12b, Walzer; frag. 12b, Ross; frag. 26, Untersteiner).

247 Sextus Empiricus, *Adversus Mathematicos* IX. 26–7 (*Adversus Physicos* I. 26–7), by way of an analogy, states that if a spectator were to observe the perfect arrays of the Greek army attacking Troy, such a spectator 'would most assuredly have arrived at the notion that there exists some one person who arranges this orderly array . . . such as Nestor. . . .' It may be argued here that the reference to a supreme commander, organizer or originator of this perfect order, as well as the reference to 'one person' and the identification of this supreme commander as a concretely identifiable person (in this instance Nestor, who to the Greek mind was a concrete person) approaches a proof for the existence of a Personal God (by way of analogy). See A.-H. Chroust (note 245), pp. 462–3.

248 Plato, *Republic* 514A ff.

249 Cicero, *De Natura Deorum* II. 37. 95–6 (frag. 12, Rose; frag. 13, Walzer; frag. 13, Ross; frag. 18, Untersteiner).

250 Sextus Empiricus, *Adversus Mathematicos* IX. 23 (*Adversus Physicos* I. 23—frag. 10, Rose; frag. 12a, Walzer; frag. 12a, Ross; frag. 14, Untersteiner).

251 Sextus Empiricus, *Adversus Mathematicos* IX. 27 (*Adversus Physicos* I. 27—frag. 11, Rose; frag. 12b, Walzer; frag. 12b, Ross; frag. 26, Untersteiner).

252 Philo of Alexandria, *Legum Allegoriarum Libri Tres* III. 32. 99 (frag. 12, Rose; frag. 13, Walzer; frag. 13, Ross; frag. 15, Untersteiner). See also *Epinomis* 982CD, where we are told that the observable perfect order within the universe proclaims the fact that this universe is governed by a supreme 'Mind.' *Epinomis* 978D relates that God created the stars and the perfect circuits of the celestial bodies in order that man may know the truth—that man may know God through His handiwork.

253 Aristotle, *Metaphysics* 982 b 12 ff.

254 It may be observed that Plato, *Theaetetus* 155D, had already pointed out that 'wonder is the feeling of the philosopher, and philosophy begins in wonder.'

255 W. Jaeger, *op. cit.*, pp. 163–4.

256 W. Jaeger, *op. cit.*, p. 164. See also *ibid.*, pp. 387 ff.

257 Jaeger argues (*op. cit.*, p. 164) that Aristotle sees the visible universe in the same manner as Plato saw the transcendent world of the Separate Ideas. It is interesting to note that Philo of Alexandria, *De Praemiis et Poenis* VII. 41–3 (frag. 13, Ross, frag. 16, Untersteiner), insists that men who, like Aristotle, find the 'way to God' through His handiwork, still proceed in an 'inferior way,' because they know God (of God's existence) only through His 'shadow,' that is, through His handiwork. The proper way of knowing God, according to Philo, is through God Himself. See also Philo of Alexandria, *De Specialibus Legibus* III. 34. 185–III. 36. 194 (frag. 13, Ross; frag. 16, Untersteiner), which calls the 'way to God' through His handiwork the 'second best way.' Needless to say, Philo assumes here a thoroughgoing Platonic position.

258 An echo of this can also be detected in Aristotle, *Metaphysics* 982 b 28 ff.:

> Accordingly, the possession of [philosophy, philosophic wisdom or of a knowledge of the divine] may also be justly regarded as being beyond human power. For in many ways human nature is in bondage. According to Simonides, 'God alone can have this privilege,' it is unfitting that man should not be content to seek the knowledge that is suited to him. If, then, there is something in what the poets say, and jealousy is natural to the divine power, it must probably occur in this case above all, and all who excelled in this knowledge would be unfortunate. But the divine power cannot be jealous . . . nor should any other science be thought more honorable than one of this sort.

See also *Epinomis* 988A: 'Let none of the Greeks fear that it is not right for mortal men to preoccupy themselves with divine matters. They must hold an entirely opposite view.' See also Plato, *Laws* 821A; Aristotle, *Nicomachean Ethics* 1177 b 31 ff.

259 This idea is also expressed in the apocryphal story about the Indian who informed Socrates that he could never know himself unless and until he knew God. See Aristoxenus, frag. 31, Müller. See also Diogenes Laertius (II. 45), who might refer to this Indian. Now we may also understand why in the *On Philosophy* Aristotle apparently discussed the meaning of the Socratic 'Know thyself.' See Plutarch, *Adversus Coloten* 20 (*Moralia* 1118C —frag. 1, Rose; frag. 1, Walzer; frag. 1, Ross; frag. 2, Untersteiner); Stobaeus, *Florilegium* III. 21. 26 (frag. 3, Rose; frag. 3, Walzer; frag. 3, Ross; frag. 4, Untersteiner); Clement of Alexandria, *Stromateis* I. 14. 60. 3 (frag. 3, Rose; frag. 3, Walzer; frag. 3, Ross; frag. 5, Untersteiner).

260 W. Jaeger, *op. cit.*, p. 166.

261 *Ibid.*, pp. 159–61.

262 *Ibid.*, p. 164.

263 *Ibid.*, p. 166.

264 Psalm 19:1.

265 Under the title of *Aristoteles' Dialog 'Über die Philosophie': ein Versuch der Wiederherstellung*, P. Wilpert intended to publish what may have amounted to a conclusive and detailed discussion and possible reconstruction of the Aristotelian *On Philosophy*. To everyone's deep sorrow, P. Wilpert died early in 1967. Recently M. Untersteiner, *Aristotele: Della Filosofia* (Rome, 1963) published a thorough and most useful 'commentary' to the several fragments credited to the *On Philosophy*.

266 See, for instance, I. Düring (note 75), *passim*. Recently W. Haase, 'Ein vermeintliches Aristotelesfragment bei Johannes Philoponos,' *Synusia* (Pfullingen, 1965), pp. 323–54, has attempted, not entirely without success, to show that the first part of Philoponus' *Comment. in Nicomachi Math. Isagogen* I. 1 (frag. 13, Rose; frag. 8, Walzer; frag. 8, Ross; frag. 1, Untersteiner) is in no way related to Aristotle's *On Philosophy*. In the past

this particular fragment had been credited to the *On Philosophy* by I. Bywater, 'Aristotle's dialogue *On Philosophy*,' *Journal of Philology*, vol. 8 (1877), p. 65; W. Jaeger, *op. cit.*, p. 137, note 1; I. Düring (see note 75), p. 131; E. Bignone, *L'Aristotele Perduto e la Formazione Filosofica di Epicuro*, vol. II (Florence, 1936), pp. 509 ff.; A. J. Festugière, *La Révélation d'Hermès Trismégiste*, vol. II (Paris, 1949), p. 222, note 1 and pp. 587–91; P. Moraux, *Les Listes Anciennes des Ouvrages d'Aristote* (Louvain, 1951), p. 30, note 12; A. Grilli, 'La posizione di Aristotele, Epicuro, Posidonio nei confronti della storia della civiltà,' *Rendiconti Class. Lettere: Istituto Lombardo di Scienze e Lettere*, vol. 86 (1953), p. 4; H. D. Saffrey, 'Le Περὶ Φιλοσοφίας d'Aristote et la théorie platonicienne des idées nombres,' *Philosophia Antiqua*, vol. VII (Leiden, 1955), pp. 9–10; P. Wilpert, 'Die aristotelische Schrift *Über die Philosophie*,' *Autour d'Aristote* (Louvain, 1955), pp. 99 ff. and pp. 113 ff.; R. Mondolfo, *La Comprensione del Soggetto Umano nell'Antichità Classica* (Florence, 1958), p. 675; E. Berti (see note 194), p. 327; M. Untersteiner (see note 265), pp. 121 ff.; K. Gaiser, *Platon's Ungeschriebene Lehre* (Stuttgart, 1963), pp. 236 ff.

267 See, for instance, J. Zürcher, *Aristoteles' Werk und Geist* (Paderborn, 1952), *passim*.

268 V. Rose, *Aristoteles Pseudepigraphus* (Leipzig, 1863), *passim*.

269 See A.-H. Chroust (see note 1), *passim*.

270 One of the paramount problems connected with Jaeger's discussion of the lost works of the young Aristotle is the following: since the days of V. Rose (*Aristotelis Librorum Ordine et Auctoritate Commentatio*, Berlin, 1854; *Aristoteles Pseudepigraphus*, Leipzig, 1863), and before that time, the Platonism of these early compositions has been recognized. This discovery raised the fundamental issue of whether the Platonism of the early works and the Aristotelianism of the later doctrinal treatises could be reconciled without denying or ignoring the Platonism of the early works; without denying the authenticity of the 'Platonizing' early works; and without denying the authenticity of the later doctrinal writings. To resolve this obvious and perhaps crucial dilemma, Jaeger, who concedes the philosophic differences between the early works and the later doctrinal treatises, develops his justly famous evolutionary thesis which in its essential features proclaims Aristotle's intellectual progression (or regression?) from an early Platonism to a later Aristotelianism. Thus, Jaeger not only recognizes the authenticity of both the early works and the later treatises, but also accepts the Platonism of the early compositions.

# Index of Ancient Authors

Simple Arabic numbers refer to the text; small Roman numerals to the Introduction. Roman numerals and Arabic numbers, separated by a comma, refer to chapter and note. References to notes in the Introduction are indicated by Intr. and Arabic numbers. Ps and Arabic numbers refer to notes in the Postscript.

Aelian
*De Natura Animalium*
(IV. 49) 77
*Varia Historia*
(V. 9) XIV, 12
(VII. 17) XVI, 11
(XI. 42) IX, 31
(XII. 30) IX, 31
Aeschines
*Oratio*
(III. 258) II, 72
Aeschylus
*Agamemnon*
(160) II, 11
Aetius
*Placita Philosophorum*
(I. 7. 9) XIV, 127
(V. 20. 1) XII, 61; XIV, 109; Ps, 211
Albinus
*Didascalicus*
(X. 7–8) XIV, 121
(XIV. 2) II, 18
Alexander of Aphrodisias
*Comment. in Arist. De Anima* 60; IV, 29
*Comment. in Arist. Metaphys.*
(56, 35 )I, 29; XII, 30
(59, 33–4) I, 29; XII, 30
(79, 3 ff.) XII, 31
(79, 7) I, 12
(85, 9 ff.) XII, 31
(85, 16 ff.) I, 29; XII, 30; XII, 31

(98, 20 ff.) XII, 31
(98, 22) I, 12
(117, 24) XII, 2; XII, 82
(250, 20) I, 29; XII, 30
(262, 19) I, 29; XII, 30
*Comment. in Arist. Meteorologica*
(13, 14) XIV, 95
*Comment. in Arist. Topic. Lib.*
(149, 9–17) 86; I, 62; VII, 2; VII, 12; VII, 56; VII, 57; VIII, 34
Alexinus
*Tarentinoi* 127; X, 6
Al-Kindi
*Cod. Taimuriyya Falsafa*
(55) V, 64
St Ambrose
*Hexameron*
(I. 1. 1–4) XIV, 130
Ammonius (Pseudo-)
*Comment. in Arist. Cat.* (Venice, 1546)
(fol. 5b) II, 83
*Comment. in Arist. Cat.*
(6, 25 ff.) III, 13; III, 14
Ammonius
*Comment. in Porphyrii Quinque Voces*
(42, 22 ff.) Ps, 187
Anaxagoras
frag. 194 B (Diels-Kranz) X, 14
Anonymous
*Proleg. to the Philosophy of Plato* (Westerink)

469

# INDEX OF ANCIENT AUTHORS

Aristotle—*continued*
(1283 a 33 ff.) II, 64
(1285 a 20 ff.) II, 86
(1287 b 26 ff.) 217
(1287 b 37–41) VI, 70
(1288 b 21 ff.) XVII, 18
(1290 b 25 ff.) XVII, 18
(1293 b 39) II, 64
(1294 a 20) II, 61
(1295 a 16–17) VI, 70
(1295 a 36 ff.) VI, 113
(1301 b 6) II, 64
(1301 b 35–6) VI, 114
(1321 a 37 ff.) II, 51
(1321 b 26 ff.) 220
(1323 a 35) XVII, 19
(1323 b 1) XVII, 26
(1323 b 7) XVII, 19
(1323 b 8 ff.) XVII, 26
(1324 a 10–12) VI, 71
(1324 a 35 ff.) VI, 71
(1325 b 38 ff.) XVII, 14; XVII, 17
(1327 a 41 ff.) XVII, 30
(1327 b 19 ff.) XIV, 97
(1327 b 23–8) VI, 91
(1329 b 25 ff.) XVI, 39; XVI, 41; Ps, 178
(1329 b 31 ff.) XVI, 15
(1329 b 34 ff.) XVI, 13
(1330 b 32 ff.) XVII, 33
(1332 b 27 ff.) VI, 64; VI, 114
(1332 b 32 ff.) XVII, 31
(1333 a 16–24) VI, 91
(1333 a 24–7) VI, 101
(1334 b 17–22) VI, 91
(1337 a 1 ff.) Ps, 97
(1338 b 2 ff.) Ps, 100
(1342 a 19 ff.) XVII, 13
*Politicus* xviii; 11–12; 14; 27; 34; 71; 73; 80; 100; 101; 113; 114; 116; 117; 134 ff.; 222; 225; 232; 233; 234; Intr., 6; I, 54; I, 84; I, 88; VI, 39; VII, 73; VIII, 16; VIII, 19; VIII, 26; VIII, 31; IX, 33; XI, 1 ff.; XI, 38; XIII, 40; XVII, 11; XVII, 18; Ps, 66; Ps, 104; Ps, 124; Ps, 132; Ps, 133; Ps, 159
*Posterior Analytics* 9; 89; I, 68; I, 75
(99 b 35 ff.) XVII, 12

*Prior Analytics* 91; 168; I, 75
(24 b 20) I, 75
(25 a 6) I, 75
(25 a 27 ff.) I, 75
(26 a 3) I, 75
(29 b 29 ff.) I, 75
(30 a 15 ff.) I, 75
(47 a 33) I, 75
(53 b 18) I, 75
(57 a 40) I, 75
(62 a 11) I, 75
*Problemata* xi; VI, 13
*Protrepticus* xii; xiii; xiv; xviii; 3; 5; 6; 7; 8–11; 12; 13; 15; 27; 34; 78; 79; 86 ff.; 105 ff.; 119 ff.; 126 ff.; 144; 147; 154; 155; 156; 178; 217–18; 224; 232; 234; 236; 240 ff.; Intr., 6; Intr., 13; Intr., 19; I, 10; I, 51; I, 62; I, 65; I, 67; I, 68; I, 77; I, 78; I, 79; I, 88; I, 93; II, 17; II, 24; II, 33; II, 47; II, 58; II, 95; III, 7; III, 73; III, 83; IV, 24; IV, 36; IV, 43; IV, 63; V, 36; VI, 39; VI, 51; VI, 102; VII, 1 ff.; VII, 8; VII, 12; VII, 15; VII, 16; VII, 21; VII, 28; VII, 38; VII, 39; VII 40; VII, 42; VII, 47; VII, 57; VII, 57; VII, 73; VII, 78; VII, 83; VII, 89; VII, 96; VII, 97; VII, 98; VII, 99; VII, 100; VIII, 1 ff.; VIII, 2; VIII, 5; VIII, 19; VIII, 22; VIII, 23; VIII, 31; VIII, 35; VIII, 37; VIII, 42; VIII, 43; IX, 1 ff.; IX, 9; IX, 11; IX, 17; IX, 18; X, 14; X, 21; X, 22; XI, 10; XI, 12; XI, 25; XII, 2; XII, 24; XII, 80; XIII, 29; XIII, 37; XIII, 40; XIV, 27; XIV, 28; XIV, 29; XIV, 123; XV, 34; XV, 37; XV, 58; XVII, 26; Ps, 32; Ps, 34; Ps, 48 ff.
*Rhetoric* VI, 13
(Books I and II) 9; 32; 89
(1354 a 11 ff.) III, 76
(1355 a 18 ff.) Ps, 166
(1355 b 6) XVII, 26
(1360 b 31 ff.) II, 58; II, 64
(1387 a 16 ff.) XIII, 53
(1390 b 15 ff.) II, 58; II, 64
(1390 b 22) II, 67

(V. 24) XIV, 67

(VI. 28–VII, 34) IV, 57; XIV, 38;
Ps, 201; Ps, 214

(VIII. 39–43) IV, 57; XII, 44; XIV,
35; XIV, 38; Ps, 201; Ps, 214; Ps,
218

(XIV. 45) XIV, 109; Ps, 211

*De Gigantibus*

(II. 7 ff.) XIV, 109; Ps, 211

*De Plantatione*

(III. 12) XIV, 109; Ps, 211

*De Praemiis et Poenis*

(VII. 40–6) XIII, 8; XIV, 41; Ps, 233

(VII. 41–3) 160; 169; XI, 46; XII, 45;
XII, 66; XIII, 8; XIII, 45; XIII, 50;
XIII, 51; XIII, 64; XIII, 68; XIV,
38; Ps, 246; Ps, 257

(VII. 43) XIII, 50; XIII, 51; XIII,
64

*De Somniis*

(I. 22. 135) XIV, 109; Ps, 211

*De Specialibus Legibus*

(III. 34. 185–III. 36. 194) XIII, 4;
XIII, 49; XIII, 64; XIII, 68; XIV,
41; Ps, 246; Ps, 257

*De Virtutibus*

(187–227 (*On Noble Birth*), V, pp.
224 ff., Cohn-Wendland) II, 58

*Legum Allegoriarum Libri Tres*

(III. 32. 97–9) 159; 168; 264–5; XI,
46; XII, 45; XII, 66; XIII, 22;
XIII, 40; XIII, 41; XIII, 64; XIV,
38; XIV, 39; Ps, 246; Ps, 252

*Quis Rerum Divinarum Heres*

(57. 283) XIV, 85; XV, 17; XV, 76;
XV, 77

Philodemus

*De Diis*

(3, col. 10, 7–11: p. 30, Diels) XIV, 7;
XIV, 113

*De Ira*

(p. 65, 31–66, 2, Wilke) XI, 57

*De Pietate*

(7 b 4–8) XII, 2; XIV, 14

*De Rhetorica: Volumina Rhetorica*

(vol. II, pp. 50 ff., Sudhaus) III, 57;
III, 63 ff.

(col. 48, 36–7: p. 50, Sudhaus) III, 63;
III, 84

(col. 48, 36–55, 44: pp. 50–61, Sudhaus) 37–9; III, 64–70

(col. 48, 36–7: pp. 50–1, Sudhaus)
III, 63

(col. 48, 37–49, 37: pp. 51–2, Sudhaus) III, 65

(col. 51, 40: p. 55, Sudhaus) III, 66

(col. 52, 41: pp. 56–7, Sudhaus) III,
67

(col. 53, 42–54, 42: pp. 58–9, Sudhaus) III, 68

(col. 54, 42: p. 59, Sudhaus) III, 69

(col. 54, 43–4: p. 60, Sudhaus) III, 70

(col. 55, 43–4: pp. 60–1, Sudhaus)
III, 64

(col. 56, 45 ff.: p. 62, Sudhaus) III, 64

(p. 175, Sudhaus) XI, 57

*Hercul. Papyr.*

(III, p. 3, col. 28) II, 50

Περὶ οἰκονομίας

(ed. Jensen, col. XXI, 28–35, pp. 59–
60) II, 50

Philolaus

(frag. 14, Diels-Kranz) Ps, 32

Philoponus

*De Aeternitate Mundi* (Rabe)

(31, 17) VI, 4

(32, 5 ff.) Ps, 157

*Comment. in Arist. Categ.*

(3, 16 ff.) III, 13

(3, 22–4) II, 90; XVII, 1

*In Arist. De Anima Comment.* IV, 29

(75, 34 ff.) I, 29; I, 31; I, 38; XII, 2;
XII, 30

(141, 21 ff.) 56–8; 65; IV, 47; V, 3;
V, 14; V, 27; Ps, 27

(141, 30 ff.) I, 57

(144 ff.) Ps, 27

(144, 24–5) V, 15; V, 28

(144, 24 ff.) I, 57

(144, 25–30) V, 16; V, 30; V, 54

(144, 30–7) V, 17; V, 29; V, 46

(145, 2 ff.) I, 57

(147, 6 ff.) I, 57; V, 20; V, 28; V, 31

(147, 7–9) V, 21

(147, 10) V, 22

(186, 25) XII, 2

*Comment. in Nicomachi Math. Isag.*

(I. 1) XII, 2; Ps, 266

# Index of Modern Authors

Tarn, W., XVII, 42
Taylor, A. E., I, 33; XII, 59
Theiler, W., 8; 99; 147; 154; 155; 182;
I, 64; I, 70; VII, 65; VII, 98; VIII, 23;
XII, 23; XII, 34; XIV, 26; XIV, 46;
XIV, 51; XIV, 58; XIV, 71; XIV,
72; XIV, 89; XV, 71
Thillet, P., 31; 32; 36; Intr., 22; I, 1;
II, 4; II, 46; III, 9; III, 12; III, 21;
III, 23; III, 38; III, 48; III, 49; III, 60
Toeplitz, O., I, 33
Torraca, L., VII, 62
Trendelenburg, F. A., I, 13
Tricot, J., XII, 1

Ueberweg, F., XII, 1
Unger, G. F., XVI, 11
Untersteiner, M., xiii; xiv; 145; 182;
202; Intr., 16; II, 1; XI, 39; XI, 41;
XI, 44; XII, 1; XII, 2; XII, 6; XII, 7;
XIII, 28; XIII, 44; XIV, 60; XIV,
68; XIV, 85; XIV, 89; XIV, 121;
XIV, 127; XV, 10; XV, 11; XV, 24;
XV, 64; XVI, 1; XVI, 4; XVI, 9;
Ps, 194; Ps, 265; Ps, 266
Usener, H., 97; VII, 13

Verbeke, G., 78; VI, 39; VI, 50
Verdenius, W. J., XIII, 50; XIII, 53
Villa, E., VII, 28

Waerden, B. L. van der, XVI, 9
Walzer, R., xiii; xiv; 102; Intr., 16;
II, 2; IV, 29; IV, 63; VI, 15; VII, 79;
VII, 83; VII, 84; VII, 85; VII, 88;
VIII, 37; XIV, 85; XIV, 127; XV, 4;
XV, 17; Ps, 114
Waszink, J. H., V, 64
Wehrli, F., 100; VII, 70; VIII, 23; VIII,
40
Weil, R., 135; 136; I, 54; II, 31; VI,
39; XI, 16; XI, 26; XVI, 41; XVII, 8
Wendland, P., Ps, 149
West, M. L., XVI, 17; XVI, 29
Westerink, E., XVI, 20
Wieland, W., VI, 39
Wilamowitz-Moellendorf, U. von, IX,
27; XII, 1; XIV, 144
Wilhelm, F., VI, 43
William of Moerbeke, II, 8
Wilpert, P., 3; 146; I, 13; I, 14; I, 17;
I, 22; I, 23; I, 26; I, 32; I, 46; II, 1;
VII, 57; VII, 63; VIII, 38; XII, 1;
XII, 2; XII, 9; XII, 14; XII, 32;
XIV, 17; XVI, 9; Ps, 265; Ps, 266
Wolfson, H. A., XIII, 41; XIII, 44
Wundt, M., XIV, 131

Zeller, E., 92; 97; 147; I, 13; VII, 31;
VII, 32; VII, 33; XII, 20; XIV, 48;
XIV, 82; XVI, 5; XVI, 8; Ps, 16;
Ps, 182
Zepf, M., XIII, 22; XIII, 24; XIII, 28;
XIII, 36
Zuntz, G., VII, 83
Zürcher, J., 8; 9; I, 69; Ps, 267